Revolutionary Patriots

of Baltimore Town
& Baltimore County, Maryland
1775-1783

Henry C. Peden, Jr.

Willow Bend Books
2003

WILLOW BEND BOOKS
AN IMPRINT OF HERITAGE BOOKS, INC.

Books, CDs, and more – Worldwide

For our listing of thousands of titles see our website
at
www.HeritageBooks.com

Published 2003 by
HERITAGE BOOKS, INC.
Publishing Division
1540 Pointer Ridge Place #E
Bowie, Maryland 20716

International Standard Book Number: 1-58549-107-1

TABLE OF CONTENTS

iii

INTRODUCTION

Students of the Revolutionary War period quickly learn that not every colonist supported the movement toward independence. Just as the patriots of 1776 objected to the laws and regulations of King and Parliament, so many of the colonists (including a great many inhabitants of Baltimore County) resisted--vocally and physically--the resolutions, decisions, and policies of the Continental Congress, the Provincial Conventions, and of the Committees of Observation. Many joined the Association of Freemen of the Province of Maryland, enrolled in the county militia, or subscribed to the Oath of Fidelity and Allegiance to the State of Maryland, and they were known respectively as Associators, Enrollers, and Jurors. On the other hand, there were many who did not join, enroll, or subscribe, and they came to be known as Non-Associators, Non-Enrollers, and Non-Jurors.

In addition to the county militia, able-bodied men were organized to join the State Flying Camp. and the Continental Line. Many of these organizations overlapped in function and organization, and most had trouble recruiting men, maintaining discipline, and obtaining supplies.

This Introduction will present a brief chronology of some of the events of the period, and at the same time attempt to explain some of the terms found in the literature of the period.

The first Provincial Convention met in Annapolis in June, 1774. Every county sent delegates, and the 92 members denounced the British blockade of Boston, suggested that the colonies break off with Great Britain, and nominated delegates to the First Continental Congress which would soon be held.[1]

Soon after the Convention, militia companies were formed. All males between the ages of 16 and 50 were required to enroll in militia companies. Even though they had the right to elect their own officers, many refused to enroll (hence the origin of the term Enrollers and Non-Enrollers).[2]

The Convention met in Annapolis again in July of 1775. Now that the Battle of Lexington had been fought, the members faced the dual tasks--each formidable in itself--of organizing the civil government, and preparing for war.[3] The Convention drew up a document entitled the Association of Freemen of Maryland. All colonists were supposed to sign before the county Committee of Observation to indicate their support for the colonial cause. Those who signed have come to be known as Associators, while those who refused (through conviction, religious beliefs, or for some other reason) were to be known as Non-Associators. At first no penalty was imposed on those who refused to sign, but by January, 1776, the Non-Associators were required to pay higher taxes, had their arms confiscated, and had to give parole for their good conduct.[4]

The Convention also organized militia companies, and called for 1,444 men to be enrolled, with proper officers, into companies to be raised immediately, for "the defense of this Province." There were to be 8 companies consisting of 68 privates, formed into a battalion, and the remainder of the troops were to be organized into companies of 100 men each. Two of these latter companies were to be trained as matrosses.[5] Hoffman, in Spirit of Dissension, points out that the non-enrollers not only refused to enroll, but refused to pay the fines, and hurled such insults at those who did enroll, that the militia men refused to serve until the fines levied against the non-enrollers were collected.[6]

In June of 1776 the Convention, in compliance with a resolution of the Continental Congress, authorized the formation of a "Flying Camp" (men ready to take arms and move quickly) to consist of 3,405 men. The Flying Camp was dissolved in December of 1776, and many of the officers and men joined the Continental Regiments.[7]

The Declaration of Independence was adopted by the Continental Congress in the first days of July, 1776, but the Declaration was not read until the end of the month. Sheriff Robert Christie, Jr., loyal to the British, refused to read the document, and fled to the countryside. Finally, it was read by William Aisquith, member of the Committee of Observation.[8] Following the reading of the Declaration, the Whig Club, a secret political organization made up of merchants and tavernkeepers, began to harrass and torment anyone who felt loyalty to the Crown, or who did not appear to support the Revolutionary cause completely. Members of the club would threaten physical violence or death to anyone who did not change his sentiments or leave the Province immediately.[9]

In November, 1776, James Bosley, collector of fines for the Baltimore Committee of Observation, went to the home of one Vincent Trapnall, who refused to pay the fine, threatened to blow Bosley's brains out, and then struck him in the head. He dared Bosley to bring the whole committee to the house, and "he would treat them the same way."[10]

The Maryland Line, under the command of Col. William Smallwood, was organized in December, 1776. The Line, which was to remain in existence until December 31, 1780, had Mordecai Gist, scion of a Baltimore County family, as Brigadier-General.[11]

Early in 1778, a law was passed requiring all men to take the Oath of Fidelity and Allegiance to the State of Maryland. Those who refused to take the Oath were to be designated as Non-Jurors. Refusal to take the Oath did not necessarily imply loyalty to the Crown. Soldiers were not required to take the Oath, and members of some religious groups, such as members of the Society of Friends, refused to take any Oaths as a matter of conscience. Unpublished sources indicate that 2,203 men of Baltimore County took the Oath, while the Minutes of the Baltimore County Court for 1778 listed 2,2:1 Non-Jurors (or Non-Associators).[12]

Discipline in the military was a recurring problem. In February, 1779, Major Nathaniel Smith wrote to Governor Thomas Sim Lee that a number of men in his command wanted to be discharged, and that one of the men had tried to kill Smith and two other officers.[13]

The War created problems for civilians also. In November, 1780, Robert Slater petitioned that one of his daughters had married one William McCarter and later had moved to New York, leaving two children with the maternal grandparents. Now the McCarters wanted to have the children join them in New York, and McCarter was requesting permission to allow the children to be escorted by a maid servant through the lines to New York. The petition was granted.[14]

In January, 1781, the Army was reformed. Smallwood remained as Major General, and Mordecai Gist continued as Brigadier General.[15]

In April, 1781, Mark Alexander and other merchants of Baltimore complained to Governor Lee that they were afraid an attack by the enemy would find Baltimore unprepared and undefended. They wanted the militia to be called out to duty, and they stated their willingness to perform garrison duty themselves. They wanted a plan established whereby the militia could be called out at a minute's notice.[16]

In October, 1782, the inhabitants of My Lady's Manor sent a petition to Daniel of St. Thomas Jenifer that the sale of the manor be postponed. Some held leases from Thomas Brerwood, and some held leases from Lord Baltimore's Agent. They asked that the State Legislature confirm all titles to the property.[17] It was incertainty over their right to the land they had farmed for years that kept some of the inhabitants from enrolling in the militia or taking the Oath of Fidelity.[18]

The hostilities came to an end with the surrender of Cornwallis at Yorktown. The Continental Congress met at Annapolis in December, 1783, when Washington resigned as Commander in Chief of the Army, and it was at Annapolis that the Congress ratified the Treaty of Paris, by which the independence of the United States was recognized.[19]

ROBERT W. BARNES

March 22, 1988

vii

INTRODUCTION NOTES

[1] *Maryland Manual 1973-1974*, compiled by Morris L. Radoff and Frank F. White, Jr. (Annapolis: Hall of Records Commission, 1974), p. 38.

[2] Neal A. Brooks and Eric G. Rockel. *A History of Baltimore County* (Towson: Friends of the Towson Library, 1979), p. 88.

[3] *Maryland Manual*, p. 38.

[4] Ronald Hoffman. *A Spirit of Dissension* (Baltimore: The Johns Hopkins Press, 1973), p. 191.

[5] Rieman A. Steuart. *The Maryland Line* (The Society of the Cincinnati of Maryland, 1969), p. 2.

[6] Hoffman, p. 192.

[7] Steuart, p. 5

[8] Brooks and Rockel, p. 87.

[9] Hoffman, pp. 190-191.

[10] *Ibid.*, p. 192.

[11] Steuart, p. 10.

[12] Brooks and Rockel, pp. 94-95.

[13] *Calendar of Maryland State Papers: Number 4, Part 3: The Red Books* (Annapolis: Hall of Records Commission, 1955), Item 349, p. 53.

[14] *Ibid.*, Item 727, p. 115.

[15] Steuart, p. 28.

[16] *Calendar*, Item 886, p. 139.

[17] *Ibid.*, Item 1257, p. 195.

[18] Brooks and Rockel, p. 93

[19] *Maryland Manual*, p. 39.

FOREWORD

It has been the ambition of the author that those who refer to this book may be able to locate a Revolutionary War ancestor in Baltimore County and Baltimore Town, Maryland, from whom they could subsequently join the Sons of the American Revolution, the Daughters of the American Revolution, as well as other patriotic and hereditary organizations.

There are over 6,000 names of men and women in this book who rendered active service in the cause of American independence during the Revolutionary War between 1775 and 1783, including the names of Non-Jurors to the Oath of Allegiance in 1778. Altogether, there are some 12,000 names within the text.

Those listed in this compilation served either as an officer, soldier, seaman, marine, militiaman, or minuteman in the armed forces of the State of Maryland, or any of the other States, and of the Continental Congress; or, served on Committees of Correspondence, Safety, Inspection and Observation; or, held a civil office such as Justice of the Peace, Judge, Mayor, Sheriff, or Legislator; or, performed overt acts of resistance to the authority of Great Britain, such as Signers and Representatives to the Association of Freemen in 1775, Signers and Members of the Sons of Liberty in 1776, Signers of the Oath of Allegiance and Fidelity to the State of Maryland in 1778 and 1781, and Members of the Baltimore Salt Committee in 1779; and, others who unfailingly opposed Great Britain during the Revolutionary War, such as men who served as militia substitutes, men and women who rendered material aid to the army and navy, and those who kept the government informed of anything suspicious regarding British activities and Loyalist movements in the area.

This book is far more than just a list of names, for careful research has been made to obtain genealogical data for many of those named. Data can vary from just one line to a full page, depending on the information at hand, and the prominence of the individual. In the case of officers, in a large majority of cases, it has been possible to establish the dates of their commissions, their promotions, their resignations, their companies, their pay certificates, their bounty lands, their dates of birth, death and marriage, and the names of their wives and children. Similar data is also included for the rank and file soldier, but all too frequently the only information available is the name on a muster or pay roll.

It should be noted that many patriots and soldiers born in Baltimore Town and Baltimore County actually served in the military from Harford County or rendered other patriotic service. Harford County was formed from Baltimore County in 1773 and the government was established in 1774, just prior to the American Revolution. In the event an ancestor cannot be found herein, it is suggested that Harford County records be checked, or refer to my Revolutionary Patriots of Harford County, Maryland, 1775-1783. Also, many patriots either married, lived or died in Baltimore Town and Baltimore County although they served in other counties and states. The same applies to those born in the Baltimore area who moved away and served elsewhere. Such patriots, when located in the course of this research, have been included in this book also. Additionally, Carroll County was formed from Baltimore County, in part, in 1837, so many patriots named herein lived and left descendants in that part of western Baltimore County which subsequently became Carroll County.

Prior to the American Revolution, in 1766, a number of Baltimoreans met in the Lodge Room of the Baltimore Mechanical Company and organized what was afterwards known as the "Sons of Liberty." They took it upon themselves to maintain order and protect property. Subsequently, these Sons enrolled for the defense of the colonies in 1775 and 1776, forming some of the earliest known militia companies (as well as the Baltimore Independent Company in 1774, prior to the start of the American Revolution). Some of those patriots are named herein.

In December, 1776, and January, 1777, in response to the resolves of the Continental Congress, a large number of men marched from Frederick, Baltimore and Harford counties, but no rolls of these companies, giving date of service, can be found. And, militia men, for the most part, were not included in the Archives of Maryland, Volume XVIII. In August, 1777, again, a large number of men marched to war from Baltimore County. These troops were present at the Battles of Paoli and Germantown in that year. As noted in the Archives of Maryland, Volume XVIII, "the loss of these rolls causes the most serious gap in the Maryland records."

In 1777 the members of the Baltimore Mechanical Company organized the rebellion against the "rule of Governor Eden and the British lion." It later became known as the "Whig Club" and became a great factor throughout the Revolution. It held its meetings in secret at the dwelling of David Rush on Market Street in Baltimore, and was regarded as one of the most pronounced rebellious and mischievous organizations in Maryland. Some of those patriots are listed herein.

In 1778 the muster roll of Capt. John Gist's Company in Col. Nathaniel Gist's Regiment of Rangers attached to the 3rd Maryland Regiment, commanded by Col. Mordecai Gist, contained names of soldiers who resided in the Maryland counties of Anne Arundel, Prince George's, Talbot, Harford and Somerset, primarily. However, there were also soldiers from Baltimore and Frederick in the 3rd Maryland Regt., but it is not readily apparent which ones. Therefore, caution was exercised before assuming that soldiers listed were actually from Baltimore. Any errors or omissions in this regard are purely unintentional.

Also, in 1778, following the resolve of the Maryland Council in 1777, every free male over the age of eighteen years was required to take the Oath of Fidelity and Allegiance to the State of Maryland. It appears that the purpose of the Oath was to primarily get a feel for the sympathies of the populace and to see who was available for military purposes if the need arose. However, the mere signing the Oath did not necessarily say that the person was a true patriot, for many signed to avoid trouble from over-zealous patriots or even perhaps the loss of their land. Therefore, additional research may be necessary on some in order to determine their status, that is, were they actually Loyalists who took the Oath just to avoid any trouble because of their British sympathies, or were non-jurors actually soldiers away on military duty at the time, or both? The Oaths were copied and published separately by Bettie Carothers and Margaret Hodges. Hodges copied them as listed by each of the Magistrates, where Carothers listed them all alphabetically; she also listed non-jurors (those who would or did not sign). In comparing the lists prepared by Hodges and Carothers, a number of discrepancies were found, although some were simple typing or spelling errors. Still, the two lists did not match. A name on Carothers' list might not appear on Hodges' list, or Carothers might list the same name three times, making it difficult to determine whether it was three separate men or one man signing three times. In fairness to Carothers, she did mention that her listing for Baltimore County was a "finding list" and included more than just patriots' names. So, in an attempt to clarify matters, the file at the Maryland Historical Society known as the Ward file was checked. These cards indicate which residents of Baltimore County did not sign the Oath of Allegiance in 1778 (as well as they who did). Those who did not sign are noted in this book as "Non-Jurors" but they may have rendered other patriotic service. Also, caution is advised for any person named in this book who took the Oath of Allegiance in 1778 and the name of the Magistrate is not given. Further documentation may be needed in order to determine whether or not they actually took the Oath.

When the artillery companies of Annapolis and Baltimore were joined into one unit in 1779, it was not readily apparent which troops were from which area. To avoid any omissions, therefore, all names have been included herein. The reader should be advised that some of those listed in the companies of Captain Richard Dorsey, Captain William Brown, and Captain James Smith were Anne Arundel County residents, but many were also from Baltimore. And, in the case of Capt. Dorsey's company, he was was at one time a prisoner of war paroled to Maryland. His company retained his name but it was actually led by Capt. James Smith from 1780 to 1783. Thus, for the most part, their two companies were actually one and the same. In May of 1780, the artillery companies of Captains Brown, Dorsey and Gale were incorporated into the Continental Army, as well as being annexed to the Virginia Company of Artillery under Colonel Harrison. Again, care has been taken to glean out the Baltimore troops from the others. Some descendants will be pleased to find that these men were at Valley Forge in the winter of 1778 with General Washington.

Throughout the revolution the names of vessels, owners and captains engaged in privateering from the port of Baltimore included men of the highest standing in the State of Maryland who actively engaged in this hazardous trade. The privateer was the "nurse of the infant navy of this country" and many of our distinguished naval officers began their careers as such. The privateer was a privately owned and armed vessel that not only involved itself in assailing the enemy's commerce, but also lent itself to many military or naval expeditions. Judging by the spirit of their commanders, they were actually vessels of war. The names of these men, their ships and their owners are included herein.

In 1779 Congress manifested an anxiety on the subject of salt. While it was their desire to secure a supply that would fulfil all their military needs, they felt an anxiety to avoid its becoming an object of monopoly in the hands of various speculators. This anxiety was equally felt by the people of Baltimore, and to prevent its falling into the hands of those who would thus make use of it, a society was formed on October 14, 1779 for purchasing all the salt that should be brought to market and sell it out to the inhabitants for such a sum as would just cover the cost. This "Baltimore Salt Committee" consisted of just a few merchants and other interested persons, and they apparently accomplished their objective because no other account of any scarcity of salt in Baltimore during the war has been found. The names of these patriots are included herein.

Also included in this book are, as noted earlier, the men and women whose services were in civil employment, which were just as valuable as the military they supported. Such patriots were providers of food, lodging, hardware, clothing and guns. They served their country faithfully and their memories are worthy of being a part hereof. They were as much patriots of the revolution as those who fought in battle or those who governed the State. The men who sat on the Baltimore Committee (whether it be Correspondence, Safety, Inspection or Observation) were directly involved in the day-to-day activities of the military as well as the government during the Revolutionary War. They were true patriots, one and all.

In accumulating the thousands of names and the respective genealogical data and historical information on the patriots of Baltimore, many sources were cited, including original records in the Maryland State Archives in Annapolis and the Maryland Historical Society Library in Baltimore. My thanks to the staffs of these institutions for their assistance. My gratitude is also extended to the Baltimore County Historical Society and its Genealogical Committee for the data they printed in their History Trails publication. They have hundreds of ancestral charts in their library for interested researchers. And thanks to the Baltimore County Genealogical Society for the use of their files in Perry Hall, Maryland. Special thanks for advice and contributions from Robert Barnes, Shirley Reightler, William Hollifield III, and Alan Virta, and my wife, Veronica Peden, who encouraged me to go on.

Additionally, information was gleaned from the tens of thousands of entries in An Inventory of Maryland State Papers, Volume I, which took many, many hours to extract the names of the Baltimore patriots. Information was also gleaned from the Archives of Maryland, Volumes 11, 12, 16, 18, 21, 43, 45, 47 and 48. Also, the 25 volumes of original applications of the Maryland Society of the Sons of the American Revolution were reviewed, page by page, and the lineages of Baltimore patriots have been included herein. And more than 30 original manuscripts and muster rolls from the aforementioned Maryland State Archives and MHS Library were similarly digested. A review of the source list used in compiling this book shows that virtually no stone was left unturned in searching for information on Baltimore's patriots, with the only exception being the National Archives in Washington, D.C. However, it has been the purpose of this book to identify Baltimore's Revolutionary War patriots and by doing so, anyone interested in additional information can thereafter use the records that are available at the National Archives, by submitting the proper forms to them, or going there personally.

It should also be mentioned that the matter of variations in the spelling of names is always puzzling in works of this kind. It is easy to confuse the early handwriting and thus misspell names. In this book, variations in spellings have been included in parenthesis after the surname. For example, one might find a name like this: WYLIE (WYLE), LUKE, or McCUBBIN (MACCUBBIN), MOSES. This simply shows that the name was spelled differently in various records. As might be expected, it is difficult to determine in some cases just how many men had the same name. Rest assured that every effort has been made to present an accurate accounting, but there may be inadvertent errors when establishing relationships. Hopefully, they have been minimized and identification of one's ancestors should not be difficult.

Finally, all entries in this book have been documented. The key to sources and documentation is a simple one: each record, manuscript or book has been assigned a letter, and it is followed by a number for the page within that record. For example, H-600 represents page 600 in Source H, which is Archives of Maryland, Volume XVIII, CCC-19 represents page 19 in Source CCC, which is McCreary's The Ancient and Honorable Mechanical Company of Baltimore, etc. The exceptions are Source A, which is divided into Source A-1 and A-2; Source YYY, which is divided into Source YYY-1 and YYY-2; and Source AAA-25, which represents the volume number and not the page. In any event, it is easy to trace the source for the documentation.

It is sincerely hoped that this book may prove to be of lasting value to the descendants of the Revolutionary War Patriots of Baltimore Town and Baltimore County, Maryland, as well as being a useful genealogical tool for subsequent research in this area.

HENRY C. PEDEN, JR.

February 14, 1988

A

ABEL, SAMUEL. Private, Capt. Howell's Company, December 30, 1775. (G-11)

ABERCROMBIE, ROBERT. Died in Baltimore County in 1784. He married Sarah or Salathiel, daughter of Jarvis and Mary BIDDISON. Salathiel died testate in Baltimore County some time after May 20, 1802. She may have married as her first husband Henry EAGLESTONE, son of Abraham EAGLESTONE and Charity JOHNES. Henry is known to have had two daughters, Charity and Mary, and when Jarvis BIDDISON made his will in 1772 he named his daughter Salathiel ABERCROMBIE and her two daughters Mary and Charity EAGLESTONE. Robert ABERCROMBIE and wife Salathiel BIDDISON were the parents of: John; Mary, married a FAULER; Robert; Elizabeth, married Joseph MANUS circa 1791; and, Charles. Robert ABERCROMBIE was a non-juror in 1778, but subsequently signed the Oath of Allegiance to Maryland in 1781. (D-7, A-1/1, QQ-104)

ABLEWHITE, JOSEPH. Recruit, Baltimore County, 1780. (H-340)

ABBOTT, WILLIAM. Oath of Allegiance, 1778, before Hon. James Calhoun (A-2/65).

ACKENHEAD (AKENHEAD), MATTHEW. Listed twice as taking the Oath of Allegiance in 1778: one before Hon. Richard Cromwell; one before Hon. Peter Shepherd. (A-1/1, A-2/46, A-2/49)

ACKERLY (AKERLY), JOHN. Private, Capt. Dorsey's Maryland Artillery, 1777. Convalescent, November 17, 1777. Gunner, Capt. Dorsey's Company at Valley Forge, June 3, 1778. (H-574, H-618, UU-231)

ACKERMAN (AKERMAN), GEORGE. Captain, Baltimore Town Battalion, September 4, 1777. Oath of Allegiance, 1778. "George AKAMAN", Captain, Baltimore Town, 1779. Died prior to January 19, 1781. (A-1/1, A-2/52, BBB-362, E-13, F-312, R-15, BBBB-29). Took Oath before Hon. George Lindenberger.

ACKLER, WOOLERY. Non-Juror to Oath of Allegiance, 1778. (A-1/1)

ACKOYD, JOHN. Oath of Allegiance before Hon. James Calhoun, 1778. (A-2/38)

ACRES, THOMAS. Enlisted at Fort Whetstone Point, Baltimore, October 4, 1779. Discharged January 27, 1780. (H-626)

ADAIR, JOHN. Applied for revolutionary pension while living in Wayne County, Kentucky, in September, 1832. He was born in County Antrim, Ireland in 1754. His father and family came to America, landing in Baltimore when he was 18 years old or a little before. They lived in Maryland for one year, moved to Pennsylvania, where they lived a year, and moved on to Sullivan County, Tennessee. John Adair lived there during the Revolution and enlisted in companies serving against the Indians who were commanded by Chief Logan. He enlisted again in 1777 or 1778 in Capt. George Brooks Company. He volunteered the following spring under Capt. James Elliott, and in the following spring, when his father was drafted, substituted for him in Capt. Samuel Brashear's Company. In 1791 he moved to what is now Knox County, Tennessee. He lived fourteen years in the Tennessee country before removing to Kentucky. Died after August 11, 1843; wife, Mary. (OO-37, JJJ-3)

ADAIR, R. Member of Sons of Liberty in Baltimore, 1776. (CCC-19)

ADAIR, WILLIAM. Ordinary Seaman, September 19, 1776. Armorer, January 11, 1777 to October 22, 1777. Armorer's Mate, October 22, 1777 to Dec. 31, 1777. Served on ship Defence. (H-654)

ADAMS, DANIEL. Account and receipt for beef in Baltimore Town, for the military, July 13, 1776. (FFF-42)

ADAMS, ENOCH. Oath of Allegiance, 1778, before Hon. William Spear. Private, Capt. McClellan's Company, Baltimore Town, September 4, 1780. (A-1/1, A-2/67, CCC-24)

ADAMS, HANS. Corporal, Capt. Brown's Company of Artillery, Nov. 22, 1777. At Valley Forge until June, 1778. At White Plains, July, 1778. At Fort Schuyler, August-September, 1780. Not listed on rolls at High Hills of the Santee, August, 1781. (UU-228)

ADAMS, JAMES. Recruit, Baltimore County, 1780. (H-340)

ADAMS, James. Sergeant, Capt. Brown's Company of Artillery, Nov. 22, 1777. At Valley Forge until June, 1778. At White Plains, July, 1778. At Fort Schuyler, August-September, 1780. Not listed on rolls at High Hills of the Santee, August, 1781. (UU-230)

ADAMS, JOHN. Born 1760. Private, Baltimore Artillery Company, October 16, 1775. Took Oath of Allegiance, 1778, before Hon. George Lindenberger. Recruit, Baltimore County, 1780. Pensioner. (G-8, A-1/1, A-2/52, H-340, YY-7)

ADAMS, JONATHAN. Non-Juror to Oath of Allegiance, 1778. (A-1/1)

ADAMS, PAUL. Non-Juror to Oath of Allegiance, 1778. (A-1/1)

ADAMS, MATTHEW. Bombardier, Capt. Brown's Company of Artillery, November 22, 1777. At Valley Forge until June, 1778. At White Plains, July, 1778. At Fort Schuyler, August-September, 1780. Not on rolls at High Hills of the Santee, 1781. (UU-228)

ADAMS, SAMUEL. Ensign, Capt. Lemmon's Company, Feb. 4, 1777. (VV-114)

ADAMS, SAMUEL. Recruit, Baltimore County, July 20, 1776. (H-53)

ADAMS, SAMUEL 2nd. Recruit, Baltimore County, July 20, 1776. (H-53)

ADAMS, WILLIAM. Private, Baltimore Artillery Company, October 16, 1775. Member of Baltimore Mechanical Company. Sergeant, in Capt. Sheaff's Company, June 16, 1777. Took Oath of Allegiance before Hon. George Lindenberger, 1778. (G-8, CCC-25, A-1/1, A-2/52, W-162)

ADAMS, WILLIAM. Enlisted, Baltimore Town, July 20, 1776. Took Oath of Allegiance before Hon. James Calhoun, 1778. (H-53, A-2/65)

ADAMSON, GEORGE. Private, Capt. Oldham's Company, 4th Maryland Rgt., December 27, 1776 to August 16, 1780. (H-80)

ADDISON, CHRISTIAN. Non-Juror to Oath of Allegiance, 1778. (A-1/1)

ADDISPEAR, FRANCIS. Non-Juror to Oath of Allegiance, 1778. (A-1/1)

ADRIAN, MATHIAS. Sergeant, Baltimore County Regt. 15, c1777. (TTT-13)

AGGIS, WILLIAM. Recruit, Baltimore County, 1780. (H-340)

AHL, JOHN PETER DR. (1748-1827) Physician, who came to Baltimore in 1772, and settled there. Surgeon's Mate to Col. Armand's Maryland Legion, 1776. Wounded at White Plains. Was in the service from 1776 to 1783, his last duty being under General Muhlenberg. Pensioner. (XX-3, YY-7)

AISQUITH, WILLIAM. Member of Sons of Liberty in Baltimore, 1766-1776. Baltimore Committee of Observation, September 23, 1775 (elected). On the Committee in 1776, and was authorized by the Continental

Congress to assign all bills of credit or money for use by Mechanical
Volunteers and others for military purposes, 1776-1782. Took Oath of
Allegiance before Hon. James Calhoun, 1778. District Naval Officer,
Baltimore, 1780. Died May 7, 1804, in his 72nd year. (ZZZ-2, CCC-19,
A-1/1, A-2/40, FF-64, GG-74, RR-47, RR-50, SS-136, CCC-18, FFF-103, 294)

AITKEN, ANDREW DR. (February 18, 1756 - April 9, 1809) Born in Paisley,
Scotland; married Elizabeth HOUSTON (June, 1762 - November 4, 1811) in
1783. They attended First Presbyterian Church in Baltimore, where the
births of their children are recorded: Ann, born August 4, 1785, married
George MONK, merchant, in 1812; Andrew, Jr., born July 17, 1787, and died
June 6, 1808; Elizabeth, born June 1, 1789; Robert, born August 31, 1790;
George, born June 11, 1792; Maria, born January 1, 1794; Eliza, born Feb.
18, 1795; James, born September 23, 1796; and, Rebecca, born January 28,
1799, and died in 1879. During the Revolutionary War, Andrew served as
a Regimental Surgeon, and a Surgeon for the U.S. Navy. He resided on
South Street in Baltimore. (ZZZ-2, D-7, D-8, XXX-114)

AKEMAN, GEORGE. Took Oath of Allegiance, 1778, before Hon. Edward Cockey.
(A-1/1, A-2/61)

ALBRIGHT, JOHN. Capt., Baltimore County Regt. 36, Vol., c1777. (TTT-13)

ALBURN, RALPH. Non-Juror to Oath of Allegiance, 1778. (A-1/1)

ALCOCK (ALCOCKE), JAMES. Took Oath of Allegiance, 1778, before Hon. William
Lux. (A-1/1, A-2/68)

ALCRAFT, JOHN. Took Oath of Allegiance, 1778, before Hon. Thomas Sollers.
(A-1/1, A-2/51)

ALDER, ROBERT. Private, Baltimore County Regt. 7, c1777. (TTT-13)

ALDRIDGE, JOHN. Took Oath of Allegiance, 1778, before Hon. James Calhoun.
(A-1/1, A-2/41)

ALDRIDGE (ALRICH), NATHANIEL. Born 1754, in Elk Ridge, Maryland. Private,
Capt. Nathaniel Smith's 1st Company of Matrosses, January 24, 1776.
Height: 5' 8¼". (H-563, H-566, QQQ-2)

ALEXANDER, CHARLES. Baltimore Privateer and Captain of the schooner Wasp
(Maryland State Vessel), which was fitted out in Baltimore with eight
guns in October, 1775. Also, Captain of ship General O'Reiley, with
fourteen guns, owned by John Meade & Co. of Phila. (III-201, III-206)

ALEXANDER, DAVID. Took Oath of Allegiance, 1778, before Hon. George
Lindenberger. (A-1/1, A-2/52)

ALEXANDER, MARK. Son of Moses Alexander of Cecil County, Maryland. Served
Baltimore Committee of Inspection, March 13, 1775. Baltimore Committee
of Correspondence, November 12, 1775. Baltimore Artillery Company, 1777.
Ensign, Capt. Richardson's Company, Baltimore Town Battalion, September 2,
1777. Took Oath of Allegiance, 1778. Baltimore Salt Committee, October
14, 1779. 2nd Lieutenant, Baltimore Town Battalion, 1779. Magistrate in
Baltimore City, 1779-1780. He recommended to Governor that he commission
Job Garretson as Sheriff of Baltimore County, February 3, 1780. Member
of Baltimore Mechanical Company. Ensign, Capt. Ridgely's Company (old
Mercantile Company), January 19, 1781. Signed a letter to Governor Lee
to provide defense for Baltimore, April 4, 1781. Mark Alexander "Jr."
requested money from Governor to facilitate his position as a recruiter
in Baltimore County, July 4, 1781. (BBB-359, BBB-541, CCC-25, CCC-26,
FFF-267, AAAA-402, FFF-408, E-13, F-312, V-368, R-15, HHH-88, S-49, RR-19,
SS-130, BBBB-61)

ALEXANDER, ROBERT. (1740-1805) Son of William Alexander of Cecil County.
Baltimore Committee of Inspection, March 13, 1775. Baltimore Comm.
of Correspondence, November 12, 1775. Baltimore Committee of Observation, September 23, 1775. Delegate to Provincial Convention,
September 23, 1775. One of the representatives from Baltimore to
the Association of Freemen, July 26, 1775. Ensign, Baltimore Co.
Militia, 1st Company under Capt. Andrew Buchanan, Dec. 19, 1775.
2nd Lieutenant, Baltimore Town Battalion, Company No. 1, under Capt.
William Buchanan, 1776. 1st Lieutenant, Baltimore Town Battalion,
under Capt. Smith, June 6, 1776. Subsequently became a Loyalist and
fled Maryland in September, 1777, having refused to sign the patriot
Oath of Allegiance. (G-10, BB-2, GG-74, RR-47, RR-19, RR-50, RR-51,
SS-130, SS-136, FFF-7, WW-457, MMM-A)

ALEXANDER, SAMUEL. Non-Juror to Oath of Allegiance, 1778. (A-1/1)

ALEXANDER, W. Took Oath of Allegiance, 1778, before Hon. Isaac VanBibber.
(A-1/1, A-2/34) Could not write; made his mark.

ALGER (ALGIER), JACOB. Non-Juror to Oath of Allegiance, 1778. (A-1/1)

ALLEN, BARTHOLAMO. Took Oath of Allegiance, 1778, before Hon. George
Lindenberger. (A-1/1, A-2/52)

ALLEN, BENJAMIN. Took Oath of Allegiance, 1778, before Hon. Isaac Van
Bibber. (A-1/1, A-2/34)

ALLEN, CHARLES. Ensign, Capt. Lemmon's Company, Upper Battalion,
August 30, 1777 - 1778. Oath Non-Juror, 1778. (A-1/1, E-14,
LL-66, BBB-350)

ALLEN, DAVID. Non-Juror to Oath of Allegiance, 1778. (A-1/1)

ALLEN, EDWARD. Private, Capt. Sheaff's Company, June 16, 1777. Took
Oath of Allegiance, 1778, before Hon. Geo. Lindenberger. (A-1/1,
A-2/52, W-162)

ALLEN, GEORGE. Enlisted, Baltimore County, August 14, 1776. (H-52)

ALLEN, HUGH. Took Oath of Allegiance, 1778, before Hon. Jesse Dorsey.
(A-1/1, A-2/63)

ALLEN, JAMES. Able Seaman, September 19, 1776. Quartermaster, January 11,
1777 to May 18, 1777. Served on ship Defence. (H-606, H-654)

ALLEN, JOHN. Took Oath of Allegiance, 1778, before Hon. James Calhoun.
One John Allen married Mary GROVER in Baltimore County on Oct. 12,
1791 (marriage proven through Maryland pension application, so it
may have been a different John Allen). (A-1/1, A-2/38, YY-109)

ALLEN, JOSEPH. Non-Juror to Oath of Allegiance 1778. (A-1/1)

ALLEN, MARY. Revolutionary War pensioner, June 1, 1840, age 75, residing
in household of Ann Allen, in Baltimore City, 5th Ward. (P-128)

ALLEN, MICHAEL. Member of Sons of Liberty in Baltimore, 1776, and the
Baltimore Mechanical Company. Oath, 1778. (A-1/1, CCC-19 & 25)

ALLEN, NICHOLAS. Took Oath of Allegiance, 1778, before Hon. William Lux.
(A-2/68)

ALLEN, RICHARD SR. Applied for revolutionary pension in Wilkes County,
North Carolina on September 4, 1832. He was born November 22, 1741
in Baltimore County, Maryland. When he was twenty-one years of age
he moved to Frederick County, Virginia, where he lived for 7 years.
He moved to Rowan County, now Wilkes County, North Carolina, in

September, 1770. In October or November, 1775, he entered the service
as a volunteer in Capt. Jesse Walton's Company, the first unit raised in
the county. He was promoted to Ensign and then to Captain. He died on
October 10, 1832; wife, Nancy LINDSAY. (OO-146, JJJ-11)

ALLEN, RICHARD. Marine, March 30 - December 31, 1777, on ship Defence. (H-654)

ALLEN, SOLOMON. Son of David and Hannah ALLEN. Born March 23, 1743/4 in
Rehobeth, Mass., and died c1820 in Baltimore County, Maryland. His wife
was Catherine Slack (or Schleich) MILLER, who died in Baltimore County in
1820. In 1791 John SCHLEICH of Baltimore County made a will naming his
grandson John ALLEN, son of Solomon. Solomon ALLEN was a Private in the
company of Capt. Hatch Dent, 2nd Md. Regt., under Lt.Col. Thos. Woolford
during the Revolutionary War. His children were: John; Charles; Lewis,
married a Miss HARDEN; Philip, married Charity PARRISH; George Washington,
married Adazillah HARDEN; Elizabeth, born Nov. 19, 1791; Mary; Margaret,
married Mr. WAYMAN; Catherine, married John T. DANNEKER; and, Solomon,
born Nov. 17, 1788. Solomon ALLEN took the Oath of Allegiance in 1778
before Hon. George Lindenberger. (A-1/1, A-2/52, D-1, JJJ-11, XXX-118)

ALLEN, W. Took the Oath of Allegiance, 1778, before Hon. Isaac Van Bibber.
Could not write; made his mark. (A-1/1, A-2/34)

ALLEN, WILLIAM. Bombardier, Capt. J. Smith's Company, Maryland Artillery,
1780-1783. Took the Oath of Allegiance subsequently. (QQ-104,H-579,YYY-2)

ALLENDER (ALLENDAR), JOSIAH. Non-Juror to Oath of Allegiance, 1778. (A-1/1)

ALLENDER, NICHOLAS. Non-Juror to Oath of Allegiance, 1778. (A-1/1)

ALLENDER, WILLIAM. (May 15, 1757 - August 26, 1838, Baltimore County) He
married Ann SOLLERS (1768-1830) on November 19, 1788. Their son (other
children unknown), Nicholas B. ALLENDER (1795-1885) married Avarilla Day
HOLLAND (1816-1898) in 1836; their son, William R. ALLENDAR (1839-1914)
married Araminta B. HOLLAND in 1874. William ALLENDER took the Oath of
Allegiance, 1778, before Hon. Jesse Dorsey (signed name and "farmer").
He also served in Capt. Benjamin Rumsey's Company No. 6 in Harford Co.,
Joppa, Maryland, September 16, 1775. (A-1/1, A-2/63, AAA-1466)

ALLENDER, WILLIAM. (November 16, 1763 - March 14 or November 14, 1843) Born in
Baltimore County; died in Baltimore City. Wife, Barbara (1775-1848) and
children: Catherine (1795-1876) married Robert NIELSON (1792-1840) in
1825, and their son Joseph NIELSON (1826-1896) married Julia A FREEBIRD
(1829-1884) in 1849; Ann, born 1798; William; Sarah, born 1801; Mary Ann,
born 1808; Martha, born 1810; Frederick, born 1812; Priscilla, born 1815;
and, Carolina, born 1818. William ALLENDER took the Oath of Allegiance,
1778, before Hon. Hercules Courtenay (name spelled "ALLANDER"). He was
also a Private, 4th Company, 2nd Battalion, Maryland Line, under Lieut.
William Adams, 1782. (H-446, A-2/37, AAA-1001, AAA-558, JJJ-11, XXX-119)

ALLER, CHRISTIAN. Non-Juror to Oath of Allegiance, 1778. (A-1/1)

ALLISON, PATRICK. Took Oath of Allegiance, 1778, before Hon. John Merryman.
(A-1/1, A-2/45)

ALLISON, RALPH. Private, Capt. Ewing's Company No. 4, 1776. (H-13)

ALLRIGHT, JOSEPH. Took Oath of Allegiance, 1778, before Hon. Jesse Dorsey.
(A-1/1, A-2/64)

ALMACK, WILLIAM. Non-Juror to Oath of Allegiance, 1778. (A-1/1)

ALMERY, JOHN. Involved in evaluation of Baltimore County confiscated
proprietary reserve lands in 1782. (FFF-548)

ALTIMUS, WILLIAM. Private, Capt. Graybill's Company, German Regiment, 1776.
(H-265)

AMBROSE, ABRAHAM. Non-Juror to Oath of Allegiance, 1778. (A-1/1)

AMBROSE, JAMES. Non-Juror to Oath of Allegiance, 1778. (A-1/1)

AMBROSE, WILLIAM. Non-Juror to Oath of Allegiance, 1778. Involved
in evaluation of Baltimore County confiscated proprietary reserve
lands in 1782. (A-1/1, FFF-543)

AMBROSE, WILLIAM JR. Non-Juror to Oath of Allegiance, 1778. Involved
in evaluation of Baltimore County confiscated proprietary reserve
lands in 1782. (A-1/1, FFF-543)

AMERICA, HUGH. Private, Capt. Howell's Company, Dec. 30, 1775. (G-11)

AMEY, NICHOLAS. Non-Juror to Oath of Allegiance, 1778. (A-1/1)

AMOS, ELIZABETH, of Baltimore City. March 5, 1834 - To receive quarterly,
half pay of a Captain, in consideration of the services rendered by
her husband (name not given) during the Revolutionary War. March 16,
1840 - A deceased pensioner, all monies due her to go to Samuel B.
HUGO, her heir, of Baltimore. (C-315)

AMOS, MORDECAI. Born 1753, Baltimore County, Maryland. Died c1842,
Harrison County, Ohio. Wife, Margaret. He served in Harford Co.,
Maryland, Militia under Capt. Benjamin AMOS and Captain HUTCHINS;
was a 2nd Lt. (Pension S2034). (AAA-2335, JJJ-13; also, see Peden's
Revolutionary Patriots of Harford County, Maryland, 1775-1783, p. 5)

AMOS, THOMAS. Took Oath of Allegiance, 1778, before Hon. Jesse Dorsey.
(A-1/1, A-2/63)

ANCKLE, PETER. Private, Capt. Keeports' Company, German Regiment.
Enlisted August 25, 1776; at Philadelphia, Sept. 19, 1776. (H-263)

ANDERSON, ABRAHAM. Took Oath of Allegiance, 1778, before Hon. John Hall.
(A-1/1, A-2/36)

ANDERSON, BENJAMIN. Took Oath of Allegiance, 1778, before Hon. Jesse
Dorsey. (A-1/1, A-2/64)

ANDERSON, GEORGE. Non-Juror to Oath of Allegiance, 1778. (A-1/1)

ANDERSON, JAMES. Took Oath of Allegiance, 1778, before Hon. William
Spear. (A-1/1, A-2/67)

ANDERSON, JOHN. Private, 7th Maryland Regiment; wounded at Battle of
Katen Island, August 22, 1777. With Capt. Deams' Company, 7th Regt.
by January 28, 1777. Listed as a Recruit in Baltimore County, 1780.
Private in the Extra Regiment at Fort Whetstone Point in Baltimore,
1781. Paid three pounds, fifteen shillings, for three months half pay
due November 12, 1788. (K-93, H-305, H-340, H-626)

ANDERSON, JOSEPH. Non-Juror to Oath of Allegiance, 1778. (A-1/1)

ANDERSON, JOSHIAH. Took Oath of Allegiance, 1778. (A-1/1)

ANDERSON, JOSHUA. Ensign, Capt. J. Talbot's Company No. 4, Baltimore,
on August 26, 1776, October 28, 1776, and December 20, 1776 rolls.
Took Oath of Allegiance, 1778, before Hon. John Hall. 2nd Lieut.,
Gunpowder Upper Battalion, October 23, 1781. Involved in evaluation
of Baltimore County confiscated proprietary reserve lands in 1782.
(PPP-2, RR-99, ZZ-541, FFF-547, A-2/36, AAAA-650)

ANDERSON, NATHAN. Non-Juror to Oath of Allegiance, 1778. (A-1/1)

ANDERSON, SAMUEL. Took Oath of Allegiance, 1778, before Hon. John Beale
Howard. (A-1/1, A-2/29)

ANDERSON, THOMAS. Died in Baltimore County before June 10, 1778. His wife's name was Mary; she was probably the Mary PURDUE who married one Thomas ANDERSON on March 26, 1744. Their children were: Theresa, married George ELLIOTT in 1769; another daughter married Daniel CURTIS; and, another one married John SHEPPARD. Thomas ANDERSON took the Oath of Allegiance, 1778, before Hon. James Calhoun. (A-1/1, A-2/42, D-1)

ANDERSON, WILLIAM. Took Oath of Allegiance, 1778, before Hon. James Calhoun. Involved in evaluation of Baltimore County confiscated proprietary reserve lands in 1782. (A-1/1, A-2/42, FFF-547)

ANDREW, WILLIAM. Took Oath of Allegiance, 1778, before Hon. George Gouldsmith Presbury. (A-1/1, A-2/48)

ANDREWS, JACOB. Non-Juror to Oath of Allegiance, 1778. (A-1/1)

ANDREWS, THOMAS DR. From Harford County, Maryland. On Committee of Safety, 1774-1775. Began practice in Baltimore Town, 1776. State prover of arms, 1776. (XX-3)

ANDREWS, WENDELL (ANDREAS, VENDELL). Private, Capt. Graybill's Company, German Regiment, 1776. (H-265, ZZ-32)

ANDS, MICHAEL. Took Oath of Allegiance, 1778, before Hon. Charles Ridgely of William. Could not write; made his mark. (A-1/1, A-2/27)

ANGUS, JOHN. Baltimore Privateer and Captain of ship Caroline with 16 guns and 60 men, owned by John Wight Stanly, of Philadelphia. (III-206)

ANTHONY (ANTHENEY), MARTAIN. Took Oath of Allegiance, 1778, before Hon. John Hall. (A-1/1, A-2/36)

APPENHAMMER, ANDREW. Non-Juror to Oath of Allegiance, 1778. (A-1/1)

APPLE (APPEL), CHRISTIAN. Private, Capt. Graybill's Company, German Regiment, 1776. Took Oath of Allegiance, 1778, before Hon. George Lindenberger. (A-1/1, A-2/52, H-265)

APPLE, CHRISTIAN JR. Non-Juror to Oath of Allegiance, 1778. (A-1/1)

APPLEBY, WILLIAM. Born 1752 in America. Private. Col. Ewing's Battalion, August, 1776; enlisted July 7, 1776 in Baltimore County. Height: 5' 6¼"; black curled hair. (H-55)

APPLEGARTH, WILLIAM. Took Oath of Allegiance, 1778, before Hon. Isaac Van Bibber. (A-1/1, A-2/34)

APPLEMAN, CONRAD. Took Oath of Allegiance, 1778, before Hon. James Calhoun. (A-1/1, A-2/39)

APPOLD, ANDREW. Born c1755 in Berks or York County, Pennsylvania. Died on October 31, 1818 in Baltimore, Maryland. Married Elizabeth ODENBAUGH on December 29, 1779. Served in Baltimore County Militia. Their children: Anna Maria, born c1784; Catherine, born 1789; George, born 1791; Deitrick, born 1793; and, Elizabeth, born 1795. (XXX-124)

ARM (ARNE), JAMES. Ordinary Seaman, and QR Gunner, on the ship Defence from September 19, 1776 through 1777. (H-654)

ARMAGRASS, CHRISTIAN. Non-Juror to Oath of Allegiance, 1778. (A-1/1)

ARMAND, TUFFIN CHARLES, MARQUIS DE LA ROUERIE. From France. Colonel of 3rd Cavalry in Pulaski's Legion, May 10, 1777. Succeeded Pulaski in command of the Legion, October 11, 1779, which became Armand's Partisan Corps on October 21, 1780. Appointed Brigadier General, Continental Army, on March 26, 1783. Recognized by Congress, February 27, 1784. Died on January 30, 1793. Men from Baltimore served in his Legion. (H-593)

ARMATAGE, JAMES. Took Oath of Allegiance, 1778. (A-1/1)

ARMOR (ARMON), JOHN. Non-Juror to Oath of Allegiance, 1778. (A-1/1)

ARMSTRONG, AQUILLA. Non-Juror to Oath of Allegiance, 1778. (A-1/1)

ARMSTRONG, DAVID. Took Oath of Allegiance, 1778, before Hon. George Lindenberger. (A-1/1, A-2/52)

ARMSTRONG, DAVID. "Bondsman." Took Oath of Allegiance, 1778. (A-1/1)

ARMSTRONG, GEORGE. Non-Juror to Oath of Allegiance, 1778. (A-1/1)

ARMSTRONG, JAMES. Marine, on ship Defence, 1777. Took Oath of Allegiance, 1778, before Hon. George Lindenberger, after which he informed him that he lived in Kent County. (H-654, A-2/52)

ARMSTRONG, JEREMIAH SR. Non-Juror to Oath of Allegiance, 1778. (A-1/1)

ARMSTRONG, JOHN. Non-Juror to Oath of Allegiance, 1778. "General John Armstrong" was a pensioner on June 1, 1840, age 83, residing in household of Horatio G. Armstrong, Baltimore County, 2nd District. (A-1/1, P-127)

ARMSTRONG, MICHAEL. Took Oath of Allegiance, 1778, before Hon. Richard Cromwell. (A-1/1, A-2/46)

ARMSTRONG, NEHEMIAH. Non-Juror to Oath of Allegiance, 1778. (A-1/1)

ARMSTRONG, SOLOMON. Non-Juror to Oath of Allegiance, 1778. (A-1/1)

ARMSTRONG, THOMAS. Took Oath of Allegiance, 1778, before Hon. James Calhoun. (A-2/65)

ARMSTRONG, WILLIAM. Took Oath of Allegiance, 1778, before Hon. James Calhoun. Stored flour for the Baltimore Town Committee in 1780. (A-1/1, A-2/40, RRR-6)

ARNOLD, BENJAMIN. Non-Juror to Oath of Allegiance, 1778. (A-1/1)

ARNOLD, EDWARD. Non-Juror to Oath of Allegiance, 1778. (A-1/1)

ARNOLD, GEORGE. Took Oath of Allegiance, 1778, before Hon. John Beale Howard. Could not write; made his mark. (A-1/1, A-2/29)

ARNOLD, JACOB. Non-Juror to Oath of Allegiance, 1778. (A-1/1)

ARNOLD, JOSEPH, Non-Juror to Oath of Allegiance, 1778. (A-1/1)

ARNOLD, JOSHIAH (JOSHUA). Non-Juror to Oath of Allegiance, 1778. (A-1/1)

ARNOLD, PETER. Non-Juror to Oath of Allegiance, 1778. (A-1/1)

ARNOLD, WILLIAM. Private, Capt. S. Smith's Company No. 8, 1st Maryland Battalion, January 15, 1776. Took Oath of Allegiance, 1778. (A-1/1) (H-640)

ARON, JOHN. Supplied plank for use at Fort Whetstone Point in Baltimore, August 26, 1776. (FFF-53)

ARTHUS (ARTIS), THOMAS. Recruit, Baltimore County, 1780. Private in the Extra Regiment, Fort Whetstone Point, Baltimore, 1781. (H-340, H-627)

ASHER, ABRAHAM. Took Oath of Allegiance, 1778, before Hon. James Calhoun. (A-1/1, A-2/40)

ASHERS, JOHN. Non-Juror to Oath of Allegiance, 1778. (A-1/1)

ASHMAN, JOHN. Took Oath of Allegiance, 1778, before Hon. James Calhoun. (A-1/1, A-2/42)

ASHMORE, JOHN. Non-Juror to Oath of Allegiance, 1778. (A-1/1)

ASHWALL, WILLIAM. Private, Capt. Deams' Company, 7th Maryland Regiment, January 1, 1777. (H-305)

ASKEW, DALRYMPLE. Non-Juror to Oath of Allegiance, 1778. (A-1/1)

ASKEW, PEREGRINE (PERREY). Matross, Capt. J. Smith's Company, Maryland Artillery, 1780-1783, and part of Capt. Dorsey's Company at "Camp Col. Scirvin's" on January 28, 1782. Private, Bounty Land Warrant No. 10932, issued February 1, 1790. (H-579, UU-232, YYY-2/3, ZZ-2).

ASKINS, WILLIAM. Marine, on ship Defence, 1777. (H-654)

ASQUEW, WILLIAM. Private, Capt. McClellan's Company, September 4, 1780. (CCC-24)

ASTON, PETER. Took Oath of Allegiance, 1778, before Hon. Peter Shepherd. (A-1/1, A-2/56)

ATHENSON, WILLIAM. Non-Juror to Oath of Allegiance, 1778. (A-1/1)

ATHERTON, JAMES SR. Took Oath of Allegiance, 1778, before Hon. George Lindenberger. (A-1/1, A-2/52)

ATHERTON, JAMES JR. Took Oath of Allegiance, 1778, before Hon. George Lindenberger. (A-1/1, A-2/52)

AUBRE, JOHN. Served on ship Defence, April 1 - July 25, 1777. (H-654)

AUCHENLECK (AUCHENTECK), HENRY. Lieutenant on ship Defence, September 19, 1776 to 1777. (H-654)

AUDET, JOSEPH. Baltimore Privateer and Captain of the schooner Resource (with 14 men), owned by John Dumost of Baltimore. (III-206)

AUGUSTINE, HENRY. Took Oath of Allegiance, 1778, before Hon. James Calhoun. (A-1/1, A-2/39)

AUSTIN, ISAAC. Private, Capt. Oldham's Company, 4th Maryland Regiment, May to August, 1780. (H-80)

AUSTON, JOHN. Took Oath of Allegiance, 1778, before Hon. James Calhoun. (A-1/1, A-2/38)

AYLER, GEORGE. Took Oath of Allegiance, 1778, before Hon. Andrew Buchanan. (A-1/1, A-2/57)

AYRES (AYERS), JEREMIAH (JR.) Took Oath of Allegiance, 1778, before Hon. Jesse Dorsey. (A-1/1, A-2/64)

AYRES, JOHN. Born 1750. Son of John and Ann Ayres of Baltimore County. Private, 5th Maryland Line, 1776-1780, and also Delaware service. Pension S45226. (D-1, H-182, YY-8, ZZ-2)

AYRES, THOMAS. Born 1755. Son of John and Ann Ayres, of Baltimore County. Private, 5th Maryland Line, 1776-1780; wounded. Bounty Land Warrant 10923 and 274-60-55, issued June 9, 1789. (D-1, H-182, YY-8, ZZ-2)

B

BACKER, JOHN. Took Oath of Allegiance, 1778, before Hon. George Lindenberger. This name appears twice on the list. (A-1/1, A-2/52)

BACKLEY, JOHN. Non-Juror to Oath of Allegiance, 1778. (A-1/1)

BACKLEY, MATTHIAS. 2nd Lt. in Capt. Showers' Co., Baltimore County Militia, August 30, 1777. Non-Juror to Oath of Allegiance, 1778. (A-1/1, BBB-350)

BACON, JOHN. Born August 20, 1743. Died c1784 in Baltimore County. Son of Martin BACON and Mary WATSON. His siblings were: William, born in 1738, went to Louisville, KY; Elizabeth, born 1741, married Edward FUGATE in 1758. John BACON married Temperance HUNT, daughter of William and Elizabeth HUNT, on August 25, 1771. She was born in 1741 and died c1799. Their children were: John, born 1768 (may have been from an earlier marriage), died 1827; Mary, born 1772, died 1831? and married Gabriel HOLMES in 1793; Martin, born 1776, died 1858, married Elizabeth LYNCH in 1813; Elizabeth, born 1779, died 1807, married c1797 Thomas PEARCE. John BACON took the Oath of Allegiance, 1778, before Hon. Jesse Dorsey. (A-1/1, A-2/64, D-2)

BACQUES (BAQUES), JACQUES (JAMES). Commissioned 1st Lt. in Capt. Dorsey's Co., Maryland Artillery, Sept. 3, 1779. Also served as 1st Lt. under Lt. Col. Ed. Carrington's Continental Artillery, May 11, 1780. Later served under Capt. J. Smith's Artillery Company and under Capt. Dorsey Artillery Company, 1782-1783. Granted 200 acres for military service; western Maryland lots 1660, 1661, 1662, 1663. (H-477, H-579, UU-231, YYY-2/5, VVV-96, DDDD-1)

BAGFORD, WILLIAM. Non-Juror to Oath of Allegiance, 1778. (A-1/1)

BAGGOTT, WILLIAM. Private, Capt. Ewing's Company No. 4. Enlisted May 29, 1776. (H-11)

BAGWELL, THOMAS. Took Oath of Allegiance, 1778, before Hon. James Calhoun. (A-2/40)

BAHON (BEHON), STEPHEN. Private, Capt. McClellan's Co., Baltimore Town, Sept. 4, 1780. Took Oath of Allegiance, 1778, before Hon. James Calhoun. (A-2/39, CCC-24)

BAILEY, ELAM. 1st Lt., Baltimore County Militia Company No. 4, December 19, 1775. Captain, Hunting Ridge Company, 39th Battalion of Militia on August 29, 1777, replacing Capt. McCubbins who resigned. Captain in Baltimore Town Battalion, 1778. Took Oath of Allegiance, 1778, before Hon. Charles Ridgely of William. Baltimore County Militia rolls show "the late Capt. Elam Barley" resigned May 17 or 18, 1779. (A-1/1, G-10, E-13, A-2/27, F-309, F-311, GGG-401, Y-61, BBB-348)

BAILEY, ELEXIS. Commissioned Ensign, Capt. Lemmon's Company, in the Upper Battalion, Baltimore County Militia, Feb. 1, 1782. (CCCC-65)

BAILEY, ENOCH. Captain during the Revolutionary War. Died April 15, 1808, age 50, in Baltimore; funeral from his residence in Market Space. His only son, Enoch Fry Bailey, died in October, 1800. (ZZZ-12)

BAILEY, GEORGE. Enlisted in Baltimore County, July 20, 1776. Took Oath of Allegiance, 1778, before Hon. Charles Ridgely of William. (A-1/1, A-2/27, H-52)

BAILEY, JAMES. This James Bailey married Christiana WEIDEMAN on Jan. 31, 1791, in Baltimore County, as proven through the Maryland pension application. One James Bailey was a Drummer in the 3rd Maryland Regt. and died in 1782; another was a Sergeant in the 6th Maryland Regt. and died in 1781. Perhaps the aforementioned James Bailey was related to them, or served in the war himself. (H-524, H-527, YY-110)

BAILEY, JOHN SR. Took Oath of Allegiance, 1778, before Hon. Charles Ridgely of William. (A-1/1, A-2/27)

BAILEY, JOHN JR. Ensign, Baltimore County Militia, 4th Co., Dec. 19, 1775. 1st Lt., Militia, Sept. 13, 1776. Entered Continental Service on Aug. 29, 1777. Took Oath of Allegiance, 1778, before Hon. Peter Shepherd. (A-1/1, A-2/50, G-10, Y-61, JJ-9)

BAILEY, MATTHIAS. 2nd Lt., Upper Battalion, 1778. (E-14)

BAILEY, PHILIP. Private, Baltimore County Militia, Enlisted August 15, 1776. (H-58)

BAILEY, THOMAS. Took Oath of Allegiance, 1778, before Hon. Peter Shepherd. (A-2/49)

BAILEY, WILLIAM. Enlisted in Baltimore County, July 25, 1776. Took Oath of Allegiance, 1778, before Hon. James Calhoun. (H-52, A-1/1, A-2/38)

BAIN, JOHN. Took Oath of Allegiance, 1778, before Hon. John Beale Howard. (A-1/1, A-2/29)

BAIN, WILLIAM. Took Oath of Allegiance, 1778, before Hon. John Beale Howard. (A-1/1, A-2/29)

BAKER, CHARLES SR. Died in Baltimore County circa 1790; wife's name not known. Children, named in his will: Elizabeth, married a Mr. TOWSON; James (father of Providence and Sarah); and, Charles (father of Ann). Took the Oath of Allegiance, 1778, before Hon. John Beale Howard. Signed with his mark "B". (A-1/1, A-2/29, D-8)

BAKER, CHARLES JR. Took Oath of Allegiance, 1778, before Hon. John Beale Howard. Son of Charles Baker, Sr. above. (A-1/1, A-2/29, D-8)

BAKER, ELAM. Took Oath of Allegiance, 1778, before Hon. Charles Ridgely of Wm. (A-1/1, A-2/28)

BAKER, ELI. Non-Juror to Oath of Allegiance, 1778. (A-1/1)

BAKER, GEORGE. Bombardier, Capt. Brown's Artillery Company. Joined November 22, 1777. At Valley Forge until June, 1778. At White Plains, July, 1778. At Fort Schuyler, August-September, 1780. Not listed at High Hills of the Santee, August, 1781. (UU-228)

BAKER, GILES. Non-Juror to Oath of Allegiance in 1778, but subsequently signed in 1781. (A-1/1, QQ-105)

BAKER, ISAIAH. Took Oath of Allegiance, 1778, before Hon. James Calhoun. (A-1/1, A-2/42)

BAKER, JAMES. Non-Juror to Oath of Allegiance, 1778. (A-1/1)

BAKER, JEREMIAH. Non-Juror to Oath of Allegiance, 1778. (A-1/1)

BAKER, JOHN. Non-Juror to Oath of Allegiance, 1778, (A-1/1)

BAKER, JOSEPH. Non-Juror to Oath of Allegiance, 1778. (A-1/1)

BAKER, MARTIN. non-Juror to Oath of Allegiance, 1778. (A-1/1)

BAKER, MASHACK. Born April 27, 1733 in Baltimore County. He may have been the Mesha Baker, son of Zebediah and Keturah Baker who was born September 27, 1733 in St. Paul's Parish. Meshack died between 1778 and 1790. His wife was named Elizabeth. Children: Samuel, born 1764; Jacob, born 1766; Maurice, born 1768; Ephraim, born 1770, married Stacey REIMEY. Meshack took the Oath of Allegiance, 1778, before Hon. Edward Cockey, Feb. 28th. (A-1/1, A-2/61, D-8, XXX-133)

BAKER, NICHOLAS. Took Oath of Allegiance, 1778, before Hon. Charles Ridgely of William. (A-1/1, A-2/28)

BAKER, PETER. Private, Capt. Graybill's Company, German Regiment, July 12, 1776. (A-265, ZZ-32)

BAKER, SAMUEL. Two men with this name were Non-Jurors to the Oath, 1778. (A-1/1)

BAKER, THOMAS. Private, Capt. Ewing's Company No. 4. Enlisted January 24, 1776. Discharged June 3, 1776. (H-12)

BAKER, WILLIAM. Member of Sons of Liberty, 1776. Drafted into Baltimore
County Regiment No. 36, circa 1777. Non-Juror to Oath of Allegiance,
1778. Maryland Line defective, October 20, 1781, Baltimore Co. res.
(COC-19, TTT-13, A-1/1, H-415)

BAKER, ZACHARIAH. Took Oath of Allegiance, 1778, before Hon. James Calhoun.
(A-1/1, A-2/39)

BALCH, AMOS. (1758-1835) Applied for revolutionary pension while living in
Bedford County, Tennessee. Born in Baltimore County, Maryland. Moved
to North Carolina and enlisted in Mechlenberg County in 1779 in Captain
Richard Simmon's Company. Attached to the regular cavalry under Gen.
Washington. In the Battle of Camden. Died in Bedford County, Tenn.
Wife was Ann PATTON. Among his children were James Calvin BALCH who
married Eliza Jane HAZLETT, and John Balch who married Sarah COOK.(OO-95)

BALDWIN, SILAS. Took Oath of Allegiance, 1778, before Hon. Jesse Dorsey.
(A-1/1, A-2/63)

BALL, DANIEL CARROLL. Trooper under Capt. Nicholas Ruxton Moore, June 25,
1781; had an eight year old black mare. (BBBB-313)

BALL, THOMAS. Non-Juror to Oath of Allegiance, 1778. (A-1/1)

BALL, WILLIAM. Took Oath of Allegiance, 1778, before Hon. Jesse Dorsey.
Involved in evaluation of Baltimore County confiscated proprietary
reserve lands in 1781. (A-1/1, A-2/63, FFF-553)

BALLARD, MICHAEL. Private, Capt. J. Cockey's Baltimore County Dragoons at
Yorktown in 1781. (MMM-A)

BALLARD, ROBERT. Colonel, Baltimore City, May 19, 1782. (FFF-511)

BALSER, WILLIAM. Non-Juror to Oath of Allegiance, 1778. (A-1/1)

BALTIMORE, THOMAS. Private, Capt. Howell's Company, Dec. 30, 1775. (G-11)

BANKS, JAMES. Non-Juror to Oath of Allegiance, 1778. (A-1/1)

BANKS, JOHN JR. Non-Juror to Oath of Allegiance, 1778. (A-1/1)

BANKSON, JAMES. Took Oath of Allegiance, 1778, before Hon.George Lindenberger. Private, Capt. McClellan's Company, Baltimore Town, Sept. 4,
1780. (A-1/1, A-2/52, COC-24)

BANKSON, COL. JOHN. Died June 4, 1814 at his late residence in Baltimore.
He entered the army at the start of the Revolution and served in Canada
as a Captain. At the end of the war he was Adjutant, Brigade Major and
Inspector General of the Pennsylvania Line. For many years he was an
inhabitant of Baltimore. (ZZZ-14)

BANNEKER, BENJAMIN. Took Oath of Allegiance, 1778, before Hon. Charles
Ridgely of William. (Z-1/1, A-2/27)

BARBER, DANIEL. There were two Non-Jurors to the Oath of Allegiance, 1778,
with this name. (A-1/1)

BARBER, THOMAS. Sergeant, Capt. Brown's Artillery Company. Joined Nov. 22,
1777. At Valley Forge until June, 1778. At White Plains, July, 1776.
At Fort Schuyler, August-September, 1780; At High Hills of the Santee,
August, 1781. At Camp Col. Scirvins, January, 1782. At Bacon's Bridge,
South Carolina, in April, 1782. (UU-228, 229)

BARBETT, FRANCIS. Recruit, Baltimore County, 1780. (H-340)

BARBIERS, NICHOLAS. Took Oath of Allegiance, 1778, before Hon. James
Calhoun. (A-1/1, A-2/40)

BARBIN, MOSES. Non-Juror to Oath of Allegiance, 1778. (A-1/1)

BARDELL, CHARLES. Non-Juror to Oath of Allegiance, 1778. (A-1/1)

BARDLEY, CHARLES. Non-Juror to Oath of Allegiance, 1778. (A-1/1)

BARGER, DEETAR. Took Oath of Allegiance, 1778, before Hon. George Lindenberger. (A-1/1, A-2/52)

BARKER, MORRIS. Took Oath of Allegiance, 1778, before Hon. John Beale Howard. Could not write; made his mark. (A-2/29)

BARKER, RICHARD. Non-Juror to Oath of Allegiance, 1778. (A-1/1)

BARKER, WILLIAM. Took Oath of Allegiance, 1778, before Hon. James Calhoun. (A-1/1, A-2/41)

BARKLEY, JOHN. Recruit, Baltimore County Militia, April 11, 1780. (H-335)

BARKLEY, MATTHIAS. 2nd Lt., Capt. Showers' Company, August 30, 1777. (LL-66)

BARNABY, ELIAS. Private, Baltimore Artillery Company, Oct. 16, 1775. (G-8)

BARNARD, JAMES. Took Oath of Allegiance, 1778, before Hon. Isaac VanBibber. (A-2/34)

BARNARD, JOHN. Took Oath of Allegiance, 1778, before Hon. Isaac VanBibber. (A-1/1, A-2/34)

BARNARD, RICHARD. Took Oath of Allegiance, 1778, before Hon. Jesse Dorsey. (A-1/1, A-2/63)

BARNES, ADAM. Born 1760/61 in either Anne Arundel or Baltimore County, Maryland. Died between May 2 and June 17, 1809 in Baltimore County. Married August 5, 1784 to Ruth SHIPLEY in Baltimore County. Children: Rachel; Adam; Naomi, born 1785 in Baltimore County and died 1873 in Carroll County, married Lloyd POOL (1781-1863) on March 17, 1807 and their daughter Martha Ann (1829-1893) married Elisha GRIFFEE (1823-1875) on March 11, 1847 in Carroll County, MD; Joshua; Robert; Zachariah; Hammutal; Polly; Henry; Josiah; Margaret; Ruthy; Sarian; Samuel; Susanna; Ann; and, Cassener. Adam took the Oath of Allegiance in 1778 before Hon. Peter Shepherd, and served in the 1st Battalion, 32nd Regt. in the Maryland Militia. He was also a Sergeant in Capt. J. Cockey's Baltimore County Dragoons at Yorktown in 1781. (A-1/1, A-2/50, AAA-1936, XXX-137, MMM-A)

BARNES, ANTHONY. Born 1754 in Virginia. Occupation: Shoemaker. Height: 5' 6". Enlisted January 31, 1776, as a Private in Capt. N. Smith's 1st Company of Matrosses. Served in Capt. Dorsey's Company of Maryland Artillery, Nov. 17, 1777. (H-565, H-567, H-574, VV-73, QQQ-2)

BARNES, ELIJAH. Married Catherine SHIPLEY on August 17, 1784 in Baltimore County. (Marriage proven through Maryland pension application). Pension No. W9717. Enlisted July 20, 1776. (H-40, YY-110, ZZ-3)

BARNES, HENRY. Served on ship Defence, May 29 - July 27, 1777. (H-654)

BARNES, JAMES. Ensign, Soldiers Delight Battalion, Company No. 3, May 13, 1776. 1st Lieutenant, Capt. E. Dorsey's Company, 1778 through at least May, 1779. (E-11, FF-64, HH-24, WW-467)

BARNES, JAMES. Private, Col. Ewing's Battalion, August, 1776. Born in 1758 in America. Sandy complexion; height: 5' 5". Enlisted July 7, 1776. (H-56)

BARNES (BARNS), JAMES OF N. Took Oath of Allegiance, 1778, before Hon. Edward Cockey. (A-1/2, A-2/61)

BARNES, JOHN. Non-Juror to Oath of Allegiance, 1778. (A-1/1)

BARNES, JOHN OF NATHANIEL. Took Oath (see "John of N." listed above), 1778.

BARNES (BARNS), N. Took Oath of Allegiance, 1778. (A-1/2)

BARNES, NATHANIEL. Took Oath of Allegiance, 1778. (A-1/1)

BARNES, PHILIMON. Took Oath of Allegiance, 1778. (A-1/1)

BARNES, PHILIP. Non-Juror to Oath of Allegiance, 1778. (A-1/1)

BARNES, RICHARD. Took Oath of Allegiance, 1778. (A-1/2)

BARNES (BARNS), SIMON. Took Oath of Allegiance, 1778, before Hon. George Lindenberger. (A-2/52)

BARNES (BARNS), WILLIAM. Private, Col. Ewings' Battalion. Enlisted July 7, 1776 in Baltimore County. Not on muster roll in August, 1776. Took the Oath of Allegiance, 1778, before Hon. Jesse Dorsey. (A-1/2, A-2/63, H-57)

BARNETT, ANDREW. Non-Juror to Oath of Allegiance, 1778. (A-1/2)

BARNETT, EDWARD. non-Juror to Oath of Allegiance, 1778. (A-1/2)

BARNETT, JOHN. Private, Baltimore County Militia. Enlisted July 5, 1776. Private, Capt. J. Cockey's Baltimore County Dragoons at Yorktown, 1781. (H-58, H-59, MMM-A)

BARNETT, WILLIAM. Private, Capt. J. Cockey's Baltimore County Dragoons at Yorktown, 1781. (MMM-A)

BARNEY, ABSALOM (SALOM). Non-Juror to Oath of Allegiance, 1778. (A-1/2)

BARNEY, ABSALOM (SALOM), JR. Non-Juror to Oath of Allegiance, 1778. (A-1/2)

BARNEY, BENJAMIN. Took Oath of Allegiance, 1778, before Hon. Geo. Lindenberger. (A-1/2, A-2/52)

BARNEY, JOHN. Took Oath of Allegiance, 1778, before Hon. William Spear. (A-1/2, A-2/66)

BARNEY, JOSHUA. Born July 6, 1759 in Baltimore and died December 1, 1818 in Pittsburgh. Son of William BARNEY and Frances HOLLAND. When he was a year old they moved to Bear Creek on Patapsco Neck about eight miles from Balto. He quit school at age 10, had various jobs in Baltimore, and at age 14 went to sea. He was one of the first officers in the Navy and engaged in many battles with the British. In Octobr, 1775, he was appointed Master's Mate 2nd Officer of the sloop Hornet. Mrs. Mary Chase Barney, in her Memoir of Commodore Barney, says: "A crew had not yet been shipped, and the duty of recruiting one was assigned to Barney. Fortunately for his purpose, just at this moment a new American flag, sent by Commodore Hopkins for the service of the Hornet, arrived from Philadelphia. Nothing could have been more opportune or acceptable. It was the first continental flag that had been seen in the State of Maryland; and, next morning at sunrise, Barney had the enviable honor of unfurling it to the music of drums and fifes, and hoisting it upon a staff, planted with his own hands at the door of his rendezvous. The heart-stirring sounds of the martial instruments, then a novel incident in Baltimore, and the still more novel sight of the rebel colors gracefully waving in the breeze, attracted crowds of all ranks and eyes to the gay scene of the rendezvous, and before the setting of the same day's sun, the young recruiting officer had enlisted a full crew of jolly rebels for the Hornet." Barney was transferred to the Wasp in March, 1776. After the capture of the British tender (ship) in the Delaware, he was made a Lieutenant in the Navy of the United Colonies. Subsequently, he was captured on April 1, 1776 by the frigate Emerald and was held on the Eastern Shore of Maryland at Sinepuxent. Following his release he became a member of the Baltimore Mechanical Company in 1777, but continued his naval service as well. In the spring of 1782 he was given command of the Hyder Ally of 16 guns and off Cape May fought and captured the British vessel General Monk of 20 guns. He left the service in July, 1784, the last officer to leave the Navy. From 1795 to 1802 he was in the French

Navy, first as Capitaine de Vaisseau, later as Capitaine de Vaisseau Premier, a rank similar to America's Commodore. He re-entered the U. S. Navy in 1813, rendered distinguished service in the War of 1812, and resigned in 1815. He died at Pittsburgh in 1818 and is buried in the Presbyterian Cemetery there. Barney married first to Ann BEDFORD and had a son, William Bedford Barney, who married first to Rebecca RIDGELY and second to Mary CHASE. Barney's second marriage was to Mrs. Harriet COLE (COALE) in April, 1809. (TT-53, UUU-7, III-201, III-202, III-203, III-209, JJJ-38, CCC-14, XXX-138, ZZZ-19)

BARNEY, MOSES. Private, Capt. Deams' Company, 7th Maryland Regiment, Dec. 21, 1776. Received 50 acres for service (lot #1360). (H-305, DDDD-6)

BARNEY, THOMAS. Enlisted in Baltimore Town, July 20, 1776. (H-53)

BARNEY, WILLIAM. Officer in the Marines in 1776; brother of Joshua Barney. (III-203)

BARNEY, WILLIAM. In 1781 a William Barney was drafted and his mother Sarah sent a petition to the Governor of Maryland to have him released. (FFF-350)

BARNITZ, DANIEL (ANNUAL?) Took Oath of Allegiance, 1778, before Hon. William Lux. (A-1/2, A-2/68)

BARNOVER, GEORGE. Private, Revolutionary Army of Baltimore County, pensioned on May 1, 1820, at $96 per year from November 13, 1814, had died Nov. 4, 1818. (C-318, O-4)

BARR, JOHN. Coxswain and Boatswain on ship Defence in 1776-1777. (H-654)

BARRANCE, JAMES. Served on ship Defence, July 5 - September 22, 1777. Took Oath of Allegiance, 1778. (A-1/2, H-654)

BARREN, JAMES. Took Oath of Allegiance, 1778, before Hon. George Lindenberger. (A-1/2. A-2/52)

BARREN, ROBERT. Took Oath of Allegiance, 1778, before Hon. George Lindenberger. (A-1/2, A-2/52)

BARRETT, JOHN. Served on ship Defence, January 25 - December 31, 1777. (H-654)

BARRETT (BARET), JOSEPH. Took Oath of Allegiance, 1778, before Hon. William Spear. Could not write; made his mark. (A-2/67)

BARRETT, JOSHUA. Private, Capt. Oldham's Company, 4th Maryland Regt., Dec. 18, 1776; Sergeant, June 1, 1779 until August 16, 1780. Received Bounty Land Warrant #10954 on February 7, 1790. Also received 50 acres (lot #101) in western Maryland. (H-87, ZZ-3, DDDD-6)

BARRETT, ROGER. Non-Juror to Oath of Allegiance, 1778. (A-1/2)

BARRETT, THOMAS. Took Oath of Allegiance, 1778, before Hon. George Lindenberger. (A-1/2, A-2/52)

BARRETT, TOBIAS. Took Oath of Allegiance, 1778, before Hon. James Calhoun. (A-1/2, A-2/42)

BARREY, EDWARD. Born 1742 in Ireland. Occupation: Silk Weaver. Height: 5' 5½" Enlisted January 25, 1776 as Private, Capt. N. Smith's 1st Company of Matrosses. (H-564)

BARREY, JAMES. Born 1742 in Ireland, Occupation: Labourer. Height: 5' 10¼" Enlisted January 27, 1776 as Private in Captain N. Smith's 1st Company of Matrosses. (H-564)

BARROW, JOHN. Took Oath of Allegiance, 1778, before Hon. Jesse Dorsey. (A-1/2, A-2/63)

BARROW, JOHN JR. Took Oath of Allegiance, 1778, before Hon. Jesse Dorsey. (A-1/1, A-2/63)

BARRY (BERRY), EDWARD. Private, Capt. N. Smith's 1st Company of Maryland
Artillery, June 29, 1776. Private, Capt. Dorsey's Company, Maryland
Artillery, November 17, 1777. Matross, Capt. J. Smith's Company of
Maryland Artillery, 1780. Matross, Capt. Dorsey's Company, Maryland
Artillery at Camp Col. Scirvins, January 28, 1782. (H-567, H-574,
H-579, UU-232, VV-73, QQQ-2)

BARRY (BERRY), JAMES. Private, Capt. N. Smith's 1st Company of Maryland
Artillery, June 29, 1776. Private, Capt. Dorsey's Company, Maryland
Artillery, November 17, 1777. Matross, Capt. Dorsey's Company at
Valley Forge, June 3, 1778. (H-566, 574, UU-231, VV-74, QQQ-2)

BARRY, MICHAEL. Took Oath of Allegiance, 1778, before Hon. James Calhoun.
(A-1/2, A-2/39)

BARRY, SAMUEL. Took Oath of Allegiance, 1778, before Hon. George Lindenberger.
(A-1/2, A-2/52)

BARTLETT, ARCHIBALD. Private, Capt. J. Gist's Company, 3rd Maryland Regiment,
February, 1778. (H-600)

BARTON, ASAEL. Non-Juror to Oath of Allegiance, 1778. (A-1/2)

BARTON, BENJAMIN. Took Oath of Allegiance, 1778, before Hon. Charles Ridgely
of William. Could not write; made his mark. (A-1/2, A-2/28)

BARTON, CHARLES. Took Oath of Allegiance, 1778, before Hon. Charles Ridgely
of William. (A-1/2, A-2/28)

BARTON, GRENNBURY. Non-Juror to Oath of Allegiance, 1778. (A-1/2)

BARTON, JAMES. Non-Juror to Oath of Allegiance, 1778. (A-1/2)

BARTON, SELAH. Non-Juror to Oath of Allegiance, 1778. (A-1/2)

BASEMAN, GEORGE. Private, Baltimore County Regiment No. 7, c1777. (TTT-13)

BASFORD, WILLIAM. Private, Capt. Ramsey's Company No. 5, 1776. (H-640)

BASIL, WILLIAM. Non-Juror to Oath of Allegiance, 1778. (A-1/2)

BASKER, MORRIS. Took Oath of Allegiance, 1778. (A-1/2)

BAST, JOHN. Private, Capt. Howell's Company in Baltimore, December 30, 1775.
Took Oath of Allegiance, 1778, before Hon. William Spear. (A-1/2, A-2/67,
G-11)

BAST, PETER. Private, Capt. Keeports German Regiment. Enlisted August 6, 1776.
At Philadelphia, September 19, 1776. (H-263)

BATCHOLOR, JAMES. Non-Juror to Oath of Allegiance, 1778. (A-1/2)

BATES, JOHN. Took Oath of Allegiance, 1778, before Hon. Peter Shepherd.
(A-1/2, A-2/49)

BATTERY, THOMAS. Non-Juror to Oath of Allegiance, 1778. (A-1/2)

BATTS, JOHN. Took Oath of Allegiance, 1778, before Hon. Charles Ridgely of
William. (A-1/2, A-2/28)

BATTY (BATTEE), FERDINAND (FERDINANDO). Non-Juror to Oath of Allegiance, 1778.
Died in Baltimore County in 1783; wife's name unknown. Children: John;
Mary; Ferdinand; Dinah; Philip; Elizabeth, married Vachel DORSEY in 1778.
(A-1/2, D-2)

BAUER, JOHN. Private, Capt. Keeeports' German Regiment. Enlisted July 23, 1776.
At Philadelphia, September 19, 1776. (H-263)

BAWMAN, ANDREW. Non-Juror to Oath of Allegiance, 1778. (A-1/2)

BAWSEL, JAMES. Non-Juror to Oath of Allegiance, 1778. (A-1/2)

BAXLEY, JOHN. Born July 15, 1743 in Yorkshire, England. Died December 2, 1799 in Baltimore County, Maryland. Married Mary SPROUL (1741-1804) of Baltimore Co. on August 10, 1763 in Wilmington, Delaware. A son, George BAXLEY (1771-1848) married Mary MERRYMAN (1775-1834) in 1793, and their son Jackson Brown BAXLEY (1814-1896) married Gertrude HYNE (1837-1891) in 1865. John Baxley served as Quartermaster of Col. Samuel Owings' Soldiers Delight Battalion of Baltimore County; commissisoned June 3, 1777. He ground a wagon load of flour at his mill on the Little Gunpowder River at Jerusalem Mills in Harford Co. (formerly part of Baltimore County) and drove the wagon to Washington himself at Valley Forge during the winter of 1777-1778. John took the Oath of Allegiance, 1778, before the Hon. James Calhoun. In 1781 his name appears on a list of owners of wagons employed in public service at the port of Baltimore by David Poe, A.D.Q.M., War Department, Washington DC. Family tradition says John Baxley took Gen. Lafayette to his home and nursed him when he was sick. (AAA-2001) (AAA-2001, JJJ-44, BBB-271, A-1/2, A-2/41)

BAXTER, JOHN. Non-Juror to Oath of Allegiance, 1778. (A-1/2)

BAXTER, JOSEPH. Elected 2nd Lt. in Capt. Ewing's Company No. 4, Maryland Troops, on January 2, 1776, but that position was vacant on January 3, 1776 (probably resigned). Served as Sheriff of Cecil County, Maryland, and died at Elkton on May 6, 1809. Obituary states "he stepped forth to command early in our Revolutionary struggle." (H-11, ZZZ-20)

BAXTER, PATRICK. Private, Capt. Ewing's Co. #4. Enlisted Jan. 24, 1776. (H-12)

BAXTER, SAMUEL. Private, Baltimore County Militia; enlisted August 15, 1776. Took Oath of Allegiance, 1778, before Hon. Robert Simmons. (A-1/2, A-2/58, H-58, H-59)

BAXTER, WILLIAM. Non-Juror to Oath of Allegiance, 1778. (A-1/2)

BAYLEY, THOMAS. Took the Oath of Allegiance, 1781. (QQ-105)

BAYLEY, WILLIAM. Took the Oath of Allegiance, 1781. (QQ-105)

BAYLISS, JAMES. Recruit, Baltimore County Militia, April 11, 1780. (H-335)

BAZIL, EZEKIEL, Took Oath of Allegiance, 1778, before Hon. Charles Ridgely of William. (A-1/2, A-2/27)

BEACHUM (BEACHAM), WILLIAM. Private, Capt. McClellan's Co., Baltimore Town, September 4, 1780. Non-Juror to Oath of Allegiance, 1778. (A-1/2, CCC-24)

BEACHUM (BEAUCHAMP), WILLIAM. Carpenter's Mate on ship Defence, 1776-1777. (H-607, H-654)

BEAL, THOMAS. Non-Juror to Oath of Allegiance, 1778. (A-1/2)

BEAM, GEORGE. Non-Juror to Oath of Allegiance, 1778. (A-1/2)

BEAM, PHILIP. Took Oath of Allegiance, 1778, before Hon. Richard Cromwell. (A-1/2. A-2/46)

BEAR, JOSEPH. Born in 1747 in Nova Scotia. Occupation: Labourer. Ht: 5' 6½" Enlisted Jan. 30, 1776 as Private, Capt. N. Smith's Matross Co. #1. (H-565)

BEARD, JOHN ADAM. Non-Juror to Oath of Allegiance, 1778. (A-1/2)

BEARD, MARTIN. Non-Juror to Oath of Allegiance, 1778. (A-1/2)

BEARD, WILLIAM DR. Practiced in Annapolis, Anne Arundel County, Maryland. Removed to Baltimore in 1776. Became Assistant Surgeon to Dr. Wiesenthal on State ship Defence, 1776. Took Oath of Allegiance, 1778, before Hon. George Lindenberger. (A-1/2. A-2/52, XX-4)

BEARHAM (BEARMAN), FREDERICK. Non-Juror to Oath of Allegiance, 1778. (A-1/2)

BEASING, JAMES. Took Oath of Allegiance, 1778, before Hon. Peter Shepherd. (A-1/2, A-2/50)

BEASMAN, JOHN. Non-Juror to Oath of Allegiance, 1778. (A-1/2)

BEASMAN, JOSEPH. Took Oath of Allegiance, 1778, before Hon. Peter Shepherd. (A-1/2, A-2/50)

BEASMAN, THOMAS. Took Oath of Allegiance, 1778, before Hon. Edward Cockey. (A-1/2, A-2/61)

BEATY, PHILOP. Private, Count Pulaski's Legion. Enlisted in Baltimore on May 11, 1778. (H-593)

BEAVER, JOHN. Took Oath of Allegiance, 1778, before Hon. Peter Shepherd. (A-1/2, A-2/49)

BECKLEY, HENRY. Took Oath of Allegiance, 1778. (A-1/2)

BECROFT (BECRAFT), JOHN. Private, Rawlings' Regiment; discharged July 1, 1779. Ordered in December, 1816, that he be paid, an old Revolutionary soldier of Baltimore County, quarterly, half pay of a Private, "as a further re- muneration to him for those services by which his country has been so essentially benefitted." (C-319, B-90)

BEDDISON, DANIEL. Non-Juror to Oath of Allegiance, 1778. (A-1/2)

BEDDISON, SHADRICK. Non-Juror to Oath of Allegiance, 1778. (A-1/2)

BEDDISON, THOMAS. Non-Juror to Oath of Allegiance, 1778. (A-1/2)

BEDDISON, THOMAS SR. Non-Juror to Oath of Allegiance, 1778. (A-1/2)

BEDDISON, THOMAS JR. Non-Juror to Oath of Allegiance, 1778. (A-1/2)

BEEDLE, WILLIAM. Took Oath of Allegiance, 1778, before Hon. James Calhoun. (A-2/65)

BEGEL, CHRISTOPHER. Private, Capt. Graybill's Germant Regiment, July 12, 1776. (ZZ-32)

BEGLEY, GEORGE. Private, Capt. Lansdale's Company, 4th Maryland Regiment, May 9, 1777 - August 16, 1780. Was a prisoner. (H-87)

BEHON, DEFFIN. Took Oath of Allegiance, 1778. (A-1/2)

BELEVIT,_____. On May 20, 1780, Matthew Ridgely of Baltimore County, wrote to the Governor of Maryland in reference to Mr. Belevit's desire to enter the military. (FFF-292)

BELL, EDWARD. Took Oath of Allegiance, 1778, before Hon. Richard Cromwell. (A-1/2, A-2/46)

BELL (BEALL), JOHN. Born 1753 in Baltimore County. Married April 6, 1773 to Catherine DOYLE (1756-1861) in Baltimore. (Marriage proven through Mary- land pension application). He served in 6th Maryland Regiment under Capt. Ghiselin, July 1, 1778 to April, 1779. He also took the Oath of Allegiance in 1778 before Hon. Richard Cromwell. He died August 11, 1826 in Baltimore County. Children: Susanna, Richard, John, Isaiah, Jehu, Jesse, Clarice, Cecilius, Edward, Mary, Harriet, and Sidney. (A-1/2, A-2/46, YY-110,XXX-149)

BELL, NATHANIEL. Non-Juror to Oath of Allegiance, 1778. (A-1/2)

BELL, RICHARD. Took Oath of Allegiance, 1778, before Hon. Richard Cromwell. (A-1/2, A-2/46)

BELL, WILLIAM SR. Took Oath of Allegiance, 1778, before Hon. Richard Cromwell. (A-1/2, A-2/46)

BELL, WILLIAM JR. Born April 6, 1744 in Baltimore County. Married Eva or Eve circa 1770. She was born in 1749 and died in 1812. William was a son of William and Sarah BELL. He took the Oath of Allegiance, 1778, before Hon. James Calhoun. Children: Richard (1774-1850) was a Sergeant in the War of 1812 and married Catharine LEAF (1781-1854) in 1799, and had a daughter Sarah Isabella (1821-1893) who married Thomas Sander CLARK (1809-1888) in 1843; William; George; Edward; Elizabeth; Mary; Rebecca; and another daughter who married a YOUNG. (A-1/2, A-2/42, AAA-1424, XXX-149)

BELLAMY, JOHN. Maryland Line defective, March 15, 1781; resident of Baltimore County. (H-415)

BELLSON (BELSON), JOHN. Took Oath of Allegiance, 1778, before Hon. Peter Shepherd. (A-1/2, A-2/50)

BELT, JAMES. Baltimore Privateer and Captain of ship Matilda with 22 guns and 70 men (owned by John Dorsey and Company of Baltimore). (III-206)

BELT, JOHN. Non-Juror to Oath of Allegiance, 1778. Involved in evaluation of Baltimore County confiscated proprietary reserve lands, 1782. (FFF-543, A-1/2)

BELT, JOSEPH. Non-Juror to Oath of Allegiance, 1778. (A-1/2)

BELT, LEONARD. Took Oath of Allegiance 1778, before Hon. James Calhoun. Involved in evaluation of Baltimore County confiscated proprietary reserve lands in 1782. (A-1/2, A-2/42, FFF-543)

BELT, NATHAN. Non-Juror to Oath of Allegiance, 1778. (A-1/2)

BELT, RICHARD. Non-Juror to Oath of Allegiance, 1778. (A-1/2)

BENDER, PHILIP. Involved in evaluation of Baltimore County confiscated proprietary reserve lands in 1782. (FFF-553)

BENNETT, BENJAMIN. Took Oath of Allegiance, 1778, before Hon. John Moale. (A-1/2, A-2/70)

BENNETT, EDWARD. Took Oath of Allegiance, 1778, before Hon. George Lindenberger. (A-1/2, A-2/52)

BENNETT, ELISAH. Took Oath of Allegiance, 1778, before Hon. John Moale. (A-1/2) (A-2/70)

BENNETT, EMUL. Took Oath of Allegiance, 1778. (A-1/2)

BENNETT, GEORGE. Private, Capt. S. Smith's Company No. 8, 1st MD Battalion, January 24, 1776. (H-641)

BENNETT, GEORGE. Served on ship Defence, May 19 - July 23, 1777. (H-654)

BENNETT, JAMES. Private, Capt. Ewing's Co. No. 4. Enlisted May 27, 1776. (H-11)

BENNETT, JOEL. Born 1753 in West New Jersey. Occupation: Shoemaker. Ht: 5' 7½" Enlisted January 24, 1776 as Private in Capt. N. Smith's 1st Co. of Matrosses in Baltimore County. Private, Capt. Dorsey's Co., Maryland Artillery, on November 17, 1777. Matross soldier in Baltimore County, May 7, 1779 (gave a deposition on enlistment terms). (H-563, H-566, H-574, VV-73, FFF-220, QQQ-2)

BENNETT (BENNIT), JOHN. Recruit in Baltimore County, 1780. Wounded in Battle of Camden, August 16, 1780. Private, 2nd Maryland Regiment. Received half-pay on August 9, 1785 (7 lbs., 10 shillings) and again on February 23, 1786. He received six more payments between February 14, 1787 and August 11, 1789. (J-215, J-244, J-260, H-340, K-2, K-31, K-51, K-75, K-96, K-120)

BENNETT, JOSHUA. Non-Juror to Oath of Allegiance, 1778. Private, Capt. McClellan Company, Baltimore Town, September 4, 1780. (A-1/2, CCC-25)

BENNETT, PETER. Took Oath of Allegiance, 1778, before Hon. John Moale. (A-2/70)

BENNETT, SAMUEL. Took Oath of Allegiance, 1778, before Hon. John Moale. (A-2/70)

BENNETT, THOMAS. Took Oath of Allegiance, 1778, before Hon. John Moale. (A-2/70)

BENNETT, WILLIAM. Non-Juror to Oath of Allegiance, 1778. (A-1/2)

BENNEX, BARNEY. Non-Juror to Oath of Allegiance, 1778. (A-1/2)

BENNEX, BARNETT. Involved in evaluation of Baltimore County confiscated proprietary reserve lands in 1782. (FFF-555)

BENNITT, WILLIAM. Non-Juror to Oath of Allegiance, 1778. (A-1/2)

BENNY, JAMES. Born 1750 in America. Long black hair; height: 5' 6". Private, Col. Ewing's Battalion; enlisted July 5, 1776, Baltimore County. (H-56)

BENNYWRIGHT, AD. Private, Capt. Cox's Company, December 19, 1776. (CCC-22)

BENSON, EDWARD. Private, Capt. Deams' Co., 7th Md., Dec. 25, 1776. (H-305)

BENTALOU, PAUL. 2nd Lt., German Regiment, September 25, 1776. 1st Lt., German Regiment, June 21, 1777. Resigned, December 10, 1777. Member of Baltimore Mechanical Company. Captain in Pulaski's Legion, April 12, 1778. Wounded at Savannah, October 9, 1779. Retired, June 1, 1781. Referred to as "Colonel" in Scharf's Chronicles of Baltimore in the list of notables welcoming Lafayette to Baltimore in 1824. Paul died at Baltimore, September 26, 1826 from a fall in a warehouse. There is a street in West Baltimore named for him. He was an Original Member of the Society of the Cincinnati in Maryland. (TT-57, CCC-25)

BENTON, THOMAS. Carpenter on ship Defence, February 11 - July 26, 1777. (H-654)

BERMINGHAM (BIRMINGHAM), CHRISTOPER. Account and receipt for board to John Burnell at Fell's Point in Baltimore on February 27, 1777. Served on ship Defence as Captain of Tender, in 1777. Took Oath of Allegiance, 1778, before Hon. James Calhoun. (A-1/2, A-2/42, H-654, FFF-92)

BERNEY, H. Sergeant in Capt. McClellan's Company, September 4, 1780. (CCC-23)

BERRY, EDWARD. Matross in Capt. Graybill's Company of Artillery, 1779-1780, and in Capt. Smith's Artillery, 1782-1783. Received 50 acres (lot #4104) in western Maryland. (DDDD-6, YYY-1/8, YYY-2/6)

BERRY, GEORGE. Born 1759 in America. Short hair; height: 5' 5". Private in Col. Ewing's Battalion; enlisted July 7, 1776, Baltimore County. Non-Juror to Oath of Allegiance, 1778. (H-55, A-1/2)

BERRY, JAMES. Marine on ship Defence, 1777. (H-654)

BERRY, JOHN. Non-Juror to Oath of Allegiance, 1778. (A-1/2)

BERRY, PATRICK. Private, Baltimore Artillery Company, Oct. 16, 1775. (G-8)

BERRY, THOMAS. Non-Juror to Oath of Allegiance, 1778. (A-1/2)

BERRY, WILLIAM. Non-Juror to Oath of Allegiance, 1778. (A-1/2)

BERRYMAN, JOHN. Gunner on ship Defence, September 19, 1776 and January 13 to December 31, 1777. (H-654)

BERSIL, JOHN. Took Oath of Allegiance, 1778, before Hon. James Calhoun. (A-2/41)

BERTHAUD, ADAM. 3rd Lt., Capt. Fulford's Matross Co., July 16, 1776. (ZZ-62)

BETSON (BETTSON), GEORGE. Born 1760 in America. Short hair; height: 5' 7". Private, Col. Ewing's Battalion; enlisted July 5, 1776, Baltimore Co. (H-57)

BETTIS, WILLIAM. Non-Juror to Oath of Allegiance, 1778. (A-1/2)

BEVAN, JESSE. Non-Juror to Oath of Allegiance, 1778. (A-1/2)

BEVAN, JOHN. Non-Juror to Oath of Allegiance, 1778. (A-1/2)

BEVIN, BENJAMIN. Non-Juror to Oath of Allegiance, 1778. (A-1/2)

BEYER, GEORGE. Took Oath of Allegiance, 1778, before Hon. George Lindenberger.
(A-1/2, A-2/52)

BIALIS, SAMUEL. Took Oath of Allegiance, 1778, before Hon. Isaac VanBibber.(A-2/34)

BIAYS (BYAS), JAMES. Born 1760 in Philadelphia. Died July 30, 1822 in Baltimore
County. Married Sarah JACKSON (1769-1845) in June, 1784. A daughter, Fanny
(1807-1871) married Henry HAMMOND (1805-1850) in 1827, and their daughter
Fanny Biays Hammond (1835-1899) married James MAHOOL (1828-1876) in 1856.
James BIAYS was a Private in Capt. Rhoads' Co., PA Line, 6th Battalion, 1777,
7th Class, and a Private, Capt. Griffith's Co., 3rd MD Regiment, 1777-1779,
and a Private, Capt. Wilmott's Co., 3rd MD Regiment, Dec., 1779 - Jan.19,1780.
Received 50 acres (lot #1139) in western MD. (AAA-690, AAA-1067, H-296,DDDD-7)

BIAYS (BYAS), JOSEPH. Born June 30, 1753 in either Philadelphia or Frederick Co.,
MD. Died July 19, 1822 in Baltimore. Married first a McMULLEN, 1777, (1758-
1796) and second to Elizabeth MAY on March 25, 1797. Daughter Susanna md. a
William BROWN, Jr. in Baltimore on June 21, 1810. Daughter Rachel md. a John
Adams WEBSTER (1787-1877) in February, 1816; he was a former Naval Captain.
Their son, John Adams WEBSTER, Jr. (1825-1875) married Amelia Ross PATTERSON
(1827-1904). Joseph BYAS signed the Oath of Allegiance, 1778, before Hon.
George Lindenberger. Also served as 3rd Lt., Baltimore Town Battalion, on
September 4, 1777. Subsequently, became a Captain; later in life referred
to as Colonel. (A-2/52, E-13, AAA-1452A, BBB-362, JJJ-57, XXX-154, ZZZ-42)

BICKHAM, JAMES. Recruit, Baltimore County, 1780. (H-340)

BIDDLE, RICHARD. Recruit, Baltimore County, 1780. Private; pension S34651.
Issued Bounty Land Warrant No. 10955-100 on March 22, 1797. (H-340, ZZ-4)

BIDWELL, RICHARD. Private, Capt. Sellman's Company, 4th Maryland Regiment, from
December 6, 1776 to December 6, 1779, when discharged after completing three
years. In December, 1816, he was paid, an old soldier of Baltimore, during
his life, half pay of a Private, quarterly, as further compensation for his
services during the Revolutionary War. (C-320, B-87)

BIGLER, JACOB. Private, Capt. Keeport's German Regiment. Enlisted August 1, 1776.
At Philadelphia, September 19, 1776. (H-263)

BIGGS, NATHAN. Enlisted July 25, 1776, in Baltimore County. (H-52)

BINTZIL, BALCHER. Took Oath of Allegiance, 1778, before Hon. James Calhoun.
(A-1/2, A-2/39)

BIRD, SAMUEL. Marine on ship Defence, April 2 to November 7, 1777. (H-654)

BIRNIE, HUGH. Took Oath of Allegiance, 1778, before Hon. George Lindenberger.
Supplied barrels and hoops for the military in 1780. (A-2/52, RRR-6)

BIRSSON, RENE. Captain who wrote to the Governor of Maryland on May 3, 1780,
requesting authorization to seize deserters in Baltimore City. (FFF-288)

BISCOE, MACKIE. Served on ship Defence, May 19 to June 1, 1777. (H-654)

BISHOP, WILLIAM. Marine on ship Defence, 1777. Non-Juror to Oath of
Allegiance, 1778, but did sign in 1781. (H-654, A-1/2, QQ-105)

BITTING, PHILIP. 4th Corpl.in Capt. Keeport's German Regiment; enlisted on
July 21, 1776; at Philadelphia, September 19, 1776. (H-262)

BLACK, CASER. Non-Juror to Oath of Allegiance, 1778. (A-1/2)

BLACK, DAVID. Took Oath of Allegiance, 1778, before Hon. James Calhoun.
(A-1/2, A-2/42)

BLACK, JOSHUA. Took Oath of Allegiance, 1778, before Hon, Charles Ridgely
of William. Could not write; made his mark. (A-1/2, A-2/27)

BLACK, MOSES SR. Oath of Allegiance, 1778, before Hon. Charles Ridgely of William. Could not write; made his mark. (A-1/2, A-2/27)

BLACK, MOSES JR. Oath of Allegiance, 1778, before Hon. Charles Ridgely of William. Could not write; made his mark. (A-1/2, A-2/27)

BLACKBURN, JOHN. Recruit, Baltimore County, 1780. (H-340)

BLACKMAN, STEPHEN. Seaman on ship Defence, Jan. 11 to Dec. 31, 1777. (H-654)

BLACKROD, HENRY. Oath of Allegiance, 1778, before Hon. James Calhoun. (A-2/39)

BLADE, JAMES. Non-Juror to Oath of Allegiance, 1778. (A-1/2)

BLADE, JOSEPH. Oath of Allegiance, 1778. (A-1/2)

BLAKE, ALEX. Private, Capt. Dorsey's Co., MD Artillery, Nov. 17, 1777. (H-574)

BLAKE, JOHN. Boatswain, January 13 to June 17, 1777, and Quartermaster, June 17 to December 31, 1777, on ship Defence. (H-654)

BLAKNEY (BLACKNEY), JOHN. Born 1756 in Ireland. Short black hair; ht: 5' 3" Private, Col. Ewing's Battalion; enlisted July 5, 1776, Baltimore Co. (H-56)

BLANG, PETER. Private, 4th MD Regt. at Ft. Whetstone Pt., Baltimore, 1776.(H-626)

BLATCHLY, THOMAS. Oath of Allegiance, 1778, before Hon. George Lindenberger. (A-1/2, A-2/52)

BLAZE, ISAAC. Non-Juror to Oath of Allegiance, 1778. (A-1/2)

BLEAK, NATHAN. Private, Capt. S. Smith's Co. No. 8, 1st MD Battalion, Jan. 24, 1776. (H-640)

BLECK (BLECH), JOSEPH. Oath of Allegiance, 1778, before Hon. George Lindenberger. (A-1/2, A-2/52)

BLITHEN, JOHN. Corporal of Marines on ship Defence, May 12 to August 13, 1777. (H-654)

BLIZZARD, JOHN. Non-Juror to Oath of Allegiance, 1778. (A-1/2)

BLIZZARD, WILLIAM. Born 1730 in Baltimore County. Married Luranah_____ (1735, France - 1816, Baltimore County) on May 19, 1751 at Fort Garrison in Baltimore County. Died in March, 1810, with burial in the Blizzard Family Cemetery at Woodensburg, Baltimore County, MD. A son, William (1774-1816) married Ruth TAYLOR (1779-1814) on May 19, 1802 in Baltimore County; their daughter, Luranah Rachel BLIZZARD (1804-1891) married John O'K. BLIZZARD (1807 - 1850, California) on November 21, 1828 in Baltimore County, MD. William Blizzard took the Oath of Allegiance, 1778, before Hon. James Calhoun. (A-1/2, A-2/42, AAA-2792, AAA-1840)

BLOCK, ANDREW. Non-Juror to Oath of Allegiance, 1778. (A-1/2)

BLOCK, JOHN. Non-Juror to Oath of Allegiance, 1778. (A-1/2)

BLUM, PETER. Oath of Allegiance, 1778, before Hon. George Lindenberger. (A-1/2, A-2/52)

BLUNT, CHARLES. Ordinary Seaman, September 19, 1776, and Marine in 1777, on ship Defence. (H-606, H-654)

BOAGER (BOGER), JACOB. Born 1755 in Pennsylvania. Occupation: Carpenter. Height: 5' 5 3/4". Enlisted January 31, 1776 as a Private in Capt. N. Smith's 1st Company of Matrosses. (H-565, H-567, VV-74, QQQ-2)

BOAS, HENRY. Oath of Allegiance, 1778, before Hon. Frederick Decker. (A-1/2, A-2/31)

BODAR, JOHN. Oath of Allegiance, 1778, before Hon. William Spear. (A-1/2, A-2/66)

BODDEN, JOHN. Private, Capt. Sheaff's Company, June 16, 1777. (W-162)

BODLEY, THOMAS. Private, Capt. McClellan's Co., September 4, 1780. (CCC-24)

BODY, STEPHEN. Private, Baltimore Co. Militia; enlisted July 19, 1776. (H-58)

BOEHLER, DANIEL. Private, Capt. Keeport's German Regiment; enlisted August 5, 1776. At Philadelphia, September 19, 1776. (H-263)

BOEHM, CONRAD. Private, Capt. Keeport's German Regiment; enlisted July 26, 1776. At Philadelphia, September 19, 1776. (H-263)

BOEHM, PHILLIP. Private, Capt. Keeport's German Regiment; enlisted July 30, 1776. At Philadelphia, September 19, 1776. (H-263)

BOES, JACOB. Non-Juror to Oath of Allegiance, 1778. (A-1/2)

BOLCHLOB, CHARLES. Recruit, Baltimore County, 1780. (H-340)

BOLTON, FRANCIS. Oath of Allegiance, 1778, before Hon. James Calhoun. (A-2/40)

BOLTON, JOHN. Recruit, Baltimore County, 1780. (H-340)

BOLTON, RICHARD. Non-Juror to Oath of Allegiance, 1778. (A-1/2)

BOLTON, THOMAS. Account and receipt for maps to Capt. George Cook in Baltimore on February 22, 1777. (FFF-91)

BOLTON, WILLIAM. Stored flour for the Baltimore Town Committee, February, 1780. Recruited in Baltimore by Samuel Chester for the 3rd Maryland Regiment, on March 2, 1780. (RRR-6, H-334)

BOMGARDNER, JOHN. Non-Juror to Oath of Allegiance, 1778. (A-1/2)

BOND,_____. Private, Baltimore County Regiment No. 7, circa 1777 (his first name was torn off the list). (TTT-13)

BOND, BENJAMIN. Oath of Allegiance, 1778, before Hon. Edward Cockey. Served also with Col. Nicholson's Troop of Horse, June 7, 1781. (A-1/2, A-2/61, BBBB-274)

BOND, CHARLES. Non-Juror to Oath of Allegiance, 1778. Involved in evaluation of Baltimore County confiscated proprietary reserve lands, 1782. (A-1/2, FFF-547)

BOND, CHRISTOPHER. Non-Juror to Oath of Allegiance, 1778. (A-1/2)

BOND, EDWARD. Non-Juror to Oath of Allegiance, 1778. Involved in evalution of Baltimore County confiscated proprietary reserve lands, 1782. (A-1/2, FFF-547)

BOND, HANNIBAL (HAMUBUL). Oath of Allegiance, 1778. (A-1/2)

BOND, HENRY. Oath of Allegiance, 1778, before Hon. Edward Cockey. (A-1/2, A-2/62)

BOND, JACOB. Born 1726. Married Fanny PARTRIDGE on December 28, 1747 in Baltimore County. Died 1780. Son of Thomas BOND of Baltimore County. Jacob served as Captain of Company No. 11 in Harford County. See Peden's Revolutionary Patriots of Harford County, Maryland, 1775-1783, page 21. (AAA-2737)

BOND, JAMES. 1st Lt., Baltimore County Troops, 1776. 1st Lt., 3rd Maryland Battalion, Flying Camp. July-December, 1776. Took Oath of Allegiance in 1778 before Hon. George G. Presbury. (A-1/2, A-2/48, H-52, B-109)

BOND, JOHN SR. Non-Juror to Oath of Allegiance, 1778. (A-1/2)

BOND, JOHN JR. Non-Juror to Oath of Allegiance, 1778. (A-1/2)

BOND, JOHN (OF RICHARD). Oath of Allegiance, 1778, before Hon. Robert Simmons. (A-1/2, A-2/58)

BOND, JOSHUA. Enlisted in Baltimore County on July 25, 1776. (H-52)

BOND, NATHANIEL. 1st Lt., Baltimore County Militia, September 13, 1776. (JJ-9, FFF-62)

BOND, NATHANIEL. Midshipman and Purser on ship <u>Defence</u>, April 15, 1777 to December 31, 1777. (H-654)

BOND, NICHODEMUS (GODEMUS). Non-Juror to Oath of Allegiance, 1778. (A-1/2)

BOND, RICHARD. Oath of Allegiance, 1778. (A-1/2)

BOND, SHADRACH. Oath of Allegiance, 1778, before Hon. Edward Cockey. (A-2/62)

BOND, SAMUEL. Non-Juror to Oath of Allegiance, 1778. (A-1/2)

BOND, THOMAS. Son of Barnet and Alice Bond. Born c1739 and died May 23, 1795 in St. James Parish, Baltimore County. On February 7, 1768 he married Sarah BOND, daughter of Benjamin BOND and Clemency TAYLOR. She was born June 13, 1748 and died September 11, 1830. (Another source states Thomas Bond married Rebecca STANSBURY on December 19, 1771, and that he was born in 1739 and died in 1787 in Harford County, MD) Their children: Thomas; Elizabeth, married Daniel REESE in 1790; Barnet; Alice, married James THOMAS and lived in White Marsh, Baltimore County, and they had a daughter Sarah Bond THOMAS (1814-1875) who married Joseph Wells PUGH (1810-1884) in 1831; Ann or Nancy, married Hugh HUGHES in 1794 at Zion Lutheran Church; Tobias; Joshua, born 1789; and, Mary. married Aaron HELKEN. Thomas Bond was enlisted by Capt. Siggond in Baltimore for Count Pulaski's Legion on May 8, 1778. He was transferred to the Invalid Regiment on Feb. 25, 1779, not being fit for camp duty. He was appointed a Corporal on June 1, 1779, and then Sergeant on January 15, 1781, and held that rank at least until June 28, 1781 when the Invalid Regiment was stationed at Philadelphia. (H-593, H0624, D-8, A-1/2 Non-Juror, AAA-2231)

BOND, THOMAS. 1st Lt., Capt. S. Gill's Company No. 6, on rolls of August 26, October 28, and December 20, 1776. Oath of Allegiance, 1778. (A-1/2, RR-99, ZZ-542, PPP-2)

BOND, WILLIAM. Non-Juror to Oath of Allegiance, 1778. Son of William BOND and Elizabeth STANSBURY, and grandson of Thomas BOND and Ann ROBINSON. (A-1/2, D-8)

BOOTMAN, JOHN. Corporal, Capt. Gale's Company of Artillery, 1779-1780. On command at Tuckissummy Plains in 1779. (YYY-1/9)

BORBONE (BORBINE), JOHN. Oath of Allegiance, 1778, before Hon. James Calhoun. (A-1/2, A-2/41)

BOREN, JOHN. Born in 1755 in Baltimore County, MD. Applied for pension while residing in Sewickley Township, Beaver County, PA on March 5, 1839, stating that while living in Baltimore County he enlisted in 1775 for three years, served as a Private in Capt. Robert Lemmon's Company of Col. Isaac Hammond's Maryland Regiment, was in the Battle of Brandywine, and was discharged a few days thereafter. He claimed he enlisted in 1778 and served six months as a substitute for his uncle, Richard DAVIS, in Capt. James Thompson's Maryland Company, and that he again enlisted in 1781 and served as a substitute for another uncle, Robert DAVIS, in Capt. Thompson's Maryland Company. He said he was at the Battle of Cowpens and was discharged a few days after the battle. His claim was rejected (#1030) as he failed to furnish proof of the alleged service as was required by the pension laws. After the Revolution, John BOREN resided in Baltimore County for 3 or 4 years, then moved to Huntingdon Co., PA where he resided for 10 years, and then moved to Beaver Co., PA. His family is referred to in his pension application, but no names are given. (I-12, YY-11)

BORING (BOREING), ABRAHAM. Non-Juror to Oath of Allegiance, 1778. (A-1/2)

BORING, ABSALOM. Involved in evaluation of Baltimore County confiscated proprietary reserve lands in 1782. (FFF-554)

BORING (BOREING), JAMES. Two Non-Jurors with this name did not take the Oath of Allegiance in 1778. (A-1/2)

* BONERS through BOONE are out of alphabetical sequence. See page 26 herein.

BORING (BOREING), JAMES JR. Non-Juror to Oath of Allegiance, 1778. (A-1/2)

BORING (BOREING), THOMAS. Non-Juror to Oath of Allegiance, 1778. (A-1/2)

BORING (BOREING), WILLIAM SR. Oath of Allegiance, 1778, before Hon. John Moale. (A-1/2, A-2/70)

BORNER (BONNER), ANDREW. Oath of Allegiance, 1778, before Hon. Geo. Lindenberger Private, Capt. McClellan's Company, September 4, 1780. (A-2/52, CCC-24)

BORNS, HYMAN. Oath of Allegiance, 1778. (A-1/2)

BOSE, HENRY. Ensign, Capt. Lemmon's Company, December 4, 1778. (GGG-257)

BOSLER, JACOB. Oath of Allegiance, 1778. (A-1/2)

BOSLEY, CALEB. Non-Juror to Oath of Allegiance, 1778. (A-1/2)

BOSLEY, CHARLES. Non-Juror to Oath of Allegiance, 1778. However. on January 7, 1777, he made a deposition as Capt. Charles Bosley, pertaining to behavior of one Vincent Trapnell. (A-1/2, FFF-83)

BOSLEY, ELIJAH. Oath of Allegiance, 1778, before Hon. Andrew Buchanan. (A-2/57)

BOSLEY, EZEKIEL. Non-Juror to Oath of Allegiance, 1778. (A-1/2)

BOSLEY, GIDEON. Oath of Allegiance, 1778, before Hon. Robert Simmons. (A-2/58)

BOSLEY, GREENBURY. Non-Juror to Oath of Allegiance, 1778. Involved in evaluation of Baltimore County confiscated proprietary reserve lands in 1782. He died in Baltimore County on April 1, 1814, in his 76th year, "for many years he had been afflicted." (A-1/2, FFF-553, ZZZ-31)

BOSLEY, JAMES. Captain in Baltimore County Militia, 7th Company (62 Privates), December 19, 1775, through 1777. Captain un Gunpowder Battalion from September 4, 1777, through 1778. Took the Oath of Allegiance, 1778, before the Hon. Edward Cockey. (A-2/61, CC-36, G-10, E-12, X-111, NN-88, BBB-362)

BOSLEY, JAMES (OF WILLIAM). Two men fit this name: one signed the Oath of Allegiance in 1778 before Hon. Richard Holliday; another signed with his mark ("B") before Hon. John Beale Howard. (A-1/2, A-2/29. A-2/60)

BOSLEY, JOHN. Two men with this name were Non-Jurors in 1778. (A-1/2, A-1/3)

BOSLEY, JOSEPH. Non-Juror to Oath of Allegiance, 1778. Died circa 1780 in Baltimore County' wife's name Ann. Children: Delilah, married Benjamin BARNEY in 1758; Diana, married Elias MAJORS in 1763; Ann; Mary; Johanna; Ruth; Gideon; Thomas; and, Greenbury. (A-1/3, D-2)

BOSLEY, JOSHIAH (JOSHUA). Non-Juror to Oath of Allegiance, 1778. (A-1/3)

BOSLEY, THOMAS. Involved in evaluation of Baltimore County confiscated proprietary reserve lands in 1782. (FFF-538)

BOSLEY, WALTER. 2nd Lt., Capt. Luke Wyle's Company No. 7, Baltimore County, on rolls of October 28 and December 20, 1776. Took Oath of Allegiance in 1778 before Hon. Richard Holliday. With Co. Nicholson's Troop of Horse, June 7, 1781. (A-1/3, A-2/60, ZZ-542, PPP-2, BBBB-274)

BOSLEY, WILLIAM. Oath of Allegiance, 1778, before Hon. John Beale Howard. (A-1/3, A-2/29)

BOSLEY, ZEBULON. Born 1756 and died 1791 in Baltimore County. Married 1778, Elizabeth BOND. Children: James Bond Bosley, and Daniel Bosley. Zebulon was commissioned Ensign in Capt. Bosley's Company, September 4, 1777 and served in the Gunpowder Battalion through 1778. Non-Juror to the Oath of Allegiance in 1778. (A-1/3, E-12, NN-88, BBB-362, JJJ-72, XXX-166)

BOSMAN, EDWARD. Non-Juror to Oath of Allegiance, 1778. (A-1/3)

BOSSELL, JAMES, Non-Juror to Oath in 1778, but signed in 1781. (QQ-105)

BONERS (BOUERS), JOHN. Oath of Allegiance, 1778, before Hon. George Lindenberger. (A-1/3, A-2/52)

BONEY, JOSEPH. Non-Juror to Oath of Allegiance. (A-1/2)

BOOKER, HENRY. Non-Juror to Oath of Allegiance. (A-1/2)

BOONE, JOHN. Non-Juror to Oath of Allegiance. (A-1/2)

BOONE, JOHN C. R. B. Non-Juror to Oath, 1778, but took it in 1781. (QQ-105)

BOONE, JOSEPH. Oath of Allegiance, 1778, before Hon. Thomas Sollers. (A-2/51)

BOONE, MOSES. Non-Juror to Oath of Allegiance, 1778. (A-1/2)

BOONE, RICHARD. Private, Capt. Deams' Co., 7th MD Regt., Dec. 21, 1776. (H-305)

BOSSOM, CHARLES. Non-Juror to Oath of Allegiance, 1778. Involved in evaluation of Baltimore County confiscated proprietary reserve lands, 1782. (A-1/2, FFF-553)

BOSTER, WILLIAM. Oath of Allegiance, 1778, before Hon. George Lindenberger. (A-1/3, A-2/52)

BOWDEN, PRESTON. Matross in Capt. Gale's Company of Artillery, September, 1779. Reported deserted at Annapolis, September 13, 1779. (YYY-1/10)

BOWEN, ABSALOM. Non-Juror to Oath of Allegiance, 1778. (A-1/3)

BOWEN, BENJAMIN. non-Juror to Oath of Allegiance, 1778. (A-1/3)

BOWEN, BENJAMIN (OF SOLOMON). Non-Juror to Oath of Allegiance, 1778. (A-1/3)

BOWEN, EDWARD. Non-Juror to Oath of Allegiance, 1778. (A-1/3)

BOWEN, HOSIAS (OF BENJAMIN). Oath of Allegiance, 1778. (A-1/3)

BOWEN, JAMES. Enlisted in Baltimore County, July 20, 1776. (H-53)

BOWEN, JEHU. Enlisted in Baltimore County, July 20, 1776. (H-53)

BOWEN, JOHN. Oath of Allegiance, 1778, before Hon. Thomas Sollers. (A-1/3, A-2/51)

BOWEN, JOSIAS. Captain in Patapsco Lower Company, May 6, 1776, and Captain in Gunpowder Battalion, 1777-1778. (E-12, X-111, EE-51, WW-413)

BOWEN, JOSIAS. Private in Capt. Talbott's Company, May 31, 1779. Took Oath of Allegiance, 1778, before Hon. Thomas Sollers. Josias Bowne, of Baltimore County, died Oct. 1, 1805 in his 52nd year. (F-301, U-90, ZZZ-32, A-2/51)

BOWEN, NATHAN. Non-Juror to Oath of Allegiance, 1778. (A-1/3)

BOWEN, SABRITT. Born December 10, 1758. Married Elizabeth HUMPHREY (1761-1847) of Pennsylvania, dughter of David HUMPHREY and Elizabeth ROBERTS. A daughter Eleanor BOWEN (1793-1874) married Robert HOLLOWAY (1786-1863) of Virginia; their daughter Katharine HOLLOWAY (1819-1901) married James A. HOOPER (1814-1898) in 1842. Sabritt married Elizabeth on January 4, 1792 in Baltimore County (Marriage proven through Maryland pension application). "Captain" Sabritt Bowen died November 11, 1811 in his 53rd year. His obituary states he took part in the Revolutionary War and was wounded at the charge on the Savannah Line under General Wayne. Also, Sabritt was a Sergeant in the 4th Maryland Continental Dragoons under Col. Stephen Moylan and Capt. David Plunkett, having enlisted on June 19, 1777. Elizabeth is listed as a war pensioner, aged 79, on June 1, 1840, residing in the household of Joseph Davenport in Baltimore City, 5th Ward. (AAA-672, AAA-1245, YY-111, ZZZ-32, AAA-1162, P-128)

BOWEN, SOLOMON. Oath of Allegiance, 1778, before Hon. John Merryman. Died in June, 1804, at his seat in Baltimore County, in his 81st year. (A-2/45, A-1/3, ZZZ-33) (There may have been another Solomon who did not sign Oath.)

BOWER, DANIEL. Oath of Allegiance, 1778, before Hon. Andrew Buchanan. (A-2/57)

BOWER, NATHANIEL. Oath of Allegiance, 1778. (A-1/3)

BOWING, JOSHUA. Private, Baltimore County Regiment No. 15, c1777. (TTT-13)

BOWLER, THOMAS. Matross, Capt. Gale's Company of Artillery, 1779. Wagoner,
at Chester, PA camp; in hospital, November-December, 1779, at Morristown
camp; sick in hospital, March 7 and April 13, 1780. Matross in Capt. J.
Smith's Co., MD Artillery, in 1780. Matross in Capt. Dprsey's Co., Maryland
Artillery, at Camp Col. Scirvin's, January 28, 1782. Matross in Capt. J.
Smith's Co., 1782-1783. (YYY-1/11, YYY-2/7, UU-232, H-579)

BOWLEY, DANIEL (II). Son of Daniel BOWLEY and Elizabeth LUX. Born June 6, 1745
in Anne Arundel County, MD. Married Ann STEWART. Children: William Lux
BOWLEY, married Mary HOLLINS; AnnLux BOWLEY, married Henry THOMPSON; Sarah
Stewart BOWLEY, married Charles WIRGMAN in 1805; Rebecca BOWLEY, married to
Peter WIRGMAN in 1811; Francis BOWLEY; Samuel BOWLEY; Elizabeth BOWLEY; and,
Daniel BOWLEY (III). Daniel Bowley, Esq., of Furley, died November 12, 1807,
in Baltimore County, MD. He served on the Baltimore County Committee of Observation, August 28, 1775. Was a member of the Whig Club, and Sons of Liberty
in 1776, as well as the Baltimore Mechanical Company. On March 14, 1776, he
purchased and shipped gunpowder for the Council of Safety. In 1776 he became
an Ensign in Capt. Sterrett's Company No. 2 of the Baltimore Town Battalion.
He was also a Baltimore Privateer, and signed the Oath of Allegiance in 1778
before the Hon. William Lux. He was on the Baltimore Salt Committee, Oct. 14,
1779. On September 25, 1780, he became 2nd Lt. in Capt. Yates' Company in the
Baltimore Town Battalion. He signed a letter to Governor Lee on April 4, 1781,
requesting a defense of Baltimore. Also, in 1781, he became a 1st Lieutenant
in Capt. J. Cockey's Baltimore County Dragoons and was stationed at Yorktown.
(III-206, GG-74, VV-303, S-49, EEEE-1726, CCC-19, CCC-25, FFF-28, HHH-88,
MMM-A, JJJ-102, A-1/3, A-2/68, XXX-169, ZZZ-33, ZZZ-357, "Bowley's Quarters")

BOWLS, GEORGE. Non-Juror to Oath of Allegiance, 1778. (A-1/3)

BOWSHER, THOMAS. Oath of Allegiance, 1778, before Hon. John Beale Howard. (A-2/29)

BOXLEY, WILLIAM. Oath of Allegiance, 1778. (A-1/3)

BOYCE, BENJAMIN. Oath of Allegiance, 1778, before Hon. James Calhoun. (A-1/3,A-2/39)

BOYCE, ROGER. With Col. Nicholson's Troop of Horse on June 7, 1781. (BBBB-274)

BOYCE, THOMAS. Non-Juror to Oath of Allegiance, 1778. (A-1/3)

BOYD, ABRAHAM. Oath of Allegiance, 1778, before Hon. James Calhoun. (A-1/3, A-2/38)

BOYD, JOHN DR. (1737-1790) Member of Baltimore County Committee of Safety, 1774;
Committee of Inspection, March 13, 1775; Committee of Observation, Sept. 23,
1775 (elected to Committee, having received 82 votes, and finishing 18th in
the balloting); and, Committee of Correspondence, November 12, 1775 to 1776.
Authorized by Congress to sign bills of credit, 1776. Took Oath of Allegiance
in 1778 before Hon. James Calhoun. Paid by the Maryland Council for medicines
for the militia, having served as a Doctor in Capt. McClellan's Company, 1780.
(FF-64, GG-74, ZZ-254, XX-4, SS-150, RR-19, RR-47, SS-136, RR-50, EEEE-1726,
A-1/3, A-2/38, CCC-23)

BOYD, MICHAEL. Born 1744 in Ireland, Sandy complexion; height: 5' 5". Enlisted
July 5, 1776 in Baltimore County; Private in Col. Ewing's Battaltion. (H-57)

BOYD, ROBERT. Non-Juror to Oath of Allegiance, 1778. (A-1/3)

BOYD, WARNAL. Oath of Allegiance, 1778. (A-1/3)

BOYER, MATHIAS. Member of Baltimore Mechanical Company of Militia, November 14,
1775. Private, Capt. Graybill's German Regiment, 1776. (F-298, H-266)

BRACKER, C. Private, Capt. Cox's Company, December 19, 1776. (CCC-21)

BRACKLEY, MATHIAS. Oath of Allegiance, 1778, before Hon. Charles Ridgely of William. (A-2/27)

BRADFORD, JAMES. Ordinary Seaman on ship Defence, 1777. (H-654)

BRADFORD, WILLIAM. Sergeant of Marines on ship Defence, 1777. (H-654)

BRADLEY, JAMES. Born 1753 in Dublin, Ireland. Occupation: Gardner. Ht: 5' 5½" Enlisted January 24, 1776, Private, Capt. N. Smith's 1st Co. of Matrosses. Private, Capt. Dorsey's Co., Maryland Artillery, November 17, 1777; listed as being "in gaol for house breaking." (H-564, H-574, H-567, QQQ-2, VV-73)

BRADLEY, THOMAS. Oath of Allegiance, 1778, before Hon. Jesse Dorsey. (A-2/64)

BRADSHAW, RICHARD. Oath of Allegiance, 1778, before Hon. James Calhoun. (A-2/40)

BRADY, JAMES. Non-Juror to Oath of Allegiance, 1778. (A-1/3)

BRADY (BRADEY), JOHN. Born 1754 in Dublin, Ireland. Occupation: Plasterer. Height: 5' 6½". Enlisted January 28, 1776 as Private, Capt. N. Smith's 1st Company of Matrosses. Private, Capt. Dorsey's Company of Maryland Artillery, November 17, 1777. Gunner, Capt. Dorsey's Company at Valley Forge, June 3, 1778. Matross, Capt. J. Smith's Co., Maryland Artillery, 1780-1783. (H-564, H-564, H-574, QQQ-2, VV-74, UU-231, H-579, YYY-2/8)

BRADY, MICHAEL. Served on ship Defence, June 20 to July 25, 1777. (H-654)

BRADY, WILLIAM. Corporal, Capt. Brown's Company of Artillery. Joined Nov. 22, 1777. At Valley Forge until June, 1778. At White Plains, July, 1778. At Fort Schuyler, August-September, 1780. At High Hills of the Santee, August, 1781. At Col. Scirvins Camp, January, 1782. At Bacon's Bridge, S. C., in April, 1782. (UU-228, UU-230)

BRAETER, JOSEPH. Private, Capt. Graybill's German Regiment, 1776. (H-265)

BRAITHWAITE, JOHN. Marine on ship Defence, April 28 to Dec. 11, 1777. (H-654)

BRAMWELL (BRANWELL), HENRY. Private, Baltimore County Regiment No. 15, c1777. Non-Juror to Oath of Allegiance, 1778. (A-1/3, TTT-13)

BRANAGIN, FELIX (PHELIX). Born 1742 in Armagh, Ireland. Occupation: Labourer. Height: 5' 6 3/4". Enlisted January 31, 1776, Private in Capt. N. Smith's 1st Company of Matrosses. (H-565, H-567, QQQ-2)

BRANGIN, JOHN. Oath of Allegiance, 1778, before Hon. Edward Cockey. (A-2/61)

BRANNAN, JAMES. Recruit, Baltimore County Militia, April 11, 1780. Non-Juror to Oath of Allegiance, 1778. (A-1/3, H-335)

BRANNAN, JOHN. Oath of Allegiance, 1778, before Hon. Edward Cockey. (A-2/61)

BRANNAN, THOMAS. Oath of Allegiahce, 1778, before Hon. Hercules Courtenay. (A-2/37)

BRANNAN, WILLIAM. Oath cf Allegiance, 1778, before Hon. Hercules Courtenay. (A-2/37)

BREAMAN, JAMES. Recruit, Baltimore County, 1780. (H-340)

BREIDENBACH (BRIDENBACH, BREITENBACH), JOHN. Private, Capt. Cox's Company, 1776. Oath of Allegiance, 1778, before Hon. William Spear. Private, Capt. McClellan Company, September 4, 1780. (A-1/3, A-2/66, CCC-21, CCC-24)

BRERETON, THOMAS. Non-Juror to Oath of Allegiance, 1778. (A-1/3)

BRESHEARS, JEREMIAH. Private, Baltimore County Regiment No. 15, c1777. (TTT-13)

BRETT, PATRICK. Non-Juror to Oath of Allegiance, 1778. (A-1/3)

BREVITT, JOHN. Born 1750-1760 in England. Married_____ SWOOP. Died July 24, 1824 in Baltimore. Ensign, 1st MD Regt., August, 1780; 2nd Lt., 4th MD Regt. September 20, 1780; Retained in Gunby's Batt., April 12, 1783, and served to

November 15, 1783. Lt. Brevitt was an Original Member of the Society of the Cincinnati of Maryland, and was last represented by PFC Gridley Barstow Strong, United States Marine Corps, 1947-1968, killed in Vietnam, April 21, 1968. Lt. John Brevitt received 200 acres (lots 3331, 3340, 3344, 3262) in western Maryland for his service in Virginia and Maryland. (TT-60, JJJ-83, DDDD-1)

BREWER, THOMAS. Private, Capt. Ramsey's Company No. 5, 1776. (H-640)

BRIAN (BRION), DANIEL. Private, Capt. J. Gist's Company, 3rd Maryland Regiment, February, 1778. Pensioner (born 1754). (H-600, YY-12)

BRIAN, DANIEL. Captain of the vessel Plater in 1781-1782. Delivered flour barrels to Baltimore County in 1781. (FFF-346, FFF-519)

BRIAN (BRIEN), DAVID. Recruit, Baltimore County, 1780. Private, Extra Regiment at Fort Whetstone Point in Baltimore, 1781. (H-340, H-626)

BRIARLY, JOHN. Private, Capt. McClellan's Co., Baltimore Town, 1780. (CCC-25)

BRICE, JOHN. Baltimore Mechanical Company of Militia, 1776. (CCC-28)

BRIDE, HENRY. Supplied oakum and brushes for the ship Defence, July 11, 1776. Oath of Allegiance, 1778, before Hon. Isaac VanBibber. (A-1/3, A-2/34, FFF-42)

BRIGHAM, JOHN. Matross, Capt. Brown's Company of Artillery. Joined Nov. 22, 1777. At Valley Forge until June, 1778. At White Plains, July, 1776. At Ft. Schuyler, August-September, 1780. At High Hills of the Santee, August, 1781. At Camp Col.Scirvins, January, 1782. At Bacon's Bridge, S.C., Apr., 1782. (UU-230)

BRIGHT, WILLIAM. Gunner, Capt. Brown's Company of Artillery. Joined Nov. 22, 1777. At Valley Forge until June, 1778. At White Plains, July, 1776. At Fort Schuyler, August-September, 1780. At High Hills of the Santee, August, 1781. At Camp Col.Scirvins, January, 1782. At Bacon's Bridge, S.C., Apr., 1782. (UU-230)

BRIMINGHAM (BRININGHAM), DAVID. Non-Juror to Oath of Allegiance, 1778. (A-1/3)

BRISCOE, JAMES. Marine on ship Defence, October 23 to December 31, 1777. (H-654)

BRISTOE, JOHN. Non-Juror to Oath of Allegiance, 1778. (A-1/3)

BRITT (BRETT), ROBERT. Born 1751 in Maryland. Occupation: Taylor. Ht: 5' 6½". Enlisted January 25, 1776, Private, in Capt. N. Smith's 1st Co. of Matrosses. Private, Capt. Dorsey's Co. of Artillery, November 17, 1777. Matross, in Capt. Dorsey's Co. at valley Forge, June 3, 1778. (H-564, H-567, H-574, VV-73, UU-231)

BRITTAIN (BRITTON), ABRAHAM. Baltimore County Committee of Observation, July 24, 1775; elected September 23, 1775, receiving 52 votes, and placing 37th in the balloting. Represented the Lower Middle River Hundred at the Association of Freemen, August 21, 1775. Took the Oath of Allegiance, 1778, before the Hon. Hercules Courtenay. (RR-47, SS-136, A-1/3, A-2/37, EEEE-1725, EEEE-1726)

BRITTAIN, EMANUEL SR. Oath of Allegiance, 1778. (A-1/3)

BRITTAIN, JOSEPH. Enlisted in Baltimore County, July 20, 1776. (H-52)

BRITTAIN, NATHANIAL. Received 45 votes for Baltimore Committee of Observation on September 12, 1775, but was not elected to serve. 2nd Lt. in Capt. Cockey's Company No. 1 on August 26 and October 28, 1776. 1st Lt., February 4, 1777. Oath of Allegiance, 1778, before Hon. Richard Holliday (spelled "Britton"). (A-1/3, A-2/60, RR-50, RR-98, PPP-2, VV-114)

BRITTAIN (BRITTON), NICHOLAS. Born January 26, 1730, and died August 1, 1792 in Baltimore County, MD. Married Alethia Kidd FINLY. A son, Richard BRITTAIN married Temperance TALBOT; their daughter, Ann MERRYMAN BRITTON married James JESSOP. Nicholas was a member of the Baltimore Committee of Observation in 1775, and represented Lower Middle River Hundred at the Association of Freemen on August 21, 1775. He was a 1st Lt. in Capt. Cockey's Company, February 4,

1777, and took the Oath of Allegiance in 1778 before Hon. Robert Simons. (A-1/3, A-2/58, BBB-114, AAA-237A, EEEE-1726, also Scharf's History of Maryland, Volume II, page 173)

BRITTAIN (BRITTEN), RICHARD. Oath of Allegiance, 1778, before Hon. Hercules Courtenay. (A-1/3, A-2/37)

BRITTAIN (BRITTON), RICHARD JR. Oath of Allegiance, 1778, before Hon. Robert Simmons. Served in Col. Nicholson's Troop of Horse, June 7, 1781. (A-1/3, A-2/58, BBBB-274)

BRITTAIN, SAMUEL SR. Oath of Allegiance, 1778, before Hon. Hercules Courtenay. (A-2/37)

BRITTAIN (BRITTON), SAMUEL JR. Oath of Allegiance, 1778, before Hon. Hercules Courtenay. (A-1/3, A-2/37)

BROME, THOMAS. Oath of Allegiance, 1778, before Hon. James Calhoun. (A-2/65)

BROMFIELD, THOMAS. Captain of Marines on ship Defence, April 25, 1777 to at least October 15, 1777. (H-654)

BROOKE, CLEMENT, Oath of Allegiance, 1778, before Hon. John Merryman. (A-2/45)

BROOKE, RICHARD. Resigned in Baltimore from the service, Oct. 15, 1777. (FFF-125)

BROOKMAN, GEORGE. Non-Juror to Oath of Allegiance, 1778. (A-1/3)

BROOKS, CHARLES. Non-Juror to Oath of Allegiance, 1778. Involved in evaluation of Baltimore County conficated proprietary reserve lands, 1782. (A-1/3, FFF-555)

BROOKS, EDWARD. Baltimore Privateer and Captain of ship Buckskin Hero (16 guns and 100 men), owned by John Crockett & Co. of Baltimore. (III-206)

BROOKS, HUMPHREY. Oath of Allegiance, 1778, before Hon. Richard Cromwell. (A-1/3, (A-2/46)

BROOKS, JAMES D. Born 1752 or 1753 in the north of England. Came to Maryland in 1768, indentured for five years to Mathew GRAYMER as a Weaver, which was his occupation at the time of his enlistment on February 3, 1776. Ht: 5' 5½". Private, Capt. N. Smith's 1st Company of Matrosses. Drummer, Capt. Brown's Maryland Artillery, having joined November 22, 1777. Was at Valley Forge in 1778; transferred to Col. Charles Harrison's Command (Virginia), May 30, 1778. He married Sidney_____, and died in 1820 in Baltimore County, Maryland. A son, Joseph BROOKS (d. 1841) married Priscilla GARDNER, and their daughter, Achsah BROOKS married James MARSDEN (1795-1846) in 1819. James Brooks is not listed as taking the Oath in 1778 (because he was on military duty at that time). (A-1/3, H-565, UU-228, UU-229, UU-230, AAA-1723)

BROOKS, JOHN JR. Oath of Allegiance, 1778, before Hon. Jesse Dorsey. (A-2/63)

BROOKS, SAMUEL SR. Non-Juror to Oath of Allegiance, 1778. (A-1/3)

BROOKS, SAMUEL JR. Non-Juror to Oath of Allegiance, 1778. (A-1/3)

BROOKS, THOMAS. Served on ship Defence, May 21 to June 28, 1777. (H-654)

BROOKS, WILLIAM. Oath of Allegiance, 1778, before Hon. Jeremiah Johnson. Could not write; made his mark. (A-1/3, A-2/33)

BROTHERS, AUSTIN. Non-Juror to Oath of Allegiance, 1778. (A-1/3)

BROTHERS, THOMAS. Non-Juror to Oath of Allegiance, 1778. (A-1/3)

BROTHERTON, WILLIAM. Non-Juror to Oath of Allegiance, 1778. (A-1/3)

BROTHROCK, ANDREW. Non-Juror to Oath of Allegiance, 1778. (A-1/3)

BROUGHAM, GEORGE. Oath of Allegiance, 1778, before Hon. James Calhoun. (A-1/3, A-2/42)

BROWN, ABEL. Two men by this name took the Oath of Allegiance, 1778: one before Hon. Peter Shepherd, and one before Hon. William Lux. (A-1/3, A-2/49. A-2/68)

BROWN, ALEXANDER. Oath of Allegiance, 1778, before Hon. James Calhoun. (A-2/41)

BROWN, BENJAMIN. Non-Juror to Oath of Allegiance in 1778, but subsequently took the Oath in 1781. (A-1/3. QQ-106)

BROWN, COLIN. Able Seaman, September 19, 1776, and Sailor in 1777, on State ship Defence. (H-654, H-606).

BROWN, CORNELIUS. Oath of Allegiance, 1778, before Hon. George Lindenberger. (A-1/3. A-2/52)

BROWN, DAVID. Oath of Allegiance, 1778, before Hon. James Calhoun. (A-1/3, A-2/40)

BROWN, DIXON. Non-Juror to Oath of Allegiance, 1778. (A-1/3)

BROWN, EDWARD. Oath of Allegiance, 1778, before Hon. William Spear. (A-1/3, A-2/67)

BROWN, GARRETT. Captain of Marines, 1776-1777, on ship Defence. (H-606, H-654)

BROWN, GEORGE. Non-Juror to Oath of Allegiance, 1778. (A-1/3)

BROWN, HENRY. Oath of Allegiance, 1778, before Hon. James Calhoun. Signed letter to Gov. Lee requesting defense of Baltimore, 1781. 1st Lt., Upper Battalion, November 5, 1781. (A-1/3, A-2/41, S-49, AAAA-662)

BROWN, ISAAC. Private, Capt. Lansdale's Company, 4th Maryland Regiment, Feb. 26, 1777. Corporal, November 1, 1778 to February 26, 1780. (H-88)

BROWN, JACOB. Private, Baltimore Artillery Company, October 16, 1775. 2nd Lt., Capt. B. Dickenson's Company (Old Mercantile Company) "in room of John Cannon, resigned & dead," on January 19, 1781 (company reorganized). Appointed 1st Lt. by Gov. Thomas Lee on September 25, 1780. Two men with this name took Oath of Allegiance in 1778: one before Hon. Peter Shepherd, and one before Hon. George Lindenberger. (A-2/49, A-2/52, F-308, G-8, R-15, AAAA-412, BBBB-29, BBBB-61)

BROWN, JAMES, Cabin Boy on ship Defence, September 19, 1776. (H-607)

BROWN, JAMES (OF ABEL). Oath of Allegiance, 177, before Hon. Andrew Buchanan. Recruit, Baltimore County, 1780. Private, Extra Regiment, at Fort Whetstone Point in Baltimore, 1781. (A-1/3, A-2/57, H-340, H-626)

BROWN, JOHN. Two men by this name took the Oath of Allegiance in 1778: one before Hon. Peter Shepherd, and one before Hon. William Lux. Military service naming John Brown (undoubtedly more then one person with this name served): Private, Baltimore Artillery Co., October 16, 1775. Private, Col. Ewing's Battalion, July 5, 1776; not on muster roll in August, 1776. Private, Capt. Keeports' Co. German Regiment; enlisted July 21, 1776; at Philadelphia, September 19, 1776. Sergeant, Capt. Sheaff's Company, June 16, 1777. Private, Capt. McClellan's Co., Baltimore Town, September 4, 1780. Recruit, Baltimore County, 1780. One was involved in evaluation of Baltimore County confiscated proprietary reserve land in 1782.(FFF-555, A-2/49, A-2/69, W-162, H-57, CCC-24, H-340, H-263, G-8)

BROWN, JOSEPH. Served on ship Defence, February 17 to March 16, 1777. (H-654)

BROWN, JUSTICE (JUSTUS). Oath of Allegiance, 1778, before Hon. William Lux. A printer of Baltimore, he died September 25, 1809 at a very advance age. His funeral was held from the house of Mr. Hugh STEWART, Duke Street, Old Town, Baltimore City. (A-1/3, A-2/68, ZZZ-41)

BROWN, LUKE. Non-Juror to Oath of Allegiance, 1778. (A-1/3)

BROWN, MICHAEL. Oath of Allegiance, 1778, before Hon. Peter Shepherd. (A-2/50)

BROWN, THOMAS. Private, 4th Maryland Regiment, September 6, 1777, and Corporal, Capt. Lansdale's Company, January 1 to July, 1780. One Thomas Brown was a Matross in Capt. Brown's Artillery Company as of August 1, 1781. Took Oath Allegiance, 1778, before Hon. George G. Presbury. (A-2/48, H-89, UU-230)

BROWN, WILLIAM. 1st Lt., Capt. Fulford's Company of Matrosses, July 5, 1776.
Captain, Independent Artillery Company, November 22, 1777; incorporated
in 1st Continental Artillery regiment, May 30, 1778. At Vallye Forge to
June, 1778. At White Plains, July, 1778. At Fort Schuyler, August and
September, 1780. Under Lt. Col. Carrington's 1st Maryland Artillery on
May 11, 1780. On Command at camden "superintending the hospital since
July 18, 1781. At High Hills of the Santee in August, 1781. At Camp
Col. Scrivins, January, 1781. At Bacon's Brigde, S.C. in April, 1782.
Major of 1st Continental Artillery on January 31, 1781. Served to June,
1783. Took Oath of Allegiance, 1778, before Hon. Richard Holliday. Major
William Brown was an Original Member of the Society of the Cincinnati of
Maryland, now represented by Capt. Arthur C. Bushey, Jr., USN (Retired).
(A-2/60, A-1/3, TT-62, H-477, UU-229, UU-230, UU-227, VVV-96)

BROWNE, HENRY. Oath of Allegiance, 1778. (A-1/3)

BROWNLE, THOMAS. Oath of Allegiance, 1778, before Hon. George Lindenberger.
(A-1/3, A-2/52)

BRUCE, JOHN. Corporal, Capt. Ramsey's Company No. 5, 1776. (H-639)

BRUEBACKER (BRUBACHER), MICHAEL. Private, Capt. Howell's Co., Dec. 30, 1775.
Private, Capt. Keeports German Regiment; enlisted July 15, 1776, and at
Philadelphia, September 19, 1776. (G-11, H-263)

BRUMICUM, JOHN. Seaman on ship Defence, May 29 to June 7, 1777. (H-655)

BRUMPS, BENJAMIN. Oath of Allegiance, 1778, before Hon. William Spear.
(A-1/3, A-2/66)

BRUMT (BRUNT), PETER. Non-Juror to Oath of Allegiance, 1778. (A-1/3)

BRUSBANKS, FRANCIS. Oath of Allegiance, 1778, before Hon. James Calhoun.
(A-1/3, A-2/40)

BRYAN (BRIAN), DENNIS. Private, Capt. Howell's Company, December 30, 1775.
Private, Capt. Sheaff's Company, June 16, 1777. (G-11, W-162)

BRYAN, JAMES. Born April 15, 1725 in Baltimore; son of Thurbo and Cecilia
BRYAN. Married October 7, 1761 to Mary DRAVER (DRAVES). Their daughter
Mary BRYAN married John HODGES (1768-1823), and their daughter Sarah
HODGES (1795-1847) married Henry G. FREEBURGER (1788-1828) in 1812. James
BRYAN was a Private in Col. Ewing's Battalion; enlisted July 5, 1776 in
Baltimore County; not on the muster roll in August, 1776. James BRIAN
died December 17, 1812 in his 89th year, a native of Baltimore County.
"At one time the deceased said he knew Baltimore when it contained one
small brick home 16 X 20 one story high, and 3 or 4 small frame houses."
(ZZZ-36, H-57, AAA-1672)

BRYAN (BRYANT), JOHN. Private, Capt. Fulford's Company, Maryland Artillery,
November 17, 1777. Matross, Capt. Dorsey's Company, at valley Forge on
June 3, 1778. (H-573, UU-231)

BRYAN, WILLIAM. Non-Juror to Oath of Allegiance, 1778. (A-1/3)

BRYANT, THOMAS. Oath of Allegiance, 1778, before Hon. Peter Shepherd. (A-2/50)

BRYSON, JAMES. Oath of Allegiance, 1778, before Hon. James Calhoun. (A-2/42)

BRYSON, JOHN. With Col. Nicholson's Troop of Horse, June 7, 1781. (BBBB-274)

BUCHANAN, ALEXANDER. Baltimore Privateer. (III-206)

BUCHANAN, ANDREW. (October 22, 1734 - March 12, 1786) Son of Dr. George
BUCHANAN and Elenor ROGERS. Married Susan LAWSON in July, 1760. She
was a daughter of Alexander LAWSON. Their children: George (Dr.) md.
Letitia McKEAN; Andrew; Eleanor; Dorothy; Alexander; Archibald; Susannah;
Lloyd; and, James. Andrew Buchanan was a very patriotic Baltimorean. He

BUCHANAN, ANDREW (continued)

served on many committees: Baltimore County Committee of Inspection, March 13, 1775; Committee of Observation, September 23, 1775; Association of Freemen, representing the Westminster Hundred, August 21, 1775; Committee of Correspondence, November 12, 1775; and the Baltimore Committee in May, 1776. He was a Captain of the Baltimore County Militia, 1st Company (63 Privates), December 19, 1775. He is listed as a Brigadier General in the Maryland Militia on January 6, 1776, as well as a Lieutenant Colonel in Pulaski's Legion in 1778. He was County Lieutenant of Baltimore County in 1776-1777, and Justice of the Orphans Court in 1777 to 1779, as well as Justice of the Peace in 1778. He administered the Oath of Allegiance in 1778, and was on the Committee of Safety as of September 2, 1776. He was also appointed by the General Assembly to receive subscriptions in Baltimore County on August 18, 1779. Earlier, on August 30, 1777, he signed the officers commissions list for the Baltimore County Upper Battalion. On October 13, 1780, he reported to Governor Lee: "You have here enclosed a list of recruits furnished in baltimore County. I have not received one shilling or loan for the State nor any probility of any." A merchant and attorney of Baltimore Town, Andrew Buchanan signed the Oath of Allegiance in 1778. (A-1/3, A-2/57, UUU-22, JJJ-96, EEEE-1726, XXX-185, CC-36, FFF-28, FFF-39, B-129, G-10, ZZ-254, H-592, EE-51, FF-64, F-303, GGG-499, LL-66, RR-19, EEEE-1725, SS-130, RR-47, SS-136, BBB-304, VV-273, GGG-242, RR-50)

BUCHANAN, ARCHIBALD. Baltimore County Committee of Inspection, March 13, 1775, and Committee of Observation, July 24, 1775. Baltimore Town Committee of Correspondence November 12, 1775. Member of the Sons of Liberty, 1776, and Baltimore Privateer. Took Oath of Allegiance before Hon. William Spear in 1778. Died the last Thursday in September, 1800. (ZZZ-43, A-1/3, A-2/66, CCC-19, III-207, RR-19, SS-130, and EEEE-1725)

BUCHANAN (BUCHANNON), GEORGE DR., of Baltimore County. Served on the Committee of Safety in 1776, and took the Oath of Allegiance before the Honorable Jesse Dorsey in 1778. A Magistrate for Baltimore for many years, he moved to Philadelphia in 1806. His obituary refers to him as "Lazaretto physician for port of Philadelphia." He died July 9, 1808. (ZZZ-43, XX-5, A-1/3, A-2/63)

BUCHANAN, GEORGE. Baltimore Privateer and Captain of brig Fox (14 guns), owned by John Dorsey & Company of Baltimore. He died in November, 1810, aged 70, in Baltimore County. (ZZZ-43, III-206, III-207)

BUCHANAN, JAMES. Baltimore Privateer and Captain of brig Ranger (14 guns, 6 swivels) owned by Matthew Ridley & Company of Baltimore; Captain of ship Venus (16 guns and 70 men) owned by Archibald Buchanan and others of Baltimore; and, Captain of ship Favorite (22 guns) owned by Wallace, Johnson, Muir & Co. of Baltimore. (III-206)

BUCHANAN, RICHARD. Offered to Benjamin Rumsey in Annapolis that he would build gondolas in Baltimore County for the use of the State, July 23, 1776. (FFF-46)

BUCHANAN, ROBERT. Baltimore County Committee of Observation, August 28, 1775. As Asst. Commissary of Purchases, Baltimore city, he wrote to the Governor requesting bread for the Army, December 29, 1778. (FFF-198, EEEE-1726)

BUCHANAN, SAMUEL. Oath of Allegiance, 1778, before Hon. William Spear. (A-2/66)

BUCHANAN, WILLIAM (1732-1804). Son of Robert BUCHANAN and Jane BOYD. Served on Baltimore County Committee of Inspection, March 13, 1775; Baltimore Representative to Association of Freemen, July 26, 1775; Committee of Observation, September 23, 1775; Baltimore Town Committee of Correspondence, November 12, 1775. 1st Lt. in Baltimore County Militia, 1st Company, December 19, 1775; Colonel, September 23, 1776 to at least May 28, 1777, Baltimore Battalion. Justice of Orphans Court in 1777 and 1779, and Justice of the Peace, 1778. Took the Oath of Allegiance, 1778, before Hon. John Beale Howard. (A-1/3, A-2/29, G-10, BB-2, GG-74, RR-19, SS-130, EEEE-1725, RR-47, SS-136, VV-273, GGG-242, RR-50, CCC-20, WW-443, FFF-59)

BUCHANAN, WILL (WILLIAM). Oath of Allegiance, 1778, before Hon. William Spear. With Capt. Moore's Troop (had a 12-year old bay gelding horse), June 25, 1781. (A-1/3, A-2/66, BBBB-313)

BUCK, BENJAMIN. (October 10, 1744 - December 24, 1807, Baltimore County, MD).
Son of John BUCK (1716-1793) who married Susanna INGRAM (1718-1793) in 1742.
Benjamin BUCK married Dorcas SUTTON (1747-1824) on February 10, 1763. Their
children: Christopher (1765-1807) married Kesiah GORSUCH (1772-1840) in
1790, and their son Benjamin BUCK (1795-1841) married Jane HERBERT in 1820;
John, born 1767; Susanna, born 1770; Sarah, born 1772; Benjamin (1776/8-
1848) married Catherine REESE (1787-1839) in 1804, and their son William
Henry BUCK (1818-1898) married Elizabeth HICKMAN (1821-1859) in 1841; Joshua,
born 1782; and, James, born 1785. Benjamin BUCK represented Lower Back River
in the Association of Freemen, August 21, 1775. He received 37 votes for the
Baltimore Committee of Observation on September 12, 1775, but was not elected.
He was a 1st Lt. in Capt. Mercer's Company, Back River Lower Hundred, in May,
1776, and recommended to be Captain on June 24, 1777 due to the death of Capt.
Mercer. Commissioned Captain, Gunpowder Battalion, August 30, 1777, and was
in military service to at least 1778. (E-11, EE-413, EE-51, X-111, BBB-350,
AA-65, RR-50, XXX-185, XXX-186, JJJ-97, AAA-1149, AAA-1683, EEEE-1726)

BUCK, JAMES. Non-Juror to Oath of Allegiance in 1778, but signed in 1781. (QQ-106)

BUCK, JOHN. Non-Juror to Oath of Allegiance, 1778. (A-1/3)

BUCK, JOSHUA. (April 5, 1756 - March, 1812, Baltimore County, MD). Son of John
BUCK (1716-1793) and Susannah INGRAM (1718-1793). Married Sarah CROOK (born
1758) on June 11, 1778. A daughter Sarah BUCK (1798-1870) married Thomas
Bayley HAMILTON (1799-1837) in 1831, and their daughter Sarah Catharine
HAMILTON (1831-1891) married Bartus TREW (1834-1918) in 1857. Joshua BUCK
was a 1st Lt. in the Gunpowder Battalion, August 30, 1777, and served to at
least 1778. (E-11, AA-65, AAA-1217, AAA-1186)

BUCK, WILLIAM. Oath of Allegiance, 1778, before Hon. John Hall. (A-1/3, A-2/36)

BUCKINGHAM, ASAEL. Non-Juror to Oath of Allegiance, 1778. (A-1/3)
BUCKINGHAM, BASIL. Non-Juror to Oath of Allegiance, 1778. (A-1/3)

BUCKINGHAM, BENJAMIN SR. Oath of Allegiance, 1778, before Hon. Peter Shepherd.
(A-1/3, A-2/49)

BUCKINGHAM, GEORGE. Non-Juror to Oath of Allegiance, 1778. (A-1/3)
BUCKINGHAM, JOHN SR. Non-Juror to Oath of Allegiance, 1778. (A-1/3)
BUCKINGHAM, JOHN JR. Non-Juror to Oath of Allegiance, 1778. (A-1/3)
BUCKINGHAM, RICHARD. Non-Juror to Oath of Allegiance, 1778. (A-1/3)

BUCKINGHAM, THOMAS. Oath of Allegiance, 1778, before Hon. George Lindenberger.
(A-1/3, A-2/52)

BUCKINGHAM, WILLIAM. Non-Juror to Oath of Allegiance, 1778. (A-1/3)

BUCKLE, ROBERT. Non-Juror to Oath of Allegiance, 1778. (A-1/3)

BUCKLEY, HENRY. Oath of Allegiance, 1778, before Hon. Frederick Decker. (A-2/31)

BUCKLEY, JOHN. Recruited in Baltimore by Samuel Chester for the 3rd Maryland
Regiment, March 2, 1780. (H-334)

BUCKLEY, THOMAS. Cabin Boy on September 19, 1776, and Marine in 1777 on ship
Defence. Took Oath of Allegiance, 1778, before Hon. William Lux. Could
not write; made his mark. (A-1/3, A-2/68, H-607, H-655)

BUDD, JOHN SR. Oath of Allegiance, 1778, before Hon. James Calhoun. (A-2/65)

BUNYAN, JOHN. Mate from May 24 to August 15, 1777, and Chief Mate from August 15,
to December 31, 1777, on ship Defence. (H-655)

BULGER, MARTIN. Oath of Allegiance, 1778, before Hon. George Lindenberger. (A-2/52)

BULL, ISAAC. Oath of Allegiance, 1778, before Hon. Jesse Dorsey. (A-1/3, A-2/63)

BULL, WILLIAM. Non-Juror to Oath of Allegiance, 1778. Involved in evaluation of
Baltimore County confiscated proprietary lands in 1782. (A-1/3, FFF-553)

BUM, JAMES. Non-Juror to Oath of Allegiance, 1778. (A-1/3)

BUM, JOHN. Non-Juror to Oath of Allegiance, 1778. (A-1/3)

BUNE, WILLIAM. Private, Capt. Deams' Co., 7th MD Regt., Dec. 11, 1776. (H-304)

BUNTING, WILLIAM. Oath of Allegiance, 1778, before Hon. James Calhoun. (A-2/39)

BURCHFIELD, CHARLES. Recruit, Baltimore County, 1780. (H-340)

BURDWISEL, JAMES. Non-Juror to Oath of Allegiance, 1778. (A-1/3)

BURFORD, GEORGE. Oath of Allegiance, 1778, before Hon. James Calhoun. (A-2/41)

BURGE, JOSEPH. Ship Steward on the Defence, September 19, 1776, as well as from January 11, 1777 through April 21, 1777. (H-607, H-655)

BURGESS, JOHN. Private, Capt. Ramsey's Co. No. 5, 1776. (H-640)

BURGESS, THOMAS. Oath of Allegiance, 1778, before Hon. George Lindenberger. (A-2/52)

BURGIN, THOMAS. Non-Juror to Oath of Allegiance, 1778. (A-1/3)

BURGLA, MICHAEL. Non-Juror to Oath of Allegiance, 1778. (A-1/3)

BURK (BURKE), ALEXANDER. Enlisted in Baltimore County, July 20, 1776. (H-53)

BURK, BARRY. Non-Juror to Oath of Allegiance, 1778. (A-1/3)

BURK, DANIEL. Oath of Allegiance, 1778, before Hon. Edward Cockey. (A-1/3, A-2/61)

BURK, DARBY. Oath of Allegiance, 1778, before Hon. William Lux. Could not write; made his mark ("C"). (A-1/3, A-2/68)

BURK, JOHN. Private, Baltimore Artillery Company, October 16, 1775. 1st Corporal, Col. Ewing's Battalion (enlisted July 6, 1776), August, 1776. Non-Juror to Oath of Allegiance, 1778. (A-1/3, G-8, H-54)

BURK, NATHANIEL, of Baltimore City. Private, Maryland Line. Nathan BURK and Mrs. Elizabeth JOHNSON, both of Baltimore, were married in October, 1804. As of March 13, 1829, he was paid, during life, quarterly, half pay of a Private, for his services during the Revolutionary War. On March 7, 1838, Elizabeth Burk, widow of Nathan, received half pay of a Private, as a further remuneration for services of her husband during her life. (C-324, C-325, ZZZ-45)

BURK, PETER. Private, Capt. Ewing's Co. No. 4, enlisted January 20, 1776. (H-12)

BURKE, FESTUS. Private, Capt. Smith's Co. No. 18, enlisted Jan. 11, 1776. (H-18)

BURKE, JACOB. Private, Capt. Graybill's German Regiment, 1776. (H-265)

BURKE, JOHN. Born 1745 in County Kerry, Ireland. Occupation: Labourer. Ht: 5' 6½". Enlisted January 26, 1776 as Private in Capt. N. Smith's 1st Co. of Matrosses. Joined Capt. Brown's Artillery Company as a Matross on November 22, 1777. Was at Valley Forge until June, 1778; at White Plains, July, 1778; at Fort Schuyler in August and September, 1780; not on rolls in August, 1781. (H-564, UU-228)

BURKE, RICHARD. Born 1753/1754 in Ireland. Died 1800 in Maryland. Married Hannah CASSELL, daughter of Jacob CASSELL (1734-1818) who was a Revolutionary patriot of Frederick County, MD. Richard's occupation was Butcher. Height: 5' 7¼". His son, Richard BURKE (1795-1842) married Mary DUNGAN (1801-1857), and their daughter Esther Louisa BURKE (1837-1904) married Thomas D. CASSELL in 1857. Richard BURKE was enlisted by Thomas Lansdale in Baltimore County on Jan. 27, 1776 and he became a Private in Capt. N. Smith's 1st Company of Matrosses. He was a Private in Capt. Dorsey's Maryland Artillery Company on Nov. 17, 1777. There is also a record of a Richard Burke re-enlisting in February, 1779, in Col. Otho H. Williams' 2nd MD Regiment. Richard Burke was also a member of the Baltimore Town Battalion of Major Thomas Jones on July 20, 1776. (Caution should be exercised that there might have been more than one Richard Burke.) He was a Matross in Capt. Gale's Artillery Co. in September, 1779 (having been

been deposed in May, 1779, regarding his enlistment terms as a Matross soldier. On October 31, 1779, he deserted near Chester, PA, but re-joined on December 10, 1779. He was at Morristown Camp on March 7 and April 13, 1780 (New Jersey duty). Federal Bounty Land Grant of 100 acres was issued (W1507) to his widow on May 11, 1829. He was not available for the Oath of Allegiance in 1778. (A-1/3, H-566, QQQ-2, H-564, VV-74, FFF-220, YYY-1/12, H-53, H-574, AAA-1413

BURKE, ULRICK. Oath of Allegiance, 1778, before Hon. Robert Simmons. Could not write; made his mark ("U"). (A-1/3, A-2/58)

BURLING, THOMAS. Baltimore Salt Committee, October 14, 1779. (HHH-88)

BURN, MICHAEL. Private, Capt. Oldham's Co., 4th MD Regt., April 26, 1778, as well as from June 1, 1779 to July, 1780. Oath of Allegiance, 1778, before Honorable James Calhoun. (A-1/3, A-2/40, H-88)

BURNELL, JOHN. Master on ship Defence on September 2, 1776, at which time he made a request for a commission as Lieutenant (at Baltimore). He was a Lieutenant from December 23, 1776 to at least March 3, 1777. (FFF-55, FFF-74, FFF-93, ZZ-254, ZZ-255, H-655)

BURNES, JOHN. Non-Juror to Oath of Allegiance, 1778. (A-1/3)

BURNET, PETER. Appears to be two Non-Jurors to the Oath with this same name. (A-1/3)

BURNHAM, JOHN. Non-Juror to Oath of Allegiance, 1778. (A-1/3)

BURNETT, CHARLES. Enlisted in Baltimore County, July 25, 1776. (H-52)

BURNHAM, JOHN. Private, Capt. J. Cockey's Baltimore County Dragoons at Yorktown in 1781. (MMM-A)

BURNIE, HUGH. Oath of Allegiance, 1778. (A-1/3)

BURNS, DAVID. Oath of Allegiance, 1778. (A-1/3)

BURNS, JOHN. Non-Juror to Oath of Allegiance, 1778. (A-1/3)

BURNS, PATRICK. Oath of Allegiance, 1778, before Hon. James Calhoun. (A-1/3, A-2/40)

BURNS, SIMON. Private, Baltimore Artillery Company, October 16, 1775. (G-8)

BURRIDGE, WILLIAM. Oath of Allegiance, 1778, before Hon. James Calhoun. (A-2/40)

BURTIS (BARTIS), SAMUEL. Private, Baltimore Artillery Company, October 16, 1775. Private, Capt. Sheaff's Company, June 16, 1777. 2nd Lieutenant in Company of Capt. Brittingham Dickinson in the Baltimore Town Battalion, September 25, 1780. Ensign, Capt. Dickinson's Company on January 19, 1781 and February 8, 1781. Took Oath of Allegiance, 1778. (A-1/3, F-305, G-8, W-162, R-15, BBBB-61)

BURTON, ISAAC. Matross, Capt. Brown's Artillery Company; joined November 22, 1777. Was at Valley Forge until June, 1778; at White Plains in July, 1778; at Fort Schuyler in August and September, 1780; at High Hills of the Santee in August, 1781. (UU-228, UU-229, UU-230)

BURTON, JOSEPH. Non-Juror to Oath of Allegiance, 1778. (A-1/3)
BURTON, THOMAS. Non-Juror to Oath of Allegiance, 1778. (A-1/3)

BUSBY, ABRAHAM. Involved in evaluation of Baltimore County confiscated proprietary reserve land in 1782. (FFF-543)
BUSBY, JOHN JR. Involved in evaluation of Baltimore County confiscated proprietary reserve land in 1782. (FFF-543)

BUSH (BURSH), ISAAC. Private, Capt. J. Gist's Company, 3rd MD Regt., January, 1778. Oath of Allegiance, 1778, before Hon. John Hall. (A-1/3, A-2/36, H-600)

BUSH, JAMES. Non-Juror to Oath of Allegiance, 1778. (A-1/3)
BUSH, SHADRACH. non-Juror to Oath of Allegiance, 1778. (A-1/3)

BUSHER, ULERK. Private, Baltimore County Regiment No. 15, circa 1777. (TTT-13)

BUSHON, PAUL. Oath of Allegiance, 1778, before Hon. James Calhoun. (A-1/3, A-2/41)

BUSHRO, JOSEPH. Non-Juror to Oath of Allegiance, 1778. (A-1/3)

BUSK, JAMES. Non-Juror to Oath of Allegiance, 1778. (A-1/3)

BUSK, JOHN. Non-Juror to Oath of Allegiance, 1778. (A-1/3)

BUSSBY, ABRAHAM. Non-Juror to Oath of Allegiance, 1778. (A-1/3)

BUSSBY, JOHN SR. Non-Juror to Oath of Allegiance, 1778. (A-1/3)

BUSSBY, JOHN JR. Non-Juror to Oath of Allegiance, 1778. (A-1/3)

BUSSEY, BENNETT. (November 8, 1745 - December 25, 1827) Married (1) Ann GREEN (2) Elizabeth SLADE. Took Oath of Allegiance in 1778 in Baltimore County before Hon. Jesse Dorsey, but was a Major in the Harford County Militia (see Peden's *Revolutionary Patriots of Harford County, MD, 1775-1783*). (JJJ-106, A-1/3, A-2/63)

BUSSEY, EDWARD. (1718-1782) Private in Maryland Militia, and took the Oath in 1778 before Hon. Jesse Dorsey. (JJJ-106, A-1/3, A-2/63)

BUSSEY, JESSE. Represented Gunpowder Upper Hundred at the Association of Freemen on August 21, 1775. Was a Justice of the Peace and administered the Oath in 1778 in Baltimore County. (GGG-242, A-1/4, A-2/44, EEEE-1726)

BUSSEY, JESSE JR. Oath of Allegiance, 1778, before Hon. Jesse Dorsey. (A-1/4, A-2/63)

BUTLER, ABRAHAM. 2nd Lt., Upper Battalion, November 5, 1781. (AAAA-662)

BUTLER, ABSALOM. Oath of Allegiance, 1778, before Hon. Andrew Buchanan. (A-2/57)

BUTLER, AMON (or AARON), SR. Oath of Allegiance, 1778, before Hon. Edward Cockey. (A-1/4, A-2/61) (Sources spelled his name differently; it probably was "Amon".)

BUTLER, AMON JR. Oath of Allegiance, 1778, before Hon. Andrew Buchanan. He died on August 4, 1804 in his 60th year, a resident of Baltimore County, leaving a wife and 9 children, and an aged mother and father. (A-1/4, A-2/57, ZZZ-47)

BUTLER, EDWARD. Non-Juror to Oath of Allegiance, 1778. (A-1/4)

BUTLER, EDWARD FERREL (or TERROL). Oath of Allegiance, 1778, before Hon. Isaac Van Bibber. (A-1/4, A-2/34)

BUTLER, HENRY. Ensign, Capt. Murray's Co., Baltimore County, Aug. 30, 1777. (BBB-350)

BUTLER, IGNATIUS. Joined Capt. Brown's Artillery Company as a Matross on Nov. 22, 1777. Was at Valley Forge until June, 1778; at White Plains in July, 1778; at Fort Schuyler in August and September, 1780; and at High Hills of the Santee in August, 1781. (UU-228, UU-229, UU-230)

BUTLER, JAMES. Served on ship *Defence*, March 6 to June 1, 1777. (H-655)

BUTLER, JOHN. Oath of Allegiance, 1778, before Hon. John Moale. (A-1/4, A-2/70)

BUTLER, JOHN (of Soldiers Delight). Oath of Allegiance, 1778, before Hon. John Moale. (A-1/4, A-2/70)

BUTLER, JONATHAN. Private, Capt. McClellan's Company, Baltimore Town, September 4, 1780. (CCC-24)

BUTLER, JOSEPH. There were two soldiers with this name in the military. One was a 1st Lieutenant in Capt. Ewing's Company No. 4, Maryland Troops, on Jan. 3, 1776, and in Smallwood's Maryland Regiment on Jan. 14, 1776. He was wounded and taken prisoner at the Battle of Long Island on Aug. 27, 1776, and died in captivity soon afterwards. (B-137, H-11). Another Joseph Butler was with Col. Nicholson's Troop of Horse on June 7, 1781. (BBBB-274)

BUTLER, NICHOLAS. Non-Juror to Oath of Allegiance, 1778. (A-1/4)

BUTLER, SAMUEL. Non-Juror to Oath of Allegiance, 1778. (A-1/4)

BUTLER, THOMAS. Non-Juror to Oath of Allegiance in 1778, but subsequently took the Oath in 1781. (A-1/4, QQ-107)

BUTLER, THOMAS AND BUTLER, HENRY. See "RUTTER." (Name sometimes mistaken for BUTLER)

BUTTERLING, WILLIAM. Non-Juror to Oath of Allegiance, 1778. (A-1/4)

BUTTERWORTH, BENJAMIN. Private, Capt. Howell's Company, December 30, 1775. Non-Juror to Oath of Allegiance, 1778. (A-1/4, G-11)

BUTTON, ELIAS. Non-Juror to Oath of Allegiance, 1778. (A-1/4)

BUTTON, OLIVER. He and his estate were seized by the British. An appeal in his behalf was made by John McClellan et al. to the Baltimore County Court on August 2, 1780. (FFF-306)

BUTTON, SAMUEL. Non-Juror to Oath of Allegiance, 1778. (A-1/4)

BUTTRIM, ISAAC. Private, Capt. Ramsey's Company No. 5, 1776. (H-640)

BUTTS, RICHARD. Oath of Allegiance, 1778, before Hon. Isaac Van Bibber. (A-2/34)

BYER, MATTHIAS, Private, Capt. Graybill's German Regiment, July 12, 1776. (ZZ-32)

BYERS, JAMES. Oath of Allegiance, 1778. (A-1/4)

BYERS, JOSEPH. Non-Juror to Oath of Allegiance, 1778. (A-1/4)

BYRAM, JOHN. Non-Juror to Oath of Allegiance, 1778. (A-1/4)

BYRNE, CHARLES. Recruit, Baltimore County, 1780. (H-340)

BYRNE, JOHN. Baltimore Artillery Company, 1777. Oath of Allegiance, 1778, before Hon. George Lindenberger. (A-1/4, A-2/52, V-368)

C

CABALL (CABEL), JACOB. Drafted in Baltimore County Regiment No. 36, circa 1777. Non-Juror to Oath of Allegiance in 1778. (A-1/4, TTT-13)

CADY, MICHAEL. Private, Capt. Ewing's Co. No. 4; enlisted Jan. 29, 1776. (H-12)

CAHAL,_____N. (part of list torn) Private, Baltimore Co. Regt. 7, c1777. (TTT-13)

CAIN, JOHN. Private, Capt. Smith's Company No. 8; enlisted Jan. 12, 1776. (H-18)

CAIN, WILLIAM. Supplied planks to Fort Whetstone Point in Baltimore, September 5, 1776. (FFF-55)

CALDER, JAMES. A native of Scotland, he died August 11, 1808 at his seat in Baltimore County, in his 79th year, leaving a wife and children. He took the Oath of Allegiance in 1778, and was involved in the evaluation of Baltimore County confiscated proprietary reserve lands in 1782. (A-1/4, FFF-542, ZZZ-48)

CALDER, JOHN. Baltimore Artillery Company, 1777. (V-368)

CALDWELL (CALWELL), JOHN. Private, Capt. Howell's Company, December 30, 1775. Enlisted July 17, 1776 in Baltimore Town, and served in the Baltimore Artillery Company in 1777. On May 17, 1779 he resigned as Ensign "in the room of Joseph Miller" and refused 2nd Lieutenant in the Baltimore Town Battalion the same day. He also took the Oath of Allegiance in 1778 before the Honorable William Spear. (A-2/66, F-310, GGG-401, F-311, G-11, V-368, H-53)

CALDWELL (CALDWEL), THOMAS. Non-Juror to Oath of Allegiance, 1778. (A-1/4)

CALEY, FREDERICK. Non-Juror to Oath of Allegiance, 1778. (A-1/4)

CALHOUN, JAMES. (1743-1816) Wife, Ann GIST (1746-1799); married in 1766. James was one of the most prominent patriots of Baltimore and served in many capacities. He was on the Committee of Inspection on March 13, 1775; the Committee of Observation on September 23, 1775 (having received the second most votes during the election); and the Committee of Correspondence on November 12, 1775. He was a member of the Sons of Liberty from 1766 to at least 1776, and a member of the Baltimore Mechanical

CALHOUN, JAMES (continued)
Company, and a Member of the Whig Club in 1777. On November 27, 1777, he was
"appointed Collector of cloathing for Baltimore County agreeable to Act of
Assembly to procure cloathing for the quota of this State of the American Army."
He was authorized by the Continental Congress to assign all bills of credit or
money for use by the Mechanical Volunteers and others for military purposes from
1776 to 1782. He was also Quartermaster of the Baltimore Town Battalion, 1776.
As a Justice of the Orphans Court and Justice of the Peace in 1778, he was one
of the administrative magistrates who gave the Oath of Allegiance. On Aug. 4,
1778 Major General James Calhoun wrote to the Governor on the hiring of wagons
to haul flour. On October 18, 1779 he was appointed by the General Assembly to
receive subscriptions in Baltimore County, and served on the Baltimore Salt Committee on October 14, 1779. He was selected general purveyor to look after the
comfort and subsistence of Count Rochambeau in Baltimore on September 9, 1781.
He was also one of the signers of a letter to Governor Lee on April 4, 1781, in
which they asked for help to defend the City of Baltimore against British attack.
He served throughout the Revolutionary War, and subsequently resigned as Justice
of the Peace on October 16, 1783. He was also a Baltimore Privateer, and, in
1797, James Calhoun became the first Mayor of Baltimore. He died on August 14,
1816, and his funeral was from his late residence on Baltimore Street. (ZZZ-49,
III-206, GGG-242, WW-443, GGG-499, CCC-26, HHH-88, EE-51, GG-74, A-1/4, A-2/38,
A-2/65, FF-64, CCC-18, S-49, FFF-616, SS-130, FFF-184, RR-19, RR-50, RR-47,
SS-136, EEEE-1725, BBB-426, CCC-1, CCC-18, CCC-19, CCC-25, III-207)

CALLAHAN, WILLIAM. Private, Capt. J. Cockey's Baltimore County Dragoons stationed
at Yorktown in 1781. (MMM-A)

CALLAHER, JOHN. Non-Juror to Oath of Allegiance, 1778. (A-1/4)

CALLENAN, JOHN. Private, Capt. Ramsey's Co. No. 5, 1776. (H-640)

CANNENDER (CALLENTER), DUVALL. Non-Juror to Oath of Allegiance, 1778. (A-1/4)

CALLOCHEN, EDWARD. Oath of Allegiance, 1778, before Hon. Peter Shepherd. (A-2/49)

CALLUMBER (COLLUMBER), THOMAS. Matross in Capt. Gale's Artillery Company, 1779.
Wagoner at Chester, PA, November 9, 1779. At Morristown Camp, March 7, 1780;
aick, April 13, 1780. Wounded (no date given) and "pay made up to January 1,
1782." (YYY-1/13)

CALVERT, JOHN. Oath of Allegiance, 1778, before Hon. James Calhoun. (A-2/42)

CALVERT, ROBERT. Private, Capt. Deams Co., 7th MD Regt., Jan. 5, 1777. (H-305)

CALVERT, WILLIAM. Oath of Allegiance, 1778, before Hon. William Lux. (A-2/68)

CALVIN, PHILIP. Oath of Allegiance, 1778, before Hon. George G. Presbury. (A-2/48)

CALWRIGHT, WILLIAM. Non-Juror to Oath of Allegiance, 1778. (A-1/4)

CAMBRIDGE, JOSEPH. Private, Capt. Howell's Company, December 30, 1775, and with
the Baltimore Artillery Company in 1777. (V-368)

CAMERON, JAMES. Non-Juror to Oath of Allegiance, 1778. (A-1/4)

CAMPBELL, ARCHIBALD. Blacksmith for Capt. J. Cockey's Baltimore County Dragoons
at Yorktown in 1781. (MMM-A)

CAMPBELL, GEORGE. 2nd Lt., Capt. Deams Co., Baltimore Town, June 6, 1776. (WW-467)

CAMPBELL, JAMES. 1st Lt., Capt. Smith's Co. No. 8, Smallwood's Maryland Regiment,
January 2 and 14, 1776. (B-141, H-17)

CAMPBELL, JAMES. Served on ship Defence, January 28 to July 15, 1777. (H-655)

CAMPBELL, JOHN. Served on Ship Defence, January 28 to December 31, 1777. (H-655)

CAMPBELL, ROBERT. Joined Capt. Brown's Artillery Company as a Matross on Nov. 22,
1777. Was at Valley Forge until June, 1778; at White Plains in July, 1778; at
at Fort Schuyler, August and September, 1780; not listed in 1781. (UUU-228, 230)

CAMPBELL, WILLIAM. 3rd Lt., Capt. Fulford's Company of Matrosses, Baltimore, March 23, 1776. 2nd Lt., July 5, 1776. May have been the same William Campbell (1756-1821) from Maryland who became a 2nd Lt. in the 6th Pennsylvania on January 1, 1777; wounded and taken prisoner at Germantown on October 4, 1777; exchanged October 25, 1780; became a Captain on January 1, 1781. Captain William Campbell was an Original Member of the Society of the Cincinnati of Maryland, now represented by Thomas Campbell Washington, Jr. (Captain, U.S.Army, W.W.II) of Virginia. (TT-64, H-570)

CAMPBLE (CAMPLE), SAMUEL. Oath of Allegiance, 1778, before Hon. James Calhoun. (A-1/4, A-2/40)

CANN, JOHN. Oath of Allegiance, 1778, before Hon. Jesse Dorsey. (A-1/4, A-2/63)

CANNADY, THOMAS. Private, 3rd Maryland Regiment, entitled to 50 acres (lot no. 1149) in western Maryland. (DDDD-9) Non-Juror to Oath in 1778. (A-1/4)

CANNIE, MICHAEL. Matross, Capt. J. Smith's Artillery Co., 1782-3. (YYY-2/9)

CANNON, JOHN. Private, Baltimore Artillery Company, October 16, 1775. Sergeant in Capt. Sheaff's Company, June 16, 1777. Ensign, Baltimore Town Battalion on August 29, 1777. Became a 2nd Lieutenant, but resigned "in the room of Caleb Shields" on May 19, 1779. Non-Juror to Oath in 1778. Deceased prior to January 19, 1781. (E-13, Z-63, BBB-348, GGG-401, F-310, F-312, BBBR-29, BBBB-61, R-15, W-162, G-8, A-1/4)

CAPEL, BENJAMIN. Non-Juror to Oath of Allegiance, 1778, (A-1/4)

CAPEL (CAPLE), JAMES. Private, Capt. Graybill's German Regiment, July 12, 1776. (ZZ-32)

CAPEL, SAMUEL. Non-Juror to Oath of Allegiance, 1778. (A-1/4)

CAPES, JOHN. Private, Capt. Keeports Co., German Regiment; enlisted July 21, 1776; at Philadelphia, September 19, 1776. (H-263)

CAPHNE, EDWARD. Oath of Allegiance, 1778, before Hon. Peter Shepherd. (A-2/49)

CAPKINS, JNO. Delivered flour for Baltimore Town Committee, 1780. (RRR-6)

CAPLES, ROBERT LEMON JR. (CAPEL). (September 29, 1717, Anne Arundel County, MD - March 21, 1801, Baltimore County, MD) Son of Robert Lemon CAPLES and wife Susannah HOLLAND, and grandson of William CAPELL. Buried in Old Caples Cem. on Hebb's Farm, Butler Road, Baltimore County. Married (2) Aliese COLE, and a son Jacob CAPLES (1773-1851) married Mary BASSETT or BENNETT in 1816, and their son Jacob Larkin CAPLES (1824-1892) married Emily Tyson SIMPERS (1828-1910) in 1845 in Baltimore County. Robert took the Oath of Allegiance in 1778 in Baltimore County's North Hundred. (AAA-2247)

CAPPELLE (CAPLE), JAMES. Private, Capt. Graybill's German Regt., 1776. (H-265)

CAPPERSTONE, GEORGE. Non-Juror to Oath of Allegiance, 1778. (A-1/4)
CARBACK, HENRY. Non-Juror to Oath of Allegiance, 1778. (A-1/4)
CARBACK, JOHN. Non-Juror to Oath of Allegiance, 1778. (A-1/4)
CARBACK, THOMAS. Non-Juror to Oath of Allegiance, 1778. (A-1/4)

CARBERRY, HENRY. Able Seaman on ship Defence, September 19, 1776. (H-606)

CARBERRY (CARBURY), RICHARD. Private, Capt. Ewing's Company No. 4; enlisted on January 29, 1776. (H-12)

CARBERRY (CORBERRY), THOMAS. Oath of Allegiance, 1778, before Hon. Isaac Van Bibber. (A-1/4, A-2/34)

CARDIFF (CARDOF), THOMAS. Recruited in Baltimore by Samuel Chester for the 3rd Maryland Regiment, March 2, 1780. (H-334)

CAREY, JOHN. Baltimore Privateer and Captain of brig Hercules (16 guns, 60 men) owned by Young, Knox & Company of Baltimore. (III-206)

CAREY, JOSHUA. Chosen as 2nd Lt., Hunting Ridge Company, 39th Battalion of Militia when John Bailey entered Continental Service, August 29, 1777. Served as 2nd Lt. in Baltimore Town Battalion, 1778-1779. (BBB-348, Y-61, E-13, F-311)

CARL, WILLIAM. Non-Juror to Oath of Allegiance, 1778. (A-1/4)

CARLINE (CARLIN), CHARLES. Oath of Allegiance, 1778. Ensign, Capt. Douglass' Co., Baltimore County Militia, May 17, 1779. (A-1/4, F-309) Source GGG-401 spells his name "Carbine" on page 401 and "Carline" on page 324.

CARMAN, ANDREW. Non-Juror to Oath of Allegiance, 1778. (A-1/4)

CARMAN, JAMES. Recruit, Baltimore County Militia, April 11, 1780. (H-335)

CARMEN, JOHN. Sergeant of Marines on ship Defence, June 1 to Nov. 22, 1777. (H-655)

CARMICHAEL, DUNCAN. Non-Juror to Oath of Allegiance, 1778. (A-1/4)

CARNAN, CHARLES. Captain of Soldiers Delight Company No. 5 (79 Privates) on May 13, 1776 and June 6, 1776. 1st Major, Soldiers Delight Battalion, June 3, 1777. Lt. Colonel under Col. Hammond, September 10, 1777 to 1781. Lt. Colonel under Col. Nicholson's Troop of Horse, June 7, 1781, and resigned later that year. Took the Oath of Allegiance, 1778, before Hon. John Moale, February 26, 1778. Died January 19, 1809, at his residence in Garrison Forest, an old inhabitant of Baltimore County. (ZZZ-51, BBBB-560, BBBB-274, SSS-110, BBB-271, WW-467, FF-64, E-10, BBB-368, A-1/4, A-2/70)

CARNAN, ROBERT NORTH. Private, Baltimore County Regiment No. 7, circa 1777 (name partially torn off list). Oath of Allegiance, 1778, before Hon. John Moale. Member of Col. Nicholson's Troop of Horse, June 7, 1781. Robert was born on August 8, 1756 and died on May 12, 1836 in Baltimore County, with burial in St.Thomas P.E. Church in Garrison Forest. He married Katherine RiSTEAU, who was born June 17, 1758 and died March 5, 1803. A son, Christopher (b. 1780) married Christiana Sim HOLLIDAY (d.1823) in 1802, and their son Charles CARNAN (1804-1835) married Keziah BISHOP (1802-1881) in 1824. A daughter, Rebecca R. NORTH married Joshua TEVIS in 1813. (ZZZ-318, TTT-13, AAA-2614, BBBB-274, A-1/4, A-2/70)

CARNES, ARTHUR. Joined Capt. Brown's Artillery Company as a Bombardier on Nov. 22, 1777. Was at Valley Forge until June, 1778; at White Plains, July, 1778; at Fort Schuyler, August and September, 1780; not listed in Aug. 1781. (UU-228)

CARNEY, CORNELIUS. Private, Capt. Furnival's Maryland Artillery Company, Nov. 17, 1777; listed as "sick - agae fever." Matross, Capt. Gale's Artillery Company in 1779; at Chester, PA camp, Nov. 9, 1779, and Morristown camp on March 7, 1780 and April 13, 1780. (H-573, YYY-1/14)

CARNEY (CARNY), JEREMIAH. Oath of Allegiance, 1778, before Hon. James Calhoun. (A-1/4, A-2/38)

CARNEY, JOHN. Born 1751 in Ireland. Sandy complexion; height: 5' 4". Enlisted July 7, 1776 as Private in Col. Ewing's Battalion, Baltimore County. (H-56)

CARNEY (CARNEE), MICHAEL. Enlisted in Baltimore County, July 20, 1776. (H-52)

CARPENTER, THOMAS. Joined Capt. Brown's Artillery Company on November 22, 1777. Was at Valley Forge until June, 1778; at White Plains, July, 1778; at Fort Schuyler, August and September, 1780; not listed in 1781. (UU-228, UU-230)

CARR, DANIEL. Oath of Allegiance, 1778. (A-1/4)

CARR, GEORGE. Oath of Allegiance, 1778, before Hon. Thomas Sollers. (A-2/51, A-1/4)

CARR, HENRY. Marine on ship Defence, September 19, 1776 to 1777. (H-607, H-654)

CARR, JOHN. Born 1738 in Germany. Full faced, black hair; height: 5' 8¼". Enlisted July 5, 1776 as Private in Col. Ewing's Battalion, Baltimore County. On March 9, 1846, Margaret Loney, formerly Margaret Carr of Baltimore County, widow of John Carr, a soldier of the Revolution, received half pay of a Private in consideration of services rendered by her former husband during the War of the Revolution. (C-327, H-56)

CARR (KARR), ROBERT. Private, Capt. Furnival's Maryland Artillery, Nov. 17, 1777 "sick - burnt arm at camp." Matross, Capt. Gale's Company, 1779; at Chester, PA camp, Nov. 9, 1779; at Morristown, NJ camp, Mar. 7, 1780 and April 13, 1780. (YYY-1/15, H-573, H-618)

CARRAGAN, EDWARD. Oath of Allegiance, 1778, before Hon. George Lindenberger. (A-1/4, A-2/52)

CARRING, ANDREW. Oath of Allegiance, 1778, before Hon. Richard Cromwell. (A-2/46)

CARRINGTON, EDWARD. Lt. Colonel from Virginia who commanded the 1st Continental Artillery from November 30, 1776 to retirement on January 1, 1783. Command included three companies of men from Baltimore, stationed there in 1780. He died October 28, 1810. (B-146, VVV-96)

CARROLL, DANIEL. Oath of Allegiance, 1778, before Hon. James Calhoun. Signed a letter to Gov. Lee in 1781 requesting a defense of Baltimore. (A-2/39, S-49)

CARROLL, HENRY ("HENERY CARROL"). Born 1754 in west of Ireland. Occupation was breeches maker. Height: 5' 5". Enlisted January 28, 1776 as Private in Capt. N. Smith's 1st Company of Matrosses. Private, Capt. Dorsey's Company of Artillery, November 17, 1777. Deposed May 7, 1779 as a Matross soldier in Baltimore County. Matross, Capt. Gale's Artillery Company, 1779; was at Chester, PA, November 9, 1779; at Morristown, NJ on March 7 and Apr. 13, 1780. (Letter dated April 20, 1922 from the Adjutant General's Office to United States Senator Selden P. Spencer verified the service of Henry Carroll, and that of a Col. Henry James Carroll.) (YYY-1/16, FFF-220, H-574, VV-74, H-564, H-567, QQQ-2)

CARROLL, JOHN. Born 1745 in Limerick, Ireland. Occupation: Butcher. Ht: 5' 6¼". Enlisted January 27, 1776 as Private in Capt. N. Smith's 1st Co. of Matrosses. Joined Capt. Brown's Artillery Company, November 22, 1777, as Fifer. Was at Valley Forge until June, 1778; at White Plains, July, 1778; at Fort Schuyler in August and September, 1780; not listed in 1781. (H-564, QQQ-2, UU-228)

CARROLL, JOSEPH. Private, Capt. Keeports German Regiment; enlisted July 21, 1776; at Philadelphia, September 19, 1776. (H-263).

CARROLL, THOMAS. Private, Capt. J. Gist's Co., 3rd MD Reg., Feb., 1778. (H-600)

CARSON, DAVID. Non-Juror to Oath of Allegiance, 1778. (A-1/4)

CARSON, HUGH. Non-Juror to Oath of Allegiance, 1778. (A-1/4)

CARSON (CORSON), JAMES. Oath of Allegiance, 1778, before Hon. George Lindenberger. (A-1/4, A-2/52)

CARSON, JOHN. 2nd Lt., Capt. Brown's Company No. 1, Maryland Artillery; commission on May 1, 1779; under Lt.Col. Carrington, May 11, 1780, stationed at Baltimore. Transferred to Capt. Singleton, January 1, 1781. (UU-229, VVV-96)

CARSON, RICHARD. Non-Juror to Oath of Allegiance, 1778. Wrote to the Governor of Maryland on April 11, 1780, about forwarding linen from Baltimore to Philadelphia. (A-1/4, FFF-283)

CARTER, DENNIS. Oath of Allegiance, 1778, before Hon. Jesse Dorsey. (A-1/4, A-2/63)

CARTER, HARRY. Private, Col. Aquila Hall's Baltimore County Regt., 1777. (TTT-13)

CARTER, JAMES. Private, Count Pulaski's Legion; enlisted in Baltimore, May 11, 1778. (H-593)

CARTER, JOHN. Born March 14, 1737 or 1757 in Baltimore County, MD. Died c1823 in Brownsville, PA. Married Hannah SCARBOROUGH on December 1, 1784, in MD.

During the Revolution he was a Private and a Corporal. Non-Juror to Oath of Allegiance, 1778. A son, John Scarborough CARTER, married Elizabeth ENSOR. (A-1/4, D-2, JJJ-117, XXX-200)

CARTER, JOSEPH. Non-Juror to Oath of Allegiance, 1778. (A-1/4)

CARTER, RICHARD. Non-Juror to Oath of Allegiance, 1778. (A-1/4)

CARTER, ROBERT. Born in February, 1728 in Northumberland, Virginia. Died on March 11, 1804, in Baltimore, Maryland. Married Frances Ann TASKER of Baltimore on April 15, 1754 in Baltimore. A daughter, Betty Landon CARTER (1764-1842) married Spencer BALL (1762-1832) in Virginia, and their daughter Adeline BALL (1799-1880) married Rev. Hezekiah BEST (1801-1878) in 1833 (Best was born in Maryland and died in Georgia). During the Revolutionary War, Robert CARTER served on the Executive Council of Virginia. (AAA-2600, JJJ-118, ZZZ-53)

CARTER, SAMUEL. (1730 - December 8, 1796). Married Mary IRONS. Private in Capt. J. Smith's Maryland Artillery, and appointed Sergeant in Capt. Gale's Artillery Company on September 3, 1779. Was at Chester, PA on November 9, 1779, and at Morristown, NJ on March 7, 180 and April 13, 1780. Sergeant in Capt. Dorsey's Maryland Artillery at Camp Col. Scirvins on January 28, 1782, and a Sergeant in Capt. Smith's Artillery in 1782-1783. (JJJ-118, UU-232, H-579, YYY-1/17, YYY-2/10)

CARTER, SOLOMON. Non-Juror to Oath of Allegiance, 1778. (A-1/4)

CARTER, THOMAS. (March 20, 1758 - June 6, 1792). Married Ann BETTS. Matross and Gunner in Capt. Brown's Artillery Company, joining November 22, 1777. Was at Valley Forge until June, 1778; at White Plains, July, 1778; at Fort Schuyler, August and September, 1780; not listed in 1781. (JJJ-118, UU-228, UU-230)

CARTER, WILLIAM. Midshipman on ship Defence, September 19, 1776, and May 1, 1777 to September 15, 1777. (H-655)

CARTWRIGHT, ABRAM. Non-Juror to Oath of Allegiance, 1778. (A-1/4)

CARTY, TIMOTHY. Private, Baltimore County Militia; enlisted Aug. 15, 1776. (H-58)

CARUTHERS, W. Oath of Allegiance, 1778. (A-1/4)

CARVER, WILLIAM. Oath of Allegiance, 1778, before Hon. James Calhoun. (A-1/4, A-2/38)

CARWIN, JAMES. Matross, Capt. Brown's Artillery Company, joining November 22, 1777. Was at Valley Forge until June, 1778; at White Plains, July, 1778; at Fort Schuyler, August and September, 1780; not listed in 1781. (UU-228, UU-230)

CASEY, JAMES. Private, Col. Ewing's Battalion; enlisted in Baltimore County on July 7, 1776; not on muster roll in August, 1776. (H-57)

CASEY, JOHN. Recruit, Baltimore County, 1780. (H-340)

CASEY, MICHAEL. Private, Capt. S. Smith's Company No. 8, 1st Maryland Battalion, January 24, 1776. (H-641)

CASKIN, WILLIAM. Private, Capt. Deams Co., 7th MD Regt., January 16, 1777. (H-305)

CASSAN, JAMES. Baltimore Mechanical Company of Militia, November 4, 1775. (F-299)

CASSEDYE, PATRICK. Oath of Allegiance, 1778, before Hon. Richard Cromwell. (A-2/46)

CASWELL, RICHARD. Non-Juror to Oath of Allegiance, 1778. (A-1/4)

CATHEL, JOSIAH. He enlisted two men into Capt. Brown's Company of Matrosses and "under Capt. Brown's promise to endeavor to procure his discharge on his so doing, he is therefore discharged from further service, November 6, 1777." (BBB-410)

CATCHLY (CATHLY), THOMAS. Oath of Allegiance, 1778, before Hon. George Lindenberger. (A-1/4, A-2/52)

CATIER, HENRY. Non-Juror to Oath of Allegiance, 1778. (A-1/4)

CATIER, STOPHEL. Non-Juror to Oath of Allegiance, 1778. (A-1/4)

CATO, JOHN. Private, Baltimore County Regiment No. 7, cicra 1777. (TTT-13)

CATTLE (COTTLE), JOHN. Private, Baltimore Artillery Company, Oct. 16, 1775. Oath of Allegiance, 1778, before Hon. Isaav VanBibber. (A-2/34, G-8)

CATZ, MICHAEL. Non-Juror to Oath of Allegiance, 1778. (A-1/4)

CAULFIELD, ROBERT. Commander of schooner Baltimore, July 26, 1779. Baltimore Privateer and Captain of brig Burling (14 guns, 50 men) owned by John Sterrett, Daniel Bowley and others of Baltimore. (GGG-480, III-206)

CAULK, SLIVER. Oath of Allegiance in 1781. (QQ-107)

CAUSY, JOHN. Oath of Allegiance in 1778. (A-1/4)

CAVENDAR, JOHN. Private, Capt. Ewing's Co. No. 4; enlisted Jan. 24, 1776. (H-12)

CAVIL, DAVID (DAVIS). Non-Juror to Oath of Allegiance, 1778. (A-1/4)

CAWTHER, ELY. Non-Juror to Oath of Allegiance, 1778. (A-1/4)

CHADDOCK, THOMAS. Oath of Allegiance, 1778, before Hon. George Lindenberger. (A-2/52)

CHADWICK, RICHARD. Oath of Allegiance, 1778. (A-1/4)

CHADWICK, THOMAS. 2nd Lt., Baltimore Town Battalion, 1779. (BBB-362, E-14, F-312)

CHAIN, ISAIAH. Matross, Capt. Gale's Artillery Company, 1779. On command at New Winsor, October, 1779; at Chester, PA, November 9, 1779; on furlough from November through March; reported deserted April 1, 1780. (YYY-1/18)

CHAMBERLAIN, JAMES. Oath of Allegiance, 1778, before Hon. Jesse Dorsey. (A-2/63)

CHAMBERLAIN, JOHN. Non-Juror to Oath of Allegiance, 1778. He was born circa 1755 in Baltimore County, a son of John CHAMBERLAIN and Margaret GITTINGS. He was married to Elizabeth LYNCH on November 22, 1780. (A-1/4, D-2)

CHAMBERLAIN, PHILLIP. Born December 12, 1746, a son of John CHAMBERLAIN and wife Margaret GITTINGS. Was a 2nd Lt., Gunpowder Upper Hundred Batt., May, 1776. Oath of Allegiance, 1778, before Hon. John B. Howard. (WW-413, EE-51, A-2/29)

CHAMBERLAIN, THOMAS. Oath of Allegiance in 1778. Born February 19, 1740, a son of John CHAMBERLAIN and Margaret GITTINGS. He married Elizabeth WILKINSON on December 9, 1764. (A-1/4, D-2)

CHAMBERLANE (CHAMBORLAM), CHARLES. Quartermaster, September 19, 1776, and Sailor, 1777, on ship Defence. (H-655)

CHAMBERS, JAMES. Oath of Allegiance, 1778, before Hon. Richard Holliday. (A-2/60)

CHAMBERS, NATHAN. Private, Capt. J. Gist's Co., 3rd MD Regt., Feb., 1778. (H-600)

CHAMEAU, SIXTE. Oath of Allegiance, 1778, before Hon. Geo. Lindenberger. (A-2/52)

CHAMPION, GEORGE. Boatswain's Yeoman on ship Defence, Feb. 26-Dec. 31, 1777.(H-655)

CHAMPLAIN, HUGH. Matross, Capt. Brown's Artillery Company; joined Nov. 22, 1777. Was at Valley Forge until June, 1778; at White Plains, July, 1778; at Fort Schuyler, August and September, 1780; not listed in 1781. (UU-228, UU-230)

CHANCE, JEREMIAH. Non-Juror to Oath of Allegiance, 1778. (A-1/4)

CHANDLEE, WILLIAM. Non-Juror to Oath of Allegiance, 1778. (A-1/4)

CHANDLER, ISAAC. Private, Capt. J. Cockey's Baltimore County Dragoons at Yorktown in 1781. (MMM-A)

CHANDLER, JOHN. Private, Capt. J. Cockey's Baltimore County Dragoons at Yorktown in 1781. (MMM-A)

CHANDLER, WILLIAM. Oath of Allegiance, 1778, before Hon. Hercules Courtenay. (A-2/37)

CHAPLIN, WILLIAM. Private, Capt. Ewing's Co. No. 4, enlisted Jan. 20, 1776. (H-12)

CHAPMAN, DANIEL. Oath of Allegiance, 1778, before Hon. Edward Cockey. (A-2/62)

CHAPMAN, JOHN. 2nd Lt., Soldiers Delight Battalion Company No. 4, May 13, 1776. 1st Lt., Capt. Philips Company, commissioned August 30, 1777. 1st Lt., Capt. Tevis' Company, May 27, 1779. Oath of Allegiance, 1778, before Hon. Peter Shepherd. (A-2/49, A-1/4, HH-24, E-11, FF-64, KK-66, BBB-350, GGG-422)

CHAPMAN, JOSHUA. 2nd Lt., Capt. Philips' Company, commissioned August 30, 1777. 2nd Lt., Soldiers Delight Battalion, 1778. 2nd Lt., Capt. Tevis' Company, May 27, 1779. Oath of Allegiance, 1778, before Hon. Peter Shepherd. (A-1/4, A-2/49, E-11, HH-24, KK-66, BBB-350, GGG-422)

CHAPMAN, LUKE. Oath of Allegiance, 1778, before Hon. Peter Shepherd. (A-1/4, A-2/50)

CHAPMAN, NATHAN. Non-Juror to Oath of Allegiance, 1778. Possibly a son of Robert and Margaret CHAPMAN, he died in 1807 in Baltimore County. His wife was Rebecca GRIFFITH. Their children: Jemima, married William HUTSON in 1780; Elizabeth, married John DETTOR; William; Rebecca, married Benjamin C. GRIFFITH; James, married Rachel MERRYMAN in 1798; Nathan; Job (1776-1840) married Ann SYKES; Helen (1774-1831)married John REISTER in 1801; Mary, married Mathias RIDER; Hannah; and, Joshua (d. 1795). (A-1/4, D-2)

CHAPMAN, REZIN. Oath of Allegiance, 1778, before Hon. Edward Cockey. (A-1/4, A-2/61)

CHAPMAN, ROBERT. Oath of Allegiance, 1778, before Hon. Peter Shepherd.(A-1/4, A-2/49)

CHAPMAN, STEPHEN. Oath of Allegiance, 1778, before Hon. Edward Cockey.(A-1/4, A-2/62)

CHAPMAN, SAMUEL. Oath of Allegiance, 1778. (A-1/4)

CHAPMAN, WILLIAM. (January 19, 1748 - June 16, 1800) married Mary GOSNELL. He was a Private, Extra Regt., at Fort Whetstone Point, Baltimore, 1781.(H-626, JJJ-125)

CHAPPEL, SAMUEL. Oath of Allegiance, 1778, before Hon. James Calhoun. Recruit in Baltimore County, 1780. (A-2/41, H-340)

CHAPPELL, JOHN. Non-Juror to Oath of Allegiance, 1778. (A-1/4)

CHARLES, CHARLES. Private, Capt. Graybill's German Regiment, 1776. (H-265)

CHASE, JEREMIAH TOWNLEY. (May 23, 1748 - May 11, 1828) Son of Richard CHASE. He represented Baltimore at the Association of Freemen on July 26, 1775; served on the Baltimore Town Committee of Correspondence, November 12, 1775, having been elected on September 23, 1775 to serve on the Committee of Observation. He was a Delegate to the Provincial Convention in 1775, and Baltimore City's Delegate to the Convention on August 7, 1776. He served as Council President in Annapolis in 1780, and was elected Council to the Governor, Nov. 16, 1782. His wife was Hester BALDWIN. Their children: Matilda, married Thomas CHASE in 1816; Catherine, married Richard J. CRABB, Esq., in 1813; Fanny, married Richard LOOCKERMAN in 1803; Richard Moale; and, Hester Ann. Jeremiah's long obituary gives details of his distinguished public career. (UUU-30, UUU-31, JJJ-126, BB-2, UUU-115, SS-130, SS-136, RR-51, RR-47, EEEE-1725, CCCC-305, FFF-263, FFF-50)

CHASE, SAMUEL. (April 17, 1741, Somerset County, MD - June 19, 1811, Baltimore). Son of Rev. Thomas CHASE and Matilda WALKER. Samuel was one of the 4 signers of the Declaration of Independence from Maryland. He also served on Baltimore County's Commission of Confiscated Property in 1782, and was partner in the Nottingham Ironworks in Baltimore County He was an Associate Judge of the U.S. Supreme Court. He married (1) Ann BALDWIN, and (2) Hannah GILES. Children: Thomas; Samuel; Matilda (1763-1835) married Judge Henry RIDGELY; Nancy; Fanny; Mary; and, Elizabeth or Eliza, married Dr. Skipwith H. COALE, and their son Samuel Chase COALE married Martha VOTAW. Hon. Samuel Chase died the night of June 17, 1811 in Baltimore, MD. (ZZZ-57, JJJ-127, AAA-252, UUU-154, FFF-468)

CHASE, THOMAS. Oath of Allegiance, 1778, before Hon. William Lux. (A-1/4, A-2/68)

CHATERTON, JNO. Private, Capt. Deams Co., 7th MD Regt., January 1, 1777. (H-305)

CHEANEY, RICHARD. Private, Capt. Ramsey's Company No. 5, 1776.)H-640)

CHEETAM, WILLIAM. Oath of Allegince, 1778, before Hon. Edward Cockey. (A-2/61)

CHENOWETH (CHINWORTH), ARTHUR SR. (1716 - April, 1802) Married Mary SMITH. Oath of Allegiance, 1778, before Hon. Andrew Buchanan. (A-2/57, JJJ-128)

CHENOWETH, ARTHUR JR. (July 16, 1752 - after 1793) Married Elspa LAWRENCE. Oath of Allegiance, 1778, before Hon. Peter Shepherd. Corporal, Rawlings' Regiment; discharged August 9, 1779. He first appeared on the rolls of Jan., 1778 at Hospital to March 15 and then on detachment with Capt. Lynch, 4th MD Regt., in April, 1778. (H-100, H-301, JJJ-128, A-1/4, A-2/49)

CHENOWETH, ARTHUR (OF RICHARD). (1737 - 1802) 1st Lt., Soldiers Delight Battn., Capt. Charles Chinworth's Co., February 7, 1782. Earlier, October 23, 1781, he was a 2nd Lt. in Capt. Marsh's Company, Gunpowder Upper Battn. His name was also spelled "Chinworth." Took Oath of Allegiance, 1778, before Honorable Richard Holliday. He married (1) Ann BEASEMAN, and (2) Deliah Bosley HELMS. (A-1/4, A-2/60, JJJ-128, CCCC-71, AAAA-650)

CHENOWETH (CHINWORTH), CHARLES. Captain, Soldiers Delight Battalion, "in the room of Benjamin Tevis," February 7, 1782. (CCCC-71)

CHENOWETH, EDWARD. Enlisted August 14, 1776, in Baltimore county. (H-52)

CHENOWETH, JOSEPH. Private, Capt. Talbot's Company, May 31, 1779. Non-Juror to Oath of Allegiance, 1778. (U-90, F-301, A-1/4)

CHENOWETH (CHINOWITH), RICHARD. (c1755 - after 1815) Married to Elinor ASKEW. 2nd Lt., Capt. J. Gist's Company, 3rd MD Regiment, commissioned April 6, 1777. On the Wilmington, DE rolls in February, 1778, but "absent contrary to orders, gone to Maryland" in March, 1778. (H-600, JJJ-128) Oath of 1778. (A-1/4)

CHENOWETH (CHINWORTH), SAMUEL. Oath of Allegiance, 1778, before Honorable Adnrew Buchanan. (A-1/4, A-2/57)

CHENOWETH, THOMAS. Ensign, Soldiers Delight Battalion, 1778 through May 27, 1779. Lieutenant, in Capt. Talbott's Company, May 31, 1779, after serving with Capt. Gosnell's Company. With Gunpowder Upper Battalion through October 23, 1781. Oath of Allegiance, 1778, before Hon. Andrew Buchanan. (A-1/4, A-2/57, HH-24, E-10, U-90, F-301, GGG-422, AAAA-651)

CHENOWETH (CHINWORTH), THOMAS. (1720 - after 1787) Married to Mary PRITCHETT. Oath of Allegiance, 1778, before Hon. James Calhoun. (A-2/38, JJJ-128)

CHENOWETH, THOMAS. Enlisted in Baltimore county on August 14, 1776. Took Oath of Allegiance, 1778, before Hon. Richard Holliday. (H-52, A-1/4, A-2/60)

CHENOWETH, WILLIAM. Born 1758 in Baltimore Co., & died there on July 20, 1820. He married Sarah BAXTER in 1793. Children: John Baxter (born 1794); Mary Eleanor (or Mary Nellie), born 1796, married Ned BOND; Charity, born 1798, married Henry BOND; Sarah, born 1800, married George EBAUGH; and, William, born 1802. William took Oath of Allegiance, 1778, before Honorable Peter Shepherd. (A-1/4, A-2/50, JJJ-128, D-2, XXX-208)

CHENOWETH, WILLIAM. Ensign, Soldiers Delight Battn., Company No. 8, May 13, 1776. 2nd Lt., Soldiers Delight Battn., June 6, 1776. 1st Lt., Soldiers Delight Battn., February 7, 1782 (name spelled "Chinworth") (FF-64, WW-468, CCCC-71) This William Chenoweth might be the William Chenoweth (1758-1820) above.

CHESHIRE, BENJAMIN. Marine on ship <u>Defence</u>, May 25 to Dec. 31, 1777. (H-655)

CHESTER, CHARLES. Private, Capt. Deams Co., 7th MD Regt., Jan. 16, 1777. (H-305)

CHESTER, DANIEL. Sergeant, Capt. N. Smith's 1st Co. of Matrosses, June 29, 1776.
(H-565, QQQ-2)

CHESTER, JOSEPH. Private, Baltimore Artillery Company, October 16, 1775, to 1777.
Oath of Allegiance, 1778, before Hon. Isaac VanBibber. (A-2/34, G-8, V-368, A-1/4)

CHESTER, SAMUEL. Captain and Recruiting Officer in Baltimore during the Revolution.
Died December 3, 1801, his funeral was "with the honors of war." (ZZZ-58, H-334)

CHESTER, SAMUEL. Private, Capt. Dorsey's Co. MD Artillery, Nov. 17, 1777. (H-574)

CHESTER, SAMUEL. Sergeant, Capt. N. Smith's 1st Company of Matrosses, Jan. 24, 1776.
Born 1749 in Shrewsbury, England. Occupation: Breeches Maker. Height: 5' 6" (H-563)

CHESTER, SAMEUL. Oath of Allegiance, 1778, before Hon. George Lindenberger. (A-2/52)
This Samuel Chester was probably the Capt. Samuel Chester, Baltimore's Recruiter.

CHESTON, SGT. Decision not to accept a commission if apointed, June 20, 1777. (FFF-111)

CHETTLER, WILLIAM. Oath of Allegiance, 1778, before Hon. John Beale Howard. (A-2/29)

CHEVER (CHEEVER, CHEVAR, CHEEVERS), JOHN. Commissioned 2nd Lt., September 3, 1778, in
Capt. Dorsey's MD Artillery Co. Served in Capt. Gale's Artillery Co., Sept. 8,
1779; at Chester, PA, Nov. 9, 1779; "in command alarm pole" Jan. 25, 1780; was at
Morristown, NJ, March 7 and April 13, 1780, in Capt. J. Smith's Co. Stationed in
Baltimore under Lt. Col. Carrington, May 11, 1780. Furloughed by General Greene
in 1780; deranged for want of command, but was a 2nd Lt. again in Capt. Dorsey's
MD Artillery in 1782. Received 200 acres for military service (lots #2326, 2327,
2328, 2329) in western Maryland. (UU-232, H-579, VVV-96, H-477, YYY-1/19, DDDD-1)

CHEVIER, JOHN. Midshipman on ship Defence, November 1 to December 31, 1777. (H-655)

CHEW, RICHARD. Oath of Allegiance, 1778, before Hon. Hercules Courtenay. (A-1/4, A-2/37)

CHILCOAT (CHILCOTT), HUMPHREY. Ensign, Capt. Vaughan's Company, August 26, 1776.
2nd Lt., Capt. Moore's Company, February 4, 1777. 1st Lt., Capt. Merryman's Co.,
August 30, 1777 into 1778. (E-14, LL-66, BBB-350, RR-98, VV-114) Non-Juror (A-1/4)

CHILDS, CUD. Marine on ship Defence, June 1 to December 31, 1777. (H-655)

CHILDS (CHILD), GEORGE. Born 1755 in Ireland. Full faced; height: 5' 3". Enlisted,
July 7, 1776, as Private in Col. Ewings' Battalion, Baltimore County. Corporal,
3rd MD Regiment, received 50 acres (lot #79) in western Maryland. Oath of Allegiance
in 1778, before Hon. George Lindenberger. (A-1/4, A-2/52, H-55, DDDD-10)

CHINA, JOHN HATTON. Took Oath of Allegiance in 1781. (QQ-107)

CHINWORTH: See "CHENOWETH."

CHIPLANE, THOMAS W. Baltimore Mechanical Company of Militia, 1776. (CCC-28)

CHOATE, RICHARD. Ensign, Soldiers Delight Battalion, Feb. 7, 1782. (CCCC-71)

CHOATE, SOLOMON. Oath of Allegiance, 1778, before Hon. James Calhoun. (A-1/4, A-2/42)

CHRISTIAN, JOHN. Non-Juror to Oath of Allegiance, 1778. (A-1/4)
CHRISTIAN, ROBERT. Non-Juror to Oath of Allegiance, 1778. (A-1/4)
CHRISTIAN, THOMAS. Non-Juror to Oath of Allegiance, 1778. (A-1/4)
CHRISTIAN, WILLIAM. Non-Juror to Oath of Allegiance, 1778. (A-1/4)

CHRISTIE, GABRIEL. Collector of the Port of Baltimore, died there on April 1, 1808 in
his 51st year, of a pulmonary complaint. "Vessels in the port honored his memory by
wearing their colours at half-mast." (ZZZ-59) Gabriel served in the military and
public service from Harford County, Maryland. For further details, see H. Peden's
Revolutionary Patriots of Harford County, Maryand, 1775-1783.

CHRISTIE, JOHN. 2nd Lt., 2nd MD Battalion of Flying Camp. July, 1776. 1st Lt., in
Baltimore County Troops, August 5, 1776. (B-154, H-52)

CHRISTIE, ROBERT SR. Non-Juror to Oath of Allegiance, 1778. (A-1/4)

CHRISTIE, ROBERT JR. Baltimore Committee of Observation, July 24, 1775. (EEEE-1725)

CHRISTOPHER, JOHN. Non-Juror to Oath of Allegiance, 1778. (A-1/4)

CHRISTY, BIRMINGHAM. Non-Juror to Oath of Allegiance, 1778. (A-1/4)

CHRISWELL, WILLIAM. Oath of Allegiance, 1778. (A-1/4)

CHURCH, JAMES. Non-Juror to Oath of Allegiance, 1778. (A-1/4)

CHURCH, SAMUEL. Surgeon's Mate on ship Defence, September 19, 1776. (H-606)

CITZINGER, WOLFGONE. Private, Capt. Graybill's German Regt., 1776. (ZZ-32)

CLAIRS, WILLIAM. Oath of Allegiance, 1778, before Hon. James Calhoun. (A-2/39)

CLARK, ARTHUR. Private, Capt. Deams Co., 7th MD Regt., Dec. 14, 1776. (H-305)

CLARK, JAMES. Matross, Capt. Brown's MD Artillery; joined November 22, 1777. Was at Valley Forge until June, 1778; at White Plains, July, 1778; at Fort Schuyler, August and September, 1780; at High Hills of the Santee, August, 1781; at Camp Col. Scirvins, January, 1782; at Bacon's Bridge, S.C., April, 1782. Gunner, in Capt. J. Smith's Artillery, 1782-83. (UU-228, 230, YY-2/11)

CLARK, JAMES. Private, Baltimore Town, 8th Company, 1st Battalion, MD Troops. Born in Baltimore County, and died there on April 21, 1798. Wife, Sophia, died August 22, 1798. A daughter, Ann CLARK married Hezekiah VEIRS (1768-1872) of Montgomery County, MD in 1790, and their daughter Sophia Clark VEIRS (1795-1849) married Dr. Charles Ross MACE of Dorchester Co., MD in 1817 (They died in Rossville, Baltimore County, MD). (AAA-1822D)

CLARK, JAMES. Marine on ship Defence, July 1 to December 31, 1777. (H-655)

CLARK, JOHN. Enlisted in Baltimore Town on July 17, 1776. Private, in Capt. Dorsey's MD Artillery, November 17, 1777 to January 28, 1782. Gunner, in Capt. J. Smith's MD Artillery, 1782-1783. Received 50 acres (lot #432), for military services, in western Maryland. (H-53, H-574, UU-232, YYY-2/12, DDDD-10)

CLARK, JOSEPH. Two men with this name took the Oath of Allegiance in 1778: one before Hon. James Calhoun, and one before Hon. George Lindenberger. (A-1/4, A-2/42, A-2/52)

CLARK, NICHOLAS. Enlisted in Baltimore Town, July 17, 1776. (H-53)

CLARK, PETER. Oath of Allegiance, 1778, before Hon. James Calhoun. (A-2/41)

CLARK, RICHARD. Oath of Allegiance, 1778, before Hon. Geo. Lindenberger. (A-2/52)

CLARK, SAMUEL. Born c1740 and died April 21, 1798 in Baltimore County, MD. Wife, Sophia. Children: William, Samuel, Ann and George. Served as Private in Capt. S. Smith's Company No. 8, Baltimore Town Battalion, January 12, 1776. (H-18, XXX-214)

CLARK, THOMAS. Oath of Allegiance, 1778, before Hon. Peter Shepherd. (A-2/50)

CLARK, WILLIAM. 2nd Lt., Capt. Mercer's Company, Gunpowder Battalion, May, 1776. (WW-413, WW-444, EE-51)

CLARK, WILLIAM. Private, Capt. Dorsey's MD Artillery, November 17, 1777. Noted that he was "in gaol for house breaking." Took Oath of Allegiance in 1778 before Hon. William Spear. (A-1/4, A-2/66, H-574)

CLARK, ZACHRIA. Recruited in Baltimore by Samuel Chester for the 3rd MD Regt., March 2, 1780. (H-334)

CLARKE,_____YAMS (part of name torn from list) Sergeant, Baltimore County Regiment No. 15, circa 1777. (TTT-13)

CLARKE, AMBROSE. Baltimore Artillery Company, 1777. Non-Juror to Oath of Allegiance, 1778. "A native of Ireland, and long an inhabitant of Baltimore, he died in September, 1810." (ZZZ-61, V-368, A-1/4)

CLARKE, BENJAMIN. Non-Juror to Oath of Allegiance, 1778. (A-1/4)

CLARKE, HENRY. Non-Juror to Oath of Allegiance, 1778. (A-1/4)

CLARKE, JAMES. Non-Juror to Oath of Allegiance, 1778. Offered to purchase produce, and to sell a schooner for State use, October 28, 1776. (A-1/4, FFF-64)

CLARKE, JOHN. Born 1754 in North Ireland. Occupation: Glover. Height: 5' 8". Enlisted January 24, 1776, as Private in Capt. N. Smith's 1st Company of Matrosses. Bombardier in Capt. Dorsey's MD Artillery at Valley Forge on June 3, 1778. Matross in Capt. J. Smith's MD Artillery in 1780. Gunner in Capt. Dorsey's Company on January 28, 1782. (H-566, QQQ-2, H-563, VV-74, H-579, UU-231, UU-232, A-1/4)

CLARKE, RICHARD. Enlisted in Baltimore Town, July 20, 1776. Non-Juror to Oath of Allegiance, 1778. (H-53, A-1/4)

CLARKE, SAMUEL. Non-Juror to Oath of Allegiance, 1778. (A-1/4)

CLARKE, WILLIAM. Supplied pork to Capt. George Keeports Baltimore County Company, June 18, 1779. (FFF-229)

CLARY, BENJAMIN. (c1725 - after June 1, 1782) Wife's name was Elinor. Record states he gave patriotic service in Maryland, but he was a Non-Juror to the Oath of Allegiance in 1778. (A-1/4, JJJ-136)

CLARY, DAVID. (born 1754) Record states he gave patriotic service to Maryland, and it appears he took to the Oath of Allegiance in 1778. (A-1/4, JJJ-136)

CLAUSS. WILLIAM. Oath of Allegiance, 1778. (A-1/4)

CLAVER, WILLIAM. Private, Capt. Sheaff's Company, June 16, 1777. (W-162)

CLAY, ABRAHAM. Oath of Allegiance, 1778, before Hon. Jesse Dorsey. (A-1/4, A-2/63)

CLAY, JOHN. Non-Juror to the Oath of Allegiance, 1778. (A-1/4)

CLAY, JONATHAN. Oath of Allegiance, 1778, before Hon. Jesse Dorsey. (A-1/4, A-2/63)

CLAY, WILLIAM. Non-Juror to Oath of Allegiance, 1778. (A-1/4)

CLAYTON, JOSEPH. Non-Juror to Oath of Allegiance, 1778. (A-1/4)

CLEGNESS, JOHN FRANCIS. Surgeon's Mate on ship Defence, Feb. 10 - Dec. 31, 1777. (H-655)

CLEMENT (CLEMENTS), JOHN. Baltimore Mechanical Company of Militia, Nov. 4, 1775. Private, Capt.Cox's Company, December 19, 1776. Oath of Allegiance, 1778, before Hon. George Lindenberger. (A-1/4, A-2/52, F-299, CCC-21)

CLEMM, WILLIAM. (1755-1809) Married Catharine SCHULTZ (1759-1835) of York County, PA in 1778. Their son, William CLEMM, Jr. (1779-1826) married (1) Harriet POE (1785-1816), daughter of Capt. George POE and Catharine DAWSON, and married (2) Maria POE, daughter of David POE (1742-1816) and Elizabeth CAIRNS. (Both POES were granddaughters of John POE (1698-1756) and Janet McBRIDE (1706-1802) of Ireland, who came to America about 1743.) William CLEMM was a meber of the Sons of Liberty in 1776. He was a 2nd Lt. in Capt. Ridgely's Company, Baltimore Town Battalion, in 1781, having first served as an Ensign before being promoted. (BBBB-29, BBBB-61, R-15, AAAA-402, CCC-19, and Maryland Historical Magazine, Vol. 37, No. 4, December, 1942, pages 420-422, "Lineage of Edgar Allan Poe," by Francis B. Culver)

CLEVERLY, THOMAS. Non-Juror to Oath of Allegiance, 1778. (A-1/4)

CLIFT, JONATHAN. Non-Juror to Oath of Allegiance, 1778. (A-1/4)

CLINE,_____. (part of name torn from list) Private, Baltimore County Regiment No. 15, circa 1777. (TTT-13)

CLIVES,_____. (first name not shown) Took Oath of Allegiance, 1778. (A-1/4)

CLOPPER (CLAPPER), CORNELIUS JR. Served on Baltimore Committee of Observation on July 24, 1775. Recommended as bicuit baker for Baltimore troops. Took the Oath of Allegiance in 1778. (EEEE-1725, FFF-12, A-1/4, A-2/52)

CLOSE (CLOES), CHARLES. (August 10, 1756, Antrim, Ireland - September 10, 1838 either in Baltimore or Harford County, Maryland). Married (1) Sarah _____ (2) Hannah WHITNEY. Occupation: Labourer. Height: 5' 7". Enlisted as a Private in Capt. N. Smith's 1st Company of Matrosses on February 3, 1776. (H-567, QQQ-2, H-565, VV-74, JJJ-139

CLOSS, CHRISTIAN. (January 1, 1758 - September 26, 1825) Married Catharine GRUNT. Private, Capt. Smith's Company No. 8, enlisted January 11, 1776. (JJJ-139, H-18)

CLOTRAUBAY (?), WILLIAM. Private, Capt. Howell's Company, December 30, 1775. (G-11)

CLOVER, JOHN. Oath of Allegiance, 1778, before Hon. Peter Shepherd. (A-1/4, A-2/49)

CLOWES (CLOWER), WILLIAM. Oath of Allegiance, 1778, before Hon. William Spear. Could not write; made his mark. (A-1/4, A-2/66)

CLURY (CLARY), JOHN. Oath of Allegiance, 1778. (A-1/4)

CLUTTER, GASPER. Private, Capt. Smith's Company No. 8, enlisted Jan. 27, 1776.(H-18)

COAAKER, JAMES. Oath of Allegiance, 1778. (A-1/4)

COALE, JOHN. Enlisted in Baltimore County, July 20, 1776. Oath of Allegiance, 1778, before Hon. Charles Ridgely of William. Ensign, Capt. Smith's Company, and then 2nd Lt., May 17, 1779, Baltimore Town Battalion. (A-2/27, F-309, F-311, F-313, GGG-401, H-52, A-1/4)

COALE, SAMUEL STRINGER DR. (1754-1798) Was employed by the State at the saltpetre works, 1776; appointed surgeon, 1776; began practice of medicine in Baltimore in 1778. Took Oath of Allegiance, 1778, before Hon. James Calhoun. Daughter, Anna Maria COALE, died January 3, 1813. Daughter, Eliza COALE, married John G. PROUD in 1804. Samuel died in September, 1798. (ZZZ-63, ZZZ-64, ZZZ-262, XX-5, A-1/4, A-2/39)

COALE, THOMAS. Recommended by William Lux for Baltimore City Artillery, July 3, 1777. (FFF-113)

COALE, WILLIAM. Oath of Allegiance, 1778, before Hon. Edward Cockey. (A-1/5, A-2/62)

COCHRAN, WILLIAM. Oath of Allegiance, 1778, before Hon. Thomas Sollers. (A-2/51)

COCKERTON, JOHN. Private, Capt. Dorsey's MD Artillery, Nov. 17, 1777. (H-574)

COCKERTON, ROBERT. Cabin Steward on ship Defence, April 28 - Dec. 31, 1777. (H-655)

COCKEY, EDWARD. (December 20, 1731 - February 1, 1795) Son of John COCKEY (1683-1746) and Elizabeth SLADE (1685-1780). Married Eleanor PINDELL in 1753, only child of Philip PINDELL of Baltimore County. (Marriage proven through Maryland pension application) Children: Urath COCKEY (1754-1824) married Charles COCKEY (1762-1823), son of Thomas, in 1786, at Garrison Forest; Joshua COCKEY, married (1) Henrietta CROMWELL and (2) Mary JONES; Thomas COCKEY, married Elizabeth OWINGS; and, William COCKEY. Edward Cockey was a Captain of Baltimore County Militia Co. No. 2 (65 Privates) on August 26, 1776. He became a Colonel in the Maryland Militia on October 12, 1776, and Colonel of Baltimore County Militia Classes 3rd and 4th, on September 17, 1777. As Colonel of the Gunpowder Upper Battalion in 1777 and 1778, he commanded 454 Privates (names not given in report). He was a Justice of the Peace, and one of the magistrates who administered the Oath of Allegiance in 1778. On October 13, 1780, he was Battalion Colonel of Baltimore County Militia, commanding 635 troops. (ZZ-337, FFF-62, A-1/5, SSS-110, F-12, BBB-379, F-303, PPP-2, RR-98, ZZ-541, GGG-242, AAA-2195, AAA-1556, JJJ-141,WWW-9)

COCKEY, JAMES. Represented the Upper Back River Hundred at the Association of Freemen on August 21, 1775. (EEEE-1726)

COCKEY, JOHN. (June 24, 1743 - February 8, 1808) Married Chloe CROMWELL. He was a son of William COCKEY and Constant ASHMAN, and grandson of John COCKEY and Elizabeth SLADE, and Sr. George ASHMAN. Children: Rebecca; Elizabeth; Ann; John, married Elizabeth ZANTZINGER; Mary; Eleanor, married Sebastian GRAFF;

William Joseph Cromwell; and Clarissa. John Cockey served on Baltimore County Committee of Inspection, March 13, 1775, and Committee of Observation, Sept. 23, 1775 (having been elected with 87 votes received). He was a Captain in militia (64 Privates) company under his uncle, Col. Edward Cockey in 1776; he was Captain of Company No. 1 in October and December, 1776, and served through October 31, 1780 when he was succeeded as a Captain in the Gunpowder Upper Battalion. He is listed again as a Captain of the Baltimore County Light Horse Dragoons at Yorktown, 1781, and serving under Col. Nicholson's Troop of Horse. He also took the Maryland Oath of Allegiance in 1778 before Hon. Edward Cockey. (A-1/5, A-2/62, RR-19, RR-47, RR-50, SS-136, PPP-2, RR-98, ZZ-542, JJJ-141, BBBB-274, MMM-A, VV-345, WWW-4)

COCKEY, JOHN (OF THOMAS). (1758-1824) Son of Thomas COCKEY III (1724-1784) and wife Prudence GILL, and grandson of John COCKEY and Elizabeth SLADE. Married Mary COALE in 1785. Children: Thomas (1787-1816); John (1788-1813); Mary; Samuel (1792-1859); William (1794-1795); Elizabeth (b.1796); and, Stephen (1797-1798). John served as a Private in Baltimore County Regiment No.7 circa 1777, and took the Maryland Oath of Allegiance in 1778, before Hon. William Spear. (A-2/67, TTT-13, WWW-4)

COCKEY, JOSHUA (OF EDWARD). Son of Col. Edward COCKEY and Eleanor PINDELL. Married (1) Henrietta CROMWELL and (2) Mary JONES. Served as Ensign, Baltimore County Militia Company No. 2, December 19, 1775, and Ensign, Soldiers Delight Company No. 1, May 13, 1776, being promoted to 2nd Lt., June 6, 1776. Took the Oath of Allegiance, 1778, before Hon. John Moale. Also served with Col. Nicholson's Troop of Horse on June 7, 1781. (WWW-9, BBBB-274, G-10, FF-64, WW-467, A-1/5, A-2/70)

COCKEY, RICHARD. Marine on ship Defence, 1777. (H-655)

COCKEY, THOMAS. (April 15, 1754 - November 10, 1813) Son of Thomas COCKEY (1724-1784) and Prudence GILL, and grandson of John COCKEY and Elizabeth SLADE. He married Ruth BROWN. Thomas was a 2nd Lt. in Capt. J. Cockey's Baltimore County Dragoons at Yorktown in 1781, and is listed as 2nd Lt., Gunpowder Upper Battalion, Oct. 23, 1781. (MMM-A, AAAA-650, JJJ-141, A-1/5, A-2/39, WWW-4)

COCKEY, THOMAS JR. Oath of Allegiance, 1778, before Hon. Edward Cockey. (A-1/5, A-2/62)

COCKEY, WARD. Oath of Allegiance, 1778. (A-1/5)

COCKEY, WILLIAM. Private, Capt. J. Cockey's Baltimore County Dragoons at Yorktown in 1781. (MMM-A)

CODY, JAMES. Marine on ship Defence, 1777. (H-655)

COE, GREENBURY. Oath of Allegiance, 1778, before Hon. Hercules Courtenay. (A-2/37)

COE, JOB. Corporal of Marines in ship Defence, Jan. 29 - Dec. 31, 1777. (H-655)

COE, MARK. Private in Col. Aquila Hall's Baltimore County Regiment, c1777. (TTT-13)

COE, WILLIAM. (November 19, 1757 - 1834) Married Mary SEARS. Served as Corporal in Maryland Line. Oath of Allegiance, 1778, before Hon. Hercules Courtenay. Could not write; made his mark ("W"). On February 12, 1820 William COE received, as a resident of Baltimore County, for life, quarterly, half-pay of a Private for his services during the Revolutionary War. On February 16, 1821, William COE, now of Annapolis, received half pay of a Private of Matross. On March 4, 1834, Mary COE, widow of William, received half-pay of a Matross in consideration of services by her husband during the Revolutionary War. (C-330, A-1/5, A-2/37, JJJ-141)

COERBY (COEXBY), JAMES. Oath of Allegiance, 1778, before Hon. George Lindenberger. (A-1/5, A-2/52)

COFFEE, _____. (first name not given) Non-Juror to Oath in 1778. (A-1/5)

COFIELD, JACOB. Non-Juror to Oath of Allegiance in 1778. (A-1/5)

COGGINS, SYLVESTER. Non-Juror to Oath of Allegiance, 1778. (A-1/5)

COHOLEN, JERRY. Private, Capt. J. Gist's Co., 3rd MD Regt., Feb., 1778. (H-600)

COLE, ABRAHAM. (January 10, 1727/8 - 1822, Baltimore County, MD) Son of Thomas and Sarah COLE. Wife's name unknown: children: Sarah, married Gideon BOSLEY in 1772; Ann, married Thomas DONOVAN; Ruth; Edith, married a HALL; Belinda, married William STANSBURY; Eleanor; Abraham,Jr.; and, James (According to a chart of the Cole family by Wilson Miles Carey at the Maryland Historical Soc. Library). Abraham Cole took the Oath of Allegiance, 1778, before Hon. James Calhoun. "Abram Cole, Sr." was a 2nd Lt. in Capt. Merryman's Company as of August 30, 1777, and of the Upper Battalion in 1778. (E-14, LL-66, BBB-350, D-8, A-1/5, A-2/42, JJJ-143) Also, an Abraham COLE md. Cecil GIST; d. 1841.

COLE, CHRISTOPHER. Non-Juror to Oath of Allegiance, 1778. (A-1/5)

COLE, CHRISTOPHER JR. Non-Juror to Oath of Allegiance, 1778. Involved in evaluation of Baltimore county confiscated proprietary lands in 1782. (FFF-542, A-1/5)

COLE, EZEKIEL. Non-Juror to Oath of Allegiance, 1778. (A-1/5)

COLE. GEORGE. Baltimore Mechanical Company of Militia, November 4, 1775. Served as 1st Corporal in Capt. Keeports German Regiment; enlisted July 15, 1776; was at Philadelphia, Septembr 19, 1776. (H-263, F-298)

COLE, HENRY. Oath of Allegiance, 1778, before Hon. James Calhoun. (A-1/5, A-2/40)

COLE, HOSHIER. Ordinary Seaman on ship Defence, September 19, 1776. (H-606)

COLE, JAMES. Matross, Capt. Brown's MD Artillery; joined November 22, 1777. Was at Valley Forge until June, 1778; at White Plains, July, 1778; at Fort Schuyler in August and September, 1780; not listed in 1781. (UU-228, UU-230)

COLE, JOHN. Baltimore Mechanical Company of Militia, November 4, 1775. Served as a Private in Capt. Keeports German Regiment; enlisted July 15, 1776 and stationed at Philadelphia on September 19, 1776. Non-Juror, 1778. (A-1/5, F-298, H-263)

COLE, MORDECAI. 1st Lt. in Capt. Lemmon's Company, Gist's Battalion, Feb. 4, 1777. Non-Juror to Oath in 1778, but subscribed in 1781. Involved in evaluation of Baltimore County confiscated proprietary reserve lands in 1782. (FFF-542, VV-114, A-1/5, QQ-107)

COLE, PATRICK. Marine on ship Defence, 1777. (H-654)

COLE, PHILIP. Non-Juror to Oath of Allegiance, 1778. (A-1/5)

COLE (COALE), RICHARD. Enlisted in Baltimore County, August 14, 1776. Non-Juror to Oath of Allegiance in 1778. (A-1/5, H-52)

COLE, SALATHIEL. Non-Juror to Oath of Allegiance, 1778. (A-1/5)

COLE, SAMUEL. Two men with this name were Non-Jurors in 1778. (A-1/5)

COLE, THOMAS. Baltimore Privateer and Captain of ship Iris (14 guns, 65 men) owned by Jeremiah Yellott and others of Baltimore. (III-206) Oath in 1781 (QQ-107).

COLE, THOMAS. Oath of Allegiance, 1778, before Hon. James Calhoun. (A-2/40)

COLE, VINCENT. Two men with this name were Non-Jurors in 1778. (A-1/5)

COLE, WILLIAM. Two men with this name were Non-Jurors in 1778. (A-1/5)

COLE, WILLIAM (OF SAMUEL). Non-Juror to Oath of Allegiance, 1778. (A-1/5)

COLEGATE, JOHN. Non-Juror to Oath of Allegiance, 1778. Served as an officer (rank is not given) with Col. Nicholson's Troop of Horse on June 7, 1781. (A-1/5, BBBB-274)

COLEGATE, RICHARD. 2nd Lt., Baltimore county Militia, 2nd Company, December 19, 1775. 2nd Lt., Soldiers Delight Battalion, 1st Company, May 13, 1776, becoming 1st Lt., June 6, 1776. Took Oath of Allegiance, 1778, before Hon. John Cradock. Served with Col. Nicholson's Troop of Horse on June 7, 1781. (BBBB-274, A-1/5, A-2/59, WW-467, FF-64, G-10)

COLEGATE, THOMAS. Ensign, Gunpowder Battalion, march 20, 1779. Took Oath of Allegiance, 1778, before Hon. Thomas Sollers. (A-1/5, A-2/51, GGG-325, ᴗ⁻ ꞁ)

COLEMAN (COLMAN), DUNCAN (DUNKIN). Oath of Allegiance, 1778, before Hon. Edward Cockey. (A-1/5, A-2/61)

COLEMAN (COLMAN), GEORGE STIBBONDS. Born 1741 in England. Short curled hair. Height: 5' 6½". Enlisted July 5, 1776, as Private in Col. Ewings Battalion, Baltimore County. (H-57)

COLEMAN (COLMAN), JOHN. Oath of Allegiance, 1778, before Hon. Charles Ridgely of William. Could not write; made his mark. (A-1/5, A-2/27)

COLEMAN (COLMAN), MATTHEW. Non-Juror to Oath of Allegiance, 1778. (A-1/5)

COLEMAN (COLMAN), PATRICK. Non-Juror to Oath of Allegiance, 1778. A9-1/5)

COLEN (COLEING). JOHN. Enlisted July 20, 1776 in Baltimore Town. Sergeant, 4th MD Regiment at Fort Whetstone Point in Baltimore, 1781. Received Federal Bounty Land Grant of 100 acres (Warrant #11026) on June 2, 1797. (YY-61, H-626, H-53)

COLEN, THOMAS. Recruit, Baltimore County Militia, April 11, 1780. (H-335)

COLGROVE, WILLIAM. Oath of Allegiance, 1778. (A-1/5)

COLINS, JAMES. Marine on ship Defence, 1777. (H-655)

COLLETT, DANIEL. Non-Juror to Oath of Allegiance, 1778. Involved in evaluation of Baltimore County confiscated proprietary lands in 1782. (A-1/5, FFF-542)

COLLETT, MOSES. Non-Juror to Oath of Allegiance, 1778. (A-1/5)

COLLINS, AMES. Oath of Allegiance, 1778. (A-1/5)

COLLINS, DAVID. Born 1755 in Ireland. Fullfaced; height: 5' 2". Enlisted July 7, 1776 as Private in Col. Ewings Battalion, Baltimore County. (H-56)

COLLINS, JAMES. (May 7, 1755 - June 8, 1828) Married (1) Sarah Elizabeth ANDERSON and (2) Mrs. Charity DEW. Oath of Allegiance, 1778 before Hon. William Spear. On August 10, 1785 James Collins, Sergeant, 1st MD Regt., wounded at seige of York in Virginia received 11 pounds, it being his half pay up to that day. He received 5 subsequent payments between February 14, 1786 and August 11, 1789. (A-2/67, JJJ-145, J-220, J-241, K-2, K-32, K-75, K-120)

COLLINS, JOHN. Private in Count Pulaski's Legion; enlisted in Baltimore, April 28, 1778. Took Oath of Allegiance, 1778, before Hon. William Spear. (A-2/66, H-592)

COLLINS, JOSEPH. Oath of Allegiance, 1778, before Hon. James Calhoun. (A-1/5, A-2/40)

COLLINS, MICHAEL. Non-Juror to Oath of Allegiance, 1778. (A-1/5)

COLLINS, THOMAS. Sergeant, Capt. Brown's MD Artillery, joined November 22, 1777. Was at Valley Forge until June, 1778; at White Plains, July, 1778; at Fort Schuyler in August and September, 1780; not listed in 1781. (UU-228, UU-230)

COLLINS, TIMOTHY.(September 23, 1754 - December 24, 1833) Married Elizabeth (Franklin) McFEE on April 21, 1778 in Baltimore County. (Marriage proven through Maryland pension application). Corporal, 4th MD Regiment, February 19, 1777, and Sergeant, Capt. Lansdale's Company, February 11, 1778 to February 12, 1780. Pensioned as a Corporal in the Maryland Line. (YY-15, H-98, YY-112, JJJ-146)

COLLINS, WILLIAM. Born 1750 in Ireland. Black hair; hight" 5' 1½". Enlisted July 7, 1776 as Private in Col. Ewing's Battalion, Baltimore County. Two men with this name took the Oath of Allegiance in 1778: one before Hon. James Calhoun, and one before Hon. Edward Cockey. (A-2/38, A-2/61, A-1/5, H-55, H-58)

COLLIS, WILLIAM. Recruit, Baltimore County, 1780. (H-340)

COLOSTON, JEREMIAH. Non-Juror to Oath of Allegiance, 1778. (A-1/5)
COLOSTON, JOSEPH. Non-Juror to Oath of Allegiance, 1778. (A-1/5)
COLOSTON, JOSHUA. Non-Juror to Oath of Allegiance, 1778. (A-1/5)
COLOSTON, WILLIAM. Non-Juror to Oath of Allegiance, 1778. (A-1/5)
COLROE, STEPHEN. Non-Juror to Oath of Allegiance, 1778. (A-1/5)

COLSON (COULSTON), JOHN. Marine on ship Defence, Jan. 30 - Dec. 31, 1777. (H-655)

COLVIN, PHILIP. 2nd Lt., Capt. Young's Company, Middle River Lower Hundred, May 6, 1776. (EE-51, WW-413)

54

COMBS, COLEMAN. Son of Coleman COMBS and Elizabeth SUTHARD of New Jersey, where he was baptized August 18, 1747. He married Mary PIERCE, daughter of John and Frances PIERCE of Baltimore County, on February 10, 1770. Moved to Washington County, MD where Coleman died in 1807. He took Oath of Allegiance, 1778, before Hon. James Calhoun. Children: John COMBS, died August 31, 1843 in Perry County, Ohio, married Eleanor_____; Lewis COMBS, died before 1807; Sarah COMBS, md. Robert DOUGLAS; Thomas COMBS; and, Mary COMBS, married an EDWARDS. (D-2, A-2/39)

COMLEY, JAMES. Non-Juror to Oath of Allegiance, 1778. (A-1/5)
COMLEY, JOHN. Non-Juror to Oath of Allegiance, 1778. (A-1/5)

COMOUR, JAMES. Oath of Allegiance, 1778, before Hon. James Calhoun. (A-2/65)

COMPTON, JAMES. (c1751 - c1832) Matross, Capt. Brown's MD Artillery; joined Nov. 22, 1777. Was at Valley Forge, until June, 1778; at White Plains, July, 1778; at Ft. Schuyler in August and September, 1780; not listed in 1781. Wife's name Frances. (JJJ-147, UU-228, UU-230)

COMPTON, JOHN. Matross, Capt. Gale's MD Artillery, 1779; at Chester, PA, Nov. 9, 1779; at Morristown, NJ, Mar. 7 and Apr. 13, 1780; on command in Pennsylvania, February, 1780. Matross, Capt. J. Smith's MD Artillery, 1780-1783, with duty in Capt. Dorsey's Company at Camp Col. Scirvins on January 28, 1782. Entitled to 50 acres (lot #1483). Reported deceased July 1, 1783. (H-579, YYY-2/13, UU-232, YYY-1/21, DDDD-11)

COMPTON, JOHN. Marine on ship Defence, March 3 to December 31, 1777. (H-655)

CONAWAY, CHARLES. Oath of Allegiance, 1778, before Hon. Peter Shepherd. (A-2/50)

CONAWAY, JOHN. Died c1799 in Baltimore County. Married Anne NORWOOD, May 14, 1744. Oath of Allegiance, 1778, before Hon. Charles Ridgely of William. The will of John CONAWAY (made January 21, 1795 and probated September 25, 1799) names ten of his eleven children and also a William BANKS and granddaughter Mary BANKS. John CONAWAY's children: Rachel (born Feb. 9, 1745); Charles (born Aug. 28, 1748); Sarah (born Dec. 21, 1750); Ruth (born March 21, 1753); Ann (born March 20, 1755); John (born July 11, 1757); Susanna (born July 12, 1760); Rebecca; America (may be the America CONAWAY who died in 1823); Samuel; and, Deborah. (D-2, A-1/5, A-2/27)

CONDON (CUNDEN), MARTIN. Born 1754 in Waterford, Ireland. Occupation: Drayman. Height: 5' 7½". Enlisted January 31, 1776 as Private in Capt. N. Smith's 1st Co. of Matrosses, and later served in Capt. Dorsey's MD Artillery, November 17, 1777. (H-565, H-566, H-574, VV-74, QQQ-2)

CONDRON, THOMAS. Gunner, Capt. Brown's MD Artillery; joined November 22, 1777. Was at Valley Forge until June, 1778; at White Plains, July, 1778; at Fort Schuyler, August and September, 1780. Corporal, at High Hills of the Santee, August, 1781; at Camp Col. Scirvins, January, 1782; at Bacon's Bridge, S.C., April, 1782. Was entitled to 50 acres (lot #1126) in western Maryland. (DDDD-11, UU-228, UU-230)

CONGLETON, DAVID. Private, Capt. Ramsey's Company No. 5, 1776. (H-640)

CONGLETON, WILLIAM. Private, 4th MD Regiment, March 17, 1778, Capt. Lansdale's Co. Died in August, 1778. (H-98)

CONNELL, BARTHOLOMEW. Oath of Allegiance, 1778, before Hon. John B. Howard. (A-2/29)

CONNELLY (CONNOLLY, CONLY), JOHN. Born 1749 in Athlone, Ireland. Occupation: Shoe-maker. Height: 5' 6½". Enlisted February 3, 1776 as Private in Capt. N. Smith's 1st Company of Matrosses. Matross, Capt. Brown's MD Artillery; joined Nov. 22, 1777. Was at Valley Forge until June 3, 1778; at White Plains, July, 1778; at Fort Schuyler in August and September, 1780; not listed in 1781. This man, or perhaps another by the same name, was a Private in Capt. J. Gist's Company, 3rd MD Regt., in Feb., 1778. (H-600, H-565, H-567, UU-228, UU-230, QQQ-2)

CONNELLY, LAWRENCE. Enlisted in Baltimore Town, July 20, 1776. (H-53)

CONNELLY, MICHAEL. MD Line defective, July 2, 1781; Baltimore County resident. (H-414)

CONNELLY (CONNOLLY), PATRICK. Recruit, Baltimore County, 1780. Pensioner, born 1757, with Maryland and Delaware service. (YY-16, H-340)

CONNELLY (CONNOLLY), TIMOTHY. Matross, Capt. Brown's MD Artillery; joined Nov. 22, 1777. Was at Valley Forge until June, 1778; at White Plains, July, 1778; at Fort Schuyler in August and September, 1780; at High Hills of the Santee, August, 1781; at Camp Col. Scirvins, January, 1782; at Bacon's Bridge, S.C., April, 1782. Was entitled to 50 acres (lot #1860) in western Maryland for being an Artillery Sergt. Federal Bound Land Grant of 100 acres (W11115), JUne 14, 1796. (YY-61, DDDD-11, UU-228, UU-230)

CONNOLLY, WILLIAM. Matross, Capt. Brown's MD Artillery; joined November 22, 1777. Was at Valley Forge until June, 1778; at White Plains, July, 1778; at Fort Schuyler in August and September, 1780; not listed in 1781. Federal Bounty Land Grant of 100 acres (W11123), February 1, 1790. (YY-61, UU-229, UU-230)

CONNER, CORNELIUS. Enlisted in Baltimore County, July 20, 1776. (H-53)

CONNER, ROBERT. Marine on ship Defence, 1777. (H-655)

CONNOR, EDWARD. Non-Juror to Oath of Allegiance, 1778. (A-1/5)

CONNOR, HENRY. Non-Juror to Oath of Allegiance, 1778. (A-1/5)

CONNOR, JAMES. Oath of Allegiance, 1778. (A-1/5)

CONNOR, MICHAEL. Matross, Capt. J. Smith's MD Artillery, 1780. Was also a Matross in Capt. Dorsey's Artillery Company at Valley Forge on June 3, 1778. Also, was at Camp Col. Scirvins on January 28, 1782. Entitled to 50 acres (lot #1307) in western Maryland. (DDDD-11, H-579, UU-231, UU-232)

CONNOR (CONNER), THOMAS. Born 1756 in Ireland. Occupation: Hatter. Height: 5' 8¼". Enlisted January 24, 1776 as Private in Capt. N. Smith's 1st Company of Matrosses. Also served in Capt. Dorsey's MD Artillery Company, November 17, 1777. (H-574, H-566, QQQ-2, H-563, VV-74)

CONRAD, JOHN. Private in Col. Aquila Hall's Baltimore County Regt., 1777. (TTT-13)

CONSTABLE, AMOS. Oath of Allegiance, 1778. (A-1/5)

CONSTABLE, JOHN. Oath of Allegiance, 1778, before Hon. James Calhoun. (A-1/5, A-2/40)

CONSTABLE, THOMAS. Oath of Allegiance, 1778, before Hon. James Calhoun. Ensign in Baltimore Town Battalion, May 23, 1781. (A-2/40, AAAA-443)

CONSTANT, EDWARD. Drafted in Baltimore County Regiment No. 36, circa 1777. (TTT-13)

CONWAY, ROBERT. Oath of Allegiance, 1778, before Hon. Geo. Lindenberger. (A-2/52)

COOK, ADAM. Stored and delivered flour for Baltimore Town Committee, 1780. (RRR-6)

COOK, ARCHIBALD. (December 20, 1761, Chester County, PA - December 30, 1834, Baltimore, MD) Wife named Martha; son, Isaac P. COOK married Hannah _____ and grandson Henry F. COOK married Catharine E. _____. Archibald Cook was a Private in a PA Regt. and wintered at Valley Forge. (AAA-405, Pennsylvania Archives, Series III, Vol. 23, page 423)

COOK, BENJAMIN. "Declaration was made in Baltimore County, Maryland, March 19, 1853, Benjamin Cook, age 91, a resident of said Baltimore City, but previous there to resided in Prince Georges County, Maryland, applied under the Act of June 7, 1852. States he enlisted in the early part of 1777 in the First Maryland Regiment under Col. Otho H. Williams, that afterwards until 1778, he again enlisted in the 2nd MD Regiment in a company of which he acted as Private and Corporal under Colonel John Gunby and served until January, 1779. In August 5, 1853, Benjamin Cook again made declaration in Howard County, Maryland, stating he is aged and infirm, made declaration in Baltimore City, MD. The reason he had not made declaration for a pension earlier, he had been living in remote places in Anne Arundel County, MD and not being able to read or write or seldom seeing a newspaper or hearing of the laws of Congress on the subject of pensions. Affidavit in Baltimore County

October 21, 1853, by Thomas CONNALLY states he is age 94, that he was born in
Pennsylvania, and well remembers Benjamin COOK, late of Elliots or Ellicotts
Mills, Howard Co., Maryland - he first became acquainted with said Benjamin
COOK about the commencement of the Revolutionary War 1776, that subsequently
he visited Baltimore City, MD and there saw Benjamin COOK under Arms in a
company attached to Col. Williams' regiment and said Benjamin COOK marched with
said company and regiment to the head of the Chesapeake Bay; that said deponent
returned to his native state and there entered the militia service and marched
to Brandywine in the Penna. service, where he again met said COOK under Arms
rendering military service in and about Brandywine, Philadelphia, and at the
head of Elk River Maryland for 6 months more. This deponent visited Baltimore
City after the Revolutionary War and saw Benjamin COOK and that he stated that
he served about two years in the Revolutionary Army. That he is well acquainted
with Martha COOK and knows they lived together as man and wife." R2248 (I-12)
Revolutionary pensioner, born 1762, Corporal, Maryland Line, Benj. Cook. (YY-16)

COOK, CHARLES. Non-Juror to Oath of Allegiance, 1778. (A-1/5)

COOK, GEORGE. Lieutenant of the ship Defence, September 12 to November 15, 1776.
Captain (Commander) from November 15 to at least December 31, 1777. "Captain
Cook, formerly of the ship Defense, which was fitted out in Baltimore at the
time of the Revolutionary War, died December 18, 1799." (ZZZ-69, H-606, H-655)
Naval Captain (c1730-c1800), married Elizabeth JOHNSON in MD. (JJJ-150, FFF-70)

COOK, GREENBERY. Non-Juror to Oath of Allegiance, 1778. (A-1/5)

COOK, HENRY. Pensioner on June 1, 1840, age 82, residing in houehold of Obed
PEARCE in Baltimore City,4th Ward. (P-128) Private, MD Line, pensioner. (YY-16)

COOK, JAMES. Non-Juror to Oath of Allegiance, 1778. (A-1/5)
COOK, JOHN. Non-Juror to Oath of Allegiance, 1778. (A-1/5)
COOK, JOHN JR. Non-Juror to Oath of Allegiance, 1778. (A-1/5)
COOK, JOHN (OF THOMAS). Non-Juror to Oath of Allegiance, 1778. (A-1/5)
COOK, JOSHUA. Non-Juror to Oath of Allegiance, 1778. (A-1/5)
COOK, NICHOLAS. Non-Juror to Oath of Allegiance, 1778. (A-1/5)

COOK, SAMUEL T. DR. Offered to serve as doctor at the fort in Baltimore, May 15,
1777. (FFF-106)

COOK, STANSBURY JOHN. Took the Oath of Allegiance in 1781. (QQ-108)

COOK, THOMAS. Two men with this name were Non-Jurors to the Oath, 1778. (A-1/5)

COOK, WILLIAM. Baltimore Mechanical Company of Militia, 1776. Non-Juror to the
Oath of Allegiance, 1778. (A-1/5, CCC-27)

COOKE, JOHN. Enlisted in Baltimore County, July 20, 1776. (H-52)

COOKSON, JOHN. Sailmaker on ship Defence, 1777. (H-655)

COOPER, CEACIL. Oath of Allegiance, 1778. (A-1/5)

COOPER, GEORGE. Born 1755 in England. Occupation: Labourer. Height: 5' 8¼".
Enlisted January 27, 1776 as Private in Capt. N. Smith's 1st Company of
Matrosses. Served in Capt. Dorsey's MD Artillery, November 17, 1777. Gave a
deposition on enlistment terms as Matross in Baltimore County, May 7, 1779.
(FFF-220, H-574, H-564, H-566, VV-73, QQQ-2)

COOPER, JAMES. Non-Juror to Oath of Allegiance, 1778. (A-1/5)

COOPER, JOHN. Private, Capt. Cox's Company, December 19, 1776. Took Oath of
Allegiance, 1778, before Hon. James Calhoun. Private, Capt. McClellan's Co.
September 4, 1780. One John COOPER married Elizabeth DURHAM post 1800 in
Baltimore County (Marriage proven through Maryland pension application).
(YY-112, CCC-21, CCC-24, A-1/5, A-2/41)

COOPER, NATHANIEL. Second Mate on ship Defence, Jan. 11 - June 1, 1777. (H-655)

COOPER, PAUL. Oath of Allegiance, 1778. (A-1/5)

COOPER, THOMAS. Oath of Allegiance, 1778, before Hon. Jeremiah Johnson. (A-2/33)
There might have been another Thomas Cooper who was a Non-Juror also. (A-1/5)

COOPER, WILLIAM. Non-Juror to Oath of Allegiance, 1778. (A-1/5)

CORBET, PATRICK. Yeoman on ship Defence, January 13 - June 1, 1777, and Marine from
June 1 - October 15, 1777. (H-655)

CORBET, WILLIAM. Drafted into Baltimore County Regiment No. 36, c1777. (TTT-13)

CORBIDY, DARBY. Private in Baltimore County Regiment No. 7, c1777. (TTT-13)

CORBIN, ABRAHAM. (September 7, 1722 - 1793/1798) Married Rachel MARSHALL, Dec. 4,
1766. Children: Abraham CORBIN married Eleanor BOSLEY in 1798; Thomas CORBIN md.
Nancy TURNER in 1790; Nicholas CORBIN; Nathan CORBIN married Sophia ENLOES in 1800;
Sarah CORBIN married Thomas MARSH, Jr. c1775; and Eleanor CORBIN married Beale MARSH
in 1797. Abraham took the Oath of Allegiance, 1778, before Hon. Richard Holliday.
(A-1/5, A-2/60, JJJ-154, and research by Shirley Reightler of Bel Air, MD, 1987)

CORBIN, BENJAMIN. (Died before March, 1815. Buried near Westminster, MD) Married
Sarah SYE or LYE. Children: Ezekiel, Nicodemus, Joseph, Elijah, Micajah, Kezia,
Achel, Benjamin Jr., and Sarah. Benjamin took the Oath of Allegiance, 1778, before
Hon. James Calhoun. (A-1/5, A-2/42, and research by Shirley Reightler, Bel Air, MD)

CORBIN, EDWARD. Oath of Allegiance, 1778, before Hon. James Calhoun. (A-1/5, A-2/42)

CORBIN, JOHN. Non-Juror to Oath of Allegiance, 1778. (A-1/5)

CORBIN, NICHOLAS. Oath of Allegiance, 1778, before Hon. James Calhoun. (A-1/5, A-2/42)

CORBIN, VINCENT. Son of William Wilkinson CORBIN who married Rachel WRIGHT on Aug. 15,
1745. Vincent took the Oath of Allegiance, 1778, before Honorable James Calhoun.
(A-1/5, A-2/42, and research by Shirley Reightler, Bel Air, MD, 1987)

CORBIN, WILLIAM. Private, Capt. S. Smith's Company No. 8, 1st MD Battalion, Jan. 18,
1776. Non-Juror to Oath of Allegiance, 1778. (H-640, A-1/5)

CORBLEY, CILLIS. Oath of Allegiance, 1778. (A-1/5)

CORBLEY, NICHOLAS. Enlisted July 26, 1776 in Baltimore County. Took the Oath of
Allegiance, 1778, before Hon. Jesse Dorsey. (A-2/63, H-53)

CORCORAN, PATRICK. Sergeant, Capt. Brown's MD Artillery; joined November 22, 1777.
Was at Valley Forge until June, 1778; at White Plains, July, 1778; at Ft. Schuyler
in August and September, 1780; not listed in 1781. (UU-228, UU-230)

CORDERIN, PHILLIP. Non-Juror to Oath of Allegiance, 1778. (A-1/5)

CORDIAL, JAMES. Non-Juror to Oath of Allegiance, 1778. (A-1/5)

CORDRAY, JAMES. Second Mate on ship Defence, Sept. 19, 1776 into 1777. (H-655)

CORNAFLEAN, WILLIAM. Midshipman on ship Defence, September 4 to September 22, 1777,
and Clerk on ship, on September 22 to December 31, 1777. (H-655)

CORNAR, AMIS. Oath of Allegiance, 1778. (A-1/5)

CORNER, THOMAS. Oath of Allegiance, 1778, before Hon. Richard Cromwell. (A-2/46)

CORNTHWAIT, JOHN. Non-Juror to Oath of Allegiance, 1778. (A-1/5)

CORNWALL, WILLIAM. Born 1745/1746 in Armagh, Ireland. Occupation: Joyner. Enlisted
January 24, 1776 as Sergeant in Capt. N. Smith's 1st Company of Matrosses. Height:
5' 10". Also, Sergeant in Capt. Dorsey's Company; convalescent, Nov. 17, 1777.
Sergeant in Capt. J. Smith's MD Artillery and Capt. Dorsey's MD Artillery through
the war. On March 6, 1779, Major N. Smith wrote the Governor of Maryland about
attempt to get Sgt. Cornwall out of prison. It apparently was successful because
he was back on duty in 1780, was at Camp Col. Scirvins on January 28, 1782, and
in service in 1783. He received 50 acres (lot #857) in Maryland. Died after 1794.

CORNWALL, WILLIAM (continued)
(H-563, H-565, H-579, H-618, QQQ-2, YYY-2/14, UU-232, FFF-209, DDDD-11, JJJ-155)

CORTLAND, NATHANIEL.   Private, Capt.Ewing's Company No. 4, enl. May 29, 1776.(H-11)

COSGROVE, EDWARD.   Private, Capt. Ewing's Company No. 4, enl. Jan. 24, 1776. (H-12)

COSGROVE, WILLIAM.   Private, Capt. McClellan's Co., Baltimore Town, Sept. 4, 1780.
Took Oath of Allegiance, 1778, before Hon. George Lindenberger. (A-2/52, CCC-25)

COSKERRY, FELIX.   Oath of Allegiance, 1778. (A-1/5)

COSKERRY, FRANCIS.   Oath of Allegiance, 1778, before Hon. Jesse Dorsey. (A-2/63)

COSKEY, FELIX.   Oath of Allegiance, 1778, before Hon. Jesse Dorsey. (A-2/63)
This is most likely the Felix Coskerry listed above.

COSLIN, CHARLES.   Oath of Allegiance, 1778, before Hon. Geo.Lindenberger. (A-2/52)

COSTELLA, PETER.   Oath of Allegiance, 1778, before Hon. John Hall. (A-1/5, A-2/36)

COSTIGIN (CASSAIGAIN), PATRICK.   Private, Capt. Howell's Company, December 30, 1775
and Capt. S. Smith's Co. No. 8, 1st MD Battn., Jan. 23, 1776. (G-11, H-640)

COSTILLO, THOMAS.   Marine on ship Defence, 1777. (H-655)

COTTERAL, JAMES.   Non-Juror to Oath of Allegiance, 1778. (A-1/5)
COTTERAL, JOHN.   Non-Juror to Oath of Allegiance, 1778. (A-1/5)
COTTERAL, THOMAS.   Two men with this name were Non-Jurors in 1778. (A-1/5)
COTTERAL, THOMAS JR.   Non-Juror to Oath of Allegiance, 1778. (A-1/5)

COTTGRAVE, JOHN.   Oath of Allegiance, 1778, before Hon. Geo.Lindenberger. (A-2/52)

COUGHLAN, EDWARD.   Private, Capt. N. Smith's Co., MD Artillery, 1776-1777 at Fort
Whetstone Point in Baltimore. Private, Capt. Dorsey's Co., MD Artillery, on
Nov. 17, 1777. Matross, Capt. Dorsey's Company at Valley Forge, June 3, 1778.
(UU-231, VV-74, H-574)

COUGHLEN, JACOB.   Oath of Allegiance, 1778, before Hon. James Calhoun. (A-2/39)

COUGHLEN, RICHARD.   Oath of Allegiance, 1778, before Hon. James Calhoun. (A-2/39)

COULSON, WILLIAM.   (c1750, York County, PA - September 23, 1826, Baltimore Co., MD)
Married (1) Rhodda KERR of York County, and (2) Hannah UNDERWOOD of Baltimore in
1807. Children by first marriage: Charles, born 1777; Mary; Rebeckah; Rhoda,
born 1792; Sarah, born 1794; and Jane, born 1795. William COULSON was Captain
in York County Militia, June 17, 1779, under Lt.Col. Samuel Nelson. (XXX-236)

COULTER, ALEXANDER.   Discrepancy in dates: born either in 1750 or 1760 in County
Down, Ireland, and died either in 1815 or October 3, 1828. Sources agree that
his wife was Esther Mifflin McCASKEY. A son, Alexander COULTER Jr., married
Eliza BARKLIE, and their son Archibald Barklie COULTER (1837-1896) married to
Helen Stocket BEATTY (1840-1903) in 1861. Alexander COULTER was a Private in
Capt. Sterrett's Independent Merchants Co., Maryland Militia, 1777. (JJJ-157,
AAA-1077)

COULTER, JOHN DR. (1751 - May 24, 1823) Married Mary McCASKEY. Came to Baltimore
from Ireland in 1773. Served as Surgeon on the Maryland ship Defence in 1776,
and as Surgeon to the Military Hospitals at Baltimore, 1776. Also, was member
of the convention to ratify the Constitution of the State. (XX-5, JJJ-157)

COUNCILMAN (COUNSELMAN), FREDERICK.   Oath of Allegiance, 1778, before Hon. Peter
Shepherd. Served with Col. Nicholson's Troop of Horse, June 7, 1781. (A-2/49,
BBBB-274)

COUNCILMAN (COUNCELMAN), GEARE.   Non-Juror to Oath of Allegiance, 1778. (A-1/5)

COUNCILMAN (COUNCELMAN), GEORGE. (c1735 - October 15, 1794) Wife named Ruth.
Oath of Allegiance, 1778, before Hon. Peter Shepherd. (JJJ-157, A-1/5, A-2/49)

COUNCILMAN (COUNCELMAN), GREG. Oath of Allegiance, 1778. (A-1/5)

COUNCILMAN, HENRY. Non-Juror to Oath of Allegiance, 1778. (A-1/5)

COUNCILMAN (COUNSELMAN), JOHN. Oath of Allegiance, 1778, before Hon. Isaac Van Bibber. (A-1/5, A-2/57)

COURSEY, PATRICK. Matross, Capt. Brown's MD Artillery; joined November 22, 1777. Was at Valley Forge until June, 1778; at White Plains, July, 1778; at Fort Schuyler, August and September, 1780; not listed in 1781. (UU-228, UU-230)

COURSEY, WILLIAM. Non-Juror to Oath of Allegiance, 1778. (A-1/5)

COURTENAY, HERCULES. (October 15, 1736, Newny, Ireland - August 21, 1816, Baltimore County, Maryland) Married Sarah DRURY (1753-1788) in 1774. A son, Henry COURTENAY (1776-1854) mrried Isabella PURVIANCE (1779-1804) in 1799, and their son, Edward Henry COURTENAY (1803-1853) married Virginia Pleasants HOWARD (1816-1852) in 1846. Hercules Courtenay was one of the most prominent men of Baltimore in the Rev. War. He was a member of the Sons of Liberty from 1766 through at least 1776. He served on the Committee of Inspection, March 13, 1775; the Committee of Observation, on July 24, 1775; and the Committee of Correspondence, November 12, 1775. Also, he was authorized by the Continental Congress to assign all bills of credit or money for use of the Mechanical Volunteers and others, for military purposes, 1776-1782. He was a Justice of the Peace, 1777-1778, and a Judge of the Orphans Court, 1778, of Baltimore County, and a Baltimore County Magistrate who administered the Oath of Allegiance in 1778; he resigned that office on December 12, 1780. He was also a Captain-Lieutenant in the 4th MD Continental Artillery, and a Captain-Lieutenant in Proctor's Battalion of the PA Artillery; and a Captain in the MD Cont. Art. Co. He served as Baltimore Town Commissioner from 1781 to 1785. (AAA-784, AAA-786, JJJ-157, CCC-18, CCC-19, A-1/5, A-2/37, A-2/47, RR-19, SS-130, EEEE-1725, B-173, BBB-96, GGG-242, FFF-340, ZZZ-72)

COURTNAY, HERCULES. Ensign, Capt. Griffith's Baltimore Town Battalion, Sept. 25, 1780. (VV-303)

COUSINS, GEORGE. Oath of Allegiance, 1778, before Hon. John Beale Howard. Could not write; made his mark. (A-1/5, A-2/29)

COUTS, MICHAEL. Non-Juror to Oath of Allegiance, 1778. (A-1/5)

COWAN (COWEN), JAMES. Oath of Allegiance, 1778, before Hon. George Lindenberger. (A-1/5, A-2/52)

COWAN, WILLIAM. Non-Juror to Oath of Allegiance, 1778. (A-1/5)

COWARD, JOHN. Oath of Allegiance, 1778, before Hon. Isaac VanBibber. (A-1/5, A-2/34)

COWELL, ROBERT. Non-Juror to Oath of Allegiance, 1778. (A-1/5)

COX, ABRAHAM. (January 1, 1752 - March 24, 1834) Married Elizabeth CLARK. Served as 2nd Lt. in Capt. Shaw's Company No. 5, appearing in records dated August 26, 1776 and October 28, 1776 and December 20, 1776. Took the Oath of Allegiance in 1778 before Hon. Robert Simmons. (JJJ-159, PPP-2, RR-99, ZZ-541, A-1/5, A-2/58)

COX, GEX. Oath of Allegiance, 1778. (A-1/5)

COX, JACOB. Non-Juror to Oath of Allegiance, 1778. (A-1/5)

COX, JAMES. (Born in New Jersey and died October 5, 1777 in Battle of Germantown in Pennsylvania) He was a member of the Sons of Liberty from 1766 through 1776. "Among the very first (if not the first) to enroll a company in Baltimore, for the defense of the colonies, was James COX. This man of warlike traits was a tailor, apparently of excellent education and training. The prominent position assumed by him in the turbulent times preceding the outbreak of war, stamps him as a man of courage and decision of character. What qualifications he may have had for organizing a company of militia cannot be said, but the fact remains that his command was noted for its discipline and bravery. But for Capt. Cox's

COX, JAMES (continued)

untimely death, there is no doubt that he and his men would have reached greater distinction." (CCC-19) He represented West Baltimore at the Association of Free Men on August 21, 1775, while serving on the Baltimore Committee of Observation at that same time. He was a captain in the Baltimore County Militia, Co. No. 3 (63 Privates) on December 19, 1775, and a Captain in the Baltimore Town Battalion on March 2, 1776. (Source AAA-1872 mistakenly states James Cox enlisted in July, 1776 as a Private in the Baltimore County Militia, and formed a company at his church on December 24, 1776, and was commissiond a Captain in January, 1777. This is essentially true, but the dates appear to be incorrect.) "Captain James Cox, by vocation a tailor, and by avocation a Baptist minister and captain of a Militia Company in Baltimore which he outfiited at his own expense, marched to Germantown, Penna. On October 4, 1777, having repulsed the enemy, driving them from their breastworks, he received a ball through his body, expired in a short time, and was buried nearby. His widow, Mrs. Mary Purviance Cox a few days later left Baltimore with two slaves, disinterred the body and brought it home. He is buried at Satter's baptist churchyard on the Falls Road about 12 miles above Baltimore." (TT-69) He actually formed and enrolled his own company on October 9, 1775, (CCC-20), and was a member of the Whig Club in 1777. Records indicate that he was a Captain at the time of his death; however, he was a Major under Colonel John Moale and Soldiers Delight Battalion by September 12, 1777 (unless reference is made to another James Cox of which this writer has no knowledge). This is further proven in pay records after his death: "April, 1778 - Pay the executors of James Cox, late Major of Baltimore Town Battalion of Militia, killed in action October 4, 1777 at German Town, PA, in service of the United States, 75 pounds curreny money." (J-17) Also, payments were made in October, 1779 (150 pounds); 1781 ($600 for 2 yrs. allowance); April 10, 1782 (431 pounds, 5 shillings); and, 1784 (225 pounds). On May 6, 1785, it was certified that "Major James Cox, deceased, left a widow and five children, (no names given): a son age 18; a daughter age 16; a son age 14; a son age 12; and a daughter age 10; to receive support of 112 pounds." (J-189) The same allowance was made on April 10, 1786. Jamex COX married Mary PURVIANCE (d. 1789) on June 7, 1772 in Londontown, Anne Arundel County, MD. A daughter, Mary COX (1776-1803) married James Lowry DONALDSON (1776-1814) in 1794 in Baltimore, and their daughter Jane DONALDSON (1796-1822) married Col. Richard JACKSON (1778-1823) of Virginia in 1812 in Baltimore, MD. Major James Cox is represented in the Society of the Cincinnati of Maryland by Donald Franklin STEWART of Baltimore. (TT-69, H-652, G-10, CCC-20, AAA-1872, CC-36, WW-197, BBB-372, SSS-110, EEEE-1726, CCC-19, CCC-26, J-17, J-41, J-61, J-69, J-115, J-189, J-249, CCC-21, CCC-22)

COX, JOHN. Private, Baltimore County Regiment No. 7, circa 1777. (TTT-13)

COX, MERRIMAN. Oath of Allegiance, 1778, before Hon. Thomas Sollers. (A-1/5, A-2/51)

COX, ROBERT JR. Baltimore Mechanical Company of Militia, November 4, 1775. (F-300)

COX, THOMAS. 2nd Lt., Gunpowder Upper Battalion, October 23, 1781. Took the Oath of Allegiance, 1778, before Hon. James Calhoun. (A-1/5, A-2/41, AAAA-651)

COX, ZEBEDIAH. Non-Juror to Oath of Allegiance, 1778. (A-1/5)

COYL, SAMUEL. Private, Capt. Furnival's Company, MD Artillery, November 17, 1777. Roll indicates "prisoner in Baltimore gaol." (H-573)

COYLE, MICHAEL. Oath of Allegiance, 1778, before Hon. James Calhoun. (A-1/5, A-2/41)

CRABTREE, ISAAC. (1757, Baltimore County, MD - 1847, Wayne County, KY) Married Sally PIKE. A son, Squire CRABTREE (born 1781 in Virginia or North Caroline) married to Chloe CRABTREE and a grandson, Isaac Haywood CRABTREE was born 1808 in Va. or N.C. Isaac CRABTREE was a scout, spy and soldier in Virginia during the war (pension no. S30972). (AAA-2251A, and A. Quisenberry's Revolutionary Soldiers in Kentucky, p.68)

CRADOCK, JAMES. Baltimore Representative to Association of Freemen on July 26, 1775. Major in 2nd MD Battalion of Flying Camp. July-December, 1776. (BB-2, H-58, B-174, TT-69)

CRADOCK, JOHN DR. (January 25, 1749 - October 4, 1794) Son of Rev. Thomas CRADOCK and Katherine RiSTEAU. Married Ann WORTHINGTON. Children: Mary, Katherine, Ann, Arthur and Elizabeth. Resident of Garrison Forest in Baltimore County. He was a member of the Baltimore Committee of Inspection on March 13, 1775 and was elected to the Baltimore Committee of Observation on September 23, 1775 (received 98 votes and was 7th in the balloting), and was a member of the Association of Freemen in 1775. He was a Major in Soldiers Delight Battalion, May 25, 1776, but resigned prior to July 1, 1776. He was a Justice of the Peace, and one of the Magistrates to take and administer the Oath of Allegiance, 1778. He was elected to the House of Delegates in 1782, and although a physician, he never practiced medicine. (XX-5, RR-19, RR-47, SS-136, RR-50, A-2/29, GGG-242, JJJ-160, WW-443, WW-539)

CRADOCK, THOMAS DR. Brother of Dr. John Cradock. On Committee of Observation of Baltimore County, 1775; Surgeon in Capt. Plunkett's Company, Continental Army; served with Col. Nicholson's Troop of Horse on June 7, 1781. Took the Oath of Allegiance, 1778, before Hon. John Moale. Was one of the founders of the Medico-Chirurgical Faculty of the State of Maryland. (XX-6, BBBB-274, A-1/5, A-2/70)

CRAFFORD, ROBERT. Private, Capt. Ewing's Company No. 4, enl. May 20, 1776. (H-11)

CRAFFORD, THOMAS. Private, Capt. Ewing's Company No. 4, enl. Jan. 27, 1776. Also, listed as a Private in Baltimore County Militia, enlisting July 5, 1776. (H-11, H-58)

CRAFORD, JOHN. Private, Baltimore Artillery Company, October 16, 1775. Also, listed as a Recruit in Baltimore County Militia, Apr. 11, 1780. (G-8, H-335)

CRAIG (CRAIGE), ALEXANDER. Born 1755 in Ireland, Occupation: Labourer. Ht: 6'. Enlisted as Corporal in Capt. N. Smith's 1st Company of Matrosses, January 24, 1776. Sergeant in Capt. Dorsey's MD Artillery, November 17, 1777. (H-573, H-566, H-563, QQQ-2)

CRAIG, JOHN. Baltimore County Committee of Observation, July 24, 1775. (EEEE-1725)

CRAIG, MICHAEL. Sergeant of Marines on ship Defence, Sept. 19, 1776. (H-606)

CRAIG, ROBERT. Private, Capt. Furnival's MD Artillery, Nov. 17, 1777. (H-573)

CRAMER, ADAM. Private, Capt. Smith's Company No. 8, enl. Jan. 24, 1776. (H-18)

CRAMER, JOHN. Non-Juror to Oath of Allegiance, 1778. (A-1/5)

CRAMER, PETER. Oath of Allegiance, 1778, before Hon. Edward Cockey. (A-1/5, A-2/62)

CRAMPTON, THOMAS. Revolutionary War pensioner, June 1, 1840, age 80, residing in household of Henry CHANEY, Baltimore County, 1st District. (P-127)

CRANDEL, WILLIAM. Private, Capt. Howell's Company, December 30, 1775. (G-11)

CRANES, MICHAEL. See "KRANER, MICHAEL."

CRANES (CRANE), PETER. Non-Juror to Oath of Allegiance, 1778. (A-1/5)

CRAPPER, JOHN. Able Seaman on ship Defence, September 19, 1776, and Sergeant of Marines in 1777. "John Craper" was a Non-Juror in 1778. (A-1/5, H-606, H-655)

CRATCHER, MATTHEW. Marine on ship Defence, July 28 to October 1, 1777. (H-655)

CRATER, MARTIN. Non-Juror to Oath of Allegiance, 1778. (A-1/5)

CRAVATH, SAMUEL OR LEMUEL. Oath of Allegiance, 1778, before Hon. William Lux. (A-2/68)

CRAWFORD, LEONARD. Non-Juror to Oath of Allegiance, 1778. (A-1/5)

CRAWLEY, JAMES. Marine on ship Defence, Oct. 23 to December 31, 1777. (H-655)

CREEBLE, JACOB. Non-Juror to Oath of Allegiance, 1778. (A-1/5)

CREEVEY, HANS. Oath of Allegiance, 1778, before Hon. James Calhoun. Also, gave an account and receipt for supplies to Capt. George Ross in Baltimore, Apr. 10, 1777. (A-1/5, A-2/38, FFF-99)

CREIGHTON, JOHN. Oath of Allegiance, 1778, before Hon.James Calhoun. (A-2/40)

CREIGHTON, THOMAS. Private, Capt. Howell's Company, December 30, 1775. (G-11)

CRESWELL, JAMES. Oath of Allegiance, 1778, before Hon. James Calhoun. (A-2/38)

CRIDER, JACOB. Baltimore Mechanical Company of Militia, Nov. 4, 1775. (F-298)

CRISSWELL, BENJAMIN. Oath of Allegiance, 1778, before Hon. Peter Shepherd. (A-2/50)

CROAKER, JAMES. Oath of Allegiance, 1778, before Hon. Richard Cromwell. (A-2/46)

CROCKET, BENJAMIN. Oath of Allegiance, 1778, before Hon. Isaac VanBibber. Signed a
letter to Governor Lee, 1781, requesting a defense of Baltimore. (S-49, A-2/34)

CROCKETT, GILBERT. Baltimore Artillery Company, 1777. (V-368)

CROCKETT, JOHN. Involved in a request for an order for tichlenburg and for the powder
and supplies saved from the Peggy, January 13, 1777. Took the Oath of Allegiance,
1778, before Hon. James Calhoun. (A-1/5, A-2/42, FFF-84)

CROMER, JAMES. Recruited in Baltimore by Samuel Chester for the 3rd Maryland Regt.,
March 2, 1780. (H-334)

CROMER, RUDOLPH. Private, Baltimore Artillery Company, October 16, 1775. (G-8)

CROMRINE, GEORGE. Non-Juror to Oath of Allegiance, 1778. (A-1/5)

CROMWELL, FRANCIS. (October 2, 1752 - after December 20, 1810) Married (1) Elizabeth
GRAY and (2) Patience STANSBURY. Signed Oath of Allegiance, 1778, before Honorable
Richard Holliday. (Source JJJ-165 indicates he was a Captain during war.) (A-2/60)

CROMWELL, JACOB. Non-Juror to Oath of Allegiance, 1778. (A-1/5)
CROMWELL, JAMES. Non-Juror to Oath of Allegiance, 1778. (A-1/5)

CROMWELL, JOHN. Baltimore County Committee of Observation, July 24, 1775. (EEEE-1725)

CROMWELL, JOHN GILES. Non-Juror to Oath of Allegianc, 1778. (A-1/5)
CROMWELL, JOSEPH. Non-Juror to Oath of Allegiance, 1778. (A-1/5)

CROMWELL, NATHAN. Served on Baltimore County Committee of Inspection, March 13, 1775
but was a Non-Juror to the Oath of Allegiance in 1778. (A-1/5, RR-19)

CROMWELL, OLIVER. Non-Juror to Oath of Allegiance, 1778. (A-1/5)
CROMWELL, PHILIMON. Non-Juror to Oath of Allegiance, 1778. (A-1/5)

CROMWELL, RICHARD. (1749-1802) Nominated for Baltimore Committee of Observation, but
did not receive enough votes to get elected on September 12, 1775. Was a 1st Lt.
in Capt. Wyle's Company No. 1 in Baltimore County by October 28, 1776. Authorized
by Continental Congress to assign bills of credit or money for use of Mechanical
Volunteers and others for military purposes, 1776-1782. Was a Justice of the Peace
in 1778 and administered the Oath of Allegiance. Served in Gunpowder Upper Battn.
as a Captain prior to October 23, 1781. (AAAA-650, RR-50, ZZ-242, PPP-2, CCC-18,
GGG-242, A-1/5, A-2/40, A-2/46)

CROMWELL, STEPHEN. (October 30, 1747 - April 10, 1793) Married Elizabeth MURRAY.
Elected to Baltimore County Committee of Observation on September 23, 1775. Took
the Oath of Allegiance, 1778, before Hon. Edward Cockey. Served as 2nd Major in
Col. E. Cockey's Gunpowder Upper Battalion, 1776-1777, and possibly longer. (RR-50,
RR-47, SS-136, SS-110, ZZ-337, JJJ-165, A-1/5, A-2/61)

CROMWELL, THOMAS. (Died before February 1, 1799) Married Hannah Henrietta SMITH.
Lieutenant in Capt. Oldham's Company, 4th MD Regt., May 20, 1777 - Dec. 10, 1779.
Officer (probably Captain) with Col. Nicholson's Troop of Horse on June 7, 1781.
(H-97, JJJ-165, BBBB-274)

CROMWELL, WILLIAM. Captain, Baltimore County Militia, December 19, 1775, commanding
69 Privates, and served as Captain in the Gunpowder Battalion at least into 1777,
if not longer. Took Oath of Allegiance, 1778, before Honorable Richard Holliday.
(X-111, WW-444, G-10, CC-36, A-1/5, A-2/60)

CRON, THOMAS. Marine on ship Defence, 1777. (H-655)

CRONOVER, JACOB. Non-Juror to Oath of Allegiance, 1778. (A-1/5)

CROOK (CROOKS), HENRY. Oath of Allegiance, 1778, before Hon. Charles Ridgely of William. Recruit, Baltimore County, 1780. (A-1/5, A-2/27, H-340)

CROOK, SAMUEL. Oath of Allegiance, 1778, before Hon. Edward Cockey. (A-1/5, A-2/61)

CROSBIE, JOSEPH. Private, Capt. Smith's Co. No. 8, enl. Jan. 13, 1776. (H-18)

CROSBY, GEORGE. Maryland line defective, July, 1780, Baltimore Co. resident.(H-414)

CROSBY, JOHN. Corporal in Capt. Lansdale's Co., 4th MD Regiment, April 6, 1777 to September 1, 1778, and Private from September 1 to November 1, 1780. (H-98)

CROSLEY, WILLIAM. Marine on ship Defence, March 16 to December 31, 1777. (H-655)

CROSS, ASAEL. Non-Juror to Oath of Allegiance, 1778. (A-1/6).
CROSS, BENJAMIN. Non-Juror to Oath of Allegiance, 1778. (A-1/6)

CROSS, HENRY. Involved in evaluation of Baltimore County cofiscated proprietary reserve lands in 1782. (FFF-542)

CROSS, ISRAEL. Non-Juror to Oath in 1778. Involved in evaluation of Baltimore County confiscated proprietary reserve lands in 1782. (A-1/6, FFF-542)

CROSS, JOHN. Non-Juror to Oath of Allegiance, 1778. (A-1/6)
CROSS, ROBERT. Non-Juror to Oath of Allegiance, 1778. (A-1/6)
CROSS, SOLOMON. Non-Juror to Oath of Allegiance, 1778. (A-1/6)
CROSS, THOMAS. Non-Juror to Oath of Allegiance, 1778. (A-1/6) However, Source JJJ-166 states he was born October 30, 1711 and died March 23, 1793, had a wife name Sophia, and rendered patriotic service in Maryland.

CROTTINGER, HENRY. Took Oath of Allegiance in 1781. (QQ-108)

CROW, JAMES. Oath of Allegiance, 1778, before Hon. Edward Cockey. (A-1/6, A-2/61)

CROW, THOMAS. Private on ship Defence, September 19, 1776. (H-607)

CROWER, RUDOLPH. Private, Capt. Graybill's German Regiment in 1776. (H-265)

CROWLEY, PATRICK. Oath of Allegiance, 1778, before Hon. William Spear. (A-2/67). There may have been another Patrick Crowley who was a Non-Juror, 1778. (A-1/6)

CROWS, FRANCIS. Non-Juror to Oath of Allegiance, 1778. (A-1/6)
CROWS, JOHN. Non-Juror to Oath of Allegiance, 1778. (A-1/6)

CROXALL, CHARLES SR. Oath of Allegiance, 1778, before Hon. Charles Ridgely of William. (A-1/6, A-2/28)

CROXALL, CHARLES MOALE. (October 7, 1756, Baltimore County, MD - November 6, 1831, Anne Arundel County, MD) Married Mary MORRIS (1763, England - 1824, New Jersey) on July 26, 1781. Children: Thomas CROXALL (1791-1861) married Mary LONG (1791-1868) in 1813, and their daughter Maria Fayetta CROXALL (1814-1887) married in 1838 to Edward JONES (1807-1864); Daniel CROXALL; Morris CROXALL (born 1799); and, Anna Maria CROXALL. Charles CROXALL was a 2nd Lt. in Baltimore County Militia on September 13, 1776, and subsequently became an Ensign in the 11th PA Regt., 2nd Lt. in the 10th PA Regt., and 1st Lt. in Col. Hartley's PA Regt. in February, 1777. After the Battle of Brandywine he became a Captain and was wounded at the Battle of Paoli, and was taken prisoner. He was kept aboard a ship and then on Long Island until exchanged on November 23, 1780. He served through November 7, 1781, and was entitled to 200 acres (lots #2363 to 2366) in western Maryland. On March 12, 1827 it was ordered to pay Charles CROXALL of Baltimore City, during his life, half yearly, half pay of a Captain of Dragoons, for his services during the Revolutionary War. On March 9, 1832 it was ordered that Claudius LEGRANDE be paid $31.67, being the sum due Charles CROXALL, a Revolutionary pensioner at his death. (C-332, DDDD-1, XXX-247, JJ-9, AAA-1145, AAA-1251, AAA-500, JJJ-167)

CROXALL, JAMES. Drafted into Baltimore County Regiment No. 36, circa 1777. Took the Oath of Allegiance, 1778, before Hon. William Lux. (A-1/6, A-2/68, TTT-13)

CROXALL, RICHARD. Two men with this name took the Oath of Allegiance in 1778: one before Hon. Richard Cromwell and one before Hon. Isaac VanBibber. (A-2/46, 2/57)

CROXALL, RICHARD JR. Oath of Allegiance, 1778, before Hon. John Moale. (A-2/70)

CROXELLS, RICHARD. Oath of Allegiance, 1778. (A-1/6) This is probably the Richard Croxall listed above (name misspelled).

CRUBLE, JACOB. Oath of Allegiance, 1778, before Hon. James Calhoun. (A-1/40)

CRUDGINTON, GEORGE. Non-Juror to Oath of Allegiance, 1778. (A-1/6)

CRUSH, PHILLIP. Non-Juror to Oath of Allegiance, 1778. (A-1/6)

CRUSINS, PHILLIP. Oath of Allegiance, 1778. (A-1/6)

CRUTCHLEY, ELIAS. Corporal, Baltimore County Regiment No. 15, circa 1777. (TTT-13)

CUDLING, WILLIAM. Non-Juror to Oath of Allegiance, 1778. (A-1/6)

CULBERTSON (COLBERTSON), WILLIAM. Born 1745 in Cork, Ireland. Occupation: Labourer. Height: 5' 5". Enlisted January 28, 1776 as Private in Capt. N. Smith's 1st Co. of Matrosses. Served with Capt. Dorsey's MD Artillery on November 17, 1777. He was deposed on enlistment terms as a Matross soldier in Baltimore County, May 7, 1779. (FFF-220, H-564, H-567, H-574, CC-74, QQQ-2)

CULLEN, JOHN. Oath of Allegiance, 1778. (A-1/6)

CULLINS, JOSHUA. Non-Juror to Oath of Allegiance, 1778. (A-1/6)

CULLINS, THOMAS SR. Non-Juror to Oath of Allegiance, 1778. Involved in evaluation of Baltimore County confiscated proprietary lands in 1782. (A-1/6, FFF-553)

CULLINS, THOMAS JR. Oath of Allegiance, 1778. (A-1/6)

CULLISON, JESSE AND WILLIAM. Both involved in evaluation of Baltimore County confiscated proprietary reserve lands in 1782. (FFF-542, FFF-543)

CULLUM, WILLIAM. Oath of Allegiance, 1778, before Hon. Jesse Dorsey. (A-1/6, A-2/63)

CULLY, ARMISTEAD. (1758, Kingston Parish, Matthews County, VA - February 18, 1839, Baltimore, MD) Married Mary Jane HIGGINS (died 1837) and their daughter Lucy Ann CULLY married Captain William FRENCH. Armistead CULLY was a Private in Col. John Peyton's Regiment, Virginia Militia, 1776-1781. (AAA-466A)

CULVERTSON, WILLIAM. Matross in Capt. gale's Artillery Company, 1779; at Chester, PA on Nov. 9, 1779 and Morristown, NJ on Mar. 7 and Apr. 13, 1780. (YYY-1/23)

CULVERTWELL, RICHARD. Non-Juror to Oath of Allegiance, 1778. (A-1/6)

CUMELL, MARTIN. Non-Juror to Oath of Allegiance, 1778. (A-1/6)

CUMMINGS, ABRM. Oath of Allegiance, 1778, before Hon. Isaac Van Bibber. (A-2/34)

CUMMINGS, ALEXANDER. Marine on ship Defence, and Carpenter's Yeoman from Feb. 17 to December 31, 1777. Took Oath of Allegiance in 1778. (A-1/6, H-655)

CUMMINGS, ROBERT. (1754, Frederick County, MD - November 14, 1825, Libertytown, MD) Buried in Fairmount Cemetery. Married Mary Allen COATES. Served as Captain in Baltimore County's Upper Battalion, August 30, 1777 to al least 1778. Took the Oath of Allegiance, 1778, before Hon. John Hall. Subsequently became Commander of the 2nd Division, MD Militia, and later referred to as Major Robert Cummings. (MMM-A, JJJ-168, BBB-350, LL-66, E-14, A-1/6, A-2/36)

CUMMINS (CUMMINGS), ANTHONY. Private, Baltimore County Militia, enlisted July 19, 1776. 1st Lt., Upper Battalion, December 4, 1778. Took Oath of Allegiance in 1778, before Hon. Jesse Dorsey. (A-1/6, A-2/63, H-58, GGG-257)

CUMMINS (CUMMINGS), CHRISTOPHER. Oath of Allegiance, 1778, before Hon. Richard Cromwell. (A-1/6, A-2/46)

CUMMINS, JOHN. Oath of Allegiance, 1778, before Hon. John Hall. (A-1/6. A-2/36)

CUMMINS, RICHARD. Private, Baltimore County Militia, enlisted July 5, 1776. Corporal, Capt. Oldham's Co., 4th MD Regt., Dec, 6, 1776 to discharge Dec. 6, 1779. (H-58,99)

CUMMINS, THOMAS. Enlisted in Baltimore County, July 20, 1776. (H-52)

CUNNINGHAM, EDWARD. Non-Juror to Oath of Allegiance, 1778. (A-1/6)

CUNNINGHAM, GEORGE. Non-Juror to Oath of Allegiance, 1778. (A-1/6)

CUNNINGHAM, JNO. Born 1752 in Charles Town, Maryland. Occupation: Labourer. Ht.: 6'. Enlisted January 24, 1776 as Private in Capt. N. Smith's 1st Company of Matrosses. (H-563, H-566, QQQ-2)

CUNNINGHAM, THOMAS. 3dr Sergeant, Capt. Ewing's Co. No. 4, enl. Jan. 13, 1776. (H-11)

CUNNINGHAM, THOMPSON. Boatswain's Mate on ship Defence, July 31-Dec. 31, 1777.(H-655)

CUNNIUS (CUNIUS), WILLIAM. Private, Capt. Graybill's German Regt., 1776. (H-266)

CURAINS, PHILIP. Oath of Allegiance, 1778, before Hon. Geo. Lindenberger. (A-2/52)

CURBY, WILLIAM. Non-Juror to Oath of Allegiance, 1778. (A-1/6)

CURDEL, WILLIAM. Oath of Allegiance, 1778, before Hon. John Beale Howard. Could not write; made his mark ("U"). (A-1/6, A-2/29)

CURLING (CUSLING), W. Oath of Allegiance, 1778, before Hon. Isaac VanBibber. (A-2/34)

CURRIER, ANTHONY. Private, Capt. Howell's Company, December 30, 1775. (G-11)

CURRIER, WILLIAM. Non-Juror to Oath of Allegiance, 1778. (A-1/6)

CURRY, MORRIS. Drafted into Baltimore County Regiment No. 36, circa 1777. (TTT-13)

CURREY (CORRY), JAMES. Born 1756 in Ireland. Fair complexion; ht.: 5' 6½". Enlisted July 5, 1776 in Baltimore County, Private, Col. Ewing's Battalion. (H-56)

CURSON (CARSON), RICHARD. Baltimore Privateer and owner of schooner Baltimore Hero. Oath of Allegiance, 1778. Baltimore Salt Committee, October 14, 1779. (HHH-88, III-206, III-207, A-1/6)

CURTEIN, JAMES. Oath of Allegiance, 1778, before Hon. Geo. Lindenberger. (A-2/52)

CURTIS, FRANCIS. Baltimore Mechanical Company of Militia, 1776. (CCC-28)

CURTIS, JOHN. Born 1742 in Bucks County, PA. Occupation: Labourer. Ht.: 5' 5". Enlisted January 27, 1776, Private in Capt. N. Smith's 1st Company of Matrosses. Private, Capt. Dorsey's MD Artillery, Nov. 17, 1777. (H-564, H-573, VV-73, VV-74, H-567, QQQ-2)

CURTIS, JOHN. Born June 6, 1750; died July 27, 1843. Married Elsie (Ealsy) WILKINS in Baltimore (marriage proven through Maryland pension application). Served as a Sergeant in Capt. Dorsey's MD Artillery, Nov. 17, 1777. (YY-112, H-574, JJJ-170)

CURTIS, JOHN. Gunner, Capt. Gale's MD Artillery, 1779; was at Chester, PA ("Sick") on November 9, 1779; at Morristown, NJ ("General's Guard") on March 7, 1780, and again on rolls of April 13, 1780. (YYY-1/24)

CURTIS, JOSEPH. Oath of Allegiance, 1778, before Hon. James Calhoun. (A-1/6, A-2/42)

CURTIS, ROBERT. Born 1748 in England. Light hair; ht.: 5' 3¼". Enlisted July 5, 1776 in Baltimore County, Private, Col. Ewing's Battalion. (H-55)

CUTHBERTH, WILLIAM. Oath of Allegiance, 1778, before Hon. Jesse Dorsey. (A-2/63)

D

DADD, JOHN. Oath of Allegiance, 1778, before Hon. Andrew Buchanan. (A-1/6, A-2/57)

DAEFNEY, JOHN. Seaman on ship Defence, August 9 to Sept. 6, 1777. (H-655)

DAEMON, CHARLES. Private, Count Pulaski's Legion; enlisted in Baltimore, May 10, 1778. (H-593)

DALBERT, JAMES. Oath of Allegiance, 1778, before Hon. Geo. Lindenberger. (A-2/52)

DALEY, JACOB. Involved in evaluation of Baltimore County confiscated proprietary reserve lands in 1782. (FFF-547)

DALLAM, BRYAN. Private in Count Pulaski's Legion; enlisted in Baltimore, Apr. 29, 1778 (H-592)

DALLIS, WALTER. Non-Juror to Oath of Allegiance, 1778. (A-1/6)

DALRYMPLE, JOHN. Private, Capt. Cox's Company, December 19, 1776. Took Oath of Allegiance, 1778, before Hon. George Lindenberger. (A-1/6, A-2/52, CCC-21)

DALY, JAMES. Private, Capt. S. Smith's Company No. 8, 1st MD Battn., January 20, 1776. (H-641)

DAMNITZ, JOHN. Born 1748 in Germany. Black hair; pock marked; height: 5' 2". Enlisted July 7, 1776, Baltimore County; Private, Col. Ewing's Battn. (H-55)

DANIEL, JOHN. Non-Juror to Oath of Allegiance, 1778. (A-1/6)

D'ANMOURS, CHEVALIER. French Consul in Baltimore, 1781-1782. (FFF-536)

DANNALLY, EDWARD. Private in Count Pulaski's Legion; enlisted in Baltimore, Apr. 10, 1778. (H-592, H-593)

DANROTH, GOTTLIEB. Private, Capt. Graybills' German Regiment, 1776. (H-265)

DANROTH, LORENTZ. Private, Capt. Graybill's German Regiment, 1776. (H-265)

DAPHNEY, JOHN. Non-Juror to Oath of Allegiance, 1778. (A-1/6)

DARE, JOHN. Private, Capt. McClellan's Company, September 4, 1780. (CCC-24)

DARLING, MANUS. Oath of Allegiance, 1778, before Hon. James Calhoun. (A-2/39)

DARLING, THOMAS. Oath of Allegiance, 1778, before Hon. Thomas Sollers. (A-2/51)

DARLINGTON, JOSEPH. Private, Baltimore County Militia, enl. July 18, 1776. (H-58)

DARNALL, HENRY. Non-Juror to Oath of Allegiance, 1778. (A-1/6)

DARNALL, HENRY BENNETT. Took Oath of Allegiance in 1781. (QQ-108)

DARNES, THOMAS. Non-Juror to Oath of Allegiance, 1778. (A-1/6)

DASHIELD (DASHIELL), BENJAMIN. Oath of Allegiance, 1778. (A-1/6)

DASHIELD, FRANCIS. ("Francis DeShields") Born 1752 in Nova Scotia. Occ: Bricklayer. Height" 5' 9 3/4". Private, Capt. Howell's Company, December 30, 1775. Enlisted February 3, 1776 as Private in Capt. N. Smith's 1st Company of Matrosses. (H-565, H-566, G-11, VV-73, QQQ-2)

DASHIELD, LEWIS ("Lewis D'Shield") Private in Capt. Howell's Company, December 30, 1775, and Private in Capt. Sheaff's Company, June 16, 1777. (G-11, W-162)

DASHIELL, WILLIAM AUGUSTUS DR. (of the Eastern Shore of Maryland) Surgeon's Mate of Gen. Smallwood's Regiment, March-December, 1776. Stationed in Baltimore Town in 1776. Surgeon in Hopsital Department, June 1, 1778. Died in Baltimore on Dec. 5, 1780 while serving with 3rd MD Regiment. (Source XX-6 erroneously states that Dr. Dashiell served in the Army until 1782.) (H-20, H-103, B-186)

DASSEN (DAFFEN), GEORGE. Oath of Allegiance, 1778, before Hon. William Lux. (A-2/68)

DAUGHERTY,_____(OF RICHARD). (part of name torn off list) Private in Baltimore County Regiment No. 7, circa 1777. (TTT-13)

DAUGHTERY (DOUGHERTY), DENNIS. Private, Capt. Deams' Company, 7th MD Regiment, as of December 24, 1776. (H-305)

DAUGHERTY (DOUGHERTY), EDWARD. Private, Capt. Lansdale's Company, 4th MD Regiment; Private, May 13, 1778; Corporal, August 1, 1779; Sergeant, January 1, 1780; and, discharged, November 1, 1780. (H-105)

DAUGHERTY, JOHN. Non-Juror to Oath of Allegiance, 1778. (A-1/6)

DAUGHERTY, JOSEPH. Non-Juror to Oath of Allegiance, 1778. (A-1/6)

DAUGHERTY, PATRICK. Oath of Allegiance, 1778, before Hon. John Beale Howard. Could not write; made his mark ("\"). (A-1/6, A-2/29)

DAUGHERTY, RICHARD. Non-Juror to Oath of Allegiance, 1778. (A-1/6)

DAUGHURST, JAMES. Non-Juror to Oath of Allegiance, 1778. (A-1/6)

DAULTON, PETER. Born 1747 in Ireland. Sandy complexion; ht.: 5' 6½". Enlisted July 5, 1776 in Baltimore County; Private, Col. Ewing's Battalion. (H-57)

DAVEY, SAMUEL. Oath of Allegiance, 1778. (A-1/6)

DAVIDSON, ANDREW. Private, Capt. Cox's Company, December 19, 1776. Non-Juror to Oath of Allegiance, 1778. (A-1/6, CCC-21)

DAVIDSON, JACOB. Oath of Allegiance, 1778, before Hon. Isaac Van Bibber. (A-2/34)

DAVIDSON, JOB (JOAB). Private, Capt.Cox's Company, December 19, 1776, and in Capt. McClellan's Company, September 4, 1780. Took Oath of Allegiance, 1778, before Hon. George Lindenberger. (A-1/6, A-2/52, CCC-21, CCC-24)

DAVIDSON, JOHN. Oath of Allegiance, 1778, before Hon. William Lux. (A-1/6, A-2/68)

DAVIDSON, PETER. Oath of Allegiance, 1778, before Hon. Geo. Lindenberger. (A-2/52)

DAVIDSON, ROBERT. Baltimore Mechanical Company of Militia, November 4, 1775. Private, Capt. Cox's Company, December 19, 1776, and Capt. McClellan's Company, September 4, 1780. Took Oath of Allegiance, 1778, before Hon. George Lindenberger. (CCC-21, CCC-24, A-1/6, A-2/52)

DAVIDSON, WILLIAM. Oath of Allegiance, 1778, before Hon. George Lindenberger. One "William Davison" was a Private in Capt. McClellan's Company, September 4, 1780. (CCC-24, A-1/6, A-2/52)

DAVIS, ABEDNIGO. Non-Juror to Oath of Allegiance, 1778. (A-1/6)

DAVIS, ALEXANDER. Ensign, Soldiers Delight Battalion, August 29, 1777 through 1779. Took Oath of Allegiance, 1778, before Hon. Peter Shepherd. (BBB-348, E-10, A-2/49)

DAVIS, CHARLES. Matross in Capt. Gale's MD Artillery, 1779-1780. (YYY-1/25)

DAVIS, CHRISTIAN. Oath of Allegiance, 1778, before Hon. Thomas Sollers. (A-2/51)

DAVIS, DANIEL. Non-Juror to Oath of Allegiance, 1778. (A-1/6)

DAVIS, EDWARD. Non-Juror to Oath of Allegiance, 1778. (A-1/6)

DAVIS, FRANCIS. Non-Juror to Oath of Allegiance, 1778. (A-1/6)

DAVIS, JAMES. Non-Juror to Oath of Allegiance, 1778. (A-1/6)

DAVIS, JOHN. Enlisted in Baltimore Town, July 17, 1776. Oath of Allegiance, 1778. (H-53, A-1/6)

DAVIS, JOHN. Corporal of Marines on ship Defence, 1777. (H-655)

DAVIS, MICHAEL. Private, Capt. Ewing's Company No. 4, 1776. (H-13)

DAVIS, NATHAN. Non-Juror to Oath of Allegiance, 1778. (A-1/6)

DAVIS, NATHANIEL SR. Oath of Allegiance, 1778, before Hon. Andrew Buchanan. (A-2/57)

DAVIS, RICHARD. 2nd Lt., Soldiers Delight Company No. 7, May 13, 1776. 1st Lt., Soldiers Delight Battalion, August 29, 1777, to at least 1778. Non-Juror to Oath of Allegiance, 1778. (A-1/6, E-10, FF-64, BBB-348)

DAVIS, RICHARD. Matross, Capt. Gale's MD Artillery, 1779; sick, 1780. (YYY-1/27)

DAVIS, PETER. Matross, Capt. Gale's MD Artillery, 1779-1780. Fifer, Capt. J. Smith's MD Artillery, 1780. Fifer, Capt. Dorsey's MD Artillery at Camp Col Scirvins on January 28, 1782. (YYY-1/26, YYY-2/15, UU-232, H-578)

DAVIS, ROBERT. Non-Juror to Oath in 1778, but subscribed in 1781. (A-1/6, QQ-108)

DAVIS, SAMUEL. (March 14, 1768 - October 15, 1834) Married Margaret BARRETT. Was a Drummer and Fifer in the Maryland Line. Originally from Kent County, Samuel DAVIS received half pay of a Sergeant for his Revolutionary War services, on March 9, 1826 while residing in Baltimore City. There must have been some discrepancy in his record because he had been stricken from the pension roll on February 12, 1823, probably to do with his reank. On March 5, 1835, his widow Margaret received half pay of Private during her life, quarterly, Samuel having died in 1834. (YY-17, C-333, JJJ-180)

DAVIS, THOMAS. Oath of Allegiance, 1778, before Hon. James Calhoun. (A-1/6, A-2/38) This, or another, Thomas Davis took the Oath in 1781 also. (QQ-108)

DAVIS, WILLIAM. Ensign, Capt. Hall's Company, August 26, 1776 and February 4, 1777. 2nd Lt., Capt. Marshall's Company, Upper Battalion, August 30, 1777 through 1781. 1st Lt., Capt. Stilts' Company, Upper Battalion, November 5, 1781. Took the Oath of Allegiance in 1778. (A-1/6, E-14, LL-66, RR-99, VV-114, BBB-350, AAAA-662)

DAVIS, WILLIAM. (Born October 16, 1756) Enlisted March 2, 1777 at Fredericktown, MD. Served as Private in Capt. Stull's Company, Col. Gunby's 7th MD Regt., and was discharged March 2, 1780 at Morristown, NJ. Was in the Battles of Princeton, Brandywine. Applied for pension from Bedford County, PA and received $8 per month from August 5, 1819 (Pension S34731 issued September 11, 1819) Stated on August 8, 1820 he was age 64, of Bedford County, PA, that his wife is about 59, and he had three married sons. On November 13, 1830 he asked that hereafter he be paid his pension from Baltimore, MD as he had moved from PA to MD. "The General Accounting Office advised that the last payment of pension fro September 4, 1842 to March 4, 1843 was made at Baltimore, March 8, 1843 to O. P. Hause, Attorney for pensioner, and March 6, 1843 the pensioner certified that he had resided in Alleghany County, MD for three years and that prior thereto he lived in Bedford County, PA." (DDD-51)

DAVIS, WILLIAM. Matross, Capt. Brown's MD Artillery; joined November 22, 1777. Was at Valley Forge until June, 1778; at White Plains, July, 1778; at Fort Schuyler in August and September, 1780; not listed in 1781. (UU-228, UU-230)

DAVIS, WILLIAM. Marine on ship Defence, 1777. (H-655)

DAVIS, WILLIAM. Two men with this name took the Oath of Allegiance in 1778: one before Hon. John Hall, and one before Hon. George Lindenberger. (A-2/36, A-2/52)

DAVISON, JACOB. Oath of Allegiance, 1778. (A-1/6)

DAVRY, WILLIAM. Private in Capt. Sheaff's Company, June 16, 1777; roll indicates he had "gone to Carolina for a short time." (W-162)

DAWE (DAW), GEORGE. Recruit in Baltimore County, 1780. Private in Extrs Regiment, Fort Whetstone Point, Baltimore, 1781. (H-340, H-627)

DAWN, THOMAS. Oath of Allegiance, 1778 before Hon. Charles Ridgely of William. Could not write; made his mark. (A-1/6, A-2/28)

DAWS, FRANCIS. Non-Juror to Oath of Allegiance, 1778. (A-1/6)

DAWSEL, RICHARD. Hauled flour for the Baltimore Town Committee in 1780. (RRR-6)

DAWSON, ISAAC. Baltimore Mechanical Company of Militia, November 4, 1775. (F-299)

DAY, EDWARD. Oath of Allegiance, 1778, before Hon. Hercules Courtenay. (A-2/37)

DAY, ISAAC. Non-Juror to Oath of Allegiance, 1778. (A-1/6)
DAY, JOHN. Non-Juror to Oath of Allegiance, 1778. (A-1/6)
DAY, MARK. Non-Juror to Oath of Allegiance, 1778. (A-1/6)
DAY, MATTHEW. Non-Juror to Oath of Allegiance, 1778. (A-1/6)

DAY, NICHOLAS. (c1750 - after July 2, 1815) Married (2) Mrs. Grace ANGELLY. Served as Private in Baltimore County Militia, enl. July 19, 1776. (JJJ-182, H-58)

DAY, WILLIAM. Sergeant in Capt. Furnival's MD Artillery, reduced to a Private on November 17, 1777. Matross in Capt. Dorsey's MD Artillery at Valley Forge as of June 3, 1778. (H-572, UU-231)

DEACON, SAMUEL. Non-Juror to Oath of Allegiance, 1778. (A-1/6)

DEACON, THOMAS. Non-Juror to Oath of Allegiance, 1778. (A-1/6)

DEADY, DANIEL. Private, Capt. McClellan's Co., baltimore Town, Sept. 4, 1780. (CCC-25)

DEAKINS, JOHN. Private, Extra Regt., Fort Whetstone Point, Baltimore, 1781. (H-626)

DEAL, HENRY. Oath of Allegiance, 1778, before Hon. George Lindenberger. (A-1/6, A-2/52)

DEAL (DEALE), JOSEPH. Matross, Capt. Brown's MD Artillery; joined November 22, 1777.
Was at Valley Forge until June, 1778; at White Plains, July, 1778; at Fort Schuyler,
August and September, 1780; not listed in 1781. (UU-228, UU-230)

DEAL, PHILIP. Non-Juror to Oath of Allegiance, 1778. (A-1/6)

DEALBY, JACOB. Oath of Allegiance, 1778, before Hon. John Hall. (A-2/36)

DEAMS (DEEMS), FREDERICK. (1740-1791) Captain, Baltimore County Militia, May 27, 1776.
Captain, 3rd Division, Baltimore Battalion under Col. Buchanan, June, 1776 (72 men in
his command). Involved with enlistment bounties, October 27, 1776. Captain, 7th MD
Regiment, December 10, 1776. Took Oath of Allegiance, 1778, before Honorable James
Calhoun. Appointed Captain of a Company formerly commanded by George Ackerman (who
had died) in the Baltimore Town Battalion of Militia in Baltimore County; commission
signed by Gov. Thomas Lee on September 25, 1780. He served as Captain at least until
January 19, 1781. (JJJ-184, H-304, FFF-64, DD-47, JJ-9, FFF-63, EE-448, R-15, BBBB-29,
F-307, A-1/6, A-2/41)

DEAN, ALEXANDER. Oath of Allegiance, 1778, before Honorable James Calhoun. (A-2/40)

DEAN, DAVID. Private, Capt. J. Gist's Co., 3rd MD Regt., February, 1778. (H-600)

DEAN, HEZEKIAH. Oath of Allegiance, 1778. (A-1/6)

DEAN, JOHN. Non-Juror to Oath of Allegiance, 1778. (A-1/6)

DEAN, MICHAEL. Oath of Allegiance, 1778. (A-1/6)

DEARLY, JACOB. Oath of Allegiance, 1778. (A-1/6)

DEARMOND, NEAL. Private, Capt. Ewing's Company No. 4, enl. January 22, 1776. (H-12)

DEAVEN, JOHN. Oath of Allegiance, 1778, before Hon. Thomas Sollers. (A-2/51)

DEAVER, JOHN. (1758 - August 23, 1813, Baltimore, MD) Married (1) Susannah TALBOT on
March 11, 1777; (2) Honor WORTH on August 4, 1789; and (3) Sarah HUNT on January 12,
1797; all in Baltimore County. Family Record: Susanna DEAVER died Sept. 9, 1787;
John Talbot DEAVER was born Sept. 9, 1787, about half an hour before his mother's
death; John DEAVER and Norah WORTH (WROTH) were married August 4, 1789; Ann DEAVER,
daughter of John and Onorah DEAVER was born January 12, 1792; Onorah DEAVER, wife of
John DEAVER, died October 14, 1793; John DEAVER and Sarah HUNT were married Jan. 12,
1797. Children: Emanuel Kent DEAVER (born May 24, 1798); Job Hunt DEAVER (Jan. 9,
1801-Aug. 18, 1801); Margaretta Hopkins DEAVER (born June 26, 1802); John Hunt DEAVER
(Apr. 9-Aug. 20, 1804); Miriam Hunt DEAVER (Aug. 22, 1805- Nov. 4, 1805); Miriam
DEAVER (Oct. 23-Oct 24, 1806). It is stated that John DEAVER, the soldier, was son of
John DEAVER, Sr., and that the former was age 19 when he married Susanna TALBOT. He
and Sarah, the widow, did not apply for a pension. She appears not to have been entitled until the Act of July 29, 1848, having married in 1797 and died in 1851. The
record states "the case of Sarah DEAVER, widow of John DEAVER of Maryland, Act of
July 29, 1848, established date of marriage, & her death & the children surviving,
but still her husband is not identified by witnesses who knew of his service, with
the service admitted to have been performed by a man of this name." Margaret Hopkins
HOLTZMAN applied March 26, 1852, age 49, and declared that she was the daughter of
Sarah DEAVER, widow of John DEAVER, who was a Lieutenant in 3rd Regt., MD Continental
Troops. He entered the service as Lieutenant, December 10, 1776 and resigned his commission April 8, 1779. He died in Baltimore, August 23, 1813, leaving a widow Sarah
DEAVER and two children: Emanuel Kent DEAVER and Margaret Hopkins DEAVER. Sarah DEAVER
died October 23, 1851, leaving only one surviving child, the affiant, widow of George

DEAVER, JOHN (continued)

HOLTZMAN, of Baltimore, MD. Said Emanuel Kent DEAVER died July 27, 1844.
(All of the foregoing family record and pension information is from source
DDD-52) Additionally, John and Sarah's son, Emanuel Kent DEAVER married
Elizabeth SHIPLEY and their granddaughter Elizabeth Ann DEAVER married Abram
Martin STILLWELL. John DEAVER's service during the Revolutionary War was
questioned at the time of his widow's pension application, but the information
about him is quite substantiated (unless there was more then one John Deaver):
Member of the Sons of Liberty, 1776; Member of the Whig Club, 1777; Member of
Baltimore County Committee of Inspection, March 13, 1775; Member of Committee
of Correspondence, November 12, 1775; 2nd Lt. in Capt. Galbraith's Company in
the Baltimore Battalion, June 6, 1776; 1st Lt., September 5, 1777; fought in
Battles of White Plains and Brunswick in 1778; took the Oath of Allegiance in
1778 before the Honorable Benjamin Rogers (could not write; made his mark); and,
Captain in Baltimore County Militia, 39th Battalion, May 17, 1779. (Note: The
Deaver name was prevalent in Baltimore and Harford Counties at the time of the
Revolution, and it appears that there was more then one John Deaver who served.
Caution should be exercised here.) John DEAVER died in August, 1813, age 55.
(ZZZ-85, DDD-52, BBB-363, AAA-229, CCC-19, CCC-26, XXX-264, JJJ-183, YY-113,
A-1/6, A-2/32, E-13, H-102, F-309, F-311, GGG-401, WW-467, GG-74, RR-19, SS-130)

DEAVER, PHILIP. Oath of Allegiance, 1778, before Hon. Peter Shepherd. (A-2/49)

DEAVER, RICHARD. Oath of Allegiance, 1778, before Hon. Richard Holliday. (A-2/60)

DEAVER, WILLIAM. (1761 - February 9, 1832) Married Phebe DEAVER. Private, MD Line
and a prisoner of war. On June 8, 1784, it was ordered that William DEAVER be
paid the sum of 7 pounds, 10 shillings, it being his half pay up to that day
as "Private of the 3rd Maryland Regiment, having lost a limb in the Battle of
Camden, August 16, 1780." He received 7 subsequent payments between December,
1784 and June, 1788. (J-156, J-173, J-210, J-237, J-252, K-21, K-47, K-70, YY-18,
JJJ-183)

DEBURY, JOHN. Non-Juror to Oath of Allegiance, 1778. (A-1/6)

DECAMP, PETER. Enlisted at Fort Whetstone Point, Baltimore, September 28, 1779;
deserted from the Recruiting Officer. (H-626)

DECKER, FREDERICK. Lt. Col. under Col. Thomas Gist, February 4, 1777. Justice of
the Peace, 1778 and one of the Magistrates who administered the Oath of Allegiance
in 1778 in Baltimore County. He died in October, 1804, in his 64th year, and his
funeral was from his residence on North Howard Street. (ZZZ-85, VV-114, GGG-242,
SSS-110, A-1/6, A-2/31)

DECKER, HENRY. Private, Capt. Graybill's German Regiment, 1776. (H-265)

DeCOURCEY, HENRY. Private, Col. Aquila Hall's Baltimore County Regt., 1777. (TTT-13)

DeCOURCEY, WILLIAM. Sergeant of Marines on ship Defence, September 19, 1776. (H-606)

DEETS, MICHAEL. Non-Juror to Oath of Allegiance, 1778. (A-1/6)

DEGGAN (DEGGON), GEORGE. Oath of Allegiance, 1778, before Hon. Frederick Decker.
(A-1/6, A-2/31)

DEITCH, JOHN BARTHOLOMEW. Private, Capt. Graybill's German Regt., 1776. (H-266)

DELAND, ROGER. Private, Baltimore County Militia; enlisted July 18, 1776. (H-58)

DELANY (DELANEY), WILLIAM. Enlisted May 29, 1776; Private in Capt. N. Smith's 1st
Company of Matrosses at Fort Whetstone Point, September 7, 1776. Private, Capt.
Dorsey's MD Artillery, November 17, 1777 "in gaol on susspion of house breaking."
Corporal, Capt. Dorsey's Co., at Valley Forge, June 3, 1778. (UU-231, H-568,
H-574, QQQ-2)

DELCHER, CHRISTIAN. Private, Capt. McClellan's Company, Sept. 4, 1780. (CCC-24)

DELCHER, JOHN. Private, Capt. Cox's Company, December 19, 1776. Private, Capt.
McClellan's Company, September 4, 1780. Oath of Allegiance, 1778, before Hon.

George Lindenberger. (A-1/6, A-2/52, CCC-21, CCC-24)

DELONG, BARTHOLOMEW. Marine on ship _Defence_, 1777. (H-656)

DELWORTH, WILLIAM. Non-Juror to Oath of Allegiance, 1778. (A-1/6)

DEMIER, ANDREW. Oath of Allegiance, 1778. (A-1/6)

DEMIER, EDWARD. Oath of Allegiance, 1778, before Hon. George Lindenberger. (A-2/52)

DEMMETT, DANSBURY. Oath of Allegiance, 1778. (A-1/6)

DEMMETT, JAMES. Oath of Allegiance, 1778, before Hon. Jesse Dorsey. (A-1/6, A-2/63)

DEMMETT, WILLIAM. Oath of Allegiance, 1778, before Hon. John Moale. (A-1/6, A-2/70)

DEMMITT, JOHN. Ensign, Baltimore Town Battalion, June 6, 1776. Oath of Allegiance, 1778, before Hon. Richard Cromwell. (A-1/6, A-2/46, WW-467)

DEMMITT (DEMMETT), STANSBURY. Oath of Allegiance, 1778, before Hon. John Moale. (A-2/70) This could be, perhaps, the "Dansbury Demmett" listed above.

DEMMITT, WILLIAM. Non-Juror to Oath of Allegiance, 1778. (A-1/6)

DEMMRIST, JOHN. Ensign, Baltimore Town Battalion, 1779. (F-312)

DEMPSEY, LUKE. Non-Juror to Oath of Allegiance, 1778. (A-1/6)

DEMPSEY, PEARCE. Non-Juror to Oath of Allegiance, 1778. (A-1/6)

DENCHOWER, GEORGE. Oath of Allegiance, 1778, before Hon. George Lindenberger. (A-2/52)

DENNEHAUGH, GEORGE. Private, Capt. Howell's Company, December 30, 1775. (G-11)

DENNERIVAY, WILLIAM. Private, Capt. Deams' Co., 7th MD Regt., Jan. 16, 1777. (H-305)

DENNIS, DANIEL. 1st Lt., Baltimore Town Battalion, May 23, 1781. Captain, Baltimore Town Battalion, August 20, 1781. (AAAA-443, AAAA-572)

DENNIS, JOSEPH. Served on ship _Defence_, January 25 to April 9, 1777. (H-656)

DENNIS, WILLIAM. Commissioned 2nd Lt., Baltimore Town Battn., May 9, 1781. (AAAA-429)

DENNY, GEORGE. Non-Juror to Oath of Allegiance, 1778. (A-1/6)

DENOS, AUGUSTINE ROUXELIN. "Chevalier of the Order of St. Louis, died January 7, 1806 at the house of his son-in-law, Mr. DeCaindry, near Baltimore, in his 65th year. He was a Captain in the Saintoge Regiment and served under General Rochambeau at the seige and taking of York. He leaves a widow and two children." (ZZZ-87)

DENTON, JOHN. Oath of Allegiance, 1778. (A-1/6)

DERE, ISAAC. Oath of Allegiance, 1778. (A-1/6)

DEVELIN, PATRICK. Private in Col. Aquila Hall's Baltimore Co. Regt., 1777. (TTT-13)

DEVILBESS, GEORGE. Oath of Allegiance, 1778, before Hon. William Spear. (A-2/66)

DeVITRE, JAMES. Oath of Allegiance, 1778, before Hon. George Lindenberger. (A-2/54)

DEVO, HENRY. Non-Juror to Oath of Allegiance, 1778. (A-1/6)

DEW, JOHN. Oath of Allegiance, 1778. (A-1/6)

DeWITT, LEVI. Signed letter to Governor Lee informing him of suspicious shipments, September 4, 1778. (II-23)

DeWITT, THOMAS. Oath of Allegiance, 1778, before Hon. James Calhoun. Signed letter to Governor Lee informing him of suspicious shipments, September 4, 1778. 1st Lt. in Mercantile Company, Baltimore Town Battalion, 1779. 1st Lt., Capt. Ridgely's Company, January 19, 1781 to at least April 18, 1781. Died July 18, 1807, age 68. (ZZZ-89, A-1/6, A-2/38, F-313, II-23, R-15, AAAA-402, BBBB-61)

DeWITT, WILLIAM. Oath of Allegiance, 1778, before Hon. George Gouldsmith Presbury. Could not write; made his mark. ("己") (A-2/48)

DEWS, EDWARD. Recruit, Baltimore County, 1780. (H-340)

DEYE, THOMAS COCKEY. (January 27, 1728 - May 17, 1807) Buried at Homestead on Padonia Road in Cockeysville, MD. Son of Thomas Cockey Deye and Penelop Deye. Represented Upper Back River Hundred at the Association of Freemen, August 21, 1775. Served on Baltimore County Committee of Observation; elected Sept. 23, 1775. Served on Committee of Correspondence, November 12, 1775. Delegate to General Assembly in 1778. Speaker of the House of Delegates, 1781-1788, and a member of Convention to frame the first State Constitution. (EEEE-1726, SS-130, RR-47, RR-50, SS-136, FFF-150, Md. Gene. Soc. Bulletin, 1986, Vol. 27, #1, p.58)

DICAS, JOHN. Oath of Allegiance, 1778, before Hon. James Calhoun. (A-1/6, A-2/41)

DICK, FREDERICK. Private, Col. Aquila Hall's Baltimore Co. Regt., 1777. (TTT-13)

DICK, HEART. Born 1752 in Scotland. Occupation: Baker. Height: 5' 7½". Enlisted January 27, 1776, Private in Capt. N. Smith's 1st Company of Matrosses. (H-564, H-566, QQQ-2)

DICK, JACOB. Private, Col. Aquila Hall's Baltimore Co. Regt., 1777. (TTT-13)

DICK, WILLIAM. Oath of Allegiance, 1778, before Hon. James Calhoun. (A-2/40)

DICKENSON, BRITTINGHAM. Served on Baltimore County Committee of Observation as of July 24, 1775. Captain-Lieutenant in Baltimore Artillery Company, October 16, 1775. Lieutenant in Capt. Sheaff's Company, June 6, 1776 to 1777. Captain in Baltimore Town Battalion, August 29, 1777 through 1781, under Col. Smith Battn. Died June 24, 1808 at Fells Point in Baltimore, age 74, leaving a widow and a daughter. (ZZZ-89, EEEE-1725, BBB-348, Z-63, E-13, F-312, GGG-401, G-8, W-162, GG-74, WW-467, R-15, BBBB-29, BBBB-61)

DICKENSON, GEORGE. Non-Juror to Oath of Allegiance, 1778. (A-1/6)

DICKENSON, W. Oath of Allegiance, 1778, before Hon. Isaac Van Bibber. (A-2/34)

DICKMAN, WILLIAM. Private, Capt. Deams Co., 7th MD Regt., Jan. 5, 1777. (H-305)

DICKS, DANIEL. Served on ship Defence, January 18 to April 12, 1777. (H-656)

DICKS, JERDA. Non-Juror to Oath of Allegiance, 1778. (A-1/6)

DICKSON, JOHN. Seaman on ship Defence, September 1 to Dec. 26, 1777. (H-656)

DICKSON (DICKESON), THOMAS. Oath of Allegiance, 1778. Supplied nails to Baltimore Town Committee in 1780. Two men by this name both died in July, 1810. (ZZZ-89, A-1/6, RRR-2)

DIDIER, HENRY. Baltimore Mechanical Company of Militia, 1776. (CCC-28)

DIFFENDEFFER (DIFFEND'R), DANIEL. Private, Capt. Cox's Company, Dec. 19, 1776. Oath of Allegiance, 1778, before Hon. James Calhoun. Private, Capt. McClellan's Company, September 4, 1780. (A-1/6, A-2/38, CCC-21, CCC-24)

DIFFENDEFFER, MIL J. ("Micl. I. Diffenderffer") Private, Capt. Cox's Company, Dec. 19, 1776. Oath of Allegiance, 1778, before Hon. William Spear. (CCC-21, A-1/6, A-2/66)

DILL, JOHN. (1759-1862) Married Mary Ellen FONDERON. Served as Private, Capt. Smith's Company No. 8, enlisted January 27, 1776. (JJJ-193, H-18)

DILLEN, MOSES. Non-Juror to Oath of Allegiance, 1778. (A-1/6)
DILLIN, ROGER. Non-Juror to Oath of Allegiance, 1778. (A-1/6)

DILLING, THOMAS. Oath of Allegiance, 1778, before Hon. Isaac VanBibber. (A-2/34)

DILLINGS, JAMES. Oath of Allegiance, 1778, before Hon. Peter Shepherd. (A-2/49)

DILLON, ANDREW. Oath of Allegiance, 1778, before Hon. Robert Simmons. Could not write; made his mark. (A-1/6, A-2/58)

DIMMETT (DIMMITT), JAMES. (c1725 - May 25, 1827) Married Rachel SINKLER. Oath of Allegiance, 1778. (A-1/6, JJJ-194)

DIMOT (DIMIT), JOHN. Non-Juror in 1778; took Oath in 1781. (A-1/6, QQ-109)

DINE, JOHN. Oath of Allegiance, 1778, before Hon. William Spear. (A-1/6, A-2/66)

DISNEY, EZEKIEL SR. Ordinary Seaman on ship Defence, 1777. (H-656)

DISNEY, EZEKIEL JR. Marine on ship Defence, 1777. (H-656)

DISTEL, SAMUEL. Oath of Allegiance, 1778, before Hon. Geo. Lindenberger. (A-2/52)

DITTO, ABRAHAM. Non-Juror ro Oath of Allegiance, 1778. (A-1/6)
DITTO, GEORGE. Non-Juror to Oath of Allegiance, 1778. (A-1/6)
DITTO, HENRY. Two with this name were Non-Jurors, 1778. (A-1/6)

DIVERS. ANNIANIAS. Oath of Allegiance, 1778, before Hon. John Beale Howard. (A-2/30)

DIVERS, CHRISTOPHER. Non-Juror to Oath of Allegiance, 1778. (A-1/6)

DIXON, JOHN. Matross, Capt. Brown's MD Artillery, joined November 22, 1777; was at
Valley Forge until June, 1778; at White Plains, July, 1778; at Fort Schuyler in
August and September, 1780; not listed in 1781. Non-Juror to Oath of Allegiance
in 1778, but subscribed in 1781. (UU-228, UU-230, A-1/6, QQ-109)

DIXON, JOHN JR. Non-Juror to Oath of Allegiance, 1778. (A-1/6)

DIXON, JOSEPH. Corporal, Capt. Ramsey's Company No. 5, 1776. (H-639)

DIXON (DICKSON), WILLIAM. Gunner, Capt. gale's MD Artillery, 1779-1780; on command at
Tuckissummy Plains, and on command at Pumpton in 1779. Gunner, Capt. J. Smith's MD
Artillery, 1780-1783, and Bombardier with Capt. Dorsey's MD Artillery at Camp Col.
Scirvins on January 28, 1782. Entitled to 50 acres (lot #3130) for services as a
Bombardier. (DDDD-13, YYY-1/28, UU-232, YYY-2/16, H-579)

DIXSON, AMOS (OR THOMAS) OF JOHN. Non-Juror to Oath of Allegiance, 1778. (A-1/6)

DIXSON, JOHN SR. Oath of Allegiance, 1778, before Hon. Jesse Dorsey. (A-1/6, A-2/63)

DOBSON, JOHN. Private, Capt. J. Gist's Co., 3rd MD Regt., January, 1778. (H-600)

DOCHTERMAN, MICHAEL. Private, Capt. Keeports German Regiment; enlisted July 17, 1776.
At Philadelphia, September 19, 1776. (H-263)

DOCKER, JOHN. Non-Juror to Oath of Allegiance, 1778. (A-1/6)

DODD, JOHN. Served in Col. Nicholson's Troop of Horse, June 7, 1781. (BBBB-274)

DODGE, SAMUEL. "Captain, a worthy of the Revolution, died July 12, 1803 in Baltimore.
For 7 years he was his post among the embattled ranks of his country's defenders."
(ZZZ-91)

DODSON, JOHN. (c1740/50 - 1816) Private in Capt. McClellan's Company, Baltimore Town
Battalion, September 4, 1780. (JJJ-197, CCC-24)

DODSON, MICHAEL. Private, Capt. Lansdale's Company, 4th MD Regiment. Private, Apr. 20,
1777; Corporal, November 1, 1778; Private, June 15, 1779; Discharged, April 20, 1780.
Revolutionary pensioner as Private in Maryland Line. (YY-18, H-104)

DOICE, DENNIS. Private, Capt. Deams Co., 7th MD Regiment, Dec. 19, 1776. (H-305)

DOLTON, EDWARD. Non-Juror to Oath of Allegiance, 1778. (A-1/6)

DOMER, CHRISTIAN. Oath of Allegiance, 1778, (A-1/6)

DONAL, JOHN. Oath of Allegiance, 1778, before Hon. George Lindenberger. (A-2/52, A-1/6)

DONALD, WILLIAM. Oath of Allegiance, 1778, before Hon. Jeremiah Johnson.(A-2/33, A-1/6)

DONALDSON, ALEXANDER. On May 9, 1780, in Baltimore County, MD, he loaned money to the
State of Maryland for forwarding troops southward to South Carolina. (FFF-289)

DONALDSON, JOHN. Non-Juror to Oath of Allegiance, 1778. (A-1/6)

DONANS, DENNIS. Private, Extra Regt., Fort Whetstone Point, Baltimore, 1781. (H-626)

DONAWAY, JOHN. Non-Juror to Oath of Allegiance, 1778. (A-1/6)

DONER, CHRISTIAN. Oath of Allegiance, 1778, before Hon. James Calhoun. (A-2/42)

DONALLY, MICHAEL. Non-Juror to Oath of Allegiance, 1778. (A-1/6)

DONNELLAN, AMOS. Oath of Allegiance, 1778. (A-1/6)

DONNELLAN (DONOLAN), THOMAS. Private, Capt. Ewing's Company No. 4, enlisting January 8, 1776. Oath of Allegiance, 1778, before Hon. James Calhoun. He delivered flour for the Baltimore Commission on January 17, 1780, and fish on June 23, 1780. Wrote to Governor on July 11, 1781, expressing need for money and provisions for recruiting in Baltimore County. (FFF-262, FFF-298, FFF-409, H-12, A-2/39)

DONOHOE (DONOHUE), BARTHOLOMEW. Enlisted in Baltimore County, July 20, 1776. Private, Capt. N. Smith's MD Artillery at Fort Whetstone Point in Baltimore, 1776-1777. (H-52, VV-74)

DONOHOE (DONOGHUE), DANIEL. Born 1753 in Cork, Ireland. Occupation: Plasterer. Height: 5' 7". Enlisted January 26, 1776 as Private in Capt. N. Smith's 1st Company of Matrosses. Gunner in Capt. Dorsey's MD Artillery at Valley Forge on June 3, 1778. (UU-231, H-564, H-567, VV-73, QQQ-2)

DONOHOE (DONNOHO), JOHN W. Baltimore Mechanical Co. of Militia, Nov. 4, 1775. (F-299)

DONOVAN, JAMES. Recruit, Baltimore County Militia, April 11, 1780. (H-315)

DONOVAN (DONAVIN), JOHN. Marine on ship Defence, 1777. (H-656)

DONOVAN (DONNOVIN), TIMOTHY. Born 1750 in Cork, Ireland. Occupation: Labourer. Height: 5' 4½". Enlisted January 31, 1776 as Private in Capt. N. Smith's 1st Company of Matrosses. Private in Capt. Dorsey's MD Artillery, November 17, 1777. Gunner in Capt. Dorsey's Company at Valley Forge on June 3, 1778. Entitled to 50 acres (lot #272) for services as Matross. (DDDD-13, H-565, QQQ-2, UU-231, VV-74)

DOONE, HENRY. Oath of Allegiance, 1778, before Hon. James Calhoun. (A-2/65)

DORAN, BARNABA. Private, Capt. Norwood's Company, 4th MD Regiment; reported missing on August 16, 1780. (H-104)

DOREN, MICHAEL ("Mitchal Doring") Recruit in Baltimore County, 1780. Private, Extra Regiment at Fort Whetstone Point in Baltimore, 1781. (H-627, H-340)

DORLING, MANNS. Oath of Allegiance, 1778. (A-1/6)

DORNBAUGH, JOHN. Ensign, Soldiers Delight Battalion, August 29, 1777. (BBB-348, Z-63)

DORSET, THOMAS. Refused 2nd Lieutenant, Baltimore Town Battalion, May 17, 1779. (F-311)

DORSEY,_____. (part of name torn off rolls) Private, Baltimore County Regiment #15, circa 1777. (TTT-13)

DORSEY, ARNOLD. Oath of Allegiance, 1778. (A-1/7)

DORSEY, BAZEL JOHN. (1762, Baltimore County - May 9, 1803, Baltimore County) Son of Francis and Anne DORSEY. He married (1) Rachel ODELL (May 19, 1759 - Feb. 12, 1786) circa December 7, 1784. She was a daughter of John ODELL and Providence BAKER. He married (2) Dorothea HAINS circa December 6, 1786. "Dolley" was a daughter of Michael and Catherine HAINS; she died May 1, 1829. Children (all by second wife): Francis DORSEY (Sept. 15, 1787 - Dec. 3, 1853) married Mary WALTERS in 1811; Catherine DORSEY (Mar. 30, 1790 - 1876) married William OURSLER (1786-1867); Anne DORSEY (b. March 3, 1792) married Joshua W. HAMILTON; Rachel DORSEY (born Sept. 3, 1794, died unmarried); and, Sarah DORSEY (born May 6, 1796, died unmarried). Bazel John DORSEY enlisted as a Private in Capt. John A. Hamilton's Company, 2nd Mounted Regiment, Maryland Line in 1782. As a result of his service he received a bounty land warrant which he sold. His family lived on "Scotchman's Desire" near Granite in Baltimore County, and they are probably buried there in the family graveyard, but there is no grave marker for him. (D-2, JJJ-199, and research by William J. Hollifield, III, of Towson, MD, 1987)

DORSEY, CHARLES. (1744 - September 12, 1814) Son of Nicholas DORSEY and Sarah GRIFFITH. On March 25, 1775 he married Anne DORSEY, widow of Owen ELDER who died in 1774, and daughter of Michael DORSEY and Ruth TODD. Anne was born January 29, 1748, in Anne

Arundel County, MD and died September 30, 1806 in Baltimore County MD. Children were: Hezekiah DORSEY (born July 12, 1776) married Mary TALBOT in 1798; Charles DORSEY (born April 30, 1778, died 1843) married Catherine WELSH in 1807; Zachariah DORSEY (born on August 20, 1780); Sarah DorSEY (born Dec. 30, 1782) married John LITCHFIELD in 1817; John DORSEY (born July 5, 1785) married Jane CONNOR and moved to Kentucky, Indiana and Nebraska; and, Nancy DORSEY (born Jan. 3, 1788) married Zachariah POULTER in 1804. Charles DORSEY was a Private in the 4th MD Line on February 19, 1777, and a Corporal on July 1, 1779; discharged February 19, 1780. Non-Juror, 1778. (A-1/6, H-105, D-8)

DORSEY, EDWARD. (c1730 - 1782) Married Deborah MACCUBIN. Edward and his brother Samuel were managers of an iron works near Elkridge, MD which manufactured cannon balls in the Revolution, and they also supplied foodstuff to help supply the armed forces from their extensive landholdings in Howard, Anne Arundel and Baltimore Counties.(AAA-1640 JJJ-199)

DORSEY, ELIAS. Major in Soldiers Delight Battalion, November 27, 1781. (CCCC-5)

DORSEY, ELISHA. (1750 - November, 1806) Married Mary SLADE. He represented the North Hundred at the Association of Freemen on August 21, 1775. Commissioned 1st Lt. of Capt. Christopher Owings' Company "in the room of Samuel Merryman, Jr.broke by court martial" in the Soldiers Delight Battalion, Baltimore County, September 11, 1777. was also involved in the evaluation of Baltimore County confiscated proprietary land in 1782. (FFF-542, JJJ-199, EEEE-1726, E-10, BBB-369) Non-Juror in 1778. (A-1/7)

DORSEY, ELY. (1744 - March 14, 1803) Married Ruth DORSEY, according to one source but the obituary of Mrs. Sarah DORSEY states she "died March 29, 1798 at Linganore, the consort of Capt. Ely DORSEY, leaving a husband and a numerous family of children." Subsequently, on January 27,1801, Capt. Ely DORSEY of Fredericksburg and Araminta CUMMINS of Anne Arundel County were married by Rev. Jones. Ely DORSEY was a Captain in Soldiers Delight Battalion on May 27, 1779 "appointed in the room of Richard Owings", but he might have been a Captain as early as 1778. He left the service in February, 1782. (JJJ-199, ZZZ-93, ZZZ-94, CCCC-71, GGG-422, HH-24, E-11) Non-Juror, the Oath of Allegiance in 1778. (A-1/7)

DORSEY, GILUS. Oath of Allegiance, 1778. (A-1/7)

DORSEY, HAROLD. Oath of Allegiance, 1778. (A-1/7)

DORSEY, JAMES. Baltimore Mechanical Company of Militia, 1776. Non-Juror to Oath of Allegiance in 1778. (CCC-28, A-1/7)

DORSEY, JESSE. Magistrate who administered the Oath of Allegiance in 1778. (A-2/63)

DORSEY, JOHN. Baltimore Privateer and member of the Baltimore Salt Committee, Oct. 14, 1779. Served on baltimore Committee of Confiscated Property in 1782. (FFF-468, HHH-88, III-207)

DORSEY, JOSEPH. Marine on ship Defence, October 23 to December 31, 1777. (H-656)

DORSEY, JOSHUA. 1st Lieutenant, Soldiers Delight Company No. 4, May 13, 1776. Took Oath of Allegiance, 1778, before Hon. Peter Shepherd. Was a contractor for horses on January 9, 1781. (A-1/7, A-2/49, FFF-353, FF-64, WW-467)

DORSEY, JOSHUA WORTHINGTON. 2nd Lt., Soldiers Delight Co. No. 6, May 13, 1776. (FF-64)

DORSEY, LARKIN (LAKIN). (1744, Maryland - 1822, Stockton Station, Kentucky) Married Elizabeth INGRAM. Served as a Cadet in the 9th Company of Smallwood's Battalion in January, 1776; 2nd Lt., Baltimore Artillery Co., November 5, 1776; Cornet in the 4th Dragoons, January 25, 1777, and Ensign; resigned September 4, 1778. Larkin was born August 17, 1744 and died February 22, 1822. Children not known, but one man named Larkin DORSEY married Miss Jane ALLISON (all of Baltimore) on November 26, 1805, by Rev. Glendy. (ZZZ-93, JJJ-199, TT-75)

DORSEY, LEAVEN (LEVIN). (1735 - October, 1781) Married Elizabeth Keene HOME. Leaven enlisted January 26, 1776 as Private in Capt. N. Smith's 1st Company of Matrosses; at Fort Whetstone Point in Baltimore on September 7, 1776. Revolutionary pensioner. (YY-18, H-569, JJJ-199)

DORSEY, NATHAN. Surgeon on ship Defence, September 19, 1776. (H-607)

DORSEY, NICHOLAS. (c1712 - 1780) Married Sarah GRIFFITH (1718-1794). He was a son of
Nicholas DORSEY (c1690-1717) and Frances HUGHES. Served on Committee of Observation, January, 1775; commissioned an Ensign in 1776, later Colonel; was also Judge
of the Orphans Court; Non-Juror to Oath of Allegiance, 1778. His children were:
Rachel DORSEY (1737-1805) married Anthony LINDSAY and moved to Kentucky; Lydia
DORSEY married Charles DORSEY of Edward, and moved to Nelson County, Kentucky;
Nicholas DORSEY, Jr. (1741-1796) married Ruth TODD in 1765; Charles DORSEY (1744-
1814) married Nancy or Anne (DORSEY) ELDER, widow of Owen ELDER; Catherine DORSEY
married Robert WOOD and moved to Ross County, Ohio; Sarah DORSEY; Henry DORSEY;
Vachel DORSEY; and Lucretia DORSEY married John WELSH of Anne Arundel County, MD.;
Frances DORSEY married Eli WARFIELD; Orlando DORSEY married Martha GAITHER; and,
Achsah DORSEY married Beal WARFIELD. (NNN-64, A-1/7)

DORSEY, ORLANDO GRIFFITH. Oath of Allegiance, 1778, before Hon. Peter Shepherd. (A-2/49)

DORSEY, RICHARD. (1754, Anne Arundel County, MD - 1799, Baltimore County, MD) (Caution
is to be exercised here because there was also a Captain Richard Dorsey, 1756-1826,
of Anne Arundel County. Accordingly further research is required to distinguish between the two.)(See sources H-568, BBB-362, ZZ-53, UU-231, PP-151, TT-75, DDDD-2)
Capt. Richard Dorsey served as a Captain in Maryland Artillery Company No. 2 under
Lt.Col. Carrington; commissioned November 14, 1777; stationed at Baltimore, May 11,
1780. His children: Edward (born 1784); Sarah (born 1787); Eudocia (born 1792);
Mary (born 1794); and, Edward John (born 1796). Richard died in May, 1799 "an old,
and respected, inhabitant of Baltimore. (ZZZ-94, VVV-96, XXX-278)

DORSEY, RICHARD. Midshipman on ship Defence, 1777. (H-656)

DORSEY, ROBERT. Oath of Allegiance, 1778, before Hon. William Lux. (A-1/7, A-2/68)

DORSEY, SAMUEL. (1741-1777) He and brother Edward Dorsey were managers of an iron works
near Elkridge, MD, which manufactured cannon balls during the Revolution. And they
also supplied foodstuff to help to supply the armed forces from their extensive
landholdings in Howard, Anne Arundel and Baltimore Counties. Samuel was born on
Dec. 7, 1741 and died Sept. 11, 1777; his wife was Margaret SPRIGG. (JJJ-199, AAA-
1640)

DORSEY, THOMAS. Non-Juror to Oath of Allegiance, 1778. (A-1/7)

DORSEY, VACHEL. (January 27, 1756 - May 14, 1813 in Baltimore, MD) Married Clementine
IRELAND (d. 1816), March 14, 1786. He was a son of Nathan DORSEY (1731-1774) and
Sophia OWINGS. His children: Elizabeth DORSEY married a HALL; John DORSEY (born
Jan. 30, 1787) married Mary GALE; James Ireland DORSEY (born Oct. 7, 1788) married
Susannah BROOKES; Louisa DORSEY (born Oct. 16, 1790) entered a convent; Andrew
DORSEY (born Nov. 4, 1792) never married; Samuel DORSEY (born November 3, 1794);
Daniel Horatio DORSEY (born Nov. 21, 1796) never married; Ezekiel Salisbury DORSEY
(Dec. 16, 1798 - 1848) married Julia Elizabeth ADAMS (1807-1860) in 1830 and their
son Ezekiel Salisbury DORSEY, II (1837-1893) married Mary Mitchelmore McFEE (1849-
1890) in 1869 in Baltimore, MD; Marcellina DORSEY (born March, 1801) entered a
convent; and, Rebecca DORSEY (born Sept. 26, 1803) married Capt. Alfred ADAMS.
Vachel Dorsey was an Ensign in the Maryland Line during the Revolution. There were
two men with this name who signed the Oath of Allegiance in 1778: one before Hon.
James Calhoun, and one before Hon. Edward Cockey. (One signed as "Vache Dorsey.")
(A-1/7, A-2/42, A-2/61, AAA-2343, JJJ-199, AAA-2257)

DORSEY, WILLIAM. (1757 - 1813) Married Catey_____. Was an Ensign in the Baltimore
Town Battalion in 1779. (JJJ-199, F-314)

DORSON, ISAAC. Private, Capt. McClellan's Company, September 4, 1780. (OOC-24)

DORSON, WILLIAM. Non-Juror to Oath of Allegiance, 1778. (A-1/7)
DOUGELS, THOMAS. Non-Juror to Oath of Allegiance, 1778. (A-1/7)

DOUGLAS, ARCHIBALD. Tender's Crew on ship Defence in 1777, having earlier been a
Midshipman on September 19, 1776. (H-656)

DOUGLAS, GEORGE. Oath of Allegiance, 1778. (A-1/7)

DOUGLAS (DOUGLASS), JAMES. Recruited in Baltimore, March 2, 1780, for the 3rd MD Regt., by Samuel Chester. (H-334)

DOUGLAS (DUGLAS), JAMES. Recruited into Baltimore County Militia, Apr. 11, 1780. (H-335)

DOUGLAS (DUGLASS), JOHN. Oath of Allegiance, 1778, before Hon. Geo. Lindenberger. (A-2/52)

DOUGLAS (DOUGHLAS), WILLIAM. Recruited in Baltimore County Militia, Apr. 11, 1780. (H-335)

DOUGLASS, GEORGE SEWELL. 2nd Lt., Capt. Richardson's Company No. 5, Baltimore Town Battn. June 6, 1776. Served in Baltimore Artillery Company in 1777. Signed Oath of Allegiance in 1778 before Hon. James Calhoun. 2nd Lt. under Capt. Richardson through 1779; became Captain in baltimore County Militia on May 17, 1779. (GGG-401, F-309, F-312, WW-467, GG-74, V-368, A-1/7, A-2/42)

DOUGLASS, WILLIAM. Midshipman on ship Defence, March 13 to April 3, 1777. (H-656)

DOVE, JOSMAS DUKE. Oath of Allegiance, 1778, before Hon. James Calhoun. (A-2/65)

DOWDE, CHARLES. Matross, Capt. Brown's MD Artillery; joined November 22, 1777. Was at Valley Forge until June, 1778; at White Plains, July, 1778; at Fort Schuyler in August and September, 1780; not listed in 1781. (UU-228, UU-230)

DOWDGE, JOSIAH. Matross, Capt. gale's MD Artillery in 1779; reported as deserted at Annapolis on September 13, 1779. (YYY-1/29)

DOWLES, SAMUEL. Oath of Allegiance, 1778, before Hon. William Lux. Hauled flour for the Baltimore Committee in 1780. (A-1/7, A-2/68, RRR-6)

DOWLEY, FRANCIS. Oath of Allegiance, 1778. (A-1/7)

DOWNES, JOSEPH. Non-Juror to Oath of Allegiance, 1778. (A-1/7)

DOWNES, THOMAS. Non-Juror to Oath of Allegiance, 1778. (A-1/7)

DOWNES, WILLIAM. Non-Juror to Oath of Allegiance, 1778. (A-1/7) There was a Private in the 4th MD Regiment who was entitled to 50 acres (lot #130) in western Maryland. It probably was the same person. (DDDD-14)

DOWNEY, BARTHOLOMEW. Private, Col. Ewing's Battalion; enlisted July 5, 1776, Baltimore County; not on muster roll in August, 1776. (H-57)

DOWNEY, FREDERICK. Private, Capt. Graybill's German Regiment, 1776. (H-266)

DOWNEY, THOMAS. Oath of Allegiance, 1778, before Hon. Robert Simmons. Appointed 2nd Lt. in Capt. Lemmon's Company, Upper Battalion, February 1, 1782. (A-1/7, A-2/58, CCCC-65)

DOWNEY, WALTER. Oath of Allegiance, 1778, before Hon. Robert Simmons. Could not write; made his mark (" O "). (A-1/7, A-2/58)

DOYLE, DENNIS, Enlisted July 26, 1776 in Baltimore County. (H-53)

DOYLE, FRANCIS. Oath of Allegiance, 1778, before Hon. Jesse Dorsey. (A-1/7, A-2/63)

DOYLE, JOHN. Applied for pension while living in Knox County, Tennessee on May 9, 1818 when he was 70 years old; therefore, he was born in 1748 (place of birth not given). He enlisted May 13, 1777 in Baltimore, Maryland and served as a Private in Captain Lynch's Company of Col. Smallwood's MD Regiment. He was in the Battles of Brandywine, Paoli, Germantown and Monmouth. He was discharged at Annapolis, MD by Lt.Col. Forrest about May 13, 1780. He moved to Tennessee and in 1826, at age 78, stated his wife Evaline was "some older tham myself." He also referred to a son named William DOYLE. John Doyle received pension S38665 at $8.00 per month from May 9, 1818. He died in Knox County, Tennessee on June 3, 1837. (YY-19, OO-66, JJJ-201, and National Gene-alogical Society Quarterly, Vol. 24, No. 2, pp. 56-57, June, 1936 ed.)

DOYLE, JONATHAN. Non-Juror to Oath of Allegiance, 1778. Involved in evaluation of Baltimore County confiscated proprietary reserve lands, 1782. (FFF-542, A-1/7)

DOYLE, RICHARD. Died c1791 in Baltimore county. Married Sarah_____ who died in 1796 and in her will she mentioned her father's estate in Bucks County, PA. Children: Margaret DOYLE, married Ephraim MURRAY in 1788 and were in Washington County, Tenn.

by 1796; Mary DOYLE, died 1792, unmarried; Elizabeth DOYLE, married Peter ARMACOST in 1792. Richard DOYLE was a Private in Capt. Ewing's Company No. 4, and enlisted January 29, 1776. Non-Juror to Oath in 1778. (A-1/7, D-2, H-12)

DOYLE, THOMAS. Private in Capt. Howell's Company, December 30, 1775. Ensign in Soldiers Delight Company No. 5 by May 13, 1776. (G-11, FF-64, WW-467)

DRAKE, FRANCIS. Oath of Allegiance, 1778, before Hon. Jesse Dorsey. In 1780, he measured wheat for the Baltimore Town Committee. (A-1/7, A-2/63, RRR-6)

DRAPER, JOHN. Non-Juror to Oath of Allegiance, 1778. (A-1/7)

DRAWBACH, ABR. Private, Capt. McClellan's Co., Baltimore Town, Sept. 4, 1780. (CCC-25)

DREWITT, WILLIAM. Enlisted July 20, 1776 in Baltimore Town. Took Oath of Allegiance in 1778. (A-1/7, H-53)

DRISKILL (DRISCOLL), JEREMIAH. Private in Baltimore County Militia on July 18, 1776. Subsequently served in the 4th MD Regiment in Capt. Oldham's Company on December 6, 1776. Served as a member of Gen. Washington's Guards from April 11, 1780. In a letter to Colonel A. Spottswood on April 30, 1777, Washington wrote, in part, about the kind of men he wanted as his personal guards, which speaks well of Jeremiah, but not by name: "I desire that none of the men may exceed in stature 5' 10", nor fall short of 5' 9", sober, young, active and well made...men of good character in the regiment...." Jeremiah Driskill was entitled to 50 acres (lot #1524) in western Maryland, and also received 100 acres by Federal Bounty Land Grant (Warrant #11142) on February 1, 1790. (YY-63, DDDD-14, H-605, H-104, H-58)

DRISKILL, JOHN. Seaman on ship Defence, 1777. (H-656)

DRISKILL, TIMOTHY. Private, Baltimore County Militia, enlisted July 5, 1776. (H-58)

DRUMBO, ADAM. Non-Juror to Oath of Allegiance, 1778. (A-1/7)
DRUMBO, JOHN. Non-Juror to Oath of Allegiance, 1778. (A-1/7)

DUCAN, ARTHUR. Oath of Allegiance, 1778, before Hon. George Lindenberger. (A-2/52)

DUCKE, GEORGE. Private, Capt. Cox's Company, December 19, 1776. (CCC-22)

DUCY, WILLIAM. Oath of Allegiance, 1778, before Hon. George Lindenberger. (A-2/52)

DUDLEY, JOHN. Oath of Allegiance, 1778, before Hon. James Calhoun. (A-1/7, A-2/39)

DUE, ISAAC. Oath of Allegiance, 1778, before Hon. Richard Holliday. (A-2/60)

DUE (DEU), ROBERT. Oath of Allegiance, 1778, before Hon. Jesse Dorsey. (A-2/63)

DUESBURY, JAMES. Oath of Allegiance, 1778, before Hon. James Calhoun. (A-1/7, A-2/42)

DUFF, BRIAN. Drafted into Baltimore County Regiment No. 36, circa 1777. (TTT-13)

DUFFEY, ALEX. Able Seaman on ship Defence, September 19, 1776, and Rated Quartermaster on October 23, 1776. (H-607)

DUFFY, JNO. (1752 - 1843) Married Margarett PHARR. Private, Capt. Deams Company, 7th MD Regiment, December 24, 1776. (JJJ-204, H-305)

DUGAN, AUTHUR. Non-Juror to Oath of Allegiance, 1778. (A-1/7)

DUGAN, CUMBERLAND. Of Baltimore. Baked bread for public use and in service to the Maryland Council, September 20, 1776. (ZZ-289, ZZ-290)

DUGGAN, PAUL. Private, Capt. J. Gist's Co., 3rd MD Regt., February, 1778. (H-600)

DUKEHART (DUKHART), HENRY. Oath of Allegiance, 1778, before Hon. James Calhoun. He died September 18, 1807, "an old inhabitant of Baltimore." (ZZZ-97, A-1/7, A-2/40)

DUKEHART, SAMUEL. Non-Juror to Oath of Allegiance, 1778. (A-1/7)

DUKEHART, VALERIUS. Listed twice as a Non-Juror to Oath of Allegiance, 1778. (A-1/7)

DUKES (DUKE), CHRISTOPHER. Non-Juror to Oath in 1778, but signed in 1781. (A-1/7, QQ-109)

DUKES, WILLIAM. Took the Oath of Allegiance in 1781. (QQ-109)

DULANY, DANIEL. Non-Juror to Oath of Allegiance, 1778. (A-1/7)

DULANY, EDWARD. Private, Baltimore County Militia; enlisted July 5, 1776. (H-58)

DUMNICK (DUNACK), JOHN. Oath of Allegiance, 1778, before Hon. John Hall. (A-1/7, A-2/36)

DUNAVAN, JAMES. Recruited by Samuel Chester for 3rd MD Regt., March 2, 1780, Baltimore. (H-334)

DUNBAR, JOSEPH. Cooper on ship Defence, September 19, 1776, and January 11, 1777 to December 31, 1777. Non-Juror to Oath of Allegiance, 1778. (A-607, H-656, A-1/7)

DUNBAR, WILLIAM JOSEPH. Involved in the receipt of tile barrels for the ship Defence, January 20, 1777, in Baltimore. (FFF-85)

DUNCAN, BENJAMIN. Non-Juror to Oath of Allegiance, 1778. (A-1/7)

DUNCAN, FRANCIS. Oath of Allegiance, 1778, before Hon. George Lindenberger. (A-2/52)

DUNCAN, JOHN. Born in Scotland, and died February 3, 1805 in Baltimore County, MD. He came to Maryland from Pennsylvania and lived in Baltimore County about four miles northwest of Owings Mills and about three miles from Reisterstown. His wife's name is not know, but their son, William DUNCAN married Ann SHIPLEY and their son Johnsie DUNCAN (1818-1858) married Julia A. GORE (1824-1896). John DUNCAN was a Private in Lt. John Smith's Company, 3rd MD Regiment. (AAA-213, AAA-889)

DUNCAN, PATRICK. Oath of Allegiance, 1778. (A-1/7)

DUNCAN (DUNKIN), WILLIAM. Baltimore Mechanical Company of Militia, November 4, 1775. Private, Capt. Cox's Company, December 19, 1776. Oath of Allegiance, 1778. (A-1/7, F-298, CCC-21)

DUNGAN, BENJAMIN. Non-Juror to Oath of Allegiance, 1778. (A-1/7)

DUNHAM, LEWIS. Oath of Allegiance, 1778, before Hon. Richard Holliday. (A-1/7, A-2/60)

DUNLAP, JAMES. Oath of Allegiance, 1778, before Hon. William Spear. (A-1/7, A-2/66)

DUNN, ARTHUR. Oath of Allegiance, 1778, before Hon. Jeremiah Johnson. Could not write; made his mark. (A-1/7, A-2/33)

DUNN, HENRY. Ensign, Baltimore County Militia, September 13, 1776. Took the Oath of Allegiance, 1778, before Hon. Richard Holliday. (JJ-9, A-1/7, A-2/60)

DUNN, JOHN. Oath of Allegiance, 1778, before Hon. George Lindenberger. "Saddler" was written beside his name. (A-1/7, A-2/52)

DUNN, SAMUEL. Oath of Allegiance, 1778, before Hon. Thomas Sollers. (A-1/7, A-2/51)

DUNNEVAN, JOHN. Private, Baltimore County Militia; enlisted July 19, 1776. (H-58)

DUNNOCKS (DUNNOCK), JOHN. 1st Lt., Capt. J. Talbot's Company No. 4 by Aug. 26, 1776. Oath of Allegiance, 1778. Involved in evaluation of Baltimore County confiscated proprietary reserve lands in 1782. (PPP-2, RR-99, ZZ-541, A-1/7, FFF-547)

DUNSON, WILLIAM. Non-Juror to Oath of Allegiance, 1778. (A-1/7)

DUNSTER, JOHN. Private, Capt. Norwood's Company, 4th MD Regiment, June 1, 1779. Discharged to Invalids Regiment, April 22, 1780. (H-104)

DUNSYRE, WILLIAM. Enlisted in Baltimore County, July 20, 1776. (H-52)

DURBIN, CHRISTOPHER. Oath of Allegiance, 1778, before Hon. James Calhoun. (A-2/43)

DURDIN, THOMAS. Served on ship Defence, March 6 to December 31, 1777. (H-656)

DURHAM, WILLIAM. (January 15, 1749 - August 28, 1820) Married Margaret BRUCE. Served as Private and Corporal in Maryland Line. (JJJ-208, H-59, 200) Another William DURHAM married Anne TOLLEY in 1786 in Baltimore County (marriage proven through Maryland pension application); however, he served in Harford County, MD. (See H. Peden's Revolutionary Patriots of Harford Co., MD, 1775-1783, page 72)

DUTER, PETER. Oath of Allegiance, 1778, before Hon. William Spear. (A-2/67)

DUTRO, GEORGE. Baltimore Mechanical Company of Militia, 1776. (CCC-28)

DUVAL (DUVAULL), GEORGE. Member of the Sons of Liberty in 1776. Recruit in the Baltimore County Militia, April 11, 1780. Entitled to 100 acres by Federal Bounty Land Grant Warrant #14098, January 28, 1795. (YY-63, CCC-19, H-335)

DWEY, SAMUEL. Oath of Allegiance, 1778, before Hon. James Calhoun. (A-2/39)

DWYER, HUGH. Oath of Allegiance, 1778, before Hon. Edward Cockey. (A-1/7, A-2/61)

DYCUS, JOHN. Drummer, Capt. Gale's MD Artillery Company, 1779-1780. (YYY-1/30)

DYER, WILLIAM. Matross, Capt. Brown's MD Artillery; joined November 22, 1777. Was at Valley Forge until June, 1778; at White Plains, July, 1778; at Fort Schuyler in August and September, 1780; not listed in 1781. (UU-228, UU-230)

E

EAGAN, HUGH. Non-Juror to Oath of Allegiance, 1778. (A-1/7)

EAGLESTONE, ABRAHAM. Oath of Allegiance, 1778, before Hon. Thomas Sollers. (A-2/51)

EAGLESTONE, JONATHAN. Oath of Allegiance, 1778, before Hon. Thomas Sollers. (A-2/51)

EARBAUGH, ADAM. Private, Capt. Graybill's German Regiment, July 12, 1776. (ZZ-32)

EARLE, JOHN (OR JAMES). Baltimore Privateer and Captain of the schooner Baltimore Hero owned by Richard Curson, June 14, 1779, with 14 guns. (GGG-453, III-206)

EARNS, JOHN. Oath of Allegiance, 1778, before Hon. Jesse Dorsey. "Shoemaker" was written beside his name. (A-2/63)

EARP, JOSHUA. (c1760 - September 30, 1811, Baltimore County, MD) Married Eleanor McKINSEY on April 21, 1785. He took the Oath of Allegiance in Anne Arundel Co. in 1778. His chidlren: Honour; Eleanor; Elizabeth; Mary; William (born 1792), married Ann READ; Joshua; Ananias; Nancy; Joseph; and Daniel. (XXX-289, D-8, JJJ-211)

EATON, WILLIAM. Private, Baltimore County Militia; enlisted July 19, 1776. Also, Private, Capt. Oldham's Co., 4th MD Regt., "left off the rolls" in April, 1778. (H-58, H-107)

EAVENSON, THOMAS. Oath of Allegiance, 1778. (A-1/7)

EBBERT, ANDREW. Non-Juror to Oath of Allegiance, 1778. (A-1/7)

EBBERT, GEORGE. Oath of Allegiance, 1778, before Hon. Peter Shepherd. (A-2/50)

EBBERT, HENRY. Non-Juror to Oath of Allegiance, 1778. (A-1/7)

EBBERT, JOHN. Oath of Allegiance, 1778, before Hon. James Calhoun. (A-1/7, A-2/42)

EBBERT, JOSEPH. Oath of Allegiance, 1778. (A-1/7)

EBERHARD, MARTIN. Oath of Allegiance, 1778, before Hon. Peter Shepherd. (A-2/49)

EBERT, PHILIP. Non-Juror to Oath of Allegiance, 1778. (A-1/7)

EBER, JOSEPH. Non-Juror to Oath of Allegiance, 1778 (A-1/7)

ECKERT, MICHAEL. Oath of Allegiance, 1778. (A-1/7)

ECKISTER, THOMAS. Recruit, Baltimore County, 1780. (H-340)

EDMONDS, JOHN. Oath of Allegiance, 1778, before Hon. Andrew Buchanan. (A-2/57)

EDMONDSTONE, GEORGE. Private, Capt. S. Smith's Company No. 8, 1st MD Battalion, January 23, 1776. (H-641)

EDMONSON, JAMES. Oath of Allegiance, 1778, before Hon. James Calhoun. (A-2/65)

EDWARDS, BENJAMIN. Non-Juror to Oath of Allegiance, 1778. (A-1/7)

EDWARDS, CHARLES. Non-Juror to Oath of Allegiance, 1778. (A-1/7)

EDWARDS, EDWARD. Non-Juror to Oath of Allegiance, 1778, but Source JJJ-215 indicates he was born June 7, 1711 and died after 1778; married (1) Jemima WELSH and (2) Elizbeth CHILTON; and that he rendered patriotic service in Maryland during the war. . (A-1/7)

EDWARDS, HENRY. Non-Juror to Oath of Allegiance, 1778. (A-1/7)

EDWARDS, ISAAC. Non-Juror to Oath of Allegiance, 1778. (A-1/7)

EDWARDS, JAMES. Member of the Whig Club in 1777. Took Oath of Allegiance in 1778 before Hon. James Calhoun. (OCC-26, A-1/7, A-2/40)

EDWARDS, JOHN. Private, Capt. S. Smith's Company No. 8, 1st MD Battalion, Jan. 24, 1776. Non-Juror to Oath of Allegiance, 1778. (H-641, A-1/7)

EDWARDS, RICHARD. Oath of Allegiance, 1778, before Hon. Charles Ridgely of William, on February 27, 1778. (A-1/7, A-2/28)

EDWARDS, WILLIAM. Non-Juror to Oath of Allegiance, 1778. (A-1/7)

EHFRT, MICHAEL. Oath of Allegiance, 1778, before Hon. Peter Shepherd. (A-2/49)

EHRMAN, JOHANNES. Oath of Allegiance, 1778, before Hon. Geo. Lindenberger. (A-2/52)

EICHELBERGER, BARNET. Served on Baltimore County Committee of Observation, August 7, 1775, and Baltimore Town Committee of Correspondence, November 12, 1775. 1st Lt., Capt. Sterrett's Company No. 2, Baltimore Town Battalion, 1776. Records indicate an account and receipt for whiskey in Baltimore City, September 16, 1776. (EEEE-1726, GG-74, SS-130, FFF-57)

EINSLER, FELERIOUS. Oath of Allegiance, 1778, before Hon. Peter Shepherd. (A-2/49)

EISELL (EYSSELL), JOHN. Private, Capt. Graybill's German Regiment, 1776. Revolutionary War pensioner, born 1756, Private, Continental Line. Ordered that he be paid on March 9, 1832, a soldier of Baltimore of the Revolutionary War, during life, half yearly, half pay of a Private for his services during the war. (C-339, YY-20, H-266)

ELBERT, JOHN L. DR. (April 12, 1760 - July 10, 1835) Possibly from Talbot County, MD. Married Elizabeth SUDLER. He was a Surgeon's Mate in 1776, and subsequently a Surgeon to a Maryland Regiment at Baltimore in 1776; Apothecary to Southern Army in 1781; in general practice in Baltimore in 1783; served in Army until 1783; and was a member of the Order of the Cincinnati of Maryland. (XX-7, JJJ-217)

ELDER, ELIJAH. Oath of Allegiance, 1778, before Hon. Edward Cockey. (A-1/7, A-2/61)

ELDER, ELY. Oath of Allegiance, 1778, before Hon. Edward Cockey. (A-1/7, A-2/61)

ELDER, JOHN. Oath of Allegiance, 1778, before Hon. Edward Cockey, (A-1/7, A-2/61)

ELLER, NICHOLAS. Oath of Allegiance, 1778, before Hon. John Beale Howard. Could not write; made his mark. (A-1/7, A-2/29)

ELLICOTT, JOHN. Oath of Allegiance, 1778. (A-1/7)

ELLIN, FREDERICK. Non-Juror to Oath of Allegiance, 1778. (A-1/7)

ELLIOTT, ARTHUR. Non-Juror to Oath of Allegiance, 1778. (A-1/7)

ELLICOTT, GEORGE. Non-Juror to Oath of Allegiance, 1778. (A-1/7)

ELLIOTT, JAMES, SR. (Died 1785/1786) Married Mary WEEKS on December 29, 1736. Children: Jemima, married Abraham ENLOES; John; James, married Mary E. ATKINSON in 1759; Mary married Henry ENLOES; Michael; Sarah, married a ROBINSON; William, married Elizabeth ATKINSON; Susanna, married James NEILL in 1784; and, possibly Kezia, who md. a HOOPER; Elizabeth, who married a McBROOM; and Karenhappuck, who married in 1782 to John McBROOM. James ELLIOTT did not take the Oath of Allegiance in 1778, but was a subscriber in 1781. (A-1/7, QQ-110, and research by Shirley Reightler of Bel Air, MD)

ELLIOTT, JAMES, JR. (Died circa 1807) Son of James ELLIOTT and Mary WEEKS. Married on March 9, 1759 to Mary Ellen ATKINSON. Children: George; Thomas; Michael; William A.; Jemina, married Clement MARSH in 1799; and, Mary, married John CAIRNES. James did not take the Oath of Allegiance in 1778, but subscribed in 1781. (A-1/7, QQ-110, and research by Shirley Reightler of Bel Air, Maryland, 1987)

ELLIOTT, JOHN. Non-Juror to Oath of Allegiance, 1778, but subscribed in 1781. (A-1/7, QQ-110)

ELLIOTT, JOSEPH. Baltimore Privateer and Captain "Joseph Elliott commanded, on the 10th of March, 1780, the schooner Molly, mounting two guns, and owned by Archibald Pattison & Co., of Dorchester County. He afterwards, on the 30th of November 1780, commanded the schooner Unity, mounting eight guns, and owned by Robert Ewing and others, of Dorchester." (III-206)

ELLIOTT, SAMUEL. (1757 - 1841) Married Keziah WEBB. Served as Private in Capt. Ramsey's Company No. 5 in 1776. (H-640, JJJ-218)

ELLIOTT, THOMAS. Of Baltimore, on March 2, 1827, he was paid, during life, half yearly, half pay of a Private, for his services during the Revolutionary War. Source YY-20 lists three men by this name who were Privates in the Maryland Line during the war: one was born 1755; one was born 1759; and one listed no dates. (C-339)

ELLIOTT, WILLIAM. Two men by this name were Non-Jurors in 1778, and at least one of them subscribed to the Oath of Allegiance in 1781. (A-1/7, QQ-110)

ELLIS, HENRY. Oath of Allegiance, 1778, before Hon. Thomas Sollers. (A-1/7, A-2/51)

ELLIS, JOHN. Private, Capt. Lansdale's Company, 4th MD Regiment, from August 23, 1777 to January 3, 1779 when he was listed as deserted. Non-Juror to the Oath of Allegiance in 1778. (A-1/7, H-107)

ELLIS, NICHOLAS. Non-Juror to Oath of Allegiance, 1778. (A-1/7)
ELLIS, OBEDIAH. Non-Juror to Oath of Allegiance, 1778. (A-1/7)

ELLIS, WILLIAM. Born 1739 in Portsmouth, England. Occupation: Labourer. Ht.: 5' 5½". Enlisted January 28, 1776 as Private in Capt. N. Smith's 1st Company of Matrosses and served in Capt. Lansdale's Company, 4th MD Regiment from January 24, 1778 to November 1, 1780. Non-Juror to Oath, 1778. (A-1/7, H-107, H-564, H-567, QQQ-2)

ELMS, STEPHEN. Oath of Allegiance, 1778, before Hon. James Calhoun. (A-1/7, A-2/38)

ELSEROTE, JOHN. Non-Juror to Oath of Allegiance, 1778. (A-1/7)

ELTON, THOMAS. Non-Juror to Oath of Allegiance, 1778. (A-1/7)

ELZEY, ARNOLD SR. Oath of Allegiance, 1778, before Hon. Geo. Lindenberger. (A-2/52)

EMICH (EMICK), PHILLIP. Oath of Allegiance, 1778, before Hon. Peter Shepherd. (A-2/49)

EMMIT, DAVID. Private, Capt. McClellan's Company, September 4, 1780. (CCC-24)

EMMITT (EMMETT), DAVID. Member of the Whig Club, 1777. (CCC-26)

EMMITT (EMMET), THOMAS. Private, Capt. Cox's Company, December 19, 1776, and Private, Capt. McClellan's Company, September 4, 1780. Took Oath of Allegiance, 1778, before Hon. James Calhoun. (A-1/7, A-2/40, CCC-22, CCC-24)

ENDERS, JACOB. Oath of Allegiance, 1778, before Hon. Geo. Lindenberger. (A-2/52)

ENGLAND, ABRAHAM. Oath of Allegiance, 1778, before Hon. Geo. Lindenberger. (A-2/52)

ENGLAND, BENJAMIN. Private, Capt. Howell's Company, December 30, 1775. Drummer in Capt. Keeports German Regiment; enlisted July 15, 1776; was at Philadelphia on September 19, 1776. (G-11, H-263)

ENGLISH, ISAAC. Recruit in Baltimore County, 1780. (H-340)

ENGLISH, ROBERT. Oath of Allegiance, 1778, before Hon. William Spear. (A-1/7, A-2/66)

ENLOES, ABRAHAM. Non-Juror to Oath of Allegiance, 1778. (A-1/7)
ENLOES, JOHN. Non-Juror to Oath of Allegiance, 1778. (A-1/7)
ENLOES (ENLOWES), HENRY. Non-Juror to Oath of Allegiance, 1778. (A-1/7)

ENLOES (ENLOWS), JAMES. (1756-1822, Harford County, MD) married Prudence MARSH.
ENLOES (ENLOWES), WILLIAM. Non-Juror to Oath of Allegiance, 1778. (A-1/7)

ENNALS, ANDREW S. Baltimore County Committee of Observations, July 24, 1775. (EEEE-1725)

ENSOR, ABRAHAM (ABRAM). Baltimore Mechanical Company of Militia in 1776. Two men with this name were Non-Jurors to the Oath of Allegiance in 1778. (OCC-28, A-1/7)

ENSOR, DARBY. Non-Juror to Oath of Allegiance, 1778. (A-1/7)

ENSOR, GEORGE. Non-Juror to Oath of Allegiance, 1778. Involved in evaluation of Baltimore County confiscated proprietary reserve land, 1782. (A-1/7, FFF-544)

ENSOR, JOHN. Non-Juror to Oath of Allegiance, 1778. (A-1/7)

ENSOR, JOHN (OF WILLIAM). Oath of Allegiance, 1778, before Hon. James Calhoun. (A-2/42)

ENSOR, JONATHAN. Non-Juror to Oath of Allegiance, 1778. (A-1/7)

ENSOR, WILLIAM. Non-Juror to Oath in 1778, but signed in 1781. (A-1/7, QQ-110)

ENSOR, WILLIAM, JR. 2nd Lt., Capt. H. Howard's Company No. 3, by August 26, 1776. 1st Lt., Capt. Marsh's Company, Gunpowder Upper Battalion, October 23, 1781. Oath of Allegiance, 1778. (A-1/7, PPP-2, RR-99, ZZ-541, AAAA-650)

ENSOR, WILLIAM (OF WILLIAM). Oath of Allegiance, 1778, before Hon. Richard Holliday. (A-1/7, A-2/60)

EPAUGH, HENRY. Non-Juror to Oath of Allegiance, 1778. (A-1/7)
EPAUGH, JACOB. Non-Juror to Oath of Allegiance, 1778. (A-1/7)

ERWIN, WILLIAM. Non-Juror to Oath in 1778, but subscribed in 1781. (QQ-110)

ETCHBERGER, WILLIAM. (1743, Berks County, PA - February 13, 1823, Baltimore, MD) Married in 1778 to Mary Magdalena SCHIFLERN (1753-1844). Their son, William ETCHBERGER (1779-1815) married Charlotte CUNNINGHAM (1780-1844) in 1803, and their son, James ETCHBERGER (1804-1893) married Frances Ann DESPEAUX (1815-1865) in 1836. William was a Private, enlisting in 1776 at Reading, PA and serving to February 1, 1778, under Captains John Spohn and Peter Decker in Colonel Robert McGaw's 5th PA Battalion; captured at Fort Washington; later exchanged in 1777; also fought at Brandywine and Germantown. (AAA-265A)

ETHERINGTON, JOSHUA. Non-Juror to Oath of Allegiance, 1778. (A-1/7)

ETHERINTON, SAMUEL. Non-Juror to Oath of Allegiance, 1778. (A-1/7)

ETTER, JACOB. Private, Capt. Graybill's German Regiment, 1776. (H-265)

ETTSPERGER, WILFGANG. Private, Capt. Graybill's German Regiment, 1776. (H-265)

ETTZINGER, WOLFGANG. Private, Capt. Graybill's German Regiment, 1776. (H-265)

EVANS, COLTER. Private in Baltimore County Regiment No. 7, circa 1777. (TTT-13)

EVANS, DANIEL. Non-Juror to Oath of Allegiance, 1778. (A-1/7)

EVANS, DAVID. 1st Lt. in Capt. Howell's Company, December 30, 1775. Subsequently, a Sergeant in Capt. Cox's Company, December 19, 1776; Ensign in Baltimore Town Battn. on March 16, 1779; and Ensign in Capt. McClellan's Company on September 4, 1780. Signed a letter to Governor of Maryland on September 4, 1778 regarding suspicious shipments from Baltimore. Oath of Allegiance, 1778. (A-1/7, F-311, F-313, G-11, II-23, OCC-21, OCC-23)

EVANS, DAVID. Baltimore Mechanical Company of Militia, November 4, 1775. Private in Capt. Deams Company, 7th MD Regiment, January 23, 1777. Took Oath of Allegiance 1778, before Hon. John Merryman. (A-2/45, F-299, H-305)

EVANS, EDWARD. Recruit in Baltimore County in 1780. One "Edward Evins" was a Private in Capt. Lansdale's Company, 4th MD Regiment, Feb. 24, 1778 to November 1, 1780. (H-340, H-107)

EVANS, ELIJAH. (1752 - 1806, Baltimore County, MD) Married Catherine SCHAEFFER in 1775; she died in 1825. Children: Henry (died unmarried); Catherine (1779-1867) married Amzi BATEMAN (1776-1816) in 1799, and their daughter Margaret Evans

BATEMAN (1815-1893) married Frederick TOMLINSON (1809-1893) in 1835; Daniel married
Nancy SPARKE; Elizabeth, died unmarried; Elias, died unmarried; and, Wesley, died
younh. Elijah EVANS was an Ensign in Stephenson's Rifle Regiment in May, 1776, and
a 2nd Lt. on August 10, 1776; was a prisoner at Fort Washington on Nov. 16, 1776;
became a Captain in Moses Rawlings' Rifle Regt. on April 10, 1778; and was declared
a supernumerary on January 1, 1781. He received Federal Bounty Land Grant Warrant
#673 of 300 acres on May 25, 1789, and was entitled to 200 acres (lots #3063, 3065,
3239 and 3240) in western Maryland for his services. He was an Original Member of
the Society of the Cincinnati of Maryland, now represented by David Weeks LEE of
Houston, Texas. (TT-79, H-301, H-350, YY-64, DDDD-2, XXX-299, B-219, JJJ-225, D-3,
AAA-677; also, Pay Certificates 89440 for $58.70, 89441 for $26.40, and 89442 for
$1,573.30. (PP-168)

EVANS, HENRY. (1755/1756 - 1815) Born in Ireland; married Dolly_____. His height
was 5' 1" and he had short black hair; round face. Enlisted July 5, 1776 as Private
in Baltimore County, Col. Ewing's Battalion. He previously served as a Private in
Baltimore Artillery Company, October 16, 1775. Subsequently, he served as a Private
in Capt. Sheaff's Company, June 16, 1777. He took the Oath of Allegiance in 1778
before Hon. George Lindenberger. (G-8, W-162, A-1/7, A-2/52, H-55, JJJ-224)

EVANS, JEREMIAH. Drafted into Baltimore County Regiment 36, circa 1777. (TTT-13)

EVANS, JOB. Non-Juror to Oath of Allegiance, 1778. (A-1/7)

EVANS, JOHN. There were two men with this name who served during the Revolutionary
War. One was born December 1, 1737 and died May 18, 1802; wife named Hannah GRIFFITH
and the other John Evans was born 1760 and died 1841; wife named Elizabeth MARSHALL.
Both were Privates: one with Capt. McClellan's Company in 1780, and the other with
Capt. Brown's MD Artillery from 1777 through 1781, with service at Valley Forge in
1778. Also, both took the Oath of Allegiance: one before Hon. Isaac Van Bibber and
one before Hon. Jesse Bussey. Obviously, further research is necessary in order to
determine which John Evans fit which category, or if there were more than two with
this name. (A-2/34, A-2/44, JJJ-224, CCC-24, DDDD-15, UU-228, UU-230)

EVANS, NATHANIEL. Private in Col. Aquila Hall's Baltimore County Regt., 1777. (TTT-13)

EVANS, ROBERT. Served on ship Defence, August 1 to October 31, 1777. (H-656) Also, he
was a Non-Juror to the Oath of Allegiance in 1778. (A-1/7)

EVANS, THOMAS. Non-Juror to Oath of Allegiance, 1778. (A-1/7)

EVANS, W. Oath of Allegiance, 1778, before Hon. Isaac Van Bibber. Could not write;
made his mark. (A-2/34)

EVANS, WILLIAM. (1753 - 1794, Queen Ann County, MD) Wife named Elizabeth_____.
Children: Tilly, Josah, Ann, William, John, Jonathan and James. William enlisted in
Baltimore Town as a Private on June 22, 1778, by Richard Cockran. (XXX-300)

EVANS, WILLIAM. "Proprietor of the Indian Queen Tavern in Baltimore, died June 28,
1807, aged 56. He was a Revolutionary soldier and fought under Gen. Samuel Smith
at Long Island." (ZZZ-106)

FVERETT, JAMES. (c1760 - c1820) Married Ann Jane MEADE. He took the Oath of Allegiance
in 1778 before Hon. James Calhoun. (A-1/7, A-2/38, JJJ-225)

EVERETT, WILLIAM. Non-Juror to Oath of Allegiance, 1778. (A-1/7)

EVERHART (EVERHARD), GEORGE. Private, Baltimore County Regiment No. 15, circa 1777.
Took the Oath of Allegiance, 1778, before Hon. Frederick Decker. 2nd Lieutenant,
Capt. Shroad's Co., Upper Battalion, Dec. 4, 1778. (TTT-13, A-2/31, A-1/7, GGG-257)

EWALT, JOHN. Oath of Allegiance, 1778, before Hon. William Lux. (A-1/7, A-2/68)

EWING, THOMAS. (1730 - after 1790) Married Margaret_____. Captain of Co. #4
in Smallwood's MD Troops, January 3, 1776. Prior thereto, he served on Baltimore
County's Committee of Inspection, March 13, 1775. On February 12, 1776 he reported
on the condition of guns in Baltimore County. Became Colonel of 3rd MD Battalion of
Flying Camp. In August, 1776, his troops had moved to Head of Elk (Cecil Co., MD).

EWING, THOMAS (continued)
On October 13, 1776 his troops were at Camp North Harlem (New York). He served until December 1, 1776. (FFF-62, JJJ-226, TT-79, B-220, RR-19, H-11, FFF-25, FFF-52)

F

FAHAY, DAVID. Enlisted in Baltimore County on July 20, 1776. (H-53)

FAIR, STOPHEL. Non-Juror to the Oath in 1778, but subscribed in 1781. (A-1/7, QQ-110)

FALCONER, JAMES. Quartermaster on ship Defence, September 19, 1776. (H-606)

FALL, PATRICK. Served on ship Defence, January 11 to May 18, 1777. (H-656)

FALLEN, JOHN. Recruit in Baltimore County in 1780. (H-340)

FALLS, MOORE DR. (Of Baltimore), 1754-1834. He married (1) Abigail BIDDLE, daughter of Hon. Edward BIDDLE, in December, 1785, at Chatsworth, the seat of George LUX. She died in January, 1789 in her 23rd year. Dr. Falls married (2) Mrs. Rebecca Neilson WILSON, widow of Stephen WILSON, on September 24, 1796. Children of Moore FALLS and Rebecca WILSON: Stephen (born July 26, 1797); Rebecca (born September 1, 1798); Jan (born September 4, 1799); Sarah (born April 27, 1801); Maria (born July 3, 1803); & Moore Neilson (November 19, 1804 - April 7, 1876), who became President of the Bay Line Steamship Company. Dr. Moore Falls was one of the petitioners for a Health Office in Baltimore in November, 1785, and he asked that John KIRWAN be made Health Officer. Any service during the Revolutionary War is not known at this time. (D-8)

FANCUTT, WILLIAM. Non-Juror to Oath of Allegiance, 1778. (A-1/7)

FANNING, JOHN. Master of the schooner Baltimore on June 8, 1778. (GGG-125)

FANNING, THOMAS. Bombardier, Capt. Brown's MD Artillery; joined November 22, 1777. Was at valley Forge until June, 1778; at White Plains, July, 1778; at Fort Schuyler, August and September, 1780; at High Hills of the Santee in August, 1781, when he was a Corporal; at Camp Col. Scirvins, January, 1782; at Bacon's Bridge, S.C. in April, 1782. Entitled to 50 acres (lot #1019) in western Maryland for his Revolutionary services as a Matross in the Artillery. (DDDD-15, UU-228, UU-229, UU-230)

FARMER, SAMUEL. Paid in Baltimore on January 11, 1780 by the Collector of Tax for his recruiting expenses; rank of Lieutenant. Became a Captain of the 3rd MD Regiment on March 2, 1780; subsequently was a wounded priosner and was discharged on August 16, 1780. (H-109, FFF-260, H-334)

FARNSWORTH, JOSEPH. Non-Juror to Oath of Allegiance, 1778. (A-1/7)

FARRARA, EMANUEL. Recruit in Baltimore County in 1780. (H-340)

FARRAJARA, JOHN. Midshipman on ship Defence, August 9 to September 8, 1777. (H-656)

FARREL (FERREL), BRYAN. Private, Capt. Furnival's MD Artillery, November 17, 1777. Matross, Capt. Dorsey's MD Artillery at Valley Forge, June 3, 1778. (UU-231, H-573)

FARREL (FARRAL), JAMES. Oath of Allegiance, 1778, before Hon. Jesse Dorsey. (A-2/63)

FARREL (FAROL), JOHN. Oath of Allegiance, 1778, before Hon. Geo.Lindenberger. (A-2/53)

FARRET, JAMES. Oath of Allegiance, 1778, before Hon. William Spear. Could not write; made his mark. (A-2/67)

FARRINGTON, SAMUEL. Matross, Capt. Gale's MD Artillery, 1779. Reported as deserted at Trenton, NJ on September 29, 1779. (YYY-1/31)

FARRON, JOSEPH. Oath of Allegiance, 1778. (A-1/7)

FARVER, ADAM. Died at Burntwoods Hundred, Baltimore County, MD in 1783. Wife's name was Elizabeth. Probably the Adam FARVER and Elizabeth KEPLAR who married in 1779 in Frederick County, MD, but if true, then Adam may have married previously since his will names his four children. Took Oath of Allegiance, 1778. (A-1/7, D-8)

FASH, JACOB. Oath of Allegiance, 1778. (A-1/7)

FASS, WILLIAM. Oath of Allegiance, 1778, before Hon. Geo. Lindenberger. (A-2/53)

FATE (FABE), TIMOTHY. Oath of Allegiance, 1778, before Hon. John Beale Howard. (A-1/7, A-2/29)

FAVIS, THOMAS. Oath of Allegiance, 1778. (A-1/7)

FAWLER, JOHN. Non-Juror to Oath of Allegiance, 1778. (A-1/7)

FAWLIT, JOSEPH. Fifer, 4th MD Regt. at Fort Whetstone Point in Baltimore, 1781. (H-626)

FEAR, IGNATIUS. Gunner's Mate on ship Defence, May 28 to Sept. 20, 1777. (H-656)

FEATHER, ADAM. Non-Juror to Oath of Allegiance, 1778. (A-1/8)

FEATHER, HENRY. Non-Juror in 1778, but subscribed to Oath in 1781. He died 1785 in Baltimore County; will does not name a wife, but a son, Philip Feather. (D-8, A-1/8, QQ-110)

FEATHER, PHILIP. Corporal in Baltimore County Regiment No. 15, circa 1777. He subscribed to the Oath of Allegiance in 1781. (TTT-13, QQ-110)

FELL, WILLIAM. (1759-1786) Son of Edward FELL and Ann BOND; never married. Served in Legislature, Baltimore Town, 1782-1783. (MMM-A)

FELLS, CHRISTOPHER. Enlisted in Baltimore County, July 20, 1776. (H-52)

FELTY, FELIX. Non-Juror to Oath of Allegiance, 1778. (A-1/8)

FENNELL, STEPHEN. Born 1748. Enlisted July 2, 1776 as Private in Capt. N. Smith's 1st Company of Matrosses; was at Whetstone Point in Baltimore, Sept. 7, 1776. Private in Capt. Dorsey's MD Artillery; convalescent on Nov. 17, 1777. Was a Matross in Dorsey's Company at Valley Forge on June 3, 1778. "Steaven Fennil" was a Private in the Extra Regiment of MD Troops at Fort Whetstone Point in Baltimore in 1781. He was a Pensioner, and was entitled to 50 acres (lot 1049) in western Maryland. (DDDD-15, H-627, H-574, H-569, VV-74, H-618, UU-231)

FENTON, CORNELIUS. Marine on ship Defence, April 1 to December 31, 1777. (H-656)

FENWICK, RICHARD. Marine on ship Defence, Oct. 23 to December 31, 1777. (H-656)

FERBER, ADAM. Took the Oath of Allegiance in 1781. (QQ-110)

FERGUS, WILLIAM. Oath of Allegiance, 1778, before Hon. James Calhoun. (A-2/41, A-1/8)

FERRER, JOSEPH. Oath of Allegiance, 1778, before Hon. James Calhoun. (A-2/42, A-1/8)

FERRILL (FEARALL), JOHN. (1740 - 1790) Married Margaret Elizabeth BAUGHMAN. He was a Matross in Capt. Brown's MD Artillery; joined November 22, 1777. Served at Valley Forge until June, 1778; at White Plains, July, 1778; at Fort Schuyler in August and September, 1780; and, not listed in 1781. Non-Juror to the Oath of Allegiance in 1778. (A-1/8, JJJ-233, UU-228, UU-230)

FETLEY, JOSEPH. Oath of Allegiance, 1778, before Hon. Edward Cockey. (A-2/61)

FIELDING, JAMES. Oath of Allegiance, 1778, before Hon. Edward Cockey. (A-2/61, A-1/8)

FIGHT, FRANCIS. Oath of Allegiance, 1778, before Hon. William Lux. (A-2/68, A-1/8)

FILE, JOHN TAYLOR. Non-Juror to Oath of Allegiance, 1778. (A-1/8)

FINLATER, ALEXANDER. Private, Baltimore Artillery Company, October 16, 1775, and Private, Capt. Sheaff's Company, June 16, 1777. Took Oath of Allegiance, 1778, before Hon. George Lindenberger. A native of Aberdeen, Scotland, he died on May 2, 1809 in Baltimore in his 66th year. (ZZZ-110, G-8, W-162, A-2/53, A-1/8)

FINLEY, DR. (of Baltimore Town). Applicant for surgeoncy, and recommended by Dr. Wiesenthal to the Maryland Council during the Revolutionary War. (XX-7)

FINLEY (FNELNY), BALZER. Baltimore Mechanical Co. of Militia, Nov. 4, 1775. (F-299)

FINLEY (FINELY), COLEMAN. Private in Capt. Norwood's Company, 4th MD Regiment, and was in service until May 3, 1778, when he was reported deserted. (H-110)

FINLEY, EBENEZER. 3rd Lt., Capt. N. Smith's Company of Matrosses, December 14, 1776. 1st Lt., Capt. Dorsey's MD Artillery in 1777. Capt.-Lt. in Capt. Brown's Company of MD Artillery, July 4, 1777 and November 24, 1777, and was at Valley Forge as of June 3, 1778. Also served as Capt.-Lt. in Capt. J. Smith's MD Artillery in 1780 and served under Lt.Col. Ed. Carrington while stationed at Baltimore on May 11, 1780. He was at Camp. Col. Scirvins with Capt. Dorsey's Company on January 28, 1782, and was a Capt.-Lt. in Capt. J. Smith's MD Artillery in 1783. Subsequently, he became Capt. and was entitled to 200 acres (lots #2214, 2215, 2216, 2217) in western Maryland, & 200 acres under Federal Bounty Land Grant Warrant #2287. (UU-230, UU-231, VVV-96, H-477, H-573, H-579, DDDD-2, YY-64, ZZ-528, YYY-2/17)

FINLEY, HUGH. Oath of Allegiance, 1778, before Hon. Peter Shepherd. (A-1/8, A-2/49)

FINLEY, PETER. Drummer, Capt. Graybill's Co., German Regiment, 1776. (H-266)

FINLEY, THOMAS. Oath of Allegiance, 1778, before Hon. Richard Holliday. (A-2/60)

FINLEY, WILLIAM. There were two men by this name who took the Oath of Allegiance in 1778: one before Hon. James Calhoun, and one before Hon. John Moale. (A-2/41,A-2/70)

FINN, PETER. Applied for pension while living in Sumner County, Tennessee. After 1832 he moved to Kentucky and later moved to Illinois. He was born in Baltimore County, Maryland on July 2, 1751, and died in Marion County, Illinois in 1837. He enlisted in Maryland troops first, but by 1779 he had moved to Washington County, N.C., now Tennessee, where he enlisted under Capt. Valentine Sevier. (OO-102, YY-21)

FINN, WILLIAM. Private, Capt. Howell's Company, December 30, 1775. Non-Juror to the Oath of Allegiance in 1778. (G-11, A-1/8)

FINNIE, ROBERT. Private, Capt. Howell's Company, December 30, 1775. (G-11)

FISHER, DAVID. Non-Juror to Oath of Allegiance, 1778. (A-1/8)

FISHER, GEORGE. Ensign, Upper Battalion, Capt. Shroads Company, December 4, 1778. Oath of Allegiance, 1778, before Hon. John Hall. (A-1/8, A-2/36, GGG-257)

FISHER, GEORGE, JR. Oath of Allegiance, 1778, before Hon. Frederick Decker. (A-2/31)

FISHER, HERMAN. Oath of Allegiance, 1778, before Hon. Peter Shepherd. (A-2/50)

FISHER, JOHN. Oath of Allegiance, 1778, before Hon. Frederick Decker. (A-2/31)

FISHER, JOSEPH. Born 1748. Private, Baltimore County Militia, enlisted July 5, 1776. Corporal, Capt. Oldham's Company, 4th MD Regiment, enlisted December 16, 1776, and was a prisoner of war from August 22, 1777 to July 16, 1778; discharged December 16, 1779. Non-Juror, 1778. Pensioner. (A-1/8, H-58, H-110, YY-21)

FISHER, LEONARD. Private, Baltimore County Regiment No. 15, circa 1777. (TTT-13)

FISHER, MICHAEL. Oath of Allegiance, 1778. (A-1/8)

FISHER, PETER SR. Oath of Allegiance, 1778, before Hon. Peter Shepherd. (A-2/49)

FISHER, PETER JR. Oath of Allegiance, 1778, before Hon. Peter Shepherd. (A-2/49)

FISHER, SAMUEL. Non-Juror to Oath of Allegiance, 1778. (A-1/8)

FISHER, THOMAS. Recruit in Baltimore County in 1780. (H-340)

FISHPAW, JOHN. Oath of Allegiance, 1778, before Hon. Edward Cockey. (A-1/8, A-2/61)

FITCHEW, RICHARD. Oath of Allegiance, 1778, before Hon. James Calhoun. (A-2/65)

FITCHEW, THOMAS. Oath of Allegiance, 1778, before Hon. James Calhoun. (A-2/65)

FITCHEW, THOMAS JR. Oath of Allegiance, 1778, before Hon. James Calhoun. (A-2/65)

FITCHEW, ZEKIEL (EZEKIEL). Oath of Allegiance, 1778, before James Calhoun. (A-2/65)

FITE, HENRY. "Heinrich Vogt" was born in the Province of Hesse-Kassel, Germany in 1722, and came to American with his brothers via Rotterdam, landing in Philadelphia, Pennsylvania on September 28, 1749. He was the founder of the Maryland family of "Fite" circa 1769. Several historical works mention that Congress met in the house of Mr. Jacob Hite, known as "Old Congress Hall", when it convened in Baltimore after leaving Philadelphia in December, 1776. Such is not the case. Henry Fite built Congress Hall in 1770, & his son, Jacob, lived there but never owned it; Jacob was not born until 1772 and was only four years old when Congress convened in Baltimore. Located at the corner of Market (now Baltimore) and Sharp and Liberty Streets, "Congress Hall" was then the farthest west building in town. Its site was marked by the Sons of the American Revolution in 1894; unfortunately, the building burned in the great Baltimore Fire of 1904. The SAR plaque was saved and rededicated, now at the site of the Baltimore Arena (old Civic Center). It was at Henry Fite's tavern (not Jacob Hite's house) that the Continental Congress met and on December 27, 1776, conferred upon General Washington extraordinary powers for the conduct of the Revolutionary War. Henry FITE died on October 25, 1789 and was buried in the old German Burying Ground in Baltimore. His wife's name is not known, but his children were: Henry; Peter; Elizabeth; Mary; Eve; Andrew; Jacob; & probably Rachel Fite, who married John FAY in 1785; and also perhaps John Fite. (Elizabeth Mitchell Stephenson Fite's The Fite Families in the United States, 1907, pages 106-108, and The Work of the Maryland Society, SAR, 1889 to 1902)

FITE, JOHN. The following Revolutionary War record, in all probability, refers to John Fite of Baltimore: "Robert Walker, late Captain Artillery, wrote to Andrew Danscomb of Richmond, Virginia, from Stafford on April 18, 1786 - I have all the men's receipts to show for receipts of same, except John Fite's, who I am pretty positive received said bounty of ten pounds of Lieutenant Hughes." (UU-106 and Elizabeth Mitchell Stephenson Fite's Fite Families in the United States, page 108)

FITES, ANDREW. Non-Juror to Oath of Allegiance, 1778. (A-1/8)

FITUS, WOOLRICH. Non-Juror to Oath of Allegiance, 1778. (A-1/8)

FITZ, ROBERT. Non-Juror to Oath of Allegiance, 1778. (A-1/8)
FITZ, THOMAS. Non-Juror to Oath of Allegiance, 1778. (A-1/8)
FITZ, WILLIAM SR. Non-Juror to Oath of Allegiance, 1778. (A-1/8)
FITZ, WILLIAM JR. Non-Juror to Oath of Allegiance, 1778. (A-1/8)

FITZGERALD, JAMES. Born 1749. Enlisted in Baltimore County, July 26, 1776. Was a Sergeant in Capt. Lansdale's Company, 4th MD Regiment, on February 12, 1777, but demoted to Private on January 1, 1779; discharged February 12, 1780. Took Oath of Allegiance in 1778 before Hon. James Calhoun. Pensioner as Private, MD Line. (YY-21, H-110, H-53, A-1/8, A-2/39)

FITZGERALD, JOHN. Private in Capt. Furnival's Company, MD Artillery, 1777. Muster roll of Nov. 17, 1777 indicates he died October 15, 1777. (H-573)

FITZGERALD, TIMOTHY. Maryland Line defective, April 1, 1781. Was a resident of Baltimore County. (H-414)

FITZGERALD, WILLIAM. Oath of Allegiance, 1778, before Hon. Geo. Lindenberger. (A-2/52)

FITZJEFFRYS, AARON. Served on ship Defence, June 21, 1777 to July 15, 1777. (H-656)

FITZLER, PHILIP. Private in Capt. Howell's Company, December 30, 1775. (G-11)

FITZPATRICK, BRYAN. Private in Capt. Norwood's Company, 4th Maryland Regiment, from May 6, 1778 to August 16, 1780. (I.-110)

FITZPATRICK, GEORGE. Non-Juror to Oath of Allegiance, 1778. (A-1/8)

FITZPATRICK, JOHN. Private, Capt. Furnival's MD Artillery, November 17, 1777. Was a Matross in Capt. Dorsey's MD Artillery at Valley Forge on June 3, 1778. Non-Juror to Oath of Allegiance in 1778. (A-1/8, H-573, UU-231)

FITZPATRICK (FITSPARTRICK), NATHAN. Born 1755. Private in Baltimore County Militia, enlisting July 19, 1776. Pensioner as Private of Flying Camp. (YY-21, H-58)

FLAHERTY, JAMES. Private, 4th MD Regiment, February 16, 1777 to February 16, 1780. Oath of Allegiance, 1780, before Hon. James Calhoun. (A-1/8, A-2/41, H-110)

FLAN, ANTHONY. Recruit in Baltimore County in 1780. (H-340)

FLANAGAN, DENNIS. (December 21, 1731 - February 26, 1800) Married Margaret O'BRIAN. Private in Capt. Furnival's MD Artillery, November 17, 1777. Matross, Capt. Dorsey MD Artillery, at Valley Forge, June 3, 1778. Entitled to 50 acres (lot #3178) in western Maryland for artillery services. (DDDD-16, JJJ-240, UU-231, H-572)

FLANAGAN, EDWARD. Oath of Allegiance, 1778, before Hon. Edward Cockey. (A-1/8, A-2/61)

FLANAGAN, HENRY. Married Lydia BUSH (BUSK) in December, 1783 in Baltimore County, MD. Marriage proven through Maryland pension application. Served in 2nd MD Regiment, from Dorchester County, from May, 1778 to April, 1779. (YY-114, H-109, H-339)

FLANAGAN (FLANNAGAN), JOHN. Served on ship Defence, June 17 to June 29, 1777. Took Oath of Allegiance, 1778, before Hon. James Calhoun. (H-656, A-1/8, A-2/39)

FLANAGAN, LEREME. Oath of Allegiance, 1778, before Hon. John Beale Howard. Could not write; made his mark (" ⸰ "). (A-2/29)

FLANAGAN, PATRICK SR. Oath of Allegiance, 1778, before Hon. John B. Howard. (A-2/29)

FLANAGAN, PATRICK JR. Oath of Allegiance, 1778, before Hon. John B. Howard. (A-2/29)

FLANAGAN, TERENCE. Oath of Allegiance, 1778. (A-1/8)

FLANERY, DANIAL. Baltimore Artillery Company, 1777. ("his marke") (V-368)

FLATTERY, JAMES. Private, Capt. McClellan's Company, Baltimore Town, September 4, 1780. Non-Juror to Oath of Allegiance in 1778. (A-1/8, CCC-25)

FLEMING, JAMES. Baltimore Mechanical Company of Militia, 1776. (CCC-28)

FLEMMING, DAVID. Private, Baltimore Artillery Company, October 16, 1775. (G-8)

FLEMMING, JOHN. Sergeant of Marines on ship Defence, 1777. (H-656)

FLEMMING, WILLIAM. Sergeant of Marines on ship Defence, 1777. (H-656)

FLETCHER, JOHN. Private, Capt. S. Smith's Company No. 8, 1st Maryland Battalion, January 13, 1776. (H-640)

FLETCHER, WILLIAM. Corporal, Capt. Gale's MD Artillery Company, 1779-1780; was on command at Mt. Hope in December, 1779. (YYY-1/32)

FLINN, JAMES. Non-Juror to Oath of Allegiance, 1778. (A-1/8)

FLINN, PHARO. Recruit in Baltimore County Militia, April 11, 1780. (H-335)

FLINN OR FLINT, RICHARD. Non-Juror to Oath of Allegiance, 1778. (A-1/8)

FLOOD, PHILIP. Non-Juror to Oath of Allegiance, 1778. (A-1/8)

FLORI, JACOB. Private, Capt. S. Smith's Co. No. 8, 1st MD Battn., January 24, 1776. (H-641)

FOARD, JEREMIAH. Captain. Died March 9, 1812 at his residence in Baltimore County, "one of the worthies of '76." (ZZZ-112)

FOARD, LOYD SR. Oath of Allegiance, 1778, before Hon. William Spear. Could not write; made his mark ("V"). (A-1/8. A-2/66)

FOARD, LOYD JR. Private, Capt. Talbott's Company, May 31, 1779. Oath of Allegiance in 1778 before Hon. William Spear. Could not write; made his mark ("X"). (A-1/8, A-2/66, F-301, U-90)

FOARD, WILLIAM. Born 1757 in Cecil County, MD. Occupation: Labourer. Ht.: 5' 7½". Enlisted January 31, 1776 as Private in Capt. N. Smith's 1st Company of Matrosses. Took Oath of Allegiance in 1778. (A-1/8. H-565)

FOLKS, JOHN. Matross, Capt. Brown's MD Artillery; joined November 22, 1777. Was at Valley Forge until June, 1778; at White Plains, July, 1778; at Fort Schuyler, in August and September, 1780; not listed in 1781. (UU-228, UU-230)

90

FOLLAN, JESSE. Private, Capt. McClellan's Co., Baltimore Town, Sept. 4, 1780. (CCC-24)

FONERDEN, ADAM. He was selected to assist in looking after the comfort and subsistence of Count Rochambeau in Baltimore, September 9, 1781. Mrs. Martha FONERDEN, consort of Adam, died in October, 1797, aged 45 years. (CCC-18, ZZZ-113)

FORBES, JAMES. Baltimore Privateer and Captain of brig Nisbett (14 guns), owned by Robert Morris and John Nisbett of Philadelphia and S. Steward of Maryland. (III-206)

FORBES, WILLIAM. Born 1750 in Ireland. Occupation: Weaver. Height: 5' 4". Enlisted January 24, 1776 as Private in Capt. N. Smith's 1st Company of Matrosses. Private, Capt. Dorsey's MD Artillery, November 17, 1777, and Matross, Capt. Dorsey's Company at Valley Forge as of June 3, 1778. (UU-231, H-564, H-567, H-568, VV-74, QQQ-2)

FORD, BARNET. Non-Juror to Oath of Allegiance, 1778. (A-1/8)

FORD, BENJAMIN. Ensign, Capt. Talbott's Company, May 31, 1779. Took Oath of Allegiance in 1778 before Hon. Richard Holliday. (F-301, U-90, A-1/8, A-2/60)

FORD, EDWARD. Corporal, Capt. Ramsey's Company No. 5, 1776. Member of Col. Nicholson's Troop of Horse, June 7, 1781. (H-639, BBBB-274)

FORD, JAMES. Matross, Capt. Brown's MD Artillery; joined November 22, 1777. Was at Valley Forge until June, 1778; at White Plains, July, 1778; at Fort Schuyler, in August and September, 1780; not listed in 1781. (UU-228, UU-230)

FORD, JOHN. Took Oath of Allegiance in 1778 before Hon. George Gouldsmith Presbury, and also in 1781. (A-1/8, A-2/48, QQ-110)

FORD, JOHN (OF WILLIAM). Oath of Allegiance, 1778, before Hon. Richard Holliday. (A-1/8, A-2/60)

FORD, JOHN HOWARD. (July 30, 1753, St. Thomas' Parish, MD - c1810, Baltimore County) Son of John FORD and Ruhama HOWARD. Took Oath of Allegiance in 1778. Name of his wife unknown; children: William; Joshua; Nicholas; John; Abraham; Charles; and, Elizabeth, who married a RUSH. (D-3, A-1/8)

FORD, JOSEPH. (c1750 - 1812) Married Mary SPINKS. Joseph was a 2nd Lt. in Capt. Smith's Company No. 8 of Smallwood's MD Regiment on January 2, 1776. Became a 1st Lt. on August 16, 1776, and a Captain on December 10, 1776; resigned as of March 6, 1778. Capt. Ford was pensioned at $120 per annum from January 1, 1803 and received $1,101.33, and died in December, 1812. (Also, pay certificate number 93546 for $51.10) On March 4, 1837, it was ordered that Mary FORD, widow of said Joseph, be paid half pay of a 2nd Lt., during her life, as a further remuneration for Joseph's services during the Revolutionary War. There were also two men by this name who took the Oath of Allegiance in 1778: one before Hon. James Calhoun, and one before Hon. Richard Holliday. (A-1/8, A-2/41, A-2/60, H-17, B-232, C-342, PP-182)

FORD, JOSEPH. Private, Baltimore County Regiment No. 7, circa 1777. Also, took the Oath of Allegiance in 1778 (see above Joseph Ford). (TTT-13, A-1/8)

FORD, JOSHUA, Non-Juror to Oath of Allegiance in 1778. (A-1/8)

FORD, MORDECAI SR. (December 19, 1727 - December, 1795) Married Ruth BARNEY. Took Oath of Allegiance, 1778, before Hon. Benjamin Rogers. Could not write; made his mark. (JJJ-244, A-1/8, A-2/32)

FORD, RALPH. Oath of Allegiance, 1778, before Hon. John Beale Howard. (A-2/29)

FORD, ROBERT. Private, Capt. Smith's Company No. 8; enlisted January 27, 1776. (c1750 - 1830) Married Elizabeth PATTERSON. (JJJ-244, H-18)

FORD STEPHEN. Possibly two men with this name took the Oath in 1778. (A-1/8)

FORD, THOMAS. (February 20, 1744, Ford's Range, Baltimore County, MD - after 1782) Married Elizabeth FORTT (or FOSTT) on November 29, 1764. Served as a Private in Capt. B. Talbott's Company in Col. E. Cockey's Battalion, May 31, 1779. Daughter Susanna (1769-1855) married Alexander PENNY. (XXX-316, F-301, U-90, JJJ-245)

FORD, THOMAS SR. Oath of Allegiance, 1778, before Hon. Richard Holliday. (A-1/8, A-2/60)

FORD, THOMAS (OF STEPHEN). Oath of Allegiance, 1778, before Hon. Richard Holliday.(A-1/8, A-2/60)

FORD, THOMAS COCKEY DEYE. Married Achsah COCKEY (1755-1811), daughter of Thomas COCKEY and Prudence GILL. Children: Achsah, Ann, Prudence Elizabeth, Thomas Cockey Deye, Cassandra Deye, Sarah Cockey, Richard, Samuel, Ruth and Nancy. Thomas took Oath of Allegiance in 1778 before Hon. Richard Holliday. He was also a Private in Captain Talbott's Company, May 31, 1779. (A-1/8, A-2/60, F-301, U-90, WWW-1A)

FORD, WILLIAM. Oath of Allegiance, 1778. (A-1/8)

FOREMAN, LEONARD. Oath of Allegiance, 1781. (QQ-110)

FOREPAUGH (TOREPAUGH), WILLIAM. Served in Baltimore Artilley Company in 1777, and then as Ensign in Capt. Richardson's Company, Baltimore Town Battalion, Sept. 4, 1777. Became a 2nd Lieutenant in 1778-1779, and 1st Lieutenant, May 17, 1779, in Captain Douglass' Company. Subsequently became 1st Lieutenant in Capt. Richard Lemmon's Company, Baltimore Town Battalion, September 25, 1780. He also took the Oath of Allegiance in 1778 before Hon. James Calhoun. (V-368, F-312, E-13, F-314, F-309, GGG-401, BBB-362, A-1/7, A-2/39, F-306)

FORGENSON, THORLES. Oath of Allegiance, 1778, before Hon. James Calhoun. (A-2/65)

FORGESON, WILLIAM. Private, Baltimore County Militia, enlisted July 19, 1776. (H-58)

FORKINBRIDGE, RICHARD. Non-Juror to Oath of Allegiance, 1778. (A-1/8)

FORMAN, JOHN. Oath of Allegiance, 1778, before Hon. Hercules Courtenay. (A-1/8,A-2/37)

FORREST, CARRICK. Non-Juror to Oath of Allegiance, 1778. (A-1/8)

FORRESTER, ALEXANDER. Born 1745 in Maryland. Occupation: Labourer. Height: 5' 5". Enlisted as Private in Capt. N. Smith's 1st Company of Matrosses, Feb. 3, 1776. Private in Capt. Dorsey's MD Artillery, "sick in the country with fevers," as of November 17, 1777. Matross soldier in Baltimore County, May 7, 1779 (deposition). Matross, Capt. Gale's Company; reported deserted at Baltimore on Sept. 14, 1779. (YYY-1/33, H-567, QQQ-2, H-565, VV-74, H-574, FFF-220)

FORRESTER, CORNELIUS. Born 1754 in Maryland. Occupation: Labourer. Height: 5' 10 3/4". Enlisted as Private in Capt. N. Smith's 1st Company of Matrosses, Feb. 3, 1776. Private, Capt. Dorsey's MD Artillery, "sick with rheumatism," as of November 17, 1777. (H-618, H-574, H-565, H-566, QQQ-2, VV-74)

FORRESTER, JOHN. Born 1747 in Maryland. Occupation: Labourer. Height: 5' 8½". Enlisted Feb. 3, 1776, as Private in Capt. N. Smith's 1st Company of Matrosses, Baltimore County. Gave deposition about enlistment term, May 7, 1779. Matross in Captain Gale's Company, 1779-1780 (deserted Oct. 31, 1779; re-joined December 10, 1779). (H-566, QQQ-2, H-565, VV-74, YYY-1/34)

FORSTER, JAMES. Ensign, Capt. Wells Company, Baltimore Town Battalion, June 6, 1776. Oath of Allegiance, 1778. (A-1/8, WW-467)

FORSTER, SAM. Oath of Allegiance, 1778, before Hon. Isaac Van Bibber. (A-2/34)

FORT, SAMUEL. Non-Juror to Oath of Allegiance, 1778. (A-1/8)

FORTUNE, JAMES. Captain, of Fells Point, Baltimore, died November 5, 1797, in his 57th year. Service in Revolutionary War not mentioned. (ZZZ-114)

FOSSETT, HENRY. Oath of Allegiance, 1778, before Hon. William Spear. (A-1/8, A-2/66)

FOSTER, BENEDICT. Non-Juror to Oath of Allegiance, 1778. (A-1/8)
FOSTER, GEORGE (OF JOHN). Non-Juror to Oath of Allegiance, 1778. (A-1/8)

FOSTER, JAMES. 3rd Lieutenant, Capt. Wells Company No. 6, Baltimore Town Artillery, 1777. Unable to serve in 1777, "being absent." (GG-74, MM-89)

FOSTER, JOHN. Non-Juror to Oath of Allegiance, 1778. (A-1/8)

FORT, LOYD. Served in Baltimore County Militia one year; moved to Tennessee. (DDD-56)

FOSTER, JOSEPH. Served in Capt. Moore's Troops, Baltimore County, June 25, 1781. He had an eight-year old bay gelding horse. (BBBB-313)

FOSTER, ROBERT. Born 1752 in England. Occupation: Bricklayer. Height: 5' 7$\frac{1}{4}$". Enlisted January 28, 1776 as Private in Capt. N. Smith's 1st Company of Matrosses. (H-564)

FOSTER, WILLIAM. Served on ship Defence, March 27 to June 1, 1777. (H-656)

FOUNTAIN, COLLIER. Oath of Allegiance, 1778, before Hon. William Spear. (A-2/67)

FOUSE, JOHN. Non-Juror to Oath of Allegiance, 1778. (A-1/8)

FOWBLE (FAWBLE), FREDERICK. Oath of Allegiance, 1781. (QQ-110)

FOWBLE (FOBLE), JACOB. Oath of Allegiance, 1778, before Hon. James Calhoun. One "Jacob Foble" was 2nd Lt., Capt. Lemmons' Company, Upper Battalion, December 4, 1778. (A-1/8, A-2/42, GGG-257)

FOWBLE, MELCHIOR. Non-Juror to Oath of Allegiance, 1778. (A-1/8)

FOWBLE, MICHAEL. Non-Juror to Oath of Allegiance, 1778. (A-1/8)

FOWBLE (FOBLE), PETER. Non-Juror to Oath in 1778, but signed 1781. (A-1/8. QQ-110)

FOWLER, JAMES. (May 9, 1758 - January 31, 1848) Married Mary OZBORNE. He served as Private in Capt. Oldham's Compnay, 4th MD Argiment, from January 28, 1777 to September 10, 1778, when discharged. (H-110, JJJ-248)

FOWLER, JNO. Private, Capt. Deams' Company, 7th MD Regiment, Dec. 19, 1776. (H-305)

FOWLER, JOSEPH. "Boy" on ship Defence, May 19, 1777 to December 31, 1777. (H-656)

FOWLER, MICHAEL. Oath of Allegiance, 1778, before Hon. Thomas Sollers. (A-2/51)

FOWLER, THOMAS. Non-Juror to Oath of Allegiance, 1778. (A-1/8)

FOX, JAMES. Matross in Capt. Gale's Company of Maryland Artillery, 1779-1780, and General's Guard, 1780. (YYY-1/37) Maryland State Papers No. 4590-96, states: "From a certificate from George P. Keeports that he some time in August, 1776, enlisted James FOX as a Private to serve for three years in the company he commanded in the German Regiment, but not being a German or the son of a German could not serve in that regiment, and at his own request was turned over to a company of matrosses in Baltimore Town, and it also appearing from a certificate given by Nathaniel Smith who commanded the matross company to which he was turned over that to his knowledge he never signed any enlistment with him. The said James FOX having served the time for which he engaged is hereby discharged." Signed by the Maryland Council in Annapolis, May 13, 1780.

FOX, THOMAS. Enlisted in Baltimore County, July 25, 1776. (H-52)

FOY, JOHN. Private in Capt. Lansdale's Company, 4th MD Regiment, from May 10, 1778 to August 16, 1780 when reported missing. (H-111)

FOY, MICHAEL. Oath of Allegiance, 1778, before Hon. William Lux. Supplied buttons to Capt. Keeports, Baltimore County, June 5, 1779. (A-1/8, A-2/68, FFF-226)

FRANCEWAY, JOHN. Marine on ship Defence, January 25, 1777 to Dec. 31, 1777. (H-656)

FRANCHER, BARNETT. Recruit in Baltimore County Militia, April 11, 1780. (H-335)

FRANCIS, WILLIAM. Oath of Allegiance, 1778. (A-1/8)

FRANCISCUS, GEORGE. Baltimore Mechanical Company of Militia, 1776. (CCC-27)

FRANK (FRONK), PETER. Non-Juror to Oath of Allegiance, 1778. (A-1/8)
FRANK (FRONK), PHILIP. Non-Juror to Oath of Allegiance, 1778. (A-1/8)

FRANKEN, JOHN. Private in Capt. Keeports German Regiment; enlisted August 18, 1776. At Philadelphia, September 19, 1776. (H-263)

FRANKFORTER, JOHN. Non-Juror to Oath of Allegiance, 1778. (A-1/8)

FRANKLIN, BENJAMIN. 2nd Lieutenant in Capt. Bosley's Company, Gunpowder Battalion, September 4, 1777. Non-Juror to Oath, 1778. (A-1/8, E-12, NN-88, BBB-362)

FRANKLIN, CHARLES. Oath of Allegiance, 1778, before Hon. Edward Cockey, (A-2/61)

FRANKLIN, CHARLES (OF THOMAS), Non-Juror to Oath of Allegiance, 1778. (A-1/8)

FRANKLIN, JAMES. (Died 1792) Son of Thomas FRANKLIN and Ruth HAMMOND. Took the Oath of Allegiance in 1778 before Hon. James Calhoun. (A-1/8, A-2/38)

FRANKLIN, THOMAS. (1706-1787) Married Ruth HAMMOND. Children: Thomas, Benjamin, Sarah, Elizabeth and James. Oath of Allegiance, 1778, before Hon. Jesse Dorsey. (A-1/8. A-2/63)

FRANKLIN, THOMAS HEATH, JR. (Died 1794) Son of Thomas FRANKLIN and Ruth HAMMOND. Oath of Allegiance, 1778, before Hon. Jesse Dorsey. (A-1/8, A-2/63)

FRANTZ, ABRAHAM. Private, Capt. Graybill's German Regt., July, 1776. (H-265, ZZ-32)

FRAZER, JOHN. Non-Juror to Oath of Allegiance, 1778. (A-1/8)

FRAZIER, DANIEL. Matross, Capt. Brown's MD Artillery; joined November 22, 1777. Was at Valley Forge until June, 1778; at White Plains, July, 1778; at Fort Schuyler in August and September, 1780; not listed in 1781. (UU-229, UU-230)

FRAZIER, SAMUEL. Private, Continental Line; Revolutionary pensioner. Married to Penelope JOHNSON on December 16, 1792 in Harford County, MD. Ordered that he be paid half-pay of a Private soldier, in Harford County, December, 1816. Ordered that Penelope FRAZIER, widow of Samuel, be paid half-pay of a Private during her life, on March 16, 1836. Ordered that Priscilla FRAZIER, executrix of Penelope FRAZIER, late of Baltimore County, deceased, be paid whatever sum may be due the estate of the said testator, at her death December 2, 1848, as a pensioner of this State, January 29, 1850. (C-344, YY-114, YY-22)

FRAZIER, WILLIAM. Took Oath of Allegiance, 1778. Ordered on February 7, 1840, that Henrietta M. Frazier, of the City of Baltimore, widow of William FRAZIER, who was a Lieutenant in the Revolutionary War, or to her order, quarterly, commencing with January 1, 1840, half-pay of a Lieutenant during her life as a further remuneration for the services of her deceased husband. (C-344) As of June 1, 1840, Henrietta FRAZIER, age 79, was residing in household of Alexander YEARLY in Baltimore City's 12th Ward. (P-128)

FRE-LADNER, JOHN. Recruit in Baltimore County, 1780. (H-340)

FREELAND, JOHN. Involved in evaluation of Baltimore County confiscated proprietary reserve lands. (FFF-547)

FREEMAN, EDWARD. Private, Capt. Ewing's Company No. 4 in 1776. (H-13)

FRENCH, JAMES. Private, Capt. Cox's Company in Baltimore, December 19, 1776. (CCC-21)

FRENCH, JAMES ORMSBY. Oath of Allegiance, 1778, before Hon. James Calhoun. (A-2/38)

FRENCH, OTTO (OTHER). Oath of Allegiance, 1778, before Hon. Hercules Courtenay. Could not write; made his mark (" OF "). (A-1/8, A-2/37)

FRENCH, THOMAS. Non-Juror to Oath of Allegiance, 1778. (A-1/8)

FRENCH, WILLIAM. (April 19, 1763 - c1822) Born in Calvert County, MD, and died in Baltimore, MD. Married Annie GIBSON, and their son, Capt. William FRENCH married Lucy Ann CULLY, and their grandson Robert Armistead FRENCH married Mary Elizabeth WOODS. William was a musician (bugler) in Lt.Col. Henry Lee's Legion of Maryland Troops, 1780-1783. "William FRANCH" of Lee's Legion was entitled to 50 acres in western Maryland (lot 1196) for his services. (DDDD-16, JJJ-252, AAA-466, H-587)

FRENSHAM, HENRY. Non-Juror to Oath of Allegiance, 1778. (A-1/8)

FREYMILLER, JACOB. Private, Capt. Graybill's German Regt., July, 1776. (H-265, ZZ-32)

FREYMILLER, JOSEPH. Oath of Allegiance, 1778, before Hon. George Lindenberger. (A-1/8, A-2/53)

FRICK, PETER. Private in Capt. Sheaff's Company, June 16, 1777, reported as having "gone to Virginia for a short time." His daughter, Harriott FRICK married Jacob NORRIS in Baltimore in May, 1803. Non-Juror to Oath of Allegiance in 1778. (A-1/8, W-162, ZZZ-239)

FRIFOGLE, STOPHEL. Non-Juror to Oath of Allegiance, 1778. (A-1/8)

FRISH, FRANCIS. Oath of Allegiance, 1778, before Hon. Peter Shepherd. (A-1/8, A-2/50)

FRIZZEL, ABSOLOM. Oath of Allegiance, 1778, before Hon. Peter Shepherd. (A-2/49)

FRIZZELL, ABRAM. Non-Juror to Oath of Allegiance, 1778. (A-1/8)
FRIZZELL, JOHN. Non-Juror to Oath of Allegiance, 1778. (A-1/8)
FRIZZELL, JACOB. Non-Juror to Oath of Allegiance, 1778. (A-1/8)
FRIZZELL, JOHN JR. Non-Juror to Oath of Allegiance, 1778. (A-1/8)

FROEPATH, WILLIAM. Private, Capt. Howell's Company, December 30, 1775. (G-11)

FROG, AUSTIN. Oath of Allegiance, 1778, before Hon. James Calhoun. (A-1/8, A-2/42)

FROLICK, CHRISTIAN. Oath of Allegiance, 1778, before Hon. William Lux. (A-2/68)

FRONK (FRANK), PETER. Non-Juror to Oath of Allegiance, 1778. (A-1/8)
FRONK (FRANK), PHILIP. Non-Juror to Oath of Allegiance, 1778. (A-1/8)

FUCHS (FUCKS), ROBERT. Non-Juror to Oath of Allegiance, 1778. (A-1/8)

FUGATE, EDWARD. Non-Juror to Oath of Allegiance, 1778. (A-1/8)
FUGATE, MARTIN. Non-Juror to Oath of Allegiance, 1778. (A-1/8)

FUHRMAN, DANIEL. Private, Capt. Keeports German Regiment; enlisted August 10, 1776. At Philadelphia, September 19, 1776. (H-263)

FULFORD, JOHN. (August 14, 1737 - October 20, 1781) Married (1) Hannah VICKERY. (2) Eleanor BODKIN. Captain of a Company of Matrosses in Baltimore Town as of March 1, 1776 (and was commissioned February 9, 1776). Captain in the Maryland Militia in 1777 and subsequently became a Major (stationed in Annapolis and in Baltimore City) in 1778. Major Fulford wrote to the Governor on June 28, 1780, requesting a commission in a new artillery company in Baltimore. Pay certificates 81317 ($80), 82134 ($43.30) and 85433 ($80) were issued to him for his services. (PP-191, FFF-298, FFF-120, B-238, C-344, H-570, JJJ-254)

FULLER, JOHN. Private in Col. Aquila Hall's Baltimore County Regiment, 1776-1777. Recruit in Baltimore County Militia on April 11, 1780. (TTT-13, H-335)

FULLER, NICHOLAS. Oath of Allegiance, 1778. (A-1/8)

FULLER, WILLIAM. Maryland Line defective, January 26, 1781. Resident of Baltimore County. (H-414)

FULLUM, GEORGE. Enlisted in Baltimore Town, July 17, 1776. Private in Capt. Deams Company, 7th Maryland Regiment, December 14, 1776. (H-53, H-305)

FUNDER, PETER. Non-Juror to Oath of Allegiance, 1778. (A-1/8)

FURBER, THOMAS. Clerk in Capt. Howell's Company, December 30, 1775. Corporal in Captain Cox's Company, December 19, 1776. Took Oath of Allegiance, 1778, before Hon. George Lindenberger. Private in Capt. McClellan's Company, September 4, 1780. (G-11, A-1/8, A-2/52, CCC-21, CCC-24)

FURLONG, BENJAMIN. Enlisted in Baltimore county on July 25, 1776. (H-52)

FURNEY, PETER. Private in Capt. Cox's Company as of December 19, 1776. (CCC-22)

FURNIVAL, ALEXANDER. (1752-1807) 2nd Lt., Capt. N. Smith's Independent Company of Artillery, Januayr 14, 1776; subsequently, 1st Lt. and then Captain on Nov. 5, 1776. Also served in Capt. N. Smith's 1st Company of Matrosses at Whetstone Point in Baltimore. Retired in July, 1779. He gave his age as 37 in a deposition in August, 1786, but his death notice stated he died in September, 1807 at "Harmony" in Baltimore County, in his 55th year. Interment was in Baltimore on Sept. 16,

1807. His wife, Elizabeth, died November 3, 1801. (ZZZ-119, J-272, III-192, H-572, B-240, H-563, H-570, TT-82)

FURNY, JOHN. Non-Juror to Oath of Allegiance, 1778. (A-1/8)

FUSHE, C. (or FUSHL, G.) Oath of Allegiance, 1778, before Hon. Isaac Van Bibber. (A-1/8, A-2/34)

FUSS, WILLIAM. Oath of Allegiance, 1778. (A-1/8)

G

GADD, JOHN. Supplied plank to Fort Whetstone Point in Baltimore, Sept. 5, 1776. (FFF-55)

GADD, NATHAN. Oath of Allegiance, 1778, before Hon. James Calhoun. (A-2/65)

GADD, ROBINSON, Oath of Allegiance, 1778, before Hon. James Calhoun. (A-2/65)

GADD, THOMAS. Born 1760. Private, Maryland Line; wounded. Issued Federal Bounty Land Grant of 100 acres (Warrant #11260), May 1, 1792. Also, entitled to 50 acres (lot # 1614) in western Maryland for services as a Private in Maryland State Troops. It was ordered in November, 1811, that he be paid a sum of money in quarterly payments equal to half pay of a Private in the Maryland Line during the Revolutionary War. He also was a Non-Juror to the Oath of Allegiance, 1778. (A-1/8, YY-22, YY-65, C-344, DDDD-17)

GADDES, JAMES. Oath of Allegiance, 1778, before Hon. George Lindenberger. (A-1/8, A-2/53)

GAGGEN (GAGAN), JAMES. Cook on ship Defence, 1776, and Feb. 20 to Dec. 31, 1777. (H-656)

GAGGEN (GAGAN), WILLIAM. Able Seaman on ship Defence on September 19, 1776, and Ordinary Sailor in 1777. (H-606, H-656)

GALBRAITH (GAILBRAITH), WILLIAM. Captain of Company No. 4 in Baltimore Town Battalion in 1776 (Division No. 2 under Col. Buchanan, June 6, 1776). Resigned May 18, 1779. Also took Oath of Allegiance, 1778, before Hon. James Calhoun. (A-1/8, A-2/40, E-13, GG-74 F-311, GGG-401, WW-467, DD-47, BBB-359, BBB-363) His Company had 72 men.

GAIN, THOMAS. Private in Baltimore County Regiment No. 15, circa 1777. (TTT-13)

GAIN, WILLIAM. Non-Juror to Oath of Allegiance, 1778. (A-1/8)

GAINER, HUGH. Enlisted in Baltimore County, August 14, 1776. For his services as a Private in 3rd MD Regiment, he was entitled to 50 acres (lot #210) in western MD. (H-52, DDDD-17)

GAINSFORD, MICHAEL. Maryland Line defective, August, 1780. Resident of Baltimore County. (H-414)

GAITHER, JOSEPH. Clerk on ship Defence, March 18 to June 1, 1777. (H-656)

GALE, ALEXANDER. Non-Juror to Oath of Allegiance, 1778. (A-1/8)

GALE, EDWARD. Captain of an Independent Company of Artillery, September 3, 1779. Died on either October 31, 1779 or November 1, 1779, in Chester, PA. He commanded one of the artillery companies of the Continental Army in Baltimore and was referred to in the Resolves of the Maryland Assembly on May 9, 1780 as the late Captain Gale. He was entitled to 200 acres (lots #2208, 2210, 2211, 2212) in western Maryland for his services. (H-578, TT-82, YYY-1/38, DDDD-2)

GALE, GEORGE DR. Surgeon to Matross Company in Baltimore Town, 1777. (XX-7)

GALE, GEORGE SR. Oath of Allegiance, 1778, before Hon. Geo. Lindenberger. (A-2/53)

GALL, MICHAEL. Involved in evaluation of Baltimore County confiscated proprietary reserve lands in 1782. (FFF-542)

GALLOWAY, AQUILA. Non-Juror to Oath in 1778, but signed in 1781. (A-1/8, QQ-111)

GALLOWAY, JAMES. There were two men by this name: One signed the Oath of Allegiance in 1778 before Hon. George Lindenberger, and one was a Non-Juror to the Oath in 1778, but signed in 1781. (A-1/8, QQ-111, A-2/53)

GALLOWAY, JOHN. Non-Juror to Oath of Allegiance, 1778. (A-1/8)

GALLOWAY, MOSES. (September 2, 1726 - July 10, 1798) Middle River Neck, Baltimore County, MD. Married (1) Mary NICHOLSON; (2) Pamelia (Parnelia) OWINGS. Children: William, born 1751; John Nicholson, born 1753; James, born 1755. Moses married Mary in 1750, and Pamelia in 1782. He served on Baltimore County's Committee of Observation, and although a Non-Juror to the Oath of Allegiance in 1778, he signed in 1781. (A-1/8, QQ-111, JJJ-258, XXX-324)

GALLOWAY, THOMAS. Oath of Allegiance, 1778, before Hon. Jesse Dorsey. (A-1/8, A-2/64)

GALLOWAY, THOMAS JR. Non-Juror to Oath of Allegiance, 1778. (A-1/8)

GALLOWAY, WILLIAM JR. (November 21, 1738 - August 14, 1801) Married on January 6, 1792 to Ann Taylor WALLER (1760-1833). Children: William, born 1794; Priscilla, born 1797. He served as an Ensign in Capt. John Tully Young's Company in Middle River Lower Hundred Militia, May, 1776, and was an Ensign in Gunpowder Battalion on May 25, 1777. He was a Non-Juror to the Oath of Allegiance in 1778, but signed in 1781. His death notice states that "William Galloway, Esq., died 15 August 1801 in Baltimore County, at his seat in Middle River Neck, in his 52nd year." There is an obvious error in his age; he was born in 1738; age 62 at death, not 52. (A-1/8, QQ-111, EE-51, WW-413, WW-444, JJJ-258, XXX-324, ZZZ-121)

GALVIN, DAVID. Born 1751 in Ireland. Private in Col. Ewing's Battalion, enlisting on July 7, 1776 in Baltimore County. Height: 5' 5"; black hair. (H-55)

GAMBLE (GAMMIL), WILLIAM. (1730 - 1791) Wife's name Mary. "William Gammil" took the Oath of Allegiance in 1778 before Hon. George Lindenberger, and a Private "William Gamble" served in Capt. Oldham's Company, 4th MD Regiment, from May, 1778 to May, 1779. (A-1/8, A-2/53, H-115, H-116, JJJ-258)

GANTS, STOFEL. Private in Baltimore County Regiment No. 7, circa 1777. (TTT-13)

GANTZ (GANSE), ADAM. Private in Capt. Cox's Company, December 19, 1776, and in Capt. McClellan's Company, September 4, 1780. Took Oath of Allegiance in 1778 before Hon. George Lindenberger. (CCC-21, CCC-24, A-1/8, A-2/53)

GANTZ, JOHN. Procured wagons and forwarded flour for the Baltimore Town Committee in 1780. (RRR-6)

GARDNER (GARNER), CLEMENT. Marine on ship Defence, May 22 to Dec. 31, 1777. (H-656)

GARDNER, GEORGE. Non-Juror to Oath of Allegiance, 1778. (A-1/8)

GARDNER, JAMES. Non-Juror to Oath of Allegiance, 1778. (A-1/8)

GARDNER (GARDINER), JOHN. (1741 - February 12, 1799, Baltimore County, MD) His wife's name was Priscilla (married 1765) and she probably was a daughter of the William HAMILTON, who died in 1787 and named the wife of John GARDNER as one of his heirs. Children of John GARDNER and Priscilla HAMILTON: Priscilla GARDNER, born 1767, married Joseph BROOKS (1764-1841) in 1786 and their daughter Achsah BROOKS married James MARSDEN in 1819; Rachel GARDNER married Thomas BUCKINGHAM in 1785; William GARDNER; and, Mary GARDNER married a PEACOCK. John GARDNER enlisted in the 1st Maryland Line on June 1, 1778, having previously taken the Oath of Allegiance before Hon. Charles Ridgely of William in 1778. He served in the Battle of Monmouth and the North Jersey Campaign until reported missing on April 5, 1779. He may have been a prisoner, for 16 months later he was discharged on August 16, 1780. (H-112, AAA-1723A, D-8, JJJ-259, A-1/8, A-2/27, XXX-326)

GARDNER (GARDINER), LUKE. Born 1753 in Killarney, Ireland. Occupation: Barber. Height: 5' 9". Enlisted as Private in Capt. Howell's Company, Dec. 30, 1775, and on January 26, 1776 in Capt. N. Smith's 1st Company of Matrosses. (G-11, H-564, H-566, QQQ-2, VV-74)

GARDNER, THOMAS. Served on ship Defence, May 22 to July 7, 1777. (H-656)

GARDNER (GARDINER), WILLIAM. 2nd Lieutenant, Capt. Stinchcomb's Company, Soldiers Delight Battalion, August 29, 1777 - 1778. Oath of Allegiance, 1778, before Hon. Edward Cockey. (A-1/8, A-2/61, E-10, Z-63, BBB-348)

GARDNER, WILLIAM JR. Oath of Allegiance, 1778, before Hon. Edward Cockey. (A-2/61)

GAREY, JOHN. Marine on ship Defence, May 26 to August 15, 1777. (H-656)

GARLETS, HENRY. Non-Juror to Oath of Allegiance, 1778. (A-1/8)

GARRETSON (GARRITSON), CORNELIUS. 2nd Lieutenant, Capt. Howell's Company, Dec. 30, 1775. Oath of Allegiance, 1778, before Hon. George Lindenberger. (G-11, A-2/53)

GARRETSON (GANETSON), JOB. Baltimore County Committee of Inspection, March 13, 1775. Represented Lower Back River Hundred at the Association of Freemen, Aug. 21, 1775. Captain, Back River Lower Hundred Company, Gunpowder Battalion, May, 1776 (63 men) through 1778. Oath of Allegiance, 1778, before Hon. William Lux. Colonel, Gunpowder Battalion, July 24, 1780. He was probably the "Colonel Ganison" who commanded 794 militia troops in Baltimore County on October 13, 1780. Sheriff of Baltimore County from 1780 to 1782. (A-1/8, A-2/68, FFF-191, E-12, WW-413, EE-51, X-111, RR-19, F-303, VV-227, FFF-267, FFF-473, EEEE-1726)

GARRETT, JESSE. Involved in evaluation of Baltimore County confiscated proprietary reserve lands in 1782. (FFF-547)

GARRETT, WILLIAM. Born in 1736 in England. Enlisted July 5, 1776 in Baltimore County as a Private in Col. Ewing's Battalion. Height: 5' 5½"; black hair. (H-57)

GARRISON, CORNELIUS. Private in Capt. Cox's Company, December 19, 1776, and Private in Capt. McClellan's Company, September 4, 1780. (CCC-21, CCC-24)

GARRISON (GARRITSON), DAVID. Born 1745 in West New Jersey. Occupation: Bricklayer. Height: 5' 5". Enlisted January 24, 1776 as Private in Capt. N. Smith's 1st Company of Matrosses. (H-563, H-566, H-568, QQQ-2)

GARRITY, JNO. Private in Capt. Furnival's MD Artillery, November 17, 1777. Matross in Capt. Gale's MD Artillery, 1779-1780. (H-573, YYY-1/39)

GARTNER, GEORGE. Oath of Allegiance, 1778, before Hon. Richard Cromwell. (A-2/46)

GARTNER, MICHAEL. Oath of Allegiance, 1778, before Hon. Richard Cromwell. (A-2/46)

GARTS (GARTZ), CHARLES. Oath of Allegiance, 1778, before Hon. William Lux. In 1777 he served under the Commissary to "deliver the salt, rations, bread and salt to the Marching Militia." (BBB-347, FFF-129, A-1/8, A-2/68) He died August 24, 1811, an old merchant of Baltimore. His son John died July 21, 1816, in his 38th year, and his son Peter, eldest of Charles, died June 17, 1808. (ZZZ-122)

GARVIN, JOHN. Private in Capt. Lansdale's Company, 4th MD Regiment, from November 20, 1777 to November 1, 1780. (H-115)

GARVIS, BENJAMIN. Non-Juror to Oath of Allegiance, 1778. (A-1/8)

GASH (GATCH), BENJAMIN. (1758 - 1814) Married Ruth TAYLOR. Children: Conduce, Nicholas, Ann, Richard, Elizabeth, Benjamin Wesley, Frank, Thomas Custeman (sea captain), and Sarah. Source XXX-327 states he took the Oath of Allegiance, 1778, but Source A-1/8 states he was a Non-Juror.

GASH (GATCH), CONDUCE (CORNJUICE). (1727, at sea - after 1790, Baltimore County, MD) Married in 1750 to Prosceliah BURGIN of Burgundy, France and MD's Eastern Shore. Children: Philip, born 1751 (Reverend); Nicholas; Benjamin, born 1758; Sarah; and Elizabeth. Source XX-327 states he took the Oath of Allegiance, 1778, but Source A-1/8 states he was a Non-Juror.

GASH, FREDERICK. Non-Juror to Oath of Allegiance, 1778. (A-1/8)

GASH, GODFREY. Private in Capt. Ramsey's Company No. 5 in 1776. (H-640)

GASH, NICHOLAS. Non-Juror to Oath of Allegiance, 1778. (A-1/8)

GASH, THOMAS. Oath of Allegiance, 1778, before Hon. James Calhoun. (A-1/8, A-2/42)

GASSAWAY, JOHN. (possibly Brice John Gassaway, 1745-1806, who married Dinah Warfield) Applied for a commission in Baltimore County, May 6, 1776. Was a Lieutenant in 1st Maryland Regiment, 1780. (JJJ-261, FFF-34, FFF-296)

GATCOMB, JOHN. Non-Juror to Oath of Allegiance, 1778. (A-1/8)

GATTING (GATHING), ROBERT. Recruited by Samuel Chester in Baltimore for the 3rd MD Regiment, March 2, 1780. (H-334)

GAVEN, ROGER. Oath of Allegiance, 1778, before Hon. George Lindenberger. (A-2/53)

GAYPOTT, MARTIN. Non-Juror to Oath of Allegiance, 1778. (A-1/8)

GEABHART, MITCHELL. Non-Juror to Oath of Allegiance, 1778. (A-1/8)

GEDDES, DAVID. Member of the Whig Club in 1777. His death notice stated that he was a Captain and an old inhabitant of Fells Point, dying their on Mar. 6, 1807. Members of the different lodges were requested to attend his funeral from his residence at Fleet and Market Streets. (ZZZ-123, CCC-26)

GEDDES, GEORGE. Oath of Allegiance, 1778, before Hon. James Calhoun. (A-2/39)

GEFF, THOMAS. Non-Juror to Oath of Allegiance, 1778. (A-1/9)

GEFFARDE, JAMES. Oath of Allegiance, 1778, before Hon. Charles Ridgely of William. Could not write; made his mark. (A-2/28)

GENT, THOMAS. Non-Juror to Oath of Allegiance, 1778. (A-1/9)

GEORGE, CALEB. Non-Juror to Oath of Allegiance, 1778. (A-1/9)

GEORGE, EDMUND. Non-Juror to Oath in 1778, but signed in 1781. (A-1/9, QQ-111)

GEORGE, PETER. Non-Juror to Oath of Allegiance, 1778.(A-1/9)

GERER, JOHN VALENTINE. Oath of Allegiance, 1778, before Hon. George Lindenberger. (A-1/9, A-2/53)

GERHART, ADAM. Non-Juror to Oath of Allegiance, 1778. (A-1/9)

GERMAN, ABRAHAM. Oath of Allegiance, 1778, before Hon.James Calhoun. (A-2/42)

GERMAN, BENJAMIN. Non-Juror to Oath of Allegiance, 1778. (A-1/9)

GERMAN, JOHN. 1st Lieutenant in Capt. Young's Middle River Lower Hundred Company, Gunpowder Battalion, May, 1776 to at least 1777. Took Oath of Allegiance, 1778, before Hon. George Lindenberger (name spelled "Germain"). (A-2/53, A-1/9, EE-51, WW-413, WW-444)

GEROCK (GERROCK), JOHN. Baltimore County Quartermaster, Nov. 14, 1777. (FFF-128)

GEROCK (GERROCK), SAMUEL. Born 1754 (gave age as 32 in an August, 1786 deposition) 1st Lieutenant in Capt. Keeports German Regiment, July 11, 1776, and 1st Lieut. in Capt. Furnival's MD Artillery; "had the fever" November 17, 1777. Samuel was a prisoner of war in August, 1781, having received a letter from his brother in Baltimore County, John S. Gerrock, expressing affection and family news. He was also a pensioner. (YY-23, FFF-419, H-572, H-262, RR-90, J-272)

GEROCK (GERROCK), SEIGFRED. Oath of Allegiance, 1778, before Hon. James Calhoun. (A-1/9, A-2/41)

GETTER, STOFEL. Non-Juror to Oath in 1778, but signed in 1781. (QQ-111)

GETZER, HENRY. Non-Juror to Oath in 1778, but signed in 1781. (QQ-111)

GHENT, GEORGE. Procured wagons and forwarded flour for the Baltimore Town Committee in 1780. (RRR-6)

GIBBONS, EDWARD. Marine on ship Defence, 1777. (H-656)

GIBBONS, JOHN. Private in Capt. Sheaff's Company, June 16, 1777, "pleads age and infirm." Oath of Allegiance, 1778, before Hon. George Lindenberger. (A-1/9, A-2/53, W-162)

GIBBONS, THOMAS. Non-Juror to Oath of Allegiance, 1778. (A-1/9)

GIBBS, AARON. Non-Juror to Oath of Allegiance, 1778. (A-1/9)

GIBSON, JOSHUA. Marine on ship Defence, May 22 to December 31, 1777. (H-656)

GIBSON, WILLIAM. (c1763, Leonardtown, St. Mary's County, MD - April 29, 1832, in Baltimore) Son of John and Elizabeth GIBSON. Married Sarah MORRIS, daughter of John and Sarah MORRIS, at St. Paul's Church in Baltimore on December 21, 1775. Their children: John GIBSON (1784-1860) married Elizabeth C. GRUNDY; Dr. William GIBSON (born 1788, was a physician in Baltimore, and in 1819 held the chair of surgery at University of Pennsylvania) married Sarah HOLLINGSWORTH and second to Sarah SMITH; James GIBSON (born 1793) married Emily GRUNDY; Edmund GIBSON; Maria GIBSON married a DIDIER; and, Harriet GIBSON married George CROSDALE. William GIBSON was a member of the Court of Admiralty in 1776, and one of those authorized to sign continental money. He took the Oath of Allegiance in Baltimore in 1778, before Honorable James Calhoun. At the time of his death in 1832, he was Clerk of the Baltimore County Court. (D-3, A-1/9, A-2/38)

GIFFARD, JAMES. Able Seaman on ship Defence, September 19, 1776. Took the Oath of Allegiance in 1778. (H-606, A-1/9)

GILBERT (GILBY?), HENRY. Ordinary Sailor on ship Defence, 1776-1777. (H-606, H-656)

GILBERT, JOHN. Non-Juror to Oath of Allegiance, 1778. (A-1/9)

GILBERT, MICHAEL. (April 19, 1741, Baltimore County, MD - November 2, 1829, Franklin County, VA) Married twice; first wife unknown; second wife was Wilmouth DAVIS. Children: Sarah GILBERT (born 1774) married Thomas HOLLAND; James GILBERT (born 1780) married Christian KEEN; Preston GILBERT (born January, 1777) married Fanny LAW; Kemuwl GILBERT married Polly SMITH; Samuel GILBERT married Susanna KEMP; Michael GILBERT married Elizabeth ASHWORTH; Martha GILBERT married Thomas LAW; Wilmouth GILBERT married Joel TAYLOR; Elizabeth GILBERT married Levi DUDLEY; and, Nancy GILBERT married John WINGO. Michael GILBERT took the Oath of Allegiance in 1778 in Pittsylvania County, VA. (XXX-330)

GILBERT (GILBY?), THOMAS. Ordinary Sailor on ship Defence, 1776-77. (H-606, H-656)

GILBERT, WILLIAM. Involved in evaluation of Baltimore County confiscated proprietary reserve lands in 1781. (FFF-542)

GILBERT FAMILY: Many Gilberts born in Baltimore County served in Harford County, MD. See H. Peden's Revolutionary Patriots of Harford County, Maryland, 1775-1783.

GILBERTHORPE, THOMAS. Non-Juror to Oath of Allegiance, 1778. (A-1/9)

GILFORD, JAMES. Ordinary Sailor on ship Defence, 1777. (H-656)

GILHAMPTON, ROBERT. Private, Baltimore County Militia; enlisted Aug. 15, 1776. (H-58)

GILHAMPTON, THOMAS. Oath of Allegiance, 1778, before Hon. James Calhoun. (A-2/42)

GILL, EDWARD DR. (July 2, 1744 - October 7, 1818, Baltimore County, MD) Son of John GILL and Mary ROGERS of St. Thomas' Parish. He married twice: (1) Leah PARRISH or PRICE, in 1770; (2) Mary C. McCLAIN of Newcastle, DE. Edward GILL was a physician and took the Oath of Allegiance in 1778 before Hon. James Calhoun. He had three children by his first wife and two by the second: John Price GILL married Providence KIRBY in 1792; Mary GILL; Mordecai GILL; Edward GILL (1788-1867) married first to Eleanor C. JOHNSON and second Julianna JOHNSON, widow of Benjamin CROMWELL; and, Agnes GILL married Stephen G. GILL. (D-3, JJJ-268, A-1/9, A-2/42)

GILL, EDWARD (OF STEPHEN) Non-Juror to Oath of Allegiance, 1778. (A-1/9)

GILL, JOHN. Born 1758. Enlisted July 7, 1776 in Baltimore County; height" 5' 2½"; light colored hair. Private in Col. Ewing's Battalion, August, 1776. Took Oath of Allegiance in 1778. (A-1/9, H-56)

GILL, JOHN JR. Born February 4, 1737, son of John GILL and Mary ROGERS. Married Sarah GORSUCH on July 20, 1758. Took Oath of Allegiance, 1778, before Honorable Jeremiah

Johnson. John GILL, Jr. was involved in evaluation of Baltimore County confiscated proprietary reserve lands in 1782. (FFF-538, D-8, A-1/9, A-2/33)

GILL, JOHN SR. (October 2, 1709 - January 15, 1797, Baltimore County, MD) Son of Stephen GILL and Elizabeth HAUBERT. Married Mary ROGERS, daughter of Nicholas and Eleanor ROGERS, born 1712, on February 26, 1730. Children: Elizabeth GILL (born 1731); Sarah GILL (1733-1744); Eleanor GILL (born 1735) married John PINDELL in 1757; William GILL (born 1739) married Ruth CROMWELL in 1760; John GILL (born 1737) married Sarah GORSUCH in 1758; Stephen GILL (born 1741) married Cassandra COLE in 1772; Edward GILL (born 1744); Sarah GILL (born 1747); Nicholas GILL (born 1750); Joshua GILL (born 1753); and Elizabeth Rogers GILL (born 1755). John GILL took the Oath of Allegiance in 1778 before Hon. Andrew Buchanan. (D-8, A-1/9, A-2/57)

GILL, JONATHAN. (1757 - 1797) Married Anne FAIRFAX. Matross in Capt. Brown's Artillery Company; joined November 22, 1777. Was at Valley Forge until June, 1778; at White Plains, July, 1778; at Fort Schuyler in August and September, 1780; not listed, 1781. Entitled to 50 acres (lot #359) in western Maryland. (JJJ-268, DDDD-17, UU-228, 230)

GILL, NICHOLAS. (May 25, 1750 - May 7, 1793, Baltimore County, MD) Son of John GILL and Mary ROGERS. Married Elizabeth GILL (born 1762). Their son Stephen GILL (1781-1846) married Phoebe OSBORNE (1774-1864) in 1800, and their son George W. GILL (1808-1876) married Rebecca ENSOR (1809-1842) in 1828. Nicholas GILL was an Ensign in Capt. S. Gill's Baltimore County Militia Company No. 6, Col. E. Cockey's Battalion, in 1776. (PPP-2, RR-99, ZZ-542, AAA-564)

GILL, STEPHEN JR. (January 1, 1741 - November 29, 1811) Son of John GILL, Sr. and Mary ROGERS. He represented North Hundred at the Association of Freemen on August 21, 1775. Served as Captain of Baltimore County Militia Company No. 6 (70 Privates) from 1776 to at least 1778, when he is listed as a Captain in the Gunpowder Upper Battalion as of August 30, 1777. (Source BBB-350 erroneously spelled his name "Stephen Giles.") He was also involved in the evaluation of Baltimore County confiscated proprietary reserve lands in 1782. His death notice stated: "Stephen Gill died 29 November 1811 at his farm in Baltimore County, aged 71 years. Any information regarding his son Benjamin Gill will be thankfully received by his brother William Gill." (ZZZ-125, EEEE-1726, E-12, KK-66, BBB-350, RR-99, ZZ-542, FFF-538) Non-Juror to Oath, 1778, (A-1/9), but Stephen Gill, of John, did take the Oath of Allegiance in 1778 before the Honorable James Calhoun. (A-2/42) There apparently was more than one Stephen Gill at the time.

GILL, WILLIAM. Oath of Allegiance, 1778, before Hon. Edward Cockey. (A-1/9, A-2/61)

GILLARD, THOMAS. Enlisted at Fort Whetstone Point in Baltimore, November 15, 1779, and was discharged January 27, 1780. (h-626)

GILLELAND, GEORGE. Non-Juror to Oath of Allegiance, 1778. (A-1/9)

GILLES (GILLIS), ROBERT. Oath of Allegiance, 1778, before Hon. Robert Simmons. (A-2/58) Born in 1732; came to America from Ireland in 1750; died September 2, 1807. Resided at "Gillis Garden" (now White Hall) in Baltimore County, MD. Buried at Bethel Church with his wife, Elizabeth SHARP. Their children: Thomas GILLIS; John GILLIS; Sarah GILLIS married William MOSSMAN; William GILLIS; Elizabeth GILLIS married Samuel Davidson; Rebecca GILLIS married John NEILSON; William Robert GILLIS; James GILLIS; David GILLIS; Hannah GILLIS (twin of David); Levinah Sharp GILLIS married Dr. James Reed MOORE. (Bethel Church Cemetery Records, Jarrettsville, Maryland, 1986)

GILLIS, JOHN. Non-Juror to Oath of Allegiance, 1778. A9-1/9)

GILLING, THOMAS SR. Oath of Allegiance, 1778. (A-1/9)

GILLIS, THOMAS. Third Mate on ship Defence, June 3, 1777 to Nov. 25, 1777. (H-656)

GILMAN, JOHN. Matross, Capt. Brown;s MD Artillery; joined January 13, 1781. Was at High Hills of the Santee in August, 1781; at Camp Col. Scirvins in January, 1782; and at Bacon's Bridge, S.C. in April, 1782. (UU-230)

GILMOR, ROBERT. Signed patriotic letter to Governor Lee on April 4, 1781, urging the calling up of the militia to protect Baltimore from the British. (S-49)

GILWORD, GEORGE. Private, Extra Regt., Ft. Whetstone Point, Baltimore, 1781. (H-627)

GINIVAN, JNO. Private, Capt. Furnival's MD Artillery, November 17, 1777. Matross, Capt. Gale's MD Artillery, 1779-1780. (H-573, YYY-1/40)

GINIVAN, PATRICK. Oath of Allegiance, 1778, before Hon. James Calhoun. (A-1/9, A-2/39)

GISLER, CHRISTOPHER. Non-Juror to Oath of Allegiance, 1778. (A-1/9)

GIST, DAVID. (April 29, 1753, Baltimore County, MD - August 3, 1820, Mt. Sterling, KY) Son of Thomas GIST and Susannah COCKEY, and grandson of Richard GIST and Zipporah MURRAY. Married March 6, 1785, Rebecca HAMMOND (died 1827), daughter of Rezin HAMMOND, and granddaughter of Major Nathan HAMMOND and Rebecca HAWKINS of Anne Arundel County, MD. Children of David GIST: Rezin Hammond GIST (born 1787); Thomas GIST (born 1789) married Ann WHEELER; and, David Richard GIST (born 1791). (Rezin Hammond GIST married Rachel DAWSON.) David GIST was a 2nd Lieutenant in Captain Murray's Company, Baltimore County, August 30, 1775, through at least 1778 in the Upper Battalion. Moved to Kentucky after the war. (WWW-10, LLL-63, E-14, LL-66, BBB-350, JJJ-270, XXX-333)

GIST, JOHN. (November 22, 1738 - July 16, 1800/1801, Baltimore County, MD) Son of Thomas GIST and Susannah COCKEY. Unmarried. Captain in Nathaniel Fist's Continental Regiment, March 9, 1777 to January 1, 1781, when declared a supernumerary. He also served in Col. Mordecai Gist's 3rd MD Regiment in 1778, and was a member of Colonel Nicholson's Troop of Horse on June 7, 1781. He received pay certificates for his services: 89138 ($116.67); 89139 ($1178.46); 89140 ($40.00); and 89141 ($1000.00). And, 200 acres (lots #2225, 2226, 2227, 2228) in western Maryland. In 1778 he took the Oath of Allegiance before Hon. James Calhoun. He also received 300 acres (warrant #857) in a Federal Bounty Land Grant. Capt. Gist was an Original Member of the Soc. of the Cincinnati of Maryland, currently represented by Walter Bedfore MOORE, III of Charlottesville, VA. (WWW-9, LLL-40, LLL-41, DDDD-2, TT-85, YY-65, BBBB-274, PP-203, H-600, B-249, A-1/9, A-2/41)

GIST, JOSEPH. (September 30, 1738 - January 18, 1830, Baltimore County, MD) Son of William GIST (1711-1794) and Violetta HOWARD. Married Elizabeth ELDER (1740-1814) on August 30, 1759. Children: John Elder GIST (born 1761) married Frances TRIPPE; Cecil GIST (daughter, born 1762, died 1847) married Abraham COLE (1757-1841), and their son Lewis Robert COLE (1796-1882) married Sarah HARRYMAN (1796-1870) in 1816; Joseph GIST (born 1764, died in infancy); Jemima GIST (born 1765); Joshua Howard GIST (born 1768); Cornelius Howard GIST (born 1770) married Clara REINECKER; William GIST and Violetta GIST (twins, born 1772); Elizabeth GIST (born 1774); James GIST (born 1776); and, Owen GIST (born 1778). Joseph GIST was a 1st Lieutenant in Soldiers Delight Company No. 6, May 13, 1776, and Quartermaster Lieutenant on May 25, 1776. He became a Major under Col. Hammond on September 10, 1777, serving through 1781. In 1778 he took the Oath of Allegiance before Hon. Edward Cockey. (A-1/9, A-2/61, SSS-110, BBB-368, E-10, FF-64, WW-443, AAA-1232, AAA-1183, XXX-333)

GIST, JOSHUA. (October 16, 1747, Baltimore County, MD - November 17, 1839, Carroll County, near Westminster, MD) Son of Thomas GIST and Susannah COCKEY. Married in 1772 to Sarah HARVEY and had 11 children (names not known at this time). Joshua was 1st Major in the Baltimore County Militia on February 4, 1777, under Col. Thomas Gist's Upper Battalion. He was also a member of Col. Nicholson's Troop of Horse on June 7, 1781. He moved to what is now Carroll County in 1782 on his "Long Farm" estate. He took the Oath of Allegiance in 1778 before Hon. James Calhoun. Colonel. (LLL-56, LLL-60, WWW-9, VV-114, A-1/9, A-2/38, SSS-110, BBBB-274)

GIST, MORDECAI. (February 22, 1742, Shawan, Baltimore County, MD - September 12, 1792, Charleston, SC; buried at St. Michael's Churchyard) Son of Thomas GIST and Susannah COCKEY, and grandson of Richard GIST and Zipporah MURRAY. He married three times: (1) Cecil CARMEN in 1769, daughter of Charles and Prudence CARMEN of London; she died giving birth; (2) Mary STERRETT on January 23, 1778; and (3) Mrs. Mary McCall CATTELL in 1783 or 1786, widow of Capt. B. Cattell of South Carolina. Children of Mordecai: Cecil Carmen GIST (born 1770, died in infancy); Independence GIST (born January 8, 1779, married Rachel GIST); States GIST (1781-1822, married Branford PACKER); and,

GIST, MORDECAI (continued)

Susanna GIST (1784-1785). Mordecai's son Independence married Rachel GIST (1780-1830), daughter of Col. Joshua GIST, and their son Mordecai GIST (1814-1890) was married to Elizabeth ORNDORFF (1830-1904) in 1848. Mordecai GIST was one of the most prominent men of Maryland during the American Revolution. He served on the Baltimore County Committee of Inspection as of March 13, 1775, and was a Captain of a Baltimore Independent Company in July, 1775. He was elected to serve on the Baltimore County Committee of Observation on September 23, 1775, and also on the Baltimore Town Committee of Correspondence on November 12, 1775. He became 2nd Major in Smallwood's MD Regiment stationed at Baltimore on January 14, 1776. At the Battle of Long Island in August, 1776, he commanded the Maryland Regiment of 400 brave Marylanders who covered the retreat of General Washington. Major Gist was considered so meritorious an officer that he was promoted to Colonel in the 3rd MD Regiment on December 10, 1776. As Colonel, he fought at the Battle of Brandywine, and sought out Tories on Maryland's Eastern Shore. He was promoted to Brigadier General on January 19, 1779, and commanded the defense of Maryland when threatened by a British invasion in 1779. He went to the south and led his 2nd Maryland Regiment at the Battle of Camden (S.C.) in August, 1779. By the act of October 14, 1780, it was resolved that "the thanks of Congress be given to Brigadier Generals Smallwood and Gist and to the officers and soldiers in the Maryland and Delaware lines, the different corps of Artillery, Col. Porterfield's and Major Armstrong's Corps of Light Infantry, and Col. Armand's Cavalry, for the bravery and good conduct displayed in the action of the 16th of August, last, near Camden in the State of South Carolina." Mordecai GIST continued in the service, an active and meritorious officer, and also joined Lafayette in 1781 on his march to Yorktown. He served as Maj. Gen. through November 15, 1783 (see the numerous references in Maryland Archives, Volumes XI, XVI, XVIII and XXI) and became the Vice President of the Maryland Society of the Concinnati on November 21, 1783. He received the following pay certificates: 93616 ($182.59); 93617 ($595.55); 93618 ($46.10); 93619 ($562.45); 93620 ($7375.00); and, Federal Bounty Land Grant #108 for 580 acres, plus 200 acres (lots #2209, 2213, 2262, 2263) in western Maryland. Both the Daughters of the American Revolution and the Sons of the American Revolution in Maryland and South Carolina have erected monumental markers at Gen. Gist's grave. (TT-85, YY-65, B-249, H-20, RR-19, SS-130, RR-47, SS-136, RR-50, PP-203, PP-204, HHH-102, DDDD-2, AAA-510, JJJ-270, LLL-42, LLL-48, LLL-53, WWW-8, XXX-334, and throughout Source H and Source FFF, plus the aforementioned Maryland Archives)

GIST, NATHANIEL. (October 15, 1733, Baltimore City - October 30, 1796, Bourbon, VA) Son of Christopher GIST and Sarah HOWARD; moved to Yadkin River in Virginia, 1745. He apparently returned to Maryland because he was a Colonel in the Maryland Line, as well as the Virginia Line, during the Revolution. He received 500 acres for his services (Federal Bounty Land Grant Warrant #1874). "General Nathaniel Gist died at his seat at Bourbon on 30 October 1796." (ZZZ-126, YY-65, LLL-26, LLL-27)

GIST, RICHARD. (September 2, 1729, Baltimore City - October 7, 1780, Killed at the Battle of King's Mountain) Oldest son of Christopher GIST and Sarah HOWARD. He was a Captin in Col. Nathaniel Gist's MD and VA Regt. Never married. (LLL-25)

GIST, THOMAS JR. (March 30, 1741 - November 22, 1813, Baltimore County, MD) Son of Thomas GIST and Susannah COCKEY. Married Penelope Deye COCKEY, daughter of Joshua, on May 9, 1792; no children. Penelope died in 1803. Thomas was very active during the war. He represented Soldiers Delight Hundred at the Association of Freemen on August 21, 1775, and was elected to the Baltimore County Committee of Observation on September 23, 1775, and served on the Baltimore Committee through at least 1776. In 1777 he raised his own company in Baltimore County and became Colonel of the Soldiers Delight Battalion (Upper Battalion) early in 1777, commanding some 405 Privates. He was also appointed Coroner of Baltimore County on April 21, 1777 and took the Oath of Allegiance before Hon. Robert Simmons in 1778. In 1780 he was in command of 469 troops in Baltimore County, as Battalion Colonel, October 13, 1780. (LLL-61, ZZZ-126, JJJ-270, FFF-102, SSS-110, LL-66, E-14, VV-114, F-303, SS-136, FF-64, RR-47, RR-50, A-1/9, A-2/58, EEEE-1726)

GIST, THOMAS. Oath of Allegiance, 1778, before Hon. John Moale. (A-2/70)

GIST, THOMAS (OF WILLIAM). Oath of Allegiance, 1778, before John Moale. (A-2/70, A-1/9)

GIST, WILLIAM. (November 11, 1711 - November 19, 1794, Baltimore County, MD) Married Violetta HOWARD on October 22, 1737. Children: Joseph GIST (born 1738) married to Elizabeth ELDER; William GIST (born 1742); Anne GIST (born 1747) married James CALHOUN; Thomas GIST (born 1750) married Ruth BOND; Elizabeth GIST (twin to Thomas) married Ramey McGEE; John GIST (born 1752); Violetta GIST (born 1755); and, Ellen GIST (born 1757). William GIST took the Oath of Allegiance in 1778 before Honorable James Calhoun. (A-1/9, A-2/40, JJJ-270, XXX-334)

GITNERE, GEORGE. Private, Capt. N. Smith's MD Artillery, 1776-1777; stationed at Fort Whetstone Point in Baltimore. (VV-74)

GITTINGER, HENRY. Non-Juror to Oath in 1778, but signed in 1781. (A-1/9, QQ-111)

GITTINGER, JOHN. Non-Juror to Oath in 1778, but signed in 1781. (A-1/9, QQ-111)

GITTINGS, JAMES. (April 23, 1735/6 - February 15, 1823, Baltimore County, MD) Son of Thomas GITTINGS and Mary LEE. Married Elizabeth BUCHANAN (1742-1818), daughter of Dr. George BUCHANAN and Eleanor ROGERS. Children: James GITTINGS (1770-1820) married Harriet STERETT in 1793; Archibald GITTINGS married Elizabeth BOSLEY in 1799; Mary GITTINGS married Thomas RINGGOLD in 1795; Elizabeth GITTINGS married Lambert SMITH; Anne GITTINGS married William PATTERSON; Thomas GITTINGS; Richard GITTINGS married Polly STERETT; Eleanor GITTINGS (1766-1796) married James CROXALL in 1788. James GITTINGS served on the Baltimore Committee of Observation, having been elected on September 23, 1775. Prior thereto he had represented Upper Gunpowder Hundred at the Association of Freemen on August 21, 1775. He served on the Baltimore Committee into 1776 and became Captain of 83 men in the Gunpowder Upper Hundred on May 6, 1776. He became 1st Major in the Gunpowder Battalion on May 25, 1776 and Lieutenant Colonel on August 30, 1777 (under Colonel Darby Lux), serving through at least 1778. He took the Oath of Allegiance in 1778 before Hon. William Spear. James GITTINGS was also member of the Maryland Assembly in 1789. (AA-65, E-11, BBB-350, SSS-110, EE-51, WW-413, D-3, FF-64, SS-136, RR-47, RR-50, EEEE-1726, X-111, WW-449, A-1/9, A-2/66)

GITTINGS, THOMAS. (1731 - c1784, Baltimore County, MD) Son of Thomas GITTINGS and Elizabeth REDGRAVE. Married Hannah CLARK, daughter of John. Children: Elizabeth GITTINGS married a WILSON; James GITTINGS; Margaret GITTINGS; Clarke GITTINGS; John GITTINGS; Benjamin GITTINGS; Jesse GITTINGS; Hannah GITTINGS; Mary GITTINGS; Susannah GITTINGS; and Sarah GITTINGS. Thomas took the Oath of Allegiance in 1778 before Hon. James Calhoun. (D-3, A-1/9, A-2/42)

GIVIN, JOHN. Non-Juror to Oath of Allegiance, 1778. (A-1/9)

GLADMAN, JOHN. Non-Juror to Oath of Allegiance, 1778. (A-1/9)

GLADMAN, MICHAEL SR. (c1716 - September 17, 1789, Baltimore County, MD) Wife named Rachel. Children: Rebecca GLADMAN (born 1728/9) married a CROSS; John GLADMAN (born 1732); Michael GLADMAN (born 1736); Thomas GLADMAN (born 1738/9); Rachel GLADMAN (born 1744). Michael took the Oath of Allegiance in 1778 before Hon. John Moale. (JJJ-270, XXX-334, A-1/9, A-2/70)

GLADMAN, MICHAEL JR. (July 3, 1736 - July 25, 1818, Baltimore County, MD) Wife named Barbara. Children: Thomas, Cassandra, Barbara, Rachel and Nancy. Michael enlisted on July 22, 1776 by Richard Talbot. He took the Oath of Allegiance in 1778 before Hon. Edward Cockey. (JJJ-270, XXX-334, A-1/9, A-2/61)

GLANCEY, ABRAHAM. Non-Juror to Oath of Allegiance, 1778. (A-1/9)

GLARE, THOMAS. Oath of Allegiance, 1778, before Hon. James Calhoun. (A-2/41)

GLASGOW, SAMUEL. Private, Capt. Ewing's Company No. 4, enlisted May 20, 1776. (H-11)

GLAVE, THOMAS. (This is probably the Thomas Glare listed above) Oath, 1778. (A-1/9)

GLEESON (GLESSIN, GLISAN), THOMAS. Private in Capt. Furnival's MD Artillery as of November 17, 1777. Matross in Capt. Gale's MD Artillery in 1779; sick in 1780.

Matross, Capt. J.Snith's MD Artillery, 1780, and in Capt. Dorsey's MD Artillery at Camp Col. Scirvins on January 28, 1782. Entitled to 50 acres (lot #266) for his services in Maryland, and 100 acres (Federal Bounty Land Grant Warrant 11284). (YY-66, DDDD-17, H-573, YYY-1/42, YYY-2/18, UU-232, H-579)

GLEVES, THOMAS. Stowed flour for the Baltimore Town Committee in 1780. (RRR-6)

GLOOCH, ELIAS. Private, Baltimore County Regiment No. 15, circa 1777. (TTT-13)

GLORY (GLOREY), WILLIAM. Private, Extra Regiment, at Fort Whetstone Point, Baltimore, 1781. Received Federal Bounty Land Grant 11257, 100 acres, in 1794. (H-626, YY-66)

GLOVER, SAMUEL. Oath of Allegiance, 1778, before Hon. Peter Shepherd. (A-1/9, A-2/49)

GODDARD, MARY KATHERINE. Printer in Baltimore who printed a copy of the Declaration of Independence, January 18, 1777, and printed blank certificates for the Baltimore Town Committee in 1780. Her death notice stated she was "late of the Maryland Journal, died August 12, 1816, aged 80 years." (ZZZ-127, FFF-85, RRR-6)

GODDARD, WILLIAM. Non-Juror to Oath of Allegiance, 1778. (A-1/9)

GODFREY, EDMUND. Private, Capt. Deams Company, 7th MD Regt., January 5, 1776. (H-305)

GODFREY, WILLIAM. Private, Capt. Deams Company, 7th MD Regt., January 16, 1777. (H-305)

GODMAN, WILLIAM. (1754, Frederick County, MD - July 10, 1825) Married Allena GARTEL. Occupation: Labourer. Height: 5' 8". Enlisted January 24, 1776 as Corporal in Capt. N. Smith's 1st Company of Matrosses. Rose to rank of Captain-Lieutenant with service in Maryland and Virginia, according to Source JJJ-272. (H-563, H-565, QQQ-2)

GODSGRACE, WILLIAM. Oath of Allegiance, 1778, before Hon. Hercules Courtenay. (A-2/37)

GOFF, RICHARD. Private, Capt. Lansdale's Company, 4th MD Regiment, from February 2, 1780 until July, 1780, when reported deserted. (H-116)

GOFFER, RICHARD. Recruit in Baltimore County Militia, April 11, 1780. (H-335)

GOGHEGAN (GEOGHEGAN), AMBM. (AMBIN). Oath of Allegiance, 1778, before Hon. Peter Shepherd. (A-1/9, A-2/49)

GOGHEGAN (GEOGHEGAN), BASIL. Enlisted in Baltimore County, July 20, 1776. (H-52)

GOGIN, JOHN. Non-Juror to Oath of Allegiance, 1778. (A-1/9)

GOLD, ROBERT. Non-Juror to Oath of Allegiance, 1778. (A-1/9)

GOLD, WILLIAM. Stowed flour for the Baltimore Town Committee, 1780. (RRR-6)

GOLDEN, WALTER. Private in Revolutionary Army of Baltimore County. Pensioned on November 10, 1814 at $30 per annum, commencing May 11, 1814. (C-347, O-6)

GOLDSBOROUGH, MARK. Matross, Capt. Brown's MD Artillery; joined November 22, 1777. Was at Valley Forge until June, 1778; at White Plains, July, 1778; at Fort Schuyler in August and September, 1780; not listed in 1781. Entitled to 50 acres (lot #289) in western Maryland. (UU-228, UU-230, DDDD-17)

GOLDSBURY, JOHN. Marine on ship Defence, October 23 to November 15, 1777. (H-656)

GOLDSBURY, STEPHEN. Marine on ship Defence, October 23 to November 15, 1777, when he was "discharged, being unfit for duty." (H-656)

GOLDSMITH, THOMAS. Oath of Allegiance, 1778, before Hon. James Calhoun. (A-2/40)

GOLLIER, JOHN. Private, Capt. Norwood's Company, 4th MD Regiment, from April 26, 1778 to August 16, 1780 when reported missing. (H-115)

GOODFELLOW, WILLIAM. Non-Juror to Oath of Allegiance, 1778. (A-1/9)

GOODMAN, JOHN. Non-Juror to Oath of Allegiance, 1778. (A-1/9)

GOODSON, WILLIAM. Private, Col. Ewing's Battalion, enlisted July 7, 1776, in Baltimore County. (H-55)

GOODWIN, JOSEPH. Non-Juror to Oath of Allegiance, 1778. (A-1/9)

GOODWIN, LOYD. Oath of Allegiance, 1778, before Hon. James Calhoun. (A-1/9, A-2/38)

GOODWIN, LYDE DR. (February 4, 1754 - August 19, 1801) Married Abby LEVY and had a son, Robert Morris GOODWIN. A resident of Baltimore Town, Dr. Goodwin was Surgeon to the Baltimore Light Dragoons; appointed April 26, 1781. He served at Yorktown with Col. Nicholas Ruxton Moore's Troop of Light Horse. The roll states that "Dr. Gooding" had two bay gelding horses (seven and nine years old) on June 25, 1781. He continued as Surgeon to the Baltimore Troops through 1783 and became a Judge of the Orphans' Ct. that same year. He was one of the founders of the Medico-Chirurgical Faculty. He was also probably the "L. Goodwin" who signed a letter to Governor Lee in 1781, requesting a defense of Baltimore against British attack. He died in 1801 and is represented in the Society of the Cincinnati of Maryland by Bernard Carter RANDALL of Baltimore, MD. (TT-86, XX-7, S-49, JJJ-275, XXX-339, ZZZ-128, BBBB-313; XX-7 gives a 1725 birth year)

GOODWIN, WILLIAM. Served on Baltimore County Committee of Inspection, March 13, 1775, and represented Westminster Hundred at the Association of Freemen on Aug. 21, 1775. He took the Oath of Allegiance in 1778 before Hon. Robert Simmons, and served on the Baltimore County Committee of Confiscated Property in 1782. (RR-19, EEEE-1726, A-1/9, A-2/58, FFF-468)

GOOSE, ADAM SR. Oath of Allegiance, 1778, before Hon. Peter Shepherd. (A-1/21, A-2/49)

GOOSE, CHRISTOPHER. Oath of Allegiance, 1778, before Hon. P. Shepherd. (A-1/9, A-2/50)

GORANE, JAMES. Oath of Allegiance, 1778. (This is probably "James Govane.") (A-2/60)

GORCHIN, ROBERT. Oath of Allegiance, 1778, before Hon. George Lindenberger. (A-2/53)

GORDON, CHARLES. Oath of Allegiance, 1778, before Hon. John Beale Howard. Could not write; made his mark ("V"). (A-1/9, A-2/29)

GORDON, ENOCH. Baltimore Artillery Company, 1777. Oath of Allegiance, 1778, before Hon. Charles Ridgely of William. (V-368, A-1/9, A-2/28)

GORDON, FRANCIS. Non-Juror to Oath of Allegiance, 1778. (A-1/9)

GORDON, ISAAC MOUNT. Baltimore Artillery Company, 1777. Sergeant of Marines on ship Defence, 1777. (V-368, H-656)

GORDON, JAMES. Born 1756 in Ireland. Enlisted July 7, 1776 as 3rd Corporal in Col. Ewing's Battalion. Height: 5' 9¼"; short light hair. Took Oath of Allegiance in 1778 before Hon. James Calhoun. (H-54, A-1/9, A-2/38)

GORDON, JOHN. Private in Baltimore Artillery Company, October 16, 1775. Private in Capt. Ewing's Company No. 4; enlisted January 29, 1776. Corporal in Capt. Sheaff's Company, June 16, 1777. Took Oath of Allegiance, 1778, before Hon. James Calhoun. (G-8, H-12, W-162, A-1/9, A-2/38) One John GORDON agreed to manufacture knapsacks and haversacks for the military, July 31, 1776. (FFF-46, FFF-48)

GORDON, WILLIAM. Oath of Allegiance, 1778. (A-1/9)

GORE (GORR), ANDREW. Private, Capt. Graybill's German Regiment, 1776. (H-266)

GORE, CHRISTIAN. Member of Col. Nicholson's Troop of Horse, June 7, 1781. (BBBB-274)

GORE, CHRISTOPHER. Non-Juror to Oath of Allegiance, 1778. (A-1/9)

GORE, GEORGE. Non-Juror to Oath of Allegiance, 1778. (A-1/9)

GORE, JACOB. Two men with this name were Non-Juror in 1778. (A-1/9)

GORE, JOHN. Oath of Allegiance, 1778, before Hon. James Calhoun. (A-1/9, A-2/65)

GORE, MICHAEL SR. (1727 - c1793) Married Sibbel CHRISTIAN. Took Oath of Allegiance in 1778 before Hon. Andrew Buchanan. (JJJ-276, A-1/9, A-2/57)

GORE, MICHAEL JR. Oath of Allegiance, 1778, before Hon. Andrew Buchanan. (A-2/57)

GORE, THOMAS. Recruit in Baltimore County Militia, April 11, 1780. (H-335)

GORMAN, ABRAHAM. Private in Baltimore Artillery Company, October 16, 1775. Took Oath of Allegiance, 1778. (G-8, A-1/9)

GORMAN (GORMON), JOHN. Born 1753 in Munster, Ireland. Occupation: Pump Borer. Height: 5' 7¼". Enlisted January 24, 1776 as Private in Capt. N. Smith's 1st Co. of Matrosses. (H-564, H-566, QQQ-2, VV-74)

GORMES, W. Oath of Allegiance, 1778, before Hon. Isaac Van Bibber. (A-2/34)

GORSUCH, BENJAMIN. Private in Col. Aquila Hall's Baltimore County Regiment, 1776-77. Non-Juror to Oath of Allegiance, 1778. Wagonmaster for Baltimore Town Committee in 1780. (TTT-13, A-1/9, RRR-6)

GORSUCH, CHARLES. Oath of Allegiance, 1778, before Hon. Richard Holliday. Private in Capt. J. Cockey's Baltimore County Dragoons at Yorktown, 1781. (A-2/60, MMM-A)

GORSUCH, CHARLES SR. (October 12, 1729 - July 3, 1792) Wife named Sarah. Took Oath of Allegiance, 1778, before Hon. Edward Cockey. Involved in evaluation of Baltimore County confiscated proprietary reserve lands in 1782. (JJJ-277, FFF-543, A-2/62)

GORSUCH, DAVID. Non-Juror to Oath in 1778, he signed in 1781. (A-1/9, QQ-111)

GORSUCH, ELISHA. Non-Juror to Oath of Allegiance, 1778. (A-1/9)

GORSUCH, JOHN. Two men with this name: one took the Oath of Allegiance, 1778, before Hon. Richard Holliday; the other was a Non-Juror. (A-1/9, A-2/60)

GORSUCH, JOHN (OF THOMAS). Oath of Allegiance, 1778, before Hon. John Merryman. Private in Capt. Talbott's Company, May 31, 1779. (F-301, U-90, A-1/9, A-2/45)

GORSUCH, JOHN SR. Non-Juror to Oath of Allegiance, 1778. (A-1/9)
GORSUCH, JOHN JR. Non-Juror to Oath of Allegiance, 1778. (A-1/9)

GORSUCH, LOVELACE. (1715 - 1783) Wife named Sarah; married 1752. Children: Chiscilla GORSUCH married Charles SHIPLEY (died 1815) and their daughter Margaretta SHIPLEY (1804-1860) married Edward JORDAN (1797-1839); Ruth GORSUCH married John WILLIAMS in 1789; and, Prudence GORSUCH married Benjamin WILLIAMS in 1791. Lovelace GORSUCH was a Quaker, but took the Oath of Allegiance in 1778 before Hon. Edward Cockey. He lived on Plantation Friendship and owned property near Baltimore line and Carroll County, MD. (A-1/9, A-2/61, JJJ-277, AAA-1661, XXX-340)

GORSUCH, LOVELACE (OF THOMAS). Oath of Allegiance, 1778, before Hon. Richard Holliday. "Loveless Gorsuch" was an Ensign in Gunpowder Upper Battalion, Capt. Marsh's Company on October 23, 1781. (A-1/9, A-2/60, AAAA-650)

GORSUCH, NATHAN. Oath of Allegiance, 1778, before Hon. Edward Cockey. (A-1/9, A-2/61)

GORSUCH, NORMAN. (Born in Baltimore County and died c1828 in Zanesville, Muskingum Co., Ohio) Son of Charles GORSUCH and Margaret HARVEY. He married Keturah GORSUCH, who was a daughter of another Charles GORSUCH. Children: Charles GORSUCH (1791-c1821) married Rachel BOND in 1817; Nicholas Norman GORSUCH (born 1795); Joshua GORSUCH; Margaret GORSUCH; Achsah GORSUCH; Rachael GORSUCH; and, Aberilla GORSUCH married Jesse BUTLER; and, Mary GORSUCH. Norman GORSUCH took the Oath of Allegiance, 1778, before Hon. Richard Holliday. He was an Ensign in Capt. Kelly's Company, Gunpowder Upper Battalion, October 23, 1781. (D-3, A-1/9, A-2/60, AAAA-1650)

GORSUCH, STEPHEN. Private in Col. Aquila Hall's Baltimore County Regiment, 1776-1777. Non-Juror to Oath of Allegiance in 1778. (TTT-13, A-1/9)

GORSUCH, THOMAS. (April 11, 1752 - November 23, 1814) Married Helen CHAPMAN (1752-1823) on February 27, 1778. Children: Lovelace GORSUCH (born 1778); Margaret GORSUCH (born 1780) married Benjamin BENNETT; Thomas GORSUCH (born 1782) married Jane HAMILTON; Nathan GORSUCH (born 1784) married Anne BUCKINGHAM; Elizabeth GORSUCH (born 1786) married Richard HALL; Sarah GORSUCH (born 1788) married Benj. GORSUCH; Prudence GORSUCH (born 1790) married Larkin BENNETT; Hannah GORSUCH (born 1792) married Obadiah BUCKINGHAM; and, George Washington GORSUCH (born 1795) married Mary GARDNER. Thomas GORSUCH took the Oath of Allegiance, 1778, before Hon. Richard Holliday. Served in Baltimore County Regiment No. 7, circa 1777, as Private, and, Drummer. (A-1/9, A-2/60, XXX-340, TTT-13)

GORSUCH, THOMAS. Oath of Allegiance, 1778, before Hon. Edward Cockey. (A-1/9, A-2/61)

GORSUCH, WILLIAM. Oath of Allegiance, 1778, before Hon. Richard Holliday. (A-2/60)

GOSLIN, SAMUEL. Private, Capt. Ewing's Company No. 4, enlisted May 31, 1776. (H-12)

GOSNELL, BENJAMIN. Non-Juror to Oath of Allegiance, 1778. (A-1/9)

GOSNELL, JOHN. Oath of Allegiance, 1778, before Hon. Peter Shepherd. (A-1/9, A-2/50)

GOSNELL, MORDECAI. Captain in Soldiers Delight Battalion, August 29, 1777 through at
least 1779. Oath of Allegiance, 1778, before Hon. Peter Shepherd. (A-1/9, A-2/50,
F-10, HH-24, Z-63, GGG-422)

GOSNELL, NICHOLAS. Non-Juror to Oath of Allegiance, 1778. (A-1/9)

GOSNELL, PETER. Non-Juror to Oath of Allegiance, 1778. May have been a Private in
Baltimore County Regiment No. 7, circa 1777; part of the muster list is missing;
all that is legible is "_____er Gosnell." (A-1/9, TTT-13)

GOSNELL, WILLIAM. Non-Juror to Oath of Allegiance, 1778. (a-1/9)
GOSNELL, ZEBEDIAH. Non-Juror to Oath of Allegiance, 1778. (A-1/9)

GOTHEROP (GORTHEROP), RICHARD. Non-Juror to Oath of Allegiance, 1778. (A-1/9)
GOTT, ANTHONY. Non-Juror to Oath of Allegiance, 1778. (A-1/9)
GOTT, EDWARD. Non-Juror to Oath of Allegiance, 1778. (A-1/9)
GOTT, RICHARD. Non-Juror to Oath of Allegiance, 1778. (A-1/9) Private in Captain
Talbott's Company, May 31, 1779. (F-301, U-90)
GOTT, RICHARD (OF SAMUEL). Non-Juror to Oath of Allegiance, 1778. (A-1/9)
GOTT, SAMUEL. Two men with this name were Non-Jurors to Oath, 1778. (A-1/9)

GOTT, WILLIAM. Oath of Allegiance, 1778, before Hon. James Calhoun. (A-2/40)

GOUGH, CALEB COURTENAY. Oath of Allegiance, 1778, before Hon. William Lux. (A-2/68)

GOUGH, HARRY DORSEY. (1745 - May, 1808, Perry Hall, Baltimore County, MD) Son of
Thomas GOUGH and Sophia DORSEY; married Prudence CARNAN; had daughter, Sophia.
Non-Juror to Oath of Allegiance, 1778. Served on Baltimore Salt Committee on
October 14, 1779. Was selected to assist in looking after the comfort and sub-
sistence of Count Rochambeau in Baltimore on September 9, 1781. (A-1/9, CCC-18,
HHH-88, ZZZ-130)

GOULD, PAUL. Oath of Allegiance, 1778, before Hon. William Spear. Could not write;
made his mark. (A-1/9, A-2/66)

GOVANE, JAMES. Oath of Allegiance, 1778, before Hon. Richard Holliday. (A-1/9)(Source
A-2/60 misspelled his name "James Gorane") He also supplied wheat to Baltimore County
on July 23, 1779. (FFF-232)

GRABLE, GASPER. Private, Capt. McClellan's Company, Baltimore Town, September 4, 1780.
(CCC-24)

GRACE, PHILIP. Private, Baltimore Artillery Company, October 16, 1775. (G-8)

GRADEY, WILLIAM. Born 1746 in Ireland. Enlisted July 7, 1776 in Baltimore County, in
Col. Ewing's Battalion. Height: 5' 4"; sandy complexion. (H-55)

GRADY, JAMES. Oath of Allegiance, 1778, before Hon. Thomas Sollers. (A-1/9, A-2/51)

GRAHAM, JAMES. Oath of Allegiance, 1778, before Hon. Peter Shepherd. (A-1/9, A-2/49)

GRAHAM, JOHN. Private in 7th MD Regiment, 1778. Died in Baltimore City. Married a
WALLACE. Son, William GRAHAM, married a McKEE, and their daughter, Elizabeth Wallace
GRAHAM married James McCURLEY. (H-211, AAA-150)

GRAHAM, WILLIAM. Private, Capt. Howell's Company, December 30, 1775. Served also in
Baltimore Artillery Company in 1777. Took Oath of Allegiance, 1778, before Hon.
George Lindenberger. Supplied clothing for Capt. George Keeports, October 12, 1779.
(G-11, V-368, A-1/9, A-2/53, FFF-245)

GRANADA, JOHN. Enlisted at Fort Whetstone Point in Baltimore on September 28, 1779 and
deserted December 1, 1779. (H-626)

GRANGER, DANIEL. Non-Juror to Oath of Allegiance, 1778. (A-1/9)

GRANGER, JOHN. Non-Juror to Oath of Allegiance, 1778. (A-1/9)

GRANGER, JOSEPH. Non-Juror to Oath of Allegiance, 1778. (A-1/9)

GRANGER (GRAINGER), THOMAS. Private in Capt. Dorsey's MD Artillery, November 17, 1777. Gunner in Capt. Dorsey's Co. at Valley Forge, June 3, 1778. (H-574, UU-231)

GRANGETT (GRANGED), ANDREW. Private in Capt. Sheaff's Company, June 16, 1777. Took Oath of Allegiance in 1778 before Hon. George Lindenberger. (W-162, A-1/9, A-2/53)

GRANT, ALEXANDER. Oath of Allegiance, 1778, before Hon. George Lindenberger. Private in Capt. McClellan's Company, September 4, 1780. (A-1/9, A-2/53, CCC-24)

GRANT, DANIEL. (1733 - July, 1816, Baltimore, MD) Oath of Allegiance, 1778, before Hon. James Calhoun. (A-1/9, A-2/39, ZZZ-131)

GRANT, FRANCIS. Served in Capt. Nicholas Ruxton Moore's Troops on June 25, 1781; had a six year old sorrell gelding horse. (BBBB-313)

GRANT, JAMES. Born September 18, 1750. Recruited in Baltimore by Samuel Chester for the 3rd MD Regiment on March 2, 1780. (H-334, JJJ-280)

GRANT, JOHN. Carpenter's Mate on ship Defence, January 14 to Dec. 31, 1777. (H-656)

GRANT, MARMADUKE. Born 1755 in Dublin, Ireland. Occupation: Canemaker. Ht: 5' 4". Enlisted January 24, 1776 as Fifer in Capt. N. Smith's 1st Company of Matrosses. (H-563, H-565, QQQ-2)

GRANT, SAMUEL. Private in Capt. Howell's Company, December 30, 1775. (G-11)

GRANT, THOMAS. Non-Juror to Oath of Allegiance, 1778. (A-1/9)

GRANTHAM, WILLIAM. Marine on ship Defence, 1777. (H-656)

GRAVES, JOHN. Non-Juror to Oath of Allegiance, 1778. (A-1/9)

GRAVES, THOMAS. Non-Juror to Oath of Allegiance, 1778. (A-1/9)

GRAVES, WILLIAM. 2nd Lt., Gunpowder Battalion, May 25, 1777. (WW-444)

GRAY, EPHRAIM. Non-Juror to Oath of Allegiance, 1778. (A-1/9)

GRAY, JAMES DR. Baltimore County Committee of Observation, 1776. (XX-7)

GRAY, JOHN. (1721 - January 15, 1817) Wife named Mary. Took Oath of Allegiance in 1778 before Hon. James Calhoun. (JJJ-281, A-1/9, A-2/38)

GRAY, SAMUEL. Recruit in Baltimore County, 1780. Entitled to 50 acres in western Maryland (lot #1945) for services as a Private in State Troops. (DDDD-18, H-340)

GRAY, THOMAS. Two men by this name took the Oath of Allegiance in 1778: one before Hon. George Lindenberger, and one before Hon. Richard Holliday. (A-2/53, A-2/60)

GRAY, WILLIAM. Oath of Allegiance, 1778. (A-1/9)

GRAY, ZACHARIAH. It was ordered in April, 1778, in Baltimore County, that Comfort GRAY, widow of Zachariah GRAY, late a soldier in the Army of the United States, killed in an engagement with the enemy near Brunswick, New Jersey, would receive ten pounds current money. Same order in February, 1779, for fifteen pounds current money. (J-13, J-30)

GRAYBILL, JACOB. Oath of Allegiance, 1778, before Hon. Peter Shepherd. (A-2/49)

GRAYBILL (GREYBILL), PHILIP. Captain of a German Regiment in Baltimore County from July 11, 1776 through April 1, 1782. Also served on the Baltimore Salt Committee on October 14, 1779. Non-Juror to Oath of Allegiance in 1778 (due to military duty, no doubt). (A-1/9, HHH-89, RR-90, FFF-42, FFF-496, ZZ-32)

GREAR, JACOB. Oath of Allegiance, 1778. (A-1/9) Source A-2/27 spelled his name as "Cacob Gwar" which is obviously in error. He could not write; made his mark. The Magistrate was Hon. Charles Ridgely of William. (A-2/27)

GREAR, JACOB JR. Non-Juror to Oath of Allegiance, 1778. (A-1/9)

GREAR, JOHN. Non-Juror to Oath of Allegiance, 1778. (A-1/9)

GREATHOUSE, HARMAN (HERMAN). Oath of Allegiance, 1778, before Hon. Peter Shepherd. (A-1/9, A-2/50)

GREATHOUSE, HARMAN JR. (1762 - 1849) Served as Private in Pennsylvania. Married Mercy BUCHE. (JJJ-282)

GREBLE (GRAYBLE), ANDREW. Private in Capt. Howell's Company, December 30, 1775, and in Capt. Sheaff's Company, June 16, 1777. (G-11, W-162)

GREBLE (GREEBLE), ANDREW JR. Oath of Allegiance, 1778, before Hon. James Calhoun. (A-1/9, A-2/39)

GREBLE, DOROTHY. Mended tents for Capt. George Keeports in Baltimore County, June 26, 1779. (FFF-229)

GREEN, ABEDNEGO. Non-Juror to Oath of Allegiance, 1778. (A-1/9)

GREEN, ABRAHAM. Private, Baltimore County Regiment No. 7, circa 1777. (TTT-13)

GREEN, BENJAMIN. Oath of Allegiance, 1778, before Hon. Thomas Sollers. (A-1/9, A-2/51)

GREEN, CLEMENT. Oath of Allegiance, 1778, before Hon. James Calhoun. (A-1/9, A-2/42)

GREEN, ELISHA. Non-Juror to Oath of Allegiance, 1778. (A-1/9)
GREEN, GEORGE. Non-Juror to Oath of Allegiance, 1778. (A-1/9)
GREEN, GREENBURY. Non-Juror to Oath of Allegiance, 1778. (A-1/9)

GREEN, HENRY. Private, 2nd MD Regiment, entitled to 50 acres (lot #1340) in western Maryland. Married Elizabeth BOERING on June 21, 1778 in Baltimore County (marriage proven through Maryland pension application). Oath of Allegiance, 1778, before Hon. James Calhoun. (YY-114, A-1/9, A-2/42, DDDD-18)

GREEN, ISAAC. Non-Juror to Oath of Allegiance, 1778. (A-1/9)
GREEN, ISAAC (OF GEORGE). Non-Juror to Oath of Allegiance, 1778. (A-1/9)
GREEN, JAMES. Non-Juror to Oath of Allegiance, 1778. (A-1/9)

GREEN, JAMES. Midshipman on ship Defence, June 24 to July 29, 1777. (H-656)

GREEN, JOB. In Baltimore, on August 28, 1776, the Baltimore Committee of Safety gave him a permit to load the vessel Two Brothers for departure to designated ports. He, or perhaps another Job Green, was a Non-Juror to the Oath in 1778. (A-1/10, FFF-54)

GREEN, JOHN. Source A-1/10 states he was a Non-Juror to the Oath of Allegiance, 1778, but Source JJJ-283 shows a John GREEN (1726-1787) who was married to Ann HARDESTY, and rendered patriotic service during the war.

GREEN, JOSEPH. Oath of Allegiance, 1778, before Hon. George Lindenberger. (A-2/53)

GREEN, JOSIAS. Non-Juror to Oath of Allegiance, 1778. (A-1/10)
GREEN, MASHACK. Non-Juror to Oath of Allegiance, 1778. (A-1/10)
GREEN, MOSES. Non-Juror to Oath of Allegiance, 1778. (A-1/10)
GREEN, NATHAN. Non-Juror to Oath of Allegiance, 1778. (A-1/10)
GREEN, NATHANIEL. Non-Juror to Oath of Allegiance, 1778. (A-1/10)
GREEN, NICHOLAS. Non-Juror to Oath of Allegiance, 1778. (A-1/10)

GREEN, PETER. Stored and delivered flour for the Baltimore Town Committee, 1780. (RRR-6)

GREEN, RICHARD. Non-Juror to Oath of Allegiance, 1778. (A-1/10)
GREEN, SAMUEL. Non-Juror to Oath of Allegiance, 1778. (A-1/10)

GREEN, SHADRACH. (c1750 - c1822, Baltimore County, MD) Wife named Rachel. Daughter Temperance GREEN (1783-1835) married John MAYS (1779-1868) in 1807, and their daughter Elizabeth Ann MAYS (1808-1892) married Robert MILLER (1797-1869) in 1830. Shadrach GREEN was an Ensign in Capt. Standiford's Company, Gunpowder Upper Battn., May 6, 1776. Non-Juror to the Oath in 1778. (A-1/10, EE-51, WW-413, AAA-2305)

GREEN, THOMAS. Private, Capt. Howell's Company, December 30, 1775. There were two men with this name who took the Oath of Allegiance in 1778: one before Hon. James Calhoun and one before Hon. Andrew Buchanan. (G-11, A-1/10, A-2/42, A-2/57)

GREEN, VINCENT. (c1750 - after March 11, 1800) Married Elizabeth EAGLESTON. Served as 2nd Lt. in the Patapsco Lower Hundred Company, May 6, 1776 and became a 1st Lt. in the Gunpowder Battalion on March 20, 1779. Took the Oath of Allegiance in 1778 before Hon. Thomas Sollers. (A-1/10, A-2/51, JJJ-284, E-12, JJ-9, EE-51, WW-413)

GREEN, VINCENT. (BLACKSMITH) Oath of Allegiance, 1778, before Hon. Thomas Sollers. (A-2/51)

GREEN, WILLIAM. Private in Baltimore County Militia; enlisted July 18, 1776. He, or perhaps another William Green, was a Non-Juror to the Oath in 1778. (A-1/10, H-58)

GREENFIELD, JAMES. Non-Juror to Oath of Allegiance, 1778. (A-1/10)

GREENFIELD, McCOGY.(?) Drafted into Baltimore County Regiment No. 36, c1777. (TTT-13)

GREENLAND, MOSES. Oath of Allegiance, 1778, before Hon. James Calhoun. (A-1/10, A-2/42)

GREENWAY, JOSEPH. Oath of Allegiance, 1778. (A-1/10)

GREENWELL, JACOB. Non-Juror to Oath of Allegiance, 1778. (A-1/10)

GREENWOOD, THOMAS. 2nd Lt. in Capt. Hurd's Company, Soldiers Delight Battalion, in 1778 to at least 1779. Oath of Allegiance, 1778. (A-1/10, F-10, GGG-422)

GREER, JAMES. Armour's Mate on September 19, 1776, and Marine in 1777 on ship Defence. (H-607, H-656)

GREER, MOSES. Marine on ship Defence, 1777. (H-656)

GREGORY, JOHN. Non-Juror to Oath of Allegiance, 1778. (A-1/10)

GREGORY, ROBERT. Private in Baltimore County Militia, July 5, 1776. Corporal in Capt. Oldham's Company, 4th MD Regiment, December 7, 1776 to December 1, 1779. (H-58, 115)

GREW (GREU), JOHN. Non-Juror to Oath of Allegiance, 1778. (A-1/10)

GREY, JAMES. Enlisted in Baltimore County on July 26, 1776. (H-53)

GREY, JOSEPH. Private in Baltimore County Militia; enlisted July 5, 1776. Private in Capt. S. Smith's Company No. 8, 1st MD Battalion, January 23, 1776. (H-58, H-641)

GRIFFEE, OWEN. Non-Juror to Oath of Allegiance, 1778. (A-1/10)
GRIFFEE, RICHARD. Non-Juror to Oath of Allegiance, 1778. (A-1/10)

GRIFFIN, CHARLES. Enlisted in Baltimore County on July 20, 1776, and took the Oath of Allegiance in 1778 before Hon. Charles Ridgely of William. Married Rebecca KELLY on July 31, 1781 (marriage proven through Maryland pension application). He was a pensioner, born 1756, with service in the Maryland Militia of the Flying Camp during the war. (YY-24, YY-115, H-52, A-1/10, A-2/28)

GRIFFIN, DANIEL. Private, Capt. Deams Company, 7th MD Regiment, Dec. 23, 1776. (H-305)

GRIFFIN, IGNATIUS. Matross, Capt. Brown's MD Artillery; joined November 22, 1777. Was at Valley Forge until June, 1778; at White Plains, July, 1778; at Fort Schuyler in August and September, 1780; not listed in 1781. (UU-228, UU-230)

GRIFFIN, JOHN. Matross, Capt. Gale's MD Artillery, 1779-1780. (YYY-1/44)

GRIFFIN, JOHN JR. Non-Juror to Oath of Allegiance, 1778. (A-1/10)
GRIFFIN, PHILIP. Non-Juror to Oath of Allegiance, 1778. (A-1/10)

GRIFFIN, THOMAS. Enlisted in Baltimore County on July 20, 1776. Oath of Allegiance in 1778 before Hon. Charles Ridgely of William (made his mark).(H-52, A-1/10, A-2/28)

GRIFFIN, THOMAS JR. Oath of Allegiance, 1778, before Hon. Charles Ridgely of William. (A-1/10, A-2/28)

GRIFFIS, ABRAHAM. Non-Juror to Oath of Allegiance, 1778. (A-1/10)

GRIFFIS, EDWARD. Oath of Allegiance, 1778, before Hon. Hercules Courtenay. (A-2/37)

GRIFFIS, HUGH. Oath of Allegiance, 1778, before Hon. Hercules Courtenay. (A-2/37)

GRIFFIS, JOHN. (c1730 - c1812) Married Nancy MOORE. Served as Ensign in the Gunpowder Battalion from August 30, 1777 to at least 1778. Oath of Allegiance, 1778. (JJJ-286, A-1/10, E-11, AA-65, BBB-350)

GRIFFIS, JOHN STONE. Oath of Allegiance, 1778, before Hon. Hercules Courtenay. (A-2/37)

GRIFFIS (GRIFFITH), KINSEY (KENSEY). 2nd Lt. in Gunpowder Battalion from Aug. 30, 1777, to at least 1778. Oath of Allegiance, 1778, before Hon. Hercules Courtenay. (A-2/37, A-1/10, E-11, AA-65, BBB-350)

GRIFFITH,_____GOE (?) Part of his name torn off muster roll. Private in Baltimore County Regiment No. 7, circa 1777. (TTT-13)

GRIFFITH, ABRAHAM. Involved in evaluation of Baltimore County confiscated proprietary reserve lands in 1782. (FFF-553)

GRIFFITH, BENJAMIN. (November 22, 1732 - after 1811) Son of Orlando GRIFFITH and Katherine HOWARD of Anne Arundel County, MD. Married Mary RIGGS on November 12, 1755; son, Orlando GRIFFITH (born 1767) married Sarah McBEE in 1812, and their daughter, Catharine GRIFFITH (1819-1854) married Job R. Hall (1814-1880) in 1836. Benjamin GRIFFITH was very prominent during the Revolutionary War. He served on the Baltimore County Committee of Inspection on March 13, 1775, and represented the East Baltimore Town at the Association of Freemen on August 21, 1775. On Sept. 23, 1775 he was elected to the Baltimore County Committee of Observation, and to the Baltimore Town Committee of Correspondence on November 12, 1775. He was a member of the Sons of Liberty in 1776 and a member of the Baltimore Mechanical Company in that same year. He was also on the Baltimore Committee of Safety on September 2, 1776. From September 2, 1777 through 1779 he was a 1st Lt. in the Baltimore Town Battalion and was its Captain on September 25, 1780. He took the Oath of Allegiance in 1778 before Hon. James Calhoun, and was a magistrate for Baltimore City in 1779 and 1780. He was also Commissary for Baltimore from April 9, 1778 through September 6, 1781. (BBB-359, CCCC-303, A-1/10, A-2/40, E-13, F-311, ZZ-254, SS-130, RR-19, RR-47,WW-136, EEEE-1725, RR-50, CCC-26, AAAA-606, CCC-19, CCC-25, JJJ-286, AAA-1486)

GRIFFITH, EVAN. Pensioner as of June 1, 1840, age 83, residing in household of James Parkinson in Baltimore City, 3rd Ward. (P-128)

GRIFFITH, GEORGE. (c1748 - after 1790) Wife named Mary. Enlisted in Baltimore Town on July 17, 1776. (H-53, JJJ-286)

GRIFFITH, GREENBURY. (December 31, 1727 - March 1, 1809) Married Ruth RIGGS. Enlisted in Baltimore Town on July 17, 1776. Took Oath of Allegiance in 1778 before Honorable Andrew Buchanan. (A-1/10, A-2/57, H-53, JJJ-286)

GRIFFITH, HENRY. 2nd Lt. in Baltimore Town Battalion, September 2, 1777. (E-13)

GRIFFITH, JAMES. There were three men who served with this name: (1) Enlisted in Baltimore Town on July 17, 1776; (2) Enlisted in baltimore County on July 20, 1776; and, (3) Served as 2nd Lt. in Soldiers Delight Battalion, August 29, 1777 to 1778. (E-10, Z-63, BBB-348, H-52, H-53)

GRIFFITH, JAMES SR. Non-Juror to Oath of Allegiance, 1778. (A-1/10)

GRIFFITH, JAMES JR. Oath of Allegiance, 1778, before Hon. Peter Shepherd. (A-2/49)

GRIFFITH, JOHN DR. Authorized by Continental Congress to assign all bills of credit or money for use by Mechanical Volunteers and others, for military purposes, 1776 to 1782. Appointed by Governor as Collector of Blankets for Baltimore City, on April 2, 1777. Took the Oath of Allegiance, 1778, before Hon. James Calhoun. Was in the hospital service in Baltimore in 1781. (XX-7, CCC-18, FFF-97, A-1/10,A-2/39)

GRIFFITH, JOHN. Oath of Allegiance, 1778, before Hon. Peter Shepherd. (A-2/49)

GRIFFITH, JOHNATHAN. Non-Juror to Oath of Allegiance, 1778. (A-1/10)

GRIFFITH, NATHAN. (March 4, 1759 - after 1836) Married Elizabeth ENSOR. Enlisted in Baltimore Town on July 17, 1776 and was a pensioner for service as a Private in the Continental Line-Flying Camp. Took Oath of Allegiance, 1778, before Hon. John Moale.

GRIFFITH, NATHAN (cont.)
(JJJ-287, H-53, A-1/10, A-2/70) Another NATHAN GRIFFITH took the Oath in 1778 before Hon. James Calhoun. He died in October, 1806, in his 67th year. (A-2/39, A-1/10, ZZZ-135)

GRIFFITH, RICHARD. Non-Juror to Oath of Allegiance, 1778. (A-1/10)
GRIFFITH, WILLIAM. Non-Juror to Oath of Allegiance, 1778. (A-1/10)
GRIGGORY, JAMES. Non-Juror to Oath of Allegiance, 1778. (A-1/10)
GRIGSON, JOHN. Non-Juror to Oath of Allegiance, 1778. (A-1/10)

GRIMES, ANTHONY. Born 1750 in England. Enlisted in Baltimore County on July 5, 1776. Height: 5' 5½"; sandy hair; pock marked. Private, Col. Ewing's Battalion. (H-55)

GRIMES, JAMES. There were two Non-Jurors to the Oath in 1778 with this name. (A-1/10)

GRIMES, JOHN. Private in Baltimore County Regiment No. 7, circa 1777. Took the Oath of Allegiance in 1778 before Hon. James Calhoun. (TTT-13, A-1/10, A-2/42)

GRIMES, NICHOLAS. Non-Juror to Oath of Allegiance, 1778. (A-1/10)

GRIMES, REASON. Non-Juror to Oath of Allegiance, 1778. (A-1/10)

GRIMES, TERRENCE. Born 1746 in Ireland. Enlisted in Baltimore County, July 7, 1776. Height: 5' 7½"; black hair; scar on his left cheek. Private in Col. Ewing's Battn. Non-Juror to the Oath of Allegiance in 1778. (H-55, A-1/10)

GRIMES, W. Oath of Allegiance, 1778. (A-1/10)

GRIMES, WILLIAM. Private in Capt. Ewing's Company No. 4; enlisted January 18, 1776. Private in Capt. Furnival's MD Artillery, November 17, 1777. Matross in Captain Dorsey;s MD Artillery at Valley Forge, June 3, 1778, and with Capt. J. Smith's MD Artillery, 1780-1783. Entitled to 50 acres (lot #1023) in western Maryland for his services as an Artillery Matross. (H-12, H-573, UU-231, H-579, YYY-2/19, DDDD-18) Oath of Allegiance in 1778 before Hon. Peter Shepherd. (A-1/10, A-2/49)

GRIMSHAW, EDWARD OR EDMUND. Non-Juror to Oath of Allegiance, 1778. (A-1/10)

GRIMSHEAR, RICHARD. Non-Juror to Oath of Allegiance, 1778. (A-1/10)

GRISLER, CHRISTOPHER. Private in Capt. Sheaff's Company, June 16, 1777. (W-162)

GRIST, GEORGE GILPIN. Oath of Allegiance, 1778, before Hon. George Lindenberger. (A-1/10, A-2/53)

GRIST (GRIEST), ISAAC. (1729 - December 5, 1802, Baltimore, MD) He was a prominent man of the Revolution. He served on the Baltimore County Committee of Inspection on March 13, 1775, and represented Deptford Hundred at the Association of Freemen on August 21, 1775. He was elected to the Baltimore County Committee of Observation on September 23, 1775, and served on the Baltimore Town Committee of Correspondence on November 12, 1775. He served on these Baltimore Committees through 1776 and 1777. He was a member of the Sons of Liberty in 1776, and the Baltimore Mechanical Company. He was appointed Quartermaster of the Militia that was ordered to march to the Head of the Bay and into actual service on August 29, 1777. Took the Oath of Allegiance in 1778 before Hon. William Spear, and served as Commissioner of Baltimore City as of February 2, 1780. He was one of the signers of a letter to the Governor on April 4, 1781, asking him to call up the militia to protect Baltimore against British attack. His death notice misspelled his name: "Major Isaac GRICE died December 5, 1802, at Fells Point in his 73rd year, who served his country during our revolution; funeral from his dwelling in George St.; interment in the Baptist burying ground." And his wife's death notice suffered the same fate: "Mary GREIST, widow of the late Major Isaac GREIST, died November 29, 1814 in her 92nd year." (ZZ-134, EEEE-1726, FFF-267, BBB-347, BBB-348, CCC-25, RR-50, SS-136, RR-47, RR-19, SS-130, CCC-19, S-49, FF-64, A-1/10, A-2/66)

GROOM, MORTON. Private in Capt. J. Cockey's Baltimore County Dragoons at Yorktown, in 1781. (MMM-A)

GROOMBRIDGE, JAMES. Non-Juror to Oath of Allegiance, 1778. (A-1/10)

GROOME, CHARLES. Matross, Capt. Brown's MD Artillery; joined November 22, 1777. **Was** at Valley Forge until June, 1778; at White Plains, July, 1778; at Fort Schuyler **in** August and September, 1780; not listed in 1781. (UU-228, UU-230)

GROOMRINE, ABRAHAM. Non-Juror to Oath of Allegiance, 1778. (A-1/10)

GROOVER, BENJAMIN. Non-Juror to Oath of Allegiance, 1778. (A-1/10)

GROOVER, GEORGE. Non-Juror to Oath of Allegiance, 1778. (A-1/10)

GROOVER, JOSIAS. Non-Juror to Oath of Allegiance, 1778. (A-1/10)

GROOVER, SAMUEL. Non-Juror to Oath of Allegiance, 1778. (A-1/10)

GROOVER (GROVER), WILLIAM. Oath of Allegiance, 1778, before Hon. Jesse Dorsey. (A-1/10, A-2/64)

GROSH (GROSS), MICHAEL. Private in Capt. Keeports German Regiment; enlisted July 15, 1776; at Philadelphia, September 19, 1776; discharged March 4, 1781. Pensioner. Entitled to 50 acres (lot #1528) in western Maryland. (DDDD-18, YY-24, H-212, H-263, H-537) "Michael GROSS" was a Non-Juror to Oath of Allegiance. (A-1/10) Michael GROSH was born in 1750 in Washington or Frederick County, MD, a son of John Conrad GROSH. He married Christiana RAYMER (ROEMER) and died after March 24, 1824. His daughter Charlotte GROSH married Jacob RAMSBURG, Jr. in 1796, and their daughter Lydia Christina RAMSBURG (1802-1884) married Edward Northcroft TRAILL (1798-1876) in 1818. (AAA-1600, JJJ-288)

GROVER, WILLIAM. 2nd Lt. in Capt. Garretson's Company, May 6, 1776. (EE-51, WW-413)

GROVES, EZEKIEL. Non-Juror to Oath of Allegiance, 1778. (A-1/10)

GROVES, JAMES. Private in Col. Ewing's Battalion. Born 1757; enlisted July 7, 1776, in Baltimore County; 5' 4" tall; short curled hair. (H-56)

GROVES, THOMAS. Oath of Allegiance, 1778, before Hon. Isaac Van Bibber. (A-2/34)

GROWLEY, MICHAEL. Private in Capt. Graybill's German Regiment, 1776. (H-266)

GRUNDY, JOHN. Non-Juror to Oath of Allegiance, 1778. (A-1/10)

GUDGEON, SUTTON. 2nd Lt. in Gunpowder Upper Hundred Battalion, May 6, 1776. Took Oath of Allegiance, 1778, before Hon. Jesse Dorsey. (EE-51, WW-413, A-2/63)

GUDGEON, THOMAS. Sergeant in Col. Aquila Hall's Baltimore County Regiment in 1777. (TTT-13)

GULLEHAN, JOHN. Served on ship Defence, March 31 to July 15, 1777. (H-656)

GULLIVER, THOMAS. There were men with this name who were Non-Jurors, 1778. (A-1/10)

GUTHRIE, JAMES. Oath of Allegiance, 1778, before Hon. James Calhoun. (A-2/41)

GUTRIDGE, EDWARD. Non-Juror to Oath in 1778, but signed in 1781. (A-1/10, QQ-112)

GUTRIDGE, JOHN. Non-Juror to Oath of Allegiance in 1778. (A-1/10)

GUTRO, ANN. In Baltimore, on April 12, 1777, she received payment for an account for lodging of Capt. George Cook. (FFF-99)

GUTRO (GUTTERO), EDWARD. Oath of Allegiance, 1778, before Hon. Isaac Van Bibber. (A-1/10, A-2/34)

GUTRO (GOTRO), JOHN. Oath of Allegiance, 1778, before Hon. William Lyx. Could not write; made his mark. (A-1/10, A-2/68)

GUTRO (GUTRELL), JOSEPH. Ensign in Capt. Galbraith's Company No. 4, Baltimore Town Battalion, 1776. 2nd Lt. in Capt. Deaver's Company as of May 19, 1779. Took Oath of Allegiance in 1778 before Hon. William Spear. (A-1/10, A-2/66, GGG-401, WW-467, GG-74, F-311)

GUTRO (GUTTEROUGH), MARTIN. Born 1747 in Nova Scotia. Occupation: Labourer. Enlisted January 27, 1776 as Private in Capt. N. Smith's 1st Company of Matrosses; height: 5' 8 3/4". Reported sick in the barracks, June 29, 1776. Earlier, on December 30, 1775, he was a Private in Capt. Howell's Company. (G-11, H-564, H-566, QQQ-2)

GUYTON, BENJAMIN SR. Non-Juror to Oath of Allegiance, 1778. (A-1/10)

GUYTON, BENJAMIN JR. Non-Juror to Oath of Allegiance, 1778. (A-1/10)

GUYTON, HENRY. Non-Juror to Oath of Allegiance, 1778. (A-1/10)

GUYTON, UNDERWOOD. Non-Juror to Oath of Allegiance, 1778. (A-1/10) He was a son of Benjamin and Catherine GUYTON and died in Baltimore County in 1824. He married on August 12, 1762 to Priscilla JACKSON. Their children: Benjamin; Henry; Isaiah; Abraham; John; Vinson; Ruth GUYTON married John WATKINS in 1796; Elizabeth GUYTON married (1) William STEWART in 1788, and (2) John COLEGATE in 1798; Nelly GUYTON married a COMBS; Sarah; and, Rebecca. (D-3)

GWIN, HUGH. Born 1756 in Ireland. Enlisted July 5, 1776 in Baltimore County, MD as Private in Col. Ewing's Battalion; height: 5' 5"; short curled hair; pitted with smallpox. (H-57)

GWIN, JOHN. (1746 - September 16, 1800) Married Julia STEEL (STULL) on Sept. 20, 1785 in Baltimore County (marriage proven through Maryland pension application). Took Oath of Allegiance in 1778 before Hon. Isaac Van Bibber. "John GWYNN" was a Sergeant in 4th MD Regiment, entitled to 50 acres (lot #1309) in wester Maryland. (DDDD-18, JJJ-291, YY-115, A-1/10. A-2/34)

GWYNN, ROBERT. Lieutenant in Col. Aquila Hall's Baltimore County Regiment, 1776-1777. (TTT-13)

H

HAASS, CHRISTIAN. Oath of Allegiance, 1778, before Hon. William Lux. (A-1/10, A-2/69)

HADLEY, JOHN. Oath of Allegiance, 1778, before Hon. John Beale Howard. Could not write; made his mark ("///"). (A-1/10, A-2/30)

HADON, WILLIAM. Non-Juror to Oath of Allegiance in 1778. (A-1/10)

HAEMMERLIN, GERRET. Oath of Allegiance, 1778. (A-1/10)

HAGAN, CHARLES. Cooper's Mate on ship Defence, Feb. 12 to Dec. 31, 1777. (H-657)

HAGAN, HENRY. Oath of Allegiance, 1778, before Hon. James Calhoun. (A-1/10, A-2/38)

HAGAN, HUGH. Private in Capt. Howell's Company, December 30, 1775. (G-11)

HAGAN, JAMES. Able Seaman on ship Defence, September 19, 1776. (H-606)

HAGER, FRANCIS. Baltimore Mechanical Company of Militia in 1776. (CCC-28)

HAGERTY, JOHN. Oath of Allegiance, 1778, before Hon. Edward Cockey. (A-1/10, A-2/61)

HAGUE, ARTHUR. Non-Juror to Oath of Allegiance, 1778. (A-1/10)

HAHN, JOHN. Oath of Allegiance, 1778, before Hon. George Lindenberger. (A-2/53)

HAHN (HANN), PAUL. Oath of Allegiance, 1778, before Hon. Frederick Decker. Served as Captain in Upper Battalion, November 5, 1781 to at least February 1, 1782. (A-1/10, A-2/31, AAAA-310, CCCC-65)

HAHN, PETER. Private in Capt. Keeports German Regiment; enlisted August 14, 1776. At Philadelphia, September 19, 1776. Oath of Allegiance, 1778, before Hon. Peter Shepherd. (A-1/10, A-2/49, H-263)

HAHN, TOCHIM (YOCHIM). Oath of Allegiance, 1778, before Hon. P. Shepherd. (A-2/49)

HAINS, ANTHONY. Oath of Allegiance, 1778, before Hon. Edward Cockey. (A-1/10, A-2/61)

HAINS, JOHN. Private, Capt. Deams Co., 7th MD Regt., December 27, 1776. (H-305)

HALDER, CHARLES. Non-Juror to Oath of Allegiance, 1778. (A-1/10)

HALE (HAILE), AMON. (June 16, 1759, North Carolina - December 4, 1843, Washington County, Tennessee) While an infant his parents moved to Baltimore County, MD. He entered the service there, volunteering under Capt. Joshua Stevenson on the

HALE (HAILE), AMON (continued)

approach of the British fleet; guarded the magazine and served one year in the militia. He married his wife Mary on September 30, 1785 and they had 10 children: Elizabeth (born September 1, 1786); Martha (born September 11, 1788); Jesse W. (born October 16, 1791); Micajah B. (born March 20, 1793); Robert G. (born November 16, 1795); Mary (born December 14, 1797); Joshua (born February 10, 1800); Prisse (born August 8, 1802); Amon C. (born March 11, 1805); and, Ruth (born November 11, 1807). The original Bible pages were in his pension application. Amon HALE (HAILE) applied for Revolutionary pension while living in Washington County, Tennessee on April 17, 1833. Certificate #7642 was issued May 8, 1833 for $40 per annum from March 4, 1831. His widow applied for pension on December 18, 1843 (aged 79 years). She was born in 1764, and died January 29, 1849, leaving 8 children (2 had pre-deceased her). Her pension was W227. Amon HALE (HAILE) also took the Oath of Allegiance in 1781. He also served with Loyd FORT in Baltimore County, who gave a statement to that effect. (OO-16, DDD-55, DDD-56, YY-25, QQ-112)

HALE (HALES), CHARLES. Oath of Allegiance, 1778, before Hon. Jeremiah Johnson. And he was a Baltimore County recruit in 1780. Unable to write, he made his mark. (A-1/10, A-2/33, H-340)

HALE (HAIL), DAVID. Non-Juror to Oath of Allegiance, 1778. (A-1/10)

HALE (HAILES), GEORGE. Oath of Allegiance 1778, before Hon. James Calhoun. (A-2/40)

HALE, GEORGE JR. Non-Juror to Oath of Allegiance, 1778. (A-1/10)

HALE, HENRY. Private in Capt. Talbott's Company, May 31, 1779. (F-301, U-90) There may have been two men with this name who were Non-Jurors in 1778. (A-1/10)

HALE, JAMES. Private in Capt. J. Cockey's Baltimore County Dragoons at Yorktown in 1781. (MMM-A)

HALE, JOHN. Chief Mate on ship Defence, September 19, 1776. (H-606) Non-Juror to Oath of Allegiance in 1778. (A-1/10)

HALE, JOSEPH. Non-Juror to Oath of Allegiance, 1778. (A-1/10)

HALE (HAILE), MESHACK. Oath of Allegiance, 1778, before Hon. Richard Holliday.(A-1/10, A-2/60)

HALE, NATHAN. Born in 1757 in North Carolina and when a child his father moved to Baltimore County, MD. He enlisted in Baltimore County in Col. Joshua Stevenson's Maryland regiment. "Nathan HALE" was a Sergeant in Capt. Talbott's Company as of May 31, 1779, and "Nathan HAILE" took the Oath of Allegiance in 1778 before Hon. Richard Holliday. His father moved to Tennessee after the Revolution, and they lived first in Washington County, and Nathan moved to Giles County, Tennessee. It appears his brother Richard also served and moved with them. (OO-17, YY-25, U-90, F-301, A-1/10, A-2/60) Also, Nathan HALE applied for pension while living in Giles County, Tennessee in November, 1832, and he subsequently received it. (OO-17, YY-25)

HALE (HAILE), NEIL (NEALE) SR. Oath of Allegiance, 1778, before Hon. Richard Holliday. (A-1/10, A-2/60)

HALE (HAILE), NEIL (NEALE) JR. Oath of Allegiance, 1778, before Hon. Richard Holliday. Was an Ensign in Capt. Talbott's Company, Gunpowder Upper Battalion, Oct. 23, 1781. (A-1/10, A-2/60, AAAA-651)

HALE (HAILE), NICHOLAS. (c1723 - after April 9, 1807) Wife named Ruth. He served as an Ensign in Capt. J. Cockey's Company, February 4, 1777. Also took the Oath of Allegiance in 1778 before Hon. John Merryman. (A-1/10, A-2/45, JJJ-294, VV-114)

HALE (HAILL), NICHOLAS (OF GEORGE). Ensign in Capt. Cockey's Company, February 4, 1777 but listed as just a Private in Capt. talbott's Company on May 31, 1779. He was a Non-Juror to the Oath of Allegiance, 1778. (A-1/10, F-302, U-90, BBB-114)

HALE (HAIL), NICHOLAS. Listed as "Nicholas Hale, Jr." as Private, Capt. Talbott's Co. on May 31, 1779. Listed as "Nicholas Hail, son of Nicholas" when he took the Oath of Allegiance, 1778, before Hon. Jesse Dorsey. (A-2/64, F-302, U-90)

HALE (HAILE), PHILIP. Signed letter to Governor of Maryland in 1781, requesting the calling up of the militia to defend Baltimore against the British. (S-49)

HALE (HAILE), RICHARD. Oath of Allegiance, 1778, before Hon. Edward Cockey. Was an Ensign in Capt. Murray's Company, Upper Battalion, December 4, 1778. Lived in Giles County, Tennessee in 1832, where he stated he served in the Revolution along with Nathan Hale in Baltimore County, MD. (GGG-257, OO-17, A-1/10, A-2/61)

HALE (HAIL), STEPHEN. Non-Juror to Oath of Allegiance, 1778. (A-1/10)

HALE, TULLY (TILLY) OF GEORGE. Non-Juror to Oath of Allegiance, 1778. (A-1/10)

HALE (HAILE) TILLEY OF MATTHEW. Son of Matthew HAILE and Rebecca ROBINSON. Was a farmer in Baltimore County; died c1812. He married Hannah BAILEY (?) who is known to have been the mother of his son Thomas, but it is not known if she was the mother of his other children or if he was married to someone else. He was the father of: John HAILE (born 1773/5, died 1852) married Martha MAYS; Rebecca HAILE; Deborah HAILE married John PARSONHAM c1817; Joshua HAILE married c1807 to Mary PARSONHAM; and, Thomas HAILE. Tilley took the Oath of Allegiance in 1778 before Hon. Robert Simmons. He was also a 1st Lt. in Capt. Gill's Company of the Gunpowder Upper Battalion, October 23, 1781. (AAAA-651, D-9, JJJ-295, A-2/58)

HALE (HAILE), WILLIAM. Oath of Allegiance, 1778, before Hon. William Lux. (A-2/68)

HALEY (HAILEY), THOMAS. Born 1752. Private in Capt. Lansdale's Company, 4th MD Rgt. Enlisted December 6, 1776; prisoner August 22, 1777; rejoined June 23, 1778; and discharged December 6, 1779. Source H-53 states he enlisted in Baltimore Town, July 17, 1776. Was a pensioner. (YY-25, H-124)

HALEY (HAILEY), THOMAS. Private in Capt. Lansdale's Company, 4th MD Regiment. He enlisted February 11, 1777 and was discharged February 11, 1780 "in room of Tobias Wilson discharged December 6, 1779". Source H-53 states he enlisted in Baltimore Town, July 17, 1776. (H-124)

HALEY (HAILEY), WILLIAM. Non-Juror to Oath of Allegiance, 1778. (A-1/10)

HALKINS, JOHN. Non-Juror to Oath of Allegiance, 1778. (A-1/10)

HALL, AQUILA (1727 - 1779) Born in that portion of Baltimore County which became Harford County, MD in 1773. Very active in political and military affairs and the most influential man of his day in Harford County. Among his many activities during the Revolutionary War, he was Colonel of two regiments in 1776-1777, one of which was in Baltimore County. (TTT-13) See H. Peden's Revolutionary Patriots of Harford County, Maryland, 1775-1783, pages 98-99.

HALL, ARON. Oath of Allegiance, 1778, before Hon. James Calhoun. (A-2/65)

HALL, CALEB. Private in Baltimore Artillery Company, October 16, 1775. Member of the Sons of Liberty in 1776, and the Whig Club in 1777. Private in Capt. Sheaff's Company, June 16, 1777. Took the Oath of Allegiance in 1778 before Honorable James Calhoun. (A-1/10, A-2/42, G-8, W-162, CCC-19, CCC-26)

HALL, CHARLES. Oath of Allegiance, 1778, before Hon. George Lindenberger. (A-2/53)

HALL, EDWARD. Non-Juror to Oath of Allegiance, 1778. (A-1/10)

HALL, ELIHU (OF ELISHA). Oath of Allegiance, 1778, before Hon. James Calhoun. (A-2/39)

HALL, ISAAC. Enlisted in Baltimore County, July 20, 1776. (H-52)

HALL, JAMES. Oath of Allegiance, 1778, before Hon. William Spear. (A-2/66, A-1/10)

HALL, JOHN. Captain in Baltimore County Militia, February 4, 1777. Was a Magistrate who took and administered the Oath of Allegiance in 1778. (A-2/36, VV-114)

HALL, JOHN. 3rd Lt. in Capt. R. Dorsey's Company of Matrosses, Baltimore Town, as of September 4, 1777. Oath of Allegiance, 1778. (A-1/10, BBB-362)

HALL, JOHN. Born 1753 in Pennsylvania. Occupation: Bricklayer. Enlisted Jan. 24, 1776 as Sergeant in Capt. N. Smith's 1st Company of Matrosses. Height: 5' 6". Earlier, he served as a Private in the Baltimore Artillery Company, Oct. 16, 1775.

He took the Oath of Allegiance in 1778 before Hon. Isaac Van Bibber. Was, in 1779, a Sergeant stationed at Fort Whetstone Point in Baltimore. (FFF-55, H-563, H-565, QQQ-2, G-8, A-1/10, A-2/34)

HALL, JOHN. 3rd Mate on ship Defence, 1777. (H-657)

HALL, JOHN (OF JOSHUA). Captain of Baltimore County Militia on August 26, 1776, and in command of 48 Privates. 2nd Major, February 4, 1777. (RR-99, VV-114)

HALL, JONATHAN. There were two men with this name who took the Oath of Allegiance in 1778: one before Hon. Thomas Sollers, and one before Hon. James Calhoun. (A-1/10, A-2/51, A-2/65)

HALL, JOSEPH. (c1750 - July, 1824) Wife named Elizabeth. Served as Private in Capt. Deams Company, 7th MD Regiment, February 4, 1777. (H-305, JJJ-296)

HALL, JOSHUA JR. Non-Juror to Oath of Allegiance, 1778. (A-1/10)

HALL, JOSHUA. (c1708 - after April 10, 1782) Married (1) Diana SPICER, and (2) Ann SPICER. Served on Baltimore County Committee of Inspection, March 13, 1775, and Baltimore County Committee of Observation, July 24, 1775. Represented the North Hundred at the Association of Freemen on August 21, 1775. Took the Oath in 1778 before Hon. Benjamin Rogers. (EEEE-1725, RR-19, JJJ-296, EEEE-1726, A-1/10, A-2/32)

HALL, JOSIAS CARVIL. (1746 - 1814) Son of John and Hannah HALL. Married Jane SMITH in 1780. Children: Benedict W. HALL and Hannah E. HALL. Occupation: Doctor. Was Colonel of 2nd MD Battalion of Flying Camp, July to December, 1776. Was Colonel of 4th MD Regiment, December 10, 1776 to retirement January 1, 1781. Also served on Committee of Observation of Harford County, 1774 and asigned the Bush Declaration in 1775. Was Lt.Col. in 9th Infantry, MD Line, 1776, and Colonel thereafter. Was a Delegate to Congress in 1785 and a member of the Governor's Council in 1786. Paid certificates 91991 ($293.00), 91992 ($78.40), 91993 ($4425.00) and 93577 ($81.15). Entitled to 200 acres (lots #3083-3086) in western Maryland, and 500 acres entitlement per Federal Bounty Land Grant #1044. He was a member of the Maryland Society of the Cincinnati. His wife died March 1, 1812, in her 60th year. He died in 1814. (ZZZ-139, XX-8, DDDD-2, YY-67, PP-223, H-122, B-268)

HALL, PHILIP. Oath of Allegiance, 1778, before Hon. James Calhoun. (A-1/10, A-2/38)

HALL, STEPHEN. Mate on ship Defence, 1777. (H-657)

HALL, THOMAS. Recruit in Baltimore County, 1780. (H-340) Non-Juror in 1778. (A-1/10)

HALL, WILLIAM. Private in Col. Aquila Hall's Baltimore County Regiment, 1776-1777. Took Oath of Allegiance, 1778, before Hon. William Lyx. Recruit in Baltimore County Militia, April 11, 1780. (TTT-13, H-335, A-1/10, A-2/68)

HALL, WILLIAM. Served on ship Defence, May 26 to July 28, 1777. (H-657)

HALLER, FRANTZ. Oath of Allegiance, 1778, before Hon. George Lindenberger. (A-2/53)

HALLER, FREDERICK WILLIAM. Private, Capt. Graybill's German Regiment, 1776. (H-265)

HALLOCK, W. Baltimore County Committee of Observation, August 14, 1775. (EEEE-1726)

HALLS, ELISHA. Oath of Allegiance, 1778. (A-1/10)

HALLS, ELISHA (OF ELISHA). Oath of Allegiance, 1778. (A-1/10)

HALMONY, JOHN. Non-Juror to Oath of Allegiance, 1778. (A-1/10)

HALY, OLIVER. Marine on ship Defence, 1777. (H-657)

HAM, THOMAS. Non-Juror to Oath of Allegiance, 1778. (A-1/10)

HAMBLETON, CHARLES. Sergeant of Marines on ship Defence, 1777. (H-657)

HAMBRIGHT (HUMBRIGHT), FREDERICK. Member of Baltimore Mechanical Company of Militia, November 4, 1775. Private, Capt. S. Smith's Company No. 8, 1st MD Battalion, on January 23, 1776. (F-299, H-641)

HAMELTON, JOHN. Oath of Allegiance, 1778, before Hon. James Calhoun. (A-1/10, A-2/38)

HAMERLIN, GERRET. Oath of Allegiance, 1778, before Hon. Geo. Lindenberger. (A-2/53)

HAMILTON, ALEXANDER. Recruit in Baltimore County in 1780. (H-340)

HAMILTON, EDWARD. Oath of Allegiance, 1778, before Hon. James Calhoun. (A-2/40)

HAMILTON, EPHRAIM. Drafted into Baltimore County Regiment 36, circa 1777. (TTT-13)

HAMILTON (HAMELTON), GEORGE. (August 2, 1754 - 1826) Married Agnes COOPER. Was a
1st Corporal in Capt. Ewing's Company No. 4; enlisted May 3, 1776. Was a Private
in Capt. Oldham's Company, 4th MD Regiment, from June 2, 1778 to December, 1779,
when listed as deserted. (H-124, H-11, JJJ-298)

HAMILTON, JAMES. (1747 - March 30, 1835, Baltimore County, MD) Married on July 1,
1796 to Caty BAILEY. Children: James B. (born 1797) married a FAUDON; Thomas
B. (born 1799(married Sarah BUCK; Mary Ann Courtney (born 1802) married Thomas
TUCKER; Eliza (born 1804); Richard (born 1808); and, Sarah (born 1811). James
was a Private, Capt. Deam's Company of MD Militia. (XXX-360) Source A-1/10 says
there were three men with this name who were Non-Jurors to the Oath in 1778.

HAMILTON, JOHN. (1753 - September 4, 1843) Married Susan TODD. Private in Capt.
Howell's Company, December 30, 1775. Enlisted in Baltimore Town on July 17, 1776
and was a member of the Baltimore Artillery Company in 1777. Non-Juror to Oath,
1778. Recruit in Baltimore County, 1780. Source YY025 states he was a Private,
Maryland Line, and pensioner, born 1753. Source JJJ-298 states he was a Sergeant,
born 1753. There may have been more than one John Hamilton, or all of the above
could apply to just one mane. (G-11, V-368, H-53, H-340, A-1/10, YY-25, JJJ-298)

HAMILTON, JOHN. "An old officer of the Revolutionary War and the oldest revenue
officer of the port of Baltimore, died May 16, 1815 (in Baltimore); funeral from
residence of Capt. Samuel Poor, Prince Street, Old Town." (ZZZ-141) Source DDDD-2
states he was Lieutenant entitled to 200 acres (lots #3214-3217), but the death
notice of his wife, Margaret, states he was a Captain, of Fells Point. She died
March 31, 1813 in her 62nd year. (ZZZ-141)

HAMILTON, JOHN AGNEW. Married Margaret SHEPHERD on August 8, 1782 or 1785 by a
minister of the Dutch Reformed Church of Baltimore, MD. He was a 2nd Lieutenant
on January 19, 1781, and a 1st Lieutenant on February 8, 1781, in Capt. Dickenson
Company "in room of Caleb Shields who is always drunk and sometimes crazy." He
was Captain-Lieutenant of a Detachment of Maryland Troops at the Garrison located
at Whetstone Point in Baltimore, in 1781, and commissioned Captain, Maryland Line
on October 25, 1781. Earlier, he was an Ensign in Capt. Lansdale's Company, 4th
MD Regiment, December 10, 1776, and promoted to Lieutenant on February 1, 1778.
He was entitled to 200 acres (lots #2482-2485) in western Maryland, and Federal
Bounty Land Grant 1047 of 300 acres on May 25, 1789. He received certificates of
pay numbers 82790 ($58.56), 82791 ($81.28), 82792 ($400.00), 82793 ($1,000.00),
82794 ($500.00), 82795 ($500.00), and 82796 ($360.00). His death notice states
"Capt. John Agnew Hamilton died in August, 1803, aged upwards of 50 years. He
was an offcer in our struggle for independence." (ZZZ-141) His widow, Margaret,
applied for pension July 15, 1836 (aged 75 years) from Baltimore, MD and received
$480 per annum from March 4, 1831 (W9478; Certificate No. 2, issued July 22, 1836)
However, Source C-350 states that Margaret Hamilton, of Baltimore, on February 25,
1824 became entitled to half-pay of a Captain, as further remuneration for her
husband, Capt. John A. Hamilton's services during the Revolutionary War. (C-350,
DDDD-2, YY-115, R-15, BBBB-61, YY-67, H-123, H-483, H-627, FFF-366, PP-225, and
National Genealogical Society Quarterly, Vol. 37, No. 3 (Sept., 1949), page 90.

HAMILTON, RALPH. Non-Juror to Oath of Allegiance, 1778. (A-1/10)
HAMILTON, SAMUEL. Non-Juror to Oath of Allegiance, 1778. (A-1/10)

HAMILTON, THOMAS. Private in Capt. Ewing's Company No. 4; enlisted May 24, 1776.
(H-11)

HAMILTON, WILLIAM. Non-Juror to Oath of Allegiance, 1778. (A-1/10)
HAMMOND (HAMMON), AMON. Non-Juror to Oath of Allegiance, 1778. (A-1/10)

HAMMOND, BENJAMIN. Two Non-Jurors with this name in 1778. (A-1/10)

HAMMOND, GEORGE. Drafted into Baltimore County Regiment 36, circa 1777. Also served in Capt. Moore's Troops, June 25, 1781 (had an eight year old sorrell gelding horse). (BBBB-313, TTT-13) Two Non-Jurors to Oath in 1778. (A-1/10)

HAMMOND, ISAAC. Captain of Soldiers Delight Company No. 8 on May 13, 1776 (in command of 75 Privates). Became 2nd Major in the Battalion on May 25, 1776. Became Colonel of the Soldiers Delight Battalion on September 10, 1777, and commanded 422 Privates. Continued as Battalion Colonel to at least Oct. 13, 1780, at which time he commanded 515 troops in Baltimore County. He also took the Oath of Allegiance in 1778 before Hon. Edward Cockey. (A-1/11, A-2/61, E-10, BBB-368, SSS-110, F-303, WW-443, FF-64)

HAMMOND, JAMES. Bombardier, Capt. gale's MD Artillery; appointed November 8, 1779. Bombardier, Capt. J. Smith's MD Artillery, 1780, and became Corporal prior to his duty at Camp Col. Scirvins on January 28, 1782 under Capt. Dorsey. Continued in service under Capt. Smith through 1783. Entitled to 50 acres (lot #4108) for his services as an Artillery Corporal. (DDDD-19, H-579, YYY-1/45, YYY-2/21, UU-232) He was a Non-Juror to the Oath of Allegiance in 1778 (A-1/11).

HAMMOND JOHN. (June 8, 1728, Anne Arundel Co., MD - 1780, Baltimore County, MD) He married Ann GAITHER (1729-1783) on May 14, 1748. They had two sons: (1) Vachel HAMMOND (1751-1821) married first to Mary HAMMOND, dughter of Nathaniel HAMMOND and Anne M. WELSH in 1776, and second to Mrs. Priscilla HOUGH in 1814, and by his first wife he had Lloyd, Upton, Elizabeth, Mary, Nathan, Carroll, Rezin, Thomas, John and Julianna, and by his second wife he had Dawson Vachel; (2) John HAMMOND, Jr. (1754-1811) married first to Tomsey SIMPSON, daughter of Francis SIMPSON and Tomasis WORTHINGTON, in 1776, and second to Rachel ROBERTS in 1801. (Indications are that Vachel HAMMOND also had a son Charles HAMMOND (1779-1819) who married in 1803 to Elizabeth HAMMOND.) John HAMMOND took the Oath of Allegiance in Baltimore County before Hon. George Lindenberger in 1778, and also was a member of Frederick County's Committee of Observation. (JJJ-299, AAA-1370A, AAA-1574A, OOO-20, OOO-25)

HAMMOND, JOHN JR. Oath of Allegiance in 1778. (A-1/11)

HAMMOND, LONS (LAWRENCE). Oath of Allegiance, 1778, before Hon. Edward Cockey. (A-2/61)

HAMMOND, MORDECAI. Captain of Soldiers Delight Company No. 7 as of May 13, 1776 (and June 6, 1776), commanding 55 Privates. (FF-64, WW-467) Non-Juror, 1778. (A-1/11)

HAMMOND, REZIN (REASON). (December 25, 1706 - c1783) Married Ann Catherine SELLMAN and/or Rebecca HAWKINS. He was a Justice of Baltimore County, 1774-1775, and was Representative of the Delaware Hundred at the Association of Freemen on August 21, 1775. He took the Oath of Allegiance in 1778 before Hon. Peter Shepherd, and served in the Baltimore County Legislature from 1778 to 1781. (EEEE-1726, JJJ-299, A-1/11, A-2/50)

HAMMOND, RICHARD. Non-Juror to Oath of Allegiance, 1778. (A-1/11)
HAMMOND, THOMAS. Non-Juror to Oath of Allegiance, 1778. (A-1/11)

HAMMOND, WILLIAM. Served on Baltimore Salt Committee of October 14, 1779. Took Oath of Allegiance, 1778. Signed letter to Governor of Maryland requesting the calling up of the militia to defend Baltimore against the British in 1787. (HHH-88, S-49, A-1/11) In fact, there were two Williams Hammond's who took the Oath in 1778: one before Hon. Jeremiah Johnson, and one before Hon. William Lux. (A-2/33, A-2/68)

HAMMOND, WILLIAM (OF BENJAMIN). Non-Juror in 1778, but signed in 1781. (A-1/11, QQ-112)

HANCOCK, JOHN. Oath of Allegiance, 1778, before Hon. Charles Ridgely of William. He could not write; made his mark. (A-1/11, A-2/27)

HANDEFORD, VINCENT. Involved in evaluation of Baltimore County confiscated proprietary reserve lands in 1782. (FFF-547)

HANDLEY, BENJAMIN. Captain of privateer Harlequin awaiting commission in Baltimore, October 11, 1776. (ZZ-336)

HANDLEY, JOHN. Recruit in Baltimore County Militia, April 11, 1780. (H-335)

HANES, MICHAEL. Non-Juror to Oath of Allegiance, 1778. (A-1/11)

HANEY, JOHN. Born 1744. Private, Capt. Ewing's Company No. 4; enlisted Jan. 29, 1776. Private, 2nd MD Regiment; wounded; pensioner. Received 50 acres for his services (lot #303) in western Maryland. (H-12, YY-25, DDDD-19)

HANEY, WILLIAM HEIN. (Died January 1, 1798) Married Susanna HAY at Zion German Lutheran Church in Baltimore on October 10, 1788. Children: John Charles HANEY (born February 28, 1789); Elizabeth HANEY (October 21, 1790 - August 2, 1832) married John Gotlieb KRIEL (1787-1835) on January 28, 1812 in Baltimore, MD and their daughter Caroline KRIEL (1820-1906) married Jacob Henry MEDAIRY (1822-1904) in Baltimore; Mary Ann HANEY (born June 1, 1797); and, Wilhelm HANEY (born Mar. 23, 1798). William HANEy was a Matross and Private in Capt. N. Smith's Maryland Artillery, August 27, 1781; subsequently transferred into the Virginia Line, and was honorably discharged on March 31, 1783. Received 50 acres near Ft. Cumberland in western Maryland (lot #1325). It was ordered on April 1, 1839 to "pay Susanna HANEY, of Baltimore City, widow of William HANEY, a soldier of the Revolutionary War, or to her order, half pay of a Private of the Revolution during her life, quarterly, commencing January 1, 1839, in consideration of her husband's service." (Pension W9049). On June 1, 1840, Susanna HANEY, pensioner, age 83, was residing in the household of Catharine WILLIAMS in Baltimore City, 8th Ward. (P-128, C-351, YY-25, YY-115, DDDD-19, AAA-1829, AAA-1829A)

HANLON (HANDLEN), JOHN. Born 1747 in Dublin, Ireland. Occupation: Taylor. Ht: 5'5". Enlisted February 1, 1776 as Private in Capt. N. Smith's 1st Co. of Matrosses, and served as a Private and Matross in Capt. Dorsey's MD Artillery from Nov. 17, 1777, with duty at Vallye Forge to June 3, 1778. Also, Matross in Capt. Smith's Co. in 1782-1783. (H-565, H-567, QQQ-2, VV-74, UU-231, YYY-2/22)

HANLY, MALCER (WALCHER?). Oath of Allegiance, 1778, before Hon. George Lindenberger. (A-1/11, A-2/53)

HANNAH, ALEXANDER. Oath of Allegiance, 1778, before Hon. James Calhoun.(A-1/11,A-2/41)

HANNAH, HUGH. Non-Juror to Oath of Allegiance, 1778. (A-1/11)
HANNAH, JOHN. Non-Juror to Oath of Allegiance, 1778. (A-1/11)
HANNAH, MICHAEL. Non-Juror to Oath of Allegiance, 1778. (A-1/11)

HANNAH, WILLIAM. Oath of Allegiance, 1778, before Hon. James Calhoun.(A-1/11,A-2/41)

HANNON, ELIAS. Non-Juror to Oath of Allegiance, 1778. (A-1/11)

HANNON, JOHN. Private in Baltimore Artillery Company, October 16, 1775. Took Oath of Allegiance in 1778 before Hon. William Lux. (A-1/11, A-2/68, G-8)

HANNON, PATRICK. Private in Baltimore Artillery Company, October 16, 1775. Was paid for tent poles at the request of Gerrard Hopkins, Baltimore City, April 18, 1777. Private in Capt. Sheaff's Company, June 16, 1777. Took Oath of Allegiance, 1778, before Hon. William Lux. (A-1/11, A-2/68, G-8, FFF-101, W-162)

HANSBURY, THOMAS. Involved in evaluation of Baltimore County confiscated proprietary reserve lands in 1782. (FFF-541)

HANSON, AMON. Baltimore Mechanical Company of Militia, November 4, 1775. Baltimore Artillery Company, 1777. Oath of Allegiance, 1778, before Hon. James Calhoun. Private, Capt. McClellan's Company, September 4, 1780. (A-1/11, A-2/43, CCC-24, F-299, V-368)

HANSON, ANTHONY. Boatswain on ship Defence, September 19, 1776. Non-Juror to Oath of Allegiance, 1778. (H-606, A-1/11)

HANSON, EDWARD. Oath of Allegiance, 1778, before Hon. William Lux. (A-1/11, A-2/68)

HANSON, ISAAC. Private in Baltimore County Militia; enlisted July 19, 1776. Became Quartermaster, 4th MD Regiment, May 1, 1777; Ensign, 4th MD Regiment, Nov. 8, 1779; and Quartermaster Lieutenant, December 15, 1779. (H-58, H-122)

HANSON, JOHN. Midshipman on ship Defence, 1777. (H-657)

HANSON, JONATHAN. Non-Juror to Oath of Allegiance, 1778. (A-1/11)

HANSON, PHILARIS. Non-Juror to Oath of Allegiance, 1778. (A-1/11)

HANSON, ROBERT. There were two Non-Jurors with this name, 1778. (A-1/11)

HARBERT (HARBEST), THOMAS. Marine on ship Defence, Jan. 15 to Nov. 15, 1777. (H-657)

HARBERT, WILLIAM. Sailor on ship Defence, 1777. (H-657)

HARDIN (HARDEN), WILLIAM. Non-Juror to Oath of Allegiance, 1778. Involved in the evaluation of Baltimore County confiscated proprietary reserve lands in 1782. (A-1/11, FFF-543)

HARDING, RICHARD. Served on ship Defence, June 18 to June 29, 1777. (H-657)

HARDING, IGNATIUS. Oath of Allegiance, 1778, before Hon. Andrew Buchanan. (A-2/57)

HARDISTY, FRANCIS. Oath of Allegiance, 1778, before Hon. Charles Ridgely of William. (A-1/11, A-2/28)

HARDISTY, LEMUEL. Non-Juror to Oath of Allegiance, 1778. (A-1/11)

HARDSTONE, JACOB. Private, Capt. Graybill's German Regiment, July 12, 1776. (ZZ-32)

HARDWICK, SOLOMON. Non-Juror to Oath of Allegiance, 1778. (A-1/11)

HARE, JOHN. Non-Juror to Oath of Allegiance, 1778. (A-1/11)

HARE, STOPHEL. Non-Juror to Oath of Allegiance, 1778. (A-1/11)

HARGERODER, HENRY. Private, Capt. Graybill's German Regiment, 1776. (H-266)

HARGIS, STEPHEN. Oath of Allegiance, 1778, before Hon. Jesse Dorsey. (A-1/11,A-2/63)

HARGREAVES, DYONISIUS. Private, Capt. Smith's Co. No. 8, January 11, 1776. (H-18)

HARIEN, JAMES. Oath of Allegiance, 1778, before Hon. James Calhoun. (A-1/11,A-2/41)

HARKER, JOHN. Non-Juror to Oath of Allegiance, 1778. (A-1/11)

HARLAN, ISAAC. Oath of Allegiance, 1778, before Hon. John Merryman. (A-1/11,A-2/35)

HARLEY, PHILIP. Private, Capt. Ramsey's Company No. 5, 1776. (H-640)

HARLING (HARLIN), CORNELIUS. Matross in Capt. Gale's MD Artillery, 1779-1780. Was on command cutting wood in 1779, and on command coaling in 1780. Was also Wagoner. Matross in Capt. Dorsey's MD Artillery at Camp Col. Scirvins on January 28, 1782. Matross in Capt. J. Smith's MD Artillery until reported deceased on June 8, 1783. Entitled to 50 acres (lot #417) in western Maryland. (DDDD-19, UU-232, H-579, YYY-1/46, YYY-2/23)

HARMAN,_____. Non-Juror to Oath of Allegiance, 1778. (A-1/11)

HARMER (HAMER), JOHN. Taylor on ship Defence, October 10 to December 31, 1777. Took the Oath of Allegiance, 1778, before Hon. William Spear. (H-567, A-1/11, A-2/66)

HARPER, DANIEL. Boatswain on ship Defence, June to November 24, 1777. (H-657)

HARPER, JOHN. Non-Juror to Oath of Allegiance, 1778. (A-1/11)

HARPER, JOSEPH. Revolutionary War Pensioner on June 1, 1840, age 94, residing in household of Joseph Harper, Baltimore County, 4th District. (P-127)

HARPER, RICHARD. Non-Juror to Oath of Allegiance, 1778. (A-1/11)

HARRAD, WILLIAM. Non-Juror to Oath of Allegiance, 1778. (A-1/11)

HARRING, JOHN. Private in Capt. Keeports German Regiment; enlisted August 18, 1776. At Philadelphia, September 19, 1776. (H-263)

HARRIAN, JOHN. Oath of Allegiance, 1778, before Hon. Charles Ridgely of William. Could not write; made his mark. (A-2/28)

HARRIS, CHARLES. Oath of Allegiance, 1778, before Hon. William Spear. (A-2/66, A-1/11)

HARRIS, DAVID. (Died November 15, 1809 in Baltimore, MD) Joined the American Army in 1775, and became a 1st Lieutenant in the Baltimore Town Battalion on Sept. 25, 1780, and Captain on November 25, 1780. Was paid for supplying sugar and rum as requested by John Randall in Baltimore City on May 18, 1780. Was also Cashier of the Office of Discount and Deposit for Baltimore City. (FFF-291, UUU-82, ZZZ-145, VV-303, AAAA-223)

HARRIS, JAMES. Oath of Allegiance, 1778, before Hon. James Calhoun. (A-2/65)

HARRIS, JOHN. Fifer in Capt. Ramsey's Company No. 5 in 1776. Non-Juror to Oath of Allegiance in 1778. (H-639, A-1/11)

HARRIS, ROBERT. Served in Capt. Nicholas R. Moore's Troops in 1781. Had a black gelding horse, eight years old. (BBBB-313)

HARRIS, WILLIAM. Private in Capt. Howell's Company, December 30, 1775, and Private in Capt. J. Gist's Company, 3rd MD Regiment in February, 1778. Took the Oath of Allegiance in 1778 before Hon. James Calhoun. (G-11, H-600, A-2/65)

HARRIS, WILLIAM. Armorer on ship Defence, February 15 to April 13, 1777. (H-657)

HARRISON, CHARLES. Baltimore Privateer and Captain of ship Jolly (14 guns), owned by Messennier and J. C. Zollickoffer of Baltimore. Non-Juror to Oath of Allegiance in 1778. (A-1/11, III-206)

HARRISON, GEORGE. Non-Juror to Oath of Allegiance, 1778. (A-1/11)

HARRISON, JOHN. Baltimore Privateer and Captain of brig Viper (14 guns, 50 men), owned by David Stewart of Baltimore. Took the Oath of Allegiance in 1778 before Hon. George Lindenberger. (A-1/11, A-2/53, III-206)

HARRISON, JOSEPH DR. Began his practice in Baltimore in 1779 and became surgeon to the galley Conqueror of the State of Maryland, also in 1779. (XX-8)

HARRISON, KINSEY. Private in Rawlings' Regiment; discharged August 9, 1779. Married Sarah SAFFLE in 1779 in Baltimore County (marriage proven through Maryland pension application). (YY-115, H-124)

HARRISON, THOMAS. (Died 1782) Baltimore Representative to the Association of Freemen on July 26, 1775. Served on the Baltimore County Committee of Observation, having been elected on September 23, 1775, and also on the Baltimore Town Committee of Correspondence on November 12, 1775. Took the Oath of Allegiance in 1778 before Hon. James Calhoun. (BB-2, FF-64, GG-74, SS-130, SS-136, RR-47, RR-50, EEEE-1725, A-1/11, A-2/38)

HARRISON, THOMAS. Recruit in Baltimore County Militia on April 11, 1780. (H-335)

HARRITT, JOHN. Oath of Allegiance, 1778, before Hon. Jesse Dorsey. (A-1/11, A-2/63)

HARRITT, RICHARD. Oath of Allegiance, 1778. (A-1/11)

HARRY, DAVID. Oath of Allegiance, 1778, before Hon. James Calhoun. (A-1/11, A-2/38)

HARRYMAN (HARRIMAN), DAVID. (c1756 - after September 10, 1845) Private in Baltimore County Militia; enlisted August 15, 1776. Non-Juror to Oath of Allegiance, 1778. (A-1/11, H-58, JJJ-305)

HARRYMAN, GEORGE. There were two Non-Jurors to the Oath of 1778 with this name. (A-1/11)

HARRYMAN, JAMES. Non-Juror to Oath of Allegiance in 1778. (A-1/11)

HARRYMAN, JOHN. (Died in Baltimore County in 1784) Married twice: (1) Elizabeth CLARK on May 1, 1752; (2) Ann_____ . Children (probably by his first wife): John; Jemima; Alice married a DAVIS; Sarah married a MATTOCKX. John took the Oath of Allegiance, 1778, before Hon. Thomas Sollers. (A-1/11, A-2/51, D-9)

HARRYMAN (HARRIMAN), JOSIAS. Non-Juror to Oath of Allegiance, 1778. (A-1/11)

HARRYMAN, ROBERT. Non-Juror to Oath of Allegiance, 1778. (A-1/11)

HARRYMAN (HARRIMAN), WILLIAM. Enlisted in Baltimore County on August 14, 1776. Took the Oath of Allegiance, 1778, before Hon. Thomas Sollers. (A-1/11, A-2/51, H-52)

HART, BENJAMIN. Resigned as Ensign in the room of John Cannon, May 18, 1779. (F-310)

HART, HENRY. Oath of Allegiance, 1778, before Hon. Hercules Courtenay. (A-1/11, A-2/37)

HART, JAMES. Oath of Allegiance, 1778, before Hon. James Calhoun. (A-1/11, A-2/40)

HART, JOHN. Appointed Quartermaster to provide for the sick of the Artillery Company in Baltimore Town, September 5, 1777. Took the Oath of Allegiance in 1778 before Hon. Peter Shepherd. (BBB-363, A-1/11, A-2/50)

HART, JOSEPH. Ensign in Capt. Beal Owing's Company of Col. Ed. Cockey's Battalion on December 20, 1776. 2nd Lt. in Capt. Harvey's Company in the Gunpowder Upper Battn. on August 30, 1777 and to at least 1778. Non-Juror to Oath of Allegiance in 1778. (A-1/11, E-12, KK-66, BBB-350, ZZ-541)

HART, LEVIN. Oath of Allegiance, 1778, before Hon. James Calhoun. (A-1/11, A-2/38)

HART, MATTHEW. Private in Capt. McClellan's Company, Baltimore Town, September 4, 1780. (CCC-24)

HART, MICHAEL. Private in Baltimore County Militia; enlisted July 18, 1776. (H-58)

HART, WILLIAM. Private in Capt. Ewing's Company No. 4 in 1776. (H-13)

HARTEGAN, WILLIAM. Oath of Allegiance, 1775, before Hon. Edward Cockey. (A-1/11, A-2/61)

HARTENSTEIN (HARDENSTEIN), JACOB. Private in Capt. Graybill's German Regiment, 1776. (H-265)

HARTFORD, JOHN. Recruit in Baltimore County in 1780. (H-340)

HARTGROVE, JOHN. Non-Juror to Oath of Allegiance, 1778. (A-1/11)

HARTIE, JAMES. Quartermaster on ship Defence in 1777. (H-657)

HARTLEY, JOHN. Oath of Allegiance, 1778. (A-1/11)

HARTLEY, WALTER. Private in Capt. J. Gist's Company, 3rd MD Regiment, February, 1778. (H-600)

HARTLYS, JAMES. Non-Juror to Oath of Allegiance, 1778. (A-1/11)
HARTMAN, FRANCIS. Non-Juror to Oath of Allegiance, 1778. (A-1/11)

HARTMAN, HENRY. (1755/1760 - before 1814) Private in Capt. Graybill's German Regt. in 1776. (H-265, ZZ-32, JJJ-309)

HARTMAN, JACOB. Oath of Allegiance, 1778, before Hon. William Spear. (A-1/11, A-2/67)

HARTMAN (HATMAN), MICHAEL. (Born 1760) Private in Capt. Myers' German regiment. Served three years; discharged July 17, 1779. Entitled to 50 acres (lot #1045) in western Maryland. Also, pensioner. (YY-26, H-271, DDDD-19)

HARTSHAM (HARTSHORN), JOSHUA. Ensign in Capt. Hudson's Company in Soldiers Delight Battalion, May 27, 1779. (E-10, GGG-422)

HARVEY, CHRISTIAN. Oath of Allegiance, 1778, before Hon. James Calhoun. (A-2/41)

HARVEY, CHRISTOPHER. Oath of Allegiance, 1778. (A-1/11)

HARVEY, FRANCIS. Non-Juror to Oath of Allegiance, 1778. (A-1/11)

HARVEY, JOHN. Oath of Allegiance, 1778, before Hon. William Lux. (A-1/11, A-2/68)

HARVEY, NICHOLAS. Oath of Allegiance, 1778, before Hon. Thomas Sollers. Served as 2nd Lieutenant in Gunpowder Upper Battalion, October 23, 1781. (A-2/51, AAAA-650)

HARVEY, NICHOLAS NORMAN. Oath of Allegiance, 1778. (A-1/11)

HARVEY, ROBERT. 2nd Corporal in Capt. Ewing's Company No. 4; enlisted May 3, 1776. (H-11)

HARVEY, THOMAS. Oath of Allegiance, 1778, before Hon. William Lux. (A-1/11, A-2/68)

HARVEY, WILLIAM. 2nd Lieutenant in Capt. E. Cockey's Company No. 2, Gunpowder Upper Battalion, August 26, 1776. 1st Lieutenant, December 20, 1776. Captain, August 30, 1777. Took the Oath of Allegiance, 1778, before Hon. Edward Cockey. (KK-66, E-12, BBB-350, RR-98, PPP-2, ZZ-541, A-1/11, A-2/61)

HASE, ABRAHAM. Non-Juror in 1778, but took the Oath in 1781. (QQ-112)

HASE, JOSEPH. Non-Juror to Oath of Allegiance, 1778. (A-1/11)

HASE (HOSE), MICHAEL. Private in Baltimore County Regiment No. 7, c1777. (TTT-13)

HASKINS, WILLIAM. Non-Juror to Oath of Allegiance, 1778. (A-1/11)

HASTY, JAMES. Quartermaster on ship Defence, September 19, 1776; disrated Oct. 23, 1776. (H-606)

HATTON, AQUILLA. Non-Juror in 1778, but took Oath in 1781. (A-1/11, QQ-112)

HATTON, CHANEY. Non-Juror to Oath of Allegiance, 1778. (A-1/11)
HATTON, HENRY. Non-Juror to Oath of Allegiance, 1778. (A-1/11)

HATTON, JAMES. Sergeant in Capt. Dorsey's Company, MD Artillery, at Camp Colonel Scirvins on January 28, 1782. (UU-232)

HATTON, JOHN. Non-Juror to Oath of Allegiance, 1778. (A-1/11)

HAUPT, ELIZABETH. Revolutionary War Pensioner on June 1, 1840, age 81, residing in Baltimore City, 12th Ward. (P-128)

HAUSSER, WILLIAM. Oath of Allegiance, 1778. (A-1/11)

HAVARD, WILLIAM. Seaman on ship Defence, March 6 to December 31, 1777. (H-657)

HAVERS, JOHN. Cooper's Crew on ship Defence, June 19 to Dec. 31, 1777. (H-657)

HAVEY, DANIEL. Matross in Capt. Brown's MD Artillery; joined November 22, 1777. Was at Valley Forge until June, 1778; at White Plains, July, 1778; at Fort Schuyler in August and September, 1780; served through 1782. (UU-228, UU-230)

HAWKE, MICHAEL. Gunner in Capt. Brown's MD Artillery; joined November 22, 1777. Was at valley Forge until June, 1778; at White Plains, July, 1778; at Fort Schuyler in August and September, 1780; at High Hills of the Santee, August 1, 1781, when he became a Corporal; at Camp Col. Scirvins in January, 1782; and, at Bacon's Bridge, S.C. in April, 1782. (UU-228, UU-229, UU-230)

HAWKINS, _____. (Part of name torn off list) Private in Baltimore County Regt. No. 15, circa 1777. (TTT-13)

HAWKINS, AARON. Non-Juror to Oath of Allegiance, 1778. (A-1/11)

HAWKINS, EDWARD. Recruit in Baltimore County in 1780. (H-340)

HAWKINS, JAMES. Yeoman on ship Defence, September 19, 1776; Midshipman, March 1 to August 15, 1777; Ship's Tender, August 15 to November 15, 1777; Skipper, November 15 to November 24, 1777. Took Oath of Allegiance in 1778 before Hon. William Spear. (A-1/11, A-2/66, H-606, H-657)

HAWKINS, JOHN. Baltimore Mechanical Company of Militia, 1776. Baltimore Artillery Company, 1777. Oath of Allegiance, 1778, before Hon. Peter Shepherd. (A-1/11, A-2/49, V-368, CCC-27)

HAWKINS, JOHN. Private in Col. Aquila Hall's Baltimore County regiment in 1777. (TTT-13)

HAWKINS, JOSEPH. Oath of Allegiance, 1778, before Hon. Peter Shepherd. (A-2/50)

HAWKINS, PHILIP. (Born 1756) Private in Capt. Smith's Company No. 8; enlisted on January 26, 1776. Revolutionary War pensioner (S41612). (YY-26, H-18)

HAWKINS, REZIN. Non-Juror to Oath of Allegiance, 1778. (A-1/11)

HAWKINS, THOMAS. Private in Col. Aquila Hall's Baltimore County Regiment in 1777. Oath of Allegiance, 1778, before Hon. Jesse Dorsey. (TTT-13, A-1/11, A-2/64)

HAWKINS, WILLIAM. Oath of Allegiance, 1778, before Hon. William Spear. (A-1/11, A-2/66)

HAWN (HOWN), JOSEPH. Private in Baltimore County Militia; enlisted Aug. 15, 1776.(H-58)

HAWN, MICHAEL. Private in Capt. Stricker's 9th Company of Light Infantry, April 10, 1776. Non-Juror to Oath of Allegiance in 1778. (H-20, A-1/11)

HAWN (HAUN), PETER. Paid in Baltimore County on January 18, 1780, by the Collector of Tax for recruiting expenses. (FFF-262)

HAY, JAMES. 1st Lieutenant in Capt. Dickenson's Company, Baltimore Militia, commission acknowledged May 27, 1781. (FFF-398, AAA-452)

HAY, JOHN. Oath of Allegiance, 1778, before Hon. William Lux. (A-1/11, A-2/68)

HAY, PATRICK. Private in Capt. Deams Co., 7th MD Regt., December 10, 1776. (H-304)

HAYES, JAMES. Oath of Allegiance, 1778, before Hon. James Calhoun. Involved in the evaluation of Baltimore County confiscated proprietary reserve lands in 1782. (A-1/11, A-2/39, FFF-548)

HAYES, JAMES JR. Oath of Allegiance, 1778, before Hon. James Calhoun. (A-1/11, A-2/39)

HAYES, WILLIAM. Oath of Allegiance, 1778, before Hon. James Calhoun. (A-1.11, A-2/42)

HAYMAN, JOHN. 2nd Lieutenant in Capt. Wells' Company No. 6, Baltimore Town Artillery, June 6, 1776. Unable to serve in 1777 "laying sick at the time." Took the Oath of Allegiance in 1778 before Hon. James Calhoun. (GG-74, WW-467, MM-89, A-1/11, A-2/41)

HAYNES, ANTHONY. Non-Juror to Oath of Allegiance, 1778. (A-1/11)

HAYNON, THOMAS. Private in Capt. Ewing's Company No. 4; enlisted May 27, 1776. (H-11)

HAYS, ABRAHAM. Non-Juror to Oath of Allegiance, 1778. (A-1/11)

HAYS, JAMES. Non-Juror to Oath of Allegiance, 1778. Maryland Line defective on November 3, 1781; resident of Baltimore County. (A-1/11, H-415)

HAYS, JOHN. Baltimore Mechanical Company of Militia, 1776. (CCC-28)

HAYS, WILLIAM. Standard Bearer, Baltimore Artillery Company, Oct. 16, 1775. (G-8)

HAYS, WILLIAM. Private, Baltimore Artillery Company, October 16, 1775. Private in Capt. Sheaff's Company, June 16, 1777. (G-8, W-162)

HAYS, WILLIAM. In Frederick County, Maryland, on October 9, 1780, he made a statement that he "acknowledges he is a Deserter, it is known that he Enlisted in Baltimore County, when first Taken said he Marched with the Militia from Baltimore, then said he belonged to the Virginia Line and now says he belongs to the Pennsylvania Line." (H-345)

HAYWOOD, JOSEPH. Non-Juror to Oath of Allegiance, 1778. (A-1/11)

HAZLETT (HASLETT), MOSES DR. (Died 1796) Began practice in Baltimore in 1775. Source XX-8 states no known military service, but a Dr. Moses Haslett served on Harford County's War Committee in 1775. (See H. Peden's Revolutionary Patriots of Harford County, Maryland, 1775-1783, page 107) He took the Oath of Allegiance in 1778 before Hon. James Calhoun in Baltimore. He died in March, 1796, "well known in Baltimore as a physician long established." (ZZZ-148, A-2/38, XX-8)

HEAD, JOHN. Born 1760. Matross in Capt. Brown's MD Artillery; joined November 22, 1777. Was at Valley Forge until June, 1778; at White Plains, July, 1778; at Fort Schuyler in August and September, 1780; at High Hills of the Santee in Aug., 1781; at Camp Col. Scirvins in January, 1782; at Bacon's Bridge, S.C. in April, 1782. He was entitled to Federal Bounty Land Grant of 100 acres on July 9, 1800, which was issued to Asahel PHELPS. Also, entitled to 50 acres (lot #920) in western Maryland for his Matross services. Pensioner. (YY-26, YY-28, UU-228, UU-230, DDDD-20)

HEADINGTON (HEDDINGTON), ABEL. Quartermaster, Baltimore County, September 1, 1777. Oath of Allegiance, 1778, before Hon. Robert Simmons. (BBB-355, A-1/11, A-2/58)

HEADINGTON, NICHOLAS. Non-Juror to Oath of Allegiance, 1778. (A-1/11)

HEADINGTON (HEDDINGTON), WILLIAM. Oath of Allegiance, 1778, before Hon. Jesse Dorsey. (A-1/11, A-2/63)

HEADINGTON, ZEBULON. (1740 - 1839) Married Sarah BOSLEY. Non-Juror to Oath of Allegiance. (A-1/11) Source JJJ-318 states he was a Soldier in Maryland Line.

HEARLY (HARLEY), JOHN. Private in Capt. Graybill's German Regiment, 1776. (H-265)

HEATON, JOHN. Maryland Line defective, August, 1780. Resident of Baltimore Co.(H-414)

HECKMAN, LORNCE. Oath of Allegiance, 1778, before Hon. Geo. Lindenberger. (A-2/53)

HEDGELY, JOHN. Recruit in Baltimore County in 1780. (H-340)

HEES, VALENTINE. Non-Juror to Oath of Allegiance, 1778. (A-1/11)

HEGNOS, THOMAS. Oath of Allegiance, 1778, before Hon. James Calhoun. (A-2/41)

HELLAM, THOMAS. Private in Capt. Norwood's Company, 4th MD Regiment, from May 16, 1778 to April 1, 1779 when reported deserted. (H-124)

HELLAR, SOLOMAN. Oath of Allegiance, 1778. (A-1/11)

HELLEN, BAZIL. Fifer in Capt. Gale's MD Artillery. Discharged Nov. 8, 1779.(YYY-1/48)

HELLEN, DAVID. Oath of Allegiance, 1778, before Hon. Geo. Lindenberger. (A-2/53)

HELLEN (HELLING), WILLIAM. Bombardier in Capt. Gale's MD Artillery, 1779-1780. He was entitled to 50 acres (lot #3112) for his services. (DDDD-20, YYY-2/49)

HELLER, FREDERICK. Sergeant in Capt. Graybill's German Regiment in 1776. (H-266)

HELM, LEONARD. (died c1794 in Baltimore County) Son of Mayberry HELM. Married to Mary HORSEMAN. Children: James; Ann; William; Mary (died 1792 and left a will); Elizabeth; and, Joseph. Leonard HELM made his will on November 13, 1792 and it was probated January 4, 1794. In addition to his children, he named his grandson Leonard HELM, son of James; his sister Mary McLELLAN; and his wife's brother John HORSEMAN. Leonard HELM took the Oath of Allegiance, 1778, before Hon. James Calhoun. (A-1/11, A-2/40, D-3)

HELM, MAYBERRY. Served on Baltimore County Committee of Inspection, March 13, 1775, and Baltimore County Committee of Observation, July 24, 1775. Represented Middlesex Hundred at the Association of Freemen on August 21, 1775. "Maybru Helm" took Oath of Allegiance before Hon. James Calhoun in 1778. (RR-19, A-2/38, EEEE-1725 & 1726)

HELMS, GEORGE. Private in Capt. Cox's Company, December 19, 1776. (CCC-21)

HENDERSON, HENRY. Private in Baltimore County Militia; enlisted July 19, 1776. (H-58)

HENDERSON, JAMES. Matross soldier, Baltimore County. Gave deposition on enlistment terms, May 7, 1779. (FFF-220)

HENDON, HENRY. Non-Juror to Oath of Allegiance, 1778. "An old inhabitant of Baltimore County, died October 2, 1810." (ZZZ-152, A-1/11)

HENDON, RICHARD. Non-Juror to Oath of Allegiance, 1778. (A-1/11)

HENDRICKSON, ABRAHAM. Non-Juror to Oath of Allegiance, 1778. (A-1/11)

HENDRICKSON, AMOS. Non-Juror to Oath of Allegiance, 1778. (A-1/11)

HENDRICKSON, JAMES. Born 1749 in Maryland. Occupation: Labourer. Enlisted as Private in Capt. N. Smith's 1st Company of Matrosses, January 31, 1776. Height: 5' 6$\frac{1}{4}$". Was a Corporal in Capt. Dorsey's MD Artillery, November 17, 1777. Appointed Bombardier, Capt. Gale's MD Artillery, November 8, 1779; on command commissary, October, 1779; served to at least 1780. Entitled to 50 acres (lot #1420) in western Maryland for his services. (DDDD-20, YYY-1/52, H-565, H-567, H-574, QQQ-2)

HENDRICKSON, JOHN. Non-Juror to Oath of Allegiance, 1778. (A-1/11)

HENDRICKSON, JOSEPH. Non-Juror to Oath of Allegiance, 1778. (A-1/11)
HENESTOPHEL, HENRY. Non-Juror to Oath of Allegiance, 1778. (A-1/11)
HENESTOPHEL, JOHN. Non-Juror to Oath of Allegiance, 1778. (A-1/11)
HENLEY, GEORGE. Non-Juror to Oath of Allegiance, 1778. (A-1/11)
HENLEY, PETER. Non-Juror to Oath of Allegiance, 1778. (A-1/11)

HENNEGH, CHRISTOPHER. Oath of Allegiance, 1778, before Hon. James Calhoun. (A-2/38)

HENNESSY, EDWARD. Matross in Capt. Brown's MD Artillery as of August 1, 1781. Was at
    High Hills of the Santee in August, 1781; at Camp Col. Scirvins in January, 1782;
    and at bacon's Bridge, S.C. in April, 1782. (UU-230)

HENNESSY, MICHAEL. Non-Juror to Oath of Allegiance, 1778. (A-1/11)

HENRY, ISAAC. Oath of Allegiance, 1778, before Hon. Charles Ridgely of William.(A-2/27)

HENRY, JAMES. Marine on ship Defence, 1777. (H-657)

HENRY, JAMES. Matross in Capt. Brown's MD Artillery; joined January 13, 1781. Was at
    High Hills of the Santee in August, 1781; at Camp Col. Scirvins in January, 1782;
    at Bacon's Bridge, S.C. in April, 1782. (UU-230)

HENREY, PETER. Oath of Allegiance, 1778, before Hon. Frederick Decker. (A-1/11,A-2/31)

HERITAGE, BENJAMIN. Private in Baltimore County Militia; enl. July 5, 1776. (H-58)

HERLIHY (HERLITY), WILLIAM. Private in Count Pulaski's Legion; enlisted in Baltimore
    on May 6, 1778. Took Oath of Allegiance, 1778, before Hon. George Lindenberger.
    (A-1/11, A-2/53, H-593)

HERNE, WILLIAM. Oath of Allegiance, 1778, before Hon. James Calhoun. (A-1/11, A-2/42)

HERRIAN, JOHN. Oath of Allegiance, 1778. (A-1/11)

HERRICK, ELIAS. Non-Juror to Oath of Allegiance, 1778. (A-1/11)
HERRING, JAMES. Non-Juror to Oath of Allegiance, 1778. (A-1/11)

HERRINGTON, JACOB. Private in Col. Aquila Hall's Baltimore County Regiment in 1777.
    (TTT-13)

HERRON (HIRON), JAMES. Private in Capt. Ewing's Company No. 4; enlisted January 18,
    1776. "James HIRON" took Oath of Allegiance in 1778 before Hon. Hercules Courtenay.
    "James HERRON" was a pensioner (Private in Revolutionary Army of Baltimore County)
    from August 8, 1814 at $96 per annum (received $343). Died September 4, 1818. (O-7,
    C-353, H-12, A-1/12, A-2/37)

HESS, PETER. Oath of Allegiance, 1778, before Hon. James Calhoun. (A-1/11, A-2/42)

HESSY, HENRY. Non-Juror to Oath of Allegiance, 1778. (A-1/11)

HESTERLING, ISAAC. Private in Capt. J. Cockey's Baltimore County Dragoons stationed
    at Yorktown in 1781. (MMM-A)

HEWITT (HEWET), EDWARD. Oath of Allegiance, 1778, before Hon. John Merryman. (A-2/70)

HEWEITT, JACOB. Oath of Allegiance, 1778, before Hon. Richard Cromwell. (A-2/46)

HEWITT, RICHARD. Oath of Allegiance, 1778, before Hon. Jesse Dorsey. (A-2/63)

HEWITT, ROBERT. Oath of Allegiance, 1778, before Hon. Richard Cromwell. (A-2/46)

HEWITT, VACHT. Oath of Allegiance, 1778, before Hon. Peter Shepherd. (A-2/50)

HICK, JOHN. Oath of Allegiance, 1778. (A-1/11)

HICKEY, OWEN. Non-Juror to Oath of Allegiance, 1778. (A-1/11)

HICKEY, THOMAS. Private in Capt. Norwood's Company, 4th MD Regiment; enlisted on
    April 26, 1778; became Corporal, April 1, 1779; deserted January 2, 1780. (H-123)

HICKINSON, WILLIAM. Matross in Capt. Brown's MD Artillery; joined Nov. 22, 1777. Was
    at Valley Forge until June, 1778; at White Plains, July, 1778; at Fort Schuyler in
    August and September, 1780; not listed in 1781. (UU-228, UU-230)

HICKS, ABRAM (ABRAHAM). 1st Lieutenant in Capt. Cummins' Company, Upper Battalion, August 30, 1777 to at least 1778. Involved in evaluation of Baltimore County's confiscated proprietary reserve lands in 1782. (FFF-544, E-14, LL-66, BBB-350) Non-Juror to Oath of Allegiance in 1778. (1-1/11)

HICKS, ELISHA. Non-Juror to Oath of Allegiance, 1778. (A-1/11)

HICKS, HENRY. Non-Juror to Oath of Allegiance, 1778. (A-1/11)

HICKS, ISAAC. There were two men with this name who took the Oath of Allegiance in 1778: one before Hon. Benjamin Rogers, and one before Hon. Robert Simmons. The latter Isaac HICKS could not write and made his mark ("/"). One of these Isaac HICKS also delivered flour in Baltimore County on January 29, 1780. (FFF-266, A-1/11, A-2/32, A-2/58)

HICKS, JACOB. Non-Juror to Oath of Allegiance, 1778. (A-1/11)

HICKS, JOHN. Oath of Allegiance, 1778, before Hon. Peter Shepherd. (A-1/11, A-2/50)

HICKS, LABAN. Non-Juror to Oath of Allegiance, 1778. (A-1/11)

HICKS, NEHEMIAH. Non-Juror to Oath of Allegiance, 1778. (A-1/11)

HICKS, RICHARD. Non-Juror to Oath of Allegiance, 1778. (A-1/11)

HICKS, STEPHEN. Oath of Allegiance, 1778, before Hon. James Calhoun. (A-1/11, A-2/42)

HICKS, THOMAS. Non-Juror to Oath of Allegiance, 1778. (A-1/11)

HIDE, HENRY. Oath of Allegiance, 1778, before Hon. James Calhoun. (A-1/11, A-2/39)

HIGGENBOTHAM, THOMAS. Recruit in Baltimore County in 1780. (H-340)

HIGGINBOTTOM, JOEL JR. Non-Juror to Oath of Allegiance, 1778. (A-1/11)

HIGGINS, DENNIS. Recruit in Baltimore County Militia, April 11, 1780. (H-335)

HIGGINS, HUGH. Non-Juror to Oath of Allegiance, 1778. (A-1/11)

HIGGINS, JOHN. Recruit in Baltimore County in 1780. (H-340)

HIGGINS, PATRICK. Oath of Allegiance, 1778, before Hon. James Calhoun. (A-1/11, A-2/39)

HIGGS, HENRY. Matross in Capt. Brown's MD Artillery; joined November 22, 1777. Was at Valley Forge until June, 1778; at White Plains, July, 1778; at Fort Schuyler in Aug. and Sept., 1780; at High Hills of the Santee in Aug., 1781; at Camp Col. Scirvins in January, 1782; at Bacon's Bridge, S.C. in April, 1782. Entitled to 50 acres for his services (lot #276) in western Maryland. (UU-228, UU-230, DDDD-20)

HIGGS, LAZARUS. Recruit in Baltimore County in 1780. Private in the Extra Regiment at Fort Whetstone Point in Baltimore, 1781. Entitled to 50 acres (lot #222) for his services as a Private in the State Troops (land in western MD).(H-340,H-626,DDDD-20)

HIGH, GEORGE. Ordinary Sailor on ship Defence, 1777. (H-657)

HIGMAN, EDWARD. Born 1758 in England. Enlisted as Private in Col. Ewing's Battalion on July 5, 1776; height: 5' 3¼"; black hair; scar on his cheek. (H-54)

HIGNOT (HEGNET), JOHN. Volunteer in Baltimore County Regt. No. 36, c1777. (TTT-13)

HIGNOT, THOMAS. Oath of Allegiance, 1778. Stored and delivered flour for Baltimore Town Committee in 1780. (A-1/11, RRR-6)

HILL, JOSEPH. Non-Juror to Oath of Allegiance, 1778. (A-1/12)

HILL, RICHARD. Private in Baltimore Artillery Company, October 16, 1775. (G-8)

HILL, SAMUEL. Non-Juror to Oath of Allegiance, 1778. (A-1/12)

HILL, THOMAS. (1759, Ireland - 1821, prob. Baltimore County, MD) Married Sarah HOWARD. Private in Capt. Ewing's Company No. 4; enlisted January 22, 1776; discharged April 26, 1776. Enlisted July 7, 1776 as 2nd Sergeant in Col. Ewing's Battn.; ht: 5' 6¼"; long black hair. Took Oath of Allegiance in 1778 before Hon. Edward Cockey. (H-54, A-1/12, A-2/61, JJJ-329, H-12)

HILL, WALTER. Non-Juror to Oath of Allegiance, 1778. (A-1/12)

HILL (HILLS), WILLIAM. Oath of Allegiance, 1778, before Hon. Jeremiah Johnson. Could not write; made his mark ("ᴎ"). (A-1/12, A-2/33)

HILLARD, CHARLES C. Oath of Allegiance, 1778, before Hon. Charles Ridgely of William. Could not write; made his mark. (A-1/12, A-2/27)

HILLEN, JOHN. (October 6, 1761 - August 11, 1840) Baltimore Mechanical Company of Militia, 1776. (CCC-28) Buried at Prospect Hill Cemetery, Towson, MD, "a witness & participant in two wars." (Baltimore Sun, Aug. 15, 1840; History Trails, Vol. 6, No. 3, 1972)

HILLEN, WILLIAM. Bombardier, Capt. Dorsey's MD Artillery, at Camp Col. Scirvins on January 28, 1782. (UU-232)

HILSON, BENGEMAN. Oath of Allegiance, 1778. (A-1/12)

HILTON, JAMES. Non-Juror to Oath of Allegiance, 1778. (A-1/12)

HILTON, JOHN. Non-Juror to Oath of Allegiance, 1778. Died in Baltimore County when he was killed by a fall from his horse in February, 1784. His wife was named Sarah and their children were Sarah, John, James, William, Abraham, Priscilla, Elinor, and Patience. (A-1/12, D-3)

HILTON, JOHN JR. Non-Juror to Oath of Allegiance, 1778. (A-1/12)
HILTON, JOSEPH. Non-Juror to Oath of Allegiance, 1778. (A-1/12)
HILTON, WILLIAM. Non-Juror to Oath of Allegiance, 1778. (A-1/12)

HILTRHIMER, FRANCIS. Private in Capt. S. Smith's Company No. 8, 1st MD Regiment, on January 13, 1776. (H-640)

HINGSTON, RICHARD. Non-Juror to Oath of Allegiance, 1778. (A-1/12)

HINLEY, GEORGE. Private in Baltimore County Militia; enlisted Aug. 15, 1776. (H-58)

HIOT, CHRISTOPHER. Non-Juror to Oath of Allegiance, 1778. (A-1/12)

HIPKINS, JOHN. Private in Baltimore County Militia; enlisted July 19, 1776. (H-58)

HIPWELLS, BENJAMIN. Born 1753 in Ireland. Enlisted July 5, 1776 as 3rd Sergeant in Col. Ewing's Battalion. Height: 5' 9"; long black hair. Took Oath of Allegiance in 1778 before Hon. George Lindenberger. (A-1/12, A-2/53, H-54)

HIRED,_____. (First name not given) Fifer in Capt. Ewing's Company No. 4, having enlisted on May 23, 1776. (H-11)

HISON (HISOR), JOHN. Oath of Allegiance, 1778, before Hon. Richard Cromwell. (A-2/40)

HISSEY, CHARLES. Non-Juror to Oath of Allegiance, 1778. (A-1/12)

HIVER, RICHARD. Private in Capt. Talbott's Company, May 31, 1779. (F-302, U-90)

HOALE, SAMUEL. Private in Capt. J. Cockey's Baltimore County Dragoons at Yorktown in 1781. (MMM-A)

HOBBES, MARK. Oath of Allegiance, 1778, before Hon. Peter Shepherd. (A-2/50)

HOBBS, WILLIAM. Private in Capt. Sheaff's Company, June 16, 1777. Non-Juror to the Oath of Allegiance in 1778. (W-162, A-1/12)

HOCKLY (HOCKELY), JOHN. Oath of Allegiance, 1778, before Hon. John Beale Howard. (A-1/12, A-2/29)

HODGES (HODGE), JOHN. Oath of Allegiance, 1778, before Hon. John Cradock. Could not write; made his mark. (A-1/12, A-2/59)

HOFFMAN, JACOB. Private in Capt. Graybill's German Regiment in 1776. A resident of Bridge Street in Baltimore, he was found dead in his cellar in January, 1810. (H-265, ZZZ-158)

HOFFMAN, W. Oath of Allegiance, 1778, before Hon. Isaac Van Bibber. (A-1/12, A-2/34)

HOFSTATTER, HENRY. Oath of Allegiance, 1778. (A-1/12)

HOGAN, JAMES. Ordinary Sailor on ship Defence, 1777. (H-657)

HOGEN, EDMUND. Oath of Allegiance, 1778, before Hon. Geo. Lindenberger. (A-2/53)

HOGG, JAMES. Private in Capt. Ramsey's Company No. 5 in 1776. (H-640)

HOLDEN, HABYCUCK. Private in Capt. Deams Co., 7th MD Regt., Dec. 1, 1776. (H-304)

HOLDEN (HOLDIN), RICHARD. Non-Juror to Oath of Allegiance, 1778. (A-1/12)

HOLDEN, WILLIAM. Non-Juror to Oath of Allegiance, 1778. (A-1/12)

HOLEBROOKE, AMOS. Non-Juror to Oath of Allegiance, 1778. (A-1/12)

HOLEBROOKE, EDWARD. Enlisted in Baltimore Town on July 20, 1776. Non-Juror to the Oath of Allegiance in 1778. (A-1/12, H-53)

HOLEBROOKE, JOHN. Non-Juror to Oath of Allegiance, 1778. (A-1/12)

HOLLAND, DANIEL. Recruit in Baltimore County Militia, April 11, 1780. (H-335)

HOLLAND, GABRIEL. Married Sarah HARRIMAN on May 5, 1773 at St. James Chapel, in that part of Baltimore County that became Harford County in 1773/1774. Gabriel was a resident of Joppa in 1768, and took the Oath of Allegiance in 1778 before Hon. James Calhoun in Baltimore. Only known child was Thomas HOLLAND, born circa 1785. Gabriel had moved to Washington County, PA by 1790 and after that he moved to Harrison County, Ohio. Also, there was a Gabriel HOLLAND who enlisted as a substitute for Frederick BRADENBURGH on April 30, 1778 in Frederick County, MD, and served under Col. Otho Holland Williams' 6th MD Regiment. (A-1/12, A-2/42, Maryland Historical Magazine, Vol. VI (1911), page 257, H-214, MMM-A, and info from Marilyn H. Opfer of Fairfax, Virginia, 1987)

HOLLAND, GEORGE. Non-Juror to Oath of Allegiance, 1778. (A-1/12)

HOLLAND, JACOB. The record of Jacob HOLLAND is given as found in pension claim R5141 based upon his service in the Revolutionary War: "Jacob HOLLAND was born in March, 1754 (place and name of parents not stated). He enlisted in Unity, Montgomery Co., Maryland on March 1, 1776 and served ten months as Private in Capt. Patrick Sims' Company of Col. William Smallwood's MD Regiment, and was in the Battles of Long Island, Harlem Heights and White Plains. He enlisted in Baltimore County, MD, in May, 1777, and served as Corporal in Capt. Vashel Denton Howard's, Nicholas Ruxton Moore's, and Peter Manifold's Companies in Col. Moylan's 4th Regt. of Continental Dragoons. He was in the battles of Brandywine and Germantown, and many skirmishes, and was discharged June, 1780. He moved from Montgomery County, MD, 1780, to VA (Berkeley County) until 1801 when he moved to Monongalia County, VA. He was allowed pension on his application July 23, 1832, still living in said county. He married 1786 in Montgomery County, MD to Mary, whose maiden name is not stated (Ed.: Source JJJ-337 states his wife was Mary SMITH). Jacob HOLLAND died September 17, 1838 while on a visit to a son in Harrison County, VA. The widow Mary HOLLAND died on April 12, 1840 in Monongalia County, VA. The following schildren of Jacob HOLLAND and wife, Mary, were alive in 1851 and were age then as follows: Allen HOLLAND was born June 14, 1787; Elizabeth HOLLAND, age 62; Daniel HOLLAND, age 57; William HOLLAND, age 52; Solomon HOLLAND, age 48. Their son Isaac HOLLAND died before his parents and left two children, Alpheus and Eliza HOLLAND." (I-46, JJJ-337)

HOLLAND, THOMAS. Private in Capt. Ewing's Company No. 4; enlisted January 29, 1776. Private in 4th MD Regiment from April 16, 1777 to March 1, 1780. (H-12, H-122)

HOLLAR, WILLIAM. Private in Capt. McClellan's Company, Baltimore Town, September 4, 1780. (CCC-24)

HOLLES, MARK. Oath of Allegiance, 1778. (A-1/12)

HOLLIDAY, JAMES. Baltimore Mechanical Company of Militia, November 4, 1775. (F-298)

HOLLIDAY, JOHN ROBERT. Served on the Baltimore County Committee of Observation on July 24, 1775, but did not receive enough votes to be elected to it again on September 12, 1775. Was a 1st Lieutenant in Capt. J. Cockey's Company No. 1 in Baltimore County, August 26, 1776. Was a Justice of the Peace in 1778, and took the Oath of Allegiance in 1778. His wife, Eleanor A., died on July 4, 1798. In Feb., 1802, he married Mary Burrows STONE. (ZZZ-158, GGG-242, EEEE-1725, RR-50, PPP-2)

HOLLIDAY, RICHARD. One of the Magistrates who administered the Oath in 1778. (A-2/60)

HOLLINGSWORTH, JESSE. (March 12, 1732, Cecil County, MD - September 30, 1810, Baltimore) Married Sinai RICKETTS (1737-1786) in 1758, and secondly to Rachel L. PERKINS. Jesse HOLLINGSWORTH was a member of the Commissary Department, served on the Baltimore Salt Committee on October 14, 1779, took the Oath of Allegiance in Baltimore County on March 19, 1778, and was active in military affairs during the Revolutionary War. His children were: Mary (born 1760) married Capt. Jeremiah YELLOTT; Zebulon (born 1762) married Elizabeth IRELAND; Horatio (born 1764; died young); George (born 1767; died young); Ann (born 1768) married Rev. Henry WILLIS; John (born 1771) married Rachel YELLOTT; and, Francis (1773-1826) married Mary YELLOTT (1783-1864) in 1801, and their son Parkin HOLLINGSWORTH (1802-1837) married Martha A. KELER (1804-1879) in 1827. (BBB-541, ZZZ-159, AAA-1242, BBB-350, FFF-51, HHH-88, JJJ-338, XXX-395)

HOLLINGSWORTH, SAMUEL. (January 17, 1757, Cecil County, MD - May 9, 1830, Baltimore, MD) Son of Zebulon HOLLINGSWORTH and Mary JACOBS. Samuel married Sarah ADAMS of Christiana, Delaware, in 1782. Their children were: Jacob, married Nancy GOODING; Samuel Jr. married Ellin Maria MOALE in 1816; Sarah, married William GIBSON; Elizabeth, married Gen. Charles S. Ridgely; Mary Ann, married James CHESTON; and, Juliana. (See J. Adger Stewart's Descendants of Valentine Hollingsworth, Sr. (1925), page 47, for details). Samuel HOLLINGSWORTH was a member of the Sons of Liberty in 1776. He also served as Lieutenant in Capt. Nicholas Ruxton Moore's 1st Baltimore Volunteers and was at the Battles of Trenton and Princeton, N.J. He was at Yorktown, VA on June 25, 1781 marching to Virginia with Lafayette's troops; he rode his six year old bay gelding horse. (BBBB-313, AAA-121, ZZZ-159, CCC-19) He is buried in St. Paul's Churchyard.

HOLLINGSWORTH, THOMAS. (1746 - September 5, 1815) He and brother Samuel HOLLINGSWORTH were merchants in Baltimore City and served on the Baltimore Salt Committee of 1779. Thomas also rode with Capt. Moore's Troops in 1781, and had a six year old sorrell gelding horse. (HHH-88, BBBB-313, ZZZ-159)

HOLLOW, NICH. Private in Capt. McClellan's Company, Baltimore Town, September 4, 1780. (CCC-24)

HOLLYDAY, ROBERT. Quartermaster for Baltimore County, October 12, 1776. (ZZ-337)

HOLMES, _____. (First name torn off list) Private in Baltimore County Regiment 15 circa 1777. (TTT-13)

HOLMES, G. Oath of Allegiance, 1778. (A-1/12)

HOLMES, JAMES. Non-Juror to Oath of Allegiance, 1778. (A-1/12)

HOLMES, THOMAS. There were two men with this name who took the Oath of Allegiance in 1778: one before Hon. George Gouldsmith Presbury, and one before Hon. James Calhoun. The former could not write; made his mark. (A-1/12, A-2/48, A-2/65)

HOLMES, WILLIAM. Two Non-Jurors with this name to the Oath in 1778. (A-1/12)

HOLTZMAN, GEORGE. Married Margaret DEAVER in Baltimore County, MD (marriage proven through Maryland pension application), per Source YY-116, but service not stated.

HOMBEY, WALTER. Non-Juror to Oath of Allegiance, 1778. (A-1/12)

HOMES, JAMES. Private in Capt. J. Gist's Company, 3rd MD Regiment, in February, 1778. May have been in the 1st MD Regiment since a James HOMES was entitled to 50 acres (lot #1317) for that service. He also received 100 acres by Federal Bounty Land Grant 11347 on March 27, 1794. Non-Juror to Oath in 1778. (H-600, YY-68, DDDD-21, A-1/12)

HOMES, JOHN. Non-Juror to Oath of Allegiance, 1778. (A-1/12)

HONEE, JAMES WALTER. Recruit in Baltimore County, 1780. (H-340)

HOOD, JAMES. (1755 - February 19, 1819) Married Kitty FRANKLIN on July 22, 1784 in Baltimore County (marriage proven through Maryland pension application). She died on January 8, 1847. Their son, John HOOD (1788-1850) married Tabitha WOLF (1792-1823) in 1809, and their son, John HOOD Jr. (1811-1892) married Mary GRIMES (1813-

1881) in 1833. James HOOD served as a Corporal in Col. J. C. Hall's 4th MD Regt. on March 5, 1777 and became Quartermaster Sergeant on May 1, 1777. His assignment to the Commissary Department, 2nd Battalion, was on August 20, 1778 and he was the Assistant Commissary. He served as Lieutenant until March 15, 1780. Pension W3816. (H-122, AAA-1785, YY-116, AAA-1681, JJJ-340)

HOOD, JOHN. Enlisted in Baltimore County on August 14, 1776. Sergeant in Captain Norwood's Company, 4th MD Regiment, from April 24, 1777 to April 24, 1780. (H-52, H-122)

HOOD, RICHARD. Enlisted in Baltimore County on August 14, 1776. (H-52) Non-Juror to Oath of Allegiance in 1778. (A-1/12)

HOOD, RICHARD SR. Non-Juror to Oath of Allegiance, 1778. (A-1/12)
HOOD, RICHARD JR. Non-Juror to Oath of Allegiance, 1778. (A-1/12)
HOOFMAN, ISAAC. Non-Juror to Oath of Allegiance, 1778. (A-1/12)
HOOFMAN, JACOB. Non-Juror to Oath of Allegiance, 1778. 9A-1/12)
HOOFMAN, JOHN. Non-Juror to Oath of Allegiance, 1778. (A-1/12)
HOOFMAN, LAWRENCE. Non-Juror to Oath of Allegiance, 1778. (A-1/12)

HOOFMAN, WILLIAM. Oath of Allegiance, 1778, before Hon. John Hall. (A-1/12, A-2/36) Source A-2/36 misspelled the name as "Hoosman" instead of "Hoofman."

HOOK (HOOKE), ANDREW. Private in Capt. Sheaff's Company, June 16, 1777, "pleads age." Non-Juror to Oath of Allegiance in 1778. (A-1/12, W-162)

HOOK, GEORGE. Oath of Allegiance, 1778, before Hon. James Calhoun. (A-1/12, A-2/39)

HOOK, JACOB. (1748 - June 16, 1815) Wife named Elizabeth. A daughter, Margaret Ann HOOK (1788- circa 1850) married John Goodshine McCLATCHIE (1778-circa 1840) in 1805 in Baltimore County, and their daughter, Elizabeth Stowers McCLATCHIE (1812-1877) married John E. COUSINS (1813-1879) in 1836 in Baltimore. Jacob HOOK took the Oath of Allegiance in 1778 before Hon. Richard Cromwell. He is buried in McKendree Churchyard on Reisterstown Road in Baltimore County. (AAA-2682, A-1/12, A-2/46)

HOOK, JACOB (OF JOSEPH). (1752, Hookstown, Baltimore County, MD - 1815/1825) Married Susannah Cockley BOONE on March 13, 1791. Their daughter Susan HOOK (born 1792) married George RICHARDSON. Jacob HOOK took the Oath of Allegiance in 1778 before Hon. Richard Cromwell. (A-1/12, A-2/46, JJJ-341, XXX-396)

HOOK, JACOB (OF RUTOLPH). Oath of Allegiance, 1778, before Hon. Richard Cromwell. (A-1/12, A-2/46)

HOOK, JOSEPH. (Born 1756) Volunteered in Baltimore County Regiment No. 36 and then as a Private in Capt. Graybill's German Regiment, 1776-1777. Became a Corporal, and Pensioner. Took the Oath of Allegiance in 1778. Marriage proven through the Maryland pension application shows one Joseph HOOK married to Anne CHANNELL, 1821, in Baltimore County. (YY-116, H-266, YY-28, TTT-13)

HOOK, RUTOLPH. Oath of Allegiance, 1778, before Hon. Richard Cromwell. (A-1/12,A-2/46)

HOOKE, JOHN. Ensign in Capt. Merryman's Company of the Upper Battalion, Nov. 5, 1781. (AAAA-662)

HOOKE, JOSEPH. 2nd Lieutenant in Capt. Deams' Company of the Baltimore Town Battalion, August 20, 1781. (AAAA-572)

HOOKER, AQUILA. 1st Lieutenant in Soldiers Delight Company No. 7, May 13, 1776. Was a Non-Juror to Oath of Allegiance in 1778. (A-1/12, FF-64, WW-467)

HOOKER, BENJAMIN. Oath of Allegiance, 1778, before Hon. James Calhoun. (A-1/12,A-2/42)

HOOKER, JACOB. Non-Juror to Oath of Allegiance, 1778. (A-1/12)

HOOKER, JOHN. Oath of Allegiance, 1778, before Hon. Robert Simmons. He also drove wagons for military supplies in 1780. (A-1/12, A-2/58, RRR-6)

HOOKER, RICHARD. Non-Juror to Oath of Allegiance, 1778. (A-1/12)

HOOKER, RICHARD SR. Non-Juror to Oath of Allegiance, 1778. (A-1/12)

HOOKER, RICHARD JR. Non-Juror to Oath of Allegiance, 1778. (A-1/12)

HOOKER, THOMAS. Non-Juror to Oath of Allegiance, 1778. (A-1/12)

HOOKS, JACOB. Non-Juror to Oath of Allegiance, 1778. (A-1/12)

HOOKS, JACOB JR. Non-Juror to Oath of Allegiance, 1778. (A-1/12)

HOOKS, MICHAEL. Non-Juror to Oath of Allegiance, 1778. (A-1/12)

HOOPER, ABRAHAM. (Born 1756) Private in 4th MD Regiment, from Baltimore County.
Discharged December 3, 1781. Wounded. Pensioner. (YY-28, Q-72)

HOOPER, ISAAC. (c1758 - c1820/30) Married Jane CRAGE. Non-Juror to Oath of Allegiance
in 1778. (A-1/12, JJJ-341) Source JJJ-341 indicates patriotic service was rendered.

HOOPER, JACOB. (c1760 - after 1836) Married MARY CORD. Enlisted in Baltimore County,
Private, July 26, 1776. Took Oath of Allegiance in 1781. (H-53, JJJ-341, QQ-113)

HOOPER, JAMES. Oath of Allegiance, 1778, before Hon. Edward Cockey. (A-1/12, A-2/62)

HOOPER, JAMES. (October 3, 1703 - November 3, 1789) Married Mary WOOLFORD. He took an
Oath of Allegiance in 1778 before Hon. James Calhoun. (A-1/12, A-2/65, JJJ-341)

HOOPER, JOHN. Private in Capt. McClellan's Company, Baltimore Town, September 4, 1780.
Non-Juror to the Oath in 1778, he signed in 1781. (A-1/12, QQ-113, CCC-24)

HOOPER, THOMAS. Was a Private in Capt. Talbott's Company as of May 31, 1779. Reported
as enlisting at Fort Whetstone Point in Baltimore on October 21, 1779, and reported
as being discharged on January 27, 1780. Shown as recruited in Baltimore for 3rd
MD Regiment by Samuel Chester on March 2, 1780. (F-301, U-90, H-334, H-626)

HOOPER, WILLIAM. Private in Capt. McClellan's Company, Baltimore Town, September 4,
1780. (CCC-24)

HOPE, ROBERT. Ordinary Sailor on ship Defence in 1777. (H-657)

HOPERLY, FREDERICK. Private in Capt. Deam's Company, 7th MD Regiment, December 10,
1776. (H-304)

HOPEWELL, THOMAS. Midshipman on ship Defence, May 15 to December 31, 1777. (H-657)

HOPKINS, DANIEL. Served in Capt. Nicholas Ruxton Moore's Troops, June 25, 1781. He
had a ten year old sorrell mare. (BBBB-313)

HOPKINS, EZEKIEL. Non-Juror to Oath in 1778, but signed in 1781. (A-1/12, QQ-113)

HOPKINS, GERARD (JERRARD) SR. (January 7, 1709 - July 3, 1777) Married Mary HALL.
Served on Baltimore Town Committee of Inspection on March 13, 1775 and Baltimore
Town Committee of Correspondence on November 12, 1775. Member of the Sons of
Liberty in 1776. Source A-1/12 lists Gerard Hopkins, Sr. as a Non-Juror to the
Oath of Allegiance in 1778, but Source JJ-342 states he died in 1777. (SS-130,
RR-19, CCC-19, JJJ-342)

HOPKINS, GERARD JR. Deputy Commissary for Baltimore City in 1776. Commissary of
Stores in Baltimore, August 24, 1776. (FFF-16, FFF-30, ZZ-237)

HOPKINS, GERARD (OF RICHARD). Oath of Allegiance, 1778, before Hon. John Merryman.
(A-1/12, A-2/45)

HOPKINS, JOSEPH. Non-Juror to Oath of Allegiance, 1778. (A-1/12)

HOPKINS, PHILIP. Non-Juror to Oath of Allegiance, 1778. (A-1/12)

HOPKINS, RICHARD. (c1760 - c1826) Married Hannah HAMMOND. Oath of Allegiance in
1778. (A-1/12, JJJ-342)

HOPKINS, ROGER. Served on ship Defence, April 28 to July 21, 1777. (H-657)

HOPKINS, WILLIAM. Private in Capt. Smith's Company No. 8; enlisted January 13, 1776.
(H-18)

HOPPAMAN, WILLIAM. Non-Juror to Oath of Allegiance, 1778. (A-1/12)

HOPSTATTER, HENRY. Oath of Allegiance, 1778, before Hon. Geo. Lindenberger. (A-2/53)

HORLLEY, JOHN. Oath of Allegiance, 1778, before Hon. Isaac Van Bibber. (A-2/34)

HORN (HORNE), THOMAS. Non-Juror to Oath of Allegiance, 1778. (A-1/12)

HORNER, GEORGE. Private in Capt. Ramsey's Company No. 5 in 1776. (H-640)

HORNIG (HOENIG), CHRISTOPHER. Oath of Allegiance, 1778, before Hon. George Lindenberger. (A-1/12, A-2/53)

HOSEL, JOHN. Enlisted in Baltimore County on August 14, 1776. (H-52)

HOSHALL, JESSE. (April 4, 1756, Holland - July 15, 1830, Baltimore County, MD) Married Mary Ellen HURST (1760-1843), daughter of Benedict HURST, on December 22, 1779. Their son, ISaac HOSHALL (1780-1867) married Sarah KEITH (1782-1835), and grand-daughter, Eleanor HOSHALL (1817-1894) married Lysander McCULLOUGH (1814-1906) in 1840. Jesse HOSHALL served as a Private in the German Battalion, enlisting in Frederick, MD in July, 1776 and serving until July, 1779, under Captains Fister and Baltzel. He was in the battles of Trenton, Princeton, Brandywine, Germantown, and Monmouth. He was discharged at Wyoming, PA. (AAA-1693, JJJ-344)

HOSIER, JOSHUA. Seaman on ship Defence, January 23, to December 31, 1777. (H-657)

HOSTETTER, FRANCIS. Non-Juror to Oath of Allegiance, 1778. (A-1/12)

HOUCK (HOUK), BARNET. (1747, Rotterdam, Holland - May 28, 1835, Baltimore (Carroll) County, MD) Married Barbara WOLF about 1780. She was born 1756 in Pennsylvania and died May 12, 1836 in Baltimore County, MD. (Ed.: Where they lived in Baltimore County became Carroll County in 1837.) Both are buried at St. Paul's Evangelical Lutheran Church, Arcadia. Barnet HOUCK's tombstone states he was a Corporal in a Pennsylvania Regiment in 1781. He served in Capt. Furrey's Company, York County, PA Militia from July 16 to September 16, 1781. The children of Barnet HOUCK and Barbara WOLF were: William HOUCK (1781-1854) married Catherine FRANK and was Captain in War of 1812; John HOUCK (born 1735) married Mary WOLFE and served in the War of 1812; Elizabeth HOUCK married Aaron STOCKSDALE; Susan HOUCK married Louis LUTZ; Catherine HOUCK married Mathias BOWERS; Jacob HOUCK; and, George HOUCK. (Elias HOUCK, 1890-1897, son of William HOUCK, married Margaret WISE in 1852 in Carroll County, MD.) Barnet HOUCK was a Non-Juror to the Oath of Allegiance in 1778, but signed the Oath in 1781. Other family notes: Capt. William HOUCK was one of the first Commissioners for Carroll Co. Dr. Jacob HOUCK donated land for the Battle Monument at North Point, Baltimore County. Ella HOUCK (Mrs. Reuben Ross HOLLOWAY) was responsible for legislation that made the Star Spangled Banner our National Anthem. The pen used by President Herbert HOOVER to sign the Act was given to her and is enshrined at Fort McHenry in Baltimore City. (AAA-1894, JJJ-345, A-1/12, QQ-113, D-4, XXX-401, and information compiled and given to the author by Dr. Charles H. Williams, a direct descendant, of Pasadena, MD, 1985)

HOUCK (HOUK), MICHAEL. Oath of Allegiance, 1778, before Hon. Frederick Decker. (A-2/31)

HOULT, THOMAS. Private in Count Pulaski's Legion; enlisted in Baltimore, May 9, 1778. (H-593)

HOULTON, JOHN. (April 19, 1756, Philadelphia, PA - July 28, 1806, Baltimore, MD) Son of William and Elizabeth HOULTON. Married Eleanor SOLES on January 17, 1786. She was born in 1762 and died in 1824. A son, John HOULTON (1790-1833) married in 1811 to Ruth BRUSBANKS (1793-1857), and their daughter Mary Ann HOULTON (1819-1871) married Thomas NORNEY (1813-1881) in 1837. John HOULTON was a Plasterer by trade, and joined Capt. N. Smith's 1st Company of Matrosses on January 24, 1776 in Baltimore. He was 6' 1/8" in height, which was quite tall for his day. (AAA-1846, H-563, VV-73, QQQ-2)

HOUSE, FILLER. Non-Juror to Oath of Allegiance, 1778. (A-1/12)

HOUSE, THOMAS. Oath of Allegiance, 1778, before Hon. George Lindenberger. (A-2/53)

HOUSER, WILLIAM. Oath of Allegiance, 1778, before Hon. James Calhoun. (A-2/39)

HOW, EDWARD. Non-Juror to Oath of Allegiance, 1778. (A-1/12)

HOW, ROBERT. Private, Baltimore County Militia; enlisted July 18, 1776. (H-58)

HOW, SAMUEL. Non-Juror to Oath of Allegiance, 1778. (A-1/12)

HOWARD, BURGES. Matross in Capt. Gale's MD Artillery, 1779-1780. Was a Wagoner, 1779. Employed by Capt. Cranger, 1780. (YYY-1/53)

HOWARD, CHARLES. Oath of Allegiance, 1778, before Hon. James Calhoun. (A-1/12, A-2/41)

HOWARD, CORNELIUS. Sergeant, 3rd MD Regiment; entitled to 50 acres (lot #1854) in western Maryland. Non-Juror to Oath of Allegiance, 1778. (A-1/12, DDDD-21)

HOWARD, HENRY. Captain of Baltimore County Militia Company No. 3 in Col. Ed. Cockey's Battalion, August 26, 1776 (commanding 69 Privates). Continued service as a Captain to at least October 31, 1780. Took the Oath of Allegiance, 1778, before Honorable Richard Holliday. (A-1/12, A-2/60, PPP-2, RR-99, ZZ-541, VV-345)

HOWARD, JAMES. Enlisted in Baltimore County on July 20, 1776. Took Oath of Allegiance in 1778 before Hon. James Calhoun. Became 2nd Lieutenant in Capt. Kraner's Company, Baltimore Town Battalion, January 19, 1781. Served also in Col. Nicholson's Troop of Horse on June 7, 1781. (H-52, R-15, AAAA-401, BBBB-61, BBBB-274, A-1/12, A-2/39)

HOWARD, JOHN. Born 1748 in Maryland. Occupation: Labourer. Enlisted January 27, 1776 as Private in Capt. N. Smith's 1st Company of Matrosses. Height: 5' 11". There were three men with this name listed as Privates who became Revolutionary War Pensioners, according to Source YY-28. One was a Private in Capt. Dorsey's Company of Maryland Artillery on November 17, 1777; one took the Oath of Allegiance in 1778 before Hon. John Beale Howard; and another John Howard (and perhaps the same one) was a Sergeant in Capt. Dorsey's MD Artillery at Valley Forge on June 3, 1778. It is not known at this time which John Howard falls into which category. (H-574, H-564, H-566, QQQ-2, UU-230, YY-28, A-1/12, A-2/29, VV-74)

HOWARD, JOHN BEALE. (1735, Maryland - July 15, 1799, Baltimore County, MD) Son of John HOWARD and Elizabeth GASSAWAY. Married Blanche Carvill HALL on April 18, 1765, and had children: Parker HOWARD (born and died 1766); Matthias HOWARD (1777-1781); John Beale HOWARD (born 1774) married Margaret WEST; Edward Aquilla HOWARD (born 1775) married (1) Charlotte RUMSEY, and (2) Agnes Young DAY; and, Elizabeth HOWARD (born 1767) married Rev. Benjamin Vincent RICHARDSON and had a son Beale Howard RICHARDSON who married Mary PETERS. John Beale HOWARD was a 1st Lieutenant in the 8th Battalion of Harford County, Capt. Cowen's Company from April 26, 1776 through April 2, 1777. He was a Justice of the Orphans Court of Baltimore County in 1777, and a Justice of the Peace in 1778. As Magistrate, he was one of the officials who administered the Oath of Allegiance in 1778. On August 18, 1779, he was appointed by the General Assembly to receive subscriptions in Baltimore County. In 1781, he was a Delegate to the Maryland Legislature from Baltimore County. (XXX-405, WW-387, WW-538, VV-273, AAA-295, JJJ-347, GGG-242, GGG-499, A-1/12, A-2/29, A-2/30, and the Maryland Archives, Volume II, page 387)

HOWARD, JOHN EAGER. (June 4, 1752, Baltimore County, MD - October 12, 1827, Baltimore Co., Maryland) A son of Cornelius HOWARD, of Garrison Forest, and Ruth EAGER, of Belvedere, he married Margaretta (or Margaret) CHEW (1761-1824) on June 18, 1787. Their children: John Eager HOWARD Jr. (1788-1822) married Cornelia READ; George HOWARD (born 1789) md. Prudence RIDGELY; Benjamin HOWARD (born 1791) md. Jane GILMORE; William HOWARD (born 1793) md. Rebecca KEY; Juliana HOWARD (born 1796) md. John McHENRY; James HOWARD (b. 1797) married (1) Sophia RIDGELY, and (2) Catherine ROSS; Sophia Catherine HOWARD (b. 1800) married William George READ, and their daughter Mary Cornelia READ married James Fenner LEE; and, Charles HOWARD (1802-1869) married Elizabeth P. KEY, and had two sons John Eager HOWARD, Esq. (born 1828) and General James HOWARD (born 1832). John Eager HOWARD was one of the most prominent men from Maryland during the Revolutionary War. He served on the Baltimore County Committee of Inspection on March 13, 1775, and was elected to the Baltimore County Committee of Observation on September 23, 1775. He represented Soldiers Delight Hundred at the Association of Freemen on August 21, 1775. On December 19, 1775, he became a 2nd Lieutenant in Baltimore County Militia Company No. 5, but left the service and continued his work on the Baltimore Committee in 1776. Subsequently, he entered the military as a Captain of the 2nd MD Battalion of Flying Camp. Baltimore County, on July 16, 1776. He distinguished himself at the Battle of White Plains, and when a number of battalions were required to be raised by a resolve

136

HOWARD, JOHN EAGER (continued)

of Congress, Capt. Howard was appointed a Major in one of the number allotted to
Maryland (4th MD Regt.) on December 10, 1776. He was with the army at Rocky Hill
near Princeton, in April, 1777, and remained with it until June when he returned
home due to the death of his father. He rejoined the army in September, 1777 and
was in the Battle of Germantown. He became Lieutenant Colonel of the 5th MD Regt.
in March, 1779. He was in the disastrous Battle of Camden, S.C. Subsequently,
in December, 1780, General Green became Commander of the southern army and Col.
Howard served under him. On January 17, 1781, Col. Howard fought in the Battle
of Cowpens, and on March 9, 1781, Congress "resolved that a medal of silver be
presented to Lt. Col. Howard of the Infantry, with emblems and mottoes descriptive
of his conduct at the battle of Cowpens, 17 January 1781." At Eutaw Springs, on
September 8, 1781, Col. Howard again distinguished himself, and at this time he
received a severe wound in the left shoulder. General Green observed of him, in
one of his letters, "Col. Howard was as good an officer as the world afforded, and
deserved a statue of gold, no less than the roman and Grecian heroes." He was in
command of the 2nd MD Regiment until deranged on January 1, 1783, and continued to
serve until retired on April 12, 1783. In November, 1788, John Eager HOWARD was
elected Governor of Maryland, serving until 1792. He became State Senator in 1795,
and succeeded Richard Potts, deceased, in the U. S. Senate in 1796 and was elected
for six more years. He declined a seat in Washington's Cabinet in 1796, but in the
anticipation of war with France in 1798, John Eager HOWARD was selected by Pres.
Washington as one of his Major Generals. During the panic in Baltimore in 1814,
susbequeent to the capture of Washington, D.C. by the British in the War of 1812,
Gen. Howard was prepared to take the field once again to defend his country. He
also received the following pay certificates for his Revolutionary War service:
80816 ($50); 82953 ($217.30; 82954 ($975.04); 82955 ($780); 82956 ($1000); 82957
($1000); 82958 ($1000); 82959 ($1425); and 85516 ($12.20). In addition, he was
entitled to 200 acres (lots #3243, 3244, 4138, 4149)in western Maryland, and he
was issued Federal Bounty Land Grant Warrant #1043 for 500 acres on Oct. 18, 1796.
John Eager HOWARD was an Original Member of the Society of the Cincinnati of Maryland (joined 1783) and served as its Vice President from 1795 to 1804 and President
from 1804 to 1827; currently represented in that Society by Dr. John Eager Howard,
of Baltimore. Gen. Howard was a candidate for Vice President of the United States
in 1816. He died at Baltimore on October 12, 1827, with burial at Old St. Paul's
Cemetery. On March 15, 1828, a preamble recited the death the past year of "Col.
John Eager Howard, a native of Maryland, one of the most distinguished officers of
the war of the revolution, formerly chief magistrate of this state, afterwards our
senator in Congress, whose courage and conduct raised the Maryland line to that
high character which our troops acquired and maintained during the struggle for
our national independence. Portrait provided for House of Delegates." In 1971
the Maryland Society of the Sons of the American Revolution named its Baltimore
City Chapter in honor of General John Eager Howard. (AAA-13, AAA-14, AAA-97,
HHH-102, HHH-103, JJJ-347, G-10, H-52, H-122, RR-50, RR-47, SS-136, B-303, RR-19,
GG-74, FF-64, EEEE-1726, PP-257, DDDD-3, YY-68, XXX-405, TT-98, C-357, UUU-96)

HOWARD, RICHARD. Non-Juror to Oath of Allegiance, 1778. (A-1/12)
HOWARD, ROBERT. Non-Juror to Oath of Allegiance, 1778. (A-1/12)
HOWARD, SIMON. Non-Juror to Oath of Allegiance, 1778. (A-1/12)

HOWARD, THOMAS. Able Seaman on ship Defence, September 19, 1776, and Midshipman from
February 2 to December 31, 1777. (H-606, H-657)

HOWARD, THOMAS GASSAWAY. (1735/1739 - August 9, 1803) Married Frances HOLLAND on
February 24, 1765. Their children: Elizabeth Gassaway HOWARD (born 1768) married
Thomas SADLER; Francis HOWARD (born 1770) married Margaret FITZGERALD; Susanna
HOWARD (born 1772) married James W. TOLLEY; Thomas HOWARD (born 1773) md. Martha
TOLLEY; John HOWARD (born 1775); Sarah HOWARD (born 1778) married (1) Edward B.
BUSEY, and (2) George PRESBURY; and, Mary HOWARD married John MUNNIKHUYSEN. On
November 12, 1775, Thomas served on Baltimore County's Committee of Observation
(styled "Captain") and took the Oath of Allegiance in 1778 before Hon. John Beale
Howard. (A-1/12, A-2/29, XXX-406, JJJ-347, ZZZ-164)

HOWARD, THOMAS HENRY DR. Of Baltimore Town. He was Surgeon's Mate in 1776 and Surgeon to the Baltimore Battery in 1776, and Surgeon to the Baltimore Town Militia Battalion in 1777, as well as Surgeon to the Matross Company at Annapolis in 1777. (XX-8, XX-9)

HOWARD, WILLIAM. There were two men with this name: one was Carpenter's Mate on ship Defence, September 19, 1776, and from August 15, 1777 to December 31, 1777; and one was a Marine on ship Defence in 1777. There were also two men (perhaps the same) who took the Oath of Allegiance in 1778: one before Hon. James Calhoun, and one before Hon. Peter Shepherd. (A-2/40, A-2/50, H-607, H-657)

HOWE, WILLIAM ROBERT. Oath of Allegiance, 1778, before Hon. Edward Cockey. (A-2/61)

HOWELL, JEHU. Captain of a Company in Baltimore on December 30, 1775. (G-11)

HOWELL, JOHN. Served in Baltimore Artillery Company in 1777. (V-368)

HOWLAND, JOHN. Private in Col. Aquila Hall's Baltimore County Regiment, 1777. (TTT-13)

HOY, JOSEPH. Enlisted in Baltimore County, 1776. Non-Juror to Oath, 1778. (A-1/12,H-53)

HOY, NICHOLAS. Oath of Allegiance, 1778, before Hon. Andrew Buchanan. (A-1/12, A-2/57)

HUBBARD, CHARLES. Non-Juror to Oath of Allegiance, 1778. (A-1/12)

HUBBARD, JAFRAY. Oath of Allegiance, 1778, before Hon. Edward Cockey. (A-1/12, A-2/61)

HUBBARD, PETER. Oath of Allegiance, 1778, before Hon. James Calhoun. (A-1/12, A-2/42)

HUBBART, JOHN. Oath of Allegiance, 1778, before Hon. Charles Ridgely of William.(A-2/28)

HUBBERT, WILLIAM. Oath of Allegiance, 1778, before Hon. John Moale. (A-1/12, A-2/70)

HUDDLESTON, ROBERT. Non-Juror to Oath of Allegiance, 1778. (A-1/12)

HUDSON,_____(First name torn off list) Private in Baltimore County Regiment No. 7, circa 1777. (TTT-13)

HUDSON (HUTSON), JOHN. Ensign in Capt. William Hudson's Company, Soldiers Delight Battn. in 1778. (HH-24)

HUDSON, JONATHAN. He wrote to the Governor of Maryland on February 25, 1778 regarding the acquisition of cannons in Baltimore County. He served on the Baltimore Salt Committee on October 14, 1779. And he wrote the Governor on February 13, 1781 about a proposal to supply fish to the State. (FFF-147, FFF-361, HHH-88)

HUDSON, ROBERT. Maryland Line defective in August, 1780; resident of Baltimore County. Non-Juror to Oath of Allegiance in 1778. (H-414, A-1/12)

HUDSON (HUTSON), WILLIAM. 1st Lieutenant in Soldiers Delight Company No. 5 on May 13, 1776. Became Captain on August 29, 1777 and served to at least May 27, 1779. (E-10, Z-63, FF-64, WW-467, BBB-348, GGG-422)

HUDSON, WILLIAM. Seaman on ship Defence, June 24, 1777 to Dec. 31, 1777. (H-657)

HUESE, R. Oath of Allegiance, 1778, before Hon. John Cradock. (A-2/59)

HUETTINGER, MICHAEL. Oath of Allegiance, 1778. (A-1/12)

HUGGARD, WILLIAM. Marine on ship Defence in 1777. (H-657)

HUGGINS, WILLIAM. Marine on ship Defence, September 6 to December 31, 1777. (H-657)

HUGHES, BENJAMIN. Non-Juror to Oath of Allegiance, 1778. (A-1/12)
HUGHES, CHARLES. Non-Juror to Oath of Allegiance, 1778. (A-1/12)

HUGHES, CHRISTOPHER. Private in Capt. J. Gist's Company, 3rd MD Regiment, January, 1778. Oath of Allegiance, 1778, before Hon. James Calhoun. (H-600, A-1/12, A-2/40)

HUGHES, DANIEL. Served on Baltimore County Committee of Observation, July 24, 1775. Wrote to Governor of Maryland on April 13, 1781, regarding responsibility for naval prisoners in Baltimore County. (FFF-381, EEEE-1725)

HUGHES, ELIJAH. Non-Juror to Oath in 1778, but signed in 1781. (A-1/12, QQ-113)

HUGHES, FRANCIS. Non-Juror to Oath of Allegiance, 1778. (A-1/12)

HUGHES, HENRY. Private, 4th MD Regiment, at Fort Whetstone Point in Baltimore, 1781. Non-Juror to Oath of Allegiance in 1778. (A-1/12, H-626)

HUGHES, HORATIO. Non-Juror to Oath of Allegiance, 1778. (A-1/12)

HUGHES, JAMES. Non-Juror to Oath in 1778, but signed in 1781. (A-1/12, QQ-113)

HUGHES, JOHN. There were two men with this name: one was born 1750 and was a Private in Baltimore County Militia, April 11, 1780; and one was born 1755 and was also a Private in the Maryland Line, Flying Camp. Both were Non-Jurors to the Oath, 1778. (A-1/12, YY-28, YY-29, H-335)

HUGHES, JOHN JR. Took the Oath of Allegiance in 1778 before Hon. Jesse Dorsey, and also took it again in 1781 (unless there were two men so named). (A-2/63, QQ-113)

HUGHES, MICHAEL. Matross in Capt. Brown's MD Artillery; joined November 22, 1777. Was at Valley Forge until June, 1778; at White Plains, July, 1778; at Fort Schuyler in August and September, 1780; not listed in 1781. Entitled to 50 acres for (lot #1933) in western Maryland. (UU-228, UU-230, DDDD-21)

HUGHES, SAMUEL. Baltimore Privateer. (III-206)

HUGHES, SOLOMON. Non-Juror to Oath of Allegiance, 1778. (A-1/12)

HUGHES, THOMAS. Oath of Allegiance, 1778, before Hon. Jesse Dorsey. Stored and delivered flour for the Baltimore Town Committee, 1780. (A-1/12, A-2/63, RRR-6)

HUGHES, WILLIAM. Oath of Allegiance, 1778, before Hon. James Calhoun. Stowed flour for the Baltimore Town Committee, 1780. (A-1/12, A-2/41, RRR-6)

HULIHANE, JOHN. Oath of Allegiance, 1778, before Hon. William Spear. (A-1/12, A-2/66)

HULING, MICHAEL. Private in Capt. Graybill's German Regiment in 1776. (H-266)

HULLER, NICHOLAS. Oath of Allegiance, 1778, before Hon. Jesse Dorsey. (A-2/63)

HULSE, R. Oath of Allegiance, 1778. (A-1/12)

HUMPHREYS, LEWIS. Served on ship Defence, June 25 to July 15, 1777. (H-657)

HUNGERFORD, THOMAS. Oath of Allegiance, 1778, before Hon. Isaac Van Bibber. (A-2/34)

HUNSON, ROBERT. Oath of Allegiance, 1778, before Hon. James Calhoun. (A-1/12, A-2/42)

HUNT, BENJAMIN. Ensign in Capt. Dickinson's Company, Baltimore Town Battalion, as of May 18, 1779. Also, took Oath of Allegiance in 1778 before Hon. James Calhoun. (A-1/12, A-2/42, F-312, GGG-401)

HUNT, JAMES. Non-Juror to Oath of Allegiance, 1778. (A-1/12)

HUNT, JOB (JOBE). (March 16, 1747 - February 18, 1809) Son of Job HUNT and Elizabeth CHEW. He married Margaret HOPKINS, daughter of Samuel HOPKINS, on Feb. 7, 1771. She was born in 1747 and died February 26, 1794. Both are buried in the Hunt Family Burying Ground off of Joppa Road in Baltimore County. Their children: Samuel (1771-1779); Elizabeth (1774-1775); Sarah (born 1777) married John DEAVER; Miriam (born 1779) married Lewis E. EvANS; Samuel (1780-1782); Elizabeth (1783-1784); Job (1785-1823) married Ann BOYD; Johns Hopkins (1787-c1827) married Susanna BOSLEY; Elizabeth (born 1789) married Rev. Daniel STANSBURY; and, Jesse (born 1793). Job HUNT was a Non-Juror to the Oath of Allegiance in 1778. (A-1/12, D-4)

HUNT, JOHN. (1750 - 1825) Married Joanna HOLBROOK. Took Oath of Allegiance, 1778, before Hon. William Spear. (A-1/12, A-2/66, JJJ-355)

HUNT, PHINEAS. Non-Juror to Oath of Allegiance, 1778. (A-1/12)

HUNT, SAMUEL. Oath of Allegiance, 1778, before Hon. James Calhoun. (A-1/12, A-2/41)

HUNT, SIMON. Non-Juror to Oath of Allegiance, 1778. (A-1/12)

HUNT, THOMAS. Involved in evaluation of Baltimore County confiscated proprietary reserve lands in 1782. (FFF-547)

HUNT, WILLIAM. Oath of Allegiance, 1778, before Hon. James Calhoun. (A-1/12, A-2/41)

HUNT, WILLIAM (OF THOMAS). Private, Col. Aquila hall's Baltimore County Regiment, 1777. (TTT-13)

HUNTER, GEORGE. Oath of Allegiance, 1778, before Hon. Jesse Dorsey. He was a Captain at Fells Point in Baltimore when he received muskets from Peter Littig on April 26, 1781. (A-1/12, A-2/64, FFF-387)

HUNTER, GEORGE JR. Non-Juror to Oath of Allegiance, 1778. (A-1/12)

HUNTER, PETER. Oath of Allegiance, 1778, before Hon. Jesse Dorsey. (A-1/12, A-2/63)

HUNTER, SAMUEL. Oath of Allegiance, 1778, before Hon. Jesse Dorsey. (A-1/12, A-2/64)

HUNTER, THOMAS. Private in Capt. Ramsey's Company No. 5 in 1776. (H-640)

HUNTER, WILLIAM. Non-Juror to Oath of Allegiance, 1787. (A-1/12)

HUNTS, JOSEPH. Oath of Allegiance, 1778. (A-1/12)

HURBERT (HURBURT), FRANCIS. Able Seaman on ship Defence, September 19, 1776, and Boatswain's Mate in 1777. (H-607, H-657)

HURBURT, WILLIAM. Able Seaman on ship Defence, September 19, 1776. (H-606)

HURD, BENNETT. "Bennett Hurd from Baltimore, substitute to serve until 10 December 1781, is hereby discharged, 29 November 1781." (CCCC-7) "Bennett Herd" enlisted in Frederick County, MD on July 29, 1776. (H-44) "Bennett Heard" enlisted in the 5th MD Regiment on April 16, 1782, by Major Davidson, for three years. (H-428)

HURD, JOHN. Oath of Allegiance, 1778, before Hon. John Moale. (A-1/12, A-2/70)

HURD, JOSHUA. Ensign in Soldiers Delight Battalion, August 29, 1777. Appointed Captain in the room of Thomas Owings, May 27, 1779 (but may have held that rank back in 1778). He left service prior to February 7, 1782. Also, took the Oath of Allegiance, 1778, before Hon. Edward Cockey. (A-1/12, A-2/61, BBB-348, Z-63, E-10, HH-24, GGG-422, CCCC-71)

HURST, CUTHBERT. Served on ship Defence, June 27 to December 31, 1777. (H0657)

HURST, SHADRICK. Private in Col. Aquila Hall's Baltimore County Regiment, 1777. (TTT-13)

HUSH (HUSCH), CONRAD. (c1757 - after 1801, Baltimore, MD) Married Eleanor PUTNEY on November 4, 1778. Their children: Samuel (born 1787) married Mary Ann LEARY; Peter (born 1791); George (born 1792); Henry (1794-1795); and, Urith (born 1795). He took the Oath of Allegiance, 1778, before Hon. Geo. Lindenberger. (XXX-414, JJJ-358, A-2/53)

HUSH, JOHN. Non-Juror to Oath of 1778, but signed in 1781. (A-1/12, QQ-113)

HUSH, PETER. Non-Juror to Oath of Allegiance, 1778. (A-1/12)

HUSH, VALENTINE. Oath of Allegiance, 1778, before Hon. James Calhoun. (A-1/12, A-2/42)

HUSK, BENEDICT. Non-Juror to Oath of Allegiance, 1778. (A-1/12)
HUSK, BENNETT. Non-Juror to Oath of Allegiance, 1778. (A-1/12)

HUSS, ISAAC. Oath of Allegiance, 1778, before Hon. James Calhoun. (A-1/12, A-2/39)

HUTCHERSON, ROBERT. Oath of Allegiance, 1778, before Hon. James Calhoun. (A-1/12, A-2/43)

HUTCHINS, JOSHUA. Non-Juror to Oath of Allegiance, 1778. (A-1/12)

HUTCHINS, NICHOLAS SR. Non-Juror to Oath of Allegiance, 1778. Delivered flour for Baltimore County, January 29, 1780. (A-1/13, FFF-266)

HUTCHINS, NICHOLAS JR. Oath of Allegiance, 1778, before Hon. Richard Cromwell. (A-2/46)

HUTCHINS, RICHARD. (January, 1741 - July 23, 1826) Buried at St. James Church, My Lady's Manor. Md. Zana Phyllis STANDIFORD. 2nd Lt., MD Line. (History Trails, Vol. 6, 1972)

HUTCHISON, THOMAS. Volunteer in Baltimore County Regiment No. 36, circa 1777. (TTT-13)

HUTIN, LAURENCE. Private in Capt. Smith's Company No. 8; enlisted Jan. 12, 1776. (H-18)

HUTSON, JOSHUA. (c1750 - before February, 1804) Married Suzanna HOOKER. Took the Oath of Allegiance, 1778, before Hon. Andrew Buchanan. (JJJ-359, A-1/13, A-2/57)

HUTSON, ROBERT. Recruit in Baltimore County Militia, April 11, 1780. (H-335)

HUTSON, SAMUEL. Revolutionary War Pensioner, June 1, 1840, age 77, residing in the household of Ed. Cleary in Baltimore City, 1st Ward. (P-128) Service not stated.

HUTSON, THOMAS. Oath of Allegiance, 1778, before Hon. Edward Cockey. (A-1/13, A-2/61)

HUTSON, WILLIAM. Oath of Allegiance in 1778 before Hon. Andrew Buchanan. (A-2/57)

HUTTENGER, MICHAEL. Oath of Allegiance, 1778, before Hon. Geo. Lindenberger. (A-2/53)

HUTTON, JAMES. Corporal in Capt. Gale's MD Artillery; appointed September 3, 1779. On command at Pumpton in 1779. Corporal in Capt. J. Smith's MD Artillery, 1780 to 1783. (H-579, YYY-1/54, YYY-2/24)

HUTTON, WILLIAM. Oath of Allegiance, 1778, before Hon. William Lux. Matross in Capt. Gale's MD Artillery, 1779, and Capt. J. Smith's Company, 1780. Corporal in Capt. Dorsey's MD Artillery at Camp Col. Scirvins, January 28, 1782, and served in that company through 1783. Entitled to 50 acres (lot #1021) in western Maryland for his services. (A-1/13, A-2/68, YYY-1/55, YYY-2/25, H-579, UU-232)

HUYER, ISAAC. Took the Oath of Allegiance in 1781. (QQ-113)

HYATT, GEORGE. Fifer in Capt. Graybill's German Regiment in 1776. (H-265, ZZ-32)

HYDE, WILLIAM. Captain in Smallwood's MD Regiment, January 14, 1776, and Lt.Col. in 2nd MD Battalion of Flying Camp, July, 1776. Men from Baltimore County served under his command. (B-312, H-53, H-59)

HYNDSON, ANTHONY. Boatswain on ship _Defence_ in 1777. (H-657)

HYNER (HYMER), NICHOLAS. Non-Juror to Oath in 1778, but signed in 1781. (A-1/13, QQ-113)

HYNES, MARTIN. Private in Baltimore County Militia; enlisted July 5, 1776. (H-58)

I

IGON, WILLIAM. Oath of Allegiance, 1778, before Hon. Peter Shepherd. (A-1/13, A-2/50)

INGLISH, JAMES. Non-Juror to Oath of Allegiance, 1778. (A-1/13)
INGS, JOHN. Non-Juror to Oath of Allegiance, 1778. (A-1/13)
INNIS, JOSHUA. Non-Juror to Oath of Allegiance, 1778. (A-1/13)
INSOR, JOSEPH. Non-Juror to Oath of Allegiance, 1778. (A-1/13)

INUMBROUGH, RAN. Baltimore Mechanical Company of Militia, November 4, 1775. (F-299)

IRELAND, JOHN. Matross in Capt. Gale's MD Artillery, 1779; employed by Capt.Lieutenant Horne in 1780. Matross in Capt. J. Smith's MD Artillery, 1780-1782. Matross in Capt. Dorsey's MD Artillery at Camp Col. Scirvins, January 28, 1782. In service to 1783. Entitled to 50 acres (lot #1203) in western Maryland, and received Federal Bounty Land Grant 11403 of 100 acres on February 7, 1790. (YYY-1/56, YYY-2/26, H-579, YY-68, DDDD-22, UU-232)

IRON, FREDERICK. Matross, Capt. Gale's MD Artillery, 1779-1780. (YYY-1/57)

ISAAC, HICKS. Oath of Allegiance, 1778. (A-1/13)

ISER, JOHN. Non-Juror to Oath of Allegiance, 1778. (A-1/13)
ISER, RICHARD. Non-Juror to Oath of Allegiance, 1778. (A-1/13)

ISGRID (ISGRIG), WILLIAM JR. Oath of Allegiance, 1778, before Hon. Jesse Dorsey. (A-2/63)

ISGRID (ISGRIG), WILLIAM SR. Non-Juror to Oath of Allegiance, 1778. (A-1/13)

ISLER, GEORGE. Oath of Allegiance, 1778, before Hon. James Calhoun. (A-1/13, A-2/38)

ISLER (ISLES), THOMAS. Non-Juror to Oath of Allegiance, 1778. (A-1/13)

ISRAEL, GILBERT SR. (Died in 1788 in Baltimore County) Wife named Prudence. Children of Gilbert Israel were named in his will and in the administration accounts of his estate filed December 11, 1790: Robert; Ely, married Ann GOLSON in 1785; John; and Gilbert; a daughter married Richard PARRISH; a daughter married Edward PARRISH; and daughter married John CLARK; and, Jemima. Gilbert Israel was a Non-Juror to Oath of Allegiance in 1778. (A-1/13, D-9)

ISRAEL, GILBERT JR. Non-Juror to Oath of Allegiance, 1778. (A-1/13)

ISRAEL, JOHN. Non-Juror to Oath of Allegiance, 1778. (A-1/13)

IVES, LUCAS. Recruited in Baltimore by Samuel Chester on March 2, 1780, for service in the 3rd MD Regiment. (H-334)

IVORY, PATRICK. Drummer in Capt. Ewing's Company No. 4; enlisted May 23, 1776. (H-11)

J

JACK, JAMES. Born in 1751 in Glasgow, Scotland. Occupation: Weaver. Enlisted Jan. 25, 1776 as Private in Capt. N. Smith's 1st Company of Matrosses. Height: 5' 4". Served as Matross in Capt. Dorsey's MD Artillery at Valley Forge, June 3, 1778. (UU-231, H-564, H-567, VV-73, QQQ-2)

JACKELEN (JAKQUELIN), FRANCIS. Cabin Steward on ship Defence, September 19, 1776, and Marine in 1777. (H-607, H-657)

JACKS, THOMAS. Non-Juror to Oath of Allegiance, 1778. (A-1/13)

JACKSON, ABRAHAM. (Died at Fells Point in Baltimore in 1787) He served as a Private in the Baltimore Artillery Company on October 16, 1775 and was a Corporal in Captain Sheaff's Company on June 16, 1777. He took the Oath of Allegiance in 1778 before Hon. Isaac Van Bibber. His children as named in his will (wife's name not included) were: William; Sarah, wife of James BIAYS; Maria; Elizabeth; Anna; Rosana, wife of John SMITH; and, Frances. (D-9, G-8, W-162, A-1/13, A-2/34)

JACKSON, ANTHONY. Recruit in Baltimore County in 1780. (H-340)

JACKSON, GEORGE. Private in Capt. McClellan's Company, Baltimore Town, September 4, 1780. Was a Non-Juror to Oath of Allegiance in 1778. (A-1/13, CCC-24)

JACKSON, HENRY. Non-Juror to Oath of Allegiance, 1778. (A-1/13)

JACKSON, JAMES. Born 1743. Sergeant, 2nd MD Regiment, at Fort Whetstone Point in Baltimore, 1781. Prisoner of war, and Pensioner. (H-626, YY-29)

JACKSON, MESHECK. Oath of Allegiance, 1778, before Hon. Richard Cromwell. (A-2/46)

JACKSON, RICHARD. Private in Capt.Deams Co., 7th MD Regt., December 15, 1776. (H-305)

JACKSON, THOMAS. Private in Baltimore County Regiment No. 7, circa 1777. (TTT-13)

JACKSON, WILLIAM. There were two men with this name who took the Oath of Allegiance in 1778 both before Hon. James Calhoun. (A-2/38, A-2/41, A-1/13)

JACOB (JACOBS), WM. Pvt. in Baltimore Artillery Company, October 16, 1775. Corporal in Capt. Sheaff's Company, June 16, 1776. Ensign in Capt. Rutter's Company, Feb. 7, 1777. 2nd Lieutenant in Baltimore Town Battalion, March 16, 1779. 1st Lieutenant in Capt. Young's Company, September 25, 1780. He wrote to Governor of Maryland, Dec. 16, 1780, requesting a commission as a Captain. He also took the Oath of Allegiance, 1778 before Hon. James Calhoun. (F-312, VV-303, G-8, W-162, BBB-121, FFF-342, A-2/38)

JACOB, WILL. Oath of Allegiance, 1778, before Hon. Isaac Van Bibber. (A-2/34)

JACOBS, JAMES. Private in Baltimore Artillery Company, October 16, 1775. (G-8)

JACOBS, JOHN. Non-Juror to Oath of Allegiance, 1778. (A-1/13)

JACOBS, ROBINSON. Private in Capt. Norwood's Company, 4th MD Regiment, from April 13, 1778 to August 16, 1780 when he was reported missing. (H-128)

JAFFREY, JAMES. Baltimore County Committee of Observation, July 24, 1775. Served with Capt. Nicholas Ruxton Moore's Troops on June 25, 1781. He had a seven year old sorrell gelding horse. (BBBB-313, EEEE-1725)

JAHN, JOCHIM. Oath of Allegiance, 1778. (A-1/13)

JAHN, JOHN. Oath of Allegiance, 1778. (A-1/13)

JALLOME (JELLOM), JOHN. Served in Capt. Furnival's Company; convalescent, Nov. 17, 1777. Matross in Capt. Dorsey's MD Artillery at Valley Forge, June 3, 1778. (H-618, UU-231)

JAMES, GEORGE. (Died in 1791 in Baltimore County) Wife named Rachel. Children in his will: Samuel; Diana, married Edward PARKINSON in 1785; Hannah, married William SLATER; Sarah, married a DAVIS; and, John. George JAMES was a Non-Juror to Oath of Allegiance in 1778, but signed in 1781. (D-9, A-1/13, QQ-114)

JAMES, ISAAC. Born 1748 in Philadelphia. Occupation: Taylor. Enlisted January 24, 1776 as Corporal in Capt. N. Smith's 1st Company of Matrosses. Height: 5' 9½". Earlier, on December 30, 1775, he was a Private in Capt. Howell's Company in Baltimore. (G-11, H-563)

JAMES, MICAJAH. Oath of Allegiance, 1778. (A-1/13)

JAMES, PHILIP. Recruit in Baltimore County Militia, April 11, 1780. (H-335)

JAMES, ROBINSON. Ensign in Upper Battalion of Baltimore County, 1778. (E-14)

JAMES, THOMAS. Non-Juror to Oath of Allegiance, 1778. (A-1/13)

JAMES, WALTER. Oath of Allegiance, 1778, before Hon. Richard Holliday. Private in Capt. Talbott's Company, May 31, 1779. (A-1/13, A-2/60, F-301, U-90)

JAMES, WATKINS. Non-Juror to Oath of Allegiance, 1778. (A-1/13)
JAMES, WILLIAM. Non-Juror to Oath of Allegiance, 1778. (A-1/13)

JARMAN, ABRAHAM. Born 1755 in America. Enlisted July 7, 1776 in Baltimore County as Private in Col. Ewing's Battalion. Height: 5' 5¼"; short black hair. (H-55)

JARMAN, JOHN. Oath of Allegiance, 1778, before Hon. George G. Presbury. (A-2/48)

JARVIS, EDWARD. Oath of Allegiance, 1778, before Hon. James Calhoun.(A-1/13,A-2/41)

JARVIS, JOHN. Private in Capt. Dorsey's MD Artillery, November 17, 1777. (H-574) Revolutionary War Pensioner, Private, Maryland Line. (YY-29)

JARVIS, MEAD. Oath of Allegiance, 1778, before Hon. Richard cromwell. (A-2/46)

JARVIS, PHILIP. Oath of Allegiance, 1778, before Hon. James Calhoun.(A-1/13,A-2/41)

JEANE (JANE), WILLIAM. Ensign in Capt. Harvey's Company, Gunpowder Upper Battalion, August 30, 1777 to at least 1778. Oath, 1778. (A-1/13, E-12, KK-66, BBB-350)

JEFFERS, JOHN. Non-Juror to Oath of Allegiance, 1778. Served with Capt. Nicholas Ruxton Moore's Troops on June 25, 1781. He had a ten year old dark bay horse. (A-1/13, BBBB-313)

JEFFERSON, EDWARD. Matross in Capt. Brown's MD Artillery; joined November 22, 1777. Was at Valley Forge until June, 1778; at White Plains, July, 1778; at Fort Schuyler in August and September, 1780; not listed in 1781. (UU-229, UU-230)

JEFFREYS, JOHN. Private in Baltimore County Militia; enlisted July 19, 1776. (H-58)

JENKINS, IGNATIOUS. Oath of Allegiance, 1778, before Hon. James Calhoun. (A-2/42)

JENKINS (JINKINS), JOHN. Oath of Allegiance, 1778, before Hon. William Spear. Pvt. in Capt. McClellan's Co., Baltimore Town, Sept. 4, 1780. (A-1/13, A-2/67, CCC-24)

JENKINS, MICHAEL. Oath of Allegiance, 1778, before Hon. James Calhoun.(A-1/13,A-2/39)

JENNETT, GREEN. Marine on ship _Defence_ in 1777. (H-657)

JENNETT (JANNETT), PETER. Born 1755 in Ireland. Enlisted July 5, 1776 in Baltimore County as Private in Col. Ewing's Battalion. Height: 5' 5"; long brown hair. (H-57)

JENNINGS, WILLIAM. Non-Juror to Oath of Allegiance, 1778. (A-1/13)

JERRIAL, JOHN. Marine on ship Defence, June 8 to August 4, 1777. (H-657)

JERVIS, HENRY. In Baltimore, March 10, 1777, he made an oath to attempt a prisoner exchange with Capt. George Cook of the Defence. (FFF-94)

JESSOP, CHARLES. Took the Oath of Allegiance in 1781. (QQ-114)

JESSOP (GESSOP), NICHOLAS. Non-Juror to Oath in 1778, but signed in 1781. (A-1/9,QQ-114)

JESSOP (GESSOP), WILLIAM JR. Non-Juror to Oath, 1778, but signed in 1781. (A-1/9, QQ-114)

JOBE, MORRIS. (May 26, 1753 - May 1, 1803) Married Lydia BOND. Private in Capt. John Cockey's Baltimore County Dragoons at Yorktown in 1781. (JJJ-369, MMM-A)

JOHNS, AQUILA. Lieutenant on ship Defence in 1777. Oath of Allegiance in 1778 before Hon. Isaac Van Bibber. Baltimore Privateer and Captain of ship Buckskin (28 guns), owned by S. & R. Purviance of Baltimore. (III-206, H-657, A-1/13, A-2/34)

JOHNS, JOHN. Oath of Allegiance, 1778, before Hon. Peter Shepherd. (A-2/49)

JOHNS, RICHARD. Oath of Allegiance, 1778, before Hon. Richard Holliday. Member of Col. Nicholson's Troop of Horse, June 7, 1781. (A-1/13, A-2/58, BBBB-274)

JOHNSON, ABM. Was Private in Capt. Norwood's Company, 4th MD Regiment; died Sept. 26, 1778. (H-128)

JOHNSON, ABSALOM. Born 1757. Lieutenant in Pennsylvania Militia, and was a pensioner from Maryland. (YY-30) Also, Non-Juror to Oath of Allegiance in 1778. (A-1/13)

JOHNSON, BENEDICT. Matross in Capt. J. Smith's MD Artillery in 1780; reported that he "lost his leg." Also listed as Matross in Capt. Dorsey's MD Artillery at Camp Col. Scirvins on January 28, 1782. Received Federal Bounty Land Grant Warrant #11404 of 100 acres on February 1, 1790. (YY-69, H-579, UU-232)

JOHNSON, DAVID. (December 4, 1744, Baltimore Co., MD - May 17, 1823, Baltimore Co., MD) Married Sarah STANDIFORD (1756-1835) on November 19, 1773. Their children: Elizabeth; Susannah; Eleanor, married a PEARCE; Charlotte; Cordelia; Benjamin; Sarah, married Moses MILES; Mary, married Charles R.WATTS; Thomas (1791-1832) married Martha JARRETT (1780-1842) in 1821 and their daughter Clara Mussard JOHNSON (1829-1906) married in 1848 to Charles Thomas PAINE; and, James. David JOHNSON took the Oath of Allegiance in 1778 before Hon. Jesse Dorsey. (There might have been two men by this name since Source A-2 lists them twice.) (A-1/13. A-2/63, A-2/64, JJJ-370, AAA-1828, XXX-425)

JOHNSON, EDWARD. Oath of Allegiance, 1778, before Hon. John Moale. (A-1/13, A-2/70)

JOHNSON, EPHRAIM. Non-Juror to Oath of Allegiance, 1778. (A-1/13)

JOHNSON (JOHNSTON), FRANCIS. Matross in Capt. Brown's MD Artillery; joined Nov. 22, 1777. Was at Valley Forge until June, 1778; at White Plains, July, 1778; at Fort Schuyler in August and September, 1780; at High Hills of the Santee in August, 1781. Received Federal Bounty Land Grant Warrant #346 for 100 acres on April 27, 1807, for his services. (UU-228, UU-230, YY-69)

JOHNSON, GEORGE. Non-Juror to Oath of Allegiance, 1778. (A-1/13)

JOHNSON, HORATIO. (1755, Baltimore County, MD - 18ι1, Anne Arundel County, MD) Son of Thomas JOHNSON and Ann RISTEAU. Married Elizabeth WARFIELD. Their son, Arthur Livingston JOHNSON (died 1860) married Margaret SMITH (died 1875) in 1822, and their grandson, Arthur Livingston JOHNSON Jr. (1832-1896) married Ruth Eugenia HASLUP in 1863. Horatio JOHNSON was an Ensign and Lieutenant in Capt. Norwood's Company, MD Line, 1776. (JJJ-370, AAA-838, WW-139)

JOHNSON, HORSFORD. Marine on ship Defence, April 28 to December 16, 1777. (H-657)

JOHNSON, JACOB. Non-Juror to Oath of Allegiance, 1778. (A-1/13)

JOHNSON, JAMES. Non-Juror to Oath of Allegiance, 1778. (A-1/13)

JOHNSON, JEREMIAH, ESQ. (1739 - 1814) Married Cassandra_____ in 1764. Their children: Sarah JOHNSON married John MERRYMAN; Elizabeth JOHNSON married Brian PHILPOT; Jeremiah JOHNSON married Ruth HOWARD; Richard JOHNSON married Eleanor JOHNSON; and Jayette JOHNSON married Elizabeth CRADDOCK. Jeremiah JOHNSON was representative for the North Hundred to the Association of Freemen on August 21, 1775. He was elected to the Baltimore County Committee of Observation on Sept. 23, 1775. He served as Judge of the Orphans Court and Justice of the Peace, Baltimore County, 1777-1778, and was one of the Magistrates who administered the Oath of Allegiance in 1778. In 1782 he was involved in the evaluation of Baltimore County confiscated proprietary reserve lands. (RR-47, RR-50, SS-136, FFF-538, XXX-426, A-1/13, A-2/33, GGG-242, JJJ-370, EEEE-1726)

JOHNSON, JOHN. Private in Col. Aquila Hall's Baltimore County Regiment, 1776-1777. Took Oath of Allegiance in 1778 before Hon. Jesse Dorsey. Recruit, Baltimore Co., 1780. Involved in evaluation of Baltimore County confiscated proprietary reserve lands in 1782. (H-340, TTT-13, FFF-547, A-1/13, A-2/63)

JOHNSON, JOHN. Seaman on ship Defence, January 11 to March 3, 1777. (H-657)

JOHNSON, JOSEPH. Non-Juror to Oath of Allegiance, 1778. (A-1/13)

JOHNSON, LUKE. Non-Juror to Oath, 1778, but signed in 1781. (A-1/13, QQ-114)

JOHNSON, MARK. Non-Juror to Oath of Allegiance, 1778. (A-1/13)
JOHNSON, MELCHISEDECK. Non-Juror to Oath of Allegiance, 1778. (A-1/13)

JOHNSON, RINNOLDO. Oath of Allegiance, 1778, before Hon. James Calhoun. (A-2/38)

JOHNSON, ROBERT. There were two men by this name who took the Oath of Allegiance in 1778: one before Hon. John Beale Howard (could not write; made his mark), and one before Hon. James Calhoun. (A-1/13, A-2/29, A-2/41)

JOHNSON, THOMAS. Represented Middlesex Hundred at the Association of Freemen on August 21, 1775. Took the Oath of Allegiance in 1778 before Hon. Isaac Van Bibber. (A-1/13, A-2/34, EEEE-1726)

JOHNSON, THOMAS. Born 1760. Private in Baltimore County Militia; enlisted July 18, 1776. Pensioner. (A-1/13, A-2/70, H-58, YY-30) Took Oath of Allegiance in 1778 before Hon. John Moale.

JOHNSON, THOMAS. Baltimore Privateer and Captain of brig Ranger (14 guns), owned by Daniel Bowley and John McLure of Baltimore. (III-206)

JOHNSON, WILLIAM. He reported to the Council of Safety on the lack of canvas for tents at Fort Whetstone Point in Baltimore, October 25, 1776. Took the Oath of Allegiance in 1778 before Hon. Isaac Van Bibber. On September 25, 1780, he was commissioned Ensign in Capt. Dickinson's Company, Baltimore Town Battalion Militia. He served until February 8, 1781, when apparently replaced; no known reason given. (A-1/13, A-2/34, F-305, BBBB-29, BBBB-61, FFF-64)

JOHNSON, WILLIAM. Matross in Capt. Brown's MD Artillery; joined November 22, 1777. Was at Valley Forge until June, 1778; at White Plains, July, 1778; at Fort Schuyler in August and September, 1780; not listed in 1781. (UU-228, UU-230)

JOHNSON, WILLIAM. Private in Baltimore County Regiment No. 15, circa 1777. Took the Oath of Allegiance in 1778 before Hon. Robert Simmons. (TTT-13, A-2/58)

JOHNSON, WILLIAM JR. Private in Capt. Sheaff's Company, June 16, 1777. Non-Juror to the Oath of Allegiance in 1778. (W-162, A-1/13)

JOHNSTON (JOHNSON), CHRISTOPHER. (1750, Moffatt, Scotland - March 6, 1819, Baltimore, Maryland) Married Susanna STITH (1759-1838) in 1779 in Northampton County, Virginia. Their son, Christopher JOHNSON II (1800, Baltimore, Maryland - 1835, Cincinnati,Ohio) married Eliza GATES in 1821, and their grandson Christopher JOHNSTON III (1822-1891) married Sarah L. C. SMITH (1835-1879) in 1855. Christopher JOHNSTON was a Private in Capt. Nicholas Ruxton Moore's Baltimore Light Dragoons in the Yorktown campaign 1781.

Christopher JOHNSON also took the Oath of Allegiance in 1778 before Hon. James Calhoun. He is buried under Westminster Church on Fayette Street in Baltimore. (AAA-2758, A-1/13, A-2/39)

JOHNSTON, JOHN. Martha JOHNSTON, widow of John JOHNSTON, applied for pension because of the Revolutionary War service of her husband in 1841 when she resided in Maury County, Tennessee. She was then 83 years of age. She stated that she married John JOHNSTON in the summer of 1774 in Baltimore, Maryland, and that shortly after their marriage they moved to York District, South Carolina, where they resided until after the close of the Revolution. She stated that her husband was in the battles of Hanging Rock and King's Mountain and that he died Octobr 5, 1818. She stated that after the close of the Revolution she and her husband and their children moved to Davidson County, Tennessee, and from there to maury County, Tennessee, where she resided from 1807. She stated that she was born in Nottongham County, Maryland (?) (Ed.: Obvious error, as there is no such county in Maryland.) in 1758 and that she was a member of the Methodist Church. They had several children whose names are not given in the application. (OO-136) There was also a John JOHNSTON who was Private in the Extra Regiment at Fort Whetstone Point in Baltimore in 1781. (H-627)

JOHNSTON, THOMAS. Oath of Allegiance, 1778, before Hon. James Calhoun. (A-2/38)

JOHNESTON, JOSEPH. Oath of Allegiance, 1778, before Hon. John Hall. (A-2/36)

JONES, ARTHUR. Oath of Allegiance, 1778. (A-1/13)

JONES, BENJAMIN. Born 1745 in Maryland. Occupation: Bricklayer. Enlisted Jan. 30, 1776 as Private in Capt. N. Smith's 1st Company of Matrosses. Earlier, on Dec. 30, 1775, he was Private in Capt. Howell's Company in Baltimore. On November 17, 1777, he was Private in Capt. Dorsey's MD Artillery and was deposed on May 7, 1779 about his enlistment terms. He also took the Oath of Allegiance in 1778 before Honorable John Merryman. On September 15, 1779 he was left as an invalid at Fort Whetstone Point in Baltimore and was subsequently discharged from service on May 8, 1781. (H-573, H-626, FFF-220, G-11, H-567, QQQ-2, H-565, VV-73, A-1/13, A-2/45)

JONES, CHARLES. Of Baltimore County. Married Elizabeth RICHARDS in 1799. Children: (all born in St. James Parish) Elizabeth Robinson (born 1800); John (born 1801); and Charles (born 1803) He was a Non-Juror to Oath in 1778. (D-4, A-1/13)

JONES, FRANCIS. Non-Juror to Oath of Allegiance, 1778. (A-1/13)

JONES, JERRY. Private in Capt. Smith's Company No. 8; enlisted January 27, 1776 and subsequently deserted. (H-18)

JONES, JOHN. (April 9, 1737/1739 - 1785, Baltimore County) Son of John JONES and wife Hannah. He married Esther _____ who died in 1787. Their children: John (born in 1760); Elisah; Ann, married John WALTON; Sophia, married Joseph HOOK; Eleanor, md. Benjamin PARKS; Joshua; Caleb; and Enoch. (Last three were under age in 1787) John JONES was a Private in either the 3rd or 7th MD Regiment durin the war, and probably was the John JONES in Capt. Deams Company on January 19, 1777, and also the one in the Extra Regiment at Fort Whetstone Point in Baltimore in 1781. There appears to have been more than one man with this name, as anothr John JONES is reported to be a a recruit in Baltimore County in 1780. His son, John JONES, was his administrator and recipient of his father's Federal Bounty Land Grant issued November 29, 1790. (D-4, H-340, H-305, H-627, AAAA-650, and Clark's Revolutionary Pensioners, p. 22)

JONES, JOHN. 2nd Lieutenant in Capt. Lane's Company, Gunpowder Upper Battalion, on October 23, 1781. Took Oath of Allegiance in 1778 before Hon. Richard Holliday. (A-1/13, A-2/60, AAAA-650)

JONES, JONAS. Non-Juror to Oath of Allegiance, 1778. (A-1/13)

JONES, JOSEPH. Marine on ship Defence in 1777. (H-657)

JONES, JOSHUA. (1735/1750 - January 9, 1811, Baltimore County, MD) Married Mary HARVEY, daughter of William HARVEY and Margaret NORMAN. Their children: Nicholas H. married Susanna GORSUCH; Joshua; Thomas; William; Elisha; John; Andrew; Elizabeth, married a PARKS; Priscilla, md. Peter PARKS. Took the Oath in 1778. (D-4, JJJ-374, A-1/13 N-J)

JONES, MICHAEL. Private in Capt. McClellan's Company, Baltimore Town, September 4, 1780. Took Oath of Allegiance, 1778, before Hon. James Calhoun. (CCC-25, A-2/41)

JONES, MORGIN. Oath of Allegiance, 1778, before Hon. James Calhoun. (A-2/65)

JONES, NATHAN. Served on ship Defence, January 25 to May 13, 1777. (H-657)

JONES, NICHOLAS. Non-Juror to Oath of Allegiance, 1778. (A-1/13) He might have been the Nicholas Jones (1751-1835) who was born in Baltimore County, enlisted in Harford County, and lived in Allegany County, receiving pension S8771. (See Raymond Clark's Maryland Revolutionary Pensioners, page 22)

JONES, PETER. (1760 - July 3, 1842) Married Mary BRANSON. Recruit in Baltimore County in 1780. (JJJ-364, H-340)

JONES, PHILIP. Born 1754 in Maryland. Occupation: Bricklayer. Enlisted January 25, 1776 as Private in Capt. N. Smith's 1st Company of Matrosses. (Source YY-30 states he was born in 1758.) Height: 5' 7". Served as Corporal in Capt. Dorsey's Company of Artillery at Valley Forge, June 3, 1778. Served as Gunner in Capt. J. Smith's MD Artillery, 1780-1783, with service as Matross in Capt. Dorsey's Company, Jan. 28, 1782. Entitled to 50 acres (lot #1099) in western Maryland for his war services. (YY-30, H-564, H-567, H-579, QQQ-2, VV-73, UU-231, UU-232, YYY-2/27, DDDD-23)

JONES, RICHARD. (Died in Baltimore County in 1791) Wife named Alice. He was a son of Richard JONES. Children: Samuel; Richard; William; Joseph; Sarah; Cassandra, married a COE; Rachel, married a TALBOTT; Lucy, married Stephen OWINGS, Jr.; and, Abraham. Richard JONES was a Non-Juror in 1778 to the Oath of Allegiance, and he was one of those who petitioned that the sale of My Lady's Manor be postponed in October, 1782. (D-9, A-1/13)

JONES, RICHARD. Sergeant in Col. Aquila Hall's Baltimore County Regiment in 1777. (TTT-13)

JONES, RICHARD. (OF ARTHUR). Oath of Allegiance, 1778, before Hon. Jesse Dorsey. He might have been the Sergeant Richard Jones mentioned previously. (A-2/63)

JONES, ROBINSON. Ensign in Capt. Merryman's Company, Upper Battalion, August 30, 1777. Oath of Allegiance, 1778, before Hon. Robert Simmons. 2nd Lieutenant as of November 5, 1781. (AAAA-662, BBB-350, LL-66, A-1/13, A-2/58)

JONES, SAMUEL. Private in Capt. Norwood's Company, 4th MD Regiment from May 19, 1778 until August 16, 1780 when reported missing. (H-128)

JONES, SOLOMON. (Died November 30, 1830) Matross in Capt. Gale's MD Artillery, 1779 to 1780; in the hospital, November, 1779 to March, 1780. Non-Juror to the Oath of Allegiance in 1778. (A-1/13, YYY-1/58)

JONES, THOMAS. (March 12, 1735, Baltimore County, MD - September 27, 1812, Baltimore) His first wife was Elizabeth BAXTER, daughter of Col. James and Elizabeth BAXTER. They married December 14, 1761. His second wife was Elizabeth McCLURE (1755-1848). Thomas JONES had two children by his first wife and seven by his second: Henrietta M. JONES married Josiah DALLAM; Elizabeth Waugh JONES married Lloyd BEALL; Philip JONES married Mary_____; Thomas Sprigg JONES married Susanna TROTTEN; Anna Barbara JONES married jacob SCHLEY; Richard Sprigg JONES; Rachel JONES; Henry JONES and, an infant. Thomas JONES served on the Baltimore County Committee of Observation on August 7, 1775, and was commissioned 2nd Major in the Baltimore Town Battn. of Militia on May 25, 1776. He took the Oath of Allegiance, 1778, before Honorable Peter Shepherd. "Hon. Thomas Jones died in September, 1812, at Fort McHenry in his 77th year." (ZZZ-178, EEEE-1726, H-53, H-58, ZZ-32, D-9, JJJ-375, A-1/13, A-2/49)

JONES, THOMAS. Private, Capt. Ewing's Company No. 4 in 1776. Oath of Allegiance in 1778 before Hon. Andrew Buchanan ("labourer" written next to his name). Might have been a pensioner since there were eight from Maryland with this name who were. (H-13, YY-30, A-2/57)

JONES, THOMAS. Recruit in Baltimore County Militia in 1780. Private in Capt. Cockey's

Baltimore County Dragoons at Yorktown, 1781. Oath of Allegiance, 1778, before Hon. William Lux. Might have been a pensioner since there were eight with this name in Maryland who were pensioned. (H-335, MMM-A, YY-30, A-2/68)

JONES, WILLIAM. There were five men with this name who were pensioners in Maryland; at least two of them were from Baltimore County. One was a Gunner in Capt. Brown's MD Artillery; joined November 22, 1777. Was at Valley Forge until June, 1778; at White Plains, July, 1778; at Fort Schuyler in August and September, 1780; and listed 1781, as a Bombardier, probably serving through April, 1782. Another William JONES served as Matross in Capt. Gale's MD Artillery, 1779-1780; reported sick at Annapolis, 1779. One of them, or perhaps a third William JONES, took the Oath of Allegiance in 1778 before Hon. James Calhoun. (A-1/13, A-2/38, YY-30, YY-31, UU-228, UU-230, YYY-1/59)

JORDAN (JORDON), FELIX. Oath of Allegiance, 1778, before Hon. James Calhoun. (A-2/38)

JORDAN, HENRY. Non-Juror to Oath of Allegiance, 1778. (A-1/13)

JORDAN (JOURDAN), JEREMIAH. Served on ship Defence, Jan. 23 to Dec. 31, 1777. (H-657)

JORDAN (JOURDAN), JOHN. Sergeant of Marines on ship Defence, Jan. 23 to Dec. 31, 1777. Took Oath of Allegiance, 1778, before Hon. George Lindenberger. (H-657, A-2/53)

JORDAN (JURDAN), MICHAEL. Oath of Allegiance, 1778, before Hon. George Lindenberger. (A-1/13, A-2/53)

JORDAN, ROBERT. Non-Juror to Oath in 1778, but signed in 1781. (A-1/13, QQ-114)

JORDAN, SAMUEL. Corporal of Marines on ship Defence, Oct. 22 to Dec. 31, 1777. (H-657)

JORDAN, THOMAS. (c1720 - after 1790) Wife named Ann. Non-Juror, 1778. (A-1/13, JJJ-377) However, Source JJJ-377 states he gave patriotic service so further research needed.

JORDAN (JORDON), WILLIAM. Born 1755 in America. Enlisted July 5, 1776 in Baltimore County as Private in Col. Ewing's Battalion; height: 5' 7½"; sandy hair. (H-56)

JOY, PETER. Non-Juror to Oath of Allegiance, 1778. (A-1/13)

JOYCE (JOICE), EDWARD. Corporal in Capt. J. Gist's Company, 3rd MD Regiment, February, 1778. (H-600)

JOYCE (JOICE), JOSEPH. Oath of Allegiance, 1778, before Hon. James Calhoun. (A-2/41)

JOYCE, STEPHEN. Private in Capt. Howell's Company, December 30, 1775. Took Oath of Allegiance, 1778, before Hon. Isaac Van Bibber. (G-11, A-1/13, A-2/34)

JOYCE, WILLIAM. Recruit in Baltimore County Militia, April 11, 1780. (H-335)

JRIAOM(?), JOHN. Oath of Allegiance, 1778. (A-1/13)

JUDAH, WILLIAM. (1724 - 1782) Wife named Mary. 2nd Lieutenant in Capt. Dorsey's MD Artillery from November 17, 1777 to at least August 30, 1779. (JJJ-377, FFF-237, H-573, TT-102)

JUDGES, WILLIAM. Ordinary Sailor on ship Defence in 1777. (H-657)

JUDY, JOHN SR. Non-Juror to Oath of Allegiance, 1778. (A-1/13)
JUDY, JOHN JR. Non-Juror to Oath of Allegiance, 1778. (A-1/13)

JUDY, NICHOLAS. Oath of Allegiance, 1778, before Hon. James Calhoun. (A-1/13, A-2/39)

JUDY, WIMBERT. Oath of Allegiance, 1778, before Hon. James Calhoun. (A-1/13, A-2/39)

JUNCK, JOHN. Oath of Allegiance, 1778, before Geo. Lindenberger. (A-1/13, A-2/53)

K

KAGEN, HENRY. Private in Baltimore County Militia; enlisted July 19, 1776. (H-58)

KALEY, JAMES. Non-Juror to Oath of Allegiance, 1778. (A-1/13)

KALLER, JOHN. Oath of Allegiance, 1778, before Hon. George Lindenberger. (A-2/53)

KANTZ (KAUTZ), PHILIP. Private, Capt. Graybill's German Regiment, 1776. (H-265, ZZ-32)

KAWTZMAR, ANDREW. Oath of Allegiance, 1778, before Hon. James Calhoun. (A-2/39)

KEAN, JAMES. Baltimore Artillery Company, 1777. (V-368)

KEEFER, VINCENT. Non-Juror to Oath of Allegiance, 1778. (A-1/13)

KEENAN, LARRONS. Private in Baltimore County Militia; enlisted July 18, 1776. (H-58)

KEENE, JANNY. Oath of Allegiance, 1778, before Hon. James Calhoun. (A-2/65)

KEENE, JOSHAM. Oath of Allegiance, 1778, before Hon. James Calhoun. (A-2/65)

KEENE, WILLIAM. Supplied plank for use at Fort Whetstone Point in Baltimore on September 5, 1776. (FFF-55)

KEENER, BARNEY. Private in Capt. Deams Co., 7th MD Regt., January 16, 1777. (H-305)

KEENER, CHRISTIAN. (August 12, 1752 - November 21, 1817) Married Susanna SWOPE on April 20, 1780. Daughter, Anna Maria KEENER (Ann Mary) married (1) John REIGART in 1799, and (2) Rev. James STEVENS. Daughter, Susan KEENER (died 1809) married Nicholas ORRICK in 1803. Christian KEENER took the Oath of Allegiance in 1778 before Hon. James Calhoun. (ZZZ-294, ZZZ-268, XXX-434, JJJ-379, A-1/13, A-2/40)

KEENER, GEORGE. Private in Capt. McClellan's Company, Baltimore Town, September 4, 1780. (CCC-25)

KEENER, JOHN. 3rd Sergeant in Capt. Keeports German Regiment; enlisted August 19, 1776. At Philadelphia, September 19, 1776. (H-262)

KEENER, MELCHIOR (MELCHER). (September 25, 1720 - August 26, 1798) Wife named Margaret. Member of the Sons of Liberty in 1776. On December 13, 1776, Melchior KEENER and the Whig Club were deemed by the Maryland Council to be getting too disorderly and in jeopardy of prejudicing the common cause against the British. The Baltimore Committee of Observation was ordered to watch these overzealous patriots and to point out anyone who acted contrary to their resolves. "Melchor Kenor" took the Oath of Allegiance in 1778 before Hon. James Calhoun. When he died in 1798 his death notice stated he was one of the oldest settlers of Baltimore and interment was in the German Presbyterian Burying Ground. (ZZZ-180, ZZ-526, JJJ-379, CCC-19, A-1/13, A-2/39)

KEENER, PETER. On September 17, 1777, he was under contract "to make 150 musquets fixed with bayonets, steel rammers, swivels priming wires, and brushed, at 3 lbs. 15 shillings each....at Baltimore Town...." (BBB-377)

KEENTS, JOSEPH. Oath of Allegiance, 1778, before Hon. Thomas Sollers. (A-2/51)

KEEPLE, JOSEPH. Oath of Allegiance, 1778, before Hon. George Lindenberger. (A-2/53)

KEEPORTS (KEYPORTS). GEORGE PETER. 3rd Lieutenant in Capt. N. Smith's 1st Company of Matrosses, January 24, 1776 in Baltimore Town (Source TT-102 erroneously states it was in Annapolis). Became Captain of the 1st German Regiment of Continental Troops commanded by Col. Nicholas Husacker, July 8, 1776. The Regiment was raised from Baltimore County (a second regiment was raised in Frederick County). He was at Philadelphia on September 19, 1776. Source TT-102 states he resigned May 4, 1777, but he was still active in the war effort because he wrote the Governor of Maryland on October 20, 1777 about the need for lead for the manufacture of musket cartridges in Baltimore. He took the Oath of Allegiance in 1778 before Hon. George Lindenberger in Baltimore, and on June 12, 1779, he was appointed Armourer at Baltimore. (GGG-452, FFF-126, III-192, TT-102, H-563, RR-90, H-262, A-1/13, A-2/53)

KEEPORTS. JACOB. (1718 - march 8, 1792) Took Oath of Allegiance, 1778, before Hon. George Lindenberger. (JJJ-379, A-1/13, A-2/53)

KEES, FREDERICK. Non-Juror to Oath of Allegiance, 1778. (A-1/13)

KEES, GEORGE. Non-Juror to Oath of Allegiance, 1778. (A-1/13)

KEES, JOHN. Non-Juror to Oath of Allegiance, 1778. (A-1/13)

KEES, MATTHIAS. Recruited into Baltimore County Militia, April 11, 1780. (H-335)

KEIP, CHARLES. Oath of Allegiance, 1778, before Hon. George Lindenberger. (A-2/53)

KEITH (KEITHS), PATRICK. Baltimore Artillery Company, 1777. Oath of Allegiance, 1778, before Hon. James Calhoun. (A-1/13, A-2/41, V-368)

KEITH, WILLIAM. Non-Juror to Oath of Allegiance, 1778. (A-1/13)

KELL, THOMAS. (1745/1747, England - 1790, Guadaloupe, West Indies) Capt. Thomas KELL was of Fell's Point in Baltimore and Kellville in Harford County, MD. He married Aliceanna BOND (c1748-April 21, 1814) on May 30, 1767, a daughter of John BOND (1712-1791), a Quaker who lived both at Fell's Point and at Kellville, and his wife Aliceanna WEBSTER (died 1765). They had fifteen children, one of whom was Pamelia KELL, and another was Judge Thomas KELL, Jr. (1772-1846) of the Baltimore County Court. Capt. Thomas KELL was a sea captain and commanded the privateers Dolphin and Little Davy in the Revolutionary War. He spent most of his life in Maryland, and died in the West Indies while on a voyage there in 1790. (JJJ-379, and Maryland Historical Magazine, Vol. 37, No. 2, June, 1942, pages 133-134)

KELLEHER (KELLIHER, KELLIKER), HENRY. Born 1757 in Cork, Ireland. Occupation: Taylor. Enlisted January 24, 1776 as Drummer in Capt. N. Smith's 1st Company of Matrosses. Height: 5' 8". Served as Drummer in Capt. Dorsey's MD Artillery, November 17, 1777 and was at Valley Forge, June 3, 1778. (H-566, H-574, QQQ-2, UU-231)

KELLER, JOSEPH. Non-Juror to Oath of Allegiance, 1778. (A-1/13)

KELLY (KELLEY), CHARLES. Enlisted in Baltimore County on August 14, 1776. Took the Oath of Allegiance, 1778, before Hon. Edward Cockey. (A-2/61, H-52, H-59)

KELLY, JAMES. Private in Capt. S. Smith's Company No. 8, 1st MD Battalion, January 18, 1776, and Private in Capt. Deams Company, 7th MD Regiment, December 15, 1776. As a Corporal, 7th MD Regiment, he received 50 acres (lot #1247) in western Maryland for his services. Took Oath of Allegiance, 1778, before Hon. James Calhoun. (DDDD-23, H-305, H-640, A-1/13, A-2/43)

KELLY, JOHN. Private in Baltimore County Militia; enlisted August 15, 1776. (H-58)

KELLY (KELLEY), JOSHUA (OF WILLIAM). Oath of Allegiance, 1778, before Honorable John Merryman. 2nd Lieutenant in Capt. Kelly's Company, Soldiers Delight Battalion, on February 7, 1782. (A-1/13, A-2/70, CCCC-71)

KELLY (KELLEY), MATTHEW. (August 1, 1734 - December 31, 1796) Wife named Jane. He enlisted August 31, 1776 as a Private in Capt. N. Smith's 1st Company of Matrosses. Stationed at Fort Whetstone Point on September 7, 1776. Private in Capt. Dorsey's MD Artillery, November 17, 1777, and Matross in that company at Valley Forge as of June 3, 1778. Private in 4th MD Regiment at Fort Whetstone Point in Baltimore in 1781. (JJJ-381, UU-231, H-627, H-574, H-569, VV-74)

KELLY (KELLEY), NICHOLAS. Ensign in Capt. Cockey's Company, Gunpowder Upper Battn.; August 29, 1777. Oath of Allegiance, 1778, before Hon. Edward Cockey. Captain in Gunpowder Upper Battalion, October 23, 1781. (AAAA-650, Z-63, E-12, BBB-348, A-2/61)

KELLY (KELLEY), PATRICK. Private in Baltimore County Regiment No. 7, circa 1777, and Recruit again in 1780, Baltimore County. (H-340, TTT-13)

KELLY, RICHARD. Private in Capt. Oldham's Company, 4th MD Regiment, from June 4, 1777 until March 4, 1779, when he was reported deserted. (H-130)

KELLY (KELLEY), THOMAS. Private in Baltimore County Militia; enlisted August 15, 1776. Stored flour for the Baltimore Town Committee in 1780. (H-58, RRR-6)

KELLY, TIMOTHY. Ordinary Seaman on ship Defence, September 19, 1776. (H-607)

KELLY (KELLEY), WILLIAM. Oath of Allegiance, 1778, before Hon. John Moale. (A-2/70)

KELLY (KELLEY), WILLIAM JR. (April 11, 1751 - February 22, 1816) Son of William KELLY and Elizabeth GORSUCH. Married Martha LOWELL (LOVELL), 1759-1851, in 1778. Children: Sarah KELLY, married John UHLER; John KELLY, married Charlotte YOUSE;

KELLY, WILLIAM JR. (continued)
Mary KELLY; Nicholas KELLY, married Mary BROMWELL; Joshua KELLY; Rachael KELLY
(1803-1880) married Edward TALBOTT (1789-1844) in 1822, and their daughter Miluna
TALBOTT (1834-1920) married William W. OURSLER (1831-1893) in 1859; and, Elizabeth
KELLY, married George W. MONROE. William KELLY was an Ensign in Capt. Christopher
Owings' Company, Soldiers Delight Battalion, August 29, 1777, and became a Captain
in Gist's Battalion. He took the Oath of Allegiance in 1778 before Honorable James
Calhoun. He is reported as Captain in Soldiers Delight Battalion in the room of
Elie Dorsey, February 7, 1782. (XXX-435, AAA-1068, AAA-1648, JJJ-381, CCCC-71,
BBB-348, Z-63, E-10, A-1/13, A-2/42)

KELSEY, WILLIAM SR. Non-Juror to Oath of Allegiance, 1778. (A-1/13)

KELSIMER, FRANCIS. Stored flour and drove a wagon for the Baltimore Town Committee in
1780. (RRR-6)

KELSO, THOMAS. (March 7, 1764/1765, Baltimore County, MD - January 29, 1847, Shelby
County, KY) Married Penelope RUTLEDGE (born May 9, 1765) in 1789 (marriage proven
through Maryland pension application). Their children: Jane (born Feb. 25, 1790);
Elijah (born Nov. 18, 1791); Ann (born June 14, 1793); William (born September 8,
1795); Abraham (born May 31, 1797); Penelope (born Mar.4, 1799); Ruth (born Jan. 17,
1802); Thomas (born Mar. 18, 1804); Russell (born Apr. 8, 1806); Elizabeth (born
Aug. 18, 1807); and, James (born July 18, 1811) Thomas KELSO enlisted in the Army
in March, 1780, under Capt. Daniel Shaw and Col. Joshua Gist. His brother-in-law
was a Captain Standiford. Received a pension also. (YY-31, D-9, YY-117)

KELTY, JOHN. (1751-1812) Captain in the Revolutionary War. His wife, Catharine QUINE
KELTY was a pensioner as of June 1, 1840, aged 64, residing in the household of one
Eliza JONES in Baltimore city, 9th Ward. (P-128, JJJ-381)

KELY, PETER. Private in Baltimore Artillery Company, October 16, 1775. (G-8)

KEMMELSTONE, WILLIAM. Private in Capt. Graybill's German Regiment, July 12, 1776.(ZZ-32)

KEMP, JAMES. Private in Baltimore County Militia in 1776. (H-59)

KEMP, JOHN. Oath of Allegiance, 1778, before Hon. Edward Cockey. (A-2/61)

KEMP, WILHELM. Private in Capt. Myers' Company, German Regiment; served three years;
discharged July 23, 1779. (H-270)

KENDERDINE (KENDERCLINE), JOHN. Marine on ship Defence in 1777. Private in Captain
Furnival's MD Artillery, November 17, 1777: "sick - shoulder burned by accident at
camp." Matross in Capt. Gale's MD Artillery, 1779-1780: "sick at Trenton, 1779."
(H-657, H-573, YYY-1/60)

KENNEDY, BENJAMIN DR. (Of Baltimore Town) Received an order from the Maryland Council
to pay him 44 lbs. for medicine furnished the troops, 1776. (XX-9)

KENNEDY, JAMES. Private, Capt. Lansdale's Company, 4th MD Regiment; enlisted May 22,
1779; Corporal, February 1, 1780; Sergeant, June 1, 1780; wounded; discharged,
November 1, 1780. Pensioner. Also took the Oath of Allegiance in 1778 before Hon.
George Lindenberger. (A-1/13, A-2/53, YY-31, H-131)

KENNEDY, MURDOCK. Oath of Allegiance, 1778, before Hon. James Calhoun.(A-1/13,A-2/40)

KENNY, THOMAS. Enlisted July 25, 1776 in Baltimore County. (H-52)

KENT, HENRY. Private in Count Pulaski's Legion; enlisted in Baltimore, April 22, 1778.
(H-592, H-593)

KEPLINGER, JOHN. Oath of Allegiance, 1778, before Hon. James Calhoun.(A-1/13, A-2/40)

KERHART, ADAM. Oath of Allegiance, 1778, before Hon. William Spear. Could not write;
made his mark. (A-1/13, A-2/66)

KERNS (KEARNS), CHRISTIAN. 4th Sergeant in Capt. Keeports German Regiment; enlisted
August 19, 1776. At Philadelphia, September 19, 1776. (H-262)

KERNS (KERN), CHRISTOPHER. Oath of Allegiance, 1778, before Hon. Richard Cromwell. (A-1/13, A-2/46)

KERNS (KEARNS, KERN), JACOB. Private in Capt. Graybill's German Regiment in 1776. Oath of Allegiance, 1778, before Hon. James Calhoun. (A-1/13, A-2/42, H-266)

KERNS (KERN), PETER. Oath of Allegiance, 1778, before Hon. Richard Cromwell. (A-2/46)

KERSEY, EDWARD. Enlisted in Baltimore County on July 25, 1776. (h-52)

KERSEY, JOHN. Oath of Allegiance, 1778, before Hon. Richard Cromwell. (A-1/13, A-2/46)

KERSHNER (KEARSHNER, KERSHER), MICHAEL. (1752, Germany - April 25, 1823, Maryland) Married Mary MOTTER and had at least one child, Mary Katherine. He was a Private in July, 1776; enlisted by Capt. Philip Graybill for his German Regiment. Source YY-32 states he was a pensioner and also that he was born in 1752; Source JJJ-384 states he was born in 1758; Source D-9 gives date as 1752. (H-265, ZZ-32, YY-32, D-9, JJJ-384)

KESEY, ROBERT. Oath of Allegiance, 1778, before Hon. William Spear. (A-1/13, A-2/66)

KETTLEMAN, BALENTINE (VALENTINE). Non-Juror to Oath of Allegiance, 1778. (A-1/13)

KEW, CHARLES. Baltimore Mechanical Company of Militia, November 4, 1775. (F-299)

KEY (KEAY), DANIEL. Born 1747 in England. Enlisted July 5, 1776 in Baltimore County. Private in Col. Ewing's Battalion. Height: 4' 11"; sandy complexion. (H-57)

KEYS, CHARLES. Oath of Allegiance, 1778, before Hon. James Calhoun. (A-1/13, A-2/38)

KEYSER, NICHOLAS. Private in Capt. Graybill's German Regiment in 1776. (H-266)

KEYSEY, JNO. Private, Capt. Deams Company, 7th MD Regiment, January 23, 1777. (H-305)

KIBBLE, JOSEPH. Non-Juror to Oath of Allegiance, 1778. (A-1/13)

KIDD, HENRY. Non-Juror to Oath of Allegiance, 1778. (A-1/13)

KIDD, JOHN. Non-Juror to Oath of Allegiance, 1778. (A-1/13)

KIDD, JOSHUA. Involved in evaluation of Baltimore County confiscated proprietary reserve lands in 1782. (FFF-542)

KIESS, CHARLES. Private in Capt. Cox's Company, December 19, 1776. Oath of Allegiance in 1778. (CCC-21, A-1/13)

KILDRAY, JOHN. Recruit in Baltimore County in 1780. (H-340)

KILLEY, CHARLES. Oath of Allegiance, 1778. (A-1/13)

KILLEY, JAMES. Recruit in Baltimore County Militia, November 11, 1780. (H-335)

KILLEY, NICHOLAS. Oath of Allegiance, 1778. (A-1/13)

KILLYHAM, BRADLEY. Private, Capt. Deams Company, 7th MD Regt., February 4, 1777. (H-305)

KIMMEL (KEMMELL), THOMAS. Private in Capt. Graybill's German Regiment in 1776. (H-266)

KINDLE, JOHN. Non-Juror to Oath of Allegiance, 1778. (A-1/13)

KING, BENJAMIN. (c1747 - September 20, 1810) Married Susannah BLAKE. Baltimore Privateer and Captain of brig Maryland (16 guns, 2 swivels), owned by Hool and Harrison and others of Maryland and Virginia. (III-206, JJJ-388)

KING, DANIEL. Recruit in Baltimore County, 1780. Deserted and taken up in Harford County on August 4, 1780. (H-340, H-344)

KING, GEORGE. Oath of Allegiance, 1778, before Hon. Robert Simmons. (A-1/13, A-2/58)

KING, JESSEY. Private in Extra Regt. at Fort Whetstone Point in 1781. (H-626)

KING, JOHN. Private in Capt. N. Ramsey's MD Artillery, 1776-1777, at Whetstone Point in Baltimore. (VV-74)

KING, WILLIAM. Able Seaman on ship Defence, September 19, 1776, and Ordinary Sailor in 1777. Oath of Allegiance, 1778, before Hon. Edward Cockey. (H-606, H-657, A-2/61)

KING, WILLIAM. Oath of Allegiance, 1778, before Hon. James Calhoun. Served in Captain Moore's Troops as Quartermaster on June 25, 1781. He had a six year old bay mare. Involved in evaluation of Baltimore County confiscated proprietary reserves land in 1782. (A-1/13, A-2/42, FFF-543, BBBB-313)

KINGSBERRY, JAMES. Oath of Allegiance, 1778, before Hon. Geo. Lindenberger. (A-2/53)

KINGSTONE, GEORGE. Non-Juror to Oath of Allegiance, 1778. (A-1/13)

KINLEY, SAMUEL. Non-Juror to Oath of Allegiance, 1778. (A-1/13)

KINSEY, SAMUEL. Ensign in Baltimore County Militia, September 13, 1776. (JJ-9)

KINSEY, THOMAS. Midshipman on ship Defence, April 9 to December 31, 1777. (H-658)

KINTZ (KEINTZ), JACOB. Private in Capt. Graybill's German Regiment, 1776. (H-265)

KIRBY, ANTHONY. Oath of Allegiance, 1778, before Hon. Thomas Sollers. (A-2/51)

KIRBY, NATHANIEL. Oath of Allegiance, 1778. (A-1/13)

KIRBY, WILLIAM. Oath of Allegiance, 1778, before Hon. Thomas Sollers. (A-2/51)

KIRK, DANIEL. Marine on ship Defence, May 28 to December 31, 1777. (H-658)

KIRKLAND, ROBERT. Although Source A-1/13 states he was a Non-Juror, Source BBB-533 states he took the Oath in Baltimore County on March 11, 1778.

KIRWIN, JOHN. Served in Capt. Nicholas Ruxton Moore's Troops on June 25, 1781. He had a six year old sorrell gelding horse. (BBBB-313)

KITCHPOLE, JOHN. Oath of Allegiance, 1778, before Hon. Edward Cockey. (A-2/61)

KITSTZELMAN, ANDREW. Oath of Allegiance, 1778, before Hon. George Lindenberger. (A-1/14, A-2/53)

KITTEN, THOMAS. Oath of Allegiance, 1778, before Hon. Benjamin Rogers. (A-2/32)

KITTLEMAN, JOHN. Non-Juror to Oath of Allegiance, 1778. (A-1/14)

KITTLEMAN, VALANTINE. Non-Juror to Oath of Allegiance, 1778. (A-1/14)

KIZER, VALENTINE. Private in Baltimore County Militia; enlisted July 5, 1776. (H-58)

KNEARY (KNERY), LORENTZ (LORANCE). Private in Capt. Graybill's German Regiment in 1776. (H-265, ZZ-32)

KNIGHT, BENJAMIN. Volunteered into Baltimore County Regiment 36 circa 1777. (TTT-13)

KNIGHT, DAVID. Volunteered into Baltimore County Regiment 36, circa 1777. (TTT-13)

KNIGHT, JACOB. Enlisted August 14, 1776 in Baltimore County. As a Private, 2nd MD Regiment, he received 50 acres (lot #4026) in western Maryland. (H-52, DDDD-23)

KNIGHT, JOHN. Volunteered into Baltimore County Regiment 36, circa 1777. Took the Oath of Allegiance in 1778 before Hon. Andrew Buchanan. Fifer in Capt. Lansdale's Company, 4th MD Regiment from May 26, 1778 to Nov. 1, 1780. (TTT-13, H-131, A-2/57)

KNIGHT, JOHN. Able Seaman on ship Defence, September 19, 1776, and Marine in 1777. (H-606, H-658)

KNIGHT, SHADRICK. Oath of Allegiance, 1778, before Hon. James Calhoun. (A-2/42)

KNIGHTSMITH, THOMAS SHAW. Non-Juror to Oath of Allegiance, 1778. (A-1/14)

KNOTT, THOMAS PERCY. (1745 - after 1790) Married Jane HART. Ensign in Capt. Deaver's Company, Baltimore Militia, 1779. (JJJ-393, F-309, F-311, GGG-242, ZZ-324)

KNOWLES, WILLIAM. (c1755 - c1815) Married Mary Ann WILSON. Private in Capt. J. Gist Company, 3rd MD Regiment, in February, 1778. (H-600, JJJ-394)

KNOWS, JOHN. Oath of Allegiance, 1778, before Hon. Isaac Van Bibber. (A-1/14, A-2/34)

KNOX, DAVID. Private in Capt. Howell's Company, December 30, 1775. Sergeant in Capt. Cox's Company, December 19, 1776. Oath of Allegiance in 1778 before Honorable Geo. Lindenberger. (A-1/14, A-2/53, G-11, CCC-21)

KNOX, WILLIAM. Oath of Allegiance, 1778, before Hon. James Calhoun. (A-1/14, A-2/41)

KOEFFLICH, JACOB. Private in Capt. Keeports German Regiment; enlisted July 21, 1776. At Philadelphia, September 19, 1776. (H-263)

KOHL, FREDERICK. Oath of Allegiance, 1778, before Hon. Geo. Lindenberger. (A-2/53)

KRABER, JACOB. Private in Baltimore Artillery Company, October 16, 1775. (G-8)

KRAFT, WILLIAM. (1753 - April 17, 1829) Married Catherine NICODEMUS. Private in Capt. Graybill's German Regiment in 1776. (H-266, JJJ-395)

KRAMER, ADAM. Oath of Allegiance, 1778, before Hon. James Calhoun. (A-1/14, A-2/40)

KRAMER, BOLSER. Oath of Allegiance, 1778, before Hon. James Calhoun. (A-1/14, A-2/40)

KRAMER (KREMER), CHRISTOPHER. Oath of Allegiance, 1778, before Hon. Peter Shepherd. (A-1/14, A-2/49)

KRAMER, GEORGE. Oath of Allegiance, 1778, before Hon. James Calhoun. (A-1/14, A-2/40)

KRAMER (KREMER), HENRY. Oath of Allegiance, 1778, before Hon. Peter Shepherd. (A-2/50)

KRAMER (KREMER, KROMER), RUDOLPH. Private in Capt. Graybill's German Regiment, as of July 12, 1776. (ZZ-32)

KRAMES, DAVID. Oath of Allegiance, 1778, before Hon. James Calhoun. (A-1/14, A-2/40)

KRANER (KRAMER, CRANES, CRANE), MICHAEL. (As noted, his name has been misspelled many ways, but the information appears to apply to just one man.) Ensign in Baltimore County Militia Company No. 5 on December 19, 1775. 1st Lieutenant in Capt. Rutter's Company on February 6, 1777. Took the Oath of Allegiance in 1778 before Hon. James Calhoun. Captain in Baltimore Town Battalion on March 16, 1779, and served under Colonel Smith to at least April 18, 1781. (G-10, BBB-120, A-1/14, A-2/39, BBBB-61, F-312, F-313, R-15, AAAA-401)

KREBS, MICHAEL. Oath of Allegiance, 1778, before Hon. William Spear. (A-1/14, A-2/66)

KRIES, PETER. Private in Capt. Keeports' German Regiment; enlisted July 20, 1776. Was at Philadelphia, September 19, 1776. Pensioner. (YY-32, H-263)

KUNIR, PETER. Oath of Allegiance, 1778, before Hon. William Spear. (A-1/14, A-2/66)

KURSMAN (KURFMAN), PETER. Oath of Allegiance, 1778, before Hon. John Hall. (A-2/36)

L

LABESIUS, JOHN DR. He began his medical practice in Baltimore Town in 1779. Source XX-10 states he had no known military service, but he did pledge to attempt a prisoner exchange with Capt. George Cook, Commander of the State ship Defence at Baltimore in March, 1777. (FFF-93, XX-10)

LACEMAN, LODOWICK. Of Baltimore. He was to serve until December 10, 1781, but "unfit for service for which he was intended, is hereby discharged Oct.30,1781." (AAAA-657)

LACEY, DANIEL. Enlisted July 17, 1776 in Baltimore Town, and recruited again in the Baltimore County Militia on April 11, 1780. (H-53, H-335)

LACI, PETER. Enlisted at Fort Whetstone Point in Baltimore on September 28, 1779, but deserted from Recruiting Officer. (H-626)

LACKEY, RICHARD. Oath of Allegiance, 1778, before Hon. Isaac Van Bibber. (A-2/34)

LAKE, JOHN. Oath of Allegiance, 1778, before Hon. Peter Shepherd. (A-1/14, A-2/50)

LAMB, JAMES. Private in Capt. Ewing's Company No. 4; enlisted May 8, 1776. (H-13)

LAMBERT, CHRISTOPHER. Private, 3rd MD Regiment, 1780-1783. Disabled by fire; invalid. Initially pensioned in Frederick County, MD, and also entitled to 50 acres (lot #99)

LAMBERT, CHRISTOPHER (continued)
in western Maryland for his services as a Private in the Maryland State Troops.
"Private, in Revolutionary Army, of Baltimore County, pensioned at $40 per annum
from March 4, 1789, under Act of June 7, 1785 (received $1085.53). Pensioned at
$64 per annum from April 24, 1816, under Act of same date (received $119.11) See
U.S. Pension Roll, 1835, page 8. Pay, as of March 21, 1838, to Christopher
Lambert, of Baltimore City, half pay of a Private during his life, as a further
remuneration for his services during the Revolutionary War." (C-363, O-8) He
is listed as a pensioner on June 1, 1840, age 89, residing in the household of
Christian COOK in Baltimore City, 8th Ward. (P-128, H-630, DDDD-24, C-363, O-8)

LAMBERT, SAMUEL. Private, Capt. Furnival's MD Artillery, November 17, 1777. (H-573)

LaMOTT, HENRY. Non-Juror to Oath of Allegiance, 1778. (A-1/14)

LAMOUNT, NEAL. Oath of Allegiance, 1778, before Hon. James Calhoun. (A-1/14, A-2/42)

LANAHAN, THOMAS. Baltimore Artillery Company, 1777. (V-368)

LAND, WILLIAM. Marine on ship Defence, April 2 to December 21, 1777. (H-658)

LANDE, JOSEPH. Oath of Allegiance, 1778. (A-1/14)

LANDEMAN, GEORGE. Oath of Allegiance, 1178, before Hon. James Calhoun.(A-1/14,A-2/43)

LANDONS, DOMANIC. Oath of Allegiance, 1778. (A-1/14)

LANDRA, JOHN. Took care of wagons and horses for Baltimore Committee, 1780. (RRR-6)

LANE, ABRAM. Non-Juror to Oath of Allegiance, 1778. (A-1/14)

LANE, DUTTON SR. (Died in Baltimore County in 1783) Son of Dutton LANE and Pretiosa
TYDINGS. He married Dinah BORING, daughter of John BORING. Their children were:
William; Thomas; Dutton, Jr.; Daniel (born 1732); Mary, married James MURRAY;
Dinah, married Peter GOSNELL, Jr.; and, John (died 1769). Dutton LANE was a
Non-Juror to the Oath of Allegiance in 1778. (A-1/14, D-4)

LANE, DUTTON JR. (Died in Baltimore County in 1785) Son of Dutton LANE and Dinah
BORING. Wife named Margaret. Their children were: Caleb; Micajah; John; Mary;
Elizabeth; Dinah; Sarah; Elisha; Richard; Anna; and, Ureth. Dutton LANE, Jr. took
the Oath of Allegiance in 1778 before Hon. Peter Shepherd. (A-1/14, A-2/50, D-4)

LANE, RICHARD. (c1738, Anne Arundel County, MD - 1785, Baltimore County, MD) Married
Providence DORSEY (born 1739). A daughtr, Sarah LANE (1776-1839) married to John
BRICE, IV (1770-1850) in 1794, and their daughter, Eliza BRICE (1803-1855) married
John Philip KRAFFT (died 1838) in 1824. Richard LANE took the Oath of Allegiance
in 1778 before Hon. James Calhoun. (A-1/14, A-2/39, AAA-1802K)

LANE, THOMAS. Oath of Allegiance, 1778, before Hon. Andrew Buchanan.(A-1/14, A-2/57)

LANE, WILLIAM. Oath of Allegiance, 1778, before Hon. Robert Simmons. Served as a
Captain in Gunpowder Upper Battalion, October 23, 1781. (A-1/14,A-2/58, AAAA-650)

LANGFORD, P. Oath of Allegiance, 1778, before Hon. Isaac Van Bibber.(A-1/14,A-2/34)

LANGRALE (LANGALE), LEVIN. Sailor on ship Defence, Sept. 19, 1776 - 1777. (H-658)

LANGTON, THOMAS. Died September 5, 1799, in his 43rd year, formerly a merchant in
Baltimore. Served on the Baltimore Salt Committee, Oct. 14, 1779.(ZZZ-188,HHH-88)

LANGWELL, ROBERT. Oath of Allegiance in 1778 before Hon. Charles Ridgely of William.
Could not write; made his mark. (A-1/14, A-2/27) His name might have been Longwall.

LANKTON, JOSEPH. Non-Juror to Oath of Allegiance, 1778. (A-1/14)

LANSDALE, THOMAS LANCASTER. (August 14, 1727 - 1785) Wife name Martha or Cornelia.
Date of death may be incorrect; Source ZZZ-189 shows a Thomas Lansdale who died
January 19, 1803 in Prince George's County, MD; Source JJJ-401 indicates he died
in 1785. Both sources agree that he was a Major and revolutionary War veteran.
Men from Baltimore County served in his 3rd and 4th MD Regiments during the war.

LANSDALE, THOMAS (continued)
He was 1st Lieutenant in 2nd MD Battalion of the Flying Camp from July, 1776 to December, 1776, when he became a Captain in the 4th MD Regiment, December 10, 1776. He also appears to have been a prisoner in March, 1780, but when and where taken is not given. He became a Major of the 3rd MD Regiment on February 19, 1781, serving to Novembr 15, 1783. He was entitled to the following pay certificates during the war: 82960 ($116.67); 82961 ($282.48); 82962 ($500); 82963 ($225); 82964 ($1000); 82965 ($1000); 82966 ($500); and, 82967 ($450). He also received 200 acres (lots 3210, 3212, 3231, 3233) in western Maryland, and 400 acres under Federal Bounty Land Grant Warrant #1227. (H-52, H-53, YYY-1/11, ZZZ-189, YY-32, YY-70, PP-301, DDDD-3, JJJ-401)

LANTHRONE, GEORGE. Oath of Allegiance in 1778 before Hon. Charles Ridgely of William. Could not write; made his mark. (A-1/14, A-2/28)

LANTIE, MARTIN. Private in Capt. Howell's Company, December 30, 1775. (G-11)

LANTZ, MARTIN. Private in Capt. Graybill's German Regiment in 1776. (H-265, ZZ-32)

LARANCE (LARRANCE), GEORGE. Oath of Allegiance, 1778. (A-1/14)

LARANCE (LARRENCE), JAMES. Oath of Allegiance, 1778, before Hon. Richard Cromwell. (A-1/14, A-2/46)

LARANCE, JOHN. Recruit in Baltimore County Militia, April 11, 1780. (H-335)

LARDONS, DOMANIE. Oath of Allegiance, 1778, before Hon. Geo. Lindenberger. (A-2/53) This is no doubt the Domanic Landons listed earlier in this text. (A-1/14)

LAREMORE, JOHN. Non-Juror to Oath in 1778, he signed in 1781. (QQ-115)

LARKAN (LARKINS), DENNIS. Able Seaman on ship Defence, September 19, 1776, and Seaman in 1777. (H-606, H-658)

LARRY, DANIEL. Private, Capt. Deams' Company, 7th MD Regt., Dec. 25, 1776. (H-305)

LARRY (LARNY), JACOB. Stored and delivered flour for the Baltimore Town Committee in 1780. (RRR-6)

LARSH, VALENTINE. Oath of Allegiance, 1778, before Hon. James Calhoun. (A-1/14,A-2/39)

LATTIMORE, JOHN. Non-Juror to Oath of Allegiance, 1778. (A-1/14)
LAUDISLAGER, GEORGE. Non-Juror to Oath of Allegiance, 1778. (A-1/14)
LAUDISLAGER, PHILIP. Non-Juror to Oath of Allegiance, 1778. (A-1/14)

LAUT, ADAM. Private in Capt. Howell's Company, December 30, 1775. (G-11)

LAVELY, WILLIAM. Private in Capt. Howell's Company, December 30, 1775. (G-11)

LAVENSON, THOMAS. Oath of Allegiance, 1778, before Hon. John Merryman. (A-2/35)

LAW, ANDREW. Oath of Allegiance, 1778, before Hon. James Calhoun. (A-2/65)

LAWDEGAR, CHRISTIAN. Oath of Allegiance, 1778, before Hon. William Spear. (A-2/66)

LAWELL, JOSEPH. Private in Capt. Howell's Company, December 30, 1775. (G-11)

LAWLEY, WILLIAM. Oath of Allegiance in 1778 before Hon. Jeremiah Johnson. Could not write; made his mark. (A-1/14, A-2/33)

LAWRENCE, BENJAMIN. (May or August 14, 1741, Baltimore County, MD - March 5, 1814, Jefferson County, KY) Son of Levin LAWRENCE and Susannah DORSEY. Married Urath Randall OWINGS (1738-1807). Their children: Samuel (died infant); Samuel; Mary; Susannah; Rebecca; Leaven or Levin; and, Elizabeth. Benjamin LAWRENCE served as 2nd Lieutenant in Capt. R. Owings' Soldier Delight Company No. 3 from May 13, 1776 to at least 1779. Took the Oath of Allegiance in 1778 before Hon. Peter Shepherd. (A-1/14, A-2/49, E-11, FF-64, JJJ-403, WW-467, KKK-378, KKK-379)

LAWRENCE, DAVID. Oath of Allegiance, 1778, before Hon. James Calhoun. (A-1/14,A-2/39)

LAWRENCE, GEORGE. Oath of Allegiance, 1778, before Hon. Richard Holliday. (A-2/60)

LAWRENCE, HENRY. Non-Juror to Oath of Allegiance, 1778. (A-1/14)

LAWRENCE, JAMES. Enlisted in Baltimore County on August 14, 1776. Took the Oath of Allegiance in 1778 before Hon. Richard Cromwell. (H-52, A-2/46)

LAWRENCE, JOSHUA. Seaman on ship Defence, July 2 to December 31, 1777. (H-658)

LAWRENCE, PETER. Matross in Capt. Brown's MD Artillery; joined November 22, 1777. Was at Valley Forge until June, 1778; at White Plains, July, 1778; at Fort Schuyler in August and September, 1780; at High Hills of the Santee in August, 1781; at Camp Col. Scirvins in January, 1782; and at Bacon's Bridge, S.C. in April, 1782. Entitled to 50 acres (lot 1316) in western Maryland. (UU-228, UU-230, DDDD-24)

LAWRENCE, WILLIAM. Private in Baltimore County Militia; enlisted July 5, 1776. (H-58)

LAWSON, JOHN. Non-Juror to Oath of Allegiance, 1778. Involved in evaluation of Baltimore County confiscated proprietary reserve lands in 1782. (A-1/14, FFF-547)

LAWSON, ROBERT. Private, Capt. Deams' Company, 7th MD Regt., Jan. 16, 1777. (H-305)

LAWYN, GABRIEL. Baltimore Artillery Company, 1777. (V-368)

LAYRING, AARON. Supplied linen to Capt. George Keeports, October 11, 1779. (FFF-244)

LEAGUE, AQUILLA. Non-Juror to Oath of Allegaince, 1778. (A-1/14)
LEAGUE, JAMES. Non-Juror to Oath of Allegiance, 1778. (A-1/14)
LEAGUE, JOHN. Non-Juror to Oath of Allegiance, 1778. (A-1/14)
LEAGUE, JOSIAS. Non-Juror to Oath of Allegiance, 1778. (A-1/14)
LEAGUE, LUKE. Non-Juror to Oath of Allegiance, 1778. (A-1/14)

LEARY, CORNELIUS. (1756 - 1785, Baltimore County, MD) Married Catherine LITZINGER. Their children were: Catherine, Julian, Peter and William. Cornelius LEARY took the Oath of Allegiance in 1778 before Hon. George Lindenberger. (A-1/14, A-2/53, JJJ-406, D-9)

LEARY, DANIEL. Private in Capt. Norwood's Company, 4th MD Regiment, from May 11, 1778 to January 4, 1780. (H-135)

LEATHER OR LEATHERWOOD, SAMUEL. Non-Juror to Oath of Allegiance in 1778. (A-1/14)

LEAVER, JOHN. Oath of Allegiance, 1778, before Hon. James Calhoun. (A-1/14, A-2/41)

LEAZENBY, THOMAS. Oath of Allegiance, 1778, before Hon. Peter Shepherd. (A-2/50)

LEDWITH (OR LEDWICK OR SEDWICK), Patrick. Source A-1/14 states Pattrick Ledwith took the Oath of Allegiance, 1778, and Source A-2/68 states Patrick Ledwick took the Oath in 1778 before Hon. William Lux.

LEE, ABRAHAM. Oath of Allegiance, 1778, before Hon. Isaac Van Bibber. Could not write; made his mark. (A-1/14, A-2/34)

LEE (LEIGH), CHRISTOPHER. Marine on ship Defence, May 20 to Dec. 31, 1777. (H-658)

LEE, EDWARD. Drafted into Baltimore County Regiment No. 36, circa 1777. (TTT-13)

LEE, FERGUS. Enlisted in Baltimore County on July 26, 1776. (H-53)

LEE, JOHN. Private, Capt. Deams' Company, 7th MD Regiment, January 5, 1777. Took Oath of Allegiance, 1778, before Hon. Peter Shepherd. Revolutionary pensioner. (A-1/14, A-2/49, H-305, YY-33)

LEE, PARKER HALL. (1759 - 1829) Born in Baltimore County, MD, but served in the war in Harford County, MD as a 1st Lieutenant in the 4th MD Regiment, 1778-1780. He married Elizabeth DALLAM and had children: Richard; Samuel; William, married Ann WILSON; Mary, married Zack BOND; Priscilla, married Dr. WAKEMAN; Fanny, married a HALL; and, Banneke (Banneker) married a HALL. (D-9, JJJ-408, YY-33, B-345, H-135) Source AAA-479 states that Parker Hall LEE had a son named Parker Hall LEE and he married Mary E. BRYARLY and had a son named James Lee (born 1848. Additional info on Parker Hall LEE may be found in H. Peden's Revolutionary Patriots of Harford County, Maryland, 1775-1783, page 137) A portrait of Parker Hall Lee hangs in the Harford County Courthouse In Bel Air, Maryland, outside the ceremonial court room.

LEE, WILLIAM. Non-Juror to Oath of Allegiance, 1778. (A-1/14)

LEECH, AMOROUS. Non-Juror to Oath of Allegiance, 1778. (A-1/14)

LEECH, BENJAMIN. Non-Juror to Oath of Allegiance, 1778. (A-1/14)

LEECH, JOHN. Non-Juror to Oath of Allegiance, 1778. (A-1/14.

LEECH, MURIAL. Non-Juror to Oath of Allegiance, 1778. (A-1/14)

LEECH, PHILIP. Of Baltimore County, he was "to serve until December 10, 1781 (but) is unfit for service for which he was intended, is hereby discharged October 30, 1781." (AAAA-656)

LEEF. JACOB. Oath of Allegiance, 1778, before Hon. Richard Cromwell. (A-1/14, A-2/46)

LEEF, JOHN. (Died 1836) Oath of Allegiance, 1778, before Hon. Richard Cromwell. (A-1/14, A-2/46, JJJ-408)

LEEG, NATHAN. Non-Juror to Oath of Allegiance, 1778. (A-1/14)

LEEKE, NICHOLAS. (September 29, 1749, London, England - January 31, 1834, Baltimore, MD) Married Mary FARRELL, daughter of William FARRELL. A daughter, Mary LEEKE, married Henry DASHIELL, and their son, Nicholas Leeke DASHIELL married Louisa TURPIN. In the war Nicholas LEEKE was a Private, Clerk and then Sergeant in the Maryland Militia, and a Marine under Major William Brogden, 1776-1777, and also Sergeant of Marines under Commodore James Nicholson on the frigate Virginia. He was assigned duty at Susquehannah Ferry (now Havre de Grace, Harford County, MD) to arrest all deserters (or suspects) attempting to cross the river ferry. He was pensioned at $8 per month from April 3, 1818. (XXX-456, AAA-296, AAA-296A, and an article from the Baltimore American, October 5, 1810, page 3, column 1)

LEEKINS, THOMAS. Non-Juror to Oath of Allegiance, 1778. (A-1/14)

LEES, VALENTINE. Oath of Allegiance, 1778. (A-1/14)

LEGGITT, BENJAMIN. Non-Juror to Oath of Allegiance, 1778. (A-1/14)

LEGGITT, JAMES. Non-Juror to Oath of Allegiance, 1778. (A-1/14)

LEGGITT, JOSHUA. Oath of Allegiance, 1778, before Hon. Robert Simmons. Delivered flour in Baltimore County for the military, February 12, 1780. (FFF-269, A-2/58)

LEGGITT, SUTTON. Non-Juror to Oath of Allegiance, 1778. (A-1/14)

LEGRAND, JOHN. Oath of Allegianec, 1778. (A-1/14)

LEIGH, WILLIAM. Surgeon's Mate on ship Defence in 1777. (h-658)

LEIGHTY (LITTIE), PETER. Private in Baltimore County Regiment No. 15, circa 1777. Oath of Allegiance in 1778. (TTT-13, A-1/14)

LEISTER, WILLIAM. Non-Juror to Oath of Allegiance, 1778. (A-1/14)

LEITH, ALEXANDER. Oath of Allegiance, 1778, before Hon. George Lindenberger. (A-2/53)

LEMANE, JOSEPH. Oath of Allegiance, 1778, before Hon. James Calhoun. (A-1/14, A-2/40)

LEMMON, ALEXIS.(Died 1786, Baltimore County, MD) His first wife was name Martha, and his second wife was Rachel COTTRELL, widow of Jacob JONES who had died in 1773, and she married Alexis LEMMON in 1777. The children of Jacob JONES and Rachel COTTRELL were John, Rachel, and a daughter who married Moses LEMMON. The children of Alexis LEMMON and wife Martha, were: John (born 1740) married Sarah STANSBURY; Ruth (born 1742) married a STANSBURY; Moses; Hannah; Mary, married Ulick BURK; Alexis (born 1746, died 1826) married rachel STANSBURY; Rebecca, married Jabez Murray TIPTON; and Eleanor, married a HEADINGTON. Alexis (Elexis) LEMMON rendered patriotic service in the Revolution by deliviering wheat on October 4, 1779. (FFF-243, JJJ-410, D-4)

LEMMON, ALEXIS JR. (March 12, 1746 - June 21, 1826) Son of Alexis and Martha LEMMON. Married Rachel STANSBURY on November 29, 1771. He was a Captain in the Baltimore County Militia on February 4, 1777 and was still in service as of February 1, 1782. (JJJ-410, VV-114, D-9, CCCC-65)

LEMMON, JACOB. Oath of Allegiance, 1778. Involved in evaluation of Baltimore County confiscated proprietary reserve lands in 1782. (A-1/14, FFF-538)

LEMMON, JOHN. (August 16 or November 6, 1740 - March 13, 1818, Baltimore County) Married Sarah STANSBURY (born 1739) on March 6, 1760. Their children: Eleanor married Luke ENSOR; Charles; Lemuel; Hannah, married a CORCORAN; Martha, md. Joshua PRICE (1759-1802) in 1784, and their daughter, Hannah PRICE married in 1827 to Benjamin BENSON (1801-1879); Alexis; Thomas; John; and, Benjamin. John LEMMON served in the Baltimore Artillery Company in October, 1775, and also as a Marine Private on the ship Defence, 1777. (JJJ-410, D-4, G-8, AAA-2120, H-658)

LEMMON, JOSHUA. Appointed Ensign in Capt. Richard Lemmon's Company in Baltimore Town Battalion of Militia, September 25, 1780. Took Oath of Allegiance, 1778, also. (A-1/14, F-308)

LEMMON, MOSES. Pension Application R6283: "Declaration made by Moses Lemon, son of Eliasas? and Martha Lemon, was born in Baltimore County, Maryland, 1759, and is now about 85 years of age; during the years 1776-1777 and 1778 he was called out as a militia man and served under Col. Thomas Guess? (Gist) in the company of a Capt. Nicholas Merryman, to the 5th Regiment of militia, and under Capt. Merryman he was not in excursion in Pennsylvania for about 3 weeks, then First Sergeant of the company and acted as Ensign in the company but no engagement took place, the enemy fled upon their approach. He was called out in said year twice to perform duty of Baltimore, Maryland when the British lay in the Bay. Col. Guess (Gist) was their Colonel, of the regiment, and Capt. Merriman in charge of the company. He also served more or less during the 3 years and until the final close of the war. When discharged he received no written discharge. He resided in Maryland to about a year 1824 when he left for State of Ohio, where he resided about 14 yrs., when he removed to Union County, Indiana, where he has resided ever since. He stated he was born in Baltimore County, Maryland 1759 about that year. Affidavit of Joshua LEMMON, son of Moses LEMON, February 1st, 1854, states and appointed a power of attorney of Washington, DC, as power of attorney to prosecute his claim. This was done in Union County, Indiana, 1854. A note in the files about a lady resident of Toronto, Canada who was inquiring whether there is not a pension due to the heirs of her grandfather, Moses LEMON, of Watertown, New York, account of this Revolutionary War service." (I-52) Source YY-33 states Moses LEMMON was a Revolutionary pensioner, but the "R" in the claim number indicates his claim was "Rejected." Same for Source ZZ-25. However, research shows that there was, in fact, a Private named "Moses LEMMEN" in Capt. Talbott's Company in Baltimore Co. on May 31, 1779. (F-302, U-90, YY-33, I-52, ZZ-25) Oath, 1778. (A-1/14)

LEMMON, RICHARD. Served on Baltimore County Committee of Observation in 1775, and was 1st Lieutenant in the Baltimore Artillery Company, October 16, 1775. Took the Oath of Allegiance in 1778 before Hon. James Calhoun, and was a magistrate in Baltimore city, 1779-1780. He also signed a letter to the Governor of Maryland on September 4, 1778, informing him of shipments of flour headed for the enemy. He was commissioned Captain, as follows: "The State of Maryland to Richard Lemmon, Esquire - Greetings. Be it known, that reposing especial trust and confidence in your fidelity, courage, good conduct, and attachment to the liberties and independence of America, you are by these presents constituted and appointed Captain of a Company formerly commanded by George Sewell Douglass in the Baltimore Town Battalion of Militia in Baltimore County. You are, therefore, carefully and diligently to discharge the trust reposed in you, by disciplining all officers and soldiers under your command, and they are hereby strictly enjoined and required to obey you as their Captain, and you are to observe and follows all such orders and directions as you shall from time to time receive according to the laws and regulations of the State, and the rules and regulations which under the authority thereof are or may be established. This commission to be in force until lawfully revoked. Given at Annapolis this 25th day of September A.D. 1780." Signed by the Governor of Maryland, Thomas S. Lee. Richard LEMMON was in service until at least September 30, 1781 when he presented a bill for clothing to George Keeports in Baltimore County. (G-8, A-1/14, A-2/38, II-23, FFF-347, CCC-26, EEEE-1725, EEEE-1726, and the above quote is from Source F-304)

EMMON, ROBERT DR. (1730 - 1817) Wife named Eleanor or Nancy. A daughter, Maria, md. Joseph KING. Dr. Lemmon served in Harford County, MD, 1775-1777, and was one of the signers of the famous Bush Declaration in March, 1775. He subsequently served as a Captain in the Baltimore County Militia on February 4, 1777, and served to at least February 1, 1782. He also took the Oath of Allegiance in 1778, and was a Justice of the Peace. He supplied nails to the Baltimore Town Committee in 1780, and was also involved in the evaluation of Baltimore County confiscated proprietary reserve lands in 1782. (JJJ-410, RRR-6, A-1/14, E-14, LL-66, VV-114, BBB-350, FFF-540, GGG-242, and CCCC-65; also listed in H. Peden's Revolutionary Patriots of Harford County, p. 137)

EMON, JOHN. Born 1745 in Northern Ireland. Occupation: Brickmaker. Height: 5' 7 3/4". Enlisted January 24, 1776 in Capt. N. Smith's 1st Company of Matrosses. Pension No. S40080: "Declaration was made in Armstrong County, Pennsylvania, by John LEMON, age 77, on October 28, 1822. It appears that John LEMON enlisted at Baltimore, Maryland, September, 1775, and served until July, 1776, as a Private and Sergeant in Captain Nathaniel Smith's Maryland Company. He enlisted in Cumberland County, Pennsylvania, September, 1776, and served 3 months in Capt. Andrew Homes' Pennsylvania Company. He enlisted December, 1777, and served until the summer of 1779 as Superintendent of the Continental Brickyard at Carlisle, Pennsylvania, under Capt. Samuel Serjeant. He entered at Baltimore, Maryland in the fall of 1779 and served to June, 1780, as a seaman on the ship Fanny, Capt. John Loxley. They captured the British ships Three Brothers, and Crown. He enlisted at Baltimore, Maryland in the fall of 1780, and served until after the surrender of Cornwallis under Capt. Hunter and manned a battery of artillery at Fells Point. There is no data on file as to his family." (YY-33, H-563, and the above information quited from Source I-51)

EMON, JOSEPH. Served in Capt. Nicholas Ruxton Moore's Troops on June 25, 1781. He had a fourteen year old bay gelding horse. (BBBB-313)

ENVERS, LEWIS. Oath of Allegiance, 1778. (A-1/14)

ENNOX, JOHN. Enlisted in Baltimore County on July 25, 1776. (H-52)

ENNOX (LINOXE, LYNOX), NATHAN. Non-Juror to Oath, 1778; signed in 1781. (A-1/15,QQ-115)

ePAGE, SAMUEL. (1730, Island of Guernsey - July 13, 1825, Baltimore, Maryland) Married Susannah DeGRAY in 1769; their children: Esther, married (1) William WELLING, and (2) to a GALA, and (3) to a VANDERLIP; and Susannah, married Dr. George ROBERTS. Samuel LePAGE was a Private in Col. Van Schoonhaven's Regiment in Albany County, New York Militia, and also in Philip Schuyler's Regiment. (XXX-460)

EPPEY (LEPPI), CONRAD. Non-Juror to Oath in 1778, he signed in 1781. (QQ-115)

EPPEY, DAVID. Oath of Allegiance, 1778, before Hon. Frederick Decker. (A-1/14, A-2/31)

ESSOM, JOHN. Non-Juror to Oath of Allegiance, 1778. (A-1/14)

ESTER, JOHN. Oath of Allegiance, 1778, before Hon. George Lindenberger. Private in Capt. Oldham's Company, 4th MD Regiment, September 14, 1779. Maryland Line defective in August, 1780 (deserted). Resided in Baltimore County. (A-1/14, A-2/53,H-414,H-136)

ET, ROBERT. Oath of Allegiance, 1778, before Hon. James Calhoun. (A-1/14, A-2/42)

EURY, JOHN. Served on ship Defence in 1777. (H-658)

EVELY, GEORGE. (1750 - April 29, 1796) Occupation: Clockmaker. Member of the Sons of Liberty in Baltimore 1in 1776. Took Oath of Allegiance in 1778 before Hon. William Spear. "George Leably" was a Private in Capt. McClellan's Company, Baltimore Town Militia, 1780. (ZZZ-193, CCC-19, CCC-24, A-1/14, A-2/67)

EVELY, HENRY. Oath of Allegiance, 1778, before Hon. James Calhoun. (A-1/14, A-2/41)

EVERING, AARON. (December 7, 1739, Philadelphia, PA - October 14, 1794, Baltimore, MD) Son of William LEVERING and Hannah CLEMENTS. Married Hannah RIGHTER on May 1, 1762. Their children: Charles, married Hester_____, and their son, Maurice Maulsby md. Mary Ann RUSSELL; Mary, married Joseph CLEMENT; and, Aaron Righter, married Ann B. LAWRASON. Aaron LEVERING was a Captain in the Flying Camp. Philadelphia County, PA in July, 1776; Major, July 13, 1776; at Battle of Brandywine and Defense of Fort

Mifflin. Aaron LEVERING was a Colonel at the time of his discharge in New Jersey, 1780. (AAA-442, JJJ-412, XXX-460, Pa. Archives, 2nd Series, Volume 13, page 558)

LEVINGTON, AARON. Member of Sons of Liberty in Baltimore, 1776. (CCC-19)

LEVINE, JAMES. Non-Juror to Oath of Allegiance, 1778. (A-1/14)

LEVY (LEVIE), ALEXANDER. Private in Capt. Lansdale's Company, 4th MD Regiment, from April 22, 1778 to November 1, 1780. (H-135)

LEVY, BENJAMIN. (1726 - February 3, 1802) Served on Baltimore County Committee of Observation, July 24, 1775. Oath of Allegiance, 1778, before Hon. William Spear. (A-1/14, A-2/66, EEEE-1725, ZZZ-193)

LEVY, DAVID. Private in Capt. Keeports' German Regiment; enlisted July 21, 1776. Was at Philadelphia, September 19, 1776. (H-263)

LEVY, NATHAN. Oath of Allegiance, 1778, before Hon. James Calhoun. Served in Capt. Nicholas Ruxton Moore's Troops, June 25, 1781. He had a six year old black gelding horse. (A-1/14, A-2/39, BBBB-313)

LEWES, EDWARD. Oath of Allegiance, 1778. (A-1/14)

LEWIN, JOHN. Private in Capt. J. Gist's Company, 3rd MD Regiment, February, 1778. He received 50 acres (lot 1409) in western Maryland for his services. (H-600, DDDD-24)

LEWIS, CHARLES. Oath of Allegiance, 1778. 2nd Lieutenant in Capt. Stinchcomb's Co., Soldiers Delight Battalion, February 7, 1782. (A-1/14, CCCC-71)

LEWIS, EDWARD. Oath of Allegiance, 1778, before Hon. James Calhoun. (A-1/14, A-2/42)

LEWIS, HENRY. Oath of Allegiance, 1778, before Hon. Charles Ridgely of William. (A-1/14, A-2/27)

LEWIS, HOWELL. Private in Capt. Furnival's Company, MD Artillery, November 17, 1777. Matross in Capt. Dorsey's MD Artillery at Valley Forge, June 3, 1778. (H-573,UU-231)

LEWIS, JOB. Enlisted in Baltimore County, July 20, 1776. 1st Lieutenant in Captain Stinchcomb's Company, Soldiers Delight Battalion, Feb. 7, 1782. (H-53, CCCC-71)

LEWIS, JOHN. Oath of Allegiance, 1778, before Hon. Charles Ridgely of William. He was 2nd Lieutenant, then 1st Lieutenant, in Capt. Smith's Company, Baltimore Co. Militia, May 17, 1779. (A-1/14, A-2/27, F-309, F-311, F-313, GGG-401)

LEWIS, JOHN. Private in Baltimore County regiment No. 7, circa 1777. (TTT-13)

LEWIS, JOHN SR. Non-Juror to Oath of Allegiance, 1778. (A-1/14)
LEWIS, JOHN JR. Non-Juror to Oath of Allegiance, 1778. (A-1/14)

LEWIS, JONATHAN. Two men with this name signed the Oath of Allegiance in 1778 before Hon. James Calhoun. (A-1/14, A-2/38, A-2/41)

LEWIS, JOSEPH. (April 17, 1753 - March 9, 1791) Married Elizabeth DUNCAN. Served as Ensign in 2nd MD Battalion, Flying Camp. Baltimore County, July, 1776. Lieutenant, 4th Regt., no date, exchanged with Lt. Adam Hoops to 2nd Canadian (Hazen's) Regt. 1st Lieutenant, 2nd Canadian Regt., November 3, 1776. Resigned November 16, 1780. (H-52, B-349, TT-105, JJJ-413)

LEWIS, RICHARD. (1749 - 1809) Married Ann WARREN. Sergeant in Capt. Furnival's Co., MD Artillery, November 17, 1777. Sergeant in Capt. Gale's Co., MD Artillery, apptd. September 3, 1779. Sergent in Capt. Dorsey's Co., MD Artillery, at Camp Col. Scirvins January 28, 1782. Matross in Capt. Smith's Co., MD Artillery, 1782-1783. Entitled to 50 acres (lot 1526) in western Maryland for his services as Sergeant of the Artillery. (DDDD-24, H-572, YYY-1/63, YYY-2/28, UU-232, JJJ-414)

LEWVEY, LEWIS. Oath of Allegiance, 1778, before Hon. Isaac Van Bibber. (A-2/34)

LEWYN, GABRIEL. Oath of Allegiance, 1778, before Hon. William Spear. (A-1/14, A-2/67)

LICHTE, CHRISTIAN. Private in Capt. Keeports' German Regiment; enlisted August 9, 1776. At Philadelphia, September 19, 1776. (H-263)

LIDY, YOUST (YOST). Oath of Allegiance, 1778, before Hon. Peter Shepherd. (A-2/49,A-1/14)

LIGHTFOOT, JOHN. Private in Col. Aquila Hall's Baltimore County Regt., 1777. (TTT-13)

LIGHTHAUSER (LEITHASUER), GEORGE. Private, Capt. Graybill's German Rgt., 1776. (H-265)

LIGHTHISER, MATTHIAS. Drafted into Baltimore County Regiment No. 36, c1777. (TTT-13)

LIJARD, JOHN. Private in Baltimore County Regiment No. 7, circa 1777. (TTT-13)

LIJARD, GEORGE. Private in Baltimore County Regiment No. 7, circa 1777. (TTT-13)

LILBURN (LILBON), WALTER. Midshipman on ship Defence, May 22 ro Nov. 24, 1777. (H-658)

LIMEBARKER, ANDREW. Oath of Allegiance, 1778, before Hon. Chas. Ridgely of Wm. (A-2/27)

LIMEBARKER, PHILIP. Oath of Allegiance, 1778, before Hon. Charles Ridgely of William. Could not write; made his mark. (A-1/14, A-2/27)

LIMEBARKER, WILLIAM. Enlisted in Baltimore County, July 20, 1776. Took the Oath of Allegiance, 1778, before Hon. Charles Ridgely of William. (H-52, A-2/27)

LIMES (?), CHRISTOPHER. Private, Baltimore Artillery Company, October 16, 1775. (G-8)

LINCH, WILLIAM. Private in Capt. Talbott's Company, May 31, 1779. (F-301, U-90)

LINDENBERGER, GEORGE. (1730 -1796) One of the most prominent men of Baltimore during the Revolution. Served on the Baltimore County Committee of Inspection, March 13, 1775, and represented West Baltimore at the Association of Freemen on Aug. 21, 1775. Served on the Baltimore Committee of Observation on July 24, 1775, but did not get enough votes to be elected on September 12, 1775. Served on the Baltimore Committee of Correspondence on November 12, 1775 (name spelled "George Lintenberger") and was in the Baltimore Mechanical Company of Militia on November 4, 1775 (name spelled "George Dindenberger"). Became 2nd Lieutenant of Baltimore County Militia Co. #3, December 19, 1775, and was a member of the Sons of Liberty in Baltimore in 1776. He was Lieutenant in Capt. Cox's Company on December 19, 1776. In 1778 he was one of the Magistrates who administered the Oath of Allegiance, and remained a Magistrate in Baltimore City until he resigned in 1782; also, Justice of the Peace. He remained a Lieutenant in the Baltimore Militia through 1779. His death notice stated that "George Lindenberger, of Baltimore, died in July, 1796, in his 66th year, an inhabi- tant of Baltimore for 37 years. In the late revolution he proved himself a friend of the principles of American liberty." (ZZZ-195, EEEE-1726, CCC-21, FFF-538, GGG-242, G-10, F-311, CCC-19, CCC-25, A-1/14, A-2/52, RR-19, F-299, SS-130, RR-50, EEEE-1725)

LINDENBERGER, JOHN. Ensign in Capt. Keeports' German Regiment in 1776. (RR-90, H-262)

LINDER, JOHN. Oath of Allegiance, 1778, before Hon. William Spear. (A-1/14, A-2/67)

LINDIFF, JOHN. Private, Baltimore County Militia; enlisted July 5, 1776. Sergeant, April 11, 1780. Sergeant Major, in Capt. Oldham's Company, 4th MD Regiment, May 1, 1780; prisoner, August 16, 1780. Previously, he was a prisoner, August 22, 1777 and rejoined his company July 16, 1778; was Quartermaster Sergeant, August 20, 1778. (H-58, H-135, H-335)

LINDSAY, ADAM. Private in Capt. Howell's Company, December 30, 1775. Took the Oath of Allegiance in 1778 before Hon. George Lindenberger. (A-1/14, A-2/53, G-11)

LINDSAY (LINSAY), ANTHONY. (1736 - 1808) Married Rachel DORSEY. Source A-1/14 states he was a Non-Juror to the Oath in 1778, but Source JJJ-416 states he was a patriot.

LINDSAY, JOHN. Oath of Allegiance, 1778, before Hon. John Merryman. (A-1/14, A-2/70)

LINGAN, JAMES McCUBBIN. (May 31, 1751 - July 28 or August 28, 1812) Married Janet HENDERSON. Served as 2nd Lieutenant in Stephenson's Rifle Regiment, July 22, 1776. Prisoner of war at Fort Washington, November 16, 1776; exchanged, October 25, 1780. Served in Capt. Rawlings' Regiment, December 10, 1778 (actually in prison at this time). Declared a supernumerary on January 1, 1781 and retired as a Captain. He received 200 acres (lots 4124 to 4127) in western Maryland for his services, and received 300 acres (Warrant 1294) under a Federal Bounty Land Grant, Mar. 19, 1792.

Captain Lingan, called General Lingan, was murdered at the Baltimore jail where he with several others had taken refuge from the mob in 1812. A detailed account is in Scharff's Chronicles of Baltimore. President Washington had appointed him Collector of the Port of Georgetown. He is buried in Washington, DC. Capt. Lingan was an Original Member of the Society of the Cincinnati of Maryland, currently represented by James Robbins Randolph of Sanbornville, New Hampshire. (TT-105, FFF-259, MMM-A, UUU-113, DDDD-3, YY-71, JJJ-417)

LINGAN, THOMAS. (1758 - May 28, 1825) Ensign in 2nd MD Battalion of Flying Camp. June, 1776, Baltimore County. 2nd Lieutenant, August, 1776 to December 1, 1776. 1st Lieut. in Rawlings' Continental Regiment and/or Stephenson's Rifle Regiment, January 26, 1777. Separation date unknown. Took Oath of Allegianc in 1778 before Honorable John Beale Howard. (A-1/14, A-2/29, H-52, B-352, TT-105, YY-33)

LINGAN, THOMAS JR. Oath of Allegiance, 1778, before Hon. James Calhoun.(A-1/14,A-2/41)

LINKENFETTER, ULRICH. 3rd Corporal, Capt. Keeports' German Regiment; enlisted July 21, 1776. At Philadelphia, September 19, 1776. (H-263)

LINVILLE, JOHN. (1755, Philadelphia, PA - April 30, 1801, Baltimore, MD) Married to Martha McALLISTER (1770-1810) on June 16, 1791, and a son, James McAllister LINVILLE (1792-1817) married Maria LONG (1800-1870). John LINVILLE was a Private in Captain John Flower's Company, Chester County, PA. (AAA-1146, and Pennsylvania Archives, 5th Series, Volume 5, pages 791, 861, 864)

LION, LEONARD. Private in Capt. Ewing's Company No. 4; enlisted May 20, 1776. (H-11)

LIONS, WILLIAM. He took an oath in Baltimore on March 10, 1777, to attempt a prisoner exchange with Capt. George Cook of the ship Defence. (FFF-94)

LIPPY, CONRAD. Non-Juror to Oath of Allegiance, 1778. (A-1/14)

LITTIG (LETTIG), JUSTIN. Private, Baltimore Artillery Company, October 16, 1775, and Private in Capt. Sheaff's Company, June 16, 1777. Took Oath of Allegiance in 1778 before Hon. George Lindenberger. (G-8, W-162, A-1/14, A-2/53)

LITTIG (LETTIG), PETER. (December 10, 1754 - April 13, 1799) Wife named Magdalena. He was a Gunsmith and repaired wagons for the military, August 27, 1776. He was under contract on September 17, 1777, "to make 150 musquets fixed with bayonets, steel rammers, swivels priming wires, and brushes, at 3 lbs. 15 shillings each... at Baltimore Town..." and was still making muskets in 1781. (BBB-377, FFF-387) He took Oath of Allegiance in 1778 before Hon. William Spear. (A-2/66, JJJ-418, FFF-54)

LITTIG (LETTIG), PHILIP. Private in Baltimore Artillery Company on October 16, 1775. Private in Capt. Sheaff's Company on June 16, 1777. Took the Oath of Allegiance in 1778 before Hon. George Lindenberger. (G-8, W-162, A-1/14, A-2/53)

LITTLE, GEORGE. Non-Juror to Oath in 1778, but signed in 1781. (A-1/14, QQ-115)

LITTLE, JAMES. Non-Juror to Oath of Allegiance, 1778. (A-1/14)

LITTLE, JOHN. Seaman on ship Defence, September 20 to December 31, 1777. (H-658)

LITTLE, THOMAS. Non-Juror to Oath of Allegiance, 1778. (A-1/14)

LITTLE, WILLIAM. Private, Capt. Ewing's Company No. 4; enlisted Jan. 29, 1776. (H-12)

LITTLEJOHN, MILES. Oath of Allegiance, 1778, before Hon. John Merryman. (A-1/14,A-2/45) "Dr. Miles Littlejohn" died in Baltimore, December 23, 1815, aged 57." (ZZZ-197)

LITTLEJOHN, THOMAS. Oath of Allegiance, 1778, before Hon. Geo. Lindenberger. (A-2/53)

LITZINGER (LITZENER, LITSINGER), GEORGE. Born 1754 in Maryland. Occupation: Bricklayer. Enlisted January 24, 1776 as Corporal in Capt. N. Smith's 1st Company of Matrosses. Height: 5' 8¼". He had been a Private in the Baltimore Artillery Company, Oct. 16, 1775. Either this George Litzinger or perhaps another by the same name was Private in Capt. Sheaff's Company on June 16, 1777 and Private in Capt. Dorsey's Company of MD Artillery on November 17, 1777. George Litzinger, Sr. took the Oath of Allegiance in 1778 before Hon. George Lindenberger. George Litzinger was a Bombardier in Capt.

Gale's MD Artillery, 1779-1780; appointed November 8, 1779; furloughed in November, 1779; deserted April 1, 1780. George Litsinger was a Matross soldier and was deposed on his enlistment terms in Baltimore county on May 7, 1779. (FFF-220, G-8, A-1/14, A-2/53, W-162, H-563, H-566, H-574, QQQ-2, YYY-1/62)

LITZINGER, HENRY. (May 3, 1735, Baltimore County, MD - December 5, 1827, Baltimore Co., MD) Married twice: (1) Mary Ann CYPRUS (1760-1786) on March 6, 1778, and their son, Joseph LITZINGER (1779-1822) married Matilda WRIGHT (1786-1869) in 1802 in Baltimore County, and their granddaughter, Elizabeth Ann LITZINGER (1806-1879) married Walter DANIELS (1802-1857) in 1826; (2) Sarah Charlotte CYPRUS. Henry LITZINGER served in Capt. Fulford's Company No. 2 of MD Artillery, Baltimore County, 1776, and under the command of Capt. Gale. He assisted in building forts at Whetstone Point in Baltimore, and on Swan River, and in Annapolis. He served on an expedition to the Eastern Shore of Maryland, remaining all winter, and in early spring marched to battle at German-town. Returned to Annapolis and remained until his pension was granted. (AAA-1950, XXX-467, JJJ-419)

LITZINGER, PETER. Oath of Allegiance, 1778, before Hon. Geo. Lindenberger. (A-2/53)

LITZINGER (LITZENER), WILLIAM. Private in Baltimore Artillery Company, October 16, 1775. Private, and then Sergeant, in Capt. Graybill's German Regiment in 1776. (G-8, H-266, ZZ-32)

LOBELE (LOEBELE), WILLIAM. Oath of Allegiance, 1778, before Hon. George Lindenberger. (A-1/14, A-2/53)

LOCK, ISAAC. Oath of Allegiance, 1778, before Hon. James Calhoun. (A-1/14, A-2/40)

LOCK, WILLIAM. Oath of Allegiance, 1778, before Hon. James Calhoun. (A-1/14, A-2/38)

LOCKARD (LOCKHARD), FRANCIS. Oath of Allegiance, 1778, before Hon. Peter Shepherd. (A-1/14, A-2/49)

LOCKARD, MATTHEW. Oath of Allegiance, 1778, before Hon. Peter Shepherd. (A-1/14, A-2/49)

LOCKARD, SAMUEL. Oath of Allegiance, 1778, before Hon. Peter Shepherd. (A-1/14, A-2/49)

LOCKISON, JOHN. Non-Juror to Oath of Allegiance, 1778. (A-1/14)

LODSECKER, SIMON. Oath of Allegiance, 1778, before Hon. William Spear. (A-1/14, A-2/66)

LOGAN, THOMAS. Non-Juror to Oath of Allegiance, 1778. (A-1/14)

LOGE (LOOGE), JOHN. Non-Juror to Oath of Allegiance, 1778. (A-1/14)

LOGIE, JAMES. Sergeant, 4th MD Regiment, December, 1776, and Sergeant Major, August 1, 1777. Capt. Oldham's Assistant F.M., February 10, 1780. (H-134)

LOGSDEN, LONS. Oath of Allegiance, 1778. (A-1/14)

LOLEME, JAMES. Oath of Allegiance, 1778, before Hon. George Lindenberger. (A-2/53)

LONDAMMON, GEORGE. On November 27, 1782, "permission given to George Londammon of Baltimore Town to solicit leave of his Excellency General Washington or the Command-ing Officer at Dobb's Ferry (the rout which he is to pursue) to go into the City of New York for the purpose of carrying necessaries to his son, a prisoner in New York with liberty to return." (CCCC-310)

LONG, CONRAD. Private in Baltimore County Regiment No. 15, circa 1777. (TTT-13)

LONG, HENRY. Non-Juror to Oath of Allegiance, 1778. (A-1/14)

LONG, JAMES. Oath of Allegiance, 1778, before Hon. George Lindenberger. He died on May 10, 1807, a resident of Baltimore for the last 44 years. (ZZZ-198, A-2/53)

LONG, JOHN (JONATHAN). 1st Lieutenant in Capt. Garretson's Company, as of May, 1776. (WW-413, WW-444, EE-51)

LONG, PETER. Married Margaret CARR, widow, in Baltimore County on August 30, 1791. (Marriage proven through Maryland pension application). No record of military duty so he might have been a son of a pensioner from Maryland. (YY-118)

LONG, ROBERT. There were two men by this name who took the Oath of Allegiance, 1778: one before Hon. Charles Ridgely of William, and one before Hon. George Lindenberger. One signed a letter to Governor Lee on April 4, 1781, calling for the militia to protect Baltimore, and another, if not the same one, procured wagons and forwarded supplies for the Baltimore Town Committee in 1780. One was a Silversmith, and one died in June, 1808, aged 76, leaving a wife and three children. Additional research is needed to distinguish between them. (A-2/28, A-2/53, S-49, RRR-6, ZZZ-198, A-1/4)

LONG, THOMAS. Private in Capt. Howell's Company, December 30, 1775. (G-11)

LONGFORD, JOHN. Oath of Allegiance, 1778, before Hon. James Calhoun. (A-1/14, A-2/40)

LONGLEY, DAVID. Non-Juror to Oath of Allegiance, 1778. (A-1/14)
LOOKES, JOHN. Non-Juror to Oath of Allegiance, 1778. (A-1/14)

LORAH (LAWRAH), HENRY. Served in Baltimore Mechanical Company of Militia, November 4, 1775. Corporal in Capt. Cox's Company, December 19, 1776. Took Oath of Allegiance in 1778 before Hon. James Calhoun. Private in Capt. McClellan's Company, Sept. 4, 1780. (A-1/14, A-2/39, F-299, CCC-21, CCC-24)

LORAH (LAWRAH), JOHN. (1747 - after 1809) Married Maria E. ZELLERS. Children: Maria Elizabeth LORAH married Casper LAUCKS, and Susan LORAH married Peter LAUCKS. John LORAH served in the Baltimore Mechanical Company of Militia, November 4, 1775, and was a Private in Capt. S. Smith's Company No. 8, 1st MD Battalion, Jan. 23, 1776. He was 1st Lieutenant in Capt. Gryabill's German Regiment from July 11, 1776 to at least September 25, 1780. (F-299, H-641, H-266, RR-90, VV-303, XXX-472)

LORD, ANDREW. (1756 - before 1828) Private in Capt. Lynch's Company, 5th MD Regiment August 28, 1777, to March 23, 1780. Pensioner. On March 12, 1828, a "grant of fifty acres vacant land, west of Fort Cumberland, Allegany County, MD, to heirs of Andrew Lord of Baltimore City, a soldier of Maryland Line during Revolutionary War, or if no heirs, then to Amelia LORD, widow of Andrew LORD, and patent without composition money." (C-367, H-223, YY-34)

LORENTZ (LORANTZ, LORANCE), FREDINAND. Private, Capt. Graybill's German Regiment from July 12, 1776 to July 22, 1779. Pensioner. On April 1, 1839, ordered "to pay to Elizabeth LORANTZ, widow of Fredinand LORANTZ, of Baltimore City, who was a soldier in the war of the revolution, or to her order, the half pay of a Private of the Revolutionary War, during her life, quarterly, commencing January 1, 1839." (C-367) Ann E. LORENTZ, pensioner, as of June 1, 1840, age 65, was residing in the 8th Ward of Baltimore City. (P-128, H-265, H-225, ZZ-32, YY-34, C-367)

LORENTZ, JACOB. Oath of Allegiance, 1778, before Hon. Geo. Lindenberger.(A-1/14,A-2/53)

LORENTZ (LAURENTZ, LORANTZ), VENDEL (WENDEL). Born 1759. Married Anne STEEL in Baltimore County on February 28, 1797. Private in Capt. Graybell's German Regiment from July 12 1776 to July 20, 1779. Pensioner. Received 215 acres under Federal Bounty Land Warrant No. 78517. On March 24, 1838, ordered that "Ann, widow of Vandel Laurentz, of Baltimore City, to receive half pay of a Private during her life, as a further remuneration of the services of her husband, a soldier of the Revolution." (C-364, ZZ-32, H-225, YY-70, YY-32, YY-117, H-265)

LORENZEE, JAMES. Oath of Allegiance, 1778. (A-1/14)

LOSBAUGH (LOSBACH), FREDERICK. Oath of Allegiance, 1778, before Hon. James Calhoun. Served as Private in Capt. McClellan's Company, Baltimore Town, September 4, 1780. (A-1/14, A-2/41, CCC-24)

LOUD, ADAM. Non-Juror to Oath of Allegiance, 1778. (A-1/14)

LOUD, CHARLES. Private in Baltimore County Militia; enlisted August 15, 1776. (H-58)

LOUDERMAN, GEORGE Jr. Non-Juror to Oath of Allegiance, 1778. (A-1/14)
LOUDERMAN, PETER. Non-Juror to Oath of Allegiance, 1778. (A-1/15)

LOUDIGER (LODIGER), CHRISTIAN. Private in Capt. Cox's Company, December 19, 1776, and Private in Capt. McClellan's Company, September 4, 1780. (CCC-21, CCC-24)

LOURE, GOTFRIED. Private in Capt. Keeports' German Regiment; enlisted August 5, 1776. At Philadelphia, September 19, 1776. (H-263)

LOVE, JOHN. Born 1735 in Scotland. Enlisted as Private in Col. Ewing's Battalion on July 5, 1776 in Baltimore County. Height: 5'5"; sandy complexion. (H-57)

LOVE, MILES. Oath of Allegiance, 1778, before Hon. Thomas Sollers. (A-1/15, A-2/51)

LOVE, THOMAS DR. (1753 - 1821) In 1776 the Maryland council ordered payment to him of the expenses of the Baltimore Committee of Safety. Took the Oath of Allegiance, 1778, before Hon. Hercules Courtenay. In 1782 he began practice in Baltimore County and was a founder of the Medico-Chirurgical Faculty. Served in the Legislature, 1801 to 1803. (XX-10, A-1/15, A-2/37)

LOVEALL, ETHAN. Oath of Allegiance, 1778, before Hon. James Calhoun. (A-1/15, A-2/42)

LOVEALL, HENRY. (c1755 - 1829) Wife named Mary. Children: Mary; Rachel, married to a BORING; Joseph; Jeremiah Godden; Eleakin; John, married Nancy LOCKERT; Rebecca, md. a LENIMAN; Zebulon; Aquila; Solloman; and, Ezekiel. Henry LOVEALL took the Oath of Allegiance in 1778 before Hon. James Calhoun. (XXX-474, JJJ-425, A-1/15, A-2/43)

LOVEALL, WILLIAM. (October 15, 1753 -   ) Wife named Mary. He took the Oath of Allegiance in 1778 before Hon. James Calhoun. Served as Ensign in Upper Battalion of Baltimore County, November 5, 1781. (A-1/15, A-2/42, JJJ-425, AAAA-662)

LOVEALL, ZEBULON. Oath of Allegiance, 1778, before Hon. James Calhoun. (A-1/15, A-2/42)

LOVELY, JOSHUA. Matross in Capt. Brown's MD Artillery; joined November 22, 1777. Was at Valley Forge until June, 1778; at White Plains, July, 1778; at Fort Schuyler in August and September, 1780; at High Hills of the Santee in August, 1781; at Camp Col. Scirvins in January, 1782; and at Bacon's Bridge, S.C. in April, 1782. Received 50 acres (lot 1791) for his services (in western Maryland). (UU-228, UU-230, DDDD-25)

LOVETT, CHARLES. Private in Baltimore County Militia; enlisted July 18, 1776. (H-58)

LOVETT, JOSEPH. Private in Capt. J. Gist's Co., 3rd MD Regt., February, 1778. (H-600)

LOVEPITTATAN (LOVEPITTSTON), PHILIP. Non-Juror to Oath of Allegiance, 1778. (A-1/15)
LOVEPITTATAN (LOVEPITTSTON), ROBERT. Non-Juror to Oath of Allegiance, 1778. (A-1/15)
LOWDEN, THOMAS. Non-Juror to Oath of Allegiance, 1778. (A-1/15)
LOWE, JOHN. Non-Juror to Oath of Allegiance, 1778. (A-1/15)

LOWE, JOHN HAWKINS. (1732 - 1820) Married a LAWSON. Captain, 3rd MD Battalion of the Flying Camp, July to December, 1776; wounded at Harlem Plains, September 16, 1776; resigned October 10, 1777. Source B-359 states he was a Captain; Source JJJ-427 states he was a Lieutenant Colonel; and Source FFF-51 states he was a General. The latter source states Gen. John Hawkins Lowe, in Baltimore, August 14, 1776, requested money needed for the march to Philadelphia. (B-359, FFF-51, JJJ-427)

LOWE, NICHOLAS. (1763, Baltimore County, MD - 1819, baltimore County, MD) He married to Katurah BAKER on April 6, 1787. Children: Merab LOWE married Samuel MILLIRON; Amos LOWE married Elizabeth WELLER; Susannah LOWE; Jeremiah LOWE; Ralph LOWE; Asanath LOWE married Thomas WORRELL; Jane LOWE married a JOHNSON; and, Alfred LOWE. Nicholas LOWE served a Private in Maryland Militia, "drafted July 12, 1781 to fill quota of men from Prince George's County, Maryland." (XXX-475)

LOWRY, JOSEPH. Private in Capt. Cox's Company, December 19, 1776. (CCC-22)

LOYAL, JOHN. Marine on ship Defence in 1777. (H-658)

LOYD, JOHN. Private in Capt. J. Gist's Co., 3rd MD Regt., January, 1778. (H-600)

LOYD, THOMAS. Oath of Allegiance, 1778, before Hon. George Lindenberger.(A-1/15,A-2/53)

LUCAS, FRANCIS. Oath of Allegiance, 1778, before Hon. William Spear. (A-1/15, A-2/67)

LUCAS, GEORGE. Oath of Allegiance, 1778, before Hon. George Lindenberger. (A-2/53)

LUCAS, JOSHUA. Non-Juror to Oath of Allegiance, 1778. (A-1/15)

LUCAS, MARGARET. In Baltimore on April 12, 1777, she submitted her account and receipt for making clothing for Captain George Cook. (FFF-99)

LUCAS, THOMAS. Oath of Allegiance 1778, before Hon. Peter Shepherd. (A-2/50)

LUCAS, WILLIAM. In Baltimore, 1780, he drove a team with continental flour. (RRR-6)

LUDLER (LUDLAR), JOHN. Oath of Allegiance, 1778, before Hon. John Beale Howard. He could not write; made his mark. (A-1/15, A-2/29)

LUDWIG, RICHARD. Non-Juror to Oath of Allegiance, 1778. (A-1/15)

LUGUARD, WILLIAM. Private, Capt. Ewing's Company No. 4 in 1776. (H-13)

LUKE, FOLIUS. Served on ship Defence, January 25 to March 31, 1777. (H-658)

LUMLEY, GEORGE. Oath of Allegiance, 1778, before Hon. William Lux. (A-1/15, A-2/68)

LUNN, NEHEMIAH. Enlisted July 20, 1776 in Baltimore Town. (H-53)

LUSBY, HENRY. Midshipman on ship Defence, October 15 to November 13, 1777, and Lieut. of Marines, November 13, 1777 to December 31, 1777. Took Oath of Allegiance, 1778, before Hon. Isaac Van Bibber. (H-658, A-1/15, A-2/34)

LUSK, ROBERT. Oath of Allegiance, 1778, before Hon. James Calhoun. (A-1/15, A-2/39)

LUSTRE, WILLIAM. Non-Juror to Oath of Allegiance, 1778. (A-1/15)

LUTES, JOHN. Non-Juror to Oath of Allegiance, 1778. (A-1/15)

LUVER, JOHN. Non-Juror to Oath of Allegiance, 1778. (A-1/15)

LUX, DARBY JR. (1737, Anne Arundel County, MD - April 10, 1795, Baltimore County, MD) Son of Capt. Darby LUX and Ann SAUNDERS. Married Rachel RIDGELY in 1764. Children: William LUX; Ann LUX married (1) George RISTEAU, and (2) Thomas Deye COCKEY; Rachel Ridgely LUX married James McCORMICK, Jr. in 1798; Darby LUX (III) married Sarah or Mary NICHOLSON in 1806; and, Eleanor Doll LUX married Dr. Robert GOLDSBOROUGH, Jr., and their son, Robert GOLDSBOROUGH III, married Araminta Sidney WINDER. Darby LUX's wife Rachel was born 1734 and died 1813. He was a very prominent man during the war. He served on the Baltimore County Committee of Inspection, March 13, 1775, and was a representative of Upper Back River Hundred at the Association of Freemen, August 21, 1775. He was elected to the Baltimore County Committee of Observation, September 23, 1775, and served on these committees until becoming militarily active in 1776. He was 2nd Colonel (Lieutenant Colonel) of the Gunpowder Battalion on May 25, 1776, becoming Colonel of the Gunpowder Battalion of Marching Militia on August 30, 1777, and Colonel of the 9th Battalion, commanding 594 Privates in 1777. He took the Oath of Allegiance in 1778 before Hon. Benjamin Rogers. He was selected on September 9, 1781 to assist in looking after the comfort and subsistence of Count Rochambeau in Baltimore. In 1782 he served on the Baltimore County Committee of Confiscated Property. (XXX-476, E-11, X-111, BBB-384, AA-65, BBB-350, FFF-120, BB-2, EE-51, RR-19, RR-47, SS-136, SSS-110, A-1/15, A-2/32, RR-50, FFF-468, ZZZ-200, ZZZ-201, ZZZ-204, JJJ-429, AAA-451, EEEE-1726)

LUX, GEORGE. (1753 - August, 1797) Son of William LUX and Agnes WALKER. Took the Oath of Allegiance, 1778, before Hon. James Calhoun. 1st Lieutenant in Capt. Deem's Company, Baltimore Town Battalion, September 25, 1780, and served as such due, in part, to the deaths of Capt. Ackerman and Lt. Wheeler. (F-307, R-15, BBBB-29, ZZZ-201, A-2/39)

LUX, ROBERT. Midshipman on ship Defence in 1777. (H-658)

LUX, WILLIAM. (c1730 - 1778) Son of Darby LUX and Ann SAUNDERS. Married Agnes WALKER, and had sons George and William. William LUX was very active in the Revolution, and quite prominent. He served on the Baltimore County Committee of Inspection, Mar. 13, 1775 and the Committee of Observation, September 23, 1775, having been elected that day. He also served on the Baltimore Town Committee of Correspondence, November 12, 1775, and the Baltimore Committee of Safety, May, 1776, serving as Vice-Chairman and then Chairman. He was a member of the Sons of Liberty in Baltimore, 1776, and also Secretary of the Committee of Observation. He took the Oath of Allegiance in 1778 before Hon. William Spear, and was also one of the Magistrates who administered the Oath in 1778. He was a Baltimore Privateer, and Continental Agent when he died, 1778. (ZZ-254, SS-130, EE-51, GG-74, RR-19, RR-47, SS-136, EEEE-1725, RR-50, CCC-19, EE-51, FFF-150, FFF-249, III-207, A-1/15, A-2/68)

LYLE (LYE), ROBERT. Oath of Allegiance, 1778, before Hon. Richard Holliday. (A-2/60)

LYNCH, BRADY. Non-Juror to Oath of Allegiance, 1778. (A-1/15) Signed, 1781. (QQ-115)

LYNCH, HUGH. Non-Juror to Oath of Allegiance, 1778. (A-1/15) Signed, 1781. (QQ-115)
Also, served in Baltimore County Militia; enlisted July 20, 1776. (H-52)

LYNCH, JAMES. Non-Juror to Oath of Allegiance, 1778. (A-1/15)

LYNCH, JOHN. Matross in Capt. Brown's MD Artillery; joined November 22, 1777. Was at
Valley Forge until June, 1778; at White Plains, July, 1778; at Fort Schuyler, August
and September, 1780; not listed in 1781. "Major John Lynch" died in Baltimore on
December 4, 1806, in his 44th year. "He took an active part in our struggle for
independence." (ZZZ-201, UU-228, UU-230, V-368)

LYNCH, LONS (LAWRENCE). Oath of Allegiance, 1778, before Hon. Andrew Buchanan. (A-2/57)

LYNCH, MATHIAS. Non-Juror to Oath of Allegiance, 1778; signed, 1781. (A-1/15, QQ-115)

LYNCH, PATRICK. Oath of Allegiance, 1778, before Hon. William Spear. (A-1/15, A-2/66)

LYNCH, ROBUCK. (July 23, 1728 - before 1797, Baltimore County, MD) Son of Patrick
LYNCH (died 1766 on Bear Creek, Baltimore County) and Martha BOWEN. He married to
Jemima STANSBURY (born 1727) on August 16, 1747, daughter of Thomas & Jane STANSBURY.
Children: Martha (born June 15, 1748); Patrick (May 17, 1750 - 1803), wife named
Elizabeth; Elizabeth (born January 14, 1752); William (c1754 - 1800) married Ruth
STANSBURY, daughter of George, born 1760; Roebuck (c1756 - 1821) married twice and
his second wife was Priscilla COLE; Jane, born c1758, married John BROWN in 1781.
Robuck (or Roebuck) LYNCH took the Oath of Allegiance, 1778, before Honorable Edward
Cockey. (A-1/15, A-2/61, D-4, AAA-2380)

LYNCH, WILLIAM. Son of Robuck LYNCH and Jemima STANSBURY. Born 1749/1754 and died in
1800. Married Ruth STANSBURY, and their son, William LYNCH (1794-1869) married Mary
Ann HOWLETT (1791-1884) in Baltimore County. William LYNCH served as a Private in
Capt. J. Cockey's Baltimore County Dragoons and was at Yorktown in 1781. He was a
Non-Juror to the Oath, 1778 (due to military duty). (AAA-2380, MMM-A, A-1/15)

LYNCH, WILLIAM. "Born in England." Took the Oath of Allegiance in 1778 before Hon.
Thomas Sollers. (A-2/51) Three others with this name were Non-Jurors. (A-1/15)

LYNN, HENRY. Matross in Capt. Gale's MD Artillery in 1779, and reported as deserted on
January 16, 1780. (YYY-1/66)

LYNTON, GEORGE. Recruit in Baltimore County in 1780. (H-340)

LYONS, PATRICK. Non-Juror to Oath of Allegiance, 1778. (A-1/15)

LYONS, ROBERT. Oath of Allegiance, 1778, before Hon. John Moale. (A-1/15, A-2/70)

LYONS (LYON), WILLIAM. Member of Sons of Liberty in 1776. Took Oath of Allegiance in
1778 before Hon. John Moale. Member of Col. Nicholson's Troop of Horse on June 7,
1781. (CCC-19, A-1/15, A-2/70, BBBB-274)

LYRCH, WILLIAM. (England) Oath of Allegiance, 1778. (A-1/15) (Ed. Note: This is most
likely the William Lynch, born in England, named above; error in spelling of name.)

LYSTON (LISTON), JAMES. Served in Baltimore Mechanical Company of Militia, Nov. 4,
1775, and a Private in Capt. Cox's Company, December 19, 1776. Took the Oath of
Allegiance, 1778, before Hon. William Spear. Private in Capt. McClellan's Company,
September 4, 1780. (F-298, CCC-21, CCC-24, A-1/15, A-2/66)

LYTEL, GEORGE. Involved in evaluation of Baltimore County confiscated proprietary
reserve land in 1782. (FFF-548)

M

MACABEE, JOHN. Non-Juror to Oath of Allegiance, 1778. (A-1/15)

MACE, W. Oath of Allegiance, 1778. (A-1/15)

MACGREGOR, PATRICK. Private in Capt. J. Cockey's Baltimore County Dragoons, and was at Yorktown in 1781. (MMM-A)

MACKANARY, SIMON. Recruit in Baltimore County in 1780. (H-340)

MACKELFRESH, DAVID. Oath of Allegiance, 1778, before Hon. Peter Shepherd. (A-2/49)

MACKENHEIMER, JOHN. (Died before October 27, 1823) Son of Gabriel and Catherine MACKENHEIMER. Married Susanna LINDENBERGER. Her death notice stated "Susanna Mackenheimer, consort of Col. John of Baltimore, died July 3, 1810 in her 46th year, leaving a husband and a large family of children and relatives." (ZZZ-209) John MACKENHEIMER was a Sergeant in Capt. Graybill's German Regiment in 1776 and John McINHEIMER was a 2nd Lieutenant in the Baltimore Town Battalion, September 25, 1780. (D-4, H-265, ZZZ-209, VV-303)

MACKENHEIMER, PETER. (Died before October 7, 1801) Son of Gabriel and Catherine Mackenheimer. Married in 1781 to Catherine LINDENBERGER. He served in the Baltimore Mechanical Company of Militia, November 4, 1775, and was a Private in Capt. Cox's Company, December 19, 1776. Took the Oath of Allegiance, 1778, before Hon. George Lindenberger. Peter McINHAMER was a Private in Capt. McClellan's Co., September 4, 1780. (F-298, CCC-21, CCC-24, D-4, A-1/15, A-2/53)

MACKENZIE, SAMUEL DR. Ordered by the Maryland Council in 1776 to procure medicines for the army. In 1777 he received orders from the Continental Congress to procure equipment for the army. Director of Military Hospitals at Baltimore, 1778. (XX-10)

MACKEY (MAKEY), HENRY. Private in Baltimore County Regiment No. 15, circa 1777, and was a Non-Juror to the Oath in 1778 (due to military duty). (TTT-13, A-1/16)

MACKEY, SAMUEL. Oath of Allegiance, 1778, before Hon. Peter Shepherd.(A-1/15,A-2/49)

MACKIE, EBENEZER. Baltimore County Committee of Observation, July 24, 1775.(EEEE-1726)

MACKLE, WILLIAM. Private, Capt. Cox's Company, December 19, 1776. (CCC-21)

MADDEN (MADDIN), CHARLES. Non-Juror to Oath of Allegiance, 1778. (A-1/15)

MADDEN, MICHAEL. Private in Capt. J. Gist's Co., 3rd MD Regt., February, 1778. (H-600)

MADDEN (MADDIN), THOMAS. Involved in evaluation of Baltimore County confiscated proprietary reserve lands in 1782. (FFF-555)

MADDOX, JOHN. Marine on ship Defence, June 3 to Octobr 15, 1777. (H-658)

MADKIN, WILLIAM JR. Oath of Allegiance, 1778, before Hon. James Calhoun. (A-2/65)

MAGARRY, JOHN. Oath of Allegiance, 1778, before Hon. Richard Cromwell. (A-2/46)

MAGAURAN (MALGAWRAN, MCGOWAN?), FRANCIS. Enlisted May 16, 1776 as Private in Captain N. Smith's 1st Company of Matrosses. At Fort Whetstone Point in Baltimore as of September 7, 1776. (H-568, H-570, QQQ-2, VV-74)

MAGEE, JAMES. Non-Juror to Oath of Allegiance, 1778. (A-1/15)
MAGEE, JOHN. Non-Juror to Oath of Allegiance, 1778. (A-1/15)

MAGNESS, JOHN. Oath of Allegiance, 1778, before Hon. John Beale Howard. Could not write; made his mark ("C"). (A-1/15, A-2/29)

MAGNESS, MOSES. Oath of Allegiance, 1778, before Hon. John Beale Howard. (A-2/29)

MAGRUDER, BLOYADE. Oath of Allegiance 1778, before Hon. James Calhoun. (A-2/38)

MAHONEY, FLORENCE. Enlisted in Baltimore County in 1776. (H-53)

MAHONEY, JAMES. Born 1745 in Ireland. Enlisted July 7, 1776 as Private in Colonel Ewing's Battalion, Baltimore County. Height: 5'1"; short black hair. (H-56)

MAHONEY, JOHN. Corporal in Capt. Furnival's Company, MD Artillery, Nov. 17, 1777. Matross in Capt. Gale's MD Artillery, 1779; commissary guard in 1780. (YYY-1/67, H-572)

MAHONEY, THOMAS. Enlisted in Baltimore County on July 25, 1776. (H-52)

MAHONEY, THOMAS. Born 1750 in Ireland. Occupation: Labourer. Enlisted January 27, 1776 as Private in Capt. N. Smith's 1st Company of Matrosses. Height: 5'7". (H-564, QQQ-2)

MAHONEY, TIMOTHY. Enlisted in Baltimore County on July 26, 1776. (H-53)

MAHONEY, WILLIAM. Oath of Allegiance, 1778, before Hon. James Calhoun. (A-1/15, A-2/38)

MAIDWELL, ALEXANDER. Oath of Allegiance, 1778, before Hon. James Calhoun. (A-1/15, A-2/42)

MAIDWELL (MAYDWELL), JAMES. Oath of Allegiance, 1778, before Hon. George Lindenberger. (A-1/16, A-2/53)

MAINEHIN, LORENCE. Oath of Allegiance, 1778. (A-1/15)

MAJOR, ALEXANDER. Oath of Allegiance, 1778, before Hon. Andrew Buchanan. (A-1/15, A-2/57)

MAJOR, JAMES. Oath of Allegiance, 1778, before Hon. Andrew Buchanan. (A-1/15, A-2/57)

MAJOR, ROBERT. Oath of Allegiance, 1778, before Hon. Andrew Buchanan. "Robert Majors" was 2nd Lieutenant, Capt. Chenowith's Company, Soldiers Delight Battalion, on Feb. 7, 1782. (A-1/15, A-2/57, OOOO-71)

MAKELWAYN, JAMES. Private in Capt. Cox's Company, December 19, 1776. (OOO-22)

MALES, JOHN. Non-Juror to Oath of Allegiance, 1778. (A-1/15)

MALLERD, JOHN. Non-Juror to Oath of Allegiance, 1778. (A-1/15)

MALLET, WILLIAM. Oath of Allegiance, 1778, before Hon. James Calhoun. (A-1/15, A-2/41)

MALLIMORE, JNO. Private, Capt. Deams' Company, 7th MD Regt., Dec. 27, 1776. (H-305)

MALLONEE, JOHN. (1728, France or Maryland - Died in Baltimore County) He married to Edith COLE on November 8, 1748. Children: James; Thomas; John, married Sallie BOND; William; Leonard, married Achsah SEWELL. John MALLONEE was a Private in Capt. John McGuire's Company of Col. William Greyson's Regt., Maryland Line. (XXX-496)

MALON, THOMAS. Non-Juror to Oath of Allegiance, 1778. (A-1/15)

MALONE, DENNIS. Non-Juror to Oath of Allegiance, 1778. (A-1/15)

MALONE, JOHN. Non-Juror to Oath of Allegiance, 1778. (A-1/15)

MALONE, MICHAEL. Non-Juror to Oath of Allegiance, 1778. (A-1/15)

MALONE, PETER. Non-Juror to Oath of Allegiance, 1778. (A-1/15)

MALONE, WILLIAM. Non-Juror to Oath of Allegiance, 1778. (A-1/15)

MALONEY, LAURENCE. Baltimore Artillery Company, 1777. (V-368)

MANGEL (MANGEE), SAMUEL. Oath of Allegiance, 1778, before Hon. William Spear. (A-2/66)

MANIKEN, LORENCE. Oath of Allegiance, 1778, before Hon. George Lindenberger. (A-2/53)

MANIKIN, WILLIAM. Oath of Allegiance, 1778, before Hon. Richard Cromwell. (A-2/46)

MANKEY, VALENTINE. Private in Baltimore County Regiment No. 15, circa 1777. (TTT-13)

MANN, FREDERICK. (March 4, 1754, Lancaster, PA - July 15, 1822, Baltimore, MD) Married Maria YOUNG, and their son, George MANN, married Amelia COOK; their grandson Benjamin Franklin MANN married Lina Amelia GILMORE. Frederick MANN was a Sergeant in Captain Jasper Yates' Company of Militia in Col. Slough's Battalion of Associators, Lancaster County, PA. (AAA-183, AAA-195, and Pennsylvania Archives, Volume 13, page 336)

MANN, ZACHARIAH. Oath of Allegiance, 1778, before Hon. William Spear. (A-1/15, A-2/67)

MANNAHAN, JAMES. Non-Juror to Oath of Allegiance, 1778. (A-1/15)

MANNAN, SAMUEL SR. Oath of Allegiance, 1778, before Hon. Peter Shepherd. (A-2/49)

MANNAN, SAMUEL JR. Oath of Allegiance, 1778, before Hon. Peter Shepherd. (A-2/49)

MANNIN, ABRAHAM. Oath of Allegiance, 1778, before Hon. Peter Shepherd. (A-1/15, A-2/50)

MANNIN, JOSEPH. Oath of Allegiance, 1778, before Hon. Peter Shepherd. (A-1/15, A-2/50)

MANNING, ROBERT. Oath of Allegiance, 1778, before Hon. Isaac Van Bibber. (A-1/16, A-2/34)

MANSEL (MANSIL), RICHARD. Private in Baltimore County Militia; enlisted July 18, 1776. Stored and delivered flour for the Baltimore Town Committee, 1780. (H-58, RRR-6)

MANSFIELD, LEVIN. Non-Juror to Oath of Allegiance, 1778. (A-1.16)

MANSFIELD, MRS. She submitted her account in Baltimore on April 12, 1777, for providing lodging for Capt. George Cook. (FFF-99)

MANSPIKER (MINSPAKER), HENRY. Oath of Allegiance, 1778, before Hon. George Lindenberger. Private, 4th MD Regiment (from Baltimore County); discharged December 3, 1781. (Q-72, A-1/16, A-2/53)

MANWARRING, JACOB. Non-Juror to Oath of Allegiance, 1778. (A-1/16)

MARCH, JOSHUA. Oath of Allegiance, 1778. (A-1/16)

MARCS, HERCULES. Oath of Allegiance, 1778, before Hon. James Calhoun. (A-1/16, A-2/42)

MARINER, EDWARD. Oath of Allegiance, 1778, before Hon. George G. Presbury. (A-2/48)

MARK, JAMES. Non-Juror to Oath of Allegiance, 1778. (A-1/16)

MARKEL, ADAM. Private in Capt. Keeports' German Regiment; enlisted July 21, 1776. Was at Philadelphia, September 19, 1776. (H-263)

MARKEY (MARKEE), JACOB. Non-Juror to Oath of Allegiance, 1778. Involved in evaluation of Baltimore County confiscated proprietary reserve lands in 1782. (FFF-542, A-1/16)

MARKEY, SAMUEL. Oath of Allegiance, 1778. (A-1/16)

MARKLAND, EDWARD. On February 25, 1824 it was ordered to "pay him, of Baltimore, half pay of a Lieutenant of the naval service, as further remuneration for his services during the Revolutionary War." On January 30, 1839, it was ordered to "pay to Alice MARKLAND, widow of Edward, during her life, quarterly, from April 1, 1838, an annual pension equal to that which her late husband received from Maryland under resolution of December session 1823, the half pay of a Lieutenant in the naval service, during the Revolutionary War." (C-372)

MARONEY (MORONEY), DAVID. Born 1753 in Cork, Ireland. Occupation: Bricklayer. He enlisted January 31, 1776 as Private in Capt. N. Smith's 1st Company of Matrosses. Height: 5'9". Private in Capt. Dorsey's MD Artillery, November 17, 1777, and was a Bombardier in that company at Valley Forge, June 3, 1778. (H-574, H-565, H-566, UU-231, VV-73, QQQ-2)

MARR, JAMES. Oath of Allegiance, 1778, before Hon. Charles Ridgely of William. Could not write; made his mark. (A-1/16, A-2/28)

MARR, JOHN. Private in Capt. Ramsey's Company No. 5 in 1776; discharged May 18, 1776. (H-640)

MARR, NICHOLAS. Private in Capt. Ramsey's Company No. 5 in 1776. (H-640)

MARR, WILLIAM. Born 1753. Married Arrcy OWINGS on June 14, 1784 in Baltimore County. (Marriage proven through Maryland pension application) Private in Capt. Ramsey's Company No. 5 in 1776. Took the Oath of Allegiance in 1778 before Honorable Charles Ridgely of William. Could not write; made his mark (" "). (A-1/16, A-2/28, H-640, YY-37, YY-118)

MARRIOTT, WILLIAM. Enlisted in Baltimore Town on July 20, 1776. (H-53)

MARSH, JOHN SR. Private in Col. Aquila Hall's Baltimore County Regiment in 1777. Took Oath of Allegiance, 1778, before Hon. James Calhoun. (TTT-13, A-1/16, A-2/42)

MARSH, JOHN JR. Oath of Allegiance, 1778, before Hon. Thomas Sollers. (A-1/16, A-2/51)

MARSH, JOSHUA. (1757 - November 5, 1825) Son of Thomas MARSH and Sophia CORBIN. He married Temperance HARRYMAN on December 9, 1783. Children: Elijah (never married); Stephen, married Eleanor Brooks MAGRUDER (OWINGS), widow, in 1822; Rebecca, married either Amon BOSLEY or an OWINGS; Grafton (never married); Dennis (never married); Josiah, married Eliza S. TAYLOR in 1826 (no issue); Ellen, married Amos MATTHEWS; Joshua (never married); Beale; Nelson; Achsah; William; and, Sarah. Joshua MARSH was a Captain in baltimore County's Gunpowder Upper Battalion, October 31, 1780. Also, he took the Oath of Allegiance in 1778 before Hon. Jesse Dorsey. (A-2/63, XXX-500,

JJJ-438, VV-345, YY-118, and data from Shirley Reightler of Bel Air, Maryland, 1987)

MARSH, RICHARD. (1750/1760 - December 13, 1797) Married Barbara LOUDENSLAGER. Their children: Richard; Solomon; Andrew, born 1786; Mary, married John HAGER; Elizabeth, married John SYKES; Henry; Catherine; George, born 1794, married Sarah GRIFFITH; Philip, born 1797, married Sarah McCOMULL. Richard MARSH served as 2nd Lieutenant in Capt. Carnan's Company No. 5 in Soldiers Delight Battalion. The Oath of Allegiance was taken by "Richard Marsh, Sr." before Hon. Charles Ridgely of William in 1778. He died in Boring, MD. (JJJ-438, WW-467, D-10, XXX-500, FF-64, A-2/27, and data from Shirley Reightler of Bel Air, Maryland, 1987)

MARSH, THOMAS. (c1720 - August, 1801) Married Sophia CORBIN on February 10, 1745. Their children: John; Joshua, married Temperance HARRYMAN in 1785; Thomas, married Sarah CORBIN circa 1775; David, married Nancy BOSLEY in 1791; Benedict; Clement, married to Jemima ELLIOTT in 1799; Temperance, married James BOSLEY in 1770; Achsah, married to Jacob STOVER in 1792; Beale, married Eleanor CORBIN in 1797; Prudence, married James ENLOWS; Sophia, married Benjamin HENDON in 1788; and, Elizabeth, married Joshua WINKS. Thomas MARSH took the Oath of Allegiance in 1778 before Hon. Jesse Dorsey. (A-1/16, A-2/63, JJJ-439, and data from Shirley Reightler of Bel Air, Maryland, 1987)

MARSH, WILLIAM. Non-Juror to Oath of Allegiance, 1778. (A-1/16)

MARSHALL, ISAAC. Oath of Allegiance, 1778, before Hon. Robert Simmons.(A-1/16, A-2/58)

MARSHALL, JACOB. Oath of Allegiance, 1778, before Hon. James Calhoun. (A-1/16, A-2/41)

MARSHALL, JAMES. Non-Juror to Oath of Allegiance, 1778. (A-1/16)

MARTIN, JOHN. Naval Captain in 1776. (FFF-67, FFF-69) Samuel MARTIN, son of Capt. John Martin, late of Baltimore, died August 24, 1809, aged 27. (ZZZ-215)

MARSHALL, JOHN. Non-Juror to Oath of Allegiance, 1778. (A-1/16)

MARSHALL, NATHAN. Matross in Capt. Gale's MD Artillery, 1779; deserted September 25, 1779 in Philadelphia. (YYY-1/68)

MARSHALL, THOMAS. 1st Lieutenant in Capt. Hall's Company, August 26, 1776, and Captain in Upper Battalion, August 30, 1777. Oath of Allegiance, 1778, before Hon. James Calhoun. Left military service prior to November 5, 1781. (AAAA-662, VV-114, RR-99, BBB-350, LL-66, E-14, A-1/16, A-2/39)

MARSHALL, WILLIAM. Oath of Allegiance, 1778, before Hon. John Hall. (A-1/16, A-2/36)

MARTIN, ANTHONY. Non-Juror to Oath of Allegiance, 1778. (A-1/16)
MARTIN, CHARLES. Non-Juror to Oath of Allegiance, 1778. (A-1/16)
MARTIN, GEORGE. Non-Juror to Oath of Allegiance, 1778. (A-1/16)

MARTIN, HUGH. Born 1752 in Pennsylvania. Occupation: Tanner and Currier. Enlisted as Private in Capt. N. Smith's 1st Company of Matrosses on January 24, 1776. His height was 5' 7 3/4". (H-563, H-566, VV-74, QQQ-2)

MARTIN, JOHN. Naval Captain, 1776. His son, Samuel, died August 24, 1809, aged 27, late of Baltimore.. (FFF-67, FFF-69, ZZZ-215)

MARTIN, JOHN. Sergeant in Capt. McClellan's Company, September 4, 1780. (CCC-23)

MARTIN, JOHN S. Baltimore Mechanical Company of Militia, 1776. (CCC-28)

MARTIN, LEWIS. Baltimore Matrosses; deserted, 1780. (H-341)

MARTIN, LUTHER, ESQ. Son of Benjamin and Hannah MARTIN. Married Mary CRESAP. He was appointed Attorney General in 1778 and settled in Baltimore. He served with Capt. Nicholas Ruxton Moore's Troops on June 25, 1781. He had a six year old bay stallion. He also represented Harford County, Maryland, at the Federal Constitutional Convention in 1787. Born in 1744, he died a distinguished patriot and jurist in New York City on July 8, 1826. (UUU-123, SS-163, FFF-137, BBBB-313, MMM-A)

MARTIN, MICHAEL. Enlisted in Baltimore County on July 25, 1776. (H-52)

MARTIN, NATHANIEL. Non-Juror to Oath of Allegiance, 1778. (A-1/16)

MARTIN, TERRENCE. Private in Capt. Ewing's Company No. 4; enlisted Jan. 8, 1776. (H-12)

MARTIN, WILLIAM. Private in Capt. Ewing's Company No. 4; enlisted May 11, 1776. Took the Oath of Allegiance, 1778, before Hon. James Calhoun. (H-11, A-2/65)

MARWOOD, ANDREW. Recruit in Baltimore County Militia, April 11, 1780. (H-335)

MARVELL (MARYELL), FRANCIS. Oath of Allegiance, 1778, before Hon. William Spear. (A-1/16, A-2/66)

MASH, JOHN. Non-Juror to Oath of Allegiance, 1778. (A-1/16)

MASHACK, PHILIP. Non-Juror to Oath of Allegiance, 1778. (A-1/16)

MASON, ABEL. Ordinary Sailor on ship Defence in 1777. (H-658)

MASON, BENJAMIN. Oath of Allegiance, 1778, before Hon.Thomas Sollers.(A-1/16, A-2/51)

MASON, JOHN. Non-Juror to Oath of Allegiance, 1778. (A-1/16)

MASON, MICHAEL. Oath of Allegiance, 1778, before Hon. Richard Cromwell. (A-2/46)

MASON, PETER SR. Non-Juror to Oath of Allegiance, 1778. (A-1/16)
MASON, PETER JR. Non-Juror to Oath of Allegiance, 1778. (A-1/16)

MASON, THOMAS. Private in Capt. Ewing's Company No. 4; enlisted January 29, 1776. Non-Juror to Oath of Allegiance, 1778. (H-12, A-1/16)

MASON (MASSON), WILLIAM. Recruit, Baltimore County, in 1780. Private in the Extra Regiment at Fort Whetstone Point in Baltimore, 1781. (H-340, H-627)

MASSEY, HENRY LEE. Midshipman on ship Defence, May 10 to December 31, 1777. (H-658)

MASTERS, JOHN. Oath of Allegiance, 1778, before Hon. Isaac Van Bibber.(A-1/16,A-2/34)

MASTERS, WATTERLY. Marine on ship Defence, 1777. (H-658)

MASTERSON (MASTUSON), PHILIP. Private in Capt. Furnival's MD Artilley, Nov. 17, 1777. Matross in Capt. J. Smith's MD Artillery, 1780, and in Capt. Dorsey's MD Artillery, at Camp Col. Scirvins, January 28, 1782; served to 1783. Entitled to 50 acres (lot 860)in western Maryland. (DDDD-27, YYY-2/29, H-573, H-579, UU-232)

MASTON, PHILIP. Non-Juror to Oath of Allegiance, 1778. (A-1/16)

MATCHET, JOHN. Private in 4th MD Regiment (from Baltimore County); discharged Dec. 3, 1781. (Q-72)

MATHIAS, JAMES. Born 1750/1751 in West New Jersey. Occupation: Labourer. Enlisted on January 28, 1776 as Private in Capt. N. Smith's 1st Company of Matrosses, Maryland. Private in Capt. Dorsey's MD Artillery; joined November 17, 1777 (note states he is "in gaol for house breaking.") Height: 5' 8½". Private in Capt. Lansdale's Co., 4th MD Regt., April 3, 1778 to November 1, 1780. Revolutionary War pensioner also. (YY-37, VV-73, H-144, H-564, H-566, H-574, QQQ-2)

MATHIAS, JOSEPH. Oath of Allegiance, 1778, before Hon. James Calhoun.(A-1/16,A-2/41)

MATHIAS, WILLIAM. Oath of Allegiance, 1778. (A-1/16)

MATHIOT, CHRISTIAN. "Died in Baltimore in February, 1816, in his 69th year, having served in the Pennsylvania Line during our Revolutionary struggle." (ZZZ-216)

MATTHEWMAN, LUKE. Baltimore Privateer and Captain of brigantine Snake (14 guns and 6 swivels). (III-206)

MATTHEWS, DANIEL. There may have been two men by this name in Baltimore. One wrote to the Governor of Maryland concerning powder in Baltimore on April 15, 1777. One enlisted at Ft. Whetstone Point in Baltimore on October 4, 1779, and deserted on October 12, 1779. They may have been the same person; maybe not. (H-626, FFF-100)

MATTHEWS, FRANCIS. Non-Juror to Oath of Allegiance, 1778. (A-1/16)

MATTHEWS, JAMES. Private, Capt. Ewing's Co. No. 4; enlisted Jan. 24, 1776. (H-12)

MATTHEWS, GEORGE. (1729 - February 7, 1811) Reported to Council of Safety on condition of cannons in Baltimore City in 1776, and contracted that same year with the State of Maryland to manufacture cannons in Baltimore. He was a Non-Juror to the Oath, 1778. His residence was near Friends Meeting House, east of Jones Falls. (ZZZ-216, III-212, FFF-14, A-1/16)

MATTHEWS, JOHN. Sweeper on ship Defence, January 25 to December 31, 1777. (H-658)

MATTHEWS, MATTHEW. Non-Juror to Oath of Allegiance 1778. (A-1/16)
MATTHEWS, MORDECAI. Non-Juror to Oath of Allegiance, 1778. (A-1/16)
MATTHEWS, OLIVER. Non-Juror to Oath of Allegiance, 1778. (A-1/16)
MATTHEWS, RICHARD. Non-Juror to Oath of Allegiance, 1778. (A-1/16)
MATTHEWS, SAMUEL. Non-Juror to Oath of Allegiance, 1778. (A-1/16)
MATTHEWS, THOMAS. Non-Juror to Oath of Allegiance, 1778. (A-1/16)

MATTHEWS, WILLIAM. Ensign in Capt. Marshall's Company, Upper Battalion, August 30, 1777, and still in service as of February 1, 1782; may have been a Captain by that time. He took the Oath of Allegiance in 1778 before Hon. Hercules Courtenay. He was involved in the evaluation of Baltimore County confiscated proprietary reserve lands in 1782. (E-14, LL-66, BBB-350, CCCC-65, FFF-542, A-1/16, A-2/47)

MATTHEWS, WILLIAM. Corporal of Marines on ship Defence, 1776-1777. Took the Oath of Allegiance in 1778 before Hon. John Hall. (H-606, H-658, A-2/36)

MATTISON (MATESON), AARON. Baltimore Mechanical Company of Militia, November 4, 1775. Corporal in Capt. Cox's Company, December 19, 1776. Oath of Allegiance, 1778, before Hon. William Spear. Signed letter to Governor of Maryland, September 4, 1778, to inform him of suspected shipments of flour to the enemy. On September 4, 1780, he was Private in Capt. McClellan's Company. (CCC-21, CCC-24, II-23, F-298, A-2/66)

MATTOX (MATTAX),_____(First name torn off list) Private in Baltimore County Regiment No. 7, circa 1777. (TTT-13)

MATTOX (MATTOCKS), JOHN. Oath of Allegiance, 1778, before Hon. Peter Shepherd. (A-2/49)

MATTOX, MICHAEL. Non-Juror to Oath of Allegiance, 1778. (A-1/16)
MATTOX, WILLIAM. Non-Juror to Oath of Allegiance, 1778. (A-1/16)

MAW, JOHN. Matross in Capt. Gale's MD Artillery, 1779; on furlough, November, 1779; deserted April 1, 1780. (YYY-1/69)

MAXEY, USHER. Oath of Allegiance, 1778. (A-1/16)

MAXFIELD, JAMES. Oath of Allegiance, 1778, before Hon. William Spear.(A-1/16,A-2/67)

MAY,_____. "Captain May, an old officer of the Revolution, and long an inhabitant of Baltimore, died March 4, 1807." (ZZZ-217)

MAY, BENJAMIN. Oath of Allegiance, 1778, before Hon. James Calhoun.(A-1/16, A-2/38)

MAY, JAMES. Non-Juror to Oath of Allegiance, 1778. (A-1/16)
MAY, JOHN. Non-Juror to Oath of Allegiance, 1778. (A-1/16)
MAYNER, CHARLES. Non-Juror to Oath of Allegiance, 1778. (A-1/16)

MAYNER (MAYNOR), PETER SR. Drummer in Capt. Brown's MD Artillery as of August 1, 1781 at High Hills of the Santee; at Camp Col. Scirvins in January, 1782; and at Bacon's Bridge, S.C. in April, 1782. Entitled to land in western Maryland: Peter Maynor, 50 acres, lot 108; Peter Maynor, Sr., 50 acres, lot 363. The former was a Fifer and the latter was a Matross. (DDDD-27, UU-229, UU-230)

MAYNER, WILLIAM. Oath of Allegiance, 1778. (A-1/16)

MAYS, JOHN. Non-Juror to Oath of Allegiance, 1778. (A-1/16)

MAYS, WILLIAM. Private, Capt. J. Gist's Company, 3rd MD Regiment, Feb., 1778. (H-600)

MAYSMAR, JACOB. Non-Juror to Oath of Allegiance, 1778. (A-1/16)
MAYSMAR, YOKLER. Non-Juror to Oath of Allegiance, 1778. (A-1/16)

McADAMS. JOHN. Armourer on ship Defence, October 22, to December 31, 1777. (H-658)

McALLISTER, JOEL. Sergeant in Capt. Oldham's Company, 4th MD Regiment, from Dec. 8, 1776 to Dec. 8, 1779. (H-142)

McALLISTER (McCOLESTER), JOHN. Served in Capt. Nicholas Ruxton Moore's Troops as of June 25, 1781. He had a five year old grey gelding horse. (BBBB-313)

McALLISTER, JOSEPH. Oath of Allegiance, 1778, before Hon. Richard Cromwell. (A-2/46)

McALLISTER (McCALLISTER), ROBERT. Non-Juror to Oath of Allegiance, 1778. (A-1/15)

McAVOY, NICHOLAS. Born 1735 in Ireland. Enlisted July 5, 1776, Baltimore County, as Private in Col. Ewing's Battn. Ht: 5' $\frac{1}{2}$"; short hair; full face. (H-55)

McBOYCE. JAMES. Oath of Allegiance, 1778, before Hon. Jesse Dorsey. (A-1/15, A-2/64)

McBRIDE, HENRY. 2nd Lt. in Capt. Galbraith's Company, Baltimore County Militia, on September 2, 1777. 1st Lt. in Capt. Deaver's Company, Baltimore Town Battalion, on May 19, 1779. (BBB-359, F-309, F-311, GGG-401)

McBRIED, ARCHEY. Oath of Allegiance, 1778, before Hon. Geo. Lindenberger. (A-2/54)

McCABE, JOHN. Recommended by Capt. Frederick Deams that he be commissioned a Lieut. on December 21, 1776, but records show John McCABE was a 1st Lieutenant in Capt. Richardson's Company No. 5, Baltimore Town Battalion, as of June 6, 1776. Also, his service with the Baltimore Artillery Company in 1777 shows no rank, but he is shown as 1st Lieutenant again in the Baltimore Town Battalion on May 19, 1779. He took the Oath of Allegiance in 1778 before Hon. James Calhoun. (A-1/15, A-2/38, F-312, V-368, GG-74, WW-467, FFF-74)

McCALL, GEORGE. Non-Juror to Oath of Allegiance in 1778. (A-1/15)

McCANDLESS, GEORGE. Oath of Allegiance, 1778, before Hon. George Lindenberger. (A-1/15, A-2/53)

McCANN, JOHN. Born 1747. Enlisted July 5, 1776 as Private in Col. Ewing's Battalion. Height: 5' 1$\frac{1}{4}$"; long black hair. "John McCANE" took the Oath of Allegiance, 1778, before Hon. James Calhoun. (A-1/15, A-2/42, H-54)

McCARNEL, CHARLES. Oath of Allegiance, 1778, before Hon. James Calhoun. (A-2/42)

McCARREN (McCARNAN), BARNEY. Recruited in Baltimore on March 2, 1780, by Samuel Chester for the 3rd Maryland Regiment. (H-334, H-335)

McCARTE, WILLIAM. Private in Baltimore Artillery Company, October 16, 1775. (G-8)

McCARTER, ARTHUR. Private in Capt. Sheaff's Company, June 16, 1777. (W-162)

McCARTER, WILLIAM. Oath of Allegiance in 1778 before Hon. George Lindenberger. (A-1/15, A-2/54)

McCARTHY, CALLEHAN. Oath of Allegiance, 1778, before Hon. Edward Cockey. (A-2/61)

McCARTY, DENNIS. Non-Juror to Oath of Allegiance, 1778. (A-1/15)

McCARTY, FLORENCE. Seaman on ship Defence, June 25 to December 16, 1777. (H-658)

McCARTY, JESSEY. Private in Capt. Deams' Company, 7th MD Regiment, Dec. 16, 1776. Private in Extra Regt., Fort Whetstone Point, Baltimore, 1781. (H-305, H-627)

McCASKEY, ALEXANDER. "Died March 14, 1798 in his 59th year; a resident of Fell's Point. He was an officer in the Revolutionary Army, a husband and parent. His remains were interred in Friends burying ground." (ZZZ-202)

McCASLIN, ELISHA. Ensign in Baltimore County Militia Company No. 7, December 19, 1775. "Elisah McCASTLIN" took the Oath of Allegiance in 1781. (QQ-116, G-10)

McCASTLIN, JACOB. Took the Oath of Allegiance in 1781. (QQ-116)

McCAULLEY, WILLIAM. Private in Capt. Ewing's Company No. 4; enlisted January 22, 1776. (H-12)

McCLAIN, ELY. Non-Juror to Oath of Allegiance, 1778. (A-1/15)

McCLALLUM, DAVID. Baltimore Mechanical Company of Militia, November 4, 1775. (F-298)

McCLAY, G. Oath of Allegiance, 1778, before Hon. Isaac Van Bibber. (A-1/15, A-2/34)

McCLELLAN, DAVID. (1740/1741 - march 3, 1790) Married Jane BUCHANAN, April 20, 1768. Their children: Mary; Elizabeth, married William MOORE; William; David, married Maria PENNYBAKER; Walter; Jane; John; Robert, married Sarah MILLER; Mary; and, Nancy. David McCLELLAN was nominated but not elected to the Baltimore Committee of Observation on September 12, 1775. He was an Ensign in Capt. Cox's Baltimore County Militia, 3rd Company, on December 19, 1775. He left the service in March, 1776, and returned to Marsh Creek, PA and became an officer in the York County Militia. Also, he was Justice of the Peace, 1776-1777, and was subsequently referred to as Colonel. He was born in York County, PA, and died there. (XXX-480, WW-197,JJJ-449,RR-50,G-10)

McCLELLAN (McLELLAN), JOHN. He represented Westminster Hundred at the Association of Freemen on August 21, 1775, and was a 1st Lieutenant in Capt. Cox's Baltimore County Militia, 3rd Company, on December 19, 1775. He was a Lieutenant of the Mercantile Company (formerly Cox's Company) and became Captain upon the death of Capt. Cox in October, 1777 at the battle of Germantown. He took the Oath of Allegiance in 1778 before Hon. James Calhoun, and signed a letter to the Governor of Maryland, Sept. 4, 1778, regarding suspicious flour shipments headed for the enemy. Capt. McClellan served throughout the war. (G-10,F-311,F-313,CCC-21,CCC-25,II-23,CCC-22,EEEE-1726)

McCLENAN (mCCLELAND), ROBERT. Marine on ship Defence, June 26 to Dec. 31, 1777. (H-658)

McCLENNAN, DAVID. Baltimore County Committee of Observation in 1775. (EEEE-1725/1726)

McCLELLAN, JOHN. Baltimore County Committee of Observation in 1775. (EEEE-1725/1726)

McCLOCKLING, JOHN. Private, Capt. Deams' Co., 7th MD Regt., December 27, 1776. (H-305)

McCLUGHAN, JAMES. Oath of Allegiance, 1778, before Hon. Thomas Sollers. (A-2/51)

McCLUNG, ROBERT. Oath of Allegiance, 1778, before Hon. Jesse Dorsey. (A-1/15, A-2/63)

McCLURE, JOHN. Non-Juror to Oath of Allegiance, 1778. Baltimore Privateer. Served on the Baltimore Salt Committee, October 14, 1779. (A-1/15, III-206, HHH-88)

McCOLLESTER, TOAL. Private in Baltimore County Militia in 1776. (H-59)

McCOMISKEY, DANIEL. Non-Juror to Oath of Allegiance, 1778. (A-1/15)

McCOMISKEY (McCORMISKEY), JOHN. Private in Baltimore County Regiment No. 15, circa 1777. Non-Juror to Oath of Allegiance in 1778. (TTT-13, A-1/15)

McCOMKY (McCONKY), JAMES. Non-Juror to Oath of Allegiance, 1778. (A-1/15)

McCONAUGHEY, ALEX. Corporal in Capt. Ramsey's Company No. 5 in 1776. (H-639)

McCONNELL, CHARLES. Oath of Allegiance, 1778. (A-1/15)

McCORMICK (McCORMACK), DENNIS. Gunner in Capt. Gale's MD Artillery, 1779-1780, and in Capt. J. Smith's MD Artillery in 1780. Bombardier in Capt. Dorsey's Company at Camp Col. Scirvins on January 28, 1782. Discharged, September, 1782. Entitled to 50 acres (lot 1349) in western Maryland, as Corporal in MD Artillery. (DDDD-25, H-579, UU-232, YYY-1/70)

McCOTTOR, JAMES. Oath of Allegiance, 1778, before Hon. James Calhoun. (A-2/65)

McCOY, GEORGE. Served on ship Defence, April 1 to December 31, 1777. (H-658)

McCOY, JOHN. Private in Col. Aquila Hall's Baltimore County Regiment, 1777. (TTT-13)

McCOY, WILLIAM. Non-Juror to Oath of Allegiance, 1778. (A-1/15)

McCRACKEN, JOHN. Oath of Allegiance, 1778, before Hon. Geo. Lindenberger. (A-2/53)

McCRACKIN, JAS. Private in Capt. Cox's Company on December 19, 1776. (CCC-21)

McCRAY, FERGIS. Served in Baltimore Artillery Company in 1777. (V-368)

McCRAE (McCRUE), NEAL. Private, Capt. Deams' Co., 7th MD Regt., Jan. 7, 1777. (H-305)

McCREARY, JOHN. Of Baltimore County; died Noevmber 23, 1830. Private in PA Line. Received pension August 26, 1830 dating from January 1, 1829 at $96 per annum. Received $161.06, U.S. Pension Roll, 1835, page 8. (C-369)

McCUBBIN, JOHN. Oath of Allegiance, 1778, before Hon. John Beale Howard. Could not write; made his mark (" "). (A-1/15, A-2/29)

McCUBBIN (MACKUBIN), MOSES. Oath of Allegiance, 1778, before Hon. Thomas Sollers. (A-1/15, A-2/51)

McCUBBIN (MACCUBBIN), WILLIAM. 1st Lieutenant, Patapsco Upper Battalion, May 25, 1776. Took Oath of Allegiance, 1778, before Hon. Thomas Sollers. Wrote to the Governor of Maryland on March 6, 1779, from Back River, about the enforcement of a law regarding delinquents. Captain in Gunpowder Battalion, March 20, 1779. (A-1/15, A-2/51, FFF-209, WW-413, EE-51, E-12, GGG-325)

McCUBBIN (MACKUBIN), ZACHARIAH SR. Oath of Allegiance, 1778, before Hon. Charles Ridgely of William. (A-1/15, A-2/27)

McCUBBIN (MACCUBBIN), ZACHARIAH JR. (1745-Nov.18, 1809) Married Sarah LANE. He represented Upper Patapsco Hundred at the Association of Freemen on August 21, 1775, and was elected to the Baltimore County Committee of Observation, Sept. 23, 1775. He was Captain of Baltimore County Militia Company No. 4 (60 Privates) on December 19, 1775, and captain of the 1st Division, Baltimore Battalion, under Col. Buchanan in June, 1776, commanding 72 men. From July to December, 1776, he was Captain in the 2nd MD Battalion of the Flying Camp. He took Oath of Allegiance in 1778 before Hon. Charles Ridgely of William. His death notice stated, in part, that "Major Zachariah MacCUBBIN died at his farm in Baltimore County on Nov. 18, 1809 in his 64th year." (ZZZ-205, EEEE-1726, JJJ-451, CC-36, G-10, DD-47, SS-136, H-52, RR-47, RR-50, A-1/15, A-2/28) (Source JJJ-451 states he was born in 1756. This must be incorrect, for he would have been a Captain at the tender age of 19; also, his death notice states he was 64 in 1809, thus making his birth in 1745.)

McCULLOUGH, JAMES. Baltimore Mechanical Company of Militia in 1776. He was a Non-Juror to Oath of Allegiance in 1778. (CCC-28, A-1/15)

McCURDY, ARTHUR. Non-Juror to Oath of Allegiance, 1778. (A-1/15)

McCUTCHIN, SAMUEL. Oath of Allegiance, 1778, before Hon. Jesse Dorsey.(A-1/15,A-2/63)

McDANIEL, FRANCIS. Oath of Allegiance, 1778. (A-1/15)

McDANIEL, JAMES. Oath of Allegiance, 1778. (A-1/15)

McDANIEL (McDONIEL), FRANCIS. Non-Juror to Oath of Allegiance, 1778. (A-1/15)

McDANIEL, JOHN. Delivered barrels for Baltimore County, January 7, 1781. (FFF-352)

McDANIEL, THOMAS. Enlisted in Baltimore County on July 20, 1776. (H-52)

McDEARMETT, JOHN. Private in Baltimore County Militia; enlisted July 18, 1776. (H-58)

McDENNY, THOMAS. Non-Juror to Oath of Allegiance, 1778. (A-1/15)

McDONALD, JOHN. Oath of Allegiance, 1778, before Hon. George Lindenberger. (A-2/53)

McDONALD, PAT. Born 1753 in Ireland. Enlisted July 7, 1776 in Baltimore County in Col. Ewing's Battalion, as a Private. Height: 5' 7½"; black hair. (H-56)

McDONALD, ROBERT. Ordinary Sailor on ship Defence, September 19, 1776 - 1777.(H-658)

McDONNOC (McDONNOCK), PATRICK. Non-Juror to Oath of Allegiance, 1778. (A-1/15)

McDONO, BARTHOLOMY. Recruit in Baltimore County in 1780. (H-340)

McDONOGH, JOHN. (1734 - March, 1809) Private in Capt. Cox's Company, December 19, 1776, and Private in Capt. McClellan's Company, September 4, 1780. Took Oath of Allegiance in 1778 before Hon. George Lindenberger. His death notice stated, in part, that he died in 1809 after a long illness, a patriotic veteran, aged 75.... "Under Washington he witnessed the terrible defeat of Braddock in 1755. Under the same immortal hero he fought for the liberty of these states. He enlisted under

Captain Cox, whom he saw die at Brandywine." (ZZZ-206, CCC-21, CCC-24, A-2/53)

McDONOGH, MATTHEW. Oath of Allegiance, 1778, before Hon. James Calhoun.(A-1/15,A-2/40)

McDONOGH, PATRICK. Oath of Allegiance, 1778, before Hon. John Moale. (A-1/15, A-2/70)

McDOWELL (McDOOLE), HUGH. Born 1747 in Newry, Ireland. Occupation: Blacksmith. Enlisted January 24, 1776 as Private in Capt. N. Smith's 1st Company of Matrosses. Ht: 5' 5¼". Private in Capt. Dorsey's MD Artillery, November 17, 1777, sick with "bilious fever." Matross in Capt. Dorsey's MD Artillery at Valley Forge, June 3, 1778. Matross in Capt. J. Smith's MD Artillery, 1780. Matross in Capt. Dorsey's MD Artillery at Camp Colonel Scirvins, January 28, 1782. Matross in Capt. J. Smith's MD Artillery in 1783. (H-564, H-567, H-574, H-579, H-618, UU-231, UU-232, VV-74, QQQ-2, YYY-2/30)

McFADDEN (McFADON), JAMES. 1st Lieutenant in Capt. Brown's MD Artillery; commissioned November 22, 1777; at Valley Forge until June, 1778; at White Plains, July, 1778. Was commissioned Captain-Lieutenant under Lt.Col. Ed. Carrington; stationed in Baltimore, May 11, 1780 (commissioned November 1, 1779). Received Federal Bounty Land Grant 1079 for 200 acres. (YY-72, H-477, UU-227, UU-230, VVV-96) Also, at the High Hills of the Santee on August 1, 1781, and in the Southern Campaign into 1782. (UU-229, UU-230)

McFADEN (McFADON), JAMES. Born 1755 in Ireland. Occupation: Labourer. Enlisted Jan. 31, 1776 as Private in Capt. N. Smith's 1st Company of Matrosses. Height: 6' 1" (which is quite tall for his day). Served in Baltimore Artillery Company in 1777. Sergeant at Fort Whetstone Point in Baltimore, September 7, 1776. (H-565, H-568, QQQ-2, V-368)

McFADON, JOHN. Oath of Allegiance, 1778, before Hon. James Calhoun. (A-1/15, A-2/40)

McFADON, SAMUEL. Private in Capt. McClellan's Company, Baltimore Town Battalion, Sept. 4, 1780. (CCC-24)

McFALL, JAMES. Private, Capt. Deams' Co., 7th MD Regt., January 17, 1777. (H-305)

McFALL, JOHN. Enlisted in Baltimore County on July 26, 1776. (H-53)

McFASON, MALCOLM. Oath of Allegiance, 1778, before Hon. George Lindenberger. (A-2/53)

McFEE, MALCOLM. Enlisted in Baltimore Town on July 17, 1776. (H-53)

McGAW, ADAM. Oath of Allegiance, 1778. (A-1/15)

McGAW (McGEAUGH), NICHOLAS. Enlisted in Baltimore County on July 15, 1776, as Private in Col. Ewing's Battalion. Not on muster roll in August, 1776. (H-57)

McGILL, JAMES. Marine on ship Defence in 1777. (H-658)

McGILL, JAMES. Recruit in Baltimore County in 1780. (H-340)

McGILL, PATRICK. Oath of Allegiance, 1778, before Hon. Jesse Dorsey. (A-1/15, A-2/64)

McGILTON, DANIEL. Private in Capt. Howell's Company, December 30, 1775. Took Oath of Allegiance in 1778 before Hon. William Spear. (G-11, A-1/15, A-2/67)

McGINNIS, JOHN. Oath of Allegiance, 1778, before Hon. James Calhoun. (A-1/15, A-2/38)

McGINNIS, WILLIAM. Private in Capt. Ewing's Company No. 4; enlisted May 24, 1776.(H-11)

McGLATHRY (McCLATHRY), JOHN. Private in Capt. Howell's Company, December 30, 1775. Oath of Allegiance, 1778, before Hon. James Calhoun. (G-11, A-1/15, A-2/38)

McGLOUGHLIN, ELISHA. Non-Juror to Oath of Allegiance, 1778. (A-1/15)
McGLOUGHLIN, HENRY. Non-Juror to Oath of Allegiance, 1778. (A-1/15)
McGLOUGHLIN, JACOB. Non-Juror to Oath of Allegiance, 1778. (A-1/15)

McGLOUGHLIN, JOHN. Corporal in Capt. Ewing's Co. No. 4; enlisted May 3, 1776. (H-11)

McGLOUGHLIN (MCGLOCHLIN), WILLIAM. Private in Capt. Ewing's Company No. 4; enlisted June 3, 1776. "William McCLOCHLIN" received Bounty Land Warrant 11488-100 for his services as a Private; issued September 24, 1789. (YY-28, H-12)

McGRAW, ADAM. Oath of Allegiance, 1778, before Hon. Jesse Dorsey. (A-2/64)

McGUIRE, DANIEL. Private, Capt. Deams' Co., 7th MD Regt., December 19, 1776. (H-305)

McGUIRE, PETER. (1763 - January 30, 1850) Married Charity SHIRLEY. Recruited in 1780 in Baltimore County as a Private. (JJJ-454, H-340)

McGUIRE, THOMAS. Private, Capt. Ewing's Company No. 4; enlisted Jan. 24, 1776. (H-12)

McHARD, ISAAC. He wrote to the Governor of Maryland on April 16, 1777, regarding the difficulties pertaining to hiring wagons in Baltimore. (FFF-100)

McHENRY, DANIEL. Non-Juror to Oath of Allegiance, 1778, but signed, 1781.(A-1/15,QQ-117)

McHENRY, JAMES DR. (1753, Ballymena, Country Antrim, Northern Ireland - May 3, 1816, Baltimore, Maryland) Son of Daniel and Agnes McHENRY. He came to Baltimore about 1771, attended Newark Academy, Delaware and studied medicine under Dr. Benjamin Rush in Philadelphia. He married Margaret CALDWELL. Their children: Grace; Daniel, md. Sophia RAMSAY (he died in July, 1814, age about 27 years, as a result of a fall from a horse); Anna, married James BOYD; John, married Juliann HOWARD; and, Margaretta. James McHENRY became Assistant Surgeon in 1775 and was sent to the Boston front. He was Surgeon of the 5th Battalion, Pennsylvania Flying Camp, in August, 1776, and was prisoner at Fort Washington, November 16, 1776; exchanged March 5, 1778. He became Assistant Secretary to General Washington, May 15, 1778, and Major in the Continental Army, May 25, 1781 to rank from October 30, 1780. He was Aide-de-Camp to the General Lafayette, October 30, 1780 to December 22, 1781. He served in the Revolutionary Army until 1783, then returned to Baltimore. He was elected to the Maryland State Senate, September 14, 1781, resigning in 1786. In 1787 he was appointed to the Congress to fill a vacancy caused by the death of Edward Giles. He was elected to the House of Delegates, 1788-1791. He also served as a member of the United States Constitutional Convenetion, 1787. He was again elected to the State Senate, 1791-1796. President Washington appointed him Secretary of War in 1796 where he remained to May, 1800, at which time he resigned. He also received 400 acres under Federal Bounty Land Grant 1480 for his war services. He died at his home in Baltimore on May 3, 1816. In his honor, Fort Whetstone Point was renamed Fort McHenry. (XX-11, YY-72, ZZZ-208, TT-109, FFF-359; see F.J.Brown's Sketch of the Life of Dr. James McHenry, MHS, Publication 10)

McHENRY, JOHN. Oath of Allegiance, 1778, before Hon. George Lindenberger. (A-2/54)

McHUGH, MATTHEW. Sergeant, Capt. J. Gist's Co., 3rd MD Regt., February, 1778. (H-600)

McILROY, FERGUS. Ensign in Capt. Richardson's Company No. 5, Baltimore Town Battalion, June 6, 1776. (WW-467, GG-74)

McILVAIN, ANDREW. (1737 - March 1, 1811, Adams County, PA) Took the Oath of Allegiance in Baltimore in 1778 before Hon. George Lindenberger. (A-1/15, A-2/53, ZZZ-208)

McILVAIN, GILBERT. Oath of Allegiance, 1778, before Hon. James Calhoun.(A-1/15, A-2/40)

McILVAIN, WILLIAM. Oath of Allegiance, 1778, before Hon. James Calhoun.(A-1/15, A-2/40)

McITEE, JOSEPH. Private in Extra Regt., Fort Whetstone Point, Baltimore, 1781. (H-627)

McINTIRE, DANIEL. Enlisted in Baltimore county on August 14, 1776. (H-52)

McINTYRE, JOHN. Ordinary Seaman on ship Defence, September 19, 1776. (H-606)

McKEAM, WILLIAM. In Baltimore County, 1779, he gave a deposition about his capture and imprisonment by the British. (FF-199)

McKENNY, JOHN. Non-Juror to Oath of Allegiance, 1778. (A-1/15)

McKENZIE, DANIEL. (1755 - September 7, 1825) Married Mary Ann CHAPMAN. Source A-1/15 lists him as a Non-Juror to Oath, 1778, but source JJJ-456 states he was a patriot.

McKENZIE, EDWARD. Private in Capt. Ewing's Company No. 4; enlisted Jan. 29, 1776. (H-12)

McKEVER, WILLIAM. Non-Juror to Oath of Allegiance, 1778. (A-1/15)

McKEY, SAMUEL. Oath of Allegiance, 1778. (A-1/15)

McKIM, ALEXANDER. (1748 - January 18, 1832) Married Catharine Sarah DAVEY. Served on Baltimore Salt Committee, October 14, 1779, and with Capt. Nicholas Ruxton Moore's Troops, June 25, 1781. He had a five year old grey gelding. (BBBB-313,JJJ-456,HHH-88)

McKIM, JOHN. Oath of Allegiance, 1778, before Hon. James Calhoun. (A-1/15, A-2/41)

McKIM, ROBERT. Oath of Allegiance, 1778, before Hon. James Calhoun. (A-1/15, A-2/40)

McKIM, THOMAS. Oath of Allegiance, 1778, before Hon. James Calhoun. (A-1/15, A-2/40)

McKINNEY, JOHN. Recruit in Baltimore County in 1780. (H-340)

McKNIGHT, JOHN. Non-Juror to Oath of Allegiance, 1778. (A-1/15)

McLAIN, THOMAS. Enlisted in Baltimore Town on July 17, 1776. (H-53)

McLAUGHLIN, BARNEY. Enlisted in Baltimore Town on July 17, 1776. (H-53)

McLAUGHLIN, JAMES. Recruit in Baltimore County Militia, April 11, 1780. (H-335)

McLAUGHLIN, MARK. Carpenter on ship Defence, August 5 to December 31, 1777. (H-658)

McLAUGHLIN (McLOUGHLIN), WILLIAM. "Schoolmaster." Took Oath of Allegiance in 1778 before Hon. John Moale. (A-1/15, A-2/70)

McLEAN, ADAM. Oath of Allegiance, 1778, before Hon. James Calhoun. Served as Private in Capt. McClellan's Company, September 4, 1780. (CCC-24, A-1/15, A-2/39)

McLEAN (McLANE), ARTHUR. Born 1752. Sergeant in 7th MD Regiment, Capt. Lynn's Company, February 10, 1780 to November 1, 1780. Sergeant in 1st MD Regiment, Capt. Beatty's Company, 1781. On January 30, 1829, it was ordered to pay to "Arthur McLEAN, of Baltimore County, during life, half yearly, half pay of a Sergeant, as further re- numeration for his services during the Revolutionary War." (C-370) "Arthur McLANE" is listed as a Pensioner on June 1, 1840, age 79, residing in household of John MOKE in the 1st District of Baltimore County. (P-127, H-234, H-388, YY-35, C-370)

McLEAN (McLANE), JOHN. Member of Sons of Liberty in 1776, and a Magistrate in 1779-80 in Baltimore City. (CCC-19, CCC-26)

McLONE (McLANE), JAMES. Private in Capt. Lansdale's Company, 4th MD Regiment; enlisted December 6, 1776; prisoner, August 22, 1777; rejoined June 23, 1778; and, discharged August 16, 1780. (H-144)

McLURE, JOHN. Oath of Allegiance, 1778, before Hon. William Lux. Signed a letter to Governor Lee of Maryland on April 4, 1781, urging the calling up of the militia to protect Baltimore from the British. (S-49, A-1/15, A-2/68)

McMAHON, JOHN. Enlisted in Baltimore County on July 26, 1776. (H-53)

McMAHON (McMAHAN), MATHEW. Private in Capt. Furnival's MD Artillery, Nov. 17, 1777. Matross in Capt. Dorsey's MD Artillery at Valley Forge, June 3, 1778. (H-573,UU-231)

McMAKEN, JAMES. Born 1742 in Ireland. Enlisted as Private in Col. Ewing's Battalion, July 5, 1776. Height: 5' 2½"; short light hair. (H-54)

McMANNIS. BARNEY. Private in Capt. Deams' Company, 7th MD Regiment, December 25, 1776. "Barney McMANUS" received 50 acres (lot 1944) for services as Private, 7th Regiment. (H-305, DDDD-26) "Barny McMANUS" was a Private on ship Defence, Sept. 19, 1776. (H-607)

McMASTERS, ALEXANDER. Non-Juror to Oath of Allegiance, 1778. (A-1/15)

McMECHEN, DAVID (1754 - July 15, 1810, Baltimore County, MD) Married in October, 1803 to Margaret CARROLL at the residence of Daniel CARROLL near Baltimore. He served on the Baltimore Town Committee of Correspondence, November 12, 1775, and prior to that he served on the Baltimore County Committee of Inspection, March 13, 1775. He was Secretary of the Baltimore Committee on October 28, 1776, and took the Oath of Allegiance in 1778 before Hon. James Calhoun. He was a Magistrate in Baltimore City 1779-1780, and signed a letter to Governor Lee of Maryland, urging the calling up of the militia to protect Baltimore. (SS-130,RR-19,PPP-2,CCC-26,S-49,ZZZ-211,A-2/40)

McMELLON, SAMUEL. 3rd Corporal, Capt. Ewing's Co. No. 4; enlisted May 26, 1776. (H-11)

McMILLAN (McMULLAN), HUGH. Oath of Allegiance, 1778, before Hon. Edward Cockey,(A-2/61)

McMILLEN, WILLIAM. Baltimore Artillery Company, 1777. "William McMELLON" was 4th Cpl. in Capt. Ewing's Company No. 4; enlisted May 26, 1776. (V-368, H-11)

McMULLEN (McMULLAIN), ALEXANDER. Born 1752 in North Ireland. Occupation: Tanner. Enlisted January 24, 1776 as Private in Capt. N. Smith's 1st Co. of Matrosses. Height: 5' 6 3/4". Private in Capt. Dorsey's MD Artillery, November 17, 1777, and Bombardier in that company at Valley Forge, June 3, 1778. Source VV-74 gives his name as "Ellack McMullin." (H-564, H-574, H-566, QQQ-2, UU-231, VV-74, and, R. Clark's Maryland Revolutionary Pensioners lists him under pension S38198 (p.28).

McMULLIN, JOHN. Non-Juror to Oath of Allegiance, 1778. (A-1/15)

McMUNN, ALEX. Private in Capt. Ramsey's Company No. 5 in 1776. (H-640)

McNAMARRA, WILLIAM. Private in Capt. Furnival's MD Artillery, November 17, 1777 but the muster roll on that date indicates he "deserted Sept. 29th," from Baltimore's Fort. He was "taken up" in Frederick County before the County Lieutenant and was "placed in public gaol" on April 25, 1778. (H-573, H-327)

McNAUGHTON, PETER. Private in 4th MD Regiment at Fort Whetstone Point in Baltimore, 1781. As Sergeant in 1st MD Regiment, he was entitled to 50 acres (lot 1722) in western Maryland. (H-626, DDDD-26)

McNEAL, JAMES. (Died December 22, 1831) Private in Baltimore County; pensioned $60 per year as of September 13, 1814, and $96 per year as of September 24, 1816. (O-8) Source A-1/15 indicates he was a Non-Juror to the Oath of Allegiance in 1778.

McNEALIS, CHARLES. Marine on ship Defence in 1777. (H-658)

McNUTT, WILLIAM. Oath of Allegiance, 1778, before Hon. Richard Holliday. (A-2/60)

McQUILLEN (McQUILLAN), ROLAND (ROWLAND). "Roland McQuillen" was a Private in the Baltimore Artillery Company on October 16, 1775. "Rowland McQuillan" was Private in Capt. Sheaff's Company on June 16, 1777. "Roland McQuillian" took the Oath of Allegiance in 1778 before Hon. George Lindenberger. (G-8, W-162, A-1/15, A-2/53)

McRALTY, JOHN. Non-Juror to Oath of Allegiance, 1778. (A-1/15)

MEADOWS, WILLIAM. (February 25, 1739 - 1778) Married Sarah HAINES. Private in the Baltimore County Militia; enlisted August 15, 1776. (H-58, JJJ-461)

MEATON, SARAH. In Baltimore on April 12, 1777, she submitted her account for lodging for Capt. George Cook. (FFF-99)

MECCY (MEECY), WILLIAM. Oath of Allegiance, 1778, before Hon. Geo. Lindenberger.(A-2/53)

MEDAIRY (MAIDERY), JACOB. (1735, Holland - March 9, 1785, Baltimore, MD) Son of Hans Jacob MEDAIRY (1704-1781) and Hester TSCHUDI. He came to America with his parents in 1739 to Philadelphia. Married Catherine BAUER (died 1800) on April 3, 1762, Baltimore County, MD. Children: Jacob MEDAIRY (1763-1845, Baltimore, MD) md. Catherine MUSSER; Margaret MEDAIRY (1764-1841, Reisterstown, MD) md. John MACKELFRESH; John MEDAIRY (1765-1839, Chambersburg, PA); Daniel MEDAIRY (1768-after 1819, Ross Co., Ohio) md. Eleanor STOCKSDALE; Catherine MEDAIRY (1770-1826, Baltimore County, MD) md. William FLEETWOOD; Susannah MEDAIRY; Maria MEDAIRY (1780-c1785?); and Charles MEDAIRY. Jacob MEDAIRY furnished shoes to the Maryland Council of Safety on Nov. 8, 1776 and February 27, 1777, and took the Oath of Allegiance in 1778 before Hon. Peter Shepherd. He is buried in old Lutheran Cemetery, Reisterstown, Baltimore County, MD. (JJJ-461, AAA-1809, A-1/15, A-2/49, and History Trails, Vol. 7, No. 4, 1974, p. 15)

MEDLICOH, SAMUEL. Non-Juror to Oath of Allegiance, 1778. (A-1/16)

MEDLEY, ENOCH. Seaman on ship Defence, October 23 to December 31, 1777. (H-658)

MEELWAIN, ANDREW. Oath of Allegiance, 1778, before Hon. Geo. Lindenberger. (A-2/53)

MEGUFFIN, ANDREW. Took Oath of Allegiance in 1781. (QQ-116)

MELONY, JOHN. Private, Capt. Deams' Company, 7th MD Regt., December 27, 1776. (H-305)

MELOY, JAMES. Enlisted in Baltimore County on July 26, 1776. (H-53)

MERCER, FRANCIS. Non-Juror to Oath of Allegiance, 1778. (A-1/16)

MERCER, HUGH. Private in Capt. Cox's Company, December 19, 1776. (CCC-22)

MERCER, JOHN. Served on Baltimore County Committee of Inspection, March 13, 1775. Was Captain of Back River Lower Company, May 6, 1776. Died prior to June 24, 1777. (He commanded 55 men; names unknown). (WW-413, EE-51, X-111, RR-19)

MERCER (MERCEER), RICHARD. (1753-1816) Married Cassandra TIVES (TEVIS). Children: Barbara; Robert T.; Margaret; Camilla; Archibald; Richard; Cornelius; Rachel; Cordelia; and, Ketruah. Richard and Cassandra were married in 1772. He took Oath of Allegiance in 1778 before Hon. George Lindenberger. (JJJ-463, XXX-512, A-2/53, A-1/16)

MERCER, STEPHEN. Served on ship Defence, January 13 to April 21, 1777. (H-658)

MERCER, WILLIAM. Non-Juror to Oath of Allegiance, 1778. (A-1/16)

MEREDITH, JOSHUA. Non-Juror to Oath of Allegiance, 1778. (A-1/16)

MEREDITH (MERIDITH), SAMUEL SR. Non-Juror to Oath of Allegiance, 1778. Served in Capt. J. Cockey's Baltimore County Dragoons at Yorktown in 1781 as a Cornet. (MMM-A, A-1/16)

MEREDITH, SAMUEL JR. Private in Col. Aquila Hall's Baltimore County Regiment in 1777. Non-Juror to the Oath of Allegiance in 1778. (TTT-13, A-1/16)

MEREDITH (MERIDETH), THOMAS. (1745, Baltimore County, MD - after 1790, Baltimore County) Married Hannah HUTCHINS on February 13, 1763. Daughter, Ann married Charles GORSUCH. Thomas MEREDITH was a Private in Capt. Dean's (Deams?) Company on July 18, 1776. He was a Non-Juror to the Oath of Allegiance in 1778. (XXX-512, A-1/16)

MERRICKS, ROBERT. Non-Juror to Oath of Allegiance, 1778. (A-1/16)

MERRIKEN, CHARLES. Oath of Allegiance, 1778, before Hon. Richard Cromwell. (A-2/46)

MERRITT, JAMES. Non-Juror to Oath of Allegiance, 1778. (A-1/16)

MERRITT, SYLVANUS. Oath of Allegiance, 1778, before Hon. Isaac Van Bibber. Measured wheat for the Baltimore Town Committee in 1780. (A-1/16, A-2/34, RRR-6)

MERRITT, WILLIAM. (1752-1795) Wife named Achsah. Served as Private in Capt.Deams' Co. in 7th MD Regt., January 7, 1777. Took Oath of Allegiance in 1778 before Hon. William Spear. (JJJ-465, H-305, A-1/16, A-2/66)

MERRYMAN, BENJAMIN. (1739 - May 30, 1814, Monkton, Baltimore County, MD) Son of John MERRYMAN and Sarah ROGERS. He married Mary BELL on February 2, 1762. Their children: Benjamin (died 1796); John (died 1794?), married Sarah JOHNSON; Joshua (died 1801); Nicholas (died 1816); William, married Ann PRESBURY; Philemon, married Elizabeth NORWOOD in 1812, and their son Benjamin Bell MERRYMAN (1813-1854) married Ellen PRICE (1813-1900) in 1834; Sarah; Catherine (1766-1799) married John BUCK of Benjamin, 1795; Mary, married William NEILL and/or Thomas TALBOTT; Eleanor, married Thomas H. HARLAND in 1821; Elizabeth (died unmarried); Martha (died unmarried, 1801); Ann (Nancy), md. her cousin Nicholas MERRYMAN, Jr.; Milcah, married Thomas CARR in 1806; and, Rebecca, married Lee TIPTON. Benjamin MERRYMAN may be the "Bengeman MERIMAN" that Samuel Baxter referred to on January 3, 1777 to the Council of Safety as follows: "I was sorey to see a set of toreys trampel the good law of the Country under foot as I am shure thare is not a man in this setelment (Monkton) but Mr. Bengeman Meriman and myself that would doe anything to suport Government, as they all are glad to heer of hour conquests (defeats) and will say they knew the English would conker." (BBB-12) Benjamin MERRYMAN took the Oath of Allegiance in 1778 before Hon. John Merryman. He also served, in 1775, on the Baltimore County Committee of Inspection. On December 4, 1778 he was commissioned a Captain in the Upper Battalion of Baltimore County Militia. He was still in service as of February 1, 1782. The tract he lived upon was known as "My Lady's Manor" & was a veritable hot-bed of Toryism, which makes Benjamin Merryman that much more an outstanding patriot. When "My Lady's Manor" was confiscated during the Revolution as British property, he was involved in its evaluation in 1782, when it was divided into smaller tracts and sold. (EEE-287, EEE-288, CCCC-65, AAA-1561A, RR-19, GGG-257, FFF-553, D-10, XXX-512, A-1/16, A-2/45, JJJ-465, ZZZ-219)

MERRYMAN, ELIJAH. (1753 - July 3, 1799) Son of Nicholas MERRYMAN. He married twice: (1) Frances ENSOR, daughter of Eleanor ENSOR, who died 1801, and (2) Elizabeth CROMWELL, who died in 1833. Children: John, died in Havana, Cuba, in August, 1801;

MERRYMAN, ELIJAH (continued)
Nicholas, died in 1823; and Eleanor died young. By his second wife, he had Thomas (1786-1819), married Priscilla BRITTON; and, Frances, married Jacob BOND in 1807. Elijah MERRYMAN took the Oath of Allegiance in 1778 before Hon. Robert Simmons. His rank is not given, but he was paid by the Western Shore Treasurer on Feb. 1, 1782 under the Act for the Emission of Bills of Credit, in the amount of 185 lbs., 2 shillings and 7 pence, of which he was given 13 shillings, 4 pence, and the rest he was to deliver and pay 9 Captains in the Upper Battalion in Baltimore County. His death notice states he was a representative of Baltimore County in the legislature. (ZZZ-219, CCCC-65, FFF-553, EEE-293, A-1/16, A-2/58)

MERRYMAN, GEORGE. Son of William and Margaret MERRYMAN. Born October 25, 1734. He was a Non-Juror to the Oath of Allegiance in 1778. (A-1/16, EEE-182)

MERRYMAN, JOHN. (February 16, 1736/1737 - February 14, 1814, Baltimore, MD) Son of John and Sarah MERRYMAN. He married Sarah ROGERS, widow of John Addison SMITH, on December 9, 1777. Their children: John (1778-1854); Benjamin Rogers (died young); Anne (1782-1785); Sarah Rogers (1784-1856) md. Dr. Ashton ALEXANDER in 1828; Elizabeth (1786-1860), unmarried; and, Nicholas Rogers (1788-1864). John MERRYMAN, Jr. moved to Baltimore Town from Hereford, Baltimore County, about 1763. He served on the Baltimore Committee of Inspection, March 13, 1775. He was not elected to the Baltimore Committee of Observation on September 12, 1775 (did not receive enough votes), but he was serving on the Baltimore Committee of Correspondence on Nov. 12, 1775, and was serving as such in 1776. He was a Magistrate and Justice of the Peace in 1778, administering the Oath of Allegiance in Baltimore. He was an Ensign in the Baltimore Town Battalion, becoming Captain on or before June 4, 1779. He was a Judge of the Orphans Court of Baltimore County in 1784. He died at his residence on Calvert Street in Baltimore in 1814, and was buried in St. Paul's (Loudon Park Cemetery) as was his wife who died in 1816. (EEE-286, EEE-287, GGG-242, ZZZ-220, GGG-401. F-311, F-313, SS-130, A-1/16, A-2/45, RR-19, EE-51, FF-54, FFF-50, RR-50, EEEE-1725)

MERRYMAN, LUKE. (Died February 12, 1813) Son of Nicholas MERRYMAN. He married, 1794, Elizabeth GORSUCH. Children: Nicholas (born 1795); Caleb (born 1798); and, Ann (b. 1813). Luke MERRYMAN (MERRIMAN) was a Private in 1st Company, 3rd MD Regiment in 1781. He married Elizabeth on January 29, 1794 in Baltimore County. He took Oath of Allegiance in 1778 before Hon. James Calhoun, and was also entitled to 50 acres (lot 910) in western Maryland for his war services. On March 16, 1836, it was ordered to "pay Elizabeth MERRYMAN, widow of Luke, a soldier of the Revolutionary War, half pay of a Private during life, in consideration of his Revolutionary services." (C-374) (YY-37, H-392, A-1/16, A-2/41, DDDD-27, EEE-291, YY-119)

MERRYMAN, MICAJAH. (July 4, 1750 - June 7, 1842) Son of Moses MERRYMAN. He married Mary ENSOR in 1780; she died in 1788. Their children: Sarah (1781-1806); Moses (1783-1819); Eleanor (1785-1832); Mary (1786-1829) married George W. TODD in 1803 and then Benjamin BUCKNELL after 1818; and, Micajah (1788-1854). The will of Micajah MERRYMAN mentioned his son Micajah, Jr.; grandsons, George W., Merryman D. and Joshua F. TODD; and granddaughters Sarah M. TAYLOR of Missouri, and Mary Ann BUCKNELL. He was commissioned on October 12, 1776, as 1st Major in Col. Edward Cockey's Gunpowder Upper Battalion of Baltimore County Militia, and was still in service as of Feb. 8, 1782. He had received votes for serving on the Baltimore Committee of Observation, but was not successfully elected. In 1778 he took the Oath of Allegiance before Hon. William Spear. (Also, his son Moses married Mary COCKEY, and his son Micajah, Jr. md. Clara MERRYMAN.) (XXX-513, EEE-289, JJJ-465, ZZ-337, SSS-110, RR-50, BBB-369, CCCC-71, A-1/16, A-2/66)

MERRYMAN, NICHOLAS. Private in Baltimore County regiment No. 7, circa 1777. Took Oath of Allegiance in 1778. (A-1/16, TTT-13)

MERRYMAN, NICHOLAS SR. (December 11, 1726 - July, 1801) Son of John MERRYMAN. He married (1) Elizabeth ENSOR, and (2) Jane _____, who died shortly after he did. Children: Elizabeth (born 1750) married Elisha BOSLEY; Nicholas, Jr. (1751-1832); Elijah (died 1799); Micajah (married; had issue); Jane (died 1819, unmarried); Mary, married Dennis BOND; Sarah, married John ORRICK; and, Ann, married Elijah BOSLEY (?).

MERRYMAN, NICHOLAS (continued)

Baltimore County Orphan's Court Proceedings (Source M-228) lists the heirs as widow Jane, and Dennis BOND, Mary Bond, his wife; Nicholas MERRYMAN, of Elijah; Elizabeth MERRYMAN, guardian of Thomas and Frances MERRYMAN; Nicholas ORRICK; and John ORRICK. His will (Source EEE-286) lists as heirs his wife Jane; a son Elijah MERRYMAN (dec'd); a son Nicholas MERRYMAN; daughters Jane MERRYMAN, Mary BOND, Elizabeth BOSLEY, and Sarah ORRICK; grandchildren, John and Nicholas MERRYMAN (sons of Elijah MERRYMAN, deceased), Elenor MERRYMAN (daughter of Nicholas, Jr.), and the children of his daughter Sarah ORRICK. Nicholas MERRYMAN, Sr. took the Oath of Allegiance in 1778. Earlier, on August 21, 1775, he represented Upper Middle River Hundred at the Association of Freemen. (EEEE-1726, M-228, A-1/16, EEE-286, JJJ-465, ZZZ-220)

MERRYMAN, NICHOLAS JR. (Called "White-headed Nickey" of Bacon Hall) (1751 - 1832) Son of Nicholas MERRYMAN and Elizabeth ENSOR. He married (1) Deborah ENSOR, daughter of Eleanor ENSOR, in 1778, and (2) Nancy (Ann) MERRYMAN, daughter of Benjamin MERRYMAN, Sr. Their chilren: John Ensor MERRYMAN (born 1781); Elijah MERRYMAN; Micajah MERRYMAN; Eleanor MERRYMAN, married James Edwards FRISBY; Nicholas MERRYMAN (1793-1823); and, by his second wife, Ann: Benjamin MERRYMAN (died infant) and Philemon MERRYMAN (died before his father). Nicholas MERRYMAN, Jr. was a 2nd Lieutenant in Capt. Vaughan's Co., August 26, 1776 and a 1st Lieutenant in Capt. Thomas Moore's Company, Feb. 4, 1777. He became a Captain in the Upper Battalion of Baltimore County, August 30, 1777, and was still in service as of February 1, 1782. He took the Oath of Allegiance in 1778 before Hon. Robert Simmons. (EEE-292, JJJ-465, BBB-113, BBB-350, LL-66, E-14, RR-98, VV-114, A-1/16, A-2/58, CCCC-65)

MERRYMAN, SAMUEL. (November 12, 1712 - September 28, 1809) Married Jane PRICE. Source JJJ-465 states he gave patriotic service, but Source A-1/16 states he was a Non-Juror in 1778 to the Oath of Allegiance.

MERRYMAN, SAMUEL. (June 17, 1745 - 1805) Son of Samuel MERRYMAN. Married Ruth PRICE ? & their children were: Mordecai MERRYMAN, married Margaret MAY; George Price MERRYMAN (died about 1834); Rachel MERRYMAN, married a CHAPMAN; Rebecca MERRYMAN, married John BLIZZARD; and, Mary MERRYMAN, married Laban WELSH. Samuel MERRYMAN was appointed by the Maryland General Assembly to be Baltimore County Collector of Blankets on May 2, 1777, & he took the Oath of Allegiance, 1778. (A-1/16, EEE-290, FFF-103)

MERRYMAN, SAMUEL JR. 2nd Lieutenant in Soldiers Delight Company No. 8, May 13, 1776. 1st Lieutenant, June 6, 1776. "Samuel MERRYMAN, Jr., broke by court martial in the Soldiers Delight Battalion, Baltimore County; replaced by 1st Lt. ELisah DORSEY on September 11, 1777." (BBB-369, FF-64, WW-467)

MERRYMAN, WILLIAM JR. (Born April 11, 1729) Son of William and Margaret MERRYMAN. Non-Juror to the Oath of Allegiance, 1778. (A-1/16, EEE-182)

MERRYMAN, WILLIAM (OF GEORGE). Non-Juror to Oath of Allegiance, 1778. (A-1/16)

MERRYMAN, WILLIAM. Son of Charles and Jane MERRYMAN, Jr. Non-Juror to Oath in 1778. (A-1/16, EEE-182)

MESSERSMITH, MATTHIAS. Oath of Allegiance, 1778, before Hon. James Calhoun. (A-2/39)

MESSERSMITH, SAMUEL. Baltimore Mechanical Company of Militia, November 4, 1775. Private, in Capt. Cox's Company, December 19, 1776, and Private in Capt. McClellan's Company September 4, 1780. Took Oath of Allegiance, 1778, before Hon. James Calhoun. A Samuel Messersmith, possibly this one, died September 25, 1803 in his 71st year, an old inhabitant of Baltimore; his residence was on Gay Street, and interment was in the Lutheran burying ground. Elizabeth, consort of Samuel, died October 15, 1802 in her 68th year. (ZZZ-220, CCC-21, CCC-24, F-298, A-1/16, A-2/39)

METZER, MICHAEL. Oath of Allegiance, 1778. (A-1/16)

MICHAEL, ABRAHAM. Non-Juror to Oath of Allegiance, 1778. (A-1/16)

MICHAEL, JOHN SR. Oath of Allegiance, 1778, before Hon. George Lindenberger. (A-2/54)

MIDDLETON, GILBERT. Apparently, he was a Naval Captain for he received Captain's pay on January 9, 1781, and goods from the vessel Molly were partly in his custody at that time. On January 25, 1823, it was ordered to pay him, of Baltimore, half pay

MIDDLETON, GILBERT (continued)
of a Captain for his services during the Revolutionary War. On February 9, 1823, it was ordered to pay Sarah MIDDLETON, of Baltimore, half pay of a Captain as a further compensation for services rendered by her husband during the Revolutionary War. (FFF-349, FFF-353, C-375)

MIDDLETON, HENRY. Enlisted in Baltimore County on August 14, 1776. (H-52)

MIEL, JOHANNES. Oath of Allegiance, 1778, before Hon. George Lindenberger. (A-2/53)

MILBURN, JOSEPH. Oath of Allegiance, 1778, before Hon. George Lindenberger. (A-2/54)

MILDEWS, AQUILA. Non-Juror to Oath of Allegiance, 1778. (A-1/16) "Aquila MILDEWS, of Fells Point, mourns the death of his six year old daughter, whose clothes caught on fire, April 18, 1800." (ZZZ-221)

MILDEWS, GRENNBURY. Non-Juror to Oath of Allegiance, 1778. (A-1/16)

MILES, JOSHUA. Oath of Allegiance, 1778, before Hon. Hercules Courtenay. Could not write; made his mark. (A-1/16, A-2/37)

MILES, THOMAS. 2nd Lieutenant in Baltimore County Militia Company No. 6, December 19, 1775. 1st Lieutenant in Gunpowder Battalion, August 30, 1777 to at least 1778. He took the Oath of Allegiance, 1778, before Hon. Hercules Courtenay. (A-1/16, A-2/37, G-10, E-11, AA-65, BBB-350)

MILEY, JACOB. Private in Capt. Graybill's German Regiment in 1776. (H-266)

MILLBERGER, HENRY. Private in Capt. Graybill's German Regiment in 1776. (H-265, ZZ-32)

MILLER, ANTHONY. Private in Capt. Graybill's German Regiment in 1776. (H-266)

MILLER, BENJAMIN. Oath of Allegiance, 1778, before Hon. Thomas Sollers. (A-1/16, A-2/51)

MILLER, DANIEL. Oath of Allegiance, 1778, before Hon. Peter Shepherd. (A-1/16, A-2/50)

MILLER, ELIZABETH. Involved in evaluation of Baltimore County proprietary reserve land in 1782. (FFF-542)

MILLER, GEORGE. (Born 1752) Private in Capt. Keeports' German Regiment; enlisted on August 19, 1776; was at Philadelphia on September 19, 1776. Took Oath of Allegiance in 1778 before Hon. Andrew Buchanan. Private in Capt. McClellan's Company, Baltimore Town, September 4, 1780. On March 2, 1827 it was ordered to pay him, of City of Baltimore, during lif, half yearly, half pay of a Private as further remuneration for his services during the Revolutionary War. (YY-38, H-263, CCC-24, C-375, A-2/57)

MILLER, HANNAH. Oath of Allegiance in 1778. (A-1/16) (Ed. Note: Only men took Oath.)

MILLER, HENRY. Non-Juror to Oath of Allegiance, 1778. (A-1/16)
MILLER, HUGH. Non-Juror to Oath of Allegiance, 1778. (A-1/16)

MILLER, JACOB. (1753 - October 18, 1829) Wife named Susanna. Private in Captain Graybill's German Regiment in 1776. (JJJ-469, H-266)

MILLER, JAMES. He applied for a pension while living in Claiborne Co., Tennessee, on April 21, 1834. He was born August 12, 1748 in Baltimore County, Maryland and lived in Shenandoah County, Virginia when he enlisted in October or November of 1780 in Capt. Jacob Rinker's Company of Col. Butler's VA Regiment. He was in the Battle of Guilford Courthouse. He again enlisted in May, 1781, in Capt. William Reagan's Co. of VA Militia. He died August 26, 1841, leaving a widow (name not stated or whether they had children). (OO-21, OO-22)

MILLER, JAMES. Non-Juror to Oath of Allegiance, 1778. (A-1/16)

MILLER, JOHN. (Died November 5, 1823) Married Rosannah ULRICH. Private in Captain Keeports' German Regiment; enlisted July 28, 1776; sick at Philadelphia, Sept. 19, 1776. Became a Sergeant; pensioned as such. In 1782 he was involved in evaluation of Baltimore County confiscated proprietary reserve lands. (JJJ-469, H-263, YY-38, FFF-542) There was also a John Miller who was a Non-Juror in 1778. (A-1/16)

MILLER, JOHN. 2nd Lieutenant in Capt. Cummins' Company, Upper Battalion, August 30, 1777. Non-Juror to Oath of Allegiance in 1778. (F-14, LL-66, BBB-350, A-1/16)

MILLER, JOHN (OF HANNAH). Private in Baltimore County Militia; enlisted on July 19, 1776. Oath of Allegiance, 1778, before Hon. Benjamin Rogers. He could not write; made his mark. (A-1/16, A-2/32, H-58)

MILLER, JOSEPH. (October 21, 1727, Anne Arundel County, MD - December 10, 1801, Baltimore County, MD. Buried in Mt. Olive Cemetery in Randallstown, MD) He married MARY OURSLER on September 11, 1759. Their children: Ely (born 1760); Rachel (born 1763), married Joshua SMITH; George (born 1766); Ruth (born 1767), married William JEAN; Elizah (born 1768)married Hannah STINCHCOMB; Catherine (born 1775); Mary (born 1778) married Ichabod JEAN; and, Marsiller (born 1783) married George ZIMMERMAN, Jr. Joseph MILLER took the Oath of Allegiance in 1778 before Hon. James Calhoun. He was 2nd Lieutenant in the Baltimore Town Battalion as of March 19, 1779. On May 17, 1779, he resigned as 2nd Lieutenant "in the room of Jno. Ornonseter, who this day refused to review his commission." (GGG-324, GGG-401, F-310, F-313, A-1/16, A-2/39, MMM-A, JJJ-469, XXX-519)

MILLER, JOSEPH. Private in Capt. Deams' Company, 7th MD Regiment, January 1, 1777. He took the Oath of Allegiance in 1778 before Hon. Richard Cromwell. (A-2/46, H-305)

MILLER, MATTHEW. Oath of Allegiance, 1778, before Hon. George Lindenberger. (A-2/53)

MILLER, MICHAEL. Private in Capt. Cox's Company, December 19, 1776. (CCC-21)

MILLER, NICHOLAS. Baltimore Mechanical Company of Militia, November 4, 1775. Took Oath of Allegiance, 1778, before Hon. George Lindenberger. (F-299, A-1/16, A-2/53)

MILLER (MILLAR), PETER. Enlisted in Baltimore County on July 25, 1776. (H-52)

MILLER, PHILIP. Sergeant in Capt. Cox's Company, December 19, 1776. Took the Oath of Allegiance in 1778 before Hon. William Spear. (CCC-21, A-2/66)

MILLER, PHILLIP. Private in Capt. Graybill's German Regiment in 1776. Took the Oath of Allegiance in 1778 before Hon. George Lindenberger. (H-265, A-1/16, A-2/53)

MILLER, PHILLIP. Seaman on ship Defence, January 15 to October 1, 1777. (H-658)

MILLER, SAMUEL. Oath of Allegiance, 1778, before Hon. George Lindenberger. (A-2/53)

MILLER, THOMAS. Private in Capt. Deams' Company, 7th MD Regiment, December 14, 1776. Non-Juror to Oath of Allegiance, 1778. (H-305, A-1/16)

MILLER, WILLIAM. Ship's Steward on ship Defence, June 2 to July 11, 1777. Seaman, July 11 to October 15, 1777; Gunner's Yeoman, October 15 to December 31, 1777. He took the Oath of Allegiance in 1778 before Hon. Richard Cromwell. (H-658, A-2/46)

MILLER, WILLIAM. Oath of Allegiance, 1778, before Hon. James Calhoun. (A-2/38) Source JJJ-471 lists a William Miller (1732-1814) who married Rebeckah BRADFORD; patriot.

MILLIMAN, CHARLES. Non-Juror to Oath of Allegiance, 1778. (A-1/16)

MILNER, FRANCIS. Private in Baltimore County Militia, Capt. ewing's Company No. 4; enlisted July 5, 1776. (H-13, H-58)

MILLS, DAVID. Oath of Allegiance, 1778, before Hon. James Calhoun. (A-2/65)

MILLS, JACOB. Baltimore Mechanical Company of Militia, November 4, 1775. (F-298)

MILLS, JONATHAN. Served on ship, Defence, May 22 to July 23, 1777. (H-658)

MILLS, LEONARD. Oath of Allegiance, 1778, before Hon. Peter Shepherd. (A-2/49)

MILLS, RICHARD. Oath of Allegiance, 1778, before Hon. John Beale Howard. (A-2/29)

MILLS, SAMUEL. Non-Juror to Oath of Allegiance, 1778. (A-1/16)
MILLS, THOMAS. Non-Juror to Oath of Allegiance, 1778. (A-1/16)

MINCEL, JOSHUA. Private in Capt. McClellan's Company, Baltimore Town, September 4, 1780. (CCC-25)

MINING, JOHN. Private in Baltimore County Militia in 1776. (H-59)

MINNEY, JOHN. Private, Baltimore County Militia; enlisted August 15, 1776. (H-58)

MINOR, DENNIS. Matross in Capt. Brown's MD Artillery; enlisted November 22, 1777. Was at Valley Forge until June, 1778; at White Plains, July, 1778; Fort Schuyler in August and September, 1780; not listed in 1781. (UU-229, UU-230)

MINSPAKER: See "MANSPIKER."

MINTSHAW, JOHN. Non-Juror to Oath of Allegiance 1778. (A-1/16)
MISER, WILLIAM. Non-Juror to Oath of Allegiance 1778. (A-1/16)
MISH, JOHN. Non-Juror to Oath of Allegiance, 1778. (A-1/16)

MITCHELL, HENRY. Oath of Allegiance, 1778, before Hon. James Calhoun. (A-2/65)

MITCHELL, JOHN. Oath of Allegiance, 1778, before Hon. William Spear. (A-2/66)

MITCHELL, ROBERT. Born 1753 in Charles Town, Maryland. Occupation: Sadler. Enlisted January 24, 1776 as Private in Capt. N. Smith's 1st Company of Matrosses. Private in Capt. Dorsey's MD Artillery, November 17, 1777, when reported to be "in gaol for house breaking." On May 4, 1779 he was Matross in Baltimore County and gave his deposition about enlistment terms. He was a Matross in Capt. Gale's MD Artillery, in 1779, and was sick in the hospital, November, 1779 to March, 1780. (YYY-1/71, FFF-220, H-563, H-567, H-574, QQQ-2, VV-74)

MITCHELL, THOMAS. (June 8, 1743, Baltimore County, MD - May, 1830, Harford County, MD) Son of Richard MITCHELL and Elizabeth WILLIAMS. He married Ann PRESTON (1744-1827), daughter of James PRESTON and Sarah PUTTEE (POTEET), on November 12, 1767 in Baltimore County. Their children: Elizabeth MITCHELL (born 1769) married Jabez Murray TIPTON; Sarah MITCHELL (born 1770) married William MITCHELL in 1796, Harford County, and their daughter Sarah Ann MITCHELL (1810-1895) married John Norris GILBERT, 1839; Richard (born 1771) married Priscilla GILBERT; Barnet (born 1774); Aberilla (born 1775) married John BOYD; John V.; Thomas, married Eleanor MORGAN; and, Mary MITCHELL. Thomas MITCHELL took the Oath of Allegiance in 1778 before Honorable James Calhoun. (XXX-522, AAA-2332N, JJJ-473, A-1/16, A-2/39, and information compiled by the author Henry C. Peden, Jr., of Bel Air, Maryland, 1987, a direct descendant of Thomas.)

MITCHELL, WILLIAM. Volunteer in Baltimore County Regiment No. 36, circa 1777. (TTT-13)

MITTER, BENJAMIN. Submitted his account and receipt for plank for use at Baltimore's Fort Whetstone Point, October 22, 1776. (FFF-63)

MITTINGER, JACOB. Baltimore Mechanical Company of Militia, November 4, 1775. (V-298)

MOALE, JOHN. (January 20, 1730/1731 - July 6, 1798, Baltimore, MD) Son of John MOALE and Rachel HAMMOND. He married Ellen NORTH (1740-1825), daughter of Robert NORTH and Frances TODD, on May 25, 1758. Her father, Robert NORTH, an Englishman from Whittington, Lancashire, came to Maryland about 1724 and was one of the commissioners who laid out Baltimore Town in 1729. John MOALE was a wealthy planter and merchant, and onf of the most prominent men of Baltimore during the Revolutionary War. His town house occupied the block bounded by Redwood (German), Hanover, Lombard and Sharp Sts. His country estate was "Green Spring," about ten miles north of Baltimore in the heart of the valley of that name. The children of John MOALE and Ellen NORTH were: Elizabeth (born 1759) married Richard CURZON in 1794; John (1761-1809) married Lucy MORTON (died 1802, age 35) in 1790; Rebecca (born 1763) married Thomas RUSSELL in 1780; Richard Halton (born 1765) married Judith Carter ARMISTEAD in 1797; Thomas (1766-1822) married Eleanor OWINGS (1772-1853) in 1793, and their daughter, Ellin North MOALE (1794-1803); William North (1768-1769); Robert (1769-1769); Robert North (born 1771) md. Frances OWINGS in 1801; Samuel (born 1773) married (1) Ann M. HOWARD, and (2) Ann G. WHITE; Rachel (1776-1776); Frances (1777-1781); William (1779-1779); George Washington, born 1780, died 1799; Randle Hulse (born 1782) married Elizabeth Smith PECK; and, Mary, born 1783, died 1787. John MOALE, son of John, and wife Lucy MORTON had one child, Ellen, who married Don Juan BERNABEAU, eldest son of Chevalier de BERNABEAU, in 1813. As noted, John MOALE was quite prominent during the Revolution. He served on the Baltimore Committee of Inspection, March 13, 1775, and was Baltimore's representative at

MOALE, JOHN (continued)
 the Association of Freemen on July 26, 1775, and also represented the Westminster
 Hundred at the Association of Freeman on August 21, 1775. He was elected to serve
 on the Baltimore County Committee of Observation on September 23, 1775, receiving
 the most votes of any of the candidates. He was also Delegate to the Provincial
 Convention in 1775, and served on Baltimore Town's Committee of Correspondence on
 November 12, 1775. He was Lieutenant Colonel of the 39th Battalion (Baltimore Town
 Battalion) as of May 25, 1776, and was Colonel of that battalion by Sept. 12, 1777,
 commanding 656 Privates (names unknown). He was Justice of the Peace, and Justice
 of the Baltimore County Orphans' Court, 1777-1778, and one of the Magistrates who
 administered the Oath of Allegiance in 1778 in Baltimore. He presided over the
 County Court of Baltimore County and, in 1781, he was chairman of the committee
 selected to meet General Washington on his way to take command of the army at
 Yorktown. (A-2/35, A-2/70, A-1/16, SS-130, SS-136, RR-50, RR-51, RR-19, E-12, D-5,
 ZZZ-225, UUU-130, JJJ-474, F-311, SSS-110, EEEE-1725, BB-2, Y-61, FFF-119, VV-273,
 GGG-242, RR-47, WW-443, EEEE-1726, and Md. Hist. Mag., Vol. 37, No. 2 (1942), p.141)

MOALE, RICHARD. Baltimore Town Committee of Correspondence, November 12, 1775, and
 Baltimore County Committee of Inspection, March 13, 1775. Member of Sons of Liberty
 in 1776. (SS-130, RR-19, CCC-19) Non-Juror to Oath of Allegiance in 1778. (A-1/16)

MOFFITT (MOFFATT), THOMAS. Born 1754 in Ireland. Enlisted July 5, 1776, in Baltimore
 County, as Private in Col. Ewing's Battalion. Height: 5'7"; black hair. (H-57)

MOLIDGE, SAMUEL. Private in 4th Maryland Regiment (from Baltimore County). Discharged
 December 3, 1781. (Q-72)

MONGOAL, FREDERICK. Private in Capt. Keeports' German Regiment; enlisted July 21,
 1776; was at Philadelphia, September 19, 1776. (H-263)

MONK, HENRY. Oath of Allegiance, 1778, before Hon. Charles Ridgely of William.
 (A-1/16, A-2/28)

MONK, WILLIAM. Oath of Allegiance, 1778, before Hon. Richard Cromwell. (A-2/46)

MONKS, MICHAEL. Non-Juror to Oath of Allegiance, 1778. (A-1/16)

MONROE, ALEXANDER. Oath of Allegiance, 1778, before Hon. James Calhoun. (A-2/40)

MONTGOMERY, ALEXANDER. Oath of Allegiance, 1778, before Hon. Charles Ridgely of Wm.
 (A-1/16, A-2/27)

MONTGOMERY, JOHN. Ship's Tender on ship Defence, June 7 to December 31, 1777. (H-658)

MONTGOMERY, JOSEPH. Private in Capt. Ewing's Company No. 4, April 26, 1776. (H-13)

MONTGOMERY, WILLIAM. Non-Juror to Oath of Allegiance, 1778. (A-1/16)
MOODE, MILES. Non-Juror to Oath of Allegiance, 1778. (A-1/16)

MOODY, MOYNES. Oath of Allegiance, 1778, before Hon. George Lindenberger. (A-2/54)

MOMMY: See "MUMMEY" and "MUMMA."

MOORE, DAVID. (1751 - May, 1807, Baltimore, MD) Took the Oath of Allegiance, 1778,
 before Hon. James Calhoun. (A-1/16, A-2/39, ZZZ-227)

MOORE, HUGH. Enlisted in Baltimore Town on July 20, 1776. (H-53)

MOORE, JAMES. There were two Non-Jurors to the Oath of Allegiance, 1778. (A-1/16)

MOORES, JAMES R. Purser on ship Defence in 1777. (H-658)

MOORE, JOHN. Private in Capt. Graybill's German Regiment in 1776. Private in 4th MD
 Regiment at Fort Whetstone Point in Baltimore in 1781. (H-265, H-626, ZZ-32)

MOORE, JOHN. Marine on ship Defence, May 10 to December 31, 1777. (H-658)

MOORE, MATHEW. Enlisted in Baltimore County on July 20, 1776. (H-52)

MOORE, MICHAEL. Non-Juror to Oath of Allegiance, 1778. (A-1/16)

MOORE, NICHOLAS RUXTON. (July 21, 1756 - October 7, 1816, Baltimore County, MD) He married Sarah KELSO, daughter of Col. J. KELSO and Rebecca HAMMOND, Dec. 25, 1793. Their children: Camilla Hammond MOORE, married William McKEAN, and their daughter, Camilla Hammond McKEAN married Gustavus Warfield RIDGELY; Gay MOORE, married Sarah CHALMERS; Rebecca MOORE; and, Smith Hollings MOORE. Nicholas Ruxton MOORE joined the Baltimore Independent Cadets in 1774, the first Maryland military unit organized for revolution. On March 1, 1776, he was commissioned 3rd Lieut. of a Company of Matrosses to be raised for the defence of the liberties of Maryland, commanded by Capt. John Fulford, as ordered by the Council of Safety at Baltimore Town. (Source TT-113 erroneously states it was in Annapolis). On March 23, 1776, he became 2nd Lieutenant of the 2nd Company of Matrosses, and was under Captain Nathaniel Smith's 1st Company of Matrosses at Fort Whetstone Point in Baltimore on September 7, 1776. On February 2, 1777, he was 2nd Lieutenant in the 4th Continental Dragoons, and subsequently became 1st Lieutenant. On March 15, 1778, he was Captain, 4th Continental Dragoons, and resigned on December 31, 1778. However, in 1780, he became Captain of a Maryland Cavalry Militia (Troop of Horse) and was in that service until at least June 25, 1781, when he commanded 35 men. At the time he had an eight year old bay stallion and a nine year old black stallion for his use. He had organized the Baltimore Light Dragoons which marched with Lafayette's troops. On April 4, 1781, he was one of the signers of a letter to the Governor calling for the militia to protect Baltimore against the British. Earlier, in 1778 he signed the Oath of Allegiance before Hon. William Lux. He was indeed "one of the worthies who so nobly achieved the independence we now enjoy." (UUU-130) Also, he took an active part in the suppression of the Whisky Rebellion in 1794. In 1801 he was elected to the Maryland House of Delegates, and in 1803 to the United States Congress. serving to 1811. He commanded the Baltimore County Cavalry at the Battle of North Point in the War of 1812, serving as Lieutenant Colonel and subsequently as Colonel. He was reelected to Congress and served 1813 to 1815. And during the War of 1812 he was appointed Commandant of the 6th Regimental Cavalry District of Maryland. He died at his farm near Ruxton and Circle Roads in Baltimore County in 1816 (grave no longer marked, but an historical marker is need the spot). Sources TT-113 and B-399 state he died March 9, 1816, but his death notice indicates it was on October 7, 1816 (ZZZ-227). On March 4, 1834 it was ordered to "pay to Sarah MOORE, widow of Nicholas R. MOORE, of Baltimore County, during life, quarterly, half pay of a Lieutenant, for services rendered by her husband." (C-376) Also, on February 7, 1840, it was ordered to "pay to Sarah MOORE, widow of Nicholas Ruxton Moore, of Baltimore City, during life, quarterly, commencing January 1, 1840, a sum equal to the half pay of a Captain of cavalry, in lieu of half pay of a Lieut. heretofore granted, in consideration of the services rendered by the husband during the Revolutionary War." (C-376) Capt. Moore was a member of the Society of the Cincinnati of Maryland, currently represented by Ruxton Moore Ridgely of Baltimore. The Baltimore County Chapter of the Maryland Society of the Sons of the American Revolution was named in honor of Nicholas Ruxton Moore in 1971. (AAA-85, JJJ-478, YY-119, A-1/16, A-2/68, TT-113, UUU-103, UUU-131, C-376, S-49, YY-38, BBBB-313, XXX-528, B-399, FFF-513, H-568, VV-230, ZZZ-227, and an Historic Roadside Marker dedicated in June, 1977, by the Col. Nicholas Ruxton Moore Chapter of the S.A.R.)

MOORE, ROBERT. 2nd Lieutenant, Baltimore Artillery Company, October 16, 1775. 2nd Lieutenant, Capt. Sheaff's Company, June 6, 1776. 1st Lieutenant, Capt. Dickinson's Company, August 29, 1777. Served in the Baltimore Town Battalion until he resigned on May 18, 1779. He also took the Oath of Allegiance in 1778 before Hon. George Lindenberger. (A-1/16, A-2/53, E-13, F-312, G-8, WW-467, GG-74, W-162, Z-63, BBB-348)

MOORE, SAMUEL. Non-Juror to Oath of Allegiance, 1778. (A-1/16)

MOORE, STEPHEN. Oath of Allegiance, 1778, before Hon. Geo. Lindenberger. (A-2/52)

MOORE, THOMAS. 1st Lieutenant in Capt. Vaughan's Company, August 26, 1776. Captain in Baltimore County Militia, February 4, 1777. Non-Juror to Oath of Allegiance in 1778. Buried in Baltimore, MD. (RR-98, VV-114, A-1/16, MMM-A)

MOORE, THOMAS. Ordinary Sailor on ship Defence in 1777. (H-658)

MOORE, WILLIAM. ("Middlesex") Oath of Allegiance, 1778, before Hon. James Calhoun. (A-1/17, A-2/42)

MOORHEAD, MICHAL. Oath of Allegiance, 1778, before Hon. William Spear. (A-2/66, A-1/17)

MOPPES, FREDERICK. 2nd Corporal in Capt. Keeports' German Regiment; enlisted July 19, 1776; at Philadelphia, September 19, 1776. (H-263)

MORAN (MOREN), JOHN. Private in Capt. Deams' Company, 7th MD Regiment, Jan. 19, 1777. Oath of Allegiance in 1778. (H-305, A-1/17)

MORAN, PATRICK. Recruited in Baltimore on March 2, 1780, by Samuel Chester for 3rd MD Regiment. (H-334)

MORAN, WILLIAM. Matross in Capt. Brown's MD Artillery as of August 1, 1781, at the High Hills of the Santee; at Camp. Col. Scirvins, January, 1782; and at Bacon's Bridge, S.C. in April, 1782. (UU-230) He might have been the William MORAN (1748-1824) who married Rebecca BARBER. (JJJ-478)

MORDIMER, THOMAS. Oath of Allegiance, 1778, before Hon. George Lindenberger. (A-2/53)

MOREL (MORIL), JAMES. Matross in Capt. Brown's MD Artillery; joined November 22, 1777. Was at Valley Forge until June, 1778; at White Plains, July, 1778; at Fort Schuyler, August and September, 1780. Gunner, as of August 1, 1781. (UU-228, UU-229, UU-230)

MORGAN, JAMES. 1st Lieutenant in Capt. Wells' Company No. 6 in the Baltimore Town Artillery in 1776. Unable to serve in 1777. (GG-74, MM-89)

MORGAN, JAMES. Private in Baltimore Artillery Company, October 16, 1775. Took Oath of Allegiance in 1778 before Hon. George Lindenberger. (A-1/17, A-2/54, G-8)

MORGAN, JOHN. Non-Juror to Oath of Allegiance, 1778. (A-1/17)
MORGAN, MADERS. Non-Juror to Oath of Allegiance, 1778. (A-1/17)
MORGAN, MICHAEL. Non-Juror to Oath of Allegiance, 1778. (A-1/17)

MORGAN, SOL. Served in Baltimore Mechanical Company of Militia in 1776. (CCC-27)

MORGAN, THOMAS. Oath of Allegiance, 1778, before Hon. George Lindenberger. (A-2/53)

MORGAN, WILLIAM. Sergeant in Capt. Dorsey's MD Artillery at Camp Col. Scirvins on January 28, 1782. (UU-232)

MORING, WILLIAM. Private in Capt. Deams' Company, 7th MD Regt., Dec. 17, 1776. (H-305)

MORRICK, THOMAS. Oath of Allegiance, 1778, before Hon. Andrew Buchanan. (A-2/57)

MORRIS, EDWARD. Private in Col. Aquila Hall's Baltimore County Regiment in 1777. Took the Oath of Allegiance in 1778 before Hon. Charles Ridgely of William. He could not write; made his mark. (A-1/17, A-2/28, TTT-13)

MORRIS, JAMES R. In Baltimore on August 27, 1776, he reported to the Council of Safety on the hiring of schooners. (FFF-54)

MORRIS, JOHN. Non-Juror to the Oath of Allegiance in 1778. Involved in evaluation of Baltimore County confiscated proprietary reserve land in 1782. (FFF-547, A-1/17)

MORRIS, JOSEPH. Non-Juror to the Oath of Allegiance in 1778. (A-1/17)

MORRIS, SAMUEL. Oath of Allegiance, 1778, before Hon. James Calhoun. Stowed flour in 1780 for the Baltimore Committee. Involved in the evaluation of Baltimore County's confiscated proprietary reserve lands in 1782. (RRR-6, FFF-547, A-1/17, A-2/40)

MORRIS, SAMUEL SR. Non-Juror to Oath of Allegiance, 1778. (A-1/17)

MORRIS, SAMUEL JR. Non-Juror to Oath of Allegiance, 1778. (A-1/17) Same source is in error in stating that his name was "Samuel J. Morris."

MORRIS, THOMAS. Oath of Allegiance, 1778, before Hon. Isaac Van Bibber. (A-2/34)

MORRIS, WILLIAM. Lieutenant of Marines on ship Defence, 1776-1777. (H-606, H-658)

MORRISON, FRANCIS. Private in Capt. J. Cockey's Baltimore County Dragoons stationed at Yorktown in 1781. (MMM-A)

MORRISON, JAMES. Non-Juror to Oath of Allegiance, 1778. (A-1/17)

MORRISON, JOHN. Oath of Allegiance, 1778, before Hon. Peter Shepherd. (A-2/50)

MORRISON, JOSEPH. Oath of Allegiance, 1778, before Hon. Richard Holliday. (A-2/60)

MORRISON, SAMUEL. Oath of Allegiance, 1778, before Hon. Peter Shepherd. (A-2/49)

MORROW, ROBERT. (1742 - after 1790) Married Margaret EWING. Served as 4th Sgt. in
    Capt. Ewing's Company No. 4, January 23 to may 3, 1776. Ensign in 2nd MD Battn.,
    Flying Camp. July to December, 1776. Cornet in 3rd Continental Dragoons, Feb. 20,
    1777. Regimental Adjutant, June 1, 1778; wounded and taken prisoner at Tappan on
    September 28, 1778. Lieutenant, January 3, 1779. Captain, 1781, and served until
    November 9, 1782. (H-11, H-52, B-403, JJJ-482)

MORTER, JACOB. Non-Juror to Oath of Allegiance, 1778. (A-1/17)

MORTON, GREENBURY. Oath of Allegiance, 1778, before Hon. Charles Ridgely of William.
    (A-1/17, A-2/27)

MORTON (MOTON), SAMUEL. Oath of Allegiance, 1778, before Hon. Charles Ridgely of Wm.
    (A-1/17, A-2/28) He could not write; made his mark.

MOSES, FRANCIS. (c1740, Berfelden Hessen, Germany--died in baltimore County, MD)
    Wife's name unknown; their son, Gedalia MOSES (1765-1858) married Breinley AUERBACH
    and their son Jacob MOSES (1809-1871) married Rose WOLF (1811-1885). Francis MOSES
    was a Private in the 6th MD Regiment, January 30, 1779. (H-228, AAA-1851)

MOTHERBY, CHARLES. Oath of Allegiance, 1778, before Hon. Edward Cockey. (A-2/62)

MUBARY, ALEXANDER. Private, Capt. Deams' Company, 7th MD Regt., Dec. 14, 1776. (H-305)

MUHLING, JOHN GODFRIED. Oath of Allegiance, 1778, before Hon. Geo. Lindenberger.
    (A-1/17, A-2/54)

MUIR, FRANCIS. Captain's Clerk and Pursor on ship Defence, Sept. 19, 1776. (H-606)

MULFORD, PATRICK. Matross in Capt. Gale's MD Artillery, 1779. Reported sick from
    November, 1789 to March, 1780. (YYY-1/72)

MULHERON, GEORGE. Oath of Allegiance, 1778, before Hon. John Beale Howard. (A-2/29)

MULIAN, JAMES. Oath of Allegiance, 1778. (A-1/17)

MULL, JACOB. Oath of Allegiance, 1778, before Hon. George Lindenberger. Private in
    Capt. McClellan's Company, Baltimore Town, September 4, 1780. (CCC-24, A-2/53)

MULLAN (MULLEN), PATRICK. (1740, County Armagh, Ireland - October 28, 1816, Baltimore,
    Maryland) Came to Maryland in 1770 with brothers John and William. He married to
    Sarah ASKEW (1760-1808), daughter of William ASKEW and Keziah HANSON, on January 1,
    1783. Their children: William (born 1783); Catherine (born 1785); Mary (born 1787);
    John (born 1790); Elizabeth (born 1792); Maria (born 1793); Sarah K. (born 1795);
    Jonathan (1797-1869) married Sarah PAINE (1803-1868) in 1824 and their son John Paine
    MULLAN (1825-1892) married (1) Sarah Jean GEDDES, and (2) Susanne Emily Adam SMALL in
    1855; Patrick (born 1799); Edward (born 1802); and, Ambrose (born 1804). Patrick was
    a Private in Capt.Norris' Company, 6th MD Regiment, May 21, 1777 to January 1, 1780.
    He also might have served in Pulaski's Legion. There is also a Patrick Mullan who
    was a defective from the Maryland Line in August, 1780; resident of Baltimore County.
    (XXX-537, H-414, JJJ-486, AAA-1528, AAA-1529, AAA-809, H-231)

MULLER, JOSEPH. Enlisted in Baltimore Town on July 17, 1776. (H-53)

MULLIBAN (MULLIKAN), PATRICK. Non-Juror to Oath of Allegiance, 1778. (A-1/17)

MULLIN, HUGH. Oath of Allegiance, 1778, before Hon. Thomas Sollers. (A-1/17, A-2/51)

MULLIN, JAMES. Oath of Allegiance, 1778, before Hon. James Calhoun. (A-1/17, A-2/40)

MULLIN, JOHN. Non-Juror to Oath of Allegiance, 1778. (A-1/17)

MUMMA, CHRISTIAN. Private in German Regiment. Died July 27, 1778. (H-267)

MUMMA, DAVID. (1751 - October 30, 1816, Baltimore County, MD) Private in Captain
Graybill's German Regiment, 1776. Took Oath of Allegiance, 1778, before Honorable
George Lindenberger. He died in 1816 at his residence on York Road, near the Hay
Scales. (ZZZ-232, H-265, ZZ-32, A-1/17, A-2/53)

MUMMEY (MOOMY, MOMMY), JOHN. (Born 1753) "John Moomy" applied for Revolutionary War
pension while living in Pickaway County, Ohio in 1829. He was then 76 years of age.
He enlisted in the service in Maryland in December, 1776. He was captured and made a
prisoner of war. After his escape he married; his wife was also 76 years old in 1829.
"John Mummey" took the Oath in 1778 before Hon. Richard Cromwell. (A-2/46, OO-154)

MUMMEY (MOMMEY), SAMUEL. Oath of Allegiance, 1778, before Hon. James Calhoun. (A-2/41)

MUNROE, ALEXANDER. Private in Capt. Sheaff's Company, June 16, 1777. Oath of Allegiance
in 1778. (W-162, A-1/17)

MUNROE, HUGH. Private in Capt. Ewing's Company No. 4 in 1776. (H-13)

MURAT (MURET), CHARLES. Matross in Capt. Brown's MD Artillery; joined Nov. 22, 1777.
Was at Valley Forge until June, 1778; at White Plains, July, 1778; at Ft. Schuyler,
August and September, 1780; at High Hills of the Santee, August, 1781; at Camp Col.
Scirvins, January, 1782; and, Bacon's Bridge, S.C. in April, 1782. (UU-228, UU-230)

MURLEY, DENNIS. Non-Juror to Oath of Allegiance, 1778. (A-1/17)
MURPHY, ASA. Non-Juror to Oath of Allegiance, 1778. (A-1/17)

MURPHY, CORNELIUS. Private in Capt. Ewing's Company No. 4 in 1776 (enlisted). (H-13)

MURPHY, DARBY. (c1740 - after 1830) Enlisted in Baltimore Town, July 17, 1776. (H-53)
(JJJ-488)

MURPHY, DAVID. Private in Capt. Lansdale's Company, 4th MD Regiment, until May 3, 1778
when reported deserted. (H-143)

MURPHY, EDWARD. Non-Juror to Oath of Allegiance, 1778. (A-1/17)

MURPHY, JAMES. "James Murphey" was a Drummer in Capt. Ramsey's Company No. 5 in 1776.
"James Murphy" was a Private in Capt. Deams' Company, 7th MD Regiment, Dec. 19, 1776.
(H-639, H-305)

MURPHY, JOHN. "John Murphy" enlisted in Baltimore County on July 26, 1776, and took
the Oath of Allegiance in 1778 before Hon. William Spear. "John Murphey" enlisted
in Baltimore County on July 20, 1776, and was a Non-Juror to the Oath of Allegiance
in 1778. (H-53, A-1/17, A-2/66)

MURPHY, JOSEPH. Oath of Allegiance, 1778, before Hon. William Spear. Could not write;
made his mark. (A-1/17, A-2/66)

MURPHY, MICHAEL. Private, Capt. Deams' Company, 7th MD Regt., Dec. 27, 1776. (H-305)

MURPHY, MORGAN. Marine on ship <u>Defence</u>, January 13 to March 23, 1777. (H-658)

MURPHY (MURPHEY), PATRICK. (1752 - 1782) Married Nancy MOORE. Recruited into the
Baltimore County Militia on April 11, 1780. (H-335, JJJ-488)

MURPHY, SAMUEL. Marine on ship <u>Defence</u> in 1777. (H-658)

MURPHY (MURPHEY), THOMAS. "Thomas Murphey" enlisted in Baltimore Town on July 17, 1776.
"Thomas Murphy" enlisted in Baltimore Town on July 20, 1776. "Thomas Murphey" also
listed as a recruit in Baltimore County in 1780. (H-53, H-340)

MURPHY (MURPHEY), TIMOTHY. (Born 1755 in Dublin, Ireland) Occupation: Labourer. He
enlisted on January 31, 1776 as a Private in Capt. N. Smith's 1st Company of Matrosses. Was Private in Capt. Dorsey's MD Artillery, November 17, 1777, and Matross
in Capt. Gale's MD Artillery, 1779-1780. Height: 5' 4½". (H-565, H-567, YYY-1/73,
VV-73, QQQ-2, H-574)

MURPHY, WILLIAM. 2nd Lieutenant in Soldiers Delight Battalion, August 29, 1777 to at
least 1778. Non-Juror to Oath in 1778. (A-1/17, E-10, Z-63, BBB-348)

MURRAY, ALEXANDER. (Died October 6, 1821) 2nd Lieutenant in Smallwood's MD Regiment, January 14, 1776. 1st Lieutenant, August, 1776. Captain, 1st MD Regt., Dec. 10, 1776 and resigned June 10, 1777, and joined the Navy. On October 20, 1777 he commanded the brig Saratoga, owned by Samuel and Robert Purviance, of Baltimore, mounting 12 carriage-guns and 8 swivels. On April 5, 1779, he commanded the brig Columbus, owned by the Purviances, mounting 10 guns and 6 swivels. On June 24, 1780, he commanded the brig Revenge, owned by John Muir and others, of Baltimore, mounting 12 guns and 2 swivels. (B-408, III-206)

MURRAY, BARNEY. Non-Juror to Oath of Allegiance, 1778. (A-1/17)

MURRAY, CHRISTOPHER. Non-Juror to Oath of Allegiance, 1778. (A-1/17)

MURRAY, EDWARD. (Born 1744) Non-Juror to Oath of Allegiance, 1778. (A-1/17, J-272)

MURRAY, FRANCIS. Non-Juror to Oath of Allegiance, 1778. (A-1/17)

MURRAY (MURREY), JABA. Private in Baltimore County Regt. 15, circa 1777. (TTT-13)

MURRAY, JAMES. Oath of Allegiance, 1778, before Hon. John Cradock. (A-1/17, A-2/59)

MURRAY, JOHN. (1747 - 1833) Married Diana COX. Children: John MURRAY, Jr., married Sarah BEASMAN (BAZEMAN), and grandson John WESLEY MURRAY married Keziah COX, and grandson Thomas Bazeman MURRAY married Catherine Ann MAURER; and, Belinda MURRAY married Stoffel ARMACOST, and granddaughter Margaret ARMACOST md. Daniel BUSH. John MURRAY was a Captain in Baltimore County's Upper Battalion, August 30, 1777 and was still in service (paid) on February 1, 1782. (LL-66, E-14, VV-114, CCCC-65, AAA-377, AAA-412, JJJ-488, BBB-350, and Source A-1/17 shows there may have been as many as three men with this name who were Non-Jurors to the Oath of Allegiance.)

MURRAY (MURRY), JOHN (OF JOSEPH OR JOSEPHUS). Private in Baltimore County Militia on July 18, 1776. Took Oath of Allegiance in 1778 before Hon. Andrew Buchanan. Was Private in Capt. Oldham's Co., 4th MD Regiment, May 1, 1778 to December, 1779. (H-58, H-144, A-1/17, A-2/57)

MURRAY, JOHN JR. Non-Juror to Oath of Allegiance, 1778. (A-1/17)

MURRAY (MURREY), JOSEPH. Oath of Allegiance, 1778. (A-1/17)

MURRAY (MURRY), JOSEPHUS. Oath of Allegiance, 1778. (A-1/17)

MURRAY (MURRY), MATTHEW. "Matthew Murray" was a Marine on ship Defence in 1777, and was an Armourer as of September 19, 1776. "Matthew Murry" was a Private in Capt. Ewing's Company No. 4, enlisting January 22, 1776. (H-658, H-12)

MURRAY, NICHOLAS. Non-Juror to Oath of Allegiance, 1778. (A-1/17)

MURRAY, SHADRACK. Non-Juror to Oath of Allegiance, 1778. (A-1/17)

MURRAY, WHEELER. Non-Juror to Oath of Allegiance, 1778. (A-1/17)

MUSE, WALKER. Ensign, Smallwood's MD Regiment, January 14, 1776; 2nd Lieutenant in May, 1776. Taken prisoner at Battle of Long Island, August 27, 1776; exchanged, December 8, 1776. 1st Lieutenant, 1st MD Regt., December 10, 1776; Captain, on January 10, 1777. Retained in Maryland battalion, April, 1783. Brevet Major, on September 30, 1783, and served to November 15, 1783. Pay certificates: 89483 ($117.86); 89484 ($155.78); 89485 ($400); 89486 ($260); and, 89487 ($2,360). He also received 200 acres (lots 2461, 2462, 2480, 2491) in western Maryland, and Federal Bounty Land Grant of 300 acres (Warrant 1485) on December 31, 1789, for his services as a Captain in the war. (B-408, YYY-12, YY-74, PP-370, DDDD-3)

MUSGROVE, STEPHEN. Non-Juror to Oath of Allegiance, 1778. (A-1/17)

MUTCHNER, CHRISTOPHER. Oath of Allegiance, 1778, before Hon. Jesse Bussey.(A-2/44)

MUTTON, JAMES. Private in Capt. Ramsey's Company No. 5 in 1776. (H-640)

MYER, GEORGE. ("Gunpowder.") Oath of Allegiance, 1778, before Hon. Robert Simmons. (A-1/17, A-2/58)

MYERS, ADAM. Private in Capt. Furnival's MD Artillery, November 17, 1777. He took the Oath of Allegiance in 1778 before Hon. James Calhoun. (H-573,A-1/17,A-2/40)

MYERS, CHARLES. Served in Capt. Nicholas Ruxton Moore's Troops on June 25, 1781. He had a seven year old gelding horse. (BBBB-313)

MYERS, CHRISTIAN (OR CHRISTOPHER). (Ed. Note: Various sources have mixed-up the name between Christian and Christoper, but the proper name appears to have been Christian) He enlisted in the Baltimore Mechanical Company of Militia on November 4, 1775. On July 11, 1776 he was 2nd Lieutenant in Capt. Graybill's German Regiment. and became Captain in the German Regiment on March 12, 1778, serving to at least July, 1779. He received 200 acres (lots 2075, 2114, 2116, 2119) in western Maryland for his service. (F-298, RR-90, H-266, UU-237, H-270, DDDD-3)

MYERS, FREDERICK. Oath of Allegiance, 1778, before Hon. William Spear.(A-1/17, A-2/66)

MYERS, GEORGE. (1755 - 1783) Wife named Elizabth. Private in Capt. Graybill's Co., German Regiment in 1776. Took Oath of Allegiance, 1778, before Hon. James Calhoun. (A-1/17, A-2/42, H-265, JJJ-489)

MYERS, ISAAC. Non-Juror to Oath of Allegiance, 1778. (A-1/17)

MYERS, JACOB. Private in Capt. Graybill's German Regiment in 1776. Took the Oath of Allegiance in 1778 before Hon. James Calhoun. Received 50 acres (lot 325) in west Maryland for his services as Private in State Troops and the 2nd MD Regiment during the war. (A-1/17, A-2/39, H-265, ZZ-32, DDDD-28)

MYERS, JACOB. (OF FELLS POINT). Supplied wire to the Council of Safety and was granted a substantial sum to continue the operation of his wire factory in Baltimore during the Revolutionary War. He took the Oath of Allegiance in 1778 before Hon. James Calhoun. (A-1/17, A-2/39, AAA-1809)

MYERS, JOHN. Oath of Allegiance, 1778, before Hon. Isaac Van Bibber. (A-1/17, A-2/34)

MYERS, LAWRENCE. He was a Non-Juror to the Oath of Allegiance in 1778, but he may have subsequently been a Lieutenant in the military because one officer by this name was entitled to 200 acres (lots 2465, 2466, 2492, 2495) in western Maryland. (DDDD-3)

MYERS, PHILIP. Private, Baltimore County Regiment No. 15, circa 1777. (TTT-13)

MYERS, ROBERT. Matross in Capt. Brown's MD Artillery, from January 1, 1781. Was at High Hills of the Santee in August, 1781; at Camp Col. Scirvins in January, 1782; and at Bacon's Bridge, D.C. in April, 1782. (UU-2320)

N

NABERTH (NABARD), SAMUEL. Oath of Allegiance, 1778, before Hon. James Calhoun. (A-2/41)

NACE, PETER. Ensign in Capt. A. Lemmon's Company on February 4, 1777. (VV-114)

NAGLE, CHRISTIAN. Volunteer in Baltimore County Regiment No. 36, circa 1777. (TTT-13)

NAGLE, HENRY. Lieutenant in Baltimore County Regiment No. 36 (Vol.), c1777. (TTT-13)

NAGLE, HENRY. (November 10, 1761, Pennsylvania - December 26, 1820, Baltimore, MD) Married Anne Catherine WARNER, and their daughter Julia A. NAGLE married John H. ROGERS, and their granddaughter, Julia A. ROGERS, married Michael WARNER. Henry NAGLE was a Private in a Company of Rangers in Northampton County, PA, and Private in a Company of Light Infantry of Foot, 1778-1783, subsequently becoming Sergeant. He is buried in Loudon Park Cemetery in Baltimore, MD. (AAA-255, and Pennsylvania Archives, 3rd Series, Vol. 23, Pages 295 and 372, and 2nd Series, Vol. 13, p. 171)

NAGLE, JOHN. Volunteer in Baltimore County Regiment No. 36, circa 1777. (TTT-13)

NAGLE (NAGILL), MICHAEL. Marine on ship Defence, Oct. 8 to Nov. 26, 1777. (H-658)

NAILOR, JOHN. Non-Juror to Oath of Allegiance, 1778. (A-1/17)

NAILOR, LUCAS. Non-Juror to Oath of Allegiance, 1778. (A-1/17)

NAILOR (NAILER), SAMUEL. Involved in evaluation of Baltimore County confiscated proprietary reserve lands in 1782. (FFF-544)

NASH, JOHN. Non-Juror to Oath of Allegiance, 1778. (A-1/17)

MASH, THOMAS. Boatswain's Mate, April 28 to August 15, 1777 and Marine on Ship Defence, August 15 to December 11, 1777. (H-658)

NEAL (NEIL, NEALE), DANIEL. Private in Capt.Furnival's MD Artillery, Nov. 17, 1777. Matross in Capt. Dorsey's MD Artillery at valley Forge, June 3, 1778. Matross in Capt. J. Smith's MD Artillery, 1780. (H-573, H-579, UU-231)

NEAL (NEALE), HUGH. Oath of Allegiance, 1778, before Hon. Andrew Buchanan. (A-2/57)

NEAL (NEALE), JAMES. Matross in Capt. Gale's MD Artillery, 1779; sick from Nov. 1779 to March 1780. Matross in Capt. Dorsey's MD Artillery at Camp Col. Scirvins on January 28, 1782, having served in 1780 in Capt. J. Smith's MD Artillery. He was discharged in September, 1782. (H-579, UU-232, YYY-1/74)

NEAL, JOHN. Enlisted in Baltimore Town on July 17, 1776. (H-53)

NEALE (NEIL), WILLIAM. Justice of the Peace in Baltimore,' 1778. Served on Baltimore Salt Committee on October 14, 1779. (GGG-242, HHH-88)

NEELEY, MATHEW. Private in Capt. Ramsey's Company No. 5 in 1776. (H-640)

NEGUIRE, PETER. Private in Count Pulaski's Legion; enlisted in Baltimore on May 8, 1778. (H-593)

NEIL, DANIEL. Matross in Capt. J. Smith's MD Artillery, 1782. (YYY-2/31) This is probably the Daniel Neal listed above.

NEIL, VALENTINE. Oath of Allegiance, 1778. (A-1/17)

NEILL, WILLIAM. Baltimore County Committee of Observation, July 24, 1775. Oath of Allegiance, 1778, before Hon. William Lux. (EEEE-1725, A-1/17, A-2/68) This is probably the William Neale (Neil) listed above.

NEILSON, THOMAS. Born 1751 in Tyrone, Ireland. Occupation: Carpenter. Enlisted as Private in Capt. N. Smith's 1st Company of Matrosses, January 31, 1776. Became a Corporal in Capt. Dorsey's MD Artillery at Valley Forge, June 3, 1778. Ht: 5' 7½". (H-565, UU-231)

NEISS, PETER. Non-Juror to Oath of Allegiance, 1778. (A-1/17)

NELLS, THOMAS. Oath of Allegiance, 1778, before Hon. Peter Shepherd. (A-1/17,A-2/50)

NELMES, LEMUEL J. Corporal in Capt. Brown's MD Artillery as of August 1, 1781. If he was with that company earlier, then he was at Valley Forge, 1778. (UU-229, 230)

NELSON, BENJAMIN. Oath of Allegiance, 1778, before Hon. Peter Shepherd. (A-2/50)

NELSON, JOHN. Non-Juror to Oath of Allegiance, 1778. (A-1/17)
NELSON, PHILIP. Non-Juror to Oath of Allegiance, 1778. (A-1/17)

NELSON, THOMAS. Private in Capt. N. Smith's 1st Company of Matrosses, June 29, 1776. Private in Capt. Dorsey's MD Artillery, November 17, 1777. (H-566, H-574, QQQ-2)

NELSON, VALENTINE. Oath of Allegiance, 1778, before Hon. Peter Shepherd. He also delivered flour for the Baltimore Committee in 1780. (RRR-6, A-1/17, A-2/49)

NELSON, WILLIAM. Oath of Allegiance, 1778, before Hon. Benjamin Rogers. (A-1/17,A-2/32)

NESBIT, THOMAS. Seaman on ship Defence, November 15 to December 31, 1777. (H-659)

NEVEN, DANIEL. Ordinary Seaman on ship Defence, September 19, 1776 - 1777. (H-606, 659)

NEVILLE, MAYS. Matross in Capt. Brown's MD Artillery; joined November 22, 1777. Was at Valley Forge until June, 1778; at White Plains, July, 1778; at Fort Schuyler in August and September, 1780; not listed in 1781. (UU-228, UU-230)

NEVIN, JAMES. Matross in Capt. Brown's MD Artillery as of August 1, 1781. (UU-230)

NEVIN, MAYS. Matross in Capt. Brown's MD Artillery as of August 1, 1781. (UU-228)

NEWBERRY, GODFREY. Non-Juror to Oath of Allegiance, 1778. (A-1/17)

NEWBERRY, SAMUEL. Oath of Allegiance, 1778. (A-1/17)

NEWBURN, SAMUEL. Non-Juror to Oath of Allegiance, 1778. (This information was found in the card file only and is not included in the names listed in A-1/17.)

NEWCOMB, ROBERT. Private in Capt. Oldham's Company, 4th MD Regiment, April 25, 1778 to December, 1779, when reported deserted. (H-147)

NEWCOMEN, ROBERT. Oath of Allegiance, 1778. (A-1/17)

NEWGIN, PATRICK. Enlisted in Baltimore Town on July 20, 1776. (H-53)

NEWLON, W. Oath of Allegiance, 1778. (A-1/17)

NEWMAN, FURMAN (OR FREEMAN). Born 1754 in Dublin, Ireland. Occupation: Labourer. He enlisted as a Private in Capt. N. Smith's 1st Company of Matrosses, Jan. 24, 1776. Served in Capt. Dorsey's MD Artillery, Nov. 17, 1777, and was a Matross in Dorsey's Company at Valley Forge, June 3, 1778. This information is listed under the name of "Freeman Newman." "Furman Newman" was a Private in the Baltimore Artillery Company on October 16, 1775. It appears that this was the service of one man, in spite of a misspelling in his first name. (G-8, H-563, H-567, H-574, VV-73, QQQ-2, UU-231)

NEWSMAN, ROBERT. Oath of Allegiance, 1778, before Hon. Jesse Dorsey. (A-2/63)

NEWTON, ROBERT. Non-Juror to Oath of Allegiance, 1778. (A-1/17)

NEWVALL, WILLIAM. Private, Capt. Deams' Co., 7th MD Regt., January 17, 1777. (H-305)

NICE, DAVID. Private in Capt. Howell's Company, December 30, 1775. Took the Oath of Allegiance in 1778 before Hon. George Lindenberger. (G-11, A-2/54) Source A-1/17 misspelled his name as "Davis Nice."

NICHOLAS, THOMAS SR. Non-Juror to Oath of Allegiance, 1778. (A-1/17)
NICHOLAS, THOMAS JR. Non-Juror to Oath of Allegiance, 1778. (A-1/17)

NICHOLL, ARCHIBALD. Private in Capt. lansdale's Company, 4th MD Regiment, August 6, 1777 to August, 1780, when reported deserted. (H-147)

NICHOLL, WILLIAM. Oath of Allegiance, 1778, before Hon. James Calhoun. (A-1/17,A-2/43)

NICHOLS, WALTER. Served on ship Defence, January 16 to August 15, 1777, and became a Quarter Gunner from August 15 to December 31, 1777. (H-659)

NICHOLSON, ALEXANDER. Able Seaman on ship Defence, September 19, 1776, and Sailor from January 11 to August 15, 1777, and Quartermaster from August 15 to December 31, 1777. Non-Juror to Oath of Allegiance in 1778. (A-1/17, H-606, H-659)

NICHOLSON, BENJAMIN. (1745 - 1792) Son of Joseph NICHOLSON and Hannah SMITH of Kent County, MD. He married Mary RIDGELY, and their children were: William; Mary, md. Darby LUX; John R., md. Matilda SMITH; Benjamin J.; Elizabeth; Eleanor; Sarah; and, Juliet. Benjamin NICHOLSON was very prominent during the Revolutionary War. He was Baltimore's Representative (or, rather, one of them) to the Association of Freemen on July 26, 1775, and then represented the Upper Back River Hundred at the Association of Freemen on August 21, 1775. He was elected to the Baltimore County Committee of Observation on September 23, 1775, and was a Delegate to the Provincial Convention. He served on the Baltimore Town Committee of Correspondence, Nov. 12, 1775, and became Captain of the Baltimore County Militia Company No. 2 on Dec. 19, 1775, commanding 62 Privates. He became Captain of Soldiers Delight Company No. 1 on May 13, 1776, and 1st Major in the Baltimore Town Battalion on May 25, 1776. On September 17, 1777, he was Lieutenant Colonel of Baltimore County Militia 3rd & 4th Classes, under Colonel John Moale. On October 13, 1780, he was Battalion Colonel, Baltimore County Militia, commanding 1,345 troops. Subsequently, he recruited a Troop of Horse in Garrison Forest at the request of the men of that area, and he even was willing to accept the lower rank of Captain (or Lieutenant Colonel) so as to command once again, June 7, 1781. He was also involved in the Baltimore Committee of Confiscated Property in 1782. He died in 1792, and Mary NICHOLSON was his named administratrix, August, 1794. (L-109, RR-47, RR-50, SS-136, WW-443, FFF-468, BBBB-274, JJJ-497, CC-36, G-10, E-13, F-311, BBB-379, BB-2, FF-64, F-303, SS-130, SSS-110, RR-51, EEEE-1726)

NICHOLSON, JAMES. (1737, Chestertown, Maryland - September 2, 1804, New York City) Son of Joseph NICHOLSON and Hannah SMITH of Kent County, MD. He married Frances WITTER, and chose the sea as his profession. He assisted in the capture of Havana in 1762, and early in 1776 he was Captain of the ship Defence, a vessel purchased and equipped by the Council of Safety and the Committee of Observation at Baltimore. He was stationed at Fell's Point in Baltimore on April 14, 1776. In June, 1776, he was appointed to commande the Virginia, and on October 10, 1776 he was put at the head of the list of captains of the continental Navy, a place he held until the close of the war. He afterwards commanded the Trumbull, of 38 guns; and on June 2, 1780 he had a severe action of three hours with The Wyatt, losing 30 men before the ships separated. In August, 1781, the Trumbull was captured off the Capes of Delaware by The Iris and General Monk, after a gallant resistance, being completed dismantled. Earlier, in 1778, he took the Oath of Allegiance before Hon. William Lux in Baltimore. After the war he resided in New York where he was United States Commissioner of Loans from 1801 until his death in 1804. His death notice refers to him as Commodore James Nicholson. (ZZZ-237, III-203, H-659, FFF-31, JJJ-497, A-1/17, A-2/68)

NICHOLSON, JOHN. Son of Joseph NICHOLSON and Hannah SMITH of Kent County, Maryland. He was a Lieutenant on the ship Defence in 1777. (H-659)

NICHOLSON, NATHAN. Oath of Allegiance, 1778, before Hon. George G. Presbury. (A-2/48)

NICHOLSON, THOMAS. (Died 1783) Son of Joseph Nicholson and Hannah Smith of Kent Co., MD. Took the Oath of Allegiance, 1778, before Hon. Richard Holliday. Served in Col. Benj. Nicholson's Troop of Horse on June 7, 1781. (BBBB-274, A-1/17, A-2/60)

NIFF, HENRY. Non-Juror to Oath of Allegiance, 1778. (A-1/17)

NIGH, JACOB JR. Oath of Allegiance, 1778, before Hon. John Hall. (Source A-1/17 shows his name as "Jacob Nighdeavow" and Source A-2/36 shows it as "Jacob Nigh Jiavour." It appears that it was actually "Jacob Nigh, Junior.")

NIGHT (KNIGHT), JOHN. Non-Juror to Oath of Allegiance, 1778. (A-1/17)
NITSER, JOHN ANTHONY. Non-Juror to Oath of Allegiance, 1778. (A-1/17)

NIXON, WILLIAM. Private in Capt. Ewing's Company No. 4; enlisted Jan. 29, 1776. (H-12)

NOCK, THOMAS. Oath of Allegiance, 1778. (A-1/17)

NODDIKER, CHRISTIAN. Private in Capt. Howell's Company, December 30, 1775. (G-11)

NOEL, SEPTIMUS. (c1737 - May 10, 1794, Baltimore County, MD) His wife, Ruth, died in April, 1787. Their children: Basil, james, Martha and Margaret. Septimus NOEL took the Oath of Allegiance in 1778 before Hon. William Lux. Earlier, on February 26, 1776, he offered the use of a vessel to the Council of Safety. (FFF-26, JJJ-498, D-10, A-1/17, A-2/68, and the Maryland Journal, April 3, 1787)

NOICE, JNO. Private in Capt. Deams' Company, 7th MD Regt., December 14, 1776. (H-305)

NOICE, RICHARD. Private, Capt. Deams' Company, 7th MD Regt., Dec. 15, 1776. (H-305)

NOLES, MICHEL. Recruit in Baltimore County Militia on April 11, 1780. (H-335)

NOON, WILLIAM. Oath of Allegiance, 1778, before Hon. John Merryman. (A-1/17, A-2/45)

NORRIS, JAMES. (February 25, 1742 - November 27, 1824) Married Mary BRADFORD. He was a 2nd Lieutenant in Capt. J. Talbott's Company No. 4, Baltimore County, 1776. (JJJ-499, PPP-2, RR-99, ZZ-541)

NORRIS, JAMES. Private in Baltimore County Militia in 1776. (H-59) There was also a Non-Juror to the Oath of Allegiance in 1778 with this name. (A-1/17)

NORRIS, JARRAD. Oath of Allegiance, 1778, before Hon. William Spear. Could not write; made his mark (" M "). (A-1/17, A-2/66)

NORRIS, JOHN. Non-Juror to Oath of Allegiance, 1778. (A-1/17)

NORRIS, JOSEPH SR. (February 6, 1725 - after 1780) Married Philizana BARTON. Source JJJ-499 states he gave patriotic service, but Source A-1/17 states he was Non-Juror to the Oath of 1778.

NORRIS, JOSEPH, JR. Non-Juror to Oath of Allegiance, 1778. (A-1/17)

NORTON, DAVID. Private in Capt. J. Gist's Co., 3rd MD Regt., February, 1778. (H-600)

NORWOOD, EDWARD. (Died October 25, 1815, Elkridge, Maryland) His wife Sally died on December 21, 1801, age 42 years. (The Norwood Cemetery at Relay in Baltimore County is included in the Baltimore County Genealogical Society's The Notebook, Number 29, September, 1985, page 2, and is where Col. Norwood and some family members are buried.) Edward NORWOOD served on the Baltimore county Committee of Observation on July 24, 1775. He was Captain in the 3rd MD Battlion of the Flying Camp, July to December, 1776, and Captain of the 4th MD Line on December 10, 1776. He was also Captain of the Baltimore County Regiment No. 36, curca 1777. He was dismissed from military service by General Smallwood on September 30, 1778. Capt. Norwood wrote the following in the Maryland Gazette on December 28, 1778: "Mr. Printer - As I have been dismissed from a service to which a love of country had attached me, and apprehensive the public would not (without evidence to the contrary) discriminate between me and those who have been dismissed for dishonorable conduct, I beg leave to assure them through your paper, that I have suffered this heavy misfortune for only saying General Smallwood was a partial man and no gentleman. The following certificate voluntarily given me, will satisfy them of the general tenor of my conduct, and I reserve myself to a proper time, to lay open to the world, the whole proceedings of the several Courts which have led to my dismission, where, I am sorry to say, such a system of despotism will appear to be springing up in our army, that an officer who does his duty ever so exactly and has neglected to pay a servile court to a haughty superior, holds his commission by a very precarious tenure. I am, Sir, yours and the public's most humble servant." It appears that Capt. Norwood's dismissal concerned many officers in the Maryland line because they wrote a letter to Brigadier General William Smallwood on March 1, 1780, as follows: "Sir - We have no doubt but the joint assertion of s small number of inferior officers will be as much credited, by that part of mankind who have spirit to think for themselves, as the mere ipse dixit of a brigadier; therefore, choose only to remark, that your scurrilous observations on the testimony we gave of our favorable opinion of Capt. Norwood, discovers the malevolence and presumption, more than the probity and liberality of your mind. With due respect, we are yours, Otho H. WILLIAMS, Benjamin PRICE, Benjamin FORD, Edward EDGERLY, John E. HOWARD, Hezekiah FOARD, Harry DOBSON, William REILY, james BRUFF, Adam HOOPS, Thomas PARRAN, John HAMILTON, R. DONOVAN, John HARTSHORN, Lil WILLIAMS, Richard PENDLETON, and John GASSAWAY. N.B.-The other gentlemen, whom you took occasion to abuse in your ungentlemanly performance of 105 pages, are out of camp." (SS-183, SS-184, ZZZ-241, TT-117, B-416, TTT-13, EEEE-1725)

NORWOOD, NICHOLAS. (Died in Baltimore county in 1786) Wife named Nancy. Children: Edward, Elizabeth, Mary and Sarah. Nicholas NORWOOD served on the Baltimore County Committee of Observation on July 24, 1775. Source V-105 and D-10 states he was a 2nd Lieutenant in Capt. William Wilkinson's Company in January, 1777, but Source JJ-9 indicates he was a captain in the Baltimore County Militia earlier, September 13, 1776. (EEEE-1725, JJ-9, D-10, V-105) He also took the Oath of Allegiance in 1778 before Hon. Thomas Sollers. (A-1/17, A-2/51)

NORWOOD, PHILIP. Enlisted in Baltimore County on July 20, 1776. (H-53)

NORWOOD, SAMUEL. Lieutenant in Baltimore County on August 31, 1777. (FFF-119)

NORWOOD, WILLIAM. Oath of Allegiance, 1778, before Hon. Richard Holliday.(A-1/17,A-2/60)

NOT, JOSEPH. Volunteer in Baltimore County Regiment No. 36, circa 1777. (TTT-13)

NOTT, THOMAS. Oath of Allegiance, 1778, before Hon. James Calhoun. (A-1/17, A-2/40)

NOWFOR (NOWFOX), WILLIAM. Oath of Allegiance, 1778, before Hon. James Calhoun. (A-2/40)

NOWLAN, THOMAS. Private in Capt. Smith's Company No. 8; enlisted Jan. 27, 1776. (H-18)

NOWLAND, JOHN. Matross in Capt. Gale's MD Artillery, 1779. Deserted September 11, 1779, in Annapolis, MD. (YYY-1/75)

NOYES, JOHN. Enlisted in Baltimore County on July 20, 1776. (H-53)

NUCUM, HENRY. Non-Juror to Oath of Allegiance, 1778. (A-1/17)

NUGENT (NUJANT), PATRICK. Private in Capt. Oldham's Company, 4th MD Regiment, from December 15, 1776 to December 16, 1779. (H-147)

NULL (NOLL), ANTHONY. Non-Juror to Oath in 1778, but signed in 1781. (A-1/17, QQ-117)

NULL (NOELL), LEMUEL. Oath of Allegiance, 1778, before Hon. William Spear. (A-2/66)

NUTBROWN, JOHN. Oath of Allegiance, 1778, before Hon. James Calhoun. (A-1/17, A-2/40)

NUTBROWN, MILES. Non-Juror to Oath of Allegiance, 1778. (A-1/17)

NUTH, THOMAS. Recruit in Baltimore County, 1780. (H-340)

O

OATS, HENRY. Non-Juror to the Oath in 1778, but signed in 1781. (A-1/17, QQ-117)

OATS, JACOB. Non-Juror to Oath of Allegiance, 1778. (A-1/17)

OATS, PETER. Non-Juror to the Oath in 1778, but signed in 1781. (A-1/17, QQ-117)

OBER, GEORGE. Non-Juror to oath of Allegiance, 1778. (A-1/17)

O'BRIAN, JAMES. Recruit in Baltimore County Militia, April 11, 1780. (H-335)

O'BRIAN (O'BRYAN), MICHAEL. Gunner in Capt. Brown's MD Artillery; joined November 22, 1777. Was at Valley Forge until June, 1778; at White Plains, July, 1778; at Fort Schuyler, August and September, 1780. Bombardier as of August 1, 1781; at High Hills of the Santee in August, 1781; at Camp Col. Scirvins, January, 1782; and, at Bacon's Bridge, S.C. in April, 1782. (UU-228, UU-229, UU-230) Also, Source DDDD-29 states that he was a Bugler in the Artillery and entitled to 50 acres (lot 37) in western MD.

O'BRIAN, PHILIP. Matross in Capt. Brown's MD Artillery; joined November 22, 1777. Was at Valley Forge until June, 1778; at White Plains, July, 1778; at Fort Schuyler, in August and September, 1780. Bombardier as of August 1, 1781; at High Hills of the Santee in August, 1781; at Camp Col. Scirvins in January, 1782; and, at Bacon's Bridge, S.C. in April, 1782. (UU-228, UU-229, UU-230) Also, Source DDDD-29 states he was a Corporal in the Artillery and entitled to 50 acres (lot 219) in western MD.

O'BRIEN, DANIEL. Sergeant in Baltimore County Militia; enlisted July 6, 1776. (H-58)

O'BRYAN, JAMES. Recruited in Baltimore on March 2, 1780 by Samuel Chester for the 3rd Maryland Regiment. (H-334)

O'CONNER, MICHAEL. Private in Capt. Furnival's MD Artillery, November 17, 1777. (H-573)

O'DANIEL, CONSTANTINE. Oath of Allegiance, 1778, before Hon. James Calhoun. (A-2/41)

O'DANIELL, JOHN. Gunner in Capt. Gale's MD Artillery, 1779-1780. (YYY-1/76)

O'DELL, ISAIAH. (1761 - March 20, 1847) Son of John and Providence O'DELL. His wife Elizabeth Buck TOWSON, died December 14, 1843, age 68 years. Isaiah O'DELL was a Private in Maryland (dates unknown), according to Source JJJ-503 and History Trails, Vol. 6, No. 3, Spring, 1972, page 10, which also states they are buried in the O'Dell family lot; inscriptions were published in the National Genealogical Society Qtrly., June, 1937)

ODLE (ODE), JOHN. Oath of Allegiance, 1778, before Hon. James Calhoun. (A-1/17, A-2/42)

ODLE, REYNOLD. Non-Juror to Oath of Allegiance, 1778. (A-1/17)

ODLE, WALTER. Oath of Allegiance, 1778, before Hon. Edward Cockey. (A-1/17, A-2/61)

ODLE, WILLIAM. Oath of Allegiance, 1778, before Hon. Edward Cockey. "William ODLE and Rachel WATERS, both of Baltimore County, were wed February 9, 1797, by Rev. Richards." (ZZZ-242, A-1/17, A-2/61)

O'DONNALLY (O'DONNOLLY), CORNELIUS. Matross, Capt. Gale's MD Artly., 1779-80.(YYY-1/78)

O'DONNELL, JOHN. Private in Capt. Furnival's MD Artillery, November 17, 1777. (H-573) One "John O'Donnel" died October 5, 1805 at his county residence in the Baltimore Barrens, age 56. He was a colonel in the militia and a delegate from Baltimore to the state legislature. (ZZZ-242)

O'DONNELL (O'DONNALD), ROGER. Born 1747 in Donegal, Ireland. Occupation: Labourer. Enlisted January 24, 1776 as Private in Capt. N. Smith's 1st Company of Matrosses. Private in Capt. Dorsey's MD Artillery, November 17, 1777, and Matross with that company at Valley Forge, June 3, 1778. Height: 5' 7". (H-567, H-574, H-564, VV-74, UU-231, QQQ-2)

O'FERRELL (O'FARRELL), MICHAEL. "Michael O'Farroll" was a Matross in Capt. Gale's MD Artillery, 1779-1780; sick, 1779; "absent since joined;" sick in Albany. "Michael O'Ferrell" was a Matross in Capt. J. Smith's MD Artillery, 1780. "Michael O'Farrell" was a matross in Capt. Dorsey's MD Artillery at Camp Col. Scirvins, January 28, 1782. "Michael O'Ferrell" died February 23, 1783. "Michael O'Farrel" was entitled to 50 acres for services as Artillery Matross (lot 869 in western Maryland). (H-579, UU-232, DDDD-29, YYY-1/80)

OFFIELD, JOHN. Private in Capt. Smith's Company No. 8; enlisted Jan. 27, 1776. (H-18)

O'FURRA, JESSE. Private in Extra Regt., at Ft. Whetstone Pt., Baltimore, 1781. (H-626)

OGG, BENJAMIN. Non-Juror to Oath of Allegiance, 1778. (A-1/17)
OGG, GEORGE. Non-Juror to Oath of Allegiance, 1778. (A-1/17)
OGG, WILLIAM. Non-Juror to Oath of Allegiance, 1778. (A-1/17)
OGG, WILLIAM HAMILTON. Non-Juror to Oath of Allegiance, 1778. (A-1/17)
OGGLE, GEORGE. Non-Juror to Oath of Allegiance, 1778. (A-1/17)

OGLEBY (OGILBY, OGLEVIE), JAMES. (1755 - May 21, 1808) He married Sarah CRISPIN. He was 2nd Lieutenant "James Ogleby" in Baltimore County Troops, 1776, and he was 2nd Lieutenant "James Ogilby" in 2nd MD Battalion of Flying Camp, Baltimore county, in July, 1776 to December, 1776, and he was 2nd Lieutenant "James Oglevie" in Captain Standiford's Company, Gunpowder Upper Battalion, on May 6, 1776. He took Oath of Allegiance, 1778, before Hon. George Lindenberger. (JJJ-503, H-52, H-58, A-1/17, A-2/54, TT-117, B-418, EE-51, WW-413)

O'GRAY, WILLIAM. Private in Capt. Sheaf's Company, June 16, 1777. (W-162)

O'HARA, JAMES. On December 8, 1776, Dr. Wiesenthal of Baltimore reported that O'Hara became sick while standing guard duty. (FFF-72)

O'LARY, JAMES. Private in Capt. ewing's Company No. 4; enlisted Jan.29, 1776. (H-12)

OLDHAM, EDWARD. (December 8, 1756, Cecil County, MD - November 4, 1798, Cecil County) Married Mary ENSOR (1764-1819) on November 21, 1784. Their children: Maria (born 1786); Elizabeth (born 1787); Edward (born 1789); Augustine H. (born 1790); George Washington (born 1792), married Susan Ann BIDDLE; Charles (born 1793); Hamet (born 1795); and, Ann. Edward OLDHAM was 1st Lieutenant in Capt. Standiford's Company in Gunpowder Upper Battalion, May 6, 1776, and 1st Lieutenant in 2nd MD Battalion of Flying Camp., July to December, 1776. He became 1st Lieutenant of the 4th MD Regt., December 10, 1776, and then Captain on May 20, 1777. He was transferred to the 5th MD Regt., January 1, 1781, and then to the 1st MD Regt., January 1, 1783. He was retained in Gunby's Battalion, April 1, 1783, and became a Brevet Major on Sept. 30, 1783, serving to November 3, 1783. He was an Original Member of the Society of the Cincinnati of Maryland, and was last represented by Charles Herman Oldham, Sr., of Washington , D.C. (1883-1967). Capt. Oldham received the following pay certificates for his war service: 82676 ($600); 82677 ($600); 82678 ($600); 82679 ($300); 82680 ($300); 82872 ($117.22); 82873 ($301.28); 82874 ($400); and, 82875 ($220). He was also entitled to 200 acres (lots 3302, 3279, 3280, 4119) in western Maryland, and 300 acres under Federal Bounty Land Grant Warrant 1110, February 19, 1825. (YY-74, DDDD-3, B-419, H-149, H-52, H-58, EE-51, WW-413, PP-380, TT-117, XXX-549, JJJ-504)

OLDHAM, JOHN. Married Anna ALBRIGHT on April 12, 1795, in Baltimore. (Marriage proven through Maryland pension application) (YY-120) Ed. Note: No record found on his military service, if any; he might have been a son of a Revolutionary pensioner.

O'LEARY, CORNELIUS. Served in Baltimore Artillery Company in 1777. (V-368)

O'LEGG, VACHEL. Private in Capt. Ewing's Company No. 4; enlisted May 20, 1776. (H-11)

OLLIVER, SAMUEL. Non-Juror to Oath of Allegiance, 1778. (A-1/17)

OMANSETTER (ORNANSETTER), JOHN. Oath of Allegiance, 1778, before Hon. George Linden-berger. 2nd Lieutenant, Baltimore Town Battalion, May 17, 1779. (A-1/17, A-2/54, F-311, F-313)

ONION, ZACHARIAH (ZACHEUS). (1743, England - 1781, Baltimore County, MD) He married Hannah BOND, and their son, William ONION, married Elizabeth DAY. Source JJJ-505 gives his name as "Zaccheus Barrett Onion." He served on the Baltimore County Com-mittee of Observation, January 16, 1775. "Zacheus Onion" was 1st Lieutenant in the Gunpowder Upper Hundred, May 6, 1776, and "Zachariah Onion" was Captain in Gunpowder Battalion from 1776 to at least 1778. (XXX-550, E-12, WW-413, EE-51, X-111, BBB-362)

O'NEAL, HUGH. Enlisted in Baltimore County on July 20, 1776. (H-53)

O'NEAL, PATRICK. Private in Capt. Deams' Co., 7th MD Regt., Dec. 14, 1776. (H-305)

O'NEILL, FELIX. Oath of Allegiance, 1778, before Hon. Jesse Dorsey. (A-1/17, A-2/63)

O'NEILL (O'NEAL), JOHN. Private in Capt. Ewing's Company No. 4; enlisted Jan. 20, 1776. Oath of Allegiance, 1778, before Hon. James Calhoun. (H-12, A-1/17, A-2/41)

O'NEILL, THOMAS. Oath of Allegiance, 1778, before Hon. James Calhoun. (A-2/65)

ORAM, BENJAMIN, Non-Juror to Oath of Allegiance, 1778. (A-1/17)

ORAM (OARAM), HENRY. Oath of Allegiance, 1778, before Hon. Charles Ridgely of William. (A-1/17, A-2/28)

ORAM (OARAM), JOHN. Enlisted in Baltimore County on July 20, 1776. Private in Capt. Godman's Co., 4th MD Regt.; discharged April 13, 1780. Non-Juror to Oath in 1778. (A-1/17, H-52, H-149)

ORAM (ORM), SAMUEL. Drummer in Capt. Smith' Company, 4th MD Regiment, April 7, 1778 to November 1, 1780. Non-Juror to Oath of Allegiance in 1778. One Samuel Oram was entitled to 50 acres (lot 1009) in western Maryland for his services as Private in 7th MD Regiment. (DDDD-29, H-149, A-1/17)

ORAM, THOMAS. Non-Juror to Oath of Allegiance, 1778. (A-1/17)

ORE, MARANE. Recruit in Baltimore County in 1780. (H-340)

ORRICK, CHARLES. Oath of Allegiance, 1778, before Hon. James Calhoun. Ensign in Capt. Young's Company, Baltimore Town Battalion, Sept. 25, 1780. (VV-303, A-1/17, A-2/42)

ORRICK, JOHN. Non-Juror to Oath of Allegiance, 1778. (A-1/17)

ORRICK, NICHOLAS SR. Oath of Allegiance, 1778, before Hon. Edward Cockey. A Nicholas Orrick married Susan KEENER on November 17, 1803 at the residence of Christian KEENER by Reverend Wells; she died in July, 1809. (ZZZ-244, A-1/17, A-2/61)

ORRIDGE, GEORGE. Recruit in Baltimore County in 1780. (H-340)

ORSBURN (OSBURN), SAMUEL. Oath of Allegiance, 1778, before Hon. Andrew Buchanan. (A-1/17, A-2/57)

OSBORN, JOSEPH. Oath of Allegiance, 1778, before Hon. Jeremiah Johnson. (A-1/17, A-2/33)

OSBURN, DANIEL. Non-Juror to Oath of Allegiance, 1778. (A-1/17)
OSBURN, JOHN. Non-Juror to Oath of Allegiance, 1778. (A-1/17)
OSLAR, ABRAM. Non-Juror to Oath of Allegiance, 1778. (A-1/17)
OSLAR, ELY. Non-Juror to Oath of Allegiance, 1778. (A-1/17)
OSLAR, WILLIAM. Non-Juror to Oath of Allegiance, 1778. (A-1/17)
OSTON, GABRIEL. Non-Juror to Oath of Allegiance, 1778. (A-1/17)
OSTON, HENRY. Non-Juror to Oath of Allegiance, 1778. (A-1/17)
OSTON, JOHN. Non-Juror to Oath of Allegiance, 1778. (A-1/17)
OSTON, LAWRENCE. Non-Juror to Oath of Allegiance, 1778. (A-1/17)

TWAY, NICHOLAS. Non-Juror to Oath of Allegiance, 1778. (A-1/18)

URSLER (ORSLER), CHARLES. (Born April 27, 1755) Married Martha McCANDLEY/McKINLEY in 1778. Oath of Allegiance, 1778, before Hon. Edward Cockey. (D-10, A-1/17, A-2/61)

URSLER, (ORSLER), EDWARD. (1710, England - April 4, 1789, Baltimore County, Maryland) Married Ruth OWINGS (OWENS) on November 21, 1734 in St. Paul's Parish. Children: Mary OURSLER (born 1738) married Joseph MILLER in 1759; Elizabeth OURSLER (b. 1739) married Benjamin JARVIS; Elam or Eli OURSLER (born 1741) married Ann PEMBERTON; Margaret OURSLER (born 1743); Edward OURSLER (born 1746); Jacob OURSLER (born 1748); Ormand OURSLER (born 1749); Abraham (born 1749, twin to Ormand); Catherine OURSLER (born 1751) married a WARE; William OURSLER (born 1753) married Mary PARKER in 1778; Charles OURSLER (born 1755) married Martha McCANDLEY/McKINLEY in 1778; John OURSLER (born 1758) married Sarah BAKER in 1782; and, Sarah OURSLER (born 1761) md. James GRIMES in 1779. Edward OURSLER took the Oath of Allegiance in 1778 before the Hon. Edward Cockey. (A-1/17, A-2/61, JJJ-508, D-10, XXX-553, XXX-554)

URSLER, WILLIAM. (July 31, 1753 - April, 1813) Married Mary Parker, Jan. 14, 1778. Son of Edward OURSLER and Ruth OWINGS. Sergeant, MD Militia. (JJJ-508, D-10)

VERCREEK, JOSEPH. Recruited, by Capt. John A. Hamilton for the Maryland Line, on January 1, 1782. (H-418)

WENS, ARTHUR. Served in Baltimore Artillery Company in 1777. (V-363)

WENS, BARTHOLAMEW. Oath of Allegiance, 1778, before Hon. James Calhoun. (A-2/65)

WENS, JOHN. Matross in Capt. Dorsey's MD Artillery at Camp Col. Scirvins, as of January 28, 1782. (UU-232)

WINGS, BEALE. (August 9, 1731 - December 30, 1781) Son of Samuel OWINGS and Urath RANDALL. Unmarried. 1st Lieutenant in Capt. Ed. Cockey's Baltimore County Co. No. 2, August 26, 1776, and Captain in Col. Cockey's Battalion, Dec. 20, 1776. Oath of Allegiance, 1778, before Hon. James Calhoun. (A-2/41, KKK-377, PPP-21, RR-98, ZZ-541)

WINGS, CALEB. (March 18, 1731 - February 26, 1816, Baltimore County, MD) Son of John OWINGS and Hannah STINCHCOMB. Married Susanna WALTERS (1742-1813) on November 20, 1768, a daughter of Alexander WALTERS of Queen Anne County, MD. Their children were: Son (stillborn); Mary; John, only son of Caleb, and proprietor of Sulphur Springs, near baltimore city, died October 9, 1804, in his 33rd year, leaving a wife and children; Achsah; Alexander (died young); Milcah; Suannah; Eleanor; and, Mary. Caleb OWINGS was Captain in the Severn Battalion, Anne Arundel County, MD, Militia, March 2, 1778 to 1783. He died at his farm in Baltimore County in 1816, and was the proprietor of Sulphur Springs. (ZZZ-245, ZZZ-246, KKK-348, KKK-349, BBB-525)

WINGS, CALEB. Oath of Allegiance, 1778, before Hon. Richard Holliday, Private, in Capt. Talbott's Company, May 31, 1779. (A-2/60, F-301, U-90)

WINGS, CHRISTOPHER. (February 16, 1744 - January 12, 1783) Son of Samuel OWINGS and Urath RANDALL. Married Elizabeth LAWRENCE circa 1769 (and she married secondly to Joseph WELLS). Children: Beale, Samuel, Christopher, Urath, Levin, Susan and Betsy. Christopher OWINGS served on the Baltimore County Committee of Inspection, March 13, 1775, and the Committee of Correspondence, January 16, 1775. He was 1st Lieutenant, Soldiers Delight Company No. 8, May 13, 1776 and Captain from August 29, 1777 until 1783. He took the Oath of Allegiance in 1778 before Hon. William Spear. (A-1/18, A-2/66, BBB-384, KKK-419, KKK-420, FF-64, E-10, Z-63, BBB-348, RR-19)

WINGS, DALE. Oath of Allegiance, 1778. (A-1/18)

WINGS, EDWARD. Non-Juror to Oath of Allegiance, 1778. (A-1/18)

WINGS, EPHRAIM. Served in Col. Nicholson's Troop of Horse, June 7, 1781. (BBBB-274)

WINGS, GEORGE. (March 14, 1747/1748 - after 1833) Son of Joshua OWINGS and Mary COCKEY. Unmarried. Private in Capt. James Winchester's Company in Col. John Gist's Regiment, 1776. Later, he was an Indian spy under General Anthony Wayne. He died in Calloway County, Kentucky. Pensioned, 1833, age 85; received $20 on Jan. 26, 1833.

(Anderson C. Quisenberry's Revolutionary Soldiers of Kentucky, page 51; KKK-508)

OWINGS, JACOB. Matross in Capt. Gale's MD Artillery, 1779-1780. Matross in Captain J. Smith's MD Artillery, 1780; "deceased November 19, 1781; paid widow one month." (H-579, YYY-1/82)

OWINGS, JOHN. (c1719, Baltimore County, MD - September 30, 1779, Baltimore County, MD) Son of Richard OWINGS. John's wife Catherine died February 5, 1826. Their children: Joshua OWINGS (born 1756); Rebecca OWINGS, married Hugh LYNCH in 1780; Ruth OWINGS, married Capt. Thomas STINCHCOMB in 1788 (she may have married a CONWAY earlier); Rachel OWINGS, married John CROOKS in 1788; Benjamin OWINGS (born 1767), married Ann Catherine ZIMMERMAN, daughter of George, in 1792; Mary OWINGS (born 1770), married Peter BARNET in 1790; Achsah OWINGS (born 1772), married Levin LAWRENCE in 1805; Israel OWINGS (born 1778); George OWINGS (1778-1864, twin to Israel), married Sarah MUMMEU in 1802. John OWINGS was a Lieutenant in Capt. Joshua Beall's Company, MD Militia, during the French and Indian War. He took the Oath of Allegiance in 1778 before Hon. Richard Cromwell. (A-1/18, A-2/46, D-10)

OWINGS, JOHN COCKEY. (January 11, 1736, Baltimore County, MD - February 3, 1810 either in Baltimore County, MD, according to Source ZZZ-245, or in Bourbon County, Kentucky, according to Source KKK-510 and Source JJJ-510) Son of Joshua OWINGS and Mary COCKEY. He married Colgate Deye COLGATE (1754-1828), daughter of Thomas COLGATE and Cassandra Cockey DEYE, on March 15, 1772. Their chidlren: Cassandra Deye, Charlotte Colgate, Thomas Deye, Mary Cockey, Churchilla Cockey Deye, Penelope Deye, and Francis Thwaites. John Cockey OWINGS was a 1st Lieutenant in Baltimore County Militia Company No. 2 on December 19, 1775, and 1st Lieutenant in Capt. Nicholson's Company No. 1 of Soldiers Delight Battalion in 1776. He became Captain on June 6, 1776 and transferred to Gunpowder Battalion, August 29, 1777. (Source BBB-348 incorrectly spelled his name as "Capt. I. Cockey Owings.") He took the Oath of Allegiance in 1778 before Hon. Edward Cockey. In October, 1781, he resigned from the military as Captain in the Gunpowder Upper Battalion. (WW-467, G-10, FF-64, E-12, Z-63, BBB-348, JJJ-510, ZZZ-245, A-1/18, A-2/61, KKK-509, KKK-510, KKK-511)

OWINGS, JOSHUA. (April 5, 1704 - April 11, 1785) Son of Capt. Richard OWINGS and wife Rachel. He married Mary COCKEY (1716-1768) in Baltimore on March 9, 1735. Children: John Cockey, Richard, Joshua, Edward, Michal, Marcella, George, Rebecca, Elizabeth, Rachel, and Ephraim. Joshua OWINGS took the Oath of Allegiance in 1778 before Hon. Richard Cromwell, and furnished supplies to the Maryland troops during the Revolution. (DAR Magazine, Vol. 118, No. 9, November, 1984, page 150; JJJ-510, KKK-506, KKK-509, A-1/18, A-2/46)

OWINGS, JOSHUA. (May 22, 1740, Maryland - January 7, 1804, Kentucky) Son of Joshua OWINGS and Mary COCKEY. He married Elizabeth HOWE, daughter of Edward HOWE, in 1776 in Baltimore. Their children: Elihu; Joshua; Mordecai, Sarah, Mary, Michal, Samuel, Edward Cockey, Thomas Cockey, John, and Richard Howe. Joshua OWINGS was a 1st Lieut. in the Maryland Militia, and was the first Owings to go to Kentucky somemtime after 1776. (JJJ-510, KKK-640, KKK-641)

OWINGS, JOSHUA. (September 3, 1756 - September 24, 1843) Son of John and Catherine OWINGS. Married Rachel CROOKS (died 1834) on October 4, 1777 at St. Paul's Church. Their children: John OWINGS, married Dorothy STINCHCOMB; Henry OWINGS (born 1783), married Achsah GOSNELL; Ephraim OWINGS, married Mary JEAN; Miche OWINGS (1787-1884) married Peter SIPES; and, Mary Ann OWINGS (1790-1861) married Thomas STINCHCOMB. Joshua OWINGS was an Ensign in Soldiers Delight Company No. 6 on May 13, 1776, and 1st Lieutenant in Capt. C. Owing's Company, Soldiers Delight Battalion, August 29, 1777 to at least 1779. (FF-64, Z-63, E-10, BBB-348, KKK-173)

OWINGS, JOSHUA. Private in Col. Aquila Hall's Baltimore County Regiment, 1777. (TTT-13)

OWINGS, JOSHUA. One of the above men by this name took the Oath of Allegiance in 1778 before Hon. Charles Ridgely of William. (A-2/28)

OWINGS, LEVIN. Private in Baltimore County Regiment No. 7, circa 1777. (TTT-13)

OWINGS, NICHOLAS. Non-Juror to Oath of Allegiance, 1778. (A-1/18)

OWINGS, NATHANIEL. (c1731 - November 4, 1788) Son of Henry OWINGS and Helen STINCHCOMB.
Married Urath KELLEY, daughter of William KELLEY and Elizabeth GORSUCH, on January 7,
1763. Children: Henry, Joshua, Elizabeth, Thomas Isaac, Michal, George Washington,
Rachel, Nicholas, John and Luther. Nathaniel OWINGS was a resident of Baltimore Co.
until 1768 when he moved to Anne Arundel County. He was an Ensign in Capt. Rigg's Co.
in the Elk Ridge Battalion, March 30, 1776, and 1st Lieutenant in Capt. Hammond's Co.
on March 2, 1778. (KKK-305, KKK-306)

OWINGS, RICHARD. (July 16, 1749, Owings Mills, Baltimore County, MD - January 21, 1819,
Clarksville, Anne Arundel County, MD) Son of Samuel OWINGS and Urath RANDALL. He
married Ruth WARFIELD (1756-1830), daughter of Dr. Joshua WARFIELD and Rachel HOWARD,
circa 1774. Children: Beal OWINGS (born 1775), married Cordelia HARRIS; Mary OWINGS
(born 1776), married William WELLING; Samuel OWINGS (born 1778), married (1) Rachel
GASSAWAY, and (2) Sarah Ann Brown HATHERLY; James OWINGS (born 1780); Joshua OWINGS;
Richard OWINGS (born 1783), married Elizabeth MUNRO; Basil OWINGS; Thomas OWINGS (b.
1788), married (1) Anna Maria WARFIELD, and (2) Sarah WOOD; Joshua Warfield OWINGS
(born 1790), married Eleanor Hood WORTHINGTON; David OWINGS; Ann OWINGS (born 1794),
married Dominic Brown JESSOP; Henry OWINGS; Basil OWINGS (born 1798), md. Eleanor
Ann GRIFFITH; and, Henry Howard OWINGS (born 1800), married (1) Sarah Harvey GIST,
and (2) Elizabeth DORSEY. Richard OWINGS was a Captain of Soldiers Delight Company
No. 3 on May 13, 1776, commanding 58 Privates. He was Captain in Baltimore County's
Marching Militia as of September 17, 1777, and Captain in Soldiers Delight Battalion
in 1778. He resigned May 27, 1779. He also took the Oath of Allegiance, 1778 before
Hon. Peter Shepherd. (JJJ-510, XXX-555, KKK-429, KKK-431, E-11, FF-64, BBB-384, GGG-
422, A-1/18, A-2/49, AAA-2916)

OWINGS, RICHARD (OF JOSHUA). Private in Capt. J. Cockey's Baltimore County Dragoons,
at Yorktown, 1781. (MMM-A) Non-Juror to Oath of Allegiance, 1778. (A-1/18)

OWINGS, RICHARD IV. (March 20, 1734, Baltimore County, Maryland - March 3, 1834,
Laurens County, South Carolina) Son of Richard OWINGS and Anna STONESTREET. He
moved to South Carolina with his parents in 1757, and married Sarah HELLAMS in 1766.
Children: Rachel, Richard, William, Archibald, Sarah, Elizabeth, Jonathan, John and
Mary. He was a Private in Capt. John Rodgers Co. & Capt. Chew's Co. (KKK-8, KKK-9)

OWINGS, ROGER. Private in Count Pulaski's Legion; enlisted in Baltimore on April 27,
1778. (H-592, H-593) Non-Juror to Oath of Allegiance, 1778. (A-1/18)

OWINGS, SAMUEL JR. (August 17, 1733 - June 11, 1803, Baltimore County, MD) Son of
Samuel OWINGS and Urath RANDALL. Married Deborah LYNCH (1746-1810), daughter of
William LYNCH and Elinor DORSEY, on October 6, 1765. Children: William OWINGS (b.
1766), married Ann HENDERSON; Urath OWINGS (born 1769), married John CROMWELL;
Samuel OWINGS (born 1770), married Ruth COCKEY; Eleanor OWINGS (born 1772) married
Thomas MOALE in 1793; Sarah OWINGS (born 1773) married James WINCHESTER in 1793;
Rebecca OWINGS (born 1776), unmarried; Deborah OWINGS (born 1777), married Peter
HOFFMAN; Frances OWINGS (born 1779), married Robert North MOALE in 1801; Rachel
OWINGS (1781-1782); Mary OWINGS (born 1784), married Richard CROMWELL; Ann OWINGS
(born 1785), married George WINCHESTER; and, Beale OWINGS (born 1791), married
Eleanor MAGRUDER. Samuel OWINGS was a Captain on May 13, 1776; Lieutenant Colonel
in 1777; and, Colonel, Soldiers Delight Battalion, June 3, 1777. He was later a
Delegate to the Maryland Legislature in 1786. Earlier, he had served on Baltimore
County's Committee of Inspection on March 13, 1775, and the Committee of Observation
on July 24, 1775. (FF-64, RR-19, EEEE-1725, D-5, JJJ-510, BBB-271, ZZZ-245, KKK-380)

OWINGS, SAMUEL (OF STEPHEN). Non-Juror to Oath of Allegiance in 1778. (A-1/18)

OWINGS, STEPHEN. Oath of Allegiance, 1778, before Hon. James Calhoun. (A-2/41)
There may have been another Stephen Owings who was a Non-Juror in 1778. (A-1/18)

OWINGS, THOMAS. (October 18, 1740 - August 23, 1822, Baltimore County, MD) Son of
Samuel OWINGS (1702-1775) and Urath RANDALL (1712-1792). He married Ruth LAWRENCE
(1745-1827) on November 27, 1760, daughter of Levin and Susan LAWRENCE. Children:
Levin Lawrence OWINGS (born 1761), married Achsah DORSEY; Samuel OWINGS (b. 1763),
married Ariana DORSEY; Thomas OWINGS (born 1765); Thomas Beale OWINGS (born 1767),

OWINGS, THOMAS (continued)

married (1) Ann JOHNSON, and (2) Cordelia Harris OWINGS; Betsy OWINGS (born 1769), married Capt. John DORSEY; Isaac OWINGS (born 1771), married (1) Achsah DORSEY, and (2) Rebecca WILLIAMS; David OWINGS (born 1773); Susannah OWINGS (born 1775) married Bazil SOLLERS; Ruth OWINGS (born 1777) married Joseph SHEETS; Jesse OWINGS (1779-1812) married Hannah HOOD (1786-1838) in 1801, and their son Thomas OWINGS (1802-1866) married Mary JENNINGS (1802-1876) in 1823; Anne OWINGS (born 1781), married Benjamin HOOD; Levin OWINGS (born 1784); Harwood OWINGS (born 1786); and, Matilda OWINGS (born 1789) married Edwin DOWNEY. Thomas OWINGS was 2nd Lieutenant, Co. 2, Soldiers Delight Battn.; May 13, 1776, and 1st Lieutenant in Capt. Wells' Company, Soldiers Delight Battn.; June 6, 1776; became Captain, August 29, 1777, serving to 1778, when he resigned his commission either on April 13 or May 27, 1778. (FFF-158, GGG-422, AAA-1573, FF-64, Z-63, BBB-348, E-10, JJJ-510, XXX-555, KKK-390, KKK-392)

OWINGS, WILLIAM. Non-Juror to Oath of Allegiance, 1778. (A-1/18)

P

PACA, ABRAHAM. Non-Juror to Oath of Allegiance, 1778. (A-1/18)

PACA, PETER SR. Non-Juror to Oath of Allegiance, 1778. (A-1/18)

PACA, PETER JR. Non-Juror to Oath of Allegiance, 1778. (A-1/18)

PAGE, JOHN. Oath of Allegiance, 1778, before Hon. John Beale Howard. Could not write; made his mark. (A-1/18, A-2/29)

PAGE, RICHARD. Matross in Capt. Brown's MD Artillery; joined November 22, 1777. Was at Valley Forge; reported deserted on January 4, 1778. (UU-229, UU-230)

PAIN, GEORGE (OR J. GEORGE). Non-Juror to Oath of Allegiance, 1778. (A-1/18)

PAINE, JOSHUA. Oath of Allegiance, 1778, before Hon. James Calhoun. (A-1/18, A-2/38)

PAKER, JOHN. Oath of Allegiance, 1778, before Hon. William Spear. Could not write; made his mark. (A-2/67)

PALFREY, EDWARD. Enlisted in Baltimore county in 1776. (H-53)

PALLAN, RICHARD. Oath of Allegiance, 1778, before Hon. Charles Ridgely of William. (A-2/28)

PALMER, GEORGE. Oath of Allegiance, 1778, before Hon. John Hall. (A-1/18, A-2/36)

PALMER, JOHN. Oath of Allegiance, 1778, before Hon. Charles Ridgely of William. Could not write; made his mark. (A-1/18, A-2/28)

PALMER, THOMAS. Marine on ship Defence, May 29 to December 31, 1777. (H-659) He was a Non-Juror to Oath of Allegiance in 1778. (A-1/18)

PANNELL, EDWARD. Oath of Allegiance, 1778, before Hon. James Calhoun.(A-1/18, A-2/40)

PANNELL, JOHN, of Fells Point, Baltimore. (Died in January, 1799) Oath of Allegiance in 1778 before Hon. James Calhoun. (A-1/18, A-2/40, ZZZ-247)

PANTEL, THOMAS. Oath of Allegiance, 1778. (A-1/18)

PANTSE, THOMAS. Oath of Allegiance, 1778, before Hon. George Lindenberger. (A-2/54)

PARKER, ALEXANDER. Oath of Allegiance, 1778, before Hon. Edward Cockey. (A-2/61)

PARKER, JOHN. Oath of Allegiance, 1778. (A-1/18)

PARKER, ROBERT. Non-Juror to Oath of Allegiance, 1778. (A-1/18)

PARKER, WALTER SMITH. Lieutenant in Hunting Ridge Company of the 39th Battalion of Militia in Baltimore County prior to August 29, 1777, for on that day he became a 1st Lieutenant (promotion); served at least to 1779. Also, took the Oath of Allegiance in 1778 before Hon. Charles Ridgely of William. (E-13, F-311, Y-61, BBB-348, A-2/27)

PARKER, WILLIAM. (1746 - 1797) Wife named Mary. Served as 2nd Lieutenant, Baltimore County Militia, 4th Company, December 19, 1775. Ensign, Capt. Hurd's Co., Soldiers Delight Battalion, 1778 to at least May 27, 1779. Oath of Allegiance, 1778, before Hon. Peter Shepherd. (G-10, F-10, GGG-422, HH-24, JJJ-516, A-2/49)

PARKER, WILLIAM SMITH. Oath of Allegiance, 1778. (A-1/18)

PARKERSON (PERKERSON), ABRAHAM. Matross in Capt. Gale's MD Artillery, 1779; sick at Annapolis, November 1779 to April, 1780. (YYY-1/89)

PARKS, AQUILLA. Non-Juror to Oath of Allegiance, 1778. (A-1/18)

PARKS (PARK), DAVID. (1742 - January 23, 1814, Baltimore County, MD) Possibly a son of William PARKS and Mary MIKLEWS. Married Elizabeth_____, and their children: Peter PARKS (1763-1854), married (1) Julia Ann RIDGELY, and (2) Priscilla JONES in 1791, daughter of Joshua JONES; Peter's son John PARKS (1796-1878) married, 1824, Margaret SWARTZ (died 1889), and Peter's son Joseph PARKS (1801-1873) married in 1831 to Rebecca COALE (1803-1894); Benjamin PARKS; David PARKS, Jr., married in 1794 to Elizabeth JONES (not TOWSON as stated in Source D-5); Mary PARKS, married James WHITELY in 1784; Rachel PARKS, married Raphel DIXON in 1791; and, William PARKS (died 1796), unmarried. David PARKS took the Oath of Allegiance in 1778 before Hon. James Calhoun. (A-1/18, A-2/40, AAA-2650, AAA-1490, JJJ-514, XXX-558, XXX-559, D-5; David's wife might have been a TOWSON, but not yet documented----Ed.)

PARKS, JOHN. Non-Juror to Oath of Allegiance, 1778. (A-1/18) Colonel Samuel Smith, Baltimore, wrote to Governor Thomas S. Lee on August 17, 1781: "John Parks is now confined in Baltimore jail on suspicion of being concerned with the Tories of Frederick. His conduct since his residence in this place has been peaceable. His wife informs that he has generally attended the militia. I am informed there is no evidence against him. I do not consider him a dangerous person and beg permission for his release." (BBBB-426) John Parks is shown as serving in Capt. Lynn's Company, 4th MD Regiment, 1781. (H-404)

PARKS, JOHN JR. Non-Juror to Oath of Allegiance, 1778. (A-1/18)
PARKS, WILLIAM SR. Non-Juror to Oath of Allegiance, 1778. (A-1/18)
PARKS, WILLIAM JR. Non-Juror to Oath of Allegiance, 1778. (A-1/18)
PARLETT, CHARLES. Non-Juror to Oath of Allegiance, 1778. (A-1/18)
PARLETT, MARTIN. Non-Juror to Oath of Allegiance, 1778. (A-1/18)
PARLETT, WILLIAM SR. Non-Juror to Oath of Allegiance, 1778. (A-1/18)
PARLETT, WILLIAM JR. Non-Juror to Oath of Allegiance, 1778. (A-1/18)

PARR, WILLIAM. Private in Capt. ewing's Company No. 4; enlisted Jan. 27, 1776. (H-12)

PARRIER (PARRIES), PETER. Oath of Allegiance, 1778, before Hon. James Calhoun.(A-2/41)

PARRISH, AQUILLA, Non-Juror to Oath of Allegiance, 1778. (A-1/18)
PARRISH, BENJAMIN. Non-Juror to Oath of Allegiance, 1778. (A-1/18)

PARRISH, EDWARD (OF EDWARD). Ensign in Soldiers Delight Company No. 7, May 13, 1776. 2nd Lieutenant, August 29, 1777 to at least 1778. (Z-63, BBB-348, E-10, FF-64) He was a Non-Juror to the Oath of Allegiance in 1778. (A-1/18)

PARRISH, EDWARD. Born 1757. Married Clemency HUGHES on May 20, 1782, in Baltimore County. (Marriage proven through Maryland pension application). Source H-52 shows Edward Parrish enlisting in Baltimore County on August 14, 1776; Source H-53 shows Edward Parish enlisting in Baltimore County on July 26, 1776. Source YY-41 states he was a Pensioner, and was a Sergeant in the Maryland Line, at one time wounded. On March 2, 1827, it was ordered to "pay to him, of Baltimore County, during life, half·yearly, half pay of a Sergeant, for his services during the Revolutionary War." On March 24, 1836, it was ordered to "pay to James NELSON, for use of Clemency PARRISH, widow of Edward, deceased, late of Baltimore County, a soldier of the Revolution, it being the amount due said Parrish for revolutionary services, at time of his decease." On March 16, 1836, it was ordered to "pay to Clemmency Parrish, widow of Edward, a soldier of the revolution, half pay of a sarjent during her life." (C-380, H-52, H-53, YY-41, YY-120) Also, one Edward PARRISH was a Non-Juror to the Oath of Allegiance in 1778. (A-1/18)

PARRISH, EDWARD (OF RICHARD). Non-Juror to Oath of Allegiance, 1778. (A-1/18)
PARRISH, JOHN. Source A-1/18 shows three Non-Jurors in 1778 with this name.
PARRISH, JOHN (OF EDWARD). Non-Juror to Oath of Allegiance in 1778. (A-1/18)
PARRISH, JOHN (OF JOHN). Non-Juror to Oath of Allegiance in 1778. (A-1/18)
PARRISH, JOHNATHAN. Non-Juror to Oath of Allegiance in 1778. (A-1/18)
PARRISH, MORDECAI. Non-Juror to Oath of Allegiance, 1778. (A-1/18)
PARRISH, NATHANIEL. Non-Juror to Oath of Allegiance, 1778. (A-1/18)
PARRISH, NICHOLAS. Non-Juror to Oath of Allegiance in 1778. (A-1/18)
PARRISH, RICHARD. Non-Juror to Oath of allegiance in 1778. (A-1/18)
PARRISH, RICHARD SR. Non-Juror to Oath of Allegiance, 1778. (A-1/18)
PARRISH, RICHARD (OF EDWARD). Non-Juror to Oath of Allegiance, 1778. (A-1/18)
PARRISH, RICHARD (OF JOHN). Non-Juror to Oath of Allegiance, 1778. (A-1/18)
PARRISH, STEPHEN. Non-Juror to Oath of Allegiance, 1778. (A-1/18)

PARRISH, WILLIAM JR. Oath of Allegiance, 1778, before Hon. Jesse Dorsey. (A-2/63)

PARRISH, WILLIAM. Ensign in Capt. Standiford's Company, Gunpowder Battalion, on
    September 3, 1777 and to at least 1778. (BBB-350, T-83, E-11) Source A-1/18
    states William Parrish, Sr. was a Non-Juror to the Oath of Allegiance in 1778.

PARRISH, WILLIAM (OF EDWARD). Non-Juror to Oath of Allegiance in 1778. (A-1/18)
PARRISH, WILLIAM (OF JOHN). Non-Juror to Oath of Allegiance, 1778. (A-1/18)

PARROT, ROGER. Oath of Allegiance, 1778, before Hon. James Calhoun.(A-1/18,A-2/40)

PARRY, JOHN. Oath of Allegiance, 1778, before Hon. Richard Cromwell.(A-1/18,A-2/46)

PARSNIP, JOHN. Non-Juror to Oath of Allegiance, 1778. (A-1/18)

PARSONS, WILLIAM. Marine on ship Defence, April 28 to December 31, 1777. (H-659)

PARTRIDGE, JOHN. Oath of Allegiance, 1778, before Hon. James Calhoun.(A-1/18,A-2/38)

PARTUS, WILLIAM. Able Seaman on ship Defence, September 19, 1776. (H-606)

PARUTHERS, W. Oath of Allegiance, 1778, before Hon. Isaac Van Bibber. He could not
    write; made his mark. (A-2/34)

PASSINGHAM, JOHN. Oath of Allegiance, 1778, before Hon. Jesse Dorsey.(A-1/18,A-2/63)

PATMORE, BENJAMIN. Matross in Capt. Brown's MD Artillery; joined November 22, 1777.
    Was at Valley Forge until June, 1778; at White Plains, July, 1778; at Ft. Schuyler
    in August and September, 1780; at High Hills of the Santee in August, 1781; at
    Camp Col. Scirvins, January, 1782; at Bacon's Bridge, SC, April, 1782. (UU-230)

PATRICK, JOHN. Oath of Allegiance, 1778, before Hon. Jesse Dorsey. (A-1/18, A-2/63)

PATRICK, JOHN JR. Non-Juror to Oath of Allegiance in 1778. (A-1/18)
PATRIDGE, DAUBNEY BUCKLEY. Non-Juror to Oath of Allegiance in 1778. (A-1/18)
PATRIDGE, JOSEPH. Non-Juror to Oath of Allegiance in 1778. (A-1/18)
PATRIDGE, ROBERT. Non-Juror to Oath of Allegiance in 1778. (A-1/18)

PATTERSON, ALEXANDER. Oath of Allegiance, 1778, before Hon. Jesse Dorsey. (A-2/63)

PATTERSON, JAMES. Oath of Allegiance, 1778, before Hon. James Calhoun. (A-2/42)

PATTERSON, JOHN. Non-Juror to Oath of Allegiance, 1778. (A-1/18)

PATTERSON, WILLIAM. (November 1, 1752 - February 7, 1835) Married Dorcas SPEAR.
    One of Baltimore's most distinguished and wealthy merchants, William Patterson
    gave the following brief sketch in his will of shipping arms and ammunition to
    America when he was a Baltimore Privateer during the Revolutionary War: "When
    the American Revolution commenced, in which I took great interest, it appeared
    to me that one of the greatest difficulties we should experience was the want of
    powder and arms, in consequence of the great precautions taken by the British
    Government to prevent there being brought to this country from other places. This
    induced me in the year 1775 to embark all the property I then possessed in parts
    of two vessels and their cargoes, destined from Philadelphia to France, for the
    sole purpose of returning with powder and arms, and in one of which I embarked

PATTERSON, WILLIAM (continued)
myself. One only of these vessels got safe back to Philadelphia, where she arrived
in the month of March, 1776, with the cargo intended, and in a most critical time,
when it was said that General Washington, then before Boston with the army, had not
powder sufficient to fire a salute." (III-207, and Scharf's Chronicles of Baltimore
page 482) Elizabeth Patterson BONAPARTE was his daughter. (JJJ-520, III-207)

PATTERSON, WIRT. Oath of Allegiance, 1778, before Hon. James Calhoun. (A-2/65)

PATTINGTON, GEORGE. Enlisted in Baltimore Town on July 17, 1776. (H-53)

PATTISON, JOHN. Non-Juror to Oath of Allegiance, 1778. (A-1/18)
PATTISON, MATTHEW. Non-Juror to Oath of Allegiance, 1778. (A-1/18)
PATTISON, WILLIAM. Source A-1/18 gives two Non-Jurors in 1778 with this name.
PATTMAN, ROBERT. Non-Juror to Oath of Allegiance, 1778. (A-1/18)

PATTON, GEORGE. Member of the Sons of Liberty, 1776, in Baltimore. (CCC-19)

PATTON, MATTHEW. He agreed to manufacture knapsacks and haversacks, July 31, 1776. He
took the Oath of Allegiance in 1778 before Hon. George Lindenberger. On June 25,
1781, he served with Capt. Nichols Ruxton Moore's Troops, and rode a bay gelding
horse. (BBBB-313, FFF-46, FFF-48, A-1/18, A-2/54)

PATTON (PATTAN), RICHARD. Oath of Allegiance, 1778. (A-1/18)

PATTON (PATTEN), THOMAS. Drummer in Capt. Dorsey's MD Artillery, at Camp Co. Scirvins
on January 28, 1782. (UU-232)

PATTON, WILLIAM. Oath of Allegiance, 1778, before Hon. James Calhoun. (A-1/18, A-2/40)

PATTY, ORRISE. Born 1751 in America. Enlisted July 5, 1776, in Baltimore County, as
a Private in Col. Ewing's Battalion. Height: 5'8"; shor black hair. (H-55)

PAULMAN, HENRY. Non-Juror to Oath of Allegiance, 1778. (A-1/18)

PAULTON, HUGH. Enlisted in Baltimore County on July 20, 1776. (H-52)

PAYNE, JOHN. Oath of Allegiance in 1778 before Hon. James Calhoun. Served as Matross
in Capt. Dorsey's MD Artillery at Camp Col. Scirvins on January 28, 1782, and with
Capt. J. Smith's MD Artillery between 1780 and 1783. He was reported deceased as of
May 22, 1783, by Capt. Smith. (H-579, UU-232, YYY-2/32, A-2/41)

PAYNE (PAYN), MICHALE (MICHAEL). Matross and Waggoner in Capt. Gale's MD Artillery,
1779-1780. (YYY-1/86)

PAYSON, HENRY. Baltimore Mechanical Company of Militia in 1776. Member of the Whig
Club in 1777. (CCC-26, CCC-28)

PEACH, WILLIAM. Private in Baltimore County Militia; enlisted July 5, 1776. (H-58)

PEACHAM, W. Oath of Allegiance, 1778, before Hon. Isaac Van Bibber. (A-1/18, A-2/34)

PEACOCK (PECOCK), JOHN. Oath of Allegiance, 1778, before Hon. Jesse Dorsey. (A-2/64)

PEACOCK, JOSEPH. Oath of Allegiance, 1778, before Hon. Peter Shepherd. (A-1/18, A-2/50)

PEACOCK (PECOCK), JOSHUA. Oath of Allegiance, 1778, before Hon. Jesse Dorsey. (A-2/64)

PEAKE, JOHN. Non-Juror to Oath of Allegiance in 1778. (A-1/18)

PEALE, ST. GEORGE. Lieutenant and Commissary of Military Stores in the Continental
Magazine at Baltimore, April 14, 1777. (FFF-100)

PEARCE, CHARLES. Oath of Allegiance, 1778, before Hon. William Lux. (A-2/68)

PEARCE, CHRISTOPHER. Oath of Allegiance, 1778. (A-1/18)

PEARCE, EZEKIEL. Private in Capt. Ramsey's Company No. 5 in 1776. Private in 1st MD
Regiment, December 10, 1776 to May 12, 1779; prisoner; discharged December 27, 1779.
(H-149, H-640)

PEARCE, JOHN. Oath of Allegiance, 1778, before Hon. William Lux. (A-1/18, A-2/68)

PEARCE, JOSEPH. Non-Juror to Oath of Allegiance, 1778. (A-1/18)

PEARCE, PHILLIP GRAFFORD. Oath of Allegiance, 1778, before Hon. Richard Holliday. Lieutenant in Capt. Talbott's Company, May 31, 1779. (F-301, U-90, A-1/18, A-2/60)

PEARCE, THOMAS. (Died in Baltimore County in 1846) Married Elizabeth CUMMINS on April 16, 1795. Children: Joshua; Thomas; Benjamin; William; Sarah, married to James BARTON; Mary, married to an ELLOTT; Josiah; Nathan; Rachel (born 1794) md. Edward MATTHEWS in 1819; Elizabeth, married Abraham SLADE; Isaiah; and, Dorcas, married a LEE. "Thomas Pearce" was Non-Juror to the Oath of Allegiance in 1778, and "Thomas Pierce" was a Matross in Capt. Dorsey's MD Artillery at Valley Forge, June 3, 1778. Also, "Thomas Pearce" was involved in the evaluation of Baltimore County confiscated proprietary reserve lands in 1782. (UU-231,D-5,FFF-547,A-1/18)

PEARCE, WALTER. Source A-1/18 gives two Non-Jurors in 1778 with this name. (A-1/18)

PEARCE, WILLIAM SR. (1738 - 1800, Baltimore County, MD) Married Elizabeth PUTNAM (1748-1844). Children: Joshua PEARCE (1768-1827), married Sophia WILEY (b. 1777); Thomas PEARCE (1772-1856), married (1) Elizabeth BACON (1779-1806), and (2) Mary MILLER (1767-1843); William PEARCE (1775-1835) married Ruth SPARKS; Joseph PEARCE (1781-1837), married Rachel SLADE; John Putnam PEARCE (1784-1861), married first, Belinda GORSUCH (born 1799), and (2) Elizabeth D. GRIFFIN (born 1804); and, Philip PEARCE (1785-1861), married Elizabeth GORSUCH. William PEARCE, Sr. took the Oath of Allegiance in 1778 before Hon. Richard Holliday. (D-5, A-1/18, A-2/60)

PEARSON (PIERSON), JOHN. Born 1745 in Pennsylvania. Occupation: Bricklayer. He enlisted January 26, 1776 as a Private in Capt. N. Smith's 1st Co. of Matrosses. Private in Capt. Dorsey's MD Artillery, November 17, 1777, and Bombardier in that company at Valley Forge, June 3, 1778 (name spelled "Pierson"). Height: 6' tall, which was quite tall for his day. John Pearson was a Non-Juror to the Oath of Allegiance in 1778, no doubt due to military duty. He was entitled to 50 acres in western Maryland (lot 2089) for his services as an Artillery Matross. (DDDD-29, H-564, H-566, H-574, VV-74, QQQ-2, UU-231, A-1/18)

PEARSON, THOMAS. Born 1747 in Philadelphia, PA. Occupation: Bricklayer. Enlisted January 28, 1776 as a Private in Capt. N. Smith's 1st Company of Matrosses. Was a Corporal in Capt. Dorsey's MD Artillery, November 17, 1777, and a Gunner with Capt. Gale's MD Artillery, 1779-1780 (on duty with General's Guard in 1779). He gave a deposition on enlistment terms as a matross soldier in Baltimore County on May 7, 1779. Height: 5'5½". (H-564, H-567, H-574, QQQ-2, FFF-220, YYY-1/88)

PEASLEY, DAVID. Non-Juror to Oath of Allegiance, 1778. (A-1/18)

PEASLEY, WILLIAM. Oath of Allegiance, 1778. (A-1/18)

PECK, NATHANIEL. Baltimore Mechanical Company of Militia in 1776. (CCC-28)

PECKHAM, JOHN. Lieutenant at Fell's Point in baltimore; ordered biscuits from baker Cumberland Dugan on December 3, 1777. He apparently served on board The Chester until he resigned from service on September 18, 1778. (FFF-130, GGG-207)

PECKLEY, HENRY. Ensign in Capt. Showers' Company, Upper Battalion, Baltimore County, August 30, 1777. (E-14, LL-66, BBB-350)

PELKONTON, THOMAS. Oath of Allegiance, 1778, before Hon. William Lux. (A-2/68)

PEMBERTON, HENRY. Non-Juror to Oath of Allegiance in 1778. (A-1/18)

PENEBAKER, PETER. Oath of Allegiance, 1778, before Hon. Peter Shepherd. (A-2/49)

PENN, JOHN. Oath of Allegiance, 1778, before Hon. Charles Ridgely of Wm. (A-2/28)

PENN, NATHAN. Non-Juror to the Oath of Allegiance in 1778. (A-1/18)

PENN, RESIN. Oath of Allegiance, 1778. (A-1/18)

PENNIFIELD, THOMAS. Born 1760. Married Esther BEANE in July, 1790, in Prince George's County, MD (Marriage proven through Maryland pension application.) Private in the Extra Regiment at Fort Whetstone Point in Baltimore in 1781. "Thomas Pennifield" received 100 acres (Federal Bounty Land Grant Warrant 11600) on March 11, 1791, and "Thomas Penefill" received 215 acres (Federal Bounty Land Grant Warrant 29741) and was a Revolutionary pensioner with Maryland Line and sea service. (H-626, YY-42, YY-75, YY-120)

PENNINGTON, DANIEL. Non-Juror to the Oath of Allegiance in 1778. (A-1/18)
PENNINGTON, JAMES. Non-Juror to the Oath of Allegiance in 1778. (A-1/18)
PENNINGTON, JOHN. Non-Juror to the Oath of Allegiance in 1778. (A-1/18)
PENNINGTON, WILLIAM. Non-Juror to the Oath of Allegiance in 1778. (A-1/18)
PENNYWIT, ADAM. Non-Juror to the Oath of Allegiance in 1778. (A-1/18)
PENNY, HENRY. Non-Juror to the Oath of Allegiance in 1778. (A-1/18)

PENTZ, PHILIP HENRY ("HENRY BENTZ"). (April 27, 1755, York, PA - February 25, 1810, Baltimore, MD) Married Catherine ROTHROCK (May 18, 1757, York, PA - May 3, 1841, Baltimore, MD) circa 1777 in York, PA. A son, John Joseph PEINTZ (1790-1853) md. Barbara GOULD (1795-1847) in Baltimore in 1810, and their son, William Hamilton PENTZ (1835-1909) married Virginia WILSON (1835-1919) in Baltimore in 1852. Philip Henry PENTZ was a Private in the York County Militia, and is buried in Old Zion Church in Baltimore City. (AAA-2864)

PERCIVAL, SAMUEL. Private in Capt. Smith's Company No. 8; enlisted January 27, 1776. (H-18)

PERDUE (PURDUE), LABAN. Non-Juror to Oath of Allegiance in 1778. (A-1/18)

PERDUE, WALTER. Oath of Allegiance, 1778, before Hon. Richard Holliday.(A-1/18,A-2/60)

PERDUE (PURDUE), WILLIAM. Oath of Allegiance, 1778, before Hon. John Hall. (A-2/36)

PERDUE (PURDUE), WILLIAM, JR. Non-Juror to Oath of Allegiance in 1778. (A-1/19)

PERES, ANTHONY. Seaman on ship Defence, August 9 to September 6, 1777. (H-659)

PERIN, WILLIAM. Oath of Allegiance, 1778, before Hon. William Spear. (A-1/18, A-2/67)

PERINE, ELISHA. Oath of Allegiance, 1778. (A-1/18)

PERINE, HENRY. Oath of Allegiance, 1778. (A-1/18)

PERINE, JAMES. Oath of Allegiance, 1778. (A-1/18)

PERINE, JOSEPH. Oath of Allegiance, 1778. (A-1/18)

PERINE (PERRIN), SIMON. (1738, Monmouth County, New Jersey - April 5, 1823, Baltimore County, Maryland) Son of William and Jane PERINE. Married Hannah MILLS on Jan. 3, 1768. A son, William PERINE (died 1826) married Susannah FOWLER (1780-1853), 1799. Simon's granddaughters, Micha PERINE and Sarah PERINE, are named in his will. Sarah PERINE (1812-1899) married William WONN in 1830. Simon PERINE took the Oath of Allegiance in Baltimore County in 1778 before Hon. Richard Holliday. He was called "Major" in later life, but no documentation on military service. (AAA-1488, A-2/60)

PERRIGOE, ELISHA. Non-Juror to Oath in 1778. (A-1/18; listed in source's card file only)

PERRIGOE, HENRY. Non-Juror to Oath in 1778. (A-1/18; listed in source's card file only)

PERRIGOE, JAMES. Non-Juror to Oath in 1778. (A-1/18; listed in source's card file only)

PERRIGOE, JOSEPH. Non-Juror to Oath in 1778. (A-1/18; listed in source's card file only)

PERRIGOE (PERRIGO), JOHN. Oath of Allegiance, 1778, before Hon. Thomas Sollers. (A-2/51)

PERRIGOE (PERRIGO), MOSES. Non-Juror to Oath of Allegiance in 1778. (A-1/18)
PERRIGOE (PERRIGO), NATHAN. Non-Juror to Oath of Allegiance in 1778. (A-1/18)
PERRIGOE (PERRIGO), WILLIAM. Non-Juror to Oath of Allegiance in 1778. (A-1/18)

PERRY, FRANCIS. Private in Capt. Lansdale's Company, 4th MD Regiment; enlisted on March 18, 1778; transferred to Col. Hall's Company on May 27, 1780. (H-153)

PERRY, RICHARD. Non-Juror to Oath of Allegiance in 1778. (A-1/18)

PETERS, DANIEL. Private in Capt. McClellan's Company, Baltimore Town, September 4, 1780. (CCC-25)

PETERS, GEORGE. Oath of Allegiance, 1778, before Hon. John Hall. (A-1/18, A-2/36)

PETERS, JACOB. Non-Juror to Oath of Allegiance in 1778. (A-1/18)

PETERS, NICHOLAS. Marine on ship Defence in 1777. (H-659)

PETERSON, JOSEPH. Non-Juror to Oath of Allegiance in 1778. (A-1/18)

PETTICOAT, _____ S. (part of name torn off list) Private in Baltimore County Regiment No. 7. circa 1777. (TTT-13)

PETTICOAT, HUMPHRY. Non-Juror to Oath of Allegiance in 1778. (A-1/18)

PETTICOAT (PEDDECOAT), WILLIAM. Oath of Allegiance, 1778, before Hon. Edward Cockey. (A-1/18, A-2/61)

PETTY, FRANCIS. Private in Capt. Smith's Company No. 8; enlisted Jan. 27, 1776. (H-18)

PETTY, JOHN. Non-Juror to Oath of Allegiance in 1778. (A-1/18)

PHELAN (PHILIN), JOHN. (July, 1745, Waterford, Ireland - September 14, 1827, Baltimore, Maryland) Married Mary HERON. He came to America in June, 1777, to take part in the war. He volunteered into Baltimore County Regiment No. 36 in 1777 and served through the war and was disbanded at Newburgh, New York on October 2, 1783. Also, his son, Matthew PHELAN, married Frances SCOTT. (XXX-574, TTT-13)

PHILE, JOHN. Oath of Allegiance, 1778, before Hon. William Lux. (A-1/18, A-2/68)

PHILIP, ISAAC. Non-Juror to Oath of Allegiance, 1778. (A-1/18)

PHILIP, WILLIAM. Oath of Allegiance, 1778, (A-1/18)

PHILLIPS, DAVID. Born 1752 in America. Enlisted July 7, 1776, Baltimore County, as a Private in Col. Ewing's Battalion. Height: 5'8"; short hair; pock marked. (H-55)

PHILLIPS, ELIZABETH. Revolutionary War pensioner as of June 1, 1840, aged 68, living in the household of James LEAGUE in Baltimore City, 10th Ward. (P-128)

PHILLIPS (PHILIPS), HENRY. Private in Capt. Sheaff's Company, June 16, 1777. Oath of Allegiance, 1778, before Hon. William Lux (made his mark). (W-162, A-1/18, A-2/68)

PHILLIPS (PHILIPS), JOHN. Born 1755 in Dublin, Ireland. Occupation: Labourer. Joined February 1, 1776, as Private in Capt. N. Smith's 1st Company of Matrosses. Height: 5' 6½". Reported as deserted in 1780. (H-565, H-567, H-341, QQQ-1)

PHILLIPS, JONAS. Matross in Capt. Gale's MD Artillery, 1779-1780. Entitled to fifty acres (lot 1429) in western Maryland for his services as Matross. (DDDD-30, YYY-1/90)

PHILLIPS, THOMAS. Captain of Soldiers Delight Company No. 4 on May 13, 1776 (commanded 77 Privates). Commissioned Captain in Soldiers Delight Battalion, August 30, 1777. Resigned May 27, 1779. Also, took the Oath of Allegiance in 1778 before Hon. Peter Shepherd. (FF-64, E-11, KK-66, BBB-350, GGG-422, A-1/18, A-2/49)

PHILLIPS, WILLIAM. Oath of Allegiance, 1778, before Hon. Richard Holliday. Private, Capt. Talbott's Company, May 31, 1779. (U-90, F-301, A-1/18, A-2/60)

PHILPOT, BRIAN (BRYAN). (1749 - April 11, 1812, Reisterstown, Baltimore County, MD) His death notice, and Source TT-119, state he died in 1812, while Sources JJJ-533 and XXX-576 state it was 1811. Also, Source TT-119 states he was born August 9, 1756, while sources JJJ-533 and XXX-576 state 1749. Source ZZZ-253 states he left a wife and six children at his death on April 11, 1812. His wife was Elizabeth JOHNSON (Source JJJ-533 states it was Elizabeth JOHNS, which is incorrect) Marriage proven through Maryland pension application, and Robert Barnes' Maryland Marriages, 1778-1800, page 177, as occurring in Baltimore County on November 16, 1796 (YY-121). Brian PHILPOT was an Ensign in Capt. Smith's Company No. 8, January 2, 1776, and in Smallwood's MD Regiment on January 14, 1776. He took the Oath of Allegiance in 1778 before Hon. Jeremiah Johnson. On June 25, 1781, he is among those serving in Capt. Nicholas Ruxton Moore's Troops; he rode a nine year old dark bay mare. On Sept. 9, 1781, he was selected to assist in looking after the comfort and subsistence of Count Rochambeau in Baltimore. He was a member of the Society of the Cincinnati of Maryland, currently represented by Blanchard Randall (President of the Maryland Society, 1952-60). (OOC-18, TT-119, JJJ-533, XXX-576, BBBB-313, H-17, B-440, A-2/33)

PHILPOT, JOHN. Represented Upper Back River Hundred at the Association of Freemen on Aug. 21, 1775. Ensign, Capt. Sterrett's Co., Baltimore Town, Battn., Aug. 30, 1777. Oath of Allegiance, 1778, before Hon. James Calhoun.(EEEE-1726,BBB-351,E-13,A-2/39)

PHINNIMORE, JOHN. Enlisted in Baltimore County on July 20, 1776. (H-53)

PHIPPS, JAMES. Oath of Allegiance, 1778, before Hon. Peter Shepherd. (A-1/18, A-2/49)

PICKARD, JOHN. Non-Juror to Oath of Allegiance, 1778. (A-1/18)

PICKARD, WILLIAM. Non-Juror to Oath of Allegiance, 1778. (A-1/18)

PICKED, CHARLES. Oath of Allegiance, 1778. (A-1/19)

PICKETT, WILLIAM. Oath of Allegiance, 1778, before Hon. Edward Cockey. (A-1/18, A-2/61)

PICKRON, JOHN. Oath of Allegiance, 1778, before Hon. James Calhoun. (A-2/65)

PICKSLER, JACOB. Non-Juror to Oath of Allegiance, 1778. (A-1/18)

PIERCY, WILLIAM. Yeoman on ship Defence, 1776, and Midshipman, 1777. (H-606, H-659)

PIERLY, CONRAD. Non-Juror to Oath of Allegiance, 1778. (A-1/19)

PIERLY, LODOWICK. Non-Juror to Oath of Allegiance, 1778. (A-1/19)

PIERPOINT, CHARLES SR. Non-Juror to Oath of Allegiance, 1778. (A-1/19)

PIERPONT, JOHN. Non-Juror to Oath of Allegiance, 1778. (A-1/19)

PIERPONT, JOSEPH. Non-Juror to Oath of Allegiance, 1778. (A-1/19)

PIKE, JOHN. Marine on ship Defence, January 21 to December 31, 1777. (H-659)

PIKE, JOHN. Maryland Line defective, Oct., 1780; resident of Baltimore County. (H-414)

PIKE, MATTHEW. Non-Juror to Oath of Allegiance, 1778. (A-1/19)

PILASH, JOSEPH. Oath of Allegiance, 1778. (A-1/19)

PILL, GEORGE. Non-Juror to Oath of Allegiance, 1778. (A-1/19)

PILLER, JAMES. Private in Baltimore Artillery Company, October 16, 1775. (G-8)

PIMBARTON, HENRY JR. Oath of Allegiance, 1778, before Hon. Edward Cockey. (A-2/61)

PINDELL, JOHN SR. (1718-1789) Son of Philip PINDELL and Elizabeth HOLLAND. His paternal grandfather was Thomas PINDELL (died 1710) of Prince George's County, MD; his maternal grandparents were Otho HOLLAND and Mehitabel LARKIN of Londontown, Anne Arundel County MD. John PINDELL purchased land in Baltimore County in 1744. The register of Saint Thomas Church indicates he married twice: (1) Eleanor BOND (died 1756), and they had Elizabeth (born 1749), Philip (born 1752), and John (1754-1817); and, (2) Eleanor GILL (died 1795), and they had: Catherine (born 1759) married Edward BOND in 1778; Mary (born 1761); Thomas (1763-1793), married Margaret GORSUCH in 1790; Sarah (born 1765) married Christopher BOND in 1787; Eleanor, married William CONOVER in 1785; John Larkin, married Susannah LOUDERMAN in 1791; Charles Ridgely, married Mary LAUDAMAN in 1800; and, Joshua, married Catherine WALKER in 1803. (Source JJJ-536 erroneously says John, Sr. was born in 1735.) John PINDELL, Sr. took the Oath of Allegiance in 1778 before Hon. Edward Cockey. (A-1/19, A-2/61, and information on the Pindell family provided by Alan Virta of Hyattsville, Maryland, 1988)

PINDELL, JOHN. Oath of Allegiance, 1778, before Hon. Richard Holliday. (A-1/19, A-2/60)

PINDELL, PHILIP. Oath of Allegiance, 1778, before Hon. Richard Holliday. Served as a 1st Lieutenant in Capt. Kelly's Company, Gunpowder Upper Battalion, Oct. 23, 1781. (A-1/19, A-2/60, AAAA-650, and information from Alan Virta of Hyattsville, MD, 1988)

PINE, FREDERICK. Enlisted May 29, 1776 as Private in Capt. N. Smith's 1st Company of Matrosses; at Fort Whetstone Point in Baltimore, September 7, 1776. Was Private in Captain Dorsey's MD Artillery, November 17, 1777, and matross with that company at Valley Forge, June 3, 1778. (UU-231, H-568, H-569, H-574, VV-74, QQQ-2)

PINES, CHARLES. Non-Juror to Oath of Allegiance in 1778. (A-1/19)

PINES, WILLIAM. Non-Juror to Oath of Allegiance in 1778. (A-1/19)

PINGLE, PETER. Oath of Allegiance, 1778, before Hon. James Calhoun. (A-1/19, A-2/42)

PINSIL (PENSIL), BALSER. Private in Capt. McClellan's Co., September 4, 1780. (CCC-24)

PINSIL (PANSIL), JOHN. Private in capt. Cox's Company, December 19, 1776, and Private in Capt. McClellan's Company, September 4, 1780. (CCC-21, CCC-24)

PIPER, WILLIAM. Oath of Allegiance, 1778, before Hon. James Calhoun. (A-1/19, A-2/40)

PITSLAND, RICHARD. Born in 1748 in South Carolina. Occupation: Labourer. Enlisted as Private in Captain N. Smith's 1st Company of Matrosses on February 3, 1776. Served as Private in Captain Dorsey's Maryland Artillery, November 17, 1777, and reported "sick in the country with bilious fever." (H-574, H-565, H-567, VV-73, QQQ-2)

PITTS, JOHN. Oath of Allegiance, 1778, before Hon. Edward Cockey. (A-1/19, A-2/61)

PITTS, LOUIS (LEWIS). Non-Juror to Oath of Allegiance, 1778. Involved in evaluation of Baltimore County confiscated proprietary lands in 1782. (FFF-543, A-1/19)

PLATT, JAMES. Non-Juror to Oath of Allegiance in 1778. (A-1/19)

PLOWMAN, EDWARD. Oath of Allegiance, 1778, before Hon. James Calhoun. (A-2/42)

PLOWMAN, JAMES. Non-Juror to Oath of Allegiance, 1778. (A-1/19)
PLOWMAN, JOHN. Non-Juror to Oath of Allegiance, 1778. (A-1/19)

PLOWMAN, JONATHAN. Merchant of Baltimore Town. Married Rebecca ARNOLD, eldest daughter of David ARNOLD, on October 7, 1762 in Calvert County, MD. Jonathan PLOWMAN took the Oath of Allegiance in 1778 before Hon. James Calhoun in Baltimore. (UUU-146, A-2/42)

PLOWMAN, RICHARD. Oath of Allegiance, 1778, before Hon. James Calhoun. Served as Ensign in Capt. Kelly's Co., Soldiers Delight Battn., Feb. 7, 1782. (CCCC-71, A-2/42)

PLUM, WILLIAM. Non-Juror to Oath of Allegiance, 1778. (A-1/19)

PLUMLY, JACOB. Pirvate in Capt. Smith's Company No. 8; enlisted Jan. 27, 1776. (H-18)

PLUNKET, DAVID. "Mr. Plunket was an active partizan officer, and had been in several battles. He was by birth an Irish gentleman, and the elder brother of the present Lord Plunket, late the chancellor of Ireland. He was the person employed by the (Baltimore) committee of 1776, to wait on congress, to receive from them the in- struction that might be given repsecting the seizure of the person of Gov. Eden." (HHH-105) "Daviot Plunket" was a 2nd Lieutenant in Company No. 5, 1st MD Regiment, in 1776. He was lost at sea in 1793. (H-639, HHH-105)

POAGUE (POGUE), JOSEPH. Matross in Capt. Brown's MD Artillery; joined Nov. 22, 1777. Was at Valley Forge until June, 1778; at White Plains, July, 1778; at Ft. Schuyler, August and September, 1780; at High Hills of the Santee, August, 1781; at Camp Col. Scirvins, January, 1782; and at Bacon's Bridge, S.C., April, 1782. (UU-228, UU-230)

POCOCK, DANIEL. Non-Juror to Oath of Allegiance, 1778. (A-1/19)

POCOCK, GEORGE. Private in Col. Aquila Hall's Baltimore County Regt., 1777. (TTT-13)

POCOCK, JAMES. Non-Juror to Oath of Allegiance, 1778. (A-1/19)

POCOCK, JOHN. (Died in Baltimore County in 1791) May have married Ruth GOTT in 1757. Children: Sutton, Susanne, George, Thomas, Joshua, John, Ashel, Diley and Elizabeth. Oath of Allegiance, 1778, before Hon. Jesse Bussey, according to Source D-10, but it appears that there was an error in the spelling of his name because "John Pecock", which could have been "John Pocock", took the Oath before Hon. Jesse Dorsey. (A-2/64) If such is the case, this "John Pocock" and the earlier "John Pecock" are the same.

POCOCK, JOSHUA. Oath of Allegiance, 1778. (A-1/19) This appears to have been the "Joshua Pecock" mentioned earlier in this book under "Joshua Peacock." (A-2/64)

POE, DAVID. (1742, Ireland - October 17, 1816, Baltimore, MD) Son of John POE (1698- 1756) and Janet McBRIDE (1706-1802) who came to America from Ireland circa 1743. David POE married Elizabeth CAIRNS (CAIRNES), 1755-1835), of Lancaster, PA. Their children: David POE, Jr. (died 1811) married Eliza HOPKINS (1792-1822) and their son, Edgar Allan POE (1809-1849), famous American short story writer, married to Virginia CLEMM (cousin); Eliza Hopkins POE married (2) Henry HERRING (1793-1870) in 1813; and, Maria POE, daughter of David, married William CLEMM, Jr. (1779-1826), a son of Lt. William CLEMM (1755-1809) and Catharina SCHULTZ (1759-1835), and their daughter, Virginia CLEMM, married Edgar Allan POE (1809-1849). William CLEMM, Jr.'s first wife was Harriet POE (1785-1816), daughter of Capt. George POE (1743-1823) and Catharine DAWSON (1742-1806). Capt. George POE was a brother of this David POE, Sr. David POE served in the Baltimore Mechanical Company of Militia on November 4, 1775. He was Sergeant in Capt. Cox's Company, December 19, 1776, and was appointed Asst. Quartermaster at Baltimore, November 19, 1777, and Quartermaster on April 8, 1778. He took the Oath of Allegiance in 1778 before Hon. James Calhoun. He was Chairman of the Whig Club in 1777. He was 2nd Lieutenant in the Baltimore Town Battalion on

POE, DAVID (continued)

March 16, 1779, and certified as Quartermaster General on February 7, 1780. He was a Lieutenant in Capt. McClellan's Company on September 4, 1780. He was Magistrate of Baltimore City, 1779-1780. "Mr. David Poe acted as quartermaster throughout the whole of the war. He was a faithful officer, and was held in great estimation by all who had business to transact with him. Such was his devotion to his country, that it was almost proverbial; and so unabated was it, long after the peace was proclaimed, that by the public sentiment, he became a breveted general, and in his latter days, was better known as General Poe, than by any other name." (HHH-106) "David Poe, the grandfather of Edgar Allan Poe, appears to have been a fighter, as well as a man of affairs, for, after serving through the Revolutionary War, a close friend of George Washington, we see his name again on the roll of officers in the Maryland Militia at the outbreak of the Second War with England." (CCC-14) David Poe also served in the War of 1812 just mentioned, having enlisted in 1814 at the age of 72. His death notice in 1816 states he had been a resident of Baltimore for the last 40 years, and a native of Ireland, active in the American Revolution. (ZZZ-256) On February 9, 1822, it was ordered to "pay to Elizabeth POE, of Baltimore, a sum of money equal to half pay of a Captain of the Maryland Line." (C-382, AAA-847, F-299, F-311, F-313, CCC-21, CCC-23, CCC-25, CCC-26, GGG-529, YY-42, FFF-268, HHH-106, ZZZ-256, CCC-14, and A-1/19, A-2/38, plus Francis B. Culver's "Lineage of Edgar Allan Poe," in Maryland Historical Magazine, Vol. 37, No. 4, December, 1942, pages 420-422) It should also be noted that Sources B-444 and TT-119 incorrectly give his year of death as 1820.)

POE, EDWARD. Non-Juror to the Oath of Allegiance in 1778. (A-1/19)

POE, GEORGE. (c1741/1743, Ireland - August 20, 1823, Walkersville, Frederick County, Maryland) Son of John POE and Janet McBRIDE, and brother of David POE. He married Catharine DAWSON in 1774; she was born in 1742 and died in Havre de Grace, Harford County, MD, in 1806. Children: Jacob POE (1775-1860) married Bridget Amelia Fitzgerald KENNEDY (1775-1844) in 1803; George POE (born 1778); Harriet POE (1785-1816) married William CLEMM, Jr. (1779-1826) and their daughter Josephine Emily CLEMM (1810-1889) married Neilson POE (1809-1884) who was a son of Harriet's brother, Jacob POE; and, Stephen POE (died in infancy). George POE was a Private in Captain Cox's Baltimore Company, December 19, 1776, and Sergeant in Capt. McClellan's Co., September 4, 1780, although Source MMM-A states he was a Captain as of June 11, 1776 in the 34th Battalion of Frederick County, MD. Also, Source RRR-6 states that he was Wagonmaster for the Baltimore Town Committee in 1780. (CCC-21, CCC-23, RRR-6, JJJ-539, XXX-580, MMM-A, ZZZ-256, and Md. Hist. Mag., Vol. 37, No. 4, Dec., 1942, Pages 420-422) George Poe also took the Oath of Allegiance in 1778 before the Hon. James Calhoun in Baltimore. (A-1/19, A-2/38)

POE, JOHN. Born 1754 in America. Enlisted in Baltimore County Mechanical Company of Militia, November 4, 1775. On July 7, 1776 he enlisted as 1st Sergeant in Colonel Ewing's Battalion. Height: 5'8"; long black hair. He took the Oath of Allegiance, 1778, before Hon. George Lindenberger. (A-1/19, A-2/54, F-299, H-54)

POE, JOSEPH. Non-Juror to the Oath of Allegiance, 1778. (A-1/19)

POE, WILLIAM. Private in Capt. McClellan's Company, September 4, 1780. (CCC-24)

POLAMUS (POLEMUS), JOSEPH. Private in Capt. Howell's Company, December 30, 1775. He was a member of the 4th MD Line (Invalid), transferred May 27, 1778, and in service at the Garrison of Philadelphia on June 19, 1781. (G-11, H-623)

POLAND, WILLIAM. Marine on ship Defence, April 1 to December 31, 1777. (H-659)

POLK, JOSIAH. He corresponded with Major Nathaniel Smith about the relocation of artillery for the defence of Baltimore City in 1777. (FFF-81)

POLLARD, WILLIAM. Oath of Allegiance, 1778, before Hon. James Calhoun. (A-2/65)

POLLICE, MARTIN. Non-Juror to Oath of Allegiance, 1778. (A-1/19)

POLLY, CHRISTOPHER. Non-Juror to Oath of Allegiance, 1778. (A-1/19)

POMPHREY, JOSHUA. Private, Capt. McClellan's Company, September 4, 1780. (CCC-24)

PONABAKER, WILLIAM. Private, Baltimore County Regiment No. 15, circa 1777. (TTT-13)

POOL, BASIL. Non-Juror to Oath of Allegiance in 1778. (A-1/19)

POOL (POOLE), JOHN. Oath of Allegiance, 1778, before Hon. Jesse Bussey. (A-2/44)

POOL, MATTHEW. Non-Juror to Oath of Allegiance, 1778. (A-1/19)
POOL, PETER. Non-Juror to Oath of Allegiance, 1778. (A-1/19)
POOL, RICHARD. Non-Juror to Oath of Allegiance, 1778. (A-1/19)

POOL, WILLIAM. Oath of Allegiance, 1778, before Hon. James Calhoun. (A-1/19, A-2/41)

POORE, JOHN. Private in Capt. Dorsey's MD Artillery Company, November 17, 1777, and reported as convalescent ("sore leg"). (H-618)

POPHAM, FRANCIS. Matross in Capt. Brown's MD Artillery; joined November 22, 1777. Was at Valley Forge until June, 1778; at White Plains, July, 1778; at Ft. Schuyler, August and September, 1780; reported "killed at Augusta" (no date given, but it may have been during the September 14 to 18, 1780 attack--Ed.Note) Francis POPHAM was entitled to 50 acres (lot 487) in western Maryland. (UU-228, UU-230, DDDD-30)

PORKAPINE, CHRISTOPHER. Non-Juror to Oath of Allegiance, 1778. (A-1/19)

PORKAPINE, WILLIAM. Oath of Allegiance, 1778. (A-1/19)

PORM, REZIN. Oath of Allegiance, 1778, before Hon. Charles Ridgely of William.(A-2/27)

PORTER, ANDREW DR. (Of Baltimore Town) "Applicant for surgeoncy to the MD Council and recommended by Dr. Wiesenthal in 1776; shortly thereafter approved by the MD Council (and) applicant for the post of Dr. Morrow who had left the American forces for Philadelphia to join the British." (XX-12)

PORTER, CHARLES. Oath of Allegiance, 1778, before Hon. Edward Cockey.(A-1/19, A-2/61)

PORTER, DANIEL. Non-Juror to Oath of Allegiance, 1778. (A-1/19)

PORTER, DAVID. (Died June 24, 1808 in New Orleans, LA) Baltimore Privateer and Naval Captain. On October 20, 1777 he commanded the sloop Delight, owned by Hugh Young & Company of Baltimore, mounting six guns. (III-206, UUU-147, ZZZ-257)

PORTER, JAMES. Oath of Allegiance, 1778, before Hon. Hercules Courtenay. (A-2/37)

PORTER, JOHN. (1737, Baltimore County, MD - 1810, Allegany County, MD) Married Ann MACKENZIE (1744-1788). Their children: Michael PORTER (born 1763) married Jane POND; Samuel PORTER (born 1765) married Sarah PORTER; Thomas PORTER (born 1767) married Susannah PORTER; Henry PORTER (born 1771) married Margaret_____; Moses PORTER (born 1773) married Rachel_____; Gabriel Mackenzie PORTER (born 1776) married Rebecca FROST; John PORTER (born 1783) married Catherine GLISSON; and Elloner PORTER (born 1786) married John MATTINGLY. John PORTER served in Capt. Pacton's Militia, Bedford County, PA. "He bought a farm believed to be in Maryland, but when the dividing line (Mason-Dixon Line) was fixed between Maryland and Pennsylvania, his farm was in Pennsylvania, so he sold it and bought a farm in Maryland." (XXX-584)

PORTER, JOSHUA. (1742 - 1811) Married Rosanna SHIPLEY. 1st Lieutenant in Soldiers Delight Company No. 3, May 13, 1776 to at least 1779. (FF-64, E-11, JJJ-542) Was a Non-Juror to the Oath of Allegiance in 1778 (probably due to military duty)(A-1/19)

PORTER, PERRY (OF NATHANIEL). Oath of Allegiance, 1778. (A-1/19)

PORTER, PETER. Non-Juror to Oath of Allegiance in 1778. (A-1/19)
PORTER, PHILIP. Non-Juror to Oath of Allegiance in 1778. (A-1/19)
PORTER, RICHARD. Non-Juror to Oath of Allegianc in 1778. (A-1/19)

PORTER, ROBERT. (1757, Baltimore County, MD - March 16, 1810, Baltimore, MD) Married Susannah BUCK (1772-1845). Their son, James PORTER (1797-1843) married Elizabeth Francis TODD (1809-1861) in 1829, and their daughter, Susannah Francis PORTER (1832-1911) married Jacob Wever HOUCK (1822-1888) in 1852. Robert PORTER lived in Back River Neck at "Porter's Bar." He was a 1st Lieutenant in the 3rd MD Regiment from February 20, 1777 (commissioned) to April 17, 1777 (resigned). (AAA-639, JJJ-542)

PORTER, THOMAS. Private in Extra Regt., Fort Whetstone Point, Baltimore, 1781. (H-627)

PORTER, WILLIAM. Sailor on ship _Defence_, 1777. (H-659)

PORTER, WILLIAM. Marine on ship _Defence_, 1777. (H-659)

PORTS (PORT), PHILIP. (Died in Baltimore County in 1810) Wife named Elizabeth Margaret. Children: John (1772-1854) married Catherine WENTZ in 1798; Adam; Jacob; Magdeline md. Francis Loutenschlager; Ann Mary (born 1766) married John BROWN; and Philip, married Anna HAYS in 1801. Philip PORTS was a Non-Juror to the Oath, 1778. (D-10, A-1/19)

PORTTEUS, ROBERT. On May 6, 1776 and June 22, 1776, he requested a commission in Baltimore County. On July 16, 1776 he was 3rd Lieutenant in Capt. N. Smith's 1st Company of Matrosses. (FFF-33, FFF-38, FFF-43, ZZ-61)

POTTER, ANTHONY. Private in Capt. Howell's Company, December 30, 1775. Private in Col. Ewing's Battalion, having enlisted in Baltimore County, July 7, 1776.(G-11,H-55)

POTTER, JOHN. Non-Juror to Oath of Allegiance, 1778. (A-1/19)

POTTER, THOMAS. Fifer in Capt. Gale's MD Artillery, 1779-1780. Fifer in Capt. Smith's MD Artillery, 1780-1783. (H-578, YYY-1/91, YYY-2/33)

POTTS, THOMAS. Private in Capt. Lansdale's Company, 4th MD Regiment; Waggoner in Wilmington; Corporal, June 1, 1778; "not heard of" after September, 1779. (H-153)

POUDER, JACOB LEONARD. (1730, on the high seas on the way to America - 1796, Baltimore (now Carroll) County, Maryland) Son of John Jacob POUDER and Miss LEONARD. Married Margaret BOONE (born 1744) circa 1760. Their son, Leonard POUDER, Sr. (1767-1833), married Elizabeth CRUSE (1777-1845), and their grandson George POUDER (1793-1837), married Mary FOWBLE (1798-1820) in 1816. Jacob POUDER was an Ensign in the 9th PA Battalion, Lancaster County, PA, through 1783. He is buried on the original Pouder farm (called "The Spinning Wheel") on New Windsor Road and Pipe Creek in Carroll Co. MD. (AAA-1136, and _PA Archives_, 5th Series, Vol. 7, pp. 906, 934, 954, 964)

POWELL, BENJAMIN. Non-Juror to Oath of Allegiance, 1778. (A-1/19)

POWELL, GILES. Recruit in Baltimore County in 1780. (H-340)

POWELL, JOHN. Matross in Capt. Gale's MD Artillery, 1779-1780. (YYY-1/92)

POWELL, SAMUEL. Enlisted at Fort Whetstone Point in Baltimore on October 2, 1779, and deserted "about the last of November, 1779." (H-626)

POWER, JOHN. Born 1739 in Ireland. Occupation: Bricklayer. Enlisted January 24, 1776 as Private in Capt. N. Smith's 1st Company of Matrosses. Private in Capt. Dorsey's MD Artillery; sick, November 17, 1777. Height: 5'8". (H-566, H-574, H-563, QQQ-2)

POWER, JOHN. Marine on ship _Defence_ in 1777. (H-659)

POWLET, SEVERN. Served on ship _Defence_, June 3 to July 23, 1777. (H-659)

PRATT, EDWARD. Ensign in Capt. Ewing's Company No. 4, Smallwood's MD Regiment, from January 3, 1776 to November, 1776. (H-11, B-450)

PRATT, ROGER H. Oath of Allegiance, 1778, before Hon. James Calhoun. (A-1/19, A-2/42)

PRATT, SARAH. Submitted her account and receipt for stockings and blankets for Lieut. Nathaniel Bond in Baltimore, 1777. (FFF-80)

PRATTEN, JOHN. Recruit in Baltimore County in 1780. (H-340)

PRATTEN, THOMAS. Oath of Allegiance, 1778, before Hon. George Lindenberger. (A-2/54)

PRESBURY, GEORGE GOULDSMITH. Recommended to be Quartermaster of Gunpowder Battalion, June, 1777. Justice of the Peace in Baltimore county, and one of the Magistrates who administered the Oath of Allegiance, 1778. (X-111, GGG-242, A-1/19, A-2/48)

PRESBURY, GEORGE GOULDSMITH JR. Oath of Allegiance, 1778, before Hon. George Gouldsmith Presbury (his father). "George G. Presbury, of Middle River Neck, died in October, 1810, age 51." (ZZZ-260, A-1/19. A-2/48)

PRESS, HENRY. Oath of Allegiance, 1778, before Hon. George Lindenberger. (A-2/54)

PRESTMAN (PRESSTMAN), GEORGE. Private in Baltimore Artillery Company, October 16, 1775. Private in Capt. Sheaff's Company, June 16, 1777. Oath of Allegiance in 1778 before Hon. William Lux. (G-8, W-162, A-1/19, A-2/69)

PRESTON, THOMAS. Private in Capt.Deams' Company, 7th MD Regiment, Dec. 10, 1776. Non-Juror to Oath of Allegiance in 1778. (H-304, A-1/19)

PRESTON, WILLIAM. Private in Capt. Ewing's Company No. 4 in 1776 (and subsequently deserted). Non-Juror to Oath of Allegiance in 1778. (H-13, A-1/19)

PREW, WILLIAM. Ship's Steward on ship Defence, July 9 to December 31, 1777. (H-659)

PRIBBLE, THOMAS JR. (1760, Baltimore County, MD - December 20, 1836, Wood County, VA (now West Virginia) Son of Thomas PRIBBLE and Elizabeth TEAGARDEN. He married Hannah ENOCH (1766-1846), daughter of Col. Henry and Sarah ENOCH, in 1784 at Red Stove Fork in Greene County, PA. They moved to Virginia from Pennsylvania in 1796. Their children: Elizabeth PRIBBLE (1785-1848) married James FOUGHT; Abram PRIBBLE (1788-1825) married Ann BUTCHER in 1823; Mary PRIBBLE (1791-1861) married Joshua DARNELL; Hiram PRIBBLE (1793-1887) married Debora BUTCHER in 1828; Hugh PRIBBLE (1796-1873) married Elizabeth Permelia JACKSON; Armanelah PRIBBLE (1798-1887) md. John FOSTER; Nancy PRIBBLE (1800-1877) married Thomas PICKERING; Hedgeman PRIBBLE (1802-1890) married Priscilla DEVAUGHN; Daniel PRIBBLE (1804-1874) married Amanda M. JACKSON; and, Thomas PRIBBLE, Jr. (1806-1840) married Delila WALKER. (Ed.Note: Although Thomas Pribble, Jr. was the son of Thomas Pribble, Jr., Thomas Pribble the Revolutionary soldier was actually Thomas Pribble III and his son was IV in a long line of Thomas Pribbles.) He served as a Spy in Pennsylvania. (AAA-2521, JJJ-548, and information from Barrett L. McKown of Edgewater, MD, 1987, a direct descendant)

PRICE, ABSALOM. 1st Lieutenant in Baltimore Town Battalion, May 6, 1778. Took Oath of Allegiance, 1778, before Hon. George Lindenberger. (WW-467, A-1/19, A-2/55)

PRICE, AMON. Non-Juror to Oath of Allegiance, 1778. (A-1/19)

PRICE, BENJAMIN. Non-Juror to Oath of Allegiance, 1778. (A-1/19)

PRICE, EDWARD. Private in Capt. Ewing's Company No. 4; enlisted May 18, 1776. (H-11)

PRICE, GEORGE. Enlisted in Baltimore County on July 25, 1776. (H-52)

PRICE, HENRY. Marine on ship Defence, May 21 to December 31, 1777. (H-659)

PRICE, JAMES. Non-Juror to Oath of Allegiance, 1778. (A-1/19)

PRICE, JOHN. Private in Capt. Ewing's Company No. 4; enlisted Jan. 29, 1776. (H-12)

PRICE, JOHN. Private in Count Pulaski's Legion; enlisted in Baltimore, May 6, 1778. (H-593)

PRICE, JOHN. Source A-1/19 lists three Non-Jurors in 1778 with this name.

PRICE, JOHN JR. Non-Juror to Oath of Allegiance, 1778. (A-1/19)

PRICE, JOHN MORDECAI. Non-Juror to Oath of Allegiance, 1778. (A-1/19)

PRICE, MERRYMAN. Non-Juror to Oath of Allegiance, 1778. (A-1/19)

PRICE, MORDECAI. Source A-1/19 lists two Non-Jurors in 1778 with this name.

PRICE, MORDECAI. Private in Col. Aquila Hall's Baltimore County Regt., 1777. (TTT-13)

PRICE, MOSES. Non-Juror to Oath of Allegiance, 1778. (A-1/19)

PRICE, PETER. Oath of Allegiance, 1778, before Hon. James Calhoun. (A-1/19, A-2/40)

PRICE, ROBERT. Private in Capt. Deams' Co., 7th MD Regt., January 1, 1777. (H-305)

PRICE, SAMUEL. Source A-1/19 lists two Non-Jurors in 1778 with this name.

PRICE, STEPHEN. SOurce A-1/19 lists two Non-Jurors in 1778 with this name.

PRICE, STEPHEN JR. Non-Juror to Oath of Allegiance in 1778. (A-1/19)

PRICE, THOMAS. Private in Capt. Furnival's MD Artillery, November 17, 1777. Took the Oath of Allegiance in 1778 before Hon. James Calhoun. (H-573, A-1/19, A-2/40)

PRICE, THOMAS (OF BENJAMIN). Non-Juror to Oath of Allegiance, 1778. (A-1/19)

PRICE, VEAZY. Non-Juror to Oath of Allegiance, 1778. (A-1/19)

PRICE, WILLIAM. Two men with this name took the Oath of Allegiance in 1778: one before Hon. George Lindenberger, and one before Hon. Edward Cockey. (A-2/54, A-2/61). Yet, Source A-1/19 lists them as taking the Oath, but the corresponding card file for it states they were Non-Jurors. Also, Source QQ-117 states they took the Oath in 1781.

PRIMROSE, DAVID. Able Seaman on ship <u>Defence</u>, September 19, 1776, and Sailor in 1777. (H-606, H-659)

PRINCE, WILLIAM. Marine on ship <u>Defence</u> in 1777. (H-659)

PRINGLE, MARK. Served on Baltimore Salt Committee, October 14, 1779. Signed letter to Governor Lee on April 4, 1781, asking for the militia to protect Baltimore from the British. He was Cornet in Capt. Nicholas Ruxton Moore's Troops on June 25, 1781 and had two horses: a 12 year old bay gelding, and a 14 year old bay gelding.   "Mark PRINGLE, merchant, and Miss Lucy STITH, both of Baltimore, were married July 6, 1797 by Rev. Mr. Ireland, at 'Willow Brook', the seat of Thorowgood SMITH." (ZZZ-261,S-49, HHH-88, BBBB-313)

PRIOR, SIMON. 1st Lieutenant in Baltimore County Militia Company No. 6, Dec. 19, 1775. Captain in Gunpowder Battalion, August 30, 1777, "Capt. Cromwell having resigned." Served through at least 1778. (E-11. AA-65, BBB-350, G-10)

PRIOR, WILLIAM. Private in Capt. Lansdale's Company, 4th MD Regiment, from May 30, 1777 to November 1, 1780. (H-153)

PRITCHARD, CHARLES. Private in Capt. Ewing's Company No. 4; enlisted May 24, 1776.(H-11) "Charles PITCHED" signed Oath of Allegiance, 1778, before Hon. Peter Shepherd.(A-2/49)

PRITCHARD, WILLIAM. Non-Juror to Oath of Allegiance, 1778. (A-1/19)

PROCTOR, JOHN. Private in Baltimore Artillery Company, October 16, 1775. Private in Capt. Sheaff's Company, June 16, 1777. Oath of Allegiance, 1778, before Hon. William Lux. (G-8, W-162, A-1/19. A-2/66)

PROCTOR, JONATHAN. Oath of Allegiance, 1778, before Hon. George Gouldsmith Presbury. Could not write; made his mark (" ⊘ "). (A-1/19, A-2/48)

PROCTOR, JOSEPH. Private in Capt. Graybill's German Regiment in 1776. (H-265)

PROCTOR, THOMAS. Born 1756 in America. Enlisted July 7, 1776, Baltimore County, as a Private in Col.Ewing's Battalion. Height: 5'5¼"; sandy hair. (H-55)

PROSSER, CHARLES. Non-Juror to Oath of Allegiance, 1778. (A-1/19)
PROSSER, ISAAC. Non-Juror to Oath of Allegiance, 1778. (A-1/19)

PROUT (PROUTE), JOHN. Matross in Capt. Gale's MD Artillery; appointed September 3, 1779 and on furlough in November, 1779. Matross in Capt. J. Smith's MD Artillery, 1780 to 1782, then with Capt. Dorsey's MD Artillery at Camp Col.Scirvins on January 28, 1782, and then back with Capt. Smith in 1782 and 1783. Entitled to 50 acres (lot 2534) in western Maryland. (DDDD-30, H-579, UU-232, YYY-1/93, YYY-2/34)

PUGH, HUGH. Private in Capt. Ewing's Company No. 4; enlisted on January 29, 1776, and subsequently deserted. (H-12)

PULASKI, CASIMIR. Polish Count. Brigadier General in Continental Army, and Chief of Dragoons, September 15, 1777. Designated as Commander of an independent corps known as the Pulaski Legion, March 28, 1778. He wrote to the Governor of Maryland and re- quested aid in setting up headquarters in Baltimore City on April 4, 1778. He had served at Brandywine and had been in charge of all the American cavalry by order of Congress, but resigned that post to form his own legion mixed with cavalry as well as infantry. Men from Baltimore served in his Legion. They fought at the Battle of Germantown, and in February, 1779, Washington sent Pulaski and his men south to serve with Gen. Benjamin Lincoln's army. Pulaski died October 11, 1779 of wounds received on October 9, 1779, while leading a part of Lincoln's unsuccessful assault on the city of Savannah, Georgia. (B-454, H-591, H-594, FFF-156, and David Brownell's 1982 booklet entitled <u>Heroes of the American Revolution</u>, page 35) Ed.Note: Part of the Route 40 highway in eastern Baltimore County was named Pulaski Hwy. in his honor.

PUMPHRY, JNO. Private in Capt. Deams' Co., 7th MD Regt., January 5, 1777. (H-305)

PUNTENAY (PUNTANY), EDWARD. Enlisted in Baltimore County on July 20, 1776. Was a Non-Juror to the Oath of Allegiance in 1778. (H-52, A-1/19)

PURTLE, JOHN. Private, Capt. Ewing's Company No. 4 in 1776. (H-13)

PURVIANCE, ROBERT. (1730/1733, County Donegal, Ireland - October 9, 1806, Baltimore, Maryland) Married Frances YOUNG (1739, County Donegal, Ireland - March 3, 1821 in Baltimore) before 1763. Their children: Richard; Isaac; Mary Elizabeth; Robert; James (born 1772); Jane (born 1773); John (born 1774); Samuel (born 1775); Jane (born 1776); Hugh (born 1777, died 1797); and, Frances (1781-1843/1848) married Andrew HAZLEHURST (1781-1819) in 1805, and their son, Samuel HAZLEHURST (1814-89) married Elizabeth G. BILSON (1817-1902) in 1840. Robert PURVIANCE was in Baltimore by 1768, and rendered civil service during the Revolutionary War. He was in business with his brother Samuel in Baltimore and supplied materials during the war. He also served on the Baltimore Salt Committee, October 14, 1779. "Mr. Robert Purviance was with his brother Mr. Samuel Purviance, appointed by Congress as an agent in the management of such concerns as were entrusted to them by their legislation. These were of a most various and multilpied character, and demanded the whole time and labor of those who had charge of them. On the adoption of the Constitution of the United States, when the new government went into operation, General Washington appointed Mr. Purviance the naval officer of the port of Baltimor, and on the death of Gen. Williams, who had been at the same time appointed the collector, he made him the collector, which office he held until his death in October, 1806. I do not violate the sanctity of private correspondence, when I say, that these offices, thus bestowed, were a testimonial of approbation for revolutionary services." (HHH-106) (HHH-88, AAA-1464, ZZZ-263, JJJ-551, FFF) He also took the Oath of Allegiance in 1778 before the Honorable William Lux. (A-1/19, A-2/68)

PURVIANCE, SAMUEL JR. (September 24, 1728, Castle Finn, County Donegal, Ireland - 1788, Killed by Indians in Ohio) Brother of Robert PURVIANCE. Married Catherine STEWART (died 1781) in 1776. Their children: Isabella PURVIANCE (1779-1804) married Henry COURTENAY (1776-1854) in 1799, and their son Edward Henry COURTENAY (1803-1853) md. Virginia Pleasants HOWARD (1816-1853) in 1846; Letitia PURVIANCE (died 1802); John; John Henry; Henry; Susanna; William: and, Samuel. (Ed. Note: If Mrs. Purviance died in 1781, and she married Samuel in 1776, then she had eight children in just five years?) Samuel PURVIANCE was quite prominent during the Revolutionary War in Baltimore. In 1775, he was Chairman of the Baltimore Committee of Inspection, the Baltimore Committee of Observation, and the Baltimore Committee of Safety, and as Chairman of the latter committee he directed the arrest of Governor Eden in 1776. He was appointed Financial Agent for Congress in 1776 in Baltimore, and he also took the Oath of Allegiance in 1778 before Hon. William Lux. "Mr Samuel Purviance, Jr. of the Baltimore Committee of Correspondence, was elected Chairman, and possessing much ardor in the cause which his excellent talents enabled him to promote in an eminent manner, so continued until the new government was formed. Mr. Purviance was the writer of the greater part of the correspondence which emanated from the committee, of which he was chairman. His fate was an untimely one. In the year 1788 he was descending the Ohio, in company with several otheers, when the boat on board which he was, was captured by a band of Indians; some of the party made their escape; it was his misfortune to have been secured by his captors, and led by them into the interior of their vast wilderness. From this moment, to him, his country, his family and friends were lost forever." (SS-130, SS-131, AAA-129, AAA-786A, CC-36, EEEE-1726, RR-50, SS-136, RR-19, RR-47, FFF-31, EE-51, FF-64, ZZ-254, HHH-88, A-1/19, A-2/68)

PUSSEY, GEORGE. Non-Juror to the Oath of Allegiance in 1778. (A-1/19)

PYE, JAMES. Non-Juror to the Oath of Allegiance in 1778. (A-1/19)

PYNE, JOHN. Oath of Allegiance in 1778. (A-1/19)

Q

QUAY (QUA), JAMES. Enlisted July 7, 1776 as a Private in Col. Ewing's Battalion, in Baltimore County. Height: 5'6"; sandy hair. Entitled to 50 acres (lot 1246) in western Maryland for services as Private, 1st MD Regt. (DDDD-31, H-56)

QUAY, JAMES. Ordinary Seaman on ship Defence, April 1 to December 31, 1777. (H-659)

QUAY (QUA), SAMUEL. Born 1758 in America. Enlisted July 7, 1776, in Baltimore County, as a Private in Col. Ewing's Battalion. Height: 5'2½"; short black hair. (H-55)

QUEEN, JOSEPH. Oath of Allegiance, 1778, before Hon. James Calhoun. (A-1/19, A-2/38)

QUINE, BENJAMIN. Enlisted in Baltimore County on July 25, 1776. (H-52)

QUINN (QUIN), BARNEY. Born 1754 in Dublin, Ireland. Occupation: Labourer. Enlisted January 24, 1776 as a Private in Capt. N. Smith's 1st Company of Matrosses. Height: 5'8". (H-564, H-566, VV-74, QQQ-2)

QUINN, JOHN. Volunteer into Baltimore County Regiment No. 36, circa 1777. (TTT-13)

QUINN (QUIN), JNO. Private in Capt. Furnival's MD Artillery, November 17, 1777. Was a Matross in Capt. Gale's MD Artillery, 1779-1780; forage guard, November, 1779; sick in hospital, March, 1780. Entitled to 50 acres (lot 1500) in western Maryland for his services as Artillery Matross. (DDDD-31, H-573, YYY-1/94)

R

RABERG (RABORG), ANDREW. (September 26, 1761, Hanover, Germany - 1824, Baltimore, MD) Son of George William RABERG and Ann Marie LUCY. Married Sarah YORK (1768-1824) on November 30, 1786, and their son, Lewis RABERG (1789-1815) married Sophia RODMAN (1782-1844) in 1806, and their granddaughter, Sophia RABERG (1815-1891) married in 1836 to George Henry HALL (1811-1859). Andrew RABERG was a Private in Pennsylvania Continental Line. (AAA-1153, AAA-1565, and PA Archives, 5th Series, V. 3, p. 900)

RABORG (REBORG), CHRISTOPHER. (1745, Germany - June 17, 1815, Baltimore, Maryland) Source JJJ-553 gives his date of birth as May 3, 1750, which happens to be the same date that Source XXX-594 gives for John RABORG. And Source ZZZ-264 states that the death notice of Christopher RABORG gives his date of death as June 17, 1815 in his 70th year (residence on Water Street), and Source JJJ-553 gives that same date but Source XXX-594 states John RABORG died in Baltimore on June 13, 1815. It appears that unless John and Christopher RABORG were twins who were born and died on about the same date, there are mistakes herein, especially when Source XXX-594 states the name of John RABORG's wife is Catherine Barbara de Ormand, and Source JJJ-553 states the name of Christopher RABORG's wife is Catherine DeVorman. Errors are apparent in the DAR lineages from which this information was taken. Christopher RABORG was a Private in Capt. Cox's Baltimore Mechanical Company, December 19, 1776. Christopher REBORG took the Oath of Allegiance in 1778 before Hon. James Calhoun. Christopher REBURGH was a Private in Capt. McClellan's Company, September 4, 1780. And marriage notices show that his daughter Rachel married Jacob WAGNER of Philadelphia in 1798, and his son John RABORG married Rebecca CHANDLEY in Havre de Grace, MD in July, 1807. (ZZZ-264, ZZZ-333, JJJ-553, CCC-21, CCC-24, CCC-25, A-1/19, A-2/38)

RABORG, JOHN. (May 3, 1750, Hanover, Germany - June 13, 1815, Baltimore, MD) See the comments made above under Christopher Raborg, as there are apparent errors in dates between John and Christopher Raborg. John RABORG was a Private in Capt. James Cox's Company, Baltimore Town Battalion, 1776-1780. His son Christopher RABORG 2nd (born 1779) married Ann GODDARD in Philadelphia in 1806, and his son Samuel RABORG (born 1788) married Henrietta WINEMILLER. (ZZZ-264, XXX-594)

RABORG (REYBERG), WILLIAM. (1749, Philadelphia, PA - December 19, 1815, Baltimore, MD) He took the Oath of Allegiance in 1778 before Hon. George Lindenberger in Baltimore. (A-1/19, A-2/54, ZZZ-264)

RABORN, JOSEPH. Oath of Allegiance, 1778, before Hon. James Calhoun. (A-2/65)

RABRECK (REBOCH) CHRISTOPHER. (This may have been Christopher RABORG who served.) Baltimore Mechanical Company of Militia, November 4, 1775, lists "Christopher Reboch." "Christopehr Rebreck" of Baltimore Town supplied the province with 1,000 primer wires and brushes on July 17, 1776. (F-298, ZZ-63)

RADCLIFF, JOHN. Bombardier in Capt. Brown's MD Artillery; joined November 22, 1777. Was at Valley Forge until June, 1778; at White Plains, July, 1778; at Fort Schuyler, Aug. and Sept., 1780; Sergeant on August 1, 1781; at High Hills of the Santee, Aug. 1781; Camp Col. Scirvins, Jan., 1782; and Bacon's Bridge, S.C., April, 1782. (UU-228,UU-230)

RADFORD, WILLIAM. Sergeant of Marines on ship Defence, September 19, 1776. (H-606)

RAGAN, RODERICK. Marine on ship Defence, August 12 to October 7, 1777. (H-659)

RAGAN, TIMOTHY. Oath of Allegiance, 1778, before Hon. Edward Cockey. (A-1/19, A-2/61)

RAHM, JACOB. Oath of Allegiance, 1778, before Hon. Geo. Lindenberger. (A-1/19, A-2/54)

RAILEY (RAYLEY), BENNET. Matross in Capt. Gale's MD Artillery, 1779-1780; on command at Mount Hope. Matross in Capt. J. Smith's MD Artillery, 1780, and with Capt. Dorsey's Company at Camp. Col. Scirvins on January 28, 1782. Matross with Capt. Smith, 1783. (UU-232, H-579, YYY-1/99, YYY-2/35)

RAIN, NICHOLAS. Non-Juror to Oath of Allegiance, 1778. (A-1/19)

RAINES, HARRY. Private in Capt. J. Cockey's Baltimore County Dragoons at Yorktown in 1781. (MMM-A)

RAMMAGE, ADAM. Non-Juror to Oath of Allegiance, 1778. (A-1/19)

RAMSAY, NATHANIEL. (May 1, 1741, Lancaster County, PA - October 24, 1817, Baltimore, MD) Married (1) Margaret Jane PEALE, and (2) Charlotte HALL, daughter of Col. Aquila HALL. Nathaniel RAMSAY was a son of James RAMSAY and Jane MONTGOMERY. From his first wife he had a son, Montesquieu. Nathaniel married Charlotte HALL (1758-1838) on Jan. 7, 1790, and had a son, William White RAMSAY (born 1792) who married Eleanor Brooke HALL, and a daughter, Sophia RAMSAY, who married Daniel MCHENRY. Nathaniel RAMSAY was a Captain, Smallwood's Battalion, 1st MD Regiment, 5th Company, on January 14, 1776, and was at Fort Whetstone Point in Baltimore on July 31, 1776. He became a Lieutenant Colonel, 3rd MD Regt., December 10, 1776, and was involved in the Battles of Long Island, N.Y., Chadd's Ford and Monmouth, N.J., where he was wounded and taken prisoner on June 28, 1778. He also was at Valley Forge. He was on parole until exchanged December 14, 1780. Declared a supernumerary, he retired January 1, 1781. Pay certificate issued to him: 86509 ($1240.64); 86510 ($1000)1 86511 ($1000); 86512 ($1000); and, 86513 ($40.22) and Col. Nathaniel Ramsey of the 30th Regiment was entitled to 200 acres in western Maryland (lots 2127, 2144, 2146, 2147) for his services. He was an Original Member of the Society of the Cincinnati of Maryland in 1783. He also received Federal Bounty Land Grant Warrant 1836 for 500 acres on February 11, 1791. And, in 1782, he served on the Baltimore County Committee of Confiscated Property. He died in Baltimore on Oct. 24, 1817 (Source JJJ-555 erroneously states 1812). (TT-121, FFF-468, PP-417, H-639, UUU-149, FFF-48, B-457, YY-76, JJJ-555, DDDD-4, XXX-594, XXX-595)

RANDALL, AQUILLA SR. (May 10, 1723 - 1801) Married Margaret BROWNE. Oath of Allegiance in 1778. (JJJ-555, A-1/19)

RANDALL, AQUILA. 1st Lieutenant in Capt.R. Owings' Company of Baltimore County Marching Militia, September 17, 1777. (BBB-384)

RANDALL, BALE. Oath of Allegiance, 1778, before Hon. William Lux. (A-1/19, A-2/68)

RANDALL, BENJAMIN. Oath of Allegiance, 1778, before Hon. Edward Cockey.(A-1/19, A-2/61)

RANDALL, CHARLES. Non-Juror to Oath in 1778, but signed in 1781. (A-1/19, QQ-118)

RANDALL, CHRISTOPHER JR. (September 25, 1729, Baltimore - April 10, 1790, Baltimore) Married Elenor CAREY on May 6, 1773. Children: John (born 1774) married Caroline HILLEN; Christopher (born 1776); Maria (born 1778) married Nathan TYCON; Katherine

(born 1780); and, Margaret (born 1782) married an EVANS of Buffalo, New York. On
January 17, 1775, Christopher RANDALL, Jr. served on the Baltimore Committee of Ob-
servation. He took the Oath of Allegiance before Hon. John Moale in 1778. (A-1/19,
A-2/70, XXX-596, JJJ-555)

RANDALL, CHRISTOPHER (OF AQUILLA). Private in Baltimore County Regiment No. 15, circa
1777. Oath of Allegiance, 1778, before Hon. John Moale. (TTT-13, A-1/19, A-2/70)

RANDALL, GEORGE. 1st Lieutenant in Capt. Garretson's Company, September, 1777. It was
requested by Nathaniel Smith to Governor Lee that George remain at Fort Whetstone
Point in Baltimore on September 3, 1777. He took the Oath of Allegiance before Hon.
Charles Ridgely of William in 1778. (FFF-119, BBB-380, A-1/19, A-2/28)

RANDALL, NICHOLAS. Oath of Allegiance, 1778, before Hon. Edward Cockey. (A-1/19, A-2/61)

RANDALL, ROGER. Non-Juror to Oath of Allegiance in 1778. (A-1/19)

RANDALL, THOMAS. (Died February 27, 1795) Married margaret HUSLING. "Thomas RANDLE"
was a Private in Capt. Furnival's MD Artillery, November 17, 1777. "Thomas RANDALL"
was a Matross in Capt. Dorsey's MD Artillery at Valley Forge, June 3, 1778, and at
Camp Col. Scirvins, January 28, 1782. He served also in Capt. J. Smith's MD Artlry.
from 1780 to 1783. He was entitled to 100 acres under Federal Bounty Land Warrant
11667 on July 25, 1797. Also, depending on his military duty assignments, this
or another Thomas Randall took the Oath of Allegiance in 1778 before Hon. Robert
Simmons in Baltimore. (UU-231,UU-232,YYY-2/36,H-579,H-573,YY-76,JJJ-556,A-2/58)

RANDALL, WILLIAM. Elected to Baltimore County Committee of Observation, September 23,
1775. Took Oath of Allegiance, 1778, before Hon. Thomas Sollers. (RR-47, RR-50, SS-
136, A-1/19, A-2/51)

RANGER, JOHN. Oath of Allegiance, 1778, before Hon. James Calhoun. (A-2/65)

RANKE, JAMES. Private in Baltimore County Regiment No. 7, circa 1777. (TTT-13)

RANSHAW, BENNET. Private in Capt. McClellan's Company, Baltimore Town, September 4,
1780. (CCC-24)

RANT, JAMES. Oath of Allegiance, 1778, before Hon. James Calhoun. (A-1/19, A-2/40)

RANTER, NATHANIEL. Oath of Allegiance, 1778, before Hon. James Calhoun. (A-2/39)

RASHE, JOHN. Private in Capt. Smith's Company No. 8; enlisted Jan. 11, 1776. (H-18)

RATCLIFF, ISAIAH. Non-Juror to Oath of Allegiance, 1778. (A-1/19)

RAUCH, WILLIAM. Oath of Allegiance, 1778, before Hon. Geo. Lindenberger. (A-2/54)

RAVIN, LUKE. Non-Juror to Oath of Allegiance, 1778. (A-1/19)

RAW, W. Oath of Allegiance in 1778 before Hon. Isaac Van Bibber. (A-2/34)

RAWLINGS, AARON (OF WILLIAM). (June 28, 1738 - July 4, 1798) Married Mary SOMERS.
Private in 2nd MD Regiment, 4th Company, 1780-1783. Non-Juror to the Oath of
Allegiance in Baltimore County in 1778. (A-1/19, H-445, H-501, H-553, JJJ-557)

RAWLINGS, AARON JR. Non-Juror to Oath of Allegiance, 1778. (A-1/19)

RAWLINGS, JACOB. Enlisted in Baltimore Town on July 20, 1776. Sergeant, 4th MD Line,
March 6, 1777; reduced December 9, 1777; back to Sergeant on June 1, 1779; and was
discharged March 6, 1780. (H-53, H-158)

RAWLINGS, RICHARD. Private in Capt. John Scott's 7th Company, Maryland Line; enlisted
January 29, 1776 and discharged April 21, 1776, having been confined in guardhouse
to be discharged (reason not stated). Non-Juror to Oath, 1778. (H-16, A-1/19)

RAWLINGS (RAWLINS), WILLIAM. (1749 - August, 1812, Federal Hill, Baltimore, Maryland)
At the time of his death he left a wife and six children. He had served as a Sgt.,
Capt. Gale's MD Artillery, appointed September 3, 1779, and on command commissary
that year. Served as Sergeant in Capt. J. Smith's MD Artillery, 1780-1783, and was
Sergeant with Capt. Dorsey's MD Artillery at Camp Col. Scirvins on January 28, 1782.
(H-579, YYY-1/96, YYY-2/37, UU-232, YY-76, ZZZ-266) Non-Juror to Oath, 1778. (A-1/19)

RAWLINS (RAWLINGS), ISAAC. Commissioned 2nd Lieutenant, September 3, 1779, under the command of Lt.Col. Ed. Carrington; stationed in Baltimore on May 11, 1780. Became 2nd Lieutenant under Capt. J. Smith's MD Artillery in 1780, served with Captain Dorsey's MD Artillery in 1782, and back with Capt. Smith in 1783. He was entitled to 200 acres (lots 3184-3187) in western Maryland ("Lt. Isaac Rawling"), and also 200 acres under Federal Bounty Land Grant Warrant 1130 "Lieut. Isaac Rawlings"). Still in service as of January 1, 1783 ("2nd Lt. Isaac Rawlins") in the Artillery. (H-477, H-579, UU-232, YYY-1/95, YY-76, DDDD-4, VVV-96)

RAY, WILLIAM. Recruit in Baltimore County Militia on April 11, 1780. (H-335)

RAYBOLT, JOHN. Non-Juror to Oath of Allegiance, 1778. (A-1/19)

RAYMAN, ANTHONY. Non-Juror to Oath of Allegiance, 1778. (A-1/19)

RAYNS, PETER. Oath of Allegiance, 1778, before Hon. Jesse Dorsey. (A-2/63)

REA, GEORGE. Private in Capt. McClellan's Company, September 4, 1780. (CCC-25)

READ, JOHN. Non-Juror to Oath of Allegiance, 1778. (A-1/19)

READ, THOMAS. Commander of the brig Baltimore on April 1, 1778. (GGG-3)

READ, WILLIAM. Born 1745 in Warwickshire, England. Occupation: Stocking Weaver. Enlisted January 28, 1776 as Private in Capt. N. Smith's 1st Company of Matrosses. Height: 5' 7½". (H-564)

READING, JOHN. Private in 4th MD Regiment, April 4, 1777. Sergeant in Capt. Oldham's Company, December 8, 1779. Prisoner, August 16, 1780. (H-158)

READS, WILLIAM. Non-Juror to Oath of Allegiance, 1778. (A-1/19)

READY, JAMES. Marine on ship Defence, May 10 to December 17, 1777. (H-659)

READY, JOHN. Oath of Allegiance, 1778, before Hon. James Calhoun. (A-1/19, A-2/42)

READY, LAWRENCE. Marine on ship Defence, May 10 to December 17, 1777. (H-659)

REB, ADAM. Oath of Allegiance, 1778, before Hon. James Calhoun. (A-1/19, A-2/38)

RECHTECKER, ADAM. Non-Juror to Oath of Allegiance, 1778. (A-1/19)
RECHTECKER, JACOB. Non-Juror to Oath of Allegiance, 1778. (A-1/19)

REDDEN: See "RODDEN."

REDMAN, ELISHA. Fifer in Capt. J. Smith's MD Artillery, 1780, and then with Captain Dorsey's Company at Camp Col. Scirvins on January 28, 1782, and then back with Capt. Smith in 1782-1783. Entitled to 100 acres under Federa; Bounty Land Grant Warrant 11663 on March 22, 1797. (H-578, UU-232, YYY-2/38, YY-76)

REDMAN, THOMAS. Matross in Capt. Gale's MD Artillery, 1779-1780, and then with Capt. J. Smith's MD Artillery in 1780, and Capt. Dorsey's Company at camp Col. Scirvins on January 28, 1782, and then back to Capt. Smith in 1782 and 1783. (H-579, YYY-1/97, YYY-2/39, UU-232)

REDMILES, WILLIAM. Oath of Allegiance, 1778, before Hon. Jesse Dorsey.(A-1/19,A-2/63)

REED, EDWARD. Matross in Capt. Gale's MD Artillery, 1779-1780; "on command threshing" and "on command alarm pole" in 1779. (YYY-1/98)

REED, HUGH. Oath of Allegiance, 1778, before Hon. Jesse Dorsey. (A-1/19, A-2/63)

REED, JAMES. Private, Capt. Ewings' Company No. 4; enlisted May 3, 1776. (H-13)

REED, JOHN. Oath of Allegiance, 1778, before Hon. Jesse Dorsey, (A-1/19, A-2/63)

REED, JOSEPH. Oath of Allegiance, 1778, before Hon. Jesse Dorsey. (A-1/19, A-2/63)

REED, PATRICK. Private in Capt. Ewings' Company No. 4; enlisted Jan. 29, 1776. (H-12)

REED, THOMAS. Private in capt. Ramsey's Company No. 5 in 1776. (H-640)

REED, WILLIAM. Private in Capt. N. Smith's 1st Company of Matrosses, June 29, 1776 to

REED, WILLIAM (continued)
   1777 at Fort Whetstone Point in Baltimore. Private in Capt. Dorsey's MD Artillery,
   November 17, 1777, and with that company at Valley Forge, June 3, 1778. (UU-231,
   VV-74, H-566, H-574, QQQ-2)

REEHM (RHEEM), CHRISTOPHER. Oath of Allegiance, 1778, before Hon. William Lux. Served
   as Private in Capt. McClellan's Company, September 4, 1780. (CCC-24, A-1/19, A-2/68)

REEDY, EDWARD. Enlisted in Baltimore County on July 26, 1776. (H-53)

REES, CHRISTIAN. Private in Capt. Sheaff's Company on June 16, 1777. (W-162)

REES, DANIEL. Oath of Allegiance, 1778, before Hon. Peter Shepherd. (A-1/19, A-2/50)

REES, DAVID. Oath of Allegiance, 1778, before Hon. George Lindenberger. Signed letter
   to Governor Lee requesting the militia to protect Baltimore against British attack,
   April 4, 1781. (S-49, A-1/19, A-2/54)

REES, GEORGE. Born 1752 in Germany. Occupation: Rope Maker. Enlisted Jan. 24, 1776,
   as Private in Capt. N. Smith's 1st Company of Matrosses. Height: 5'7". In 1780 he
   supplied nails to the Baltimore Committee. (RRR-6, VV-74, H-563, H-567, QQQ-2)

REES, HENRY. Born 1737 in Germany. Occupation: Weaver. Enlisted January 24, 1776 as
   Private in Capt. N. Smith's 1st Company of Matrosses. Height: 5' 11", which was
   quite tall for his time. (H-563, H-567, QQQ-2)

REESE, ADAM. Non-Juror to the Oath of Allegiance in 1778. (A-1/19)
REESE, CHRISTOPHER. Non-Juror to oath of Allegiance, 1778. (A-1/19)

REESE, DAVID. Served with Capt. Nicholas Ruxton Moore's Troops on June 25, 1781, and
   rode an eight year old black gelding horse. (BBBB-313)

REESE, JOHN. Non-Juror to Oath of Allegiance in 1778. (A-1/19)
REEVES, JOSIAS. Non-Juror to oath of Allegiance in 1778. (A-1/19)
REEVES, THOMAS. Non-Juror to oath of Allegiance in 1778. (A-1/19)

REGELE (REGLE), CHRISTOPHER. Private, Capt. Graybill's German Regt., 1776. (H-265)

REID, JOHN. Oath of Allegiance, 1778, before Hon. Edward Cockey. (A-1/19, A-2/61)

REILLY (RIELEY), CHARLES. "Charles Rieley" was a Private in Capt. Ewing's Co. No. 4;
   enlisted January 24, 1776. "Charles Reilly" took the Oath of Allegiance in 1778
   before Hon. William Spear. (H-12, A-1/19, A-2/67)

REILLY (RIELEY), JOHN. Private in Capt. Ewings' Company No. 4; enlisted January 24,
   1776. (H-12)

REILY, GEORGE. Oath of Allegiance, 1778, before Hon. James Calhoun. (A-1/19, A-2/40)

REILY, JOHN. 2nd Lieutenant in Baltimore county Militia, 7th Company, December 19,
   1775. Oath of Allegiance, 1778, before Hon. Jesse Dorsey. (G-10, A-1/19, A-2/63)

REILY (REILEY, RILEY), WILLIAM. (1751, Baltimore, MD - July 8, 1824, Washington, DC)
   Married (1) Rebecca HARVEY, and (2) Barbara HODGKIN on September 28, 1791 (marriage
   proven through Maryland pension application). He was 1st Lieutenant in Baltimore
   County Militia, 7th Company, December 19, 1775. Became 2nd Lieutenant in 2nd MD
   Line, Flying Camp, July 24, 1776, and 1st Lieutenant in 4th MD Line, December 10,
   1776, and Captain, 4th MD, October 15, 1777. Transferred to 1st MD Line, Jan. 1,
   1781 and served to April or August, 1783. He received a Federal Bounty Land Grant
   of 200 acres (Warrant 1839) on July 18, 1789, and 200 acres (lots 1457 to 1460) in
   western Maryland. Pay certificates received: 86387 ($117.22); 86388 ($221.29);
   86389 ($400); 86390 ($260); 86391 ($1000); 86392 ($1000); and, 86393 ($360) during
   the war. He was an Original Member of the Society of the Cincinnati of Maryland,
   currently represented by Philip Key Reily of Washington, DC. Capt. Reily is buried
   in Congressional Cemetery, Washington, DC. (TT-123, JJJ-571, YY-121, YY-43, YY-76,
   G-10, H-52, H-352, B-463, PP-243, DDDD-4)

REISTER (RISTER), JOHN. Oath of Allegiance, 1778, before Hon. Andrew Buchanan.(A-2/57)

REISTER (RISTER), JOHN JR. Oath of Allegiance, 1778,before Hon.Andrew Buchanan.(A-2/57)

REISTER (RISTER), PHILIP. (1748 - 1791) 1st Lieutenant in Soldiers Delight Battalion, August 29, 1777, and served at least to 1778. Took Oath of Allegiance, 1778 before Hon. Peter Shepherd. He is buried in the Lutheran Cemetery in Reisterstown, MD. (Z-63, E-10, BBB-348, A-2/49, A-1/20, History Trails, Vol. 7 No. 4 (1974), page 15)

REITZ, CONRAD. Private in Capt. Keeports' German Regiment; enlisted July 21, 1776. At Philadelphia, September 19, 1776. (H-263)

RENNER, TOBIAS. Non-Juror to Oath of Allegiance, 1778. (A-1/19)

RENTFORD, HENRY. Sailor on ship Defence, February 1 to March 11, 1777, and was the Gunner's Mate on September 19, 1776. (H-606, H-659)

RERESLY, JOHN. Non-Juror to Oath of Allegiance, 1778. (A-1/19)

RETHER, MICHAEL. Took the Oath of Allegiance in 1781. (QQ-118)

REVERTY, JAMES. Oath of Allegiance, 1778, before Hon. James Calhoun. (A-1/19, A-2/38)

REYNOLDS, FRANCIS. Private, Capt.Deams' Co., 7th MD Regt., Dec. 21, 1776. (H-305)

REYNOLDS, JAMES. (1756, Queen Anne County, MD - 1814, Baltimore, MD) Son of John REYNOLDS. Married (1) Martha SETH, and (2) Ruth EMBERT; son, JOHN REYNOLDS married Ellen_____. James REYNOLDS (RAYNOLDS) was a Private in Capt. Levin Spedden's gunboat flotilla and was reported injured during the war. (AAA-105, H-615)

REYNOLDS, JOHN. Matross in Capt. Brown's MD Artillery; joined November 22, 1777. Was at Valley Forge until June, 1778; at White Plains, July, 1778; at Fort Schuyler in August and September, 1780; at High Hills of the Santee, August, 1781; at Camp Col. Scirvins, January, 1782; and Bacon's Bridge, S.C., April, 1782. (UU-228, UU-230)

REYNOLDS, WILLIAM. Oath of Allegiance, 1778, before Hon. George Lindenberger. (A-2/54)

RHEIMS, JOHN. Non-Juror to Oath of Allegiance, 1778. (A-1/19)
RHEIMS, NICHOLAS. Non-Juror to Oath of Allegiance, 1778. (A-1/19)
RHINEHART, FREDERICK. Non-Juror to Oath of Allegiance, 1778. (A-1/19)
RHOAD, LEWIS. Non-Juror to Oath of Allegiance, 1778. (A-1/20)

RHODES, GEORGE. Private in Col. Aquila Hall's Baltimore County Regt., 1777. (TTT-13)

RHODES, JOHN. Matross in Capt. Brown's MD Artillery; joined November 22, 1777. Was at Valley Forge until June, 1778; at White Plains, July, 1778; at Fort Schuyler in August and September, 1780; not listed in 1781. (UU-228, UU-230)

RHODES, RICHARD. Involved in evaluation of Baltimore County confiscated proprietary reserve lands in 1782. (FFF-543)

RHUME, CHARLES JACOB. Private in Capt.Cox's Company, December 19, 1776. (CCC-21)

RIBBLE, JOHN. Non-Juror to Oath of Allegiance, 1778. (A-1/20)

RICE, JAMES. Born in Baltimore County, MD. Wife named Elizabeth J._____. Their son, Henry Davenport RICE, Sr. (1802-1835) married Eliza PRIESTLY (1808-1884), and their granddaughter, Mary R. P. RICE (1824-1913) married William Leonidas RILEY in 1844. James RICE enlisted as a Private in Capt. N. Smith's 1st Company of Matross on April 3, 1776, and was at Fort Whetstone Point in Baltimore on September 7, 1776. He was a Sergeant in Capt. Dorsey's 2nd MD Artillery Company at Valley Forge, as of June 3, 1778. James RICE also took the Oath of Allegiance in 1778 before Honorable Jesse Dorsey. (A-1/20, A-2/63, H-566, H-568, QQQ-2, VV-73, UU-230, AAA-1588)

RICE, WOOLRICK. Non-Juror to Oath of Allegiance, 1778. (A-1/20)

RICH, JOHANNES. Oath of Allegiance, 1778, before Hon. George Lindenberger. (A-2/54)

RICH, JOHN. Private in Capt. Graybill's German Regiment, July 12, 1776. (ZZ-32)

RICHARDS, HAMMOND. Private in Capt. Sheaff's Company, June 16, 1777. "Hammond Richard" took the Oath of Allegiance in 1778 before Hon. James Calhoun. (W-162, A-2/41)

RICHARDS, ISAAC. Non-Juror to Oath of Allegiance in 1778. (A-1/20)
RICHARDS, JOHN. Non-Juror to Oath of Allegiance in 1778. (A-1/20)
RICHARDS, NICHOLAS. Non-Juror to Oath of Allegiance in 1778. (A-1/20)

RICHARDS, PAUL. Non-Juror to Oath of Allegiance in 1778. (A-1/20)

RICHARDS, PETER. Born 1752 in Nova Scotia. Occupation: Labourer. Enlisted Jan. 28, 1776 as Private in Capt. N. Smith's 1st Company of Matrosses. Height: 5'9". He was in Capt. Dorsey's MD Artillery on Nov. 17, 1777. (H-564, H-566, H-574, VV-74, QQQ-2)

RICHARDS, RICHARD. (1718 - 1811) Married Maria Ann VAUGHAN. Source JJJ-567 indicates he gave patriotic service, but Source A-1/20 states he was a Non-Juror to Oath, 1778.

RICHARDS, RICHARD JR. Non-Juror to Oath of Allegiance, 1778. (A-1/20)

RICHARDSON, ALEXANDER. Served on ship Defence, February 15 to May 15, 1777. (H-659)

RICHARDSON, AUBREY. Private in Capt. Howell's Company, December 30, 1775. "Awbry Richardson" took Oath of Allegiance, 1778, before Hon. James Calhoun. (G-11, A-2/38)

RICHARDSON, DANIEL. Non-Juror to Oath of Allegiance, 1778. (A-1/20)

RICHARDSON, DAVID. Revolutionary War Pension S31324: "Maryland Service, applied in Mercer County, Kentucky, September 2, 1833, age 77, served in Wayne's Indian War and War of 1812. States he entered service 1776 under Capt. Oldham in Baltimore County, MD, near the city of Baltimore, for 18 months and joined a regiment of the flying camp under Col. Howard of the said state and marched to Lancaster to Phila-delphia and through Jersey State. This was our Northern tour. We were then ordered to the south and marched through the State of Virginia and North Carolina and into South Carolina and back to Maryland and was discharged after having served fifteen months near Baltimore. During this tour, we were kept constantly on the march fol-lowing from one place to another as fast as we could travel. We think he was dis-charged about the last of Sept. or first of Oct. 1777 and in 2 or 3 days after he returned home he was drafted in his cousin's Capt. John STANDIFORD's Company, a tour of 3 months and joined the regiment, commanded by the same Col. Harrod (ed.--Howard) and marched into the state of Pa. and joined the main army under command of General Washington near Germantown where we had a sever battle and was badly defeated. We retreated and took post at a place called the White Marsh Mills where we were sta-tioned until sometime in December when the main army went into winter Quarters at Valley Forge and we were discharged and returned home during the tour--we suffered a great deal for the want of clothing--shoes and provisions, again July 1778, he was drafted for a tour of 6 months in Capt. Daniel Shaw's Company and marched to Balti-more. The enemie's shipping appeared in the river and it was thought advisable to move the magazine about 18 miles out in the country for security and our company was detached as guard for that purpose. The magazine was placed in a protestant church near Slades old tavern where we were stationed until the enemy disappeared and the magazine moved back to Baltimore. He states he entered the army young.----Captain Oldham came into his father's harvest field and he joined him and marched forth with him, states he was in service 2 years and suffered more during the 3 months until in which the battle of Germantown was fought than in all the balance of his service, he makes another application and states he joined on the General Wayne's army and marched against the Indians and was one of the spies at the time he de-feated the Indians and marched with Shelby to Canada---he and his wife were both old." (Data copied in History Trails, Vol. 17, No. 3, Spring, 1983, pp. 10-11, a publication of the Baltimore County Historical Society)

RICHARDSON, GEORGE. (1762 - after 1789) Married Mary GRIZZELLE. Private in Captain McClellan's Company, Baltimore Town, September 4, 1780. (JJJ-568, CCC-25)

RICHARDSON, JAMES. Oath of Allegiance in 1778. (A-1/20)

RICHARDSON, JOHN. There were two men with this name who served. One was born 1752 in Pennsylvania, and was a carpenter by trade. He joined as a Private in Capt. Smith's 1st Company of Matrosses on February 3, 1776. Height: 5'8¼". Another was a Private in Capt. J. Cockey's Baltimore County Dragoons at Yorktown in 1781. Both signed an Oath of Allegiance in 1778: one before Hon. Benjamin Rogers (could not write; made his mark), and another before Hon. John Hall. (H-565, MMM-A, A-2/32, A-2/36, A-1/20)

RICHARDSON, SAMUEL. Sergeant in Col. Aquila Hall's Baltimore County Regiment, 1777. (TTT-13)

RICHARDSON, THOMAS (OF JAMES). Oath of Allegiance, 1778, before Hon. Benjamin Rogers. Could not write; made his mark (" C "). (A-1/20, A-2/32)

RICHARDSON, WILLIAM (WILL). Oath of Allegiance, 1778, before Hon. George Lindenberger. Captain of Baltimore Town Company No. 5 in 1776, commanding 71 men. "The late Capt. Richardson" resigned May 17, 1779. (GGG-401, F-309, GG-74, E-13, BBB-359, A-2/54)

RICHARDSON, WILLIAM. Served in baltimore Artillery Company, 1777. Private in Captain Furnival's MD Artillery; November 17, 1777 muster roll indicates "absent--wounded by accident." Left as an invalid at Fort Whetstone Point in Baltimore, September 15, 1779; discharged May 8, 1781. (H-626, H-573, V-368)

RICHARDSON, ZACHARIAH. Non-Juror to Oath of Allegiance in 1778. (A-1/20) "Zaccheus Richardson" was involved in evaluation of Baltimore County confiscated proprietary reserve lands in 1782. (FFF-547)

RICHART. ABRAM. Non-Juror to Oath of Allegiance in 1778. (A-1/20)

RICHART (RICHERT), JOHN. Drafted into Baltimore County Regiment 36, circa 1777.(TTT-13)

RICHART (RICHARTS), MICHAEL. Oath of Allegiance, 1778, before Hon. Charles Ridgely of William. (A-1/20, A-2/27)

RICHEY (RITCHEY), JOHN. Private in Capt. Cox's Company, December 19, 1776. Private in Capt. McClellan's Company, September 4, 1780. (CCC-21, CCC-24)

RICHEY, WILLIAM. Oath of Allegiance, 1778. (A-1/20)

RICK, JOHN. Private in Capt. Graybill's German Regiment in 1776. (H-265) "Johannes Rick" took Oath of Allegiance in 1778. (A-1/20)

RICK, ROBERT. Oath of Allegiance, 1778, before Hon. Charles Ridgely of Wm. (A-2/27)

RICKETTS, DAVID. Oath of Allegiance, 1778, before Hon. George Lindenberger. (A-2/54)

RICKETTS, NICHOLAS. Private in Capt. N. Smith's 1st Company of Matrosses, June 29, 1776. Sergeant in Capt. Dorsey's MD Artillery, November 17, 1777. 2nd Lieutenant in Capt. Dorsey's Company No. 2, commissioned December 31, 1777. Was at valley Forge, June 3, 1778. 2nd Lieutenant in Capt. J. Smith's MD Artillery, 1780, and serving under Lt.Col. Ed. Carrington on May 11, 1780, stationed at Baltimore. He was still in service as of January 28, 1782. Entitled to 200 acres (lots 2870, 2872, 2873, 2874) in western Maryland for his services as a Lieutenant. (DDDD-4, H-566, H-573, H-579, QQQ-2, VVV-96, UU-230, UU-231, H-477)

RICKETTS, THOMAS. (November 23, 1753 - August 22, 1828) Married (1) Ruth ADAMSON, and (2) Martha WILSON. Oath of Allegiance, 1778. (JJJ-570, A-1/20)

RICKEY, WILLIAM. Oath of Allegiance, 1778, before Hon. John Moale. (A-2/70)

RICKHART, JOHN. Non-Juror to Oath of Allegiance in 1778. (A-1/20)

RID, JAMES. Private in Capt. Dorsey's MD Artillery, November 17, 1777. (H-574)

RIDDELL, WILLIAM. Oath of Allegiance, 1778, before Hon. George Lindenberger. (A-2/54)

RIDDLE, ALEXANDER. Non-Juror to Oath of Allegiance in 1778. (A-1/20)

RIDDLE, ROBERT. Oath of Allegiance, 1778, before Hon. James Calhoun. (A-1/20, A-2/40)

RIDENBOCK, JNO. Served in Baltimore Mechanical Company of Militia, Nov. 4, 1775.(F-300)

RIDENOUR (RIDENHOUR), NICHOLAS. Oath of Allegiance, 1778, before Hon. Thomas Sollers. Private in Capt. McClellan's Company, September 4, 1780. (CCC-24, A-1/20, A-2/51)

RIDER, JOHN. Non-Juror to Oath of Allegiance in 1778. (A-1/20)

RIDGELY, CHARLES CAPTAIN (OF "HAMPTON"). Son of Charles RIDGELY and Rachel HOWARD. Served on baltimore Committee of Inspection (March, 1775), Baltimore Committee of Correspondence (November, 1775), and Baltimore Committee of Observation (elected September 23, 1775. He was born 1733, and died 1790. His wife, Rebecca, died in September, 1812, and her funeral was at "Hampton" on September 29th. Her maiden name was Dorsey. (ZZZ-272) Her parents were Caleb and Priscilla DORSEY. Charles RIDGELY served in the House of Delegates, 1773 to 1789. (A. Parran's Register of

Md.'s Heraldic Families, Vol. I, 308) Capt. Ridgely was also a Baltimore Privateer and served on the Baltimore Committee of Confiscated Property in 1782. His beautiful "Hampton" mansion stands today in Towson, Baltimore County, MD. (III-207, FFF-648, SS-130, RR-19, RR-47, SS-136, RR-50)

RIDGELY, CHARLES (OF JOHN). Son of John RIDGELY and Mary DORSEY. He died in Baltimore on December 15, 1786. His wife, Rebecca LAWSON, died November 15, 1801, in her 49th year. Their children: Charles, Elizabeth, Rachel, Rebecca, and Dorothy. Charles served on the Baltimore County Committee of Observation, 1774-1775, but did not get enough votes to be elected in September, 1775 to that committee. (ZZZ-272, RR-50) Source D-5 states he took the Oath of Allegiance in Baltimore County.

RIDGELY, CHARLES (OF WILLIAM). (1735, Anne Arundel County, MD - 1810, Baltimore County) Son of Capt. William RIDGELY and Elizabeth DUVALL, and grandson of Charles RIDGELY and Deborah DORSEY. He married Ruth NORWOOD in 1774; their children: Samuel RIDGELY married Deborah DORSEY; Dr. Charles Carnan RIDGELY married Elizabeth DORSEY; William A. RIDGELY married Elizabeth DUMESTE (OR DUMENT?); Thomas P. RIDGELY married Maria SOLENO; Robert RIDGELY; John RIDGELY; Washington RIDGELY; Frank RIDGELY; Elizabeth RIDGELY married Robert Ridgely RICHARDSON; Julia RIDGELY married Dr. Alexander BARRON; Ruth RIDGELY married Dr. John BALTZELL; and, Susan RIDGELY married a THOMPSON. Charles RIDGELY of William was a prominent man during the Revolution. He represented Upper Patapsco Hundred at the Association of Freemen in July and August, 1775, and served on the Baltimore Committee of Observation, having been elected September 23, 1775. He was a Justice of the Peace and one of the Magistrates who administered the Oath of Allegiance in Baltimore County in 1778. He also was a member of the Constitution Convention, House of Delegates, and Senate of Maryland. (EEEE-1726, XXX-609, RR-50, XXX-610, ZZZ-271, JJJ-570, AAA-85A, RR-47, SS-136, GGG-242, BB-2, FF-64, A-1/20, A-2/27)

RIDGELY, CHARLES JR. Baltimore County Committee of Inspection, March 13, 1775. (RR-19)

RIDGELY, FREDERICK DR. (May 25, 1757, Elk Ridge, Anne Arundel County, MD - November 12, 1824, Dayton, Ohio) Son of Greenberry RIDGELY (1736-1783) and Lucy STRINGER. Married Elizabeth SHORT (died 1822) on March 16, 1790; a son, Thomas Graham RIDGELY (1826-98) married Deborah Ridgely BAER (1831-1926) in 1850, and a grandson, Joseph Graham RIDGELY (1857-1906) married Mary Hodges FISHER (1854-1925) in 1883. DR. RIDGELY began the practice of medicine in Baltimore Town in 1775. He was surgeon to the 4th MD Regiment under Major Alex. Roxbury in 1777. He also served in the Yorktown campaign. (XX-12. XX-13, AAA-1474, H-288)

RIDGELY, GREENBERRY. (July 4, 1754, Anne Arundel County, MD - March 17, 1843, Baltimore) Son of William RIDGELY III and Mary ORRICK. He married Rachel RYAN (1755-1818) on May 1, 1774; their chidlren: Lloyd (born 1775); Noah (born 1778); Lot (twin to Noah); Silas (born 1779); Mary (born 1781); Susan (born 1783); Rhoada (born 1785); Sarah (born 1787); Ann (born 1789); Greenberry (1790-1875) married Harriet TALBOTT (1792-1872) in 1814, and their son, Charles Washington RIDGELY (1815-1896) married Mary Louisa HOPPER (1824-1905) in 1843; Isaiah (born 1792); James (born 1795); and, Nicholas (born 1800). Greenberry RIDGELY took the Oath of Allegiance in 1779 in Anne Arundel County, MD. (XXX-610, JJJ-570, AAA-1489)

RIDGELY, JOHN (OF WILLIAM). Oath of Allegiance, 1778, before Charles Ridgely of William. (A-2/27)

RIDGELY, RICHARD. (1755-1824) Son of Greenbury RIDGELY and Elizabeth WARFIELD of Anne Arundel County, MD. Married Elizabeth DORSEY; their children: Edward, Richard, Ann, Deborah, Sophia, Daniel, Elizabeth and Matilda. Richard RIDGELY was a Captain in Col. Smith's Baltimore Town Battalion (formerly the Mercantile Company) on Jan. 19, 1781. He signed a letter to Governor Lee on April 4, 1781, requesting the calling of the militia to protect Baltimore. (R-15, BBBB-61, S-49, MMM-A)

RIDGELY, WILLIAM. (1703/04 - 1780) Married Mary ORRICK. Took Oath of Allegiance in 1778. (JJJ-570, A-1/20)

RIDGEWAY, WILLIAM. Oath of Allegiance, 1778, before Hon. Charles Ridgely of William. Could not write; made his mark. (A-1/20, A-2/28)

RIDLEY, MATTHEW, ESQ. Served on the Baltimore Salt Committee on October 14, 1779. "Of the House of Ridley and Pringle, was authorised to borrow and negotiate a loan in Holland for the use of the State of Maryland in 1780." (SS-184) He signed a letter on April 4, 1781 to Governor Lee, requesting the calling of the militia to protect Baltimore. On June 25, 1781 he served with Capt. Nicholas Ruxton Moore's Troops, and rode and five year old bay gelding horse. (BBBB-313, HHH-88, S-49)

RIEF, DANIEL. Private in Capt. Deams' Co., 7th MD Regt., January 28, 1777. (H-305)

RIELEY (RIELY), JOHN. Private in Baltimore County Militia; enlisted July 5, 1776. Private in Capt. Oldham's Co., 4th MD Regt., Dec. 1, 1776 to Nov.1, 1780. (H-158, H-58)

RIERDAN, MICHAEL. Private in Baltimore Artillery Company, October 16, 1775. (G-8)

RIFFETT, NICHOLAS. Oath of Allegiance, 1778, before Hon. William Lux.(A-1/20,A-2/69)

RIGDON, WILLIAM. Non-Juror to Oath of Allegiance, 1778. (A-1/20)
RIGHT, CHRISTOPHER. Non-Juror to oath of Allegiance, 1778. (A-1/20)
RIGHT, JAMES. Non-Juror to Oath of Allegiance, 1778. (A-1/20)
RIGHT, THOMAS. Non-Juror to Oath of Allegiance, 1778. (A-1/20)
RILEY, DENNIS. Non-Juror to Oath of Allegiance, 1778. (A-1/20)
RILEY, JAMES. Non-Juror to Oath of Allegiance, 1778. (A-1/20)

RILEY, MICHAEL. Marine on ship Defence in 1777. (H-659)

RILEY, STEPHEN. Married Mary HOOK on January 2, 1783 in Baltimore County, MD. Source YY-121 states marriage proven through Maryland pension application, but no service stated for Stephen; perhaps his father served.

RILEY, TIM. Ordinary Sailor on ship Defence in 1777. (H-659)

RIM, NICHOLAS. Enlisted in Baltimore Town on July 17, 1776. (H-53)

RIMMER, JOHN. Oath of Allegiance, 1778. (A-1/20)

RINEHART (REINHART), SIMON. Private in Capt. Graybill's German Regt., 1776. (H-266)

RINGFIELD, JAMES. Private in Capt. Deams' Co., 7th MD Regt., Dec. 27, 1776. (H-305)

RISTEAU, ABRAHAM. Oath of Allegiance in 1778 before Hon. Richard Holliday. He wrote to the Governor on August 1, 1780, about the purchase of provisions for Baltimore. (FFF-305, A-1/20, A-2/60)

RISTEAU, GEORGE. (1735-1792) Son of John and Katherine RISTEAU. He married Frances TODD; their children: Katherine, Eleanor, Thomas, John, Francis and Rebecca. He served on the Baltimore County Committee of Inspection, March 13, 1775, and repre-sented Soldiers Delight Hundred at the Association of Freemen on August 21, 1775. He was elected to the Baltimore County Committee of Observation on September 23, 1775, and took the Oath of Allegiance in 1778 before Hon. John Moale. (EEEE-1726, Rr-19, RR-47, RR-50, SS-136, A-1/20, A-2/70)

RISTEAU, THOMAS. Served in Col. Nicholson's Troop of Horse on June 7, 1781.(BBBB-274)

RISTON (RISTEN), BENJAMIN. Non-Juror to Oath, 1778; signed in 1781. (A-1/20, QQ-119)

RISTON, JOHN. Non-Juror to Oath of Allegiance in 1778. (A-1/20)

RITCHIE, MATTHEW. Private, Capt. Smith's Company No. 8; enlisted Jan. 27, 1776.(H-18)

RITTER, ANTHONY. Oath of Allegiance, 1778, before Hon. Richard Cromwell. (A-2/46)

RITTER, JOHN. Oath of Allegiance in 1778 before Hon. George Lindenberger. (A-2/54, A-1/20) Source QQ-119 states he took the Oath in 1781 (unless it was another man by this name).

RITTER, LODOWICK. Non-Juror to Oath of Allegiance, 1778. (A-1/20)
RITTER, MICHAEL. Non-Juror to Oath of Allegiance, 1778. (A-1/20)

RITTER, THOMAS. Private in Baltimore County Regiment No. 7, circa 1777. Took the Oath of Allegiance in 1778 before Hon. Richard Cromwell. (TTT-13, A-1/20, A-2/46)

RITTER, WILLIAM. (1750 - after 1787) 2nd Lieutenant in Capt. Keeports' German Regiment on July 11, 1776. (RR-90, H-262, JJJ-572)

RITTLEM'ER, GEORGE. Private in Capt. Graybill's German Regiment in 1776. (H-265)

ROACH (REACH), JOHN. Private in Baltimore County Militia; enlisted July 5, 1776. (H-58)

ROACH, THOMAS. Volunteered into Baltimore County Regiment 36, circa 1777. (TTT-13)

ROAD, WILLIAM. Oath of Allegiance, 1778, before Hon. Richard Holliday. (A-2/60)

ROADS, CHRISTOPHER. Non-Juror to the Oath of Allegiance in 1778. (A-1/20)

ROAN, DANIEL. Oath of Allegiance, 1778, before Hon. John Beale Howard. (A-1/20, A-2/29)

ROANE, EDWARD. Oath of Allegiance, 1778, before Hon. Edward Cockey. (A-1/20, A-2/61)

ROBBINS, PHILIP. Non-Juror to Oath of Allegiance, 1778. (A-1/20)

ROBERSON, GEORGE. Oath of Allegiance, 1778. (A-1/20)

ROBERTS, BENJAMIN. Oath of Allegiance, 1778, before Hon. James Calhoun. (A-1/20, A-2/41)

ROBERTS, JOHN. Oath of Allegiance, 1778, before Hon. James Calhoun. (A-1/20, A-2/41)

ROBERTS, PATRICK HENRY. (March 1, 1758 - March 23, 1839) Married Catherine AUSTIN, on June 20, 1810 in Baltimore County, MD (Marriage proven through Maryland pension application). Private in Maryland Line. (JJJ-574) Nothing on his service in YY-121.

ROBERTS, RICHARDS. Oath of Allegiance, 1778, before Hon. James Calhoun. (A-1/20, A-2/40)

ROBERTS, THOMAS. Drummer in Capt. Ewing's Company No. 4 in 1776. Drummer on State Ship Defence, September 19, 1776. Marine on Defence, 1777. (H-13, H-606, H-659)

ROBERTS, ZACHARIAH. Corporal in 1st MD Regiment; enlisted March 31, 1777, and served in Q.M. Dept.; discharged May 2, 1780. Pensioner. On February 24, 1823, it was ordered to "pay to Peter LEVERING, of Baltimore, or his executors, the half pay of a corporal, for the support and maintenance of Zachariah ROBERTS during his life as compensation for services rendered in Revolutionary War." (C-386, H-155, YY-44)

ROBERTSON, GEORGE. Surgeon on ship Defence, May 20 to December 31, 1777. Took Oath of Allegiance in 1778 before Hon. James Calhoun. (H-659, A-2/40)

ROBERTSON, THOMAS. Served in Capt. Dorsey's MD Artillery, November 17, 1777, when he was reported "convalescent - intermittent fever." (H-618)

ROBERTSON, WILLIAM. Volunteered into Baltimore County Regiment 36, circa 1777. (TTT-13)

ROBINSON, CHARLES. Married Mephyteca GALLOWAY on June 30, 1787, in Baltimore County. (Marriage proven through Maryland application). There was a Charles ROBINSON who was a Private in the 9th Company of the Maryland Line in 1783. (YY-122, H-499)

ROBINSON, GEORGE. (Died in Baltimore County in 1784). Wife name Rebecca in his will, but his executrix was Elizabeth Robinson. Children: George, Robert, and William. A Captain George Robinson was mentioned in a letter of William Johnson of Fells Point to the Council of Safety. Non-Juror to Oath of Allegiance, 1778. (A-1/20, D-10)

ROBINSON, JAMES. Non-Juror to Oath of Allegiance in 1778. Recruited in Baltimore by Samuel Chester on March 2, 1780 for the 3rd MD Regiment. Pensioner; Private, MD Line. (YY-45, H-340, H-334, A-1/20)

ROBINSON, JOHN. Corporal in Capt. Gale's MD Artillery, 1779; sick in hospital from November, 1779 to March, 1780. Oath of Allegiance in 1778 before Honorable Charles Ridgely of William. (A-1/20, A-2/28, YYY-1/100)

ROBINSON, JOSEPH. Oath of Allegiance, 1778, before Hon. Richard Holliday. (A-1/20, A-2/60)

ROBINSON, PETER. Matross in Capt. Brown's MD Artillery, as of August 1, 1781. Was at High Hills of the Santee; at Camp Col.Scirvins, January, 1782; and, at Bacon's Bridge S.C., April, 1782. (UU-230)

ROBINSON, ROGER. Oath of Allegiance, 1778, before Hon. Charles Ridgely of William. (A-1/20, A-2/28)

ROBINSON, SOLOMON. Oath of Allegiance, 1778. (A-1/20)

ROBINSON, STANDLY. It was ordered on February 25, 1824, to "pay Standly Robinson, of Baltimore, half pay of a Private as further remuneration for his services on board the Dolphin during the Revolutionary War." (C-386)

ROBINSON, THOMAS. Born 1754 in Harford County, MD. Occupation: Blacksmith. Ht.: 6', which was quite tall for his day. He enlisted February 3, 1776 as a Private in Capt. N. Smith's 1st Company of Matrosses. This or perhaps another Thomas Robinson joined the militia in Baltimore County on July 20, 1776. On November 17, 1777, he is listed as Private in Capt. Dorsey's MD Artillery, "sick." (H-574, H-52, H-565, VV-74, QQQ-2) Oath of Allegiance in 1778 before Hon. Charles Ridgely of William. (A-1/20, A-2/28)

ROBINSON, WILLIAM. Enlisted at Fort Whetstone Point in Baltimore, September 23, 1779; discharged January 27, 1780. He was a Non-Juror to the Oath of Allegiance in 1778, but signed in 1781. (H-626, A-1/20, QQ-119)

ROBOSSON, CHARLES. Born 1758. It was ordered on February 27, 1839, to "pay to Rebecca Robosson, of City of Baltimore, widow of Charles Robosson, a 1st Lieutenant in the Revolutionary War, half pay of a 1st Lieutenant of the army, during her life, quarterly, commencing January 1, 1839." (C-386, YY-45)

ROBY, ADAM. Served in Baltimore Mechanical Company of Militia, Nov. 4, 1775. (F-300)

ROCK, FIDDLE. Non-Juror to Oath of Allegiance, 1778. (A-1/20)
ROCK, GEORGE. Non-Juror to Oath of Allegiance, 1778. (A-1/20)
ROCK, SAMUEL. Non-Juror to Oath of Allegiance, 1778. (A-1/20)
ROCKHOLD, ASAEL. Non-Juror to Oath of Allegiance in 1778 in Baltimore County (A-1/20), but he did sign the Oath in 1778 in Harford County, MD (See H. Peden's Revolutionary Patriots of Harford County, Maryland, 1775-1783, page 193)

ROCKHOLD, CHARLES. Oath of Allegiance, 1778, before Hon. John Beale Howard. Could not write; made his mark (" R "). Also involved in evaluation of Baltimore County confiscated proprietary reserve lands in 1782. (A-1/20, A-2/29, FFF-547)

ROCKHOLD, JACOB. Involved in evaluation of Baltimore County confiscated proprietary reserve lands in 1782. (FFF-547)

ROCKWELL, ISAH (ISAIAH), Non-Juror to Oath of Allegiance, 1778. (A-1/20)

RODDEN (REDDEN), DANIEL. Corporal in Capt. Furnival's MD Artillery, November 17, 1777, when reported "sick - putrid fever." Matross in same company at Valley Forge as of June 3, 1778, and at Camp Col. Scirvins on January 28, 1782. He also served as a Matross in Capt. J. Smith's MD Artillery in 1780, and 1782-1783. (H-618, H-572, H-579, UU-231, UU-232, YYY-2/40)

RODDIN, JOHN. Non-Juror to Oath of Allegiance in 1778. (A-1/20)

RODGERS, JAMES JR. Oath of Allegiance, 1778, before Hon. William Lux. (A-1/20, A-2/68)

RODGERS, JOHN. Private in Col. Ewing's Battalion; enlisted July 7, 1776 in Baltimore County; not on muster roll in August, 1776. (H-57)

RODGERS, W. Corporal in Capt.Cox's Company, December 19, 1776, and Sergeant in Capt. McClellan's Company, September 4, 1780. (CCC-21, CCC-23)

RODWALL, GODFREY. Private in Capt. Deams' Co., 7th MD Regt., Dec. 11, 1776. (H-304)

ROE, FREDERICKS. Drafted into Baltimore County Regiment 36, circa 1777. (TTT-13)

ROE, MARMA (MANNA). Private in Baltimore County Militia in 1776. Took the Oath of Allegiance in 1778 before Hon. George Lindenberger. (H-59, A-1/20, A-2/54)

ROE, WALTER. (1748 - October 31, 1808) Merchant in Baltimore. Signed a letter to Governor Lee on April 4, 1781, requesting the calling of the militia to protect Baltimore. At his death, he left four sons and a daughter. (ZZZ-277, S-49)

ROE, WILLIAM. Non-Juror to Oath of Allegiance in 1778. (A-1/20)

ROEBUCK, WILLIAM. Corporal in Capt. Brown's MD Artillery; joined November 22, 1777.

ROEBUCK, WILLIAM (continued)
Was at Valley Forge until June, 1778; at White Plains, July, 1778; at Ft. Schuyler, August and September, 1780; not listed as of August 1, 1781. (UU-228, UU-230)

ROGERS, BENJAMIN, ESQ. Represented Upper Middle River Hundred at the Association of Freemen on August 21, 1775. Quartermaster of Gunpowder Battalion in May, 1776 and recommended to be Major in June, 1776. Justice of the Orphans Court of Baltimore County, 1777, and Justice of the Peace, 1778. Was one of the Magistrates in 1778 who administered the Oath of Allegiance. (X-111,VV-273,GGG-242,EFEE-1726, A-2/32)

ROGERS, CHARLES. (1741 - January, 1806, Baltimore County, MD) Married Sarah HOPKINS (died 1808). Children: Sarah ROGERS married a BAILEY; Ann ROGERS married a MARTIN; Mary ROGERS married a LEE; and, Catherine ROGERS. Charles ROGERS took the Oath of Allegiance in 1778 before Hon. Benjamin Rogers. (D-10, ZZZ-277, A-1/20, A-2/32)

ROGERS, DAVID. Oath of Allegiance, 1778, before Hon. James Calhoun. (A-2/65)

ROGERS, JAMES. Non-Juror to Oath of Allegiance, 1778. (A-1/20)

ROGERS, JOHN. Baltimore Privateer and Captain. He commanded the schooner General Smallwood, mounting four guns, and owned by the State. He was commissioned Oct. 20, 1777. Afterwards, on March 13, 1777, he commanded the brig Black Prince, mounting twelve guns and four swivels, with a crew of forty men. In 1778, John ROGERS took the Oath of Allegiance before Hon. James Calhoun. III-206, A-1/20, A-2/38)

ROGERS, JOHN. 2nd Lieutenant of Marines on ship Defence, Mar. 11 to Dec. 31, 1777. (H-659)

ROGERS, JOSEPH. Private in Capt. Lansdale's Co., 4th MD Regiment, from March 17, 1778 to December 29, 1779 when reported deserted. He took the Oath of Allegiance before Hon. George Lindenberger in 1778. (H-158, A-1/20, A-2/54)

ROGERS, JOSHUA. Recruit in Baltimore County Militia, April 11, 1780. (H-335)

ROGERS, NICHOLAS. (October 7, 1753, Baltimore, MD - January 2, 1822, Baltimore, MD) He was a fourth generation Baltimorean who inherited a mercantile fortune from his father. He married Eleanor BUCHANAN (1757-1812) and their son, Lloyd Nicholas ROGERS married Eliza LAW and their son was Edmund Law ROGERS (born 1818). Nicholas ROGERS aided Commissioners Silas Dean, John Jay and Benjamin Franklin in Paris at the outbreak of the Revolution, and was diplomatic courier from France to Congress. He was Major and Aide-de-Camp, May 12, 1777, to Generals Coudray and DeKalb at Valley Forge and on December 10, 1778 he was brevetted Lieutenant Colonel, Continental Army, and retired from service. After the Revolution he continued the business as a merchant and flour miller, and was active in organizing the Maryland Insurance Fire Company in 1792, the Bank of Baltimore in 1795, and the Library Company of Baltimore in 1796. He was Criminal Court Justice, 1784-1801, Orphans Court Judge, 1792-1793, and served on the Baltimore City Council, 1797-1805. He was gentleman-architect of Baltimore, and a member of the Society of the Cincinnati of Maryland, represented currently by Edmund Law Rogers Smith. (TT-125, AAA-175, ZZZ-277, and Robert Alexander's "Nicholas Rogers, Gentleman-Architect of Baltimore," Md. Hist. Mag., V. 78, #2, 1983, p. 85ff)

ROGERS, PHILIP. Baltimore Town Committee of Correspondence, November 12, 1775. Was a Non-Juror to Oath of Allegiance in 1778. (A-1/20, SS-130)

ROGERS, RUTH. In Baltimore County, December 26, 1777, she asked the Governor for an advance on account for support due to her husband being taken by the British; name of husband not given. (FFF-134)

ROGERS, THOMAS. Oath of Allegiance, 1778, before Hon. John Hall. (A-1/20, A-2/36)

ROGERS, WILLIAM. (1742 - March 25, 1784) Wife named Sarah; son, Jacob ROGERS married Elizabeth LIMES. He served in Baltimore Mechanical Company of Militia, November 4, 1775, and was a Private in Capt. Winder's Company, 1st MD Regiment, under Col. John Stout, 1776-1779. Took Oath of Allegiance in 1778 before Hon. William Spear. He was born in Baltimore. (XXX-619, F-299, A-1/20, A-2/66)

ROHRBACK, ADAM. Oath of Allegiance in 1778 before Hon. James Calhoun. "Adam Rohebuck" served in Baltimore Mechanical Company of Militia, Nov. 4, 1775. "Adam Rohrbach or

Rohhbaugh" was a Private in Capt. Graybill's German Regiment in 1776. (H-265, F-299, A-1/20, A-2/39

ROLAND, JOHN. Oath of Allegiance, 1778, before Hon. Peter Shepherd. (A-1/20, A-2/49)

ROLAND, THOMAS. Involved in evaluation of Baltimore County confiscated proprietary reserve lands in 1782. (FFF-554)

ROLES, DAVID. Non-Juror to Oath of Allegiance, 1778. (A-1/20)
ROLES, JACOB. Non-Juror to Oath of Allegiance, 1778. (A-1/20)
ROLES, THOMAS. Non-Juror to Oath of Allegiance, 1778. (A-1/20)

ROLLINGS, RICHARD. Private, Baltimore County Militia; enlisted Aug. 15, 1776. (H-58)

ROLPH, WILLIAM. Private in Count Pulaski's Legion; enlisted in Baltimore, April 22, 1778. (H-592, H-593)

ROMMELSEM, WILLIAM. Sergeant in Capt. Graybill's German Regiment in 1776. (H-265)

RONEY (RANY), JAMES. (Born 1752 in Leinst'r, Ireland) Occupation: Breeches Maker. Height: 5'7". Enlisted January 24, 1776 as Private in Capt. N. Smith's 1st Company of Matrosses. Took Oath of Allegiance in 1778 before Hon. Jesse Dorsey. (A-1/20, A-2/64, H-564, VV-73)

ROOD, WILLIAM. Oath of Allegiance, 1778. (A-1/20)

ROODS, CHRISTOPHER. Oath of Allegiance, 1778, before Hon. Peter Shepherd. (A-2/50)

ROOK, GEORGE. Non-Juror to Oath of Allegiance, 1778. (A-1/20)
ROOK, JACOB. Non-Juror to Oath of Allegiance, 1778. (A-1/20)
ROOK, MARTIN. Non-Juror to Oath of Allegiance, 1778. (A-1/20)

ROONEY, JOHN. Oath of Allegiance, 1778, before Hon. Jesse Dorsey. (A-1/20, A-2/64)

ROSE, WILLIAM. (c1745 - c1808) Married Elizabeth MARTIN. Took Oath of Allegiance in 1778 before Hon. George Lindenberger. (JJJ-581, A-1/20, A-2/54)

ROSS, GEORGE. 1st Lieutenant of Marines on ship Defence, March 18 to Dec. 31, 1777. (H-659)

ROSS, GEORGE. Private in Baltimore Artillery Company, October 16, 1775. Took Oath of Allegiance in 1778 before Hon. James Calhoun. (G-8, A-1/20, A-2/41)

ROSS, JAMES. Non-Juror to Oath of Allegiance, 1778. (A-1/20)

ROSS, NATHAN. Served on ship Defence in 1777. (H-659)

ROSS, PETER. Oath of Allegiance, 1778, before Hon. James Calhoun. (A-1/20, A-2/38)

ROSS, WOOLEY. Private in Capt. Howell's Company, December 30, 1775. (G-11)

ROSSITER, THOMAS. Oath of Allegiance, 1778, before Hon. Richard Holliday. (A-2/60)

ROUSE, JAMES. Non-Juror to Oath of Allegiance in 1778. James Rouse made his escape from the British at Portsmouth and "he has ever conducted himself as a friend to the cause of America, always turning out with the militia on every alarm and that credit may be given to his deposition." Signed by George Lindenberger, Justice of the Peace, Baltimore County, August 24, 1781. (AAAA-675, A-1/20)

ROWAN, JOHN. Private in Capt. Smith's Company No. 8; enlisted Jan. 24, 1776. (H-18)

ROWDON, JOHN. Oath of Allegiance, 1778. (A-1/20)

ROWE, JOHN. Served on ship Defence, January 16 to July 23, 1777. (H-659)

ROWELL, JAMES. Non-Juror to Oath of Allegiance in 1778. (A-1/20)

ROWEN, GEORGE. Master At Arms on ship Defence in 1777. (H-659)

ROWLAND, SAMUEL. Oath of Allegiance, 1778, before Hon. Robert Simmons.(A-1/20,A-2/58)

ROWLAND, THOMAS. Oath of Allegiance, 1778, before Hon. Robert Simmons.(A-1/20,A-2/58)

ROWLAND, WILLIAM. Private in Capt. Lansdale's Company, 4th MD Regiment, from April 23, 1777 to March 1, 1780. (H-158)

ROWLES, ASA. Non-Juror to Oath of Allegiance, 1778. (A-1/20)

ROWLES (ROWLS), ELY. Drafted into Baltimore County Regiment No. 36, circa 1777. (TTT-13)

ROWLES (ROWLS), JOHN. Oath of Allegiance, 1778, before Hon. Edward Cockey. (A-2/61)

ROWLES, RICHARD. Non-Juror to Oath of Allegiance, 1778. (A-1/20)

ROWNS, JAMES. Midshipman on ship Defence, 1776 and 1777. (H-606, H-659)

ROYNORLD, THOMAS. Recruit in Baltimore County Militia, April 11, 1780. (H-335)

ROYSTON, JAMES. (November 22, 1756 - after 1781) Married Mary GOAN. Matross in Capt. Brown's MD Artillery; joined November 22, 1777. Was at Valley Forge until June, 1778; at White Plains, July, 1778; at Fort Schuyler, August and September, 1780; promoted to Corporal on August 1, 1781, and may have seen duty in the southern campaign in 1782. Source JJJ-584 mistakenly gives his date of death in 1780. (UU-228, UU-229, UU-230)

ROYTSON, THOMAS (OF JOHN). Oath of Allegiance, 1778, before Hon. John Hall. (A-2/36)

RUBOTHAM, THOMAS. ("Weaver") Oath of Allegiance, 1778, before Hon. John Moale. (A-2/70)

RUBY (RUBEY), JOHN. Non-Juror to Oath of Allegiance, 1778. (A-1/20)

RUBY (RUBEY, ROBEY), THOMAS. Oath of Allegiance, 1778, before Hon. George Lindenberger. "Thomas ROBEY" was Ensign in Upper Battalion, December 4, 1778. "Thomas RUBEY" was involved in evaluation of Baltimore County confiscated proprietary reserve lands in 1782. (FFF-542, GGG-257, A-1/20, A-2/54)

RUBY (RUBEY), THOMAS SR. Non-Juror to Oath of Allegiance, 1778. (A-1/20)

RUMFIELD, HENRY. Private in Capt. Graybill's German Regiment in 1776. (H-265)

RUPPERT, JACOB. Private in Capt. Graybill's German Regiment in 1776. (H-266)

RUPPERT (RUPERT), JOHN. Non-Juror to Oath of Allegiance, 1778. (A-1/20)

RUSH, WILLIAM. Non-Juror to Oath of Allegiance, 1778. (A-1/20)

RUSHO, JOHN. Non-Juror to Oath of Allegiance, 1778. (A-1/20)

RUSK, DAVID. Baltimore Mechanical Company of Militia, and Sons of Liberty, in 1776. Member of the Whig Club in 1777; secret metings were held at his dwelling on Market Street in Baltimore. Oath of Allegiance, 1778, before Hon. James Calhoun. (CCC-19, CCC-25, CCC-26, A-1/20, A-2/39)

RUSK, RICHARD. Oath of Allegiance, 1778, before Hon. George Lindenberger. (A-2/54)

RUSK, THOMAS. Oath of Allegiance, 1778, before Hon. George Lindenberger. (A-2/54)

RUSK, WILLIAM. Oath of Allegiance, 1778, before Hon. George Lindenberger. (A-2/54)

RUSSELL, ANDREW. Recruit in Baltimore County in 1780. (H-340)

RUSSELL, THOMAS. Served on Baltimore Salt Committee, October 14, 1779. Also, took the Oath of Allegiance in 1778 before Hon. James Calhoun. Was a Lieutenant in Baltimore Light Horse Company, July 26, 1780, and Lieutenant in Capt. Nicholas Ruxton Moore's Troops as of June 25, 1781. He rode a seven year old dark chesnut stallion, and also had an eight year old grey mare. He signed a letter to Governor Lee on April 4, 1781 requesting the calling of the militia to protect Baltimore. (HHH-89, S-49, VV-230, BBBB-313, A-1/20, A-2/41)

RUSSELL, WILLIAM. (1739 - April, 1805, Baltimore, MD) He signed a letter to Governor Lee on April 4, 1781, requesting the calling of the militia to protect Baltimore against the British. (S-49, ZZZ-281)

RUTH, WILLIAM. Oath of Allegiance, 1778, before Hon. William Spear. (A-2/66)

RUTLEDGE, ABRAM (ABIM). Non-Juror to Oath of Allegiance, 1778. (A-1/20)

RUTLEDGE, ABRAM (ABIM), JR. Non-Juror to Oath of Allegiance, 1778. (A-1/20)

RUTLEDGE, ELIJAH. Captain in Col. Aquila Hall's Baltimore County Regiment, 1776-1777. (TTT-13)

RUTLEDGE, EPHRAIM. Non-Juror to Oath of Allegiance, 1778. (A-1/20)

RUTLEDGE, JOHN. Non-Juror to Oath of Allegiance, 1778. (A-1/20)

RUTLEDGE, JOSHUA. (1759-1825) Son of Abraham and Penelope RUTLEDGE. Joshua married Augustine Ann BIDDLE (1774-1819) on November 10, 1792 in Baltimore, MD. He was a Lieutenant in Harford County during the Revolution. (JJJ-588, AAA-2828, and see H. Peden's Revolutionary Patriots of Harford County, MD, 1775-1783, page 197)

RUTLEDGE, MICHAEL. Non-Juror to Oath of Allegiance, 1778. (A-1/20)

RUTLEDGE, PETER. Private in Col. Aquila Hall's Baltimore County Regiment in 1777. (TTT-13)

RUTLEDGE, THOMAS. Involved in evaluation of Baltimore County confiscated proprietary reserve lands in 1782. (FFF-547)

RUTLEDGE, WILLIAM. Non-Juror to Oath of Allegiance, 1778. (A-1/20)

RUTTER, HENRY. Ensign in Capt. Murray's Company, Baltimore Town Battalion, Aug. 30, 1777 (Note: His name appears to be "Butler" but it is actually "Rutter.") Became 2nd Lieutenant in 1778, and then 1st Lieutenant, March 16, 1779. Took the Oath of Allegiance in 1778 before Hon. Richard Cromwell. (A-2/46, LL-66, E-14, F-312/314)

RUTTER, MOSES. Private in Baltimore County Militia; enlisted August 15, 1776. Also served in Baltimore Artillery Company, 1777. Oath of Allegiance, 1778, before Hon. James Calhoun. (A-1/20, A-2/40, V-368, H-58)

RUTTER, RICHARD. Oath of Allegiance, 1778. (A-1/20)

RUTTER, THOMAS. Represented Middlesex Hundred at the Association of Freemen, Aug. 21, 1775. Captain of Baltimore County Militia Company No. 5, December 19, 1775 (commanded 62 Privates). Candidate for Baltimore Committee of Observation, Sept. 12, 1775, but not elected. Served on Baltimore Committee of Safety, May 13, 1776, and Captain of 4th Division in Baltimore Battalion under Col. Buchanan in June, 1776, commanding 72 men. Promoted to Major, Mar. 16, 1779 (Note: His name appears to be "Butler" but it is actually "Rutter.") "Thomas Rutter, Sr." took Oath of Allegiance in 1778 before Hon. Richard Cromwell. (EEEE-1726, RR-50, DD-47, FF-64, ZZ-254, G-10, CC-36, F-312, F-313, A-1/20, A-2/46

RUTTER, THOMAS (OF RICHARD). Private in Baltimore County Militia; enlisted Aug. 15, 1776. Oath of Allegiance, 1778, before Hon. Richard Cromwell. (H-58, A-1/20,A-2/46)

RUTURT, JACOB. Private in Capt. Graybill's German Regiment, July 12, 1776. (ZZ-32)

RUXTON, ELSWORTH. Private in Capt. J. Cockey's Baltimore County Dragoons at Yorktown in 1781. (MMM-A)

RYAN, ANTHONY. Served in Baltimore Artillery Company in 1777. (V-368)

RYAN, EDMON. Oath of Allegiance, 1778, before Hon. Jesse Dorsey. (A-1/20, A-2/63)

RYAN, JAMES. Born 1746 in Ireland. Enlisted July 5, 1776 in Baltimore County as a Private in Col. Ewing's Battalion. Height: 5' 7¼"; fullfaced. Recruited for the 3rd MD Regiment by Samuel Chester in Baltimore on March 2, 1780. On November 5, 1781 it was "ordered that the Commissary of Issues at Baltimore deliver to Auty RYAN, wife of James RYAN, a soldier in the 3rd MD Regiment, one ration per day until further orders or she can receive the allowance made her by the Orphans Court of Baltimore County." (AAAA-661, H-57, H-334)

RYAN, JAMES. Married Eleanor GREEN in March, 1774, in Baltimore County. Served in Capt. Moore's Troops, June 25, 1781; rode a six year old bay gelding horse. Was a Revolutionary pensioner, and received Federal Bounty Land Grant 1120 for 100 acres, April 15, 1825. (BBBB-313, YY-45, YY-122, YY-77)

RYAN, JAMES. Signed a letter to Governor Lee on April 4, 1781, requesting that the militia be called up to protect Baltimore from the British. (S-49)

RYAN, JOHN. Recruit in Baltimore County in 1780. (H-340)

RYAN (RYON), THOMAS. Recruit in Baltimore County Militia, April 11, 1780. (H-335)

RYAN (RIAN), WILLIAM. Born 1750 in America. Enlisted July 5, 1776 as a Private in
Col. Ewing's Battalion. Height: 5' 7¼"; black hair. Was a Private in Capt. Gist's
Company, 3rd MD Regiment in February, 1778. Took Oath of Allegiance in 1778 before
Hon. George Lindenberger. (H-54, H-600, A-1/20, A-2/54)

RYANT, JAMES. Private in Baltimore County Militia; enlisted July 19, 1776. (H-58)

RYE, HENRY. Non-Juror to Oath of Allegiance, 1778. (A-1/20)

RYLAND, NICHOLAS. Private in Count Pulaski's Legion; enlisted in Baltimore on May 8,
1778. Took Oath of Allegiance, 1778, before Hon. William Spear. (A-2/67, H-593)

RYSTON, ABRAHAM. Oath of Allegiance, 1778, before Hon. Jesse Dorsey. (A-1/20, A-2/64)

S

SADLER (SADDLER), JOSEPH. Oath of Allegiance, 1778, before Hon. James Calhoun. (A-2/38)

SADLER (SADDLER), SAMUEL. 3rd Lieutenant in Capt. Furnival's MD Artillery; commissioned
January 5, 1776, and still with that company on November 17, 1777. Commissioned as
Captain-Lieutenant, September 3, 1779, in MD Artillery Company No. 3 under Lt. Col.
Ed. Carrington. Served in Capt. Gale's MD Artillery, 1779; on furlough, Nov., 1779,
to Feb., 1780. Source YYY-1/101 states he was AWOL on April 13, 1780, while Source
VVV-96 states he resigned prior to May 11, 1780. Either way, he was back in service
as 1st Lieutenant in Capt. Tool's Company, Baltimore Town Battalion, April 26, 1781.
(H-572, FFF-129, VVV-96, YYY-1/101, AAAA-416)

SADLER, THOMAS. (1745, Queen Anne County, MD - 1794, Baltimore County, MD) He married
Ann LONG on January 1, 1765, and their children: Thomas SADLER (born 1765) married
Elizabeth HOWARD; Mary Ann SADLER (born 1767) married Thomas ROBERTS; and Sewell Long
SADLER (born 1769). Thomas was a Private in Col. Richard Graves' Kent County Militia
in the 13th Battalion, 2nd Company, 7th Class, in June, 1778. (XXX-625, XXX-626)

SADLER, WILLIAM. Non-Juror to Oath of Allegiance, 1778. (A-1/20)

SALMON, GEORGE. Died in Septembr, 1807, at his residence on Calvert Street in Baltimore.
His wife, Rebecca MERCER, died September 21, 1797, age 47. Their son, Captain George
SALMON, of the 2nd U.S. Regiment, died at Fort Wilkinson on December 20, 1803. George
SALMON (Sr.) was a Baltimore Privateer, took the Oath of Allegiance in 1778 before
Hon. James Calhoun, and quartered horses in his home, September 7, 1782. (ZZZ-282,
FFF-545, III-207, A-1/20, A-2/42)

SAMPSON, ABRAM. Non-Juror to Oath of Allegiance in 1778. (A-1/20)
SAMPSON, DAVID. Non-Juror to Oath of Allegiance in 1778. (A-1/20)
SAMPSON, EMANUEL. Non-Juror to Oath of Allegiance in 1778. (A-1/20)

SAMPSON, ISAAC. Private in Col. Aquila Hall's Baltimore County Regiment, 1777. Was a
Non-Juror to Oath of Allegiance, 1778. (TTT-13, A-1/20)

SAMPSON, ISAAC SR. Non-Juror to Oath of Allegiance, 1778. Involved in evaluation of
Baltimore County confiscated proprietary reserve lands in 1782. (A-1/20, FFF-547)

SAMPSON, ISAAC JR. Non-Juror to Oath of Allegiance, 1778. (A-1/20)
SAMPSON, RICHARD. Non-Juror to Oath of Allegiance, 1778. (A-1/20)
SAMPSON, RICHARD (OF ISAAC). Non-Juror to Oath of Allegiance, 1778. (A-1/20)

SAMUEL, MASHECK. Private in Capt. Howell's Company, December 30, 1775. (G-11)

SANDALL (SANDLE), JNO. Private in Capt. Furnival's MD Artillery, November 17, 1777.
Matross in Capt. J. Smith's MD Artillery, 1780. Earlier, he was a Matross in Capt.
Dorsey's MD Artillery at Valley Forge on June 3, 1778, and was with that company at
Camp Col. Scirvins on January 28, 1782. Entitled to 50 acres (lot 1133) in western
Maryland for his services as Artillery Matross. (DDDD-31, H-573, H-579, UU-231/232)

SANDERS, BENJAMIN. Non-Juror to Oath of Allegiance, 1778. (A-1/21)
SANDERS, JOHN. Non-Juror to oath of Allegiance, 1778. (A-1/21)

SANDERS, ROBERT. Recommended by William Lux to the Baltimore Council of Safety on July 15, 1776, that he be commissioned a Captain of Militia. (FFF-43)

SANDERSON, FRANCIS. Served on baltimore Town Committee of Correspondence, and the Baltimore County Committee of Inspection in 1775. "Francis A. Sanderson" took Oath of Allegiance in 1778 before Hon. James Calhoun. (SS-130, RR-19, A-2/38)

SANDERSON, JOSEPH. Oath of Allegiance, 1778, before Hon. George Lindenberger. (A-1/21, A-2/54)

SANDLANT, WILLIAM. Enlisted July 7, 1776 in Baltimore county as a Private in Colonel Ewing's Battalion; not on muster roll in August, 1776. (H-57)

SANK, GEORGE. Volunteered into Baltimore County Regiment No. 36, circa 1777. (TTT-13)

SANK, JOHN. Oath of Allegiance, 1778, before Hon. Thomas Sollers. (A-1/21, A-2/51)

SANK, ZACHARIAH. Non-Juror to Oath in 1778, but signed in 1781. (QQ-119)

SANSBURY, JOHN. On February 7, 1840, it was ordered to "pay to Sarah SANSBURY, of Baltimore City, widow of John, a Private Marine in Revolutionary War, or to her order, quarterly, commencing January 1, 1840, half pay of a Private during her life, in consideration of her husband's services." (C-388)

SAPP, DANIEL. Non-Juror to Oath of Allegiance in 1778. (A-1/21)
SAPP, FRANCIS. Non-Juror to Oath of Allegiance in 1778. (A-1/21)

SAPPINGTON, FRANCIS B. Oath of Allegiance, 1778, before Hon. George Lindenberger. (A-1/21, A-2/54)

SARA, DOMINICK. Enlisted at Fort Whetstone Point in Baltimore on September 28, 1779, but deserted from the Recruiting Officer. (H-626)

SARGEANT, AQUILLA. Non-Juror to Oath of Allegiance, 1778. (A-1/21)
SARGEANT, SAMUEL. Non-Juror to Oath of Allegiance, 1778. (A-1/21)
SARGEANT, WILLIAM. Non-Juror to Oath of Allegiance, 1778. (A-1/21)

SATER (SAYTER), CHARLES. Married Mary OGG in 1781. Was a Private in Capt. Cox's Co. December 19, 1776, and Capt. McClellan's Company, September 4, 1780. Took Oath of Allegiance in 1778 before Hon. James Calhoun. (A-1/21, A-2/41, CCC-22, CCC-24, and History Trails, Vol. 9, page 24, 1975)

SATER, HENRY. (April 27, 1745 - 1788) Married Hannah StANSBURY. Took the Oath of Allegiance in 1778 before Hon. James Calhoun. (A-1/21, A-2/40, JJJ-593)

SATER (SAYTER), JOSEPH. Married Hannah STANSBURY. Served in Baltimore Mechanical Company of Militia, November 4, 1775. Private in Capt. Cox's Company, Dec. 19, 1776. Took Oath of Allegiance in 1778 before Hon. James Calhoun. Joseph was born in 1753 and died in 1833. (A-1/21, A-2/40, CCC-21, F-298, and History Trails, Vol. 9, page 24, 1975)

SAUBLE, MICHAEL. Private in Baltimore County Regiment No. 15, circa 1777. (TTT-13)

SAUER (SAUR), JOHN. Oath of Allegiance, 1778, before Hon. Peter Shepherd. (A-2/50)

SAUERBREY, GEORGE. Oath of Allegiance, 1778, before Hon. George Lindenberger. (A-2/54)

SAUNDERS, EDWARD. Private in Capt. Howell's Company, December 30, 1775. Private in Capt. Cox's Company, December 19, 1776. (CCC-21, G-11)

SAUNDERS, JOHN. Matross in Capt. Brown's MD Artillery; joined November 22, 1777. At Valley Forge until June, 1778; at White Plains, July, 1778; at Fort Schuyler in August and September, 1780; not listed in 1781. (UU-228, UU-230)

SAVAGE, HILL. Non-Juror to oath of Allegiance in 1778. (A-1/21)

SAVATEER, JOHN. Oath of Allegiance, 1778, before Hon. William Lux. Stored flour in 1780 for the Baltimore Town Committee. (RRR-6, A-1/21, A-2/68)

SAWLEY, HENRY. Oath of Allegiance, 1778. (A-1/21)

SAWYER, GEORGE. Recruited in Baltimore by Samuel Chester for the 3rd MD Regiment on March 2, 1780. (H-334)

SAYCHAS. THOMAS. Private in Baltimore County Regiment No. 7, circa 1777. (TTT-13)

SAYLERS, WILLIAM. Private in Baltimore County Militia; enlisted July 18, 1776. (H-58)

SCARFF, JOHN. Non-Juror to Oath of Allegiance in 1778. (A-1/21)

SCARFF (SCARF, SCHARF), WILLIAM. (1749-1778) Married Elizabeth HARRISON, and their son William SCARF, Jr. married Susannah CHRISTOPHER (1782-1866) in 1808, and their grandson Thomas George SCHARF (1816-1886) married Anna Maria McNULTY (1820-1889) in 1837. William was an Ensign in Capt. E. Cockey's Company No. 2 as of August 26, 1776, and 2nd Lieutenant, December 20, 1776. He was 1st Lieutenant in Capt. Harvey's Company, Gunpowder Upper Battalion, August 30, 1777. Took the Oath of Allegiance, in 1778, before Hon. Edward Cockey. He was still in service in 1778 when he died (cause not stated). (E-12, KK-66, BBB-350, PPP-2, RR-98, ZZ-541, AAA-513, JJJ-596, A-2/61)

SCARFFSON, JOHN (OF JOHN). Took Oath of Allegiance in 1781. (QQ-119)

SCASEBRICK, DANIEL. Private in Baltimore Artillery Company, October 16, 1775. (G-8)

SCHAEFER, H. Member of Baltimore Mechanical Company of Militia during War. (CCC-25)

SCHAEFFER, ADAM. Private in Capt. Keeports' German Regiment; enlisted July 21, 1776. Was at Philadelphia, September 19, 1776. (H-263)

SCHESLER, GEORGE. Private in Capt. Keeports' German Regiment; enlisted Aug. 10, 1776. Was at Philadelphia, September 19, 1776. (H-263)

SCHLEY (SHLEY), JOHN. Born 1749 in Bucks County, Pennsylvania. Occupation: Brickmaker. Height: 5' 10¼". Enlisted January 24, 1776 in Capt. N. Smith's 1st Company of Matrosses. Private in that artillery at Fort Whetstone Point in Baltimore, January 24, 1777. (H-566, H-564, VV-74, QQQ-2)

SCHOFFEIL, JOHN. Non-Juror to Oath of Allegiance, 1778. (A-1/21)

SCHOOLING, WILLIAM. Enlisted in Baltimore County on July 20, 1776. (H-53)

SCHORCHT, JOHN. Private in Capt. Keeports' German Regiment; enlisted August 8, 1776. Was at Philadelphia, September 19, 1776. (H-263)

SCHRACH, ANDREW. On March 12, 1829, it was ordered to pay him, "of Baltimore City, during life, half yearly, half pay of a Private for his services during the war." (C-389) This man might be the same as Andrew Shrink (Shrike) contained herein.

SCHREOGLY (SHREAGLEY), MICHAEL. (1749 - September, 1801, Fell's Point, Baltimore, MD) "Michael Schrily" was a Private in Baltimore Artillery Company, October 16, 1775. "Michael Schreogly" took Oath of Allegiance, 1778, before Hon. George Lindenberger. "Michael "Shreagley" died in Baltimore in 1801. (ZZZ-291, G-8, A-1/21, A-2/54)

SCHRIER, MATHIAS. Private in Capt. Keeports' German Regiment; enlisted July 21, 1776. Was at Philadelphia, September 19, 1776. (H-263)

SCHÜTZ, JACOB. Private in Capt. Keeports' German Regiment; enlisted August 11, 1776. Was at Philadelphia, September 19, 1776. (H-263)

SCHWARTZ, JACOB. Oath of Allegiance, 1778, before Hon. Geo. Lindenberger. (A-2/54)

SCONE, CHARLES. Served on ship Defence, March 6 to June 30, 1777. (H-659)

SCOTT, ABRAHAM (ABRAM). Source A-1/21 states two Non-Jurors had this name, 1778.

SCOTT, AMOS. Non-Juror to Oath of Allegiance in 1778. (A-1/21)

SCOTT, ANDREW. Oath of Allegiance, 1778, before Hon. James Calhoun. (A-1/21, A-2/40)

SCOTT, BENJAMIN. Drafted into Baltimore County Regiment 36, circa 1777. (TTT-13)

SCOTT, JAMES. Born 1740 in Antrim, Ireland. Occupation: Shoemaker. Height: 5' 9¼". Enlisted January 31, 1776 as Private in Capt. N. Smith's 1st Company of Matrosses. Reported dead or deserted, June 13, 1776. (H-565, H-568, QQQ-2)

SCOTT, JAMES. In Baltimore on March 10, 1777, he made an oath to attempt a prisoner exchange with Capt. George Cook of the State Ship Defence. (FFF-94)

SCOTT, JOHN. Non-Juror to Oath of Allegiance, 1778. (A-1/21)

SCOTT, MATTHEW. Oath of Allegiance, 1778, before Hon. James Calhoun. (A-1/21, A-2/39)

SCOTT, MOSES. Ordinary Seaman on ship Defence, 1776, and Marine, 1777. (H-607, H-659)

SCOTT, REUBEN. Matross in Capt. Brown's MD Artillery; joined November 22, 1777. Was at Valley Forge until June, 1778; at White Plains, July, 1778; at Fort Schuyler in August and September, 1780; at High Hills of the Santee, August, 1781; at Camp Col. Scirvins, January, 1782; and at Bacon's Bridge, S.C., April, 1782. (UU-228, UU-230)

SCOTT, SAMUEL. Non-Juror to Oath of Allegiance, 1778. (A-1/21)

SCOTT, STOFEL. Oath of Allegiance, 1778. (A-1/21)

SCOTT, WILLIAM. Private in Baltimore Artillery Company, October 16, 1775. Took Oath of Allegiance, 1778, before Hon. Thomas Sollers. (A-1/21, A-2/51, G-8)

SCROGGIN, PHILIP. Bombardier in Capt. Gale's MD Artillery, Nov. 8, 1779. (YYY-1/104)

SEAGREAVE, PATRICK. Served on ship Defence, May 21 to July 28, 1777. (H-659)

SEALS (SEARLS), JOHN. Source A-1/21 states "John Searls" took the Oath of Allegiance in 1778, and Source A-2/54 states "John Seals."

SEBRICH, WILLIAM. Oath of Allegiance, 1778. (A-1/21)

SEEA, JOHN. Marine on ship Defence, 1777. (H-659)

SEGESSER (SEGAUER), MARTIN. Private in Capt. Cox's Company, December 19, 1776. Took Oath of Allegiance in 1778 before Hon. James Calhoun. Private in Capt. McClellan's Company, September 4, 1780. (CCC-21, CCC-24, A-1/21, A-2/41)

SEGMAN, PETER. Private in Capt. Graybill's German Regiment in 1776. (H-266)

SEHIEL, CARL. Oath of Allegiance, 1778, before Hon. George Lindenberger. (A-1/21, A-2/54)

SEIDENSTRICKER, FREDERIC D. Baltimore Mechanical Company of Militia, 1776. (CCC-28)

SEITH, JOHN. Private in Capt. J. Cockey's Baltimore County Dragoons at Yorktown in 1781. (MMM-A)

SELBY, JOHN. Oath of Allegiance, 1778, before Hon. Peter Shepherd. (A-2/49)

SELBY, VINCENT JAMES. Non-Juror to Oath of Allegiance, 1778. (A-1/21)

SELDIS, JOHN. Oath of Allegiance, 1778, before Hon. James Calhoun. (A-2/38)

SELLER, THOMAS. Matross in Capt. Gale's MD Artillery, 1779. Deserted September 29, 1779 at Trenton. (YYY-1/105)

SELLERS, PAUL. Non-Juror to Oath of Allegiance, 1778. (A-1/21)
SELLERS, WILLIAM. Non-Juror to Oath of Allegiance, 1778. (A-1/21)

SELLMAN (SILLMAN), JOHN. Oath of Allegiance in 1778 before Hon. Peter Shepherd. Was a Matross in Capt. Brown's MD Artillery as of January 1, 1781; at High Hills of Santee in August, 1781; at Camp Col. Scirvins in January, 1782; at Baocn's Bridge, S.C., in April, 1782. Entitled to 50 acres (lot 1341) in western Maryland for his services. (UU-230, DDDD-32, A-1/21, A-2/49)

SELLMAN, JOHNSEY. "Johnce Sellman" took the Oath of Allegiance in 1778 before Hon. William Lux. "Johnsy Selman" was a 2nd Lieutenant in Soldiers Delight Battn., 1778. "Johnsey Sellman" was 2nd Lieutenant in Capt. E. Dorsey's Company, May 27, 1779, of the Soldiers Delight Battalion, and 2nd Lieutenant in Capt. Young's Company, Sept.25, 1780, of the Baltimore Town Battalion. On May 20, 1814, George M. SELLMAN, son of "Johnzee Sellman," died in his 29th year, leaving a wife and child. (ZZZ-287, E-11, GGG-422, VV-303, HH-24, A-1/21, A-2/68)

SELLMAN, JONATHAN. (1753/1757, Annapolis, MD - September 9, 1817, Baltimore, MD) Son of Jonathan SELLMAN and Elizabeth BATTEE, and grandson of William SELLMAN and Ann

SELLMAN, JONATHAN (continued)
SPARROW, and Ferdinand and Elizabeth BATTEE. There appears to have been two men by this name during the Revolution. Source XXX-639 lists one who married Elizabeth DAWSON in 1783 and was a Patriot (service not stated), and had daughters, Charlotte SELLMAN who married Charles CROOK, and Polly or Patty SELLMAN who married Robert WELCH. Parran's Register of Maryland's Heraldic Families (Vol. II, pp. 321-323) also gives a Jonathan SELLMAN who married (1) Rachel LUCAS in 1783, and (2) Ann Elizabeth HARWOOD, daughter of Col. Richard HARWOOD of Anne Arundel County. This source states Jonathan Sellman was a Major and General of the 3rd MD Regiment, with military duty at Valley Forge, and a member of the Order of the Cincinnati. His children were John, Alfred, Richard, Elizabeth, Margaret, and Ann. Major Sellman was also entitled to 200 acres (lots 3893, 3894, 3895, 2525) in western Maryland for his services.(DDDD-4)

SELLMAN, JOSEPH. Non-Juror to Oath of Allegiance, 1778. (A-1/21)

SELLMAN, THOMAS. (November 29, 1727 - 1794) Married Ruth SHIPLEY. Took the Oath of Allegiance in 1778 before Hon. Edward Cockey. (A-1/21, A-2/61, JJJ-604)

SELLMAN, WILLIAM. (c1720 - 1796) Married Charity SPARROW. Took Oath of Allegiance, 1778, before Hon. Edward Cockey. (A-1/21, A-2/61, JJJ-604)

SELLY, JOHN. Private in Baltimore County Militia; enlisted July 18, 1776. (H-58)

SENCY, WILLIAM. Served on ship Defence, April 28 to August 15, 1777. (H-659)

SENN, JOHN MICHAEL. Oath of Allegiance, 1778. (A-1/21)

SENSE, ADAM. Non-Juror to Oath of Allegiance, 1778. (A-1/21)
SENSE, CHRISTIAN. Non-Juror to Oath of Allegiance, 1778. (A-1/21)
SENSE, CHRISTOPHER. Non-Juror to Oath of Allegiance, 1778. (A-1/21)

SENSE (SENCE), JOHN. Private, Baltimore County Regiment 15, circa 1777. (TTT-13)

SENSE, PETER. Non-Juror to Oath of Allegiance, 1778. (A-1/21)

SERJANT, JOHN. Oath of Allegiance, 1778, before Hon. Thomas Sollers. (A-1/21, A-2/51)

SERMON, LEONARD. Served on ship Defence, January 23 to April 11, 1777. (H-659)

SERVITEER, SAMUEL. Non-Juror to Oath of Allegiance, 1778. (A-1/21)

SETTLEMIRES, CHRISTIAN. Private in Capt. Keeports' German Regiment; enlisted July 17, 1776. Was at Philadelphia, September 19, 1776. (H-263)

SEWELL, WILLIAM. Oath of Allegiance, 1778, before Hon. James Calhoun.(A-1/21, A-2/38)

SHADLEY, JACOB. Private, Capt. Deams' Co., 7th MD Regt., December 27, 1776. (H-305)

SHADWICK, REUBIN. Oath of Allegiance, 1778, before Hon. Charles Ridgely of Wm. (A-2/27)

SHAFER, BALTZEL. Baltimore Mechanical Company of Militia in 1776. (CCC-28)

SHAFFER, FREDERIC. Baltimore Mechanical Company of Militia in 1776. (CCC-28)

SHAFFER, JACOB. Oath of Allegiance, 1778, before Hon. James Calhoun. (A-1/21, A-2/42)

SHAFFER, JOHN. (January 11, 1753 - August 11, 1823) Wife named Ann Maria. He served as Private in Capt. Graybill's German Regiment in 1776, and took the Oath of Allegiance in 1778 before Hon. James Calhoun. (JJJ-606, H-265, ZZ-32, A-1/21, A-2/42)

SHAKESPEARE, SAMUEL. Non-Juror to Oath of Allegiance in 1778. (A-1/21)
SHAKLE, WILLIAM. Non-Juror to Oath of Allegiance in 1778. (A-1/21)
SHALL (SHAUL), JOSEPH. Non-Juror to Oath of Allegiance in 1778. Involved in evaluation of Baltimore County confiscated proprietary reserve land in 1782. (FFF-543, A-1/21)

SHANE (SHEAN), ARTHUR. Born 1756 in America. Enlisted July 5, 1776 in Baltimore County as Private in Col. Ewing's Battalion. Height: 5'5¼"; long light colored hair. (H-57)

SHANE (SHEAN), HENRY. Enrolled by Lt. Joshua Miles on January 27, 1776. On March 12, 1828 it was ordered to pay him, "of Baltimore County, during life, half yearly, half pay of a Private, as further remuneration for his services during Revolutionary War." (name spelled "Shean") On February 7, 1830, it was ordered to "pay to Henry W. Shane money due his father, Henry Shane, a Revolutionary soldier at time of his decease." (C-390, H-60)

SHANGLET, JOHN. Non-Juror to oath of Allegiance in 1778. (A-1/21)

SHANLEY, JACOB. Private in Baltimore County Militia; enlisted July 5, 1776. (H-58)

SHARMILLER, GODDLIB. Oath of Allegiance, 1778, before Hon. Charles Ridgely of William. (A-1/21, A-2/27)

SHARP, GEORGE. Non-Juror to Oath of Allegiance, 1778. (A-1/21)

SHARP, JACOB (CACOB). Oath of Allegiance, 1778, before Hon. James Calhoun. (A-2/41)

SHARP, JOHN SR. There were two men with this name (or else the same man signed twice): One before Hon. Robert Simmons, and one before Hon. Jesse Dorsey, took the Oath of Allegiance in 1778. (A-2/58, A-2/63, A-1/21)

SHARP, JOHN JR. 1st Lieutenant in Capt. Shaw's Company No. 5 as of August 26, 1776. (PPP-2, RR-99, ZZ-541)

SHARP, PETER. Midshipman on ship Defence, September 19, 1776 - 1777. (H-606, H-659)

SHARP, WILLIAM. Oath of Allegiance, 1778, before Hon. Robert Simmons. "Wm. Sharpe" was in the Baltimore Mechanical Company of Militia in 1776. (CCC-28,A-1/21,A-2/58)

SHARPER, ENOCH. Non-Juror to Oath of Allegiance, 1778. (A-1/21)

SHAUGHNESS, PATRICK. Born 1754 in Dublin, Ireland. Occupation: Breeches Maker. Enlisted January 31, 1776 as Private in Capt. N. Smith's 1st Company of Matrosses. Private in capt. Dorsey's MD Artillery, November 17, 1777, and a Matross in that company at Valley Forge, June 3, 1778. (UU-231, H-565, H-567, H-574, VV-74, QQQ-2)

SHAVER, JACOB JR. Non-Juror to Oath of Allegiance in 1778. (A-1/21)

SHAVER, JOHN. Ensign in Capt. Hahn's Co., Upper Battalion, Nov. 5, 1781. (AAAA-662)

SHAW, ALEXANDER. Private in Capt. S. Smith's Co. No. 8, 1st MD Battn., January 23, 1776. (H-640)

SHAW, ARCHIBALD. (1755, County Derry, Ireland - June 22, 1845, Baltimore, Maryland) Son of John SHAW. Married (1) Mary_____ (2) Priscilla_____ (3) Agnes_____. Children: Evelina (1780-1843) married (1) John THOMPSON, and (2) Joseph FORD (1765-1843) of Kent County, MD, and their daughter, Mary Evelyn FORD (1819-1895) married James Jackson COCKRILL (1815-1878) in 1838 in Baltimore; Daniel A. SHAW (1783-1855) married Margaret_____, and their son Robert (1816-1869) married (1) Barbary STROBEL, and (2) Elizabeth JOHNSON, in Baltimore; Richard (born 1784); Margaret (born 1786); and, Mary SHAW, married an EMMERSON. Archibald's first wife died in York County, PA circa 1781. He is buried in Govans Presbyterian Church in Baltimore. He served in Col. hartley's Regiment in February, 1776, and in Col. Rankin's Regiment in November, 1777. (XXX-642, AAA-2569, AAA-1822C, JJJ-608, XXX-642, XXX-643)

SHAW, DANIEL. Captain of Baltimore County Militia Company No. 5 as of August 26, 1776, commanding 95 Privates, under Col. Ed. Cockey's Battalion. Took Oath of Allegiance, 1778, before Hon. Jesse Dorsey. (ZZ-541, PPP-2, RR-99, A-1/21, A-2/63)

SHAW, JOHN. Non-Juror to Oath of Allegiance in 1778. (A-1/21)
SHAW, NATHAN. Non-Juror to Oath of Allegiance in 1778. (A-1/21)

SHAW, PETER. Oath of Allegiance, Baltimore County, March 19, 1778. (BBB-541)

SHAW, ROBERT. Non-Juror to Oath of Allegiance in 1778. (A-1/21)

SHAW, THOMAS. (July, 1745 - December 22, 1829, Patapsco Neck, Baltimore County, MD) His wife, Ann, died March 14, 1814, aged 87. They are buried in the Shaw family cemetery on North Point Road. Thomas SHAW married Ann HORTON in 1778. He took the Oath of Allegiance in 1778 before Hon. James Calhoun. He was a member of the Methodist Church for 40 years, a Revolutionary War patriot, and held a commission as an Ensign. (See History Trails, Vol. 6, No. 3, p. 10, 1972; Baltimore Gazette and Daily Advertiser, January 16, 1830; A-1/21, A-2/42

SHAW, THOMAS KNIGHTSMITH. Oath of Allegiance, 1778, before Hon. James Calhoun. (A-1/21, A-2/42) "Thomas Nightsmith Shaw" married Sarah STANSBURY on December 31, 1777, in Baltimore County. (R. Barnes' Maryland Marriages, 1634-1777, page 162)

SHAWN, DANIEL. Oath of Allegiance, 1778. (A-1/21)

SHAWNESEY, TIMOTHY. Private in Baltimore County Militia; enlisted Aug. 15, 1776. (H-58)

SHEAFF, HENRY. Captain, Baltimore Artillery Company, October 16, 1775. Selected to be Ensign in Capt. Howell's Company, December 30, 1775, but a note explains that "Ensign Sheaff was chosen Captain of the Artillery Company in Baltimore." (G-11) Captain of Baltimore Town Company No. 3 in 1776 and served in the militia through 1781. Signed the Oath of Allegiance in 1778 before Hon. William Lux. Commanded 65 men in 1776-77 and requested payment for services, November 13, 1780. Also, made an agreement to supply Maryland officers captured in New York, January 23, 1781. (FFF-357, FFF-334, GG-74, FFF-4, G-8, G-11, FFF-110, W-162, A-1/21, A-2/68)

SHEDBOTTLE, WILLIAM. Non-Juror to Oath of Allegiance in 1778. (A-1/21)

SHEEHAN, PATRICK. Private in Baltimore County Militia; enlisted July 5, 1776. (H-58)

SHEEHAN, TIMOTHY. Private in Baltimore County Militia; enlisted July 18, 1776. (H-58)

SHEETS, ADAM. Recruited in Baltimore, March 2, 1780, for 3rd MD Regiment by Samuel Chester. (H-334)

SHEIDEL, EHRHARD. Oath of Allegiance, 1778, before Hon. George Lindenberger. (A-2/54)

SHEILD, WILLIAM. (1760, Kent County, MD - September 2, 1816, Baltimore, MD) Married Rachel BALL (1766-1857), daughter of James BALL and Elizabeth KEMP, in 1786. Their daughter Elizabeth (1790-1865) married John APPLEBY (1789-1834) in 1814, and their granddaughter Susan APPLEBY (1815-1877) married Matthew McCLINTOCK (1806-1885) in 1832. William SHEILD was a Private in Capt. Veazey's Company, Eastern Shore's 13th Battalion, 1776-1779; fought at battles of Long Island, Germantown, and camped at Valley Forge. (AAA-591A, and Kent County Muster Roll at Md. Hist. Soc. Library)

SHEKKORD, ADAM. Quartermaster, Soldiers Delight Battalion in 1778. (HH-24)

SHELLER, JOHN. Drummer, Capt. Sheaff's Company, June 16, 1777. (W-162)

SHELMERDINE, CHARLES. Oath of Allegiance, 1778, before Hon. James Calhoun. (A-2/41)

SHELMERDINE, STEPHEN. Enlisted in Baltimore County on July 20, 1776. Was Lieutenant in Capt. Deams' Baltimore Town Company, April 12, 1781. Member of Col. Nicholson's Troop of Horse, June 7, 1781. (H-53, AAAA-393, BBBB-274)

SHEPHERD, ADAM. Oath of Allegiance, 1778, before Hon. Andrew Buchanan. (A-1/21, A-2/57)

SHEPHERD, JOHN. Oath of Allegiance, 1778, before Hon. Robert Simmons. (A-1/21, A-2/58)

SHEPHERD (SHEPPARD), MICHAEL. Private, Capt. McClellan's Co., Sept. 4, 1780. (CCC-25)

SHEPHERD (SHEPPARD), NATHANIEL (NATHAN). Private in Col. Aquila Hall's Baltimore County Regiment in 1777. Oath of Allegiance, 1778, before Hon. Hercules Courtenay. (A-2/47) (TTT-13) Source A-1/21 indicates there was also one by this name who was Non-Juror.

SHEPHERD, PETER. (Died 1787) Justice of the Peace in Baltimore County, 1778. He was one of the Magistrates who administered the Oath of Allegiance in 1778. (A-1/21, A-2/49, A-2/56, GGG-242)

SHEPHERD (SHEPARD), THOMAS. Baltimore Artillery Company in 1777. (V-368)

SHEPHERD, WILLIAM. Private in Col. Aquila Hall's Baltimore County Regiment in 1777. (TTT-13)

SHERRAD, MATTHIAS. Volunteered into Baltimore County Regiment 36, circa 1777. (TTT-13)

SHERWOOD, NICHOLAUS (NICHOLAS). (c1746 - 1794) Wife named Susannah. Took Oath of Allegiance, 1778, before Hon. George Lindenberger. (A-1/21, A-2/54, JJJ-612)

SHIELDS, ABRAHAM. Oath of Allegiance, 1778, before Hon. James Calhoun. (A-1/21, A-2/42)

SHIELDS, CALEB. Private in Baltimore Artillery Company, October 16, 1775. Ensign in Capt. Sheaff's Company, June 6, 1776. 2nd Lieutenant in Capt. Dickenson's Company, August 29, 1777, Baltimore Town Battalion, 1778. Took Oath of Allegiance in 1778, before Hon. James Calhoun. Resigned as "1st Lieutenant in the room of Robt. Moss", May 18-19, 1779. He apparently returned to the service because on Feb. 8, 1781, in Capt. Dickenson's Company, he was "replaced by Lt. John Hamilton because he is always drunk and sometimes crazy." (BBBB-61, E-13, Z-63, BBB-348, F-310, F-312, GGG-401, G-8, GG-74, WW-467, W-162, A-1/21, A-2/40)

SHIELDS, CHARLES. Private, Capt. McClellan's Company, September 4, 1780. (CCC-24)

SHIELDS, DAVID. (1737 - October 3, 1811, Baltimore, MD) Member of the Sons of Liberty in 1776. Took Oath of Allegiance in 1778 before Hon. James Calhoun. Signed letters to Governor of Maryland: one on April 4, 1781, requesting the calling of the militia to protect Baltimore from the British, and another on September 4, 1778, informing the government of suspicious flour shipments possibly heading for the enemy. (II-23, S-49, CCC-19, A-1/21, A-2/38) He died at his residence on Gay Street. (ZZZ-291)

SHIELDS, JOHN. Oath of Allegiance, 1778, before Hon. Robert Simmons. (A-1/21, A-2/58)

SHIELDS, PHILIP. Non-Juror to Oath of Allegiance in 1778. (A-1/21)

SHIELDS, WILLIAM. Oath of Allegiance, 1778, before Hon. William Lux. (A-1/21, A-2/68)

SHILLING, CHRISTIAN. Non-Juror to Oath of Allegiance, 1778. (A-1/21)

SHILLING, MICHAEL. Oath of Allegiance, 1778, before Hon. George Lindenberger. (A-2/54) Source A-1/21 mistakenly shows his name as "J. Michael Shilling."

SHINE, JOHN. Oath of Allegiance, 1778, before Hon. Geo. Lindenberger. (A-1/21, A-2/54)

SHIPLEY, ABSALOM. Oath of Allegiance, 1778, before Hon. Peter Shepherd. (A-2/49)

SHIPLEY, ADAM. Oath of Allegiance, 1778. (A-1/21)
SHIPLEY, ADAM C. Oath of Allegiance, 1778. (A-1/21)

SHIPLEY, BENJAMIN. (1750, Baltimore County, MD - July 28, 1828, Anne Arundel County, (now Howard County), MD. Married (2) Amelia HOBBS on August 13, 1791. Children: Hanwital SHIPLEY married O'Neal ROBOSSON; Betsy SHIPLEY married Seth WARFIELD; Rachel SHIPLEY married Mams BECKLEY; Eliza SHIPLEY married Charles HIPSLEY; Mary SHIPLEY married Freedom HIPSLEY; Amelia SHIPLEY married Samuel HIPSLEY; Mararet ShIPLEY married Thomas ROBOSSON; Henry SHIPLEY (born 1792); Lucy SHIPLEY married Denton DIVERS; and, Nathan SHIPLEY (1797-1884) married Maria HAWKINS. Benjamin took the Oath of Allegiance, 1778, before Hon. And.Buchanan. (A-2/64, A-1/21, XXX-646, XXX-647)

SHIPLEY, BENJAMIN. (1751 - February 22, 1812, Baltimore County, MD) His son Caleb died one week earlier, age 21 years. (ZZZ-291) Benjamin took Oath of Allegiance in 1778 before Hon. Jesse Dorsey. (A-1/21, A-2/57)

SHIPLEY, BENJAMIN JR. Oath of Allegiance, 1778, before Hon. Jesse Dorsey. (A-2/64)

SHIPLEY, CHARLES. Non-Juror to Oath of Allegiance, 1778. (A-1/21)

SHIPLEY, EDWARD. Oath of Allegiance, 1778, before Hon. Jesse Dorsey. (A-1/21, A-2/64)

SHIPLEY, GREENBURY. On February 28, 1778, Hon. Andrew Buchanan received a certificate from Hon. Robert Mereweather of Anne Arundel County, that Greenbury Shipley took an Oath of Allegiance before him. (A-2/57) Source A-1/21 gives two men with this name.

SHIPLEY, HENRY. (1759 - February 11, 1828) Married Ruth HOWARD in August, 1782, in Baltimore County (Marriage proven through Maryland pension application). He was a Private in the Maryland Line; received bounty land warrant 38579-160-55; and his wife, Ruth, received pension W6046. (YY-122, JJJ-613, and Raymond Clark's Maryland Revolutionary Pensioners, page 35)

SHIPLEY, JOHN. Private in Baltimore County Militia; enlisted July 19, 1776. Oath of Allegiance, 1778, before Hon. Jesse Dorsey. (H-58, A-1/21, A-2/64)

SHIPLEY, PETER. Drafted into Baltimore County Regiment No. 36, circa 1777. Took Oath of Allegiance, 1778, before Hon. Jesse Dorsey. (TTT-13, A-1/21, A-2/64)

SHIPLEY, PETER (OF ADAM). Non-Juror to Oath of Allegiance in 1778. (A-1/21)

SHIPLEY, PETER (OF SAMUEL). Oath of Allegiance, 1778, before Hon. Andrew Buchanan. (A-1/21, A-2/57)

SHIPLEY, RICHARD SR. (1730-1787) Wife named Christina. Ensign in Capt. Philips' Co., Soldiers Delight Company No. 4, May 13, 1776. Oath of Allegiance, 1778, before Hon. Edward Cockey. (JJJ-613, FF-64, WW-467, A-1/21, A-2/61)

SHIPLEY, RICHARD JR. Oath of Allegiance, 1778. (A-1/21)

SHIPLEY, SAMUEL. Oath of Allegiance, 1778, before Hon. Jesse Dorsey. (A-2/64) Source A-1/21 states there were three men with this name (two Non-Jurors?)

SHIPLEY, SAMUEL SR. In 1778, Hon. Andrew Buchanan received a certificate from Honorable Robert Mereweather of Anne Arundel County, that Samuel Shipley Sr. had taken the Oath of Allegiance before him. (A-2/57, A-1/21)

SHIPLEY, SAMUEL JR. Oath of Allegiance, 1778, before Hon. Andrew Buchanan. (A-2/57) Source A-1/21 states there were two men with this name.

SHIRE, NICHOLAS. Private, Capt. J. Gist's Co., 3rd MD Regt., February, 1778. (H-600)

SHIRTAIL, MICHAEL. Private in Baltimore County Regiment No. 7, circa 1777. (TTT-13)

SHIRWELL, WILLIAM. Oath of Allegiance, 1778, before Hon. Charles Ridgely of William. Could not write; made his mark. (A-2/27)

SHLIFE, JOHN. Baltimore Mechanical Company of Militia, November 4, 1775. Private in Capt. Graybill's German Regiment, July 12, 1776. (F-299, H-265, ZZ-32)

SHOLL, PHILIP. Oath of Allegiance, 1778, before Hon. Peter Shepherd. (A-1/21, A-2/49)

SHOOK, PETER. Non-Juror to Oath of Allegiance in 1778. (A-1/21)

SHORT, CHRISTOPHER. Able Seaman on ship Defence, 1776, and Sailor, 1777. (H-606, H-659)

SHORT, PATRICK. Non-Juror to Oath of Allegiance in 1778. (A-1/21)

SHOWERS (SHOURS), JOHN. Captain in Upper Battalion, August 30, 1777. Took Oath of Allegiance, 1778, before Hon. William Spear. Left service prior to November 5, 1781. (A-1/21, A-2/66, LL-66, E-14, VV-114, AAAA-662, BB-350)

SHOWERS, THOMAS. Non-Juror to Oath of Allegiance, 1778. (A-1/21)

SHRACK, PITER. Oath of Allegiance, 1778. (A-1/21)

SHRANK, JOHN. (Died in Baltimore County circa 1784) Wife named Catherine. Children: Catherine, John (born 1772), and Elizabeth. "John Shrank" took the Oath of Allegiance in 1778 before Hon. James Calhoun (A-2/39), but Source A-1/21 spells his name "John Shrunk." (D-10)

SHRIACK (SHRIOCK, SHRYOCK), JOHN MICHAEL. Born 1752. Private in Capt. Graybills' Co., German Regiment, July 12, 1776. Oath of Allegiance, 1778, before Hon. James Calhoun. (A-1/21, A-2/42, H-265, ZZ-32, YY-47)

SHRIACK (SHRIOCK, SHRYOCK), MICHAEL. Private in Capt. McClellan's Company, Baltimore Town, September 4, 1780. Took Oath of Allegiance, 1778, before Hon. James Calhoun. (A-1/21, A-2/41, CCC-24)

SHRIACK, MICHAEL SR. Non-Juror to oath of Allegiance in 1778. (A-1/21)

SHRIER, LODOWICK. Non-Juror to Oath of Allegiance in 1778. (A-1/21)

SHRIM, JOHANNES. Oath of Allegiance, 1778, before Hon. Geo. Lindenberger. (A-2/54)

SHRIM, JOHN. Corporal in Capt. Cox's Company, December 19, 1776. (CCC-21)

SHRIM, JOHN SR. Private in Capt. McClellan's Company, September 4, 1780. (CCC-24)

SHRIM, JOHN JR. Private in Capt. McClellan's Company, September 4, 1780. (CCC-25)

SHRINK (SHRIKE), ANDREW. Born 1758 in Pennsylvania. Occupation: Turner. Enlisted January 28, 1776 as Private in Capt. N. Smith's 1st Company of Matrosses. Height: 5' 6 3/4". Private in Capt. Dorsey's MD Artillery, November 17, 1777, and served as a Matross with that company at Valley Forge, June 3, 1778. Matross in Capt. J. Smith's MD Artillery, 1780-1781, and Matross with Capt. Dorsey's Company at Camp Col. Scirvins, January 28, 1782; served to 1783. Entitled to 50 acres (lot 3046) in western Maryland, and 100 acres under Federal Bounty Land Grant Warrant 11740, April 7, 1791. (DDDD-32, YY-78, ZZ-35, H-564, VV-74, QQQ-2, UU-231, UU-232, H-573, H-579, H-567, YYY-2/42) Also, see "Andrew Schrach" contained herein.

SHRIVER, JACOB. Non-Juror to oath of Allegiance in 1778. (A-1/21)

SHROAD, JACOB. Private, Col. Aquila Hall's Baltimore County Regt., 1777. (TTT-13)

SHROAD, STOPHEL. 1st Lieutenant in Capt. Showers' Company, Upper Battalion, Aug. 30, 1777. (E-14, LL-66, BBB-350)

SHROAD, VALENTINE. Captain in the Upper Battalion, December 4, 1778. (GGG-257)

SHROVER, PETER. Private in Capt. Myers' Company of the German Regiment; served for three years; discharged July 29, 1779. (H-270)

SHRTS (?), JOHN. Baltimore Mechanical Company of Militia, November 4, 1775. (F-299)

SHUBUT, CHRISTR. Recruit in Baltimore County in 1780. (H-340)

SHUE, CHARLES. Baltimore Mechanical Company of Militia, November 4, 1775. (F-299)

SHUGART (SHUGARTH, SUGART), MARTIN. Ensign in Capt. Graybill's German Regiment in 1776. Lieutenant; commissioned May 25, 1778. (UU-237, RR-90, H-266)

SHUSTER, JOSHUA. Non-Juror to Oath of Allegiance, 1778. (A-1/21)

SHUTE, JOHN H. (October 19, 1752/1753, Berlin, Germany - May 4, 1848, Baltimore, MD) Married Mary ASHER in 1781 in New York. Their daughter, Ann Sophia SHUTE, married Benjamin OREM, and their grandson John H. OREM married Margaret E. STRATTNER; and, daughter, Hannah M. SHUTE (born 1782) married John MESSEROLE. John H. SHUTE was a Lieutenant, 1777-1780, in Col. Proctor's PA Artillery, and fought in the battles of Brandywine and Germantown. (XXX-649, AAA-313, AAA-331, and Pennsylvania Archives 2nd Series, Volume XI, page 204)

SHY, JOHN. Matross soldier in Baltimore County. Enlistment deposition, 1779. (FFF-220)

(SIBLE through SILISTER are out of sequence. Information on them is on page 252.)

SILVER, JAMES. Private in Capt. Lansdale's Company, 4th MD Regiment, May 9, 1778 to August 16, 1780. (H-166)

SILVER, JOHN. Non-Juror to Oath of Allegiance, 1778. 9A-1/21)

SILVESTER, JOHN. There were two men with this name who took the Oath of Allegiance in 1778: one before Hon. James Calhoun, and one before Hon. George Lindenberger. (A-1/21, A-2/41, A-2/54)

SIM, JANE. Involved in evaluation of Baltimore county confiscated proprietary reserve lands in 1782. (FFF-547)

SIMISTER, THOMAS. Maryland Line defective, May 4, 1781; resident of Baltimore County. (H-414)

SIMMONS, ALEXIS SR. Oath of Allegiance, 1778, before Hon. Robert Simmons. Could not write; made his mark (" Ξ "). (A-2/58)

SIMMONS, ALEXIS JR. Oath of Allegiance, 1778, before Hon. Robert Simmons. (A-2/58)

SIMMONS, JACOB. Oath of Allegiance, 1778, before Hon. Robert Simmons. (A-2/58)

SIMMONS (SIMMONDS), JAMES. (June 20, 1741 - September 5, 1829) Married Rebecca SHEKELLS. Gunner in Capt. Brown's MD Artillery; joined November 22, 1777. Was at Valley Forge until June, 1778; at White Plains, July, 1778; at Fort Schuyler, in August and September, 1780; Matross at High Hills of the Santee, August 1, 1781; at Camp Col. Scirvins, January, 1782; and at Bacon's Bridge, S.C., in April, 1782.

SIMMONS, JAMES (continued)
   "James Simonds" received 50 acres for his services as Artillery Matross (lot 442 in western Maryland). (UU-228, UU-230, JJJ-617, DDDD-32)

SIMMONS, JOHN. Oath of Allegiance, 1778, before Hon. Robert Simmons. Private in Capt. Oldham's Co., 4th MD Regiment; Private, May 20, 1778; Corporal, February 10, 1780; Private, May 1, 1780; subsequently deserted. (A-2/58, H-167)

SIMMONS, JOSHUA. Oath of Allegiance, 1778, before Hon. Robert Simmons. (A-2/58)

SIMMONS, MOSES. Oath of Allegiance, 1778, before Hon. Robert Simmons. (A-2/58)

SIMMONS, ROBERT. One of the Magistrates who administered the Oath of Allegiance in 1778 in Baltimore County. (A-2/58)

SIMMONS, THOMAS. Private, Capt. Deams' Co., 7th MD Regt., January 19, 1777. (H-305)

SIMMONS, WILLIAM. Married Sarah DARTON on August 9, 1796 in Baltimore County (Marriage proven through Maryland pension application). Private in 3rd MD Regiment. Entitled to bounty land grant 304022-55; wife Sarah received pension W17861. (YY-123, H-393, and Raymond Clark's Maryland Revolutionary Pensioners, page 35)

SIMMS, CHARLES. Private in Capt. S.Smith's Company No. 8, 1st MD Battalion, Jan. 18, 1776. (H-640)

SIMMS, THOMAS. Non-Juror to oath of Allegiance in 1778. (A-1/21)

SIMPSON, ANN. Submitted her account for board and lodging for Lt. Ritter of the State Ship Defence, in Baltimore, on April 8, 1777. (FFF-76)

SIMPSON, BENJAMIN. Boatswain on ship Defence, Sept. 19, 1776 - 1777. (H-606, H-659)

SIMPSON (SIMSON), JAMES. Recruit, Baltimore County Militia, April 11, 1780. (H-335)

SIMPSON, JOHN. ("Tayler.") Oath of Allegiance, 1778, before Hon. John Moale. (A-2/70)

SIMPSON, MRS. Submitted her account for boarding ill people for Capt. George Cook of the State Ship Defence, in Baltimore, April 12, 1777. (FFF-99) See "Ann" above.

SIMPSON, WILLIAM. Oath of Allegiance, 1778, before Hon. Peter Shepherd.(A-1/21,A-2/49)

SINCLAIR, EDWARD. Sergeant in Capt. Ramsey's Company No. 5 in 1776. (H-639)

SINCLAIR (SINCLARE), WILLIAM SR. Oath of Allegiance, 1778, before Hon. Benjamin Rogers. Could not write; made his mark. Delivered flour in Baltimore County, March 2, 1780. (A-1/21, A-2/32, FFF-273) Source A-1/21 also gives "William Sinkclear" in 1778.

SINDELL, DAVID. Died in Baltimore County in 1794, probably the son of Jacob SINDALL and wife Elizabeth, who was born July 20, 1757. A David SINDALL married Delilah PERRIGOE in 1781, and at the time of his death David was married to Ureth COOK whom he had married in 1791. Children: Samuel, Rebecca, Nathan, and David. (D-5) Source A-1/21 indicates "David SINDELL" was a Non-Juror to the Oath of Allegiance in 1778.

SINDELL, JACOB. Non-Juror to oath of Allegiance, 1778. (A-1/21)
SINDELL, PHILIP. Non-Juror to Oath of Allegiance, 1778. (A-1/21)
SINDELL, SAMUEL SR. Non-Juror to oath of Allegiance, 1778. (A-1/21)
SINDELL, SAMUEL JR. Non-Juror to Oath of Allegiance, 1778. (A-1/21)
SINGERY, CHRISTIAN. Non-Juror to Oath of Allegiance, 1778. (A-1/21)

SINGLETON, JOSEPH. Oath of Allegiance, 1778, before Hon.Jesse Dorsey. (A-1/21, A-2/63)

SINKLAIR, MOSES. Oath of Allegiance, 1778, before Hon. George G. Presbury. (A-2/48)

SINKLE, NATHANIEL. Non-Juror to Oath of Allegiance in 1778. (A-1/21)

SITTLER, MATHIAS. Oath of Allegiance, 1778, before Hon. James Calhoun. (A-1/21, A-2/39)

SIZLER, JOHN. Private in Capt. Sheaff's Company, June 16, 1777. (W-162)

SIZLER (SITZLER, SITZLEY), PHILIP. Born 1745 in Pennsylvania. Occupation: Breeches Maker. Enlisted January 24, 1776 as Private in Capt. N. Smith's 1st Company of Matrosses. Height: 5'7". Gave his deposition as a Matross soldier in Baltimore County, concerning enlistment terms, May 7, 1779. On February 29, 1829, ordered to

SIZLER, PHILIP (continued)
"pay to Philip Sizler, of Baltimore city, a soldier of the Revolutionary War,
during life, half yearly, half pay of a Sergeant in the artillery, in consideration of his services during Revolutionary War." (C-392, FFF-220, H-567, VV-74,
H-563, H-569, QQQ-2)

SKERRITT, CLEMENT. Served in Baltimore Artillery Company in 1777. Commissioned a
2nd Lieutenant in Capt. Brown's MD Artillery, Company No. 1, February 5, 1778.
Appointed Quartermaster, December 6, 1779. Was at Valley Forge until June, 1778;
at White Plains, July, 1778. Served under Lt.Col. Ed. Carrington, stationed at
Baltimore, May 11, 1780. On August 1, 1781 he was on furlough from South Carolina
to Maryland. As Captain, he was entitled to 200 acres (lots 2723, 2732, 2733 and
2735) in western Maryland, and also Federal Bounty land Grant Warrant 2047, for
200 acres, July 14, 1789. (YY-78, V-368, UU-227, UU-230, H-477, UU-229, VVV-96,
DDDD-4)

SKIFFINGTON, MATHEW. Enlisted in Baltimore County on July 20, 1776. (H-52)

SKIFFINGTON, ROGER. Marine on ship Defence, January 20 to December 31, 1777. (H-660)

SKINNER, FRANCIS. Prize Master on ship Defence, Sept. 15 to Dec. 31, 1777. (H-660)

SKINNER, JOHN. He notified the Council that the furnace had blown out at Nottingham
Iron Works in Baltimore County "while casting some small cannons for use of the
province, on July 16, 1776." He also took the Oath of Allegiance in 1778 before
Hon. John Beale Howard. (A-1/22, A-2/29, FFF-43, ZZ-61)

SKINNER, THOMAS. Oath of Allegiance, 1778, before Hon. Isaac Van Bibber. (A-2/34)

SKIPPER, JAMES. Non-Juror to Oath of Allegiance in 1778. (A-1/22)
SKIPPER, THOMAS. Non-Juror to Oath of Allegiance in 1778. (A-1/22)

SKULL, WILLIAM. Oath of Allegiance, 1778, before Hon. Edward Cockey.(A-1/22,A-2/61)

SLACK, HENRY. (c1738 - 1820/1825) Wife named Sarah. Sergeant in Capt. Brown's MD
Artillery; joined November 22, 1777. Was at Valley Forge until June, 1778; at
White Plains, July, 1778; at Fort Schuyler in August and September, 1780; at High
Hills of the Santee, August, 1781; at Camp Col. Scirvins, January, 1782; and, at
Bacon's Bridge, S.C., April, 1782. Entitled to 50 acres (lot 491) in western MD
and 100 acres under Federal Bounty Land Grant 1048, July 16, 1822. (DDDD-32,
YY-78, JJJ-620, UU-228, UU-229, UUU-230)

SLACK, JOHN. (1757 - June 3, 1827) Married Maria Margaret AURMAN. Matross in Capt.
Brown's MD Artillery; joined November 22, 1777. Was at Valley Forge until June,
1778; at White Plains, July, 1778; at Fort Schuyler, August and September, 1780;
Sergeant on August 1, 1781, at High Hills of the Santee; at Camp Col. Scirvins in
January, 1782, and at Bacon's Bridge, S.C. in April, 1782. Entitled to 50 acres
(lot 1926) in western Maryland, and Federal Bounty Land Grant 11732 of 100 acres
was issued March 31, 1797 to James DeBAUFRE, Assignee. His wife, Margaret, also
received pension W6072. (YY-78, DDDD-32, UU-228, UU-229, UU-230, JJJ-620, and
Raymond Clark's Maryland Revolutionary Pensioners, page 35)

SLADE, NICHOLAS. (1755-1756, Baltimore County, MD - after 1799, Wilkes County, GA)
Married Martha (Polly) AMOS. Administration papers in Wilkes County show that on
August 5, 1806, Mauldin AMOS and Polly SLADE were administrators of Nicholas SLADE.
Children: Polly, Belinda, Nancy (married Newberry YORK), Sally, Patsy, Charlotte,
Susanna (married Jeptha YORK), Rebeckah, and Josiah. Nicholas SLADE took the Oath
of Allegiance in 1778 before Hon. John Hall, while another Nicholas Slade took the
Oath before Hon. William Lux. (A-1/22, A-2/36, A-2/68, D-10, JJJ-621)

SLADE, WILLIAM. (c1726 - after 1790, Baltimore County, MD) Married Elizabeth DULANY.
Daughter, Belinda SLADE, married Thomas TALBOT, and then Edmund StANSBURY. William
SLADE took the Oath of Allegiance in 1778 before Hon. Jesse Bussey. (XXX-654,
A-1/22, A-2/44, JJJ-621)

SLADE, WILLIAM JR. (1746 - February 27, 1795, Baltimore County, MD) Married Elizabeth
STANSBURY. Children: Dixon, Josias (married Surena MORGAN), Mary (married John

SLADE, WILLIAM JR. (continued)
TALBOTT), William (married Elizabeth ANDERSON), Penelope (married Hosea BROWN), Belinda (married Robert MOORE), Mathilda (married George MULLEN), and Elizabeth (married Dr. George PATTERSON. William SLADE, Jr. took the Oath of Allegiance in 1778 before Hon. Jesse Dorsey. (A-1/22, A-2/63, JJJ-621, XXX-654)

SLAGELL, CHRIS. Non-Juror to Oath of Allegiance in 1778. (A-1/22)

SLAGLE, PETER. Non-Juror to Oath of Allegiance in 1778. (A-1/22)
SLAKER, HENRY. Non-Juror to Oath of Allegiance in 1778. (A-1/22)
SLARP, PETER. Non-Juror to Oath of Allegiance in 1778. (A-1/22)

SLATER, ROBERT. Oath of Allegiance, 1778, before Hon. William Spear. (A-1/22, A-2/67)

SLATER, WILLIAM. Oath of Allegiance, 1778, before Hon. Thomas Sollers. (A-2/51)

SLAYMAKER, JOHN. Lieutenant on ship Defence in 1777. (H-660)

SLIDE, NICHOLAS. Non-Juror to Oath of Allegiance in 1778. (A-1/22)
SLIDER, CHRIST. Non-Juror to Oath of Allegiance in 1778. (A-1/22)

SLOCAM, ELEZER. Oath of Allegiance, 1778, before Hon. James Calhoun. (A-1/22, A-2/38)

SLUPS, STEPHEN. Private, Capt. Deams' Co., 7th MD Regt., December 24, 1776. (H-305)

SLUTS, JOHN. Oath of Allegiance, 1778. (A-1/22)

SLY, JOHN. Private in Capt. Dorsey's MD Artillery, November 17, 1777; reported "sick - peupneumony." Oath of Allegiance, 1778, before Hon. William Spear. (A-1/22, A-2/66, H-574, H-618)

SLYSER, JNO. Private, Capt. Deams' Co., 7th MD Regt., January 7, 1777. (H-305)

SMALL, CONRAD. Oath of Allegiance, 1778, before Hon. James Calhoun. (A-2/38)

SMETHEREST, ROBERT. Enlisted in Baltimore Town on July 17, 1776. (H-53)

SMILIE, JOHN. "Representative in Congress from Pennsylvania, died in Baltimore, age 74, December 31, 1812. A native of Ireland, he served in our Revolutionary War in both civilian and military capacities." (ZZZ-295)

SMITH, ADAM. Oath of Allegiance, 1778, before Hon. George Lindenberger.(A-1/22,A-2/54)

SMITH, ANDREW. (1736 - July 1, 1811, Baltimore County, MD) Wife name Elizabeth (1743-October 30, 1815). Buried at farm called "Prague" off of Belfast and Yeoho Road near Wheeler Lane. Took Oath of Allegiance in 1778 before Hon. Robert Simmons. (A-1/22, A-2/58, and History Trails, Vol. 7, No. 4, page 15, 1974)

SMITH, AQUILA. Private, 7th MD Regiment. Married Catherine CONWAY, September 6, 1785 in Baltimore City (Marriage proven through Maryland pension application). Non-Juror to Oath of Allegiance in 1778. Entitled to 50 acres (lot 2023) in western Maryland for his services. (DDDD-33, YY-123, A-1/22)

SMITH, BILL. Oath of Allegiance, 1778. (A-1/22)

SMITH, CHARLES. Non-Juror to Oath of Allegiance in 1778. (A-1/22)

SMITH, CLEMENT. (1724 - 1792) Married Barbara SIM. In Baltimore, on February 22, 1777, he submitted his account and receipt for supplies and salary as Surgeon's Mate on the State Ship Defence. (FFF-91) Source JJJ-624 states he was a Deputy Commissary in MD.

SMITH, CONRAD. (1742, Baltimore, MD - January 16, 1826, Dickenson Twp., Cumberland Co., PA) Wife named Annie (died September 5, 1843) received Rev. pension W3309. Conrad enlisted in Baltimore and served as Private in 4th MD Regiment. Entitled to 50 acres (lot 1299) in western Maryland, and Bounty Land Warrant 2408-100. (DDDD-33, and Raymond Clark's Maryland Revolutionary Pensioners, page 35)

SMITH, DANIEL. Private, Col. Aquila Hall's Baltimore County Regiment, 1777. (TTT-13)

SMITH, DAVID. Baltimore Mechanical Company of Militia, November 4, 1775. Private in Capt. S. Smith's Company No. 8, 1st MD Battalion, January 24, 1776. (H-641, F-298)

SMITH, EDWARD. Born 1757 in Baltimore County, MD. Resided in Gorham, Ontario Co., New York, in 1818. Enlisted in Baltimore County on July 25, 1776. Received war pension S42323. (H-52, YY-48, and Raymond Clark's MD Rev. Pensioners, page 36)

SMITH, ELIJAH. Born 1752. Resident of Dorchester County, MD. Resided in 1818 in Baltimore County, MD, and died there March 10, 1825. Married Priscilla ABBOTT in 1785 in Dorchester County, MD (Marriage proven through Maryland pension application). Private in 4th MD Regiment, April 22, 1778 to April 2, 1780. Also received Federal Bounty Land Grant 11684 for 100 acres, February 7, 1790, and 50 acres (lot 2017) in western Maryland. In December, 1817, it was ordered to pay him "of Baltimore, an old soldier, during life, quarterly, half pay of a Private for his services during Revolutionary War." On March 9, 1826, it was ordered to "pay to Mrs. Priscilla Smith of Baltimore, whatever balance may be due to her late husband, Elijah Smith, as a pensioner of the state." On April 1, 1839, it was ordered to "pay to Priscilla Smith of Baltimore County, widow of Elijah, a soldier of the revolution, or her order, half pay of a Private of the revolution, quarterly, during her life." (C-393, YY-48, DDDD-33, H-167, YY-79, YY-123, and Raymond Clark's Maryland Revolutionary Pensioners, page 36)

SMITH, EPHRAIM. On February 2, 1843, it was ordered to pay him "of Baltimore City, during life, quarterly, half pay of a Private, in consideration of his services during the Revolutionary War." (C-393)

SMITH, FRANCIS. Died in September, 1789. Wife named Alice. Children: Francis, Margaret and John. Francis SMITH was a Private in Capt. Sheaff's Company; on June 16, 1777, reported he was "really sick." Took the Oath of Allegiance in 1778 before Hon. George Lindenberger. (W-162, D-10, A-1/22, A-2/54)

SMITH, HENRY. Born 1750 in Lancaster, PA. Enlisted in Baltimore, MD as a Private, Capt. Graybill's German Regiment, 1776. Non-Juror to Oath of Allegiance, 1778. Resided in 1842 in Anne Arundel County, MD. received pension S14504. (YY-48, H-266, A-1/22, and Raymond Clark's Maryland Revolutionary Pensioners, page 36)

SMITH, HUGH. Private in Col. Aquila Hall's Baltimore County Regt., 1777. (TTT-13)

SMITH, JACOB. 1st Sergeant in Capt. Keeports' German Regiment; enlisted July 15, 1776. At Philadelphia, September 19, 1776. Non-Juror to Oath of Allegiance in 1778. (A-1/22, H-262)

SMITH, JAMES. Commissioned Captain-Lieutenant in Capt. Brown's MD Artillery, Nov. 22, 1777. Was at Valley Forge until June, 1778; at White Plains, July, 1778. (James Smith, perhaps this one, was a Lieutenant in Capt. Lansdale's Co., 4th MD Regiment and resigned June 20, 1779.) Commissioned Captain, Maryland Artillery, on Nov. 1, 1779, and served under Lt.Col. Ed. Carrington; stationed in Baltimore, May 11, 1780. Served again with Brown's MD Artillery at the High Hills of the Santee, August 1, 1781. Then, joined Capt. Dorsey's MD Artillery, December 24, 1781, ans served as Captain-Lieutenant at Camp Col. Scirvins, January 28, 1782. In 1782 and 1783 he was Captain of Maryland Artillery under command of Major General Greene in the southern campaign. Received 200 acres (lots 2970, 2972, 3138, 3139) in western Maryland for his services, and Federal Bounty Land Grant 2046 for 300 acres. (DDDD-4, YYY-2/44, VVV-96, UU-227, UU-229, UU-230, UU-231, H-477, H-578, YY-78, TT-132, H-166, H-365)

SMITH, JAMES. Private in Capt. Graybill's German Regiment in 1776. Entitled to 50 acres (lot 1439) in western Maryland. Took Oath of Allegiance in 1778 before Hon. Hercules Courtenay. (H-266, DDDD-33, A-1/22, A-2/37)

SMITH, JAMES. Marine on ship Defence, October 22 to December 31, 1777. Took Oath of Allegiance in 1778 before Hon. James Calhoun. (H-660, A-1/22, A-2/40)

SMITH, JOB. Ensign in Capt. Bowen's Company, May 6, 1776. 2nd Lieutenant in Captain McCubbin's Company, Gunpowder Battalion, March 20, 1779. Took Oath of Allegiance in 1778 before Hon. Thomas Sollers. (WW-413, EE-51, E-12, GGG-325, A-1/22, A-2/51)

SMITH, JOHN. "Tayler." Private in Capt. Oldham's Company, 4th MD Regiment; enlisted March 14, 1779; AWOL, Jan. & Feb., 1780; left out March, 1780. (H-167)

SMITH, JOHN. (February, 1722, Ireland - June, 1794, Baltimore, MD) He married Mary
BUCHANAN and their children were: Robert (married Margaret SMITH), Samuel (married
Margaret SPEAR), John, James, Mary, Elizabeth, Margaret and Esther. John SMITH was
very active during the Revolution. Served on Baltimore county Committee of Inspection
on March 13, 1775, Baltimore county Committee of Observation (elected September 23,
1775, and Baltimore Town Committee of Correspondence, November 12, 1775. Became a 2nd
Lieutenant in Baltimore county Militia, 1st Company, December 19, 1775, and 2nd Lieut.
in 2nd Battalion, Flying Camp of Baltimore county, July 15, 1776. Became a 1st Lieut.
in 3rd MD Regiment, December 10, 1776. (Source GG-74 states a John Smith was 1st Lieut.
in Capt. Buchanan's Company No. 1, Baltimore Town Battalion, in 1776, & Source WW-467
states a John Smith was Captain in Baltimore Town Battalion on June 6, 1776.) Lt. John
Smith became Captain in the 3rd MD Regiment on January 1, 1777. He was wounded on Oct.
9, 1779 at Savannah. (Source F-309 and source GGG-401 state John Smith was Captain in
Baltimore County Militia, Baltimore Town Battalion, on May 17, 1779.) John Smith was
wounded and taken prisoner at Camden on August 16, 1780. He was transferred to 5th MD
Regiment on January 1, 1781, and was a prisoner on parole to the close of the war. He
was Brevet Major on September 30, 1783. He received 200 acres as Captain, 3rd MD Rgt.
(lots 2958, 2959, 2961, 2963) in western Maryland, and Federal Bounty Land Grant 2045
for 300 acres on January 26, 1792. (Ed. Note: With such a common name as John Smith it
is possible that the foregoing may or may not apply to more than one Capt. John Smith)
(YY-78, G-10, H-52, BBB-359, F-309, F-311, GGG-401, B-504, TT-132, C-393, E-13, GG-74,
SS-130, WW-467, RR-19, RR-47, RR-50, SS-136, XXX-659, DDDD-4, PP-468, PP-469)

SMITH, JOHN. The following references were found with respect to the name of John Smith:
(1) Pierce's Register lists 35 pay certificates to the John Smith's in Maryland (PP-
468, PP-469); (2) Four John Smith's received Federal Bounty Land Grants between 1789
and 1790 (YY-78); (3) Three John Smith's were susbcribers to the Oath of Allegiance
in Baltimore in 1778: one before Hon. James Calhoun, one before Hon. Thomas Sollers,
and one before Hon. George Lindenberger (A-2/41, A-2/51, A-2/54). Source A-1/22 also
indicates there may have been four other John Smith's who were Non-Jurors in 1778 as
well; (4) Nine John Smith's were Revolutionary War pensioners (YY-48); (5) Seven
John Smith's received 50 acres each for their military service (lots 892, 1078, 1306,
1782, 2003, 2013, and 2022) in western Maryland; (6) Two John Smith's enlisted on
the saem day (August 15, 1776) in Baltimore County's Militia as Privates (H-58); (7)
John Smith was a 1st Sergeant in Capt. Ewing's Company No. 4, enlisted Jan. 8, 1776;
(8) John Smith was a Private in Col. Ewing's Battalion, born 1738 in America, height
5'10", with short hair, enlisted in Baltimore County (H-57); (9) John Smith was a
Private in Capt. Keeports' German Regiemtn, enlisted July 30, 1776, and was serving
at Philadelphia, September 19, 1776 (H-263, H-266); (10) John Smith was recruited
in Baltimore on March 2, 1780 by Samuel Chester for the 3rd MD Regiment; (11) John
Smith was recruited on April 11, 1780 for the Baltimore County Militia (H-334, 335);
(12) John Smith was a Matross in Capt. J. Smith's MD Artillery in 1780, & discharged
September, 1782 (H-579); (13) John Smith was a Matross in Capt. Dorsey's MD Artillery
at Camp Col. Scirvins on January 28, 1782 (UU-232); (14) John Smith was a Matross and
Wagoner in Capt. Gale's MD Artillery, 1779-1780 (YYY-1/106); (15) John Smith enlisted
in Fredericktown, MD, and resided in Baltimore in 1818, age 67; and, (16) John Smith
had sea service and enlisted in Baltimore, and resided in Beaver County, PA in 1835.
(Raymond Clark's Maryland Revolutionary Pensioners, p. 36; DDDD-33, & above sources)

SMITH, JOHN (OF JOHN). Private in Baltimore County Militia in 1776. Private in Captain
Lansdale's Company, 4th MD Regiment, May 29, 1778 to March 1, 1779. (H-59, H-167)

SMITH, JOHN ADDISON. Gunner on ship Defence in 1777. (H-660)

SMITH, JONATHAN. Oath of Allegiance, 1778, before Hon. Robert Simmons.(A-1/22, A-2/58)

SMITH, JOSEPH. (1735, Prince George's County, MD - 1801, Baltimore County, MD) Married
Lucy SMITH and their children were: William (married Middleton BELT), Elizabeth (md.
William MARLOW), Walter (married Harriet SMITH), Lucy, John, Cecia, and Anthony (md.
Middleton Belt SMITH, widow). Joseph SMITH was a Captain in Nathaniel Gist's Conti-
nental Regiment, May 31, 1777, and declared supernumerary on January 1, 1781. He re-
ceived 300 acres under Federal Bounty Land Grant 2041 on June 19, 1789. He was an
Original Member of the Society of the Cincinnati of MD. (TT-132, YY-79, XXX-659)

SMITH, JOSEPH. Born 1740 in America. Enlisted July 5, 1776 in Baltimore County as a Private in Col. Ewing's Battalion. Height: 5' 4½"; short curled hair. (H-57, H-59)

SMITH, JOSEPH. Private in Capt. Howell's Company, December 30, 1775. Private in Capt. Graybill's German Regiment in 1776, and Private in Capt. McClellan's Company in the Baltimore Town Militia, September 4, 1780. (G-11, H-265, CCC-25)

SMITH, JOSEPH. Lieutenant of Marines on ship Defence, 1776-1777. (H-606, H-660)

SMITH, MICHAEL. Drummer and Fifer in Capt. J. Gist's Company, 3rd MD Regiment, in February, 1778. Revolutionary pensioner as a Drummer in Continental Line. (YY-48, H-600) A Michael SMITH was a Private, Capt. McClellan's Co., in 1780. (CCC-25)

SMITH, NATHANIEL. Captain of an Independent Company of Baltimore Artillery, Jan. 14, 1776. Captain of the 1st Company of Matrosses, Fort Whetstone Point in Baltimore, September 7, 1776. (Source TT-133 mistakenly states he was in Annapolis in 1776 and that no other records exist on him.) There are several mentionings about him in Volume XVIII of the Maryland Archives (Source H herein). Also, the following: "Mr. Nathaniel Smith of Baltimore Town, under the appointment of Mr. Daniel Hughes, had done the business of Deputy Commissary of Prisoners at Baltimore Town, since January, 1779, and recompence ought to be made for his services. The emoluments of the office at present are four rations and pay equal to a Major's." (CCCC-301, Nov. 27, 1782, and CCCC-368, Feb. 25, 1783) On February 22, 1823 it was ordered to "pay to Sarah SMITH, of Baltimore, half pay of a Cpatain, during life, as a further remuneration for her husband, Capt. Nathaniel Smith's services during the Revolutionary War." It was ordered on March 9, 1827 to "pay to Sarah SMITH, of Baltimore city, during life, half yearly, half pay of a Major, in lieu of half pay of a Captain which she now receives, as a further remuneration for her late husband, Nathaniel Smith's services during the Revolutionary Wat." (C-394) Major Smith was also an Original Member of the Society of the Cincinnati of Maryland. (FFF-81, III-192, B-506, H-563, H-565, TT-133, H-570, CCCC-310, CCCC-368, C-394)

SMITH, NICHOLAS. (c1750 - after 1803) Wife named Barbara. Source JJJ-628 states he rendered patriotic service, but Source A-1/22 indicates he was a Non-Juror in 1778.

SMITH, PATRICK. (December 23, 1760 - August 30, 1823) Married Nancy BISHOP (1773-1860) and their son, James Hawkins SMITH (1798-1836) married Nancy SMITH (1800-1881), and their granddaughter Laura Ellen SMITH (1829-1910) married Sweetser LINTHICUM (1824-1905) in 1847. Patrick Smith was a Private in Continental Army (MOntgomery County) in 1780, and a Private in the Extra Regiment at Fort Whetstone Point in Baltimore in 1781. (AAA-1210, AAA-1211, JJJ-628, H-627)

SMITH, PETER. Oath of Allegiance, 1778, before Hon. James Calhoun. (A-1/22, A-2/39) Private in capt. Ewing's Company No. 4, enlisted January 24, 1776; Private in Capt. Cox's Company, December 19, 1776; Private in Capt. Deam's Company, 7th MD Regiment, January 7, 1777; and Private in Capt. McClellan's Company, September 4, 1780. The foregoing may or may not pertain to more than one Peter Smith. (H-12, H-305, CCC-21, CCC-24, A-1/22, A-2/39)

SMITH, PHIL. Oath of Allegiance, 1778, before Hon. George Lindenberger. (A-2/54)

SMITH, RICHARD. Private in Baltimore County Militia; enlisted July 19, 1776. (H-58)

SMITH, RICHARD. Enlisted July 22, 1782 to serve on the Barge Fearnought under Captain Edward Spedden (only sailor from Baltimore). Born in Baltimore county; last resided in Baltimore Town; height 5'8"; fair complexion. (H-612)

SMITH, ROBERT. Matross in Capt. Brown's MD Artillery; joined November 22, 1777. Was at Valley Forge until June, 1778; at White Plains, July, 1778; at Fort Schuyler in August and September, 1780; at High Hills of the Santee in August, 1781; at Camp Col. Scirvins in January, 1782; and at Bacon's Bridge, S.C. in April, 1782. As a Matross he received 50 acres (lot 2538) in western Maryland. (DDDD-33, UU-228, 230)

SMITH, ROBERT. There were two men with this name who took the Oath of Allegiance in 1778: one before Hon. George Lindenberger, and one before Hon. Jesse Dorsey. (A-1/22, A-2/54, A-2/63)

SMITH, ROBERT JR. Oath of Allegiance, 1778, before Hon. James Calhoun. (A-1/22, A-2/39)

SMITH, ROLAND (ROWLAND) SR. Died in Baltimore County in 1784. Wife named Mary. Their children: Margaret (married a WELCH), Mary Magdalen (married John BRACKETT, and then William BROOKS), Katherine (married a HOKE, and then Henry DARE/DOER), and Roland Jr. (married Catherine REISTER). Roland signed the Oath of Allegiance in 1778 before Hon. James Calhoun. (D-10, D-11, A-1/22, A-2/40)

SMITH, ROLAND JR. Died prior to 1781. Married Catherine REISTER. Served in Baltimore Mechanical Company of Militia, November 4, 1775. Private in Capt. Graybill's German Regiment, July 12, 1776. Private in Capt. McClellan's Company, September 4, 1780. (F-299, H-265, ZZ-32, CCC-24, D-11)

SMITH, SAMUEL. (July 27, 1752, Lancaster County, PA - April 22, 1839, Baltimore, MD) Son of John Spear SMITH and Cary Anne NICHOLAS. His parents moved to Carlisle, PA in 1756 and to Baltimore, MD in 1760. He was educated in Carlisle and at an Academy in Elkton. At age 14 he was taken into his father's counting house and at age 19 in May, 1772 he embarked in one of his father's vessels as supercargo for Havre. He traveled in Europe and on his return home engaged with his father in the family shipping business. At the outbreak of the Revolutionary War he was appointed Captain of Company 8, 1st MD Battalion, January 1, 1776. (He may have been the Samuel Smith who served as a Private in the Baltimore Artillery Company on October 16, 1775.) He became a Major in the 4th MD Regiment, December 10, 1776, and Lieutenant Colonel on February 22, 1777. He was engaged in watching the movements of Sir William Howe, near Philadelphia, and was stationed with part of his regiment at Mud Fort (Fort Mifflin) on the Delaware, when the British fleet was ascending that river. His gallant defense of that fort, during which he was wounded, won him the reputation of a skillful and gallant officer and as a testimonial of his bravery, Congress presented him with a sword. By the Act of November 4, 1777 it was "resolved that Congress have a high sense of the merit of Lt. Col. Smith and the officers and men under his command, in their late gallant defense of Fort Mifflin (October 23, 1777), on the river Delaware, and that an elegant sword be provided by the Board of War and presented to Lt. Col. Smith." He retired from the Army some time after this battle, but did not withdraw from the service of his country. In Baltimore, he took command of a regiment of militia, and continued doing duty in this command during the whole of the war. (Source B-506 erroneously states he resigned May 22, 1779.) He also served on the Baltimore Salt Committee on October 14, 1779. He was Colonel of the Baltimore Town Battalion by September 25, 1780, serving through 1781. After the war he was elected to the House of Representatives, 1793-1803, and served in the U. S. Senate, 1803-1815. He was a Representative from 1816 to 1822, and a Senator from 1822-1835. Earlier, in 1793, he was made a Brigadier General and commanded a brigade from Maryland in the expedition of 1794 to suppress the "Whiskey Rebellion" in western Pennsylvania. As Major General of the Third Division of Maryland Militia, he defended Baltimore during the War of 1812. The repulse of the British Army in its attack upon Baltimore, was the result of his judicious management of the campaign. A statue of him is in Sam Smith Park on the water front. At the age of 83 he was Mayor of Baltimore, seving from 1835 to 1839. He retired and died a few months later. His wife was Margaret SPEAR. Samuel SMITH was an Original Member of the Society of the Cincinnati of Maryland and is currently represented by Robert Carter of Richmond, Virginia. (TT-133, TT-133, G-8, XXX-661, R-15, MMM-A, HHH-104, III-207, FFF-102, UUU-169, B-506, B-507, H-17, H-640, HHH-89, JJJ-629, VV-303, BBBB-29)

SMITH, THOMAS. Born 1755 in Maryland. Occupation: Carpenter. Enlisted January 27, 1776 as Private in Capt. N. Smith's 1st Company of Matrosses. Height: 5' 6 3/4". Private in Capt. Dorsey's MD Artillery and Capt. Brown's MD Artillery, November 17, 1777. Was at Valley Forge until June, 1778; at White Plains, July, 1778; at Fort Schuyler, August and September, 1780; at High Hills of the Santee in August, 1781; at Camp Col. Scirvins, January, 1782; and Bacon's Bridge, S.C., April, 1782. As a Matross he was entitled to 50 acres (lot 1533) in western Maryland. (DDDD-33, VV-74, H-564, H-574, H-567, UU-228, UU-230, UU-231, QQQ-2)

SMITH, THOMAS. Recruit in Baltimore County in 1780. Baltimore County resident. He was a Maryland Line defective, February 14, 1781. (H-340, H-414)

SMITH, THOMAS KNIGHT. Oath of Allegiance, 1778. (A-1/22)

SMITH, THOROUGHGOOD. Baltimore Privateer, and member of Capt. Nicholas R. Moore's Troops on June 25, 1781; he rode a seven year olf iron grey gelding horse. His death notice stated that "Thorowgood Smith, President of Baltimore Insurance Co., and late Mayor of Baltimore, died August 13, 1810 in his 67th year." (ZZZ-299, III-207, BBBB-313)

SMITH, VALENTINE. Private in Capt. Ewing's Company No. 4; enlisted January 22, 1776. (H-12)

SMITH, WILLIAM. Chairman of the Baltimore Committee of Observation, July 24, 1775, and elected to serve again on September 23, 1775. Also, served on the Baltimore Committee of Inspection, March 13, 1775, and Committee of Correspondence, Nov.12, 1775. On October 2, 1776, he requested aid from the Governor in supplying food to the French fleet under Count D'Estaing. He was a Baltimore Privateer, served with the Baltimore Salt Committee, October 14, 1779, took the Oath of Allegiance, 1778, before Hon. James Calhoun, and served in the Continental Congress, from February to December, 1777. His wife was Elizabeth BUCHANAN and their daughter Margaret, married Robert SMITH. William Smith died March 27, 1814 in his 86th year at his residence on Calvert Street in Baltimore, MD. He was a native of Pennsylvania. (III-206, ZZZ-299, HHH-88, SS-130, RR-19, RR-47, SS-136, EEEE-1725, FFF-60, RR-50, A-2/38)

SMITH, WILLIAM. There were six Revolutionary Pensioners from Maryland with this name (YYY-48, YYY-49), and those who served from Baltimore were: (1) Recruit in 1780 in Baltimore County (H-340); (2) Drummer in 4th MD Regiment at Fort Whetstone Point in Baltimore in 1781 (H-626); (3) Sergeant in Capt. Oldham's Company, 4th MD Rgt. from January 28, 1777 to his death in February, 1779 (H-165); and, two who signed the Oath of Allegiance in 1778: one before Hon. James Calhoun, and one before Hon. Richard Cromwell. (A-1/22, A-2/41, A-2/46). Also, a William Smith signed a letter to the Governor requesting the calling of the militia to protect Baltimore from the British on April 4, 1781. (S-49)

SMITHSON, DANIEL. (1723 - February 22, 1798) Married (2) Susannah TAYLOR. Took Oath of Allegiance in 1778 before Hon. Richard Cromwell. (JJJ-630, A-1/22, A-2/46)

SMOLL, CONRAD (DR.) Surgeon in Capt. Howell's Company, December 30, 1775. (G-11)

SMOOT, EDWARD. Oath of Allegiance in 1778 before Hon. Isaac Van Bibber.(A-1/22,A-2/34)

SMYLEY, JOHN. Ordinary Seaman on ship Defence, September 19, 1776. (H-607)

SMYTH, DANIEL. Enlisted July 20, 1776 in Baltimore Town. Revolutionary pensioner as Private in Maryland Line. (H-53, YY-49)

SMYTH, JOHN. 1st Lieutenant and Captain, Baltimore Town Battn., 1779. (F-311, F-313)

* SIBLE, LUDWICK. Private in Capt. Howell's Company, December 30, 1775. (G-11)

* SIDDAN, JOHN. Non-Juror to Oath of Allegiance in 1778. (A-1/21)

* SIEGLER, JOHN. Oath of Allegiance, 1778, before Hon. George Lindenberger. (A-2/54)

* SIGLER, HENRY. Baltimore Mechanical Company of Militia, November 4, 1775. (F-298)

* SIGNER, GEORGE. Non-Juror to Oath of Allegiance in 1778. (A-1/21)

* SILISTER (SELISTER), ANTHONY. Born 1738 in Nova Scotia. Occupation: Labourer. He enlisted as Private in Capt. N. Smith's 1st Company of Matrosses on Feb. 1, 1776. On June 29, 1776 he was reported "sick in barracks." Earlier, on December 30, 1775 he was a Private in Capt. Howell's Company. (Ht: 5'4") (G-11, H-565, H-568, QQQ-2)

(* The above six names with an asterisk next to them are out of sequence. See page 244.)

SNAPP, PETER JR. Non-Juror to Oath of Allegiance in 1778. (A-1/22)

SNAPP, PETER SR. 2nd Lieutenant in Capt. R. Lemmon's Company, Feb. 4, 1777. (VV-114)

SNIDER, ABRAM. Non-Juror to Oath of Allegiance in 1778. (A-1/22)

SNIDER, FREDERICK. Non-Juror to Oath of Allegiance, 1778. (A-1/22)

SNIDER, HENRY. Oath of Allegiance, 1778, before Hon. Peter Shepherd. (A-1/22, A-2/50)

SNIDER, JOHN. Private in Capt. McClellan's Company, September 4, 1780. (CCC-25)

SNIDER, MARTIN. Non-Juror to Oath of Allegiance, 1778. (A-1/22)

SNIDER, MICHAEL. Non-Juror to Oath of Allegiance, 1778. (A-1/22)

SNIDER, VALENTINE. Private in Capt. Sheaff's Company, June 16, 1777. Comment on muster
roll states he had "gone to Carolina for a short time." Also, took Oath of Allegiance
in Baltimore County in 1778 before Hon. William Spear. (W-162, A-1/22, A-2/66)

SNOW, WILLIAM. Recruited on April 11, 1780 in Baltimore County Militia. (H-335) This, or
another William Snow reported deserted from the 4th MD Regiment in 1780 also. (H-341)

SNOWDEN, FRANCIS. (1757 - February, 1812, Baltimore County, MD) Wife name Eleanor, died
June 7, 1812, age 63. Oath of Allegiance, 1778, before Hon. James Calhoun. (ZZZ-300,
A-1/22, A-2/39)

SNOWDEN, JOHN BAPTIST. Non-Juror to Oath of Allegiance, 1778. (A-1/22)

SNYDER, CHARLES. Private in capt. McClellan's Company, September 4, 1780. (CCC-24)

SNYDER, JOHN. Born in Baltimore; died in Frederick, MD. Wife unknown; their son,
Jacob SNYDER married Mary OTT, and grandson Daniel Ott SNYDER married Mary Ann
CRONEY. John SNYDER was a Private in Capt. S. Smith's Company No. 8, 1st MD Battn.,
January 23, 1776. Corporal, MD Flying Camp; wounded at White Plains, New York; and,
pensioned December 1, 1776 to November 1, 1789. (AAA-694/696, H-640, H-630/631)

SOHAN, WILLIAM. Marine on ship Defence in 1777. (H-660)

SOLLERS, BENJAMIN. Oath of Allegiance, 1778, before Hon. Thomas Sollers. (A-2/51)

SOLLERS, FRANCIS. Oath of Allegiance, 1778, before Hon. Edward Cockey. (A-1/22, A-2/62)

SOLLERS, FREDERICK. Corporal, Capt. Graybill's German Regiment in 1776. (h-266)

SOLLERS, JOHN. Oath of Allegiance, 1778, before Hon. James Calhoun. Private in Capt.
Talbott's Company, May 31, 1779. (A-2/42, F-302, U-90)

SOLLERS, JOSEPH. Non-Juror to Oath of Allegiance, 1778. (Source A-1/22 card file only)

SOLLERS, PAUL. Non-Juror to Oath of Allegiance, 1778; subscribed in 1781. (QQ-120)

SOLLERS, SABRIT. 1st Lieutenant in Capt. Wilkinson's Company, February 4, 1777. Took
Oath of Allegiance in 1778 before Hon. Thomas Sollers. (A-1/22, A-2/51, VV-114)

SOLLERS, THOMAS. (c1730 - January 3, 1783, Baltimore County, MD) Married Arian DORSEY
on May 29, 1766. She was born c1749, a daughter of Basil DORSEY and Sarah WORTHINGTON.
Ariana SOLLERS married (2) Jacob WALTERS in 1785, and died in 1798, Baltimore County.
Children of Thomas and Arianna SOLLERS: Thomas SOLLERS (b. 1767) married in 1797 to
Sarah PENNINGTON; Sarah SOLLERS (b. 1770) married John TROTTEN in 1793; Sabritt
SOLLERS (b. 1772) married Mary DORSEY; Basil SOLLERS (b. 1774) married in 1800 to
Susanna OWINGS; Mary SOLLERS (b. 1776); Dennis SOLLERS (b. 1778); Arianna SOLLERS
(b. 1780) married Rev. Tobias StANSBURY in 1799; Basil SOLLERS (1768-1771); and,
Eleanor SOLLERS (b. 1782). Thomas SOLLERS was very active during the Revolutionary
War. In 1775 he served on the Baltimore County Committee of Inspection and on the
Baltimore County Committee of Observation, and also represented Lower Patapsco Hundred
at the Association of Freemen in August of that year. In May, 1776, he was 2nd Major,
Gunpowder Battalion, and Major under Colonel Darby Lux in 1777-1778. He was a Justice
of the Peace and a Justice of the Orphans Court of Baltimore county, 1777-1778, and
one of the Magistrates who administered the Oath of Allegiance in Baltimore County in
1778. (There must have been two men with this name because in 1778 one Thomas Sollers
took the Oath before Hon. James Calhoun, and one took the Oath before Hon. William Lux
and signed his name followed by "Naval Officer", which this Thomas Sollers was from
1778 to 1782) Source AAA-1135 states he was born April 16, 1706, which must be wrong,
because he would be 43 years older than his wife and fathered his first child at 61.
(A-1/22, A-2/42, A-2/68, A-2/51, EEEE-1726, SSS-110, FF-64, GG-74, EE-51, E-11, AA-65,
BBB-350, RR-19, RR-47, RR-50, SS-136, FFF-512, XXX-667, GGG-242, JJJ-632,VV-273,SS-184)

SOLLERS, WILLIAM. Enlisted in Baltimore County on July 26, 1776. (H-53)

SOLOMON, EXICAEL (EZEKIEL). Private in Capt. Deams' Company, 7th Meryland Regiment, December 19, 1776. (H-305)

SOLOMON (SOLLOMAN), ROBERT. Oath of Allegiance, 1778, before Hon. William Lux.(A-2/68)

SOMERVILL, GEORGE. Oath of Allegiance, 1778, before Hon. James Calhoun. (A-2/41)

SOMETTER, BARNET. Oath of Allegiance, 1778, before Hon.James Calhoun.(A-1/22, A-2/38)

SOMMERS, JACOB. Served on ship Defence, April 3, 1777 to Oct. 15, 1777. (H-660)

SOMMERS, JOHN. Quartermaster on ship Defence, Feb. 15 to Dec. 11, 1777. (H-660)

SOUNDER, WILLIAM ALLENDER. Oath of Allegiance, 1778. (A-1/22)

SPALDING, DANIEL. It was ordered on March 7, 1826 to pay to Daniel Spalding, resident "of Baltimore, half pay of a Private for his Revolutionary War services." It was ordered on March 9, 1848, to "pay to Samuel Spalding, of Baltimore, $19.06, being balance of pension due the late Daniel Spalding, a revolutionary soldier, at time of his death; provided the said treasurer is satisfied that the said Samuel is the only heir to receive the same." (C-395)

SPARKS, ELIJAH. Private in Col. Aquila Hall's Baltimore County Regt., 1777. (TTT-13)

SPARKS, FRANCIS. 2nd Sergeant in Capt. J. Cockey's Baltimore County Dragoons serving at Yorktown in 1781. Involved in evaluation of Baltimore County confiscated proprietary reserve lands in 1782. (MMM-A, FFF-547)

SPARKS, JOHN. Non-Juror to Oath of Allegiance, 1778. (A-1/22 card file only)

SPARKS, JOSIAS. Oath of Allegiance, 1778, before Hon. Jesse Dorsey. (A-1/22, A-2/63)

SPEAR, JACOB. Oath of Allegiance, 1778, before Hon. John Beale Howard. Could not write; made his mark. (A-1/22, A-2/29) Also, Source A-1/22 states "Jacob Spears" was a Non-Juror in 1778.

SPEAR, JOHN. Served in Capt. Nicholas Ruxton Moore's Troops, June 25, 1781. He rode a five year old bay gelding horse. (BBBB-313) Source A-1/22 states "John Spears" was a Non-Juror to Oath of Allegiance in 1778.

SPEAR, WILLIAM. Served on Baltimore Committee of Inspection, March 13, 1775, and the Committee of Correspondence, November 12, 1775. Was a Baltimore Privateer and was a member of the Sons of Liberty and Baltimore's Mechanical Company in 1776. Was a Justice of the Peace and one of the Magistrates who administered the Oath of Allegiance in 1778. Served as a Justice of the Orphans Court of Baltimore County, 1777-1779. (A-1/22, A-2/66, III-206, GGG-242, CCC-19, CCC-25, VV-273, RR-19, SS-130) Also, Source A-1/22 states "William Spears" was a Non-Juror to the Oath in 1778.

SPEAR, WILLIAM JR. Oath of Allegiance, 1778, before Hon. William Spear. (A-2/66)

SPECK, HENRY. 2nd Sergeant, Capt. Keeports' German Regiment; enlisted July 30, 1776. Was at Philadelphia, September 19, 1776. Ensign, Capt. Graybill's Company in the Baltimore Town Battalion, September 25, 1780. One Henry Speck died in Baltimore on January 29, 1800, in his 45th year. (ZZZ-303, VV-303, H-262)

SPECK, JOHN. Private in capt. Cox's Company, December 19, 1776. Private in Captain McClellan's Company, September 4, 1780. Oath of Allegiance, 1778, before Honorable James Calhoun. (A-1/22, A-2/40, CCC-21, CCC-24)

SPECK, WILLIAM. Private in Capt. Graybill's German Regiment in 1776. Took the Oath of Allegiance in 1778 before Hon. George Lindenberger. (A-1/22, A-2/54, H-266)

SPEDDEN, EDWARD. Lieutenant on the barge Fearnought under Capt. Levin Spedden, 1782. On February 12, 1820 it was ordered to pay Edward Spedden, "of Baltimore City, an old revolutionary soldier, for life, quarterly, half pay of a 2nd Lieutenant for his services during the Revolutionary War." On February 22, 1823, it was ordered to "pay to Ann Spedden, of Baltimore, half pay of a Lieutenant, as a remuneration for her late husband, Edward Spedden's services during Rev. War." (C-395, H-611)

SPELEY, DARBY. Matross in Capt. Brown's MD Artillery; joined November 22, 1777. Was at Valley Forge until June, 1778; at White Plains, July, 1778; at Fort Schuyler, August and September, 1780; not listed in 1781. (UU-228, UU-230)

SPENCER, BENJAMIN. (1745, Pennsylvania or Delaware - October, 1805, Baltimore, MD) Occupation: Bricklayer. Enlisted January 30, 1776 as a Private in Capt. N. Smith's 1st Company of Matrosses. Height: 5' 5½". Earlier, he served in Capt. Howell's Co., December 30, 1775. The muster roll of Capt. Smith's Company reported him "dead or deserted" on June 18, 1776. Yet, in 1778, a Benjamin Spencer took Oath of Allegiance before Hon. George Lindenberger. His death notice stated that "Benjamin Spencer, bricklayer, a native of Delaware, but for the last 35 years an inhabitant of Fell's Point, died in October, 1805, over 60 years old." (ZZZ-303, H-564, H-567, QQQ-2, G-11, A-1/22, A-2/54)

SPENCER, JOHN. Oath of Allegiance, 1778, before Hon. William Spear. (A-1/22, A-2/66)

SPENCER, TAMER (TAMERLANE, TAMOLIN). Bombardier in Capt. Brown's MD Artillery; joined November 22, 1777. Was at Valley Forge until June, 1778; at White Plains in July, 1778; at Fort Schuyler in August and September, 1780; at High Hills of the Santee in August, 1781, and became a Corporal; at Camp Col. Scirvins in January, 1782; and, at Bacon's Bridge, S.C. in April, 1782. Entitled to 50 acres (lot 1405) in western MD for his artillery services. (DDDD-33, UU-228, UU-229, UU-230)

SPENCER, WILLIAM. Private in Baltimore Artillery Company, October 16, 1775. Clerk in Capt. Sheaff's Company, June 16, 1777. Oath of Allegiance, 1778, before Hon. James Calhoun. (G-8, W-162, A-1/22, A-2/38)

SPENGLE, HENRY. Private in Capt. Graybill's German Regiment in 1776. (H-266)

SPICER, ABRAHAM. Oath of Allegiance in 1778 before Hon. John Moale. (A-1/22, A-2/70)

SPICER, JAMES. Non-Juror to Oath of Allegiance in 1778. (A-1/22)

SPICER, JOHN. There were three men with this name who took the Oath of Allegiance in 1778 before Honorable James Calhoun. (A-1/22, A-2/39, A-2/65)

SPICER, VALENTINE. Oath of Allegiance, 1778, before Hon. Richard Cromwell. Ensign in the Baltimore Town Battalion, March 16, 1779. (A-1/22, A-2/46, F-312, F-314)

SPILLARD (SPILLIARDS), MATTHIAS. Recruit in Baltimore County Militia, April 11, 1780. Maryland Line defective, August 16, 1780. Baltimore Co. resident. (H-335, H-415)

SPINDLE, GEORGE. Non-Juror to Oath of Allegiance, 1778. (A-1/22)
SPINDLE, JACOB. Non-Juror to Oath of Allegiance, 1778. (A-1/22)

SPINKS, RAWLEIGH (RAWLEY). Private in Capt. Howell's Company, December 30, 1775. Was Matross in Capt. Gale's MD Artillery, September to November, 1779; appointed Corpl., November 8, 1779; forage guard, November to December, 1779; deserted April 13, 1780, but returned. He is reported as Corporal in Capt. J. Smith's MD Artillery in 1780, and "deceased November 28, 1781." Yet, he is listed as Corporal on Jan. 28, 1782 in Capt. Dorsey's MD Artillery as it stood at Camp Col. Scirvins. "Rawling Spinks" was entitled to 50 acres (lot 1219) in western MD. (DDDD-33, YYY-1/107,UU-232,H-579,G-11)

SPITLER, GEORGE. Non-Juror to Oath of Allegiance in 1778. (A-1/22)

SPITLER, JOHN. Non-Juror to Oath in 1778, but subscribed in 1781. (A-1/22, QQ-120)

SPLITSTONE, JACOB. Non-Juror to Oath of Allegiance, 1778. Involved in evaluation of Baltimore County confiscated proprietary reserve lands in 1782. (A-1/22, FFF-542)

SPONSELLER (SPONSELLOR), JOHN. (1755-1825, Frederick County, MD) Married in 1786 to Elizabeth LAMBRECHT (1761-1807); Source JJJ-638 states his wife was named Christina. Their children: Elizabeth, Catherine, Rachel, John Adam. Jacob and Frederick. A son John Jacob SPONSELLER (1791-1873) married Catherine SHOPE (1793-1870) in 1814, and their daughter Margarita SPONSLLER (1818-1887) married Joshua SHIPLEY (1815-1851) in 1836. John SPONSELLER was a Private in Capt. J. Gist's Company, 3rd MD Regiment, in February, 1778. (H-600, XXX-673, AAA-1975, JJJ-638)

SPRATT, DANIEL. Private, Capt. J. Gist's Co., 3rd MD Regt., February, 1778. (H-600)

SPRIGG, THOMAS. Sea Captain of Prince George's County, MD who later settled in Washington County. (c1765 - July 10, 1810) Son of Joseph SPRIGG (1736-1800) who held various public offices in Prince George's and Frederick Counties. It seems probable that the Captain Thomas SPRIGG who married in Baltimore on April 26, 1803 to Harriet MINSKY, was this man. (MD Hist. Magazine, Vol. 37, #2, p. 144, 1942)

SPRIM, JOHN. With Baltimore Mechanical Company of Militia, November 4, 1775. (F-299)

SPROSSON, JOHN. Private, Capt. McClellan's Co., Baltimore Town, Sept. 4, 1780.(CCC-25)

SPURRIER, GREEN. Oath of Allegiance, 1778. (A-1/22)

SPURRIER, LEVIN. Oath of Allegiance, 1778. (A-1/22)

SPURRIER, THOMAS. Private in Baltimore County Regiment No. 15, circa 1777. (TTT-13)

SQUIB, JOHN. Marine on ship Defence in 1777. (H-660)

SQUIRES, PETER. Oath of Allegiance, 1778, before Hon. Jesse Dorsey. (A-1/22, A-2/64)

STACY, ROBERT. Private in Capt. Lansdale's Company, 4th MD Regiment, from April 27, 1778 to November 1, 1780. (H-166)

STACEY (STACY), WILLIAM. Baltimore Mechanical Company of Militia, November 4, 1775. Oath of Allegiance, 1778, before Hon. James Calhoun. (F-298, A-1/22, A-2/38)

STACK, JOHN. Oath of Allegiance, 1778, before Hon. Charles Ridgely of Wm. (A-2/27)

STAFFORD, JOHN. Oath of Allegiance, 1778, before Hon. Peter Shepherd.(A-1/22,A-2/49)

STAHL, GEORGE. Oath of Allegiance, 1778, before Hon. George Lindenberger. (A-2/45)

STAHL, WILLIAM. Oath of Allegiance, 1778. (A-1/22)

STAINS, THOMAS. Non-Juror to Oath of Allegiance, 1778. (A-1/22)

STALEN, JOHN. Oath of Allegiance, 1778, before Hon. William Spear. (A-1/22, A-2/66)

STALKER, WILLIAM. Matross in Capt. Brown's MD Artillery; joined August 1, 1781, but may have served earlier. Entitled to 50 acres (lot 1055) in western Maryland for his services. (DDDD-34, UU-230)

STALLING (STALLINGS), THOMAS. Private in Baltimore Artillery Company, October 16, 1775. Oath of Allegiance, 1778, before Hon. George Lindenberger. (A-2/54, G-8)

STANDIFER, SAMUEL. Ensign, Col. Aquila Hall's Baltimore County Regt., 1777.(TTT-13)

STANDIFORD, ABRAHAM. Non-Juror to Oath in 1778, but subscribed in 1781. (QQ-120)
STANDIFORD, C. Non-Juror to Oath of Allegiance in 1778. (A-1/22)   (A-1/22)

STANDIFORD, JACOB. Non-Juror to Oath of Allegiance in 1778. (A-1/22)

STANDIFORD, JOHN. Captain in Gunpowder Upper Battalion, May 6, 1776 through 1778, commanding 53 men; may have served longer. Oath of Allegiance, 1778. (A-1/22, X-111, WW-413, EE-51, E-11, T-83, BBB-359)

STANDIFORD, JOHN (OF JOHN). Oath of Allegiance, 1778, before Hon. Benjamin Rogers. Could not write; made his mark ("ℐS"). (A-1/22, A-2/32)

STANDIFORD, JOHN (OF SKELTON). Oath of Allegiance, 1778, before Honorable Jesse Dorsey. (A-1/22, A-2/63)

STANDIFORD, NATHANIEL. Lieutenant in Col. Aquila Hall's Baltimore County Regiment, 1776-1777. (TTT-13)

STANDIFORD, SKELTON. Non-Juror to Oath of Allegiance in 1778. (A-1/22)

STANDIFORD, SKELTON SR. Non-Juror to Oath of Allegiance in 1778. (A-1/22)

STANDIFORD, SKELTON JR. Oath of Allegiance, 1778, before Hon. Benjamin Rogers. Could not write; made his mark ("➘"). (A-1/22, A-2/32)

STANDIFORD, VINCENT. Non-Juror to Oath of Allegiance in 1778. (A-1/22)

STANLEY (STANDLEY), JOHN. Matross in Capt. Gale's MD Artillery, 1779-1780, and Matross with Capt. Dorsey's MD Artillery at Camp Col. Scirvins on January 28, 1782. Matross in Capt. J. Smith's MD Artillery, 1782-1783, and reported "deceased April 24, 1783." (YYY-1/109, YYY-2/45, H-579, UU-232) Source DDDD-34 states "John Stanley, Jr." was a Matross entitled to 50 acres (lot 2560) in western Maryland.

STANLEY (STANDLEY), THOMAS. Cadet in Capt. Brown's MD Artillery as of August 1, 1781, at High Hills of the Santee; reported deceased August 6, 1781. (UU-230) Source DDDD-34 states Thomas Stanley was a Matross entitled to 50 acres (lot 929) in MD.

STANSBURY, ABRAHAM. Non-Juror to Oath of Allegiance in 1778. (A-1/22)

STANSBURY, BENJAMIN. Ensign, Capt. Mercer's Company, May 6, 1776. Took the Oath of Allegiance in 1778 before Hon. Richard Holliday. (WW-413, EE-51, A-1/22, A-2/60)

STANSBURY, CALEB. (c1760-c1843) Married (1) Rebecca COOK, and (2) Mary_____. Oath of Allegiance in 1778 before Hon. James Calhoun. (JJJ-641, A-1/22, A-2/41)

STANSBURY, CHARLES. Non-Juror to Oath of Allegiance in 1778. (A-1/22)

STANSBURY, DANIEL. Non-Juror to Oath of Allegiance in 1778. Private in Captain Talbott's Company, May 31, 1779. (A-1/22, F-301, U-90)

STANSBURY, DAVID. Non-Juror to Oath in 1778, but subscribed in 1781. Private in Capt. Talbott's Company, May 31, 1779. (A-1/22, QQ-120, F-301, U-90)

STANSBURY, DIXON. (December 6, 1720 - 1805) Married Penelope BODY on January 4, 1741. Children: Dixon, Jr. (born 1744); Edmund (born 1746), married Belinda S. TALBOTT; Elizabeth (born 1749), married William SLADE; and, James (born 1751) married Jemima GORSUCH. Oath of Allegiance, 1778, before Hon. Jesse Dorsey.(XXX-675,JJJ-641,A-2/63)

STANSBURY, DIXON JR. (Born July 22, 1744) Son of Dixon STANSBURY and Penelope BODY. He represented Mine Run Hundred at the Association of Freemen on August 21, 1775. Took Oath of Allegiance in 1778 before Hon. Jesse Dorsey. Was a 2nd Lieutenant in Capt. J. Cockey's Baltimore County Dragoons at Yorktown in 1781. (EEEE-1726, MMM-A, XXX-675, A-1/22, A-2/63)

STANSBURY, EDMUND. (October 6, 1746 - 1801, baltimore County, MD) Married Belinda Slade TALBOTT. Son of Dixon STANSBURY and Penelope BODY. Edmund's son, Dixon, married (1) Sophia LEVY and (2) Sarah McCOMAS. Edmund's daughter Elizabeth married Aquila MILES. Edmund STANSBURY represented Mine Run Hundred at the Association of Freemen on August 21, 1775. He was a 1st Lieutenant in Capt. Standiford's Company, Gunpowder Battalion in Baltimore County, September 3, 1777 to 1778. Took Oath of Allegiance, 1778, before Hon. Jesse Dorsey. (XXX-676, EEEE-1726, BBB-359, JJJ-641, T-83, E-11, A-1/22, A-2/63)

STANSBURY, GEORGE. (1732-1789) Oath of Allegiance, 1778, before Thomas Sollers.(A-2/51)

STANSBURY, ISAAC. Non-Juror to Oath of Allegiance in 1778. (A-1/22)

STANSBURY, JOHN. Non-Juror to Oath in 1778, but subscribed in 1781. (A-1/22, QQ-120)

STANSBURY, JOSEPH. (1745-1798) Ensign in Capt. Garretson's Company, May 6, 1776. Was a Non-Juror to Oath of Allegiance in 1778. Involved in evaluation of Baltimore County confiscated proprietary reserve lands in 1782. (A-1/22, FFF-540, WW-413, EE-51)

STANSBURY (STANDSBURY, STANSBERRY), LUKE. Non-Juror to Oath of Allegiance in Maryland in 1778. (A-1/22) Revolutionary pensioner; Private in militia; North Carolina (YY-49) Private in Capt. Blount's Company, Hillsborough District, N.C.; enlisted for 3 years on June 12, 1779. (Roster of Soldiers from North Carolina in the American Revolution, published by the North Carolina D.A.R. in 1932, page 162)

STANSBURY, NATHANIEL. Oath of Allegiance, 1778, before Hon. Thomas Sollers. (A-2/51)

STANSBURY, RICHARD. (1725-1791) Oath of Allegiance, 1778, before Hon. James Calhoun. (A-1/22, A-2/41)

STANSBURY, RICHARDSON. (1723-1797) Non-Juror to Oath of Allegiance, 1778. (A-1/22) Married Mary RAVEN. (History Trails, Vol. 9, page 24, 1975)

STANSBURY, RICHARDSON JR. Non-Juror to Oath of Allegiance in 1778. (A-1/22)

STANSBURY, SAMUEL. Oath of Allegiance, 1778, before Hon. Thomas Sollers. (A-2/51)

STANSBURY (STANDSBURY), THOMAS. Oath of Allegiance in 1778. (A-1/22)

STANSBURY, THOMAS JR. (OF THOMAS). (1741 - December 3, 1816) Married (1) Ruth GHANT and (2) Deborah_____. 2nd Lieutenant in Capt. A. Lemmon's Company, Feb. 4, 1777. Oath of Allegiance, 1778, before Hon. John Hall. (JJJ-641, VV-114, A-2/36)

STANSBURY (STANDSBURY), THOMAS (OF JOHN). Oath of Allegiance, 1778, before Honorable James Calhoun. (A-1/22, A-2/41)

STANSBURY, TOBIAS EMERSON. (1757/1758 - October 25, 1849) Married (1) Mary BUFFINGTON, (2) Ann (Nancy) DEW, and (3) Mrs. Anna D. STEINBECK. His first wife Mary, died April 21, 1809, age 49, leaving five children. "General Tobias E. Stansbury, late Speaker of the House of Delegates, and Miss Nancy DEW, of Green Street, Old Town, were married by Rev. Fidler, in January, 1811." (ZZZ-305) He served in the Navy during the American Revolution, was also a Captain of Militia and served in the War of 1812. Also took the Oath of Allegiance in 1778 before Hon. Thomas Sollers. Received pension S14604. (JJJ-641, ZZZ-305, YY-49, A-1/22, A-2/51, and Raymond Clark's Maryland Revolutionary Pensioners, page 37)

STANSBURY, WILLIAM (OF JOHN). Non-Juror to Oath of Allegiance in 1778. (A-1/22)

STANSBURY, WILLIAM. (January 20, 1716 - November 3, 1788) Son of Daniel STANSBURY and wife Elizabeth. William married Elizabeth ENSOR, daughter of John, in 1739. She was born July 12, 1721 and died September 10, 1799. Children: William (born 1746) married Belinda COLE; Abraham (died 1811); Isaac (1752-1792); Jacob (1755-1812); Elijah; John Ensor 91760-1841); Ruth (1744-1804), married James EDWARDS in 1775; and, Elizabeth. (D-11) Source A-1/22 indicates William was a Non-Juror to the Oath of Allegiance in 1778, but Source JJJ-641 states he gave patriotic service.

STANSBURY, WILLIAM. (April 4, 1746 - 1825, Baltimore County, MD) Son of William STANSBURY and Elizabeth ENSOR. He married Belinda COLE, daughter of Abraham. She died April 7, 1830 and both are buried at Taylor's Chapel Methodist Church on Hillen Road in Baltimore City. Their children: Abraham (married Rebecca_____); Micajah; Elizabeth (married Samuel DEVILBISS; then JOSHUA STEVENSON); Sarah, 1783-1834 (married Josiah BROWN in 1805); Ann (married a SPROUL); Ruth (married Nicholas H. BROWN in 1809); Charity (married William ALDERSON); William; Belinda; Daniel; Elijah (died 1813, married Elizabeth BCK in 1802. (D-11) William was a Non-Juror to the Oath of Allegiance in 1778. (A-1/22)

STANTON, ALEXANDER. Corporal of Marines, September 19, 1776, on State Ship Defence. Armorer, Jan. 11 to Aug. 15, 1777, and Master at Arms to Dec. 31, 1777. (H-660)

STANTRE (STANTRO), GEORGE. Non-Juror to oath of Allegiance in 1778. (A-1/22)

STAPLES, JOHN. (May 18, 1754 - February 2, 1843) Married Margaret TEEPLE. Was a Sergeant in capt. Brown's MD Artillery; joined November 22, 1777. Was at Valley Forge until June, 1778; at White Plains, July, 1778; at Fort Schuyler in August and September, 1780; not listed in August, 1781. (UU-228, UU-230, JJJ-642)

STARNER, JOHN. Non-Juror to Oath of Allegiance in 1778. (A-1/22)

STARNER, WILLIAM. Private in Baltimore County Regiment 15, circa 1777. (TTT-13)

STARR, OBEDIAH. Baltimore Mechanical Company of Militia in 1776. (CCC-28)

STATIA (STACIA), WILLIAM. Corporal in Capt. Cox's Company, December 19, 1776, and Private in Capt. McClellan's Company, September 4, 1780. Also, supplied nails, hoops and cork for military use in 1780. (CCC-21, CCC-24, RRR-6)

STATTON, HENRY ADAMS. Oath of Allegiance in 1778 before Hon. John Hall. (A-2/36)

STAUFFER, GEORGE. Corporal in Capt. Graybill's German Regiment in 1776. (H-265)

STAYTER, WILLIAM. Oath of Allegiance in 1778. (A-1/22)

STEAD, WILLIAM. Private in Capt. Oldham's Company, 4th MD Regiment; joined in June,

1780; missing August 16, 1780. (H-167)

STEEL, JAMES. Recruited in Baltimore on March 2, 1780, by Samuel Chester for the 3rd Maryland Regiment. (H-334)

STEEL, JOHN. 2nd Lieutenant in Capt. Wells' Company, Baltimore Town Battalion, on Sept. 4, 1777. (MM-89, E-13, BBB-362) There were three men with this name who were signed to the Oath of Allegiance in Baltimore County in 1778: one before Hon. Isaac Van Bibber, one before Hon. James Calhoun, and one before Hon. John Merryman. (A-1/22, A-2/34, A-2/38, A-2/45)

STEEL, WILLIAM. Oath of Allegiance, 1778, before Hon. Peter Shepherd. (A-1/22, A-2/50)

STEELE, GEORGE. Oath of Allegiance, 1778, before Hon. James Calhoun. (A-1/22, A-2/38)

STEIN, JACOB. Private in Capt. Keeports' German Regiment; enlisted August 7, 1776. Was at Philadelphia on Septembre 19, 1776. (H-263)

STELL, BENJAMIN. Oath of Allegiance, 1778, before Hon. Richard Holliday. (A-2/60)

STELL, GABRIEL. Oath of Allegiance, 1778, before Hon. Richard Holliday. (A-2/60)

STENHOUSE, A. Baltimore County Committee of Observation, July 24, 1775. (EEEE-1725)

STENSON, WILLIAM. Oath of Allegiance, 1778, before Hon. James Calhoun. (A-1/22, A-2/39)

STEPHEN, NATHAN. Non-Juror to Oath of Allegiance in 1778. (A-1/22)

STEPHENS, ABRAHAM (ABRAM). Non-Juror to Oath of Allegiance in 1778. (A-1/22)

STEPHENS, EDWARD. Non-Juror to Oath of Allegiance in 1778. (A-1/23)

STEPHENS, EPHRAIM. Non-Juror to Oath of Allegiance in 1778. (A-1/23)

STEPHENS (STEVENS), REZIN. Non-Juror to oath of Allegiance in 1778 (A-1/23).

STEPHENS (STEPHEN), THOMAS. Enlisted in Baltimore County on July 20, 1776. (H-53)

STEPHENSON (STEVENSON), JOHN. Elected to Baltimore County Committee of Observation on September 23, 1775. Captain of 2nd MD Battalion of Flying Camp, July to December, 1776, according to Source B-519, but Sources TT-135 and H-52 state he had resigned prior to July 19, 1776 and was succeeded by Capt. Thomas Yates. (RR-50, SS-136)

STEPLETON, RICHARD. Private, Capt. Deams' Co., 7th MD Regt., Jan. 28, 1777. (H-305)

STERET (STERAD), MATTHIAS. Volunteered into Baltimore Co. Regt. 36 in 1777. (TTT-13)

STERRETT, JAMES. Married Mary RIDGELY. James moved from Lancaster, Pennsylvania to Baltimore in 1761. His daughter Mary married Gen. Mordecai GIST, and James also had three sons, James, William and John, who served as officers in MD Regiments. James STERRETT served in the Baltimore Mechanical Company and Sons of Liberty in 1776. He submitted his accounts with the ships Defence and Resolution between June 30 and September 13, 1776, for supplying beer. He served in the MD General Assembly in 1783. (FFF-40, CCC-19, CCC-25, LLL-51)

STERRETT, JOHN. (February 1, 1751 - January 1, 1787) Married Deborah RiDGELY in 1771. Children: Andrew; John; Mary; Harriet; Juliet; Eliza; Sophia; Charles (1782-1847) married Elizabeth Ruth HOLLINGSWORTH in 1804; and, James, married Maria HARRIS. John STERRETT was very active during the Revolution. He served on the Baltimore Committee of Inspection, March 13, 1775, and the Baltimore Committee of Observation in 1776. He was a member of the Sons of Liberty in 1776, and was a Baltimore Privateer. He was Captain of Company No. 2 in the Baltimore Town Battalion in 1776, and Captain of an Independent Company of 60 Privates in 1777. He was Captain of Militia Company in Continental Service, and was prisoner at Eutaw Springs, Sept. 8, 1781. He took the Oath of Allegiance in 1778 before Hon. William Lux, and served on the Baltimore Salt Committee on October 14, 1779. (A-1/23, A-2/68, E-13, SSS-110, RR-19, GG-74, TT-135, XXX-679, JJJ-646, AAA-1638, CCC-19, FFF-468, HHH-89, III-207)

STERRETT, WILLIAM. Oath of Allegiance in 1778. (A-1/23)

STEUART, JOHN. Served with Capt. Nicholas Ruxton Moore's Troops on June 25, 1781. He rode a five year old grey gelding horse. (BBBB-313)

STEUART, WILLIAM. (February 25, 1760, Anne Arundel County, MD - July 16, 1846, Baltimore, MD) Married Mary SCOTT. Ensign in 4th Battalion of the Flying Camp, Cecil County, September 28, 1776. 2nd Lieutenant, 6th MD Regt., Dec. 10, 1776. Transferred to 3rd MD Regt., Jan. 1, 1781. Served to close of war. Lt. Steuart was a contractor and builder in Baltimore, a Justice of the Peace, and Commissioner of the Western District in 1836. His portrait hangs in the Maryland Historical Soc. He was a member of the Society of the Cincinnati, of Maryland, currently represented by Rieman Steuart. William is buried in Old St. Paul's Cemetery in Baltimore, MD. (TT-135, JJJ-649)

STEVENS, DAVID. 2nd Lieutenant in Baltimore Town Battalion in 1779. (F-311)

STEVENS (STEPHENS), JOHN. "John Stevens" was a Private, MD Line, born 1758, and Rev. war pensioner. "John Stephens" was a Private in Capt. Deams' Co., 7th MD Regiment, Jan. 1, 1777. "John Stevens" took the Oath of Allegiance in 1778 before Andrew Buchanan ("Delaware Hundred"). (A-1/23, A-2/57, H-305, YY-49)

STEVENS, NATHANIEL. Oath of Allegiance in 1781. (QQ-120)

STEVENS, REZIN. (September 9, 1742, Baltimore County, MD - April 10, 1826) Married Sarah HOOD in 1775 in Baltimore City. Children: James (born 1776) married Barbara MERCIER; Elizabeth (born 1779) married a PIERCE; Ann (born 1782; died young); Sarah (born 1785) married a HOBBS; Leah (born 1789) married Bazil BANKS; William (born 1792; died young); Rezin (born 1795); Matilda (born 1799) married Samuel BANKS; and, Thomas Hood (born 1801) married Mary WEAVER. Rezin STEVENS took the Oath of Allegiance in 1778 in Annapolis, MD. (XXX-680)

STEVENS, SAMUEL. Drafted into Baltimore County Regiment No. 36 in 1777. Took Oath of Allegiance in 1778 before Hon. James Calhoun. (TTT-13, A-2/65)

STEVENS, WILLIAM. Oath of Allegiance, 1778, before Hon. James Calhoun. Private in Capt. Oldham's Co., 4th MD Regt., May 6, 1778 to July, 1779. (H-167, A-2/65)

STEVENSON, BARNABAS. Oath of Allegiance, 1778, before Hon. James Calhoun. (A-2/39)

STEVENSON, HENRY. (1737-1816) Married Rachel OWINGS. Served on Baltimore Committee of Observation, July 24, 1775, but was not elected again on September 12, 1775. (RR-50, EEEE-1726) Source A-1/23 states he took the Oath of Allegiance in 1778. (Also, see History Trails, Vol. 9, p. 24, 1975)

STEVENSON, HENRY. Private, Baltimore Artillery Company, October 16, 1775. (G-8)

STEVENSON, JOHN. (1739-1804) Son of Edward and Susanna STEVENSON. Married in 1763 to Esther WYLE. Had sons. Joshua and Josias. John represented Mine Run Hundred at the Association of Freemen on August 21, 1775, and served in the Baltimore County legislature, 1776-1785. (EEEE-1726, MMM-A)

STEVENSON, JOSHUA. He rejected the commission of Captain by the Council of Safety on July 6, 1776. By October 12, 1776 he was a Lieutenant Colonel under Col. Cockey's Gunpowder Upper Battalion. He took the Oath of Allegiance in 1778 before Hon. John Merryman, and in 1780 served on the Baltimore Committee. "Col. Joshua Stevenson died suddenly on May 20, 1799 at his residence in Baltimore County at an advanced age. He was an active officer in our late conflict with Great Britain, and at the time of his death was in public office." (ZZZ-308, SSS-110, ZZ-337, FFF-41, FFF-266, A-1/23, A-2/45)

STEVENSON, JOSHIAS. (1757-1832) Non-Juror to Oath of Allegiance in 1778. (A-1/23)
STEVENSON, NICHOLAS. Non-Juror to Oath of Allegiance in 1778. (A-1/23)
STEVENSON, SATER. (1740-1817) Non-Juror to Oath of Allegiance in 1778. (A-1/23)

STEVENSON, THOMAS. Private in Col. Ewing's Battalion; enlisted July 5, 1776, in Baltimore County; not on muster roll in August, 1776. (H-57)

STEVENSON, WILLIAM. Non-Juror to Oath of Allegiance in 1778. (A-1/23)

STEWARD, CHARLES. Corporal in Capt. Brown's MD Artillery; joined November 22, 1777. Was at Valley Forge until June, 1778; at White Plains, July, 1778; at Ft. Schuyler

STEWARD, CHARLES (continued)
in August and September, 1780; Sergeant on August 1, 1781, at High Hills of Santee; at Camp Col. Scirvins', January, 1782; at Bacon's Bridge, S.C., April, 1782. (UU-228, UU-229, UU-230)

STEWARD, ELEXANDER. Private, Extra Regt., Fort Whetstone Point, Baltimore, 1781. (H-627)

STEWARD, GEORGE. Sergeant in Capt. Gale's MD Artillery, 1779; "on command alarm post" in January, 1780. (YYY-1/110)

STEWARD, JOHN. Oath of Allegiance, 1778, before Hon. George Lindenberger. (A-1/23,A-2/54)

STEWART, CHARLES. Oath of Allegiance, 1778, before Hon. James Calhoun. (A-1/23, A-2/41)

STEWART, DAVID. Baltimore Privateer, and member of the Baltimore Salt Committee, 1779. 2nd Lieutenant in Capt. Smith's Company, February 1, 1777, and 1st Lieutenant in Capt. Yates' Company, September 25, 1780. Took Oath of Allegiance in 1778 before Honorable William Lux. David Stewart, Jr. signed a letter to Governor Lee of Maryland, requesting the calling of the militia to protect Baltimore on April 4, 1781, from the British. "Mr. David Stewart was appointed by Congress to discharge the duties of marshall for the State of Maryland. These duties were performed with a zeal that seems to have been peculiar to the patriots of those days. This occupation was no sinecure, as indeed were none of the officers created by Congress. When the was was over, he resumed his commercial business, and united himself in it with Mr. David Plunket. He continued in that connexion, until the unfortunate loss of Mr. Plunket at sea, in the year 1793. Mr. Stewart died in 1817." (HHH-105, HHH-89, III-207, BBB-106, VV-303, A-2/68, S-49)

STEWART, HUGH. Oath of Allegiance in 1781. (QQ-120)

STEWART, ISAAC. Non-Juror to Oath of Allegiance in 1778. (A-1/23)

STEWART (STUART), JAMES DR. (1755-1845) Of Annapolis. Inoculated with Drs. Murray and Tootel for smallpox at Annapolis, 1782; moved to Baltimore, 1782. (XX-14)

STEWART, JOHN. (SR.) Oath of Allegiance, 1778, before Hon. Jesse Dorsey. Another John Stewart took the Oath in 1778 before Hon. William Lux. One of these men was a 1st Lt. in Capt. J. Cockey's Baltimore County Dragoons at Yorktown in 1781, and served was in Capt. Dennis' Company on August 20, 1781. (MMM-A, AAAA-572, A-1/23, A-2/63, A-2/68)

STEWART, JOHN JR. Non-Juror to Oath of Allegiance in 1778. (A-1/23)
STEWART, MITCHELL. Non-Juror to Oath of Allegiance in 1778. (A-1/23)

STEWART, ROBERT. Born 1747, Private, MD Line, and Revolutionary pensioner. Served in Capt. Deams' Company, 7th MD Regiment, January 14, 1777. Took Oath of Allegiance in 1778 before Hon. Charles Ridgely of William. (This, or another Robert Stewart, took the Oath in 1781.) (A-1/23, A-2/28, QQ-120, H-305, YY-50)

STEWART, STEPHEN. Served on the Baltimore Salt Committee, October 14, 1779, and was a member of the Baltimore Mechanical Company of Militia during the war. (CCC-25, HHH-88)

STIGER, ANDREW. Oath of Allegiance, 1778, before Hon. William Spear. (A-1/23, A-2/66)

STILES, JOHN. Non-Juror to Oath of Allegiance in 1778. (A-1/23)

STILES, SOLOMON. Pilot on ship Defence, May 22 to December 31, 1777. (H-660)

STILLWILL, OBADIAH. Private in Capt. Howell's Company, December 30, 1775. Private in Capt. S. Smith's Company No. 8, 1st MD Battalion, January 23, 1776. (G-11, H-640)

STILTS, PHILIP. (c1740 - c1811) Wife named Rachel. 2nd Lieutenant in Capt. Hall's Co., August 26, 1776, and 1st Lieutenant in Capt. Marshall's Co., August 30, 1777. Served in Upper Battalion in 1778. Captain by November 5, 1781 and served at least to Feb., 1782. Took Oath of Allegiance in 1778 before Hon. John Hall. (A-1/23, A-2/36, E-14, CCCC-65, AAAA-662, BBB-350, LL-66, RR-99, VV-114, JJJ-650)

STINCHCOMB, AQUILLA. Non-Juror to Oath of Allegiance in 1778. (A-1/23) Source YY-50 states he served in Maryland Militia and was a Revolutionary War pensioner.

STINCHCOMB, CHRISTOPHER. Married Magdaline ZIMMERMAN on October 16, 1793 in Baltimore County. Oath of 1778, Baltimore, before Hon. Wm. Lux. Sergeant, Delaware service.

STINCHCOMB, CHRISTOPHER (continued) (YY-50, YY-123, A-1/23, A-2/68)

STINCHCOMB. DAVID. Drafted into Baltimore County Regt. #36, c1777. (TTT-13)

STINCHCOMB, GEORGE. Non-Juror to Oath of Allegiance in 1778. (A-1/23)

STINCHCOMB, JOHN. Oath of Allegiance in 1778. (A-1/23)

STINCHCOMB, JOHN SR. Oath of Allegiance, 1778, before Hon. Richard Cromwell. (A-2/46)

STINCHCOMB, JOHN JR. Oath of Allegiance, 1778, before Hon. William Lux.(A-1/23,A-2/68)

STINCHCOMB, MCLAIN. Non-Juror to Oath of Allegiance in 1778. (A-1/23)

STINCHCOMB (STINCHICOMB), NATHANIEL. Oath of Allegiance, 1778, before Hon. Ed. Cockey.
Captain in Soldier's Delight Company No. 6, May 13, 1776 (commanded 76 Privates). By
November 27, 1781 he was Lieutenant Colonel in the Soldiers Delight Battalion. (E-10,
Z-63, BBB-348, A-1/23, A-2/61, FF-64, CCCC-5)

STINCHCOMB, NATHANIEL JOHN. Non-Juror to Oath of Allegiance in 1778. (A-1/23)

STINCHCOMB, THOMAS. (September 19, 1757 - October 3, 1827) Married Ruth OWINGS (1760-
1840) on April 11, 1778. They are buried on the Lineberger-Stinchcomb Cemetery off
Rice's Lane near Windsor Mill Road in Baltimore County. (Discrepancy in marriage
date: Source D-10 states it was April 23, 1788; History Trails, Vol. 6, No. 3, 1972,
page 10, states it was April 11, 1778; and Robert Barnes' Maryland Marriages, 1778-
1800, page 218, states it was April 23, 1778.) Thomas Stinchcomb was an Ensign in
Soldiers Delight Battalion on August 29, 1777, and became Captain on February 7, 1782
"in the room of Joshua Hurd." (CCCC-71, E-10, Z-63, BBB-348, JJJ-650, D-10)

STINCHCOMB, WILLIAM. Oath of Allegiance, 1778, before Hon. Richard Cromwell. (A-2/46)

STINER, JACOB. Non-Juror to Oath of Allegiance in 1778. (A-1/23)

STIRLING, JAMES. (1751, Stirling, Scotland - June 25, 1820, Baltimore, Maryland) He
married Elizabeth GIBSON in Baltimore on May 21, 1782. She was born in Carlisle, PA
in 1765 and died August 30, 1817 in Baltimore, a daughter of Andrew GIBSON and wife
Elizabeth CARNES. James and Elizabeth STIRLING are buried at Westminster Presbyterian
Church in Baltimore. Their children: Jane STIRLING (c1783-1834; unmarried); James
STIRLING (1784-Sept. 2, 1821; unmarried); William STIRLING (1787-1838) married Mary
GREENWOOD in 1800; John STIRLING (1789-1816); Elizabeth STIRLING (1792-1884) md. to
Franklin ANDERSON in 1831; Thomas STIRLING (1794-c1820); Archibald STIRLING (1798-
1888) married Elizabeth Ann WALSH in 1830; Isabella Maria STIRLING (born 1803) md.to
William H. MURRAY in 1839; and, Robert STIRLING (1800-1875) married Ann SUTTON (1800-
1845) in White Hall, MD. James STIRLING took the Oath of Allegiance in 1778 before
Hon. William Spear. He served in Capt. Nicholas Ruxton Moore's Troops as of June 25,
1781, and had a seven year old iron grey gelding horse. He was at Yorktown, and was
decorated for bravery by General Greene. (D-11, AAA-2254, BBBB-313, A-1/23, A-2/67,
and History Trails, Vol. 9, page 24, 1975)

STITT, BENJAMIN. Oath of Allegiance in 1778. (A-1/23)

STITT, GABRIEL. Oath of Allegiance in 1778. (A-1/23)

STOAKES, BENJAMIN. Non-Juror to Oath of Allegiance in 1778. (A-1/23)
STOAKES, DAVID. Non-Juror to Oath of Allegiance in 1778. (A-1/23)

STOAKES, JAMES. Oath of Allegiance, 1778, before Hon. Isaac Van Bibber.(A-1/23,A-2/34)

STOCK, RICHARD. Non-Juror to Oath of Allegiance in 1778. (A-1/23)
STOCK, WILLIAM. Non-Juror to Oath of Allegiance in 1778. (A-1/23)
STOCKEY, CHRISTIAN. Non-Juror to Oath of Allegiance in 1778. (A-1/23)
STOCKS, WILLIAM. Non-Juror to Oath of Allegiance in 1778. (A-1/23)
STOCKSDALE, EDWARD SR. Non-Juror to Oath of Allegiance in 1778. (A-1/23)
STOCKSDALE, EDWARD JR. Non-Juror to Oath of Allegiance in 1778. (A-1/23)

STOCKSDALE, EDWARD HOWARD. Non-Juror to Oath of Allegiance in 1778. Private, c1777,
in Baltimore County Regiment 15 (name partially missing on list). (TTT-13, A-1/23)

STOCKSDALE, JOHN. Non-Juror to Oath in 1778, but signed in 1781. (A-1/23, QQ-120)

STOCKSDALE, SOLOMAN. Non-Juror to Oath of Allegiance in 1778. 9A-1/23)
STOCKSDALE, THOMAS. Non-Juror to Oath of Allegiance in 1778. (A-1/23)

STODDERT (STODDER), DAVID. Signed letter to Governor Lee on April 4, 1781, requesting the calling of the militia to protect Baltimore against the British. Also involved in evaluation of Baltimore County confiscated proprietary reserve lands in 1782. (S-49, FFF-538)

STOLER, JOHN. Private in Capt. Howell's Company, December 30, 1775. (G-11)

STONE, RICHARD. Non-Juror to Oath of Allegiance in 1778. (A-1/23)

STONE, WILLIAM. (c1739-1821) Married Hannah OWINGS. Captain of the vessel Hornet, which was fitted out in Baltimore in October, 1775. Non-Juror to Oath of Allegiance in 1778. (A-1/23, III-201/202, and History Trails, Vol. 9, page 24, 1975)

STONEHOUSE, JOHN. Private in Capt. Furnivals' MD Artillery. Muster roll of November 17, 1777 indicates he "deserted September 20th." (H-573)

STOOL, JOHN. Oath of Allegiance, 1778. (A-1/23)

STOONCLOSER, FRANCIS ANTHONY. Recruit in Baltimore County Militia, Apr. 11, 1780. (H-335)

STOPHEL, HENRY. Non-Juror to Oath of Allegiance in 1778. (A-1/23)

STORK (STORKE), JOHN. Private in Capt. Sheaff's Company, June 16, 1777, "pleads infirm and doctors certificate." Oath of Allegiance in 1778 before Honorable James Calhoun. (W-162, A-1/23, A-2/38)

STORM, GEORGE. Non-Juror to Oath of Allegiance in 1778. (A-1/23)
STORM, JACOB. Non-Juror to Oath of Allegiance in 1778. (A-1/23)
STORY (STOREY), JAMES. Non-Juror to Oath of Allegiance in 1778. (A-1/23)

STORY, RALPH. 1st Lieutenant, Capt.Wells' Co., Baltimore Town Battalion, September 4, 1777. Oath of Allegiance in 1778 before Hon. George Lindenberger. (A-1/23, A-2/54, BBB-362, E-13, MM-89)

STORY (STOREY), THOMAS. Non-Juror to Oath of Allegiance in 1778. (A-1/23)
STOUT, CHARLES. Non-Juror to Oath of Allegiance in 1778. (A-1/23)

STOVER, GEORGE. Served in Baltimore Mechanical Company of Militia, Nov. 4, 1775. (F-298)

STOWIE, JACOB. Enlisted in Baltimore Town on July 20, 1776. (H-53)

STRACHEN, WILLIAM. Oath of Allegiance, 1778, before Hon. George Lindenberger. (A-2/54)

STRACK, PETER. Oath of Allegiance, 1778, before Hon. George Lindenberger.(A-2/54)

STRAWBRIDGE, GEORGE. Private in Baltimore County Regiment No. 7, circa 1777. (TTT-13)

STREET, JAMES. Oath of Allegiance in 1778 before Hon. William Spear. (A-2/66)

STREET, SAMUEL. Fifer in Capt. Norwood's Company, 4th MD Regiment, from March 31, 1778 to July, 1780. (H-166)

STREIB, DAVID. Private in Capt. Keeports' German Regiment; enlisted July 21, 1776. Was at Philadelphia, September 19, 1776. (H-263)

STRETT, WILLIAM. Oath of Allegiance in 1778 before Hon. James Calhoun. (A-2/39)

STRICKER, JOHN. (February 15, 1759, Frederick County, MD - June 23, 1825, Baltimore, MD) Son of Lt.Col. George STRICKER (1732-1810) of the German Regiment, and wife Catherine SPRINGER. John STRICKER was a Cadet in the German Regiment in 1776, and became a Sergeant in the 4th Continental Artillery in January, 1777, one month before his 18th birthday; 3rd Lieutenant, April 1, 1777; 2nd Lieutenant, May 13, 1779; 1st Lieutenant, June 3, 1779; and, Captain-Lieutenant, February 11, 1780 (only four days before his 21st birthday). He served unt.l June 17, 1783, and moved to Philadelphia, returning to Baltimore in 1798. He was appointed Brigadier General commanding the 3rd Brigade at the Battle of North Point in the War of 1812. (A secondary school in Dundalk, Maryland is named in his honor.) His portrait hangs in the Maryland Historical Society. He was an Original Member of the Society of the Cincinnati of Pennsylvania, transferring to MD in 1798; represented now by John Kenneth Hurd. (H-266, TT-137, TT-138, JJJ-656)

STRICKLIN, THOMAS. Non-Juror to Oath of Allegiance in 1778. (A-1/23)

STRICKLIN, WILLIAM. Non-Juror to Oath of Allegiance in 1778. (A-1/23)

STRITER, JACOB. Private in Capt. Graybill's Co., German Regiment, 1776. (H-265)

STRITTER, JOSEPH. Private, Capt. Graybill's Co., German Regiment, 1776. (ZZ-32)

STRONG, ABRAM. Marine on ship _Defence_ in 1777. (H-660)

STROTHER, DAVID. Member of the Whig Club in Baltimore, 1777. (CCC-26)

STROUBLE, ZACHARIAH. Oath of Allegiance, 1778, before Hon. Jesse Dorsey. (A-2/64)

STROUP (STRAUP), JACOB. Born 1756 in America. Enlisted July 5, 1776 in Baltimore County; height: 5'4¼". Private in Col. Ewing's Battalion. (H-57)

STUART, JOHN. Private in Baltimore Artillery Company, October 16, 1775. (G-8)

STUART, RICHARD. Private in Baltimore Artillery Company, October 16, 1775. (G-8)

STUART, RICHARDSON. Oath of Allegiance, 1778, before Hon. Geo. Lindenberger. (A-2/54)

STULLER, JOHN. Oath of Allegiance in 1781. (QQ-121)

STULS, JOHN. Private in Capt. Cox's Company, December 19, 1776. (CCC-21)

STURGIS, DANIEL. Oath of Allegiance, 1778, before Hon. James Calhoun.(A-1/23,A-2/38)

SULLENDER, JAMES SMITH. Oath of Allegiance, 1778, before Hon. James Calhoun.(A-2/65)

SULLIVAN, BRIGHT. Sailmaker on ship Defence, July 15, 1777 to December 31, 1777. On October 27, 1781, Bright Sullivan of Baltimore was "recommended as proper object for discharge (and) is therefore discharged from the service for which intended." (AAAA-654, H-660)

SULLIVAN, CORNELIUS. (1749 - September 10, 1816) Married Catherine BOHN. Private, Capt. Deams' Company, 7th MD Regiment, December 25, 1776. (H-305, JJJ-659)

SULLIVAN, DARBY. (c1760 - 1841) Non-Juror to Oath of Allegiance, 1778. (A-1/23) Source JJJ-659 states he was a Private in Maryland service and died in 1841; yet, Source H-245 indicates Private Darby Sullivan, of Lt. Hamilton's Company, 5th MD Regiment, enlisted June 6, 1778 and died September 15, 1779.

SULLIVAN (SWILLIVAN), JEREMIAH. Born 1744 in Ireland. Enlisted July 5, 1776 as 2nd Corporal in Col. Ewing's Battalion; height: 5'7" with short black hair. He was a Corporal in Capt. Furnival's MD Artillery on November 17, 1777, and a Matross in Capt. Gale's MD Artillery in 1779; deserted October 31, 1779; returned December 10, 1779; and, died December 14, 1779. (YYY-1/11, H-54, H-572) Yet, Source H-340 states that a Jeremiah Sullivan was a Recruit in Baltimore County in 1780.

SULLIVAN (SULLAVAN), JOHN. Oath of Allegiance in 1778 before Hon. John Hall. Matross in Capt. Gale's MD Artillery, 1779; deserted Oct. 31, 1779. (YYY-1/112, A-2/36)

SULLIVAN (SULLIVANE), PATRICK. Soldier in the 7th MD Regiment, wounded at Battle of Camden, August 16, 1780. It was ordered that he be paid 3 lbs., 15 shillings, on February 16, 1786, for 3 months pay due him; he received 3 subsequent payments in 1786. (J-242, J-255, J-260, J-285) There was also a Patrick Sullivan who served in the 3rd MD Regiment, 1778-1781, and it may or may not be the same person. (H-395)

SULLIVAN, PHILIP. Private in 7th MD Regiment, wounded at Battle of Camden, August 16, 1780. He received 10 payments of 3 lbs., 15 shillings each, while residing in Baltimore County between February 13, 1787 and August 11, 1789. (K-2, K-23, K-32, K-46, K-52, K-72, K-82, K-99, K-112, K-120) Source H-248 states he was a Corporal.

SULLIVAN (SWILLIVAN), THOMAS. Born 1749 in Ireland. Enlisted July 7, 1776 as 4th Cpl. in Col. Ewing's Battalion; height: 5'7"; much pock marked. Took Oath of Allegiance, 1778, before Hon. George Lindenberger. (H-54, A-1/23, A-2/54)

SULLIVAN, TIMOTHY. Private in Capt. J. Gist's Company, 3rd MD Regiment, January, 1778. (H-600) Source A-1/23 states there were two Non-Jurors to the Oath of Allegiance, in 1778.

SULLIVAN (SULIVAN), WILLIAM. Born 1747 in America. Enlisted July 7, 1776 in Baltimore County, as Private in Col. Ewings' Battalion. Height: 5'6", with long hair. (H-55) Source A-1/23 indicates William Sulivan/Swillivan was a Non-Juror to the 1778 Oath.

SUMMERS, JOHN. ("Blacksmith.") Private in Capt. Graybill's German Regiment in 1776. Took Oath of Allegiance in 1778 before Hon. John Moale. Served in Col. Nicholson's Troop of Horse, June 7, 1781. (A-1/23, A-2/70, H-266, BBBB-274)

SUMMERTON, JOHN. Oath of Allegiance, 1778, before Hon. James Calhoun. (A-1/23, A-2/41)

SUTER, JOSHUA. Appointed a 2nd Lieutenant in Capt. Richard Lemmon's Company in the Baltimore Town Battalion of Militia in Baltimore County, September 25, 1780. (F-306)

SUTHERLAND (SOUTHERLAND), DAVID. Ensign in Soldiers Delight Company No. 2, May 13, 1776 and 1st Lieutenant under Capt. Owings, August 29, 1777 through at least 1778. He took the Oath of Allegiance, 1778, before Hon. Andrew Buchanan. (A-1/23, A-2/57, BBB-348, FF-64, E-10, Z-63)

SUTTER, THOMAS. Source F-311 states Major Thomas Sutter resigned, March 16, 1779. (Ed. Note: This appears to be an error because Major Thomas Rutter was promoted that day.)

SUTTON, BENJAMIN. Marine on ship Defence in 1777. (H-660)

SUTTON, CHARLES. Corporal in Capt. Brown's MD Artillery; joined November 22, 1777. Was at Valley Forge until June, 1778; at White Plains, July, 1778; at Fort Schuyler in August and September, 1780; Matross, as of August 1, 1781, at High Hills of Santee; Camp Col.Scirvins, January, 1782; Bacon's Bridge, S.C., April, 1782. Subsequently, became a Sergeant, entitled to 50 acres (lot 1145) in western Maryland for his duty as an Artillery Sergeant. (UU-228, UU-230, DDDD-34)

SUTTON, HENRY ADAM. Oath of Allegiance in 1778. (A-1/23)

SUTTON, HENUS (HEMES). Oath of Allegiance, 1778, before Hon. Andrew Buchanan. (A-2/57)

SUTTON, JACOB. Marine on ship Defence in 1777. (H-660)

SUTTON, JAMES. Oath of Allegiance in 1778. (A-1/230

SUTTON, JOSEPH JR. Oath of Allegiance, 1778, before Hon. John Hall. (A-1/23, A-2/36)

SUTTON, JOSEPH SR. Oath of Allegiance, 1778, before Hon. John Hall. Also, involved in evaluation of Baltimore County confiscated proprietary reserve lands in 1782. (FFF-547, A-1/23, A-2/36)

SUTTON, RICHARD. Marine on ship Defence in 1777. (H-660)

SUTTON, SAMUEL. Born June 10, 1733. Married Ruth CANTWELL. Source A-1/23 states he was a Non-Juror to the Oath of Allegiance, 1778, but source JJJ-661 states he was a patriot.

SWAILES, ROBERT. Marine on ship Defence, October 23 to December 31, 1777. (H-660)

SWAIN, JAMES. Non-Juror to Oath of Allegiance in 1778. (A-1/23)

SWAIN, JERE. (JEREAMIA). Private in Capt. Cox's Company, December 19, 1776. Took the Oath of Allegiance in 1778 before Hon. George Lindenberger. (CCC-21,A-1/23, A-2/54)

SWAN, JOHN. (November 27, 1750, Dumfries, Scotland - August 21, 1821, Baltimore, MD) Married Elizabeth MAXWELL, and their son, James SWAN, married Elizabeth DONNELL, and their granddaughter, Elizabeth SWAN, married (1) a KEY, and (2) Robert A. DOBBIN. (Data from Source AAA-271, but Source JJJ-661 states John married Elizabeth TRIPPE.) Captain of 3rd Continental Dragoons (Baltimore Light Dragoons), April 26, 1777. He was wounded near Morristown, N.J. in 1777, and taken prisoner at Tappan, September 28, 1778. Became Major of 1st Continental Dragoons, October 21, 1780, having earlier that year (May 21st) contracted for purchasing and transporting provisions in Baltimore Co. He was at Yorktown in 1781 when Cornwallis surrendered, and was retained in Baylor's Regiment of Dragoons on November 9, 1782, and served to the close of the war in 1783. Entitled to 400 acres by Federal Bounty Land Grant Warrant 2058 on May 11, 1792. He was an Original Member of the Society of the Cincinnati of Maryland, now represented by George Washington Dobbin, Jr. of Baltimore. (TT-138,FFF-288,YY-80,AAA-271,JJJ-661)

SWAN, MATTHEW. (1743 - January 6, 1795, Baltimore, MD) Married Ann McKEAN (McCAIN) on September 7, 1784. Children: Matthew (c1785-1830); William (born 1787) md. to Martha KNOX; John E. (born 1789) married Maria SMITH of Gettysburg, PA; Thomas, (1791-1794); Elizabeth D. (1793-1795); and, Mary. Matthew SWAN was a Clerk in Capt. McClellan's Company, September 4, 1780, and Continental Storekeeper and Food Supplier, 1780-1781. (CCC-23, XXX-691)

SWAN, SAMUEL. There appears to have been two men in the militia with this name: (1) Sergeant at Fort Whetstone Point in Baltimore; appointed October 6, 1779, and discharged November 19, 1780; (2) Private in Capt. McClellan's Company, Sept. 4, 1780. (H-626, CCC-25)

SWARTSWALTER, JACOB. Non-Juror to Oath of Allegiance in 1778. (A-1/23)

SWEATMAN, JAMES. Oath of Allegiance, 1778. (A-1/23)

SWEETING, EDWARD. Non-Juror to Oath of Allegiance in 1778. (A-1/23)
SWEETING, ROBERT. Non-Juror to Oath of Allegiance in 1778. (A-1/23)

SWEINEY, CHARLES. Private in Baltimore County Militia; enlisted July 19, 1776. (H-58)

SWINDELL, PETER. Oath of Allegiance, 1778, before Hon. George Lindenberger. (A-2/54)

SWISHER, LODORWICK. Non-Juror to Oath of Allegiance in 1778. (A-1/23)

SWOPE (SWOOPE), BENEDICT. (September, 1732 - March 30, 1811) Married Susanna WELKER. Oath of Allegiance, 1778, before Hon. Peter Shepherd. (A-1/23, A-2/49, JJJ-663)

SWOPE (SWOOPE), BENEDICT JR. Oath of Allegiance, 1778, before Hon. Jeremiah Johnson. (A-1/23, A-2/33)

SWOPE (SWOOPE), GEORGE. (September 1, 1758 - c1830) Married Margaret HUFFHEINS. Oath of Allegiance, 1778, before Hon. James Calhoun. (A-1/23, A-2/39, JJJ-663)

SWOPE (SWOOPE), JACOB SR. Oath of Allegiance, 1778, before Hon. Peter Shepherd. (A-1/23, A-2/50)

SWOPE, JOHN. In Baltimore, on March 26, 1776, he applied as Surgeon on the schooner Resolution. (FFF-29) In 1778, John Swope/Swoope took the Oath of Allegiance before Hon. Jeremiah Johnson. (A-1/23, A-2/33)

SYBEARD, JOHN. Volunteered into Baltimore County Regiment No. 36, c1777. (TTT-13)

SYERS, BENJAMIN. Non-Juror to Oath of Allegiance in 1778. (A-1/23)
SYERS, JOSEPH. Non-Juror to Oath of Allegiance in 1778. (A-1/23)

SYKES, WILLIAM. Oath of Allegiance in 1778, (A-1/23)

T

TALBOTT, BENJAMIN. (February 11, 1750, near Warren, Baltimore County, Maryland - January 5, 1816, Baltimore County) Married Sarah WILMOTT (1749-1815). Children: Catherine (born 1778) married cousin Joshua TALBOTT; Aquila Wilmott (born 1781); Mary (born 1783) married cousin Vincent TALBOTT; Eleanor (born 1786); Sarah (born 1788); and, Harriet (born 1792) married Dr. Greenberry RIDGELY. Benjamin TALBOTT was an Ensign in Capt. J. Cockey's Company No. 1, Baltimore County Militia, as of August 26, 1776; 2nd Lieutenant, by February 4, 1777; and, Captain in Col. Edward Cockey's Battalion, May 31, 1779, serving through at least October 31, 1780. He also took the Oath of Allegiance in 1778. There were two Benjamin Talbott's who took the Oath: one before Hon. Richard Holliday (signer) and one before Hon. John Beale Howard (made his mark; could not write). (A-1/23, A-2/60, A-2/29, JJJ-664, XXX-693, F-301, U-90, VV-345, PPP-2, RR-98, VV-114)

TALBOTT, BENJAMIN ROBINSON. (1750 - before 1805) Married Martha DEAVERS. Enlisted in Baltimore Town on July 20, 1776. Took the Oath of Allegiance in 1778 before Hon. Thomas Sollers. (H-53, A-2/51, JJJ-664)

TALBOTT, EDWARD. (July 15, 1723, Anne Arundel County, MD - August 29, 1797, Baltimore County, MD) Married Temperance MERRYMAN (1720-1813) on May 28, 1745. Their children: John TALBOTT (born 1748) married Hannah BOSLEY; Benjamin TALBOTT (born 1750) married Sarah WILMOTT; Vincent TALBOTT (born 1752) married Elizabeth BOSLEY; Mary TALBOTT (born 1757) married Benjamin BOWEN; Temperance TALBOTT (1760-1818) married Richard BRITTON (1762-1818) in 1782, and their daughter, Ann Merryman BRITTON (1796-1832) md. James JESSOP (1799-1836) in 1824; and, Edward TALBOTT (1764-1801) married Frances TWAITES (1763-1845) in 1795, and their son Joshua Frederick Cockey TALBOTT (1796-1869) married Eliza DENMEAD (1801-1842) in 1818. Edward TALBOTT served on the Committee of Observation, Committee of Safety, and Pronvincial Convention (Back River Upper Hundred) in 1775 and 1776. He took the Oath of Allegiance in 1778 before Hon. Edward Cockey.
(A-1/23, A-2/61, ZZ-254, JJJ-664, AAA-1094, AAA-1186, AAA-237, XXX-693)

TALBOTT, EDWARD. Oath of Allegiance, 1778, before Hon. Richard Holliday.(A-1/23,A-2/60)

TALBOTT, HENRY. (c1745 - c1816) Married (1) Hannah KING, and (2) Barbara WHALEY. He took the Oath of Allegiance, 1778, before Hon. Jesse Dorsey. (A-1/23, A-2/64,JJJ-664)

TALBOTT, JAMES. Non-Juror to Oath of Allegiance in 1778. (A-1/23)

TALBOTT, JEREMIAH. Non-Juror to Oath of Allegiance in 1778. (A-1/23)

TALBOTT, JOHN. (July 13, 1748, Baltimore County, MD - Oct., 1830, Scott County, KY) Son of Edward TALBOTT and Temperance MERRYMAN. Married Hannah BOSLEY of Monkton, MD, on June 15, 1780. Children: William TALBOTT (born 1781) married Polly HOUSTON; Temperance TALBOTT (1782-1793); Rebecca TALBOTT (1783-1789); Susanna TALBOTT (born 1785) married Huet NUTTER; Sarah TALBOTT (born 1787) married Joshua DIMMITT; Richard TALBOTT (born 1788) married Martha CLAVE; Rebecca TALBOTT (born 1791) married Geo. A. PHELPS; Benjamin TALBOTT (born 1792) married Mary WOODGATE; Temperance TALBOTT (born 1795) married William NUTTER; and Edward TALBOTT (born 1797) married Mary Merrett LANING. By August 26, 1776, John Talbott was Captain of Baltimore County Militia Company No. 4 commanding 60 Privates, and was still in service in the Upper Battalion as of Feb. 1, 1782. He also took the Oath of Allegiance in 1778 before Hon. Richard Holliday, and was involved in evaluation of Baltimore County confiscated proprietary reserve lands in 1782. He moved to Bourbon County, KY in 1795, and died in Scott County in 1830.
(A-2/60, XXX-693, PPP-2, RR-99, ZZ-541, XXX-693, AAA-1094, JJJ-664, CCCC-65, FFF-542)

TALBOTT, JOHN. Enlisted in Baltimore Town on July 17, 1776. Private in Capt. Benjamin Talbott's Company, May 31, 1779. Took Oath of Allegiance in 1778 before Hon. John Hall. (H-53, F-301, U-90, A-1/23, A-2/36)

TALBOTT, RICHARD. Non-Juror to the Oath of Allegiance in 1778. (A-1/230

TALBOTT, TOBIAS. Ensign in Capt. E. Dorsey's Company, Soldiers Delight Battalion, by 1778 and serving to at least May 27, 1779. (GGG-422, HH-24, E-11)

TALBOTT, VINCENT. (October 15, 1752 - December 26, 1819) Wife, Elizabeth, died May 12, 1822. They are buried in the Ridgely Family Cemetery in Baltimore County, MD. Vincent took the Oath of Allegiance in 1778 before Hon. Richard Holliday. He was Sergeant in Capt. Benjamin Talbott's Company of Baltimore County Militia, May 31, 1779, and a 1st Lieutenant in the Gunpowder Upper Battalion, October 23, 1781. (A-1/23, A-2/60, U-90, F-301, AAAA-651, and History Trails, Vol. 7, No. 4, page 10, 1974)

TALL, ANTHONY JR. Oath of Allegiance, 1778, before Hon. James Calhoun. (A-2/65)

TALL, JAMES. Oath of Allegiance, 1778, before Hon. James Calhoun. (A-2/65)

TALLON, THOMAS. Born 1751 in Ireland. Enlisted July 5, 1776 in Baltimore County, MD. Private in Col. Ewing's Battalion. Height: 5'4"; full faced, pitted with smallpox. (H-57)

TALOR, JOHN. Oath of Allegiance, 1778. (A-1/23)

TALT, WILLIAM. Oath of Allegiance, 1778, before Hon. James Calhoun. (A-2/65)

TANNER, CHRISTOPHER. Non-Juror to Oath of Allegiance in 1778. (A-1/23)

TANNER, GEORGE. Non-Juror to Oath of Allegiance in 1778. (A-1/23)

TANNER, ISAAC. Non-Juror to Oath of Allegiance in 1778. (A-1/23)

TARINGS, JNO. Private, Capt. Deams' Co., 7th MD Regt., January 7, 1777. (H-305)

TARSON, EZEKIEL. Oath of Allegiance, 1778, before Hon. Richard Holliday. (A-2/60)

TATE, TIMOTHY. Enlisted in Baltimore County on July 26, 1776. (H-53)

TAVEY, JOHN. Oath of Allegiance, 1778, before Hon. William Spear. Could not write; made his mark. (A-1/23, A-2/66)

TAYLOR, AQUILA. Private in capt. Howell's Company, December 30, 1775. Private in Capt. S. Smith's Company No. 8, 1st MD Battn., January 23, 1776. (G-11, H-640)

TAYLOR, EDWARD. Private, Extra Regt., Ft. Whetstone Point, Baltimore,1781. (H-627)

TAYLOR, HENRY. Non-Juror to Oath of Allegiance in 1781. (A-1/23)

TAYLOR, HUGH. Oath of Allegiance, 1778, before Hon. George Lindenberger. (A-2/54)

TAYLOR, ISAAC. Baltimore Mechanical Company of Militia in 1776. (CCC-27)

TAYLOR, JACOB. Oath of Allegiance, 1778, before Hon. George Lindenberger. (A-2/54)

TAYLOR, JAMES. Matross in Capt. Brown's MD Artillery; joined November 22, 1777. At Valley Forge until June, 1778; at White Plains, July, 1778; at Fort Schuyler in August and September, 1780; not listed in 1781. (UU-228, UU-230) Non-Juror to Oath of Allegiance in 1778. (A-1/23)

TAYLOR, JOHN. Private in Capt. Cox's Company, December 19, 1776. Baltimore Artillery Company, 1777. Private in Capt. Furnival's MD Artillery, November 17, 1777. Was a Matross in Capt. Dorsey's MD Artillery at Valley Forge, June 3, 1778. Source YY-51 states there were 3 Revolutionary pensioners by this name: a Private, born 1750; a Private, born 1765; and, a Sergeant. Source A-1/23 indicates two signers to Oath of Allegiance in 1778: one before Hon. Richard Cromwell (A-2/46), and one before Hon. James Calhoun (A-2/39). (CCC-21, V-368, H-572, UU-231, YY-51, A-1/23)

TAYLOR, JOSEPH. Non-Juror to Oath of Allegiance in 1778. (A-1/23)

TAYLOR, KNOTLIFF. Enlisted in Baltimore County on July 26, 1776. (H-53)

TAYLOR, LUDO. Private in Capt. Smith's Company No. 8; enlisted Jan. 25, 1776. (H-18)

TAYLOR, RICHARD. (February 6, 1738 - 1821, Baltimore County, MD) Son of Thomas TAYLOR and Sarah PRICE. Married Anne STEVENSON. Children: Richard TAYLOR (1768-1853) md. Catherine STANSBURY in 1806; Sarah TAYLOR (1770-1849) married Joseph DAUGHADAY, 1790; Mary TAYLOR, married John PICKETT in 1808; Rachel TAYLOR, married Laban WELSH, 1804; Thomas Wilkinson TAYLOR (died 1834), married Ruth STANSBURY in 1799; Jemima TAYLOR, married Aquila CARROLL in 1806; Ann TAYLOR, married Jesse POTEET in 1811; Gen. Joshua TAYLOR (1779-1866) married Lydia RICHARDS; Ruth TAYLOR (c1780), married Benj. GATCH, 1794; and, Samuel TAYLOR. Richard Taylor was a Non-Juror to the Oath of Allegiance, 1778. (A-1/23, D-11)

TAYLOR (TAYLER), ROBERT. Recruit in Baltimore County Militia, Apr. 11, 1780. (H-335)

TAYLOR, SAMUEL. (April 1, 1740 - January 1, 1789, Baltimore County, MD) Son of Thomas TAYLOR and Sarah PRICE. Married Patience TIPTON (c1740-1821) on April 21, 1763, and their children were: Joseph TAYLOR (born 1764); Samuel TAYLOR (born 1765); Richard TAYLOR (born 1767); Patience TAYLOR (born 1770); Isaac TAYLOR (born 1772); Sarah TAYLOR (born 1778); Lilliam TAYLOR (born 1779); Jacob TAYLOR (born 1782); Ann TAYLOR (born 1784); and, Elijah TAYLOR (born 1786) married Sarah HISS. Samuel Taylor took the Oath of Allegiance in 1778 before Hon. James Calhoun. (A-1/23, A-2/39, JJJ-668, XXX-697, D-11)

TAYLOR, THOMAS. Born 1753 in Baltimore County, MD. Married Elizabeth EVANS on February 19, 1778. Children: Ruth TAYLOR (born 1779) married Benjamin TAYLOR; Samuel TAYLOR; and, Joseph TAYLOR married Sarah GATCH. Thomas TAYLOR served in 2nd MD Rgt. in Capt. Eccleston's Company, under Col. James Price, in 1778. (XXX-697; however, it was not James Price; it was Col. Thomas Price; see Source H-293/294 for muster roll) Thomas Taylor also stored and delivered flour for the Baltimore Town Committee, 1780. (RRR-6)

TAYLOR, WILLIAM. Private in Capt. Deams' Company, 7th MD Regiment, December 26, 1776. Took Oath of ALlegiance in 1778 before Hon. James Calhoun. Signed a letter to Gov. Lee on April 4, 1781, requesting the calling of the militia to protect Baltimore from the British. Served in Capt. Nicholas Ruxton Moore's Troops on June 25, 1781; had a six year old bay gelding horse. (BBBB-313, H-305, S-49, A-1/23, A-2/39)

TAYLOR, WILLIAM. Baltimore Privateer and Captain of brig Duke of Leinster (16 guns, 2 swivels, and 60 men), owned by William Neill of Baltimore. (III-206, III-207)

TEAL (TEALE), ASSA. Oath of Allegiance in 1781. (QQ-121)

TEAL (TEALE), CHARLES. Non-Juror in 1778; took Oath in 1781. (A-1/23, QQ-121)

TEAL (TEALE), EDWARD. Born 1737. Married Sarah STINCHCOMB. Non-Juror to the Oath of Allegiance in 1778; subscribed in 1781. (A-1/23, QQ-121, and History Trails, Vol. 9, page 24, 1975)

TEAL, EMANUEL. Born 1713. Married Kathrine JOHNSON. Non-Juror to Oath of Allegiance, 1778; signed in 1781. (A-1/23, QQ-121, and History Trails, Vol. 9, page 24, 1975)

TEAL (TEALE), GEORGE. Born 1743. Oath of Allegiance, 1778, before Honorable Richard Holliday. (A-1/23, A-2/60)

TEAL, JOHN. Non-Juror to Oath of Allegiance in 1778. (A-1/23)
TEAL, LOYD. Non-Juror to Oath of Allegiance in 1778. (A-1/23)

TEAMS, GEORGE. Oath of Allegiance, 1778, before Hon. Richard Cromwell. (A-1/23, A-2/46)

TEDFORD, JOHN. Private in Count Pulaski's Legion. Enlisted in Baltimore, May 12, 1778. (H-293)

TEES, VALENTINE. Oath of Allegiance, 1778, before Hon. James Calhoun. (A-2/39)

TEHUDY, MARTAIN. Oath of Allegiance, 1778, before Hon. William Spear. (A-2/67)

TENNIS, ABRAHAM. Private in Capt. Ewings' Company No. 4 in 1776. (H-13) "Abraham Tennes" enlisted on July 17, 1776 in Baltimore Town. (H-53)

TERRELL, MICHAEL S. Matross in Capt. J. Smith's MD Artillery in 1783. Reported dead on February 23, 1783. (YYY-2/46)

TERRY, CASPER. Volunteered in Baltimore County Regiment No. 36, circa 1777. (TTT-13)

TERRY, JOHN. Volunteered in Baltimore County Regiment No. 36, circa 1777. (TTT-13)

TETLEY, JOSEPH. Oath of Allegiance, 1778. (A-1/23)

TETRUDY, MARTAIN. Oath of Allegiance, 1778. (A-1/23) See "Martain Tehudy" above.

TEVIS (TEVES), BENJAMIN. (1755 - Octobr 18, 1802, Baltimore County, MD) Took the Oath of Allegiance in 1778 before Hon. Andrew Buchanan. He was appointed Captain "in room of Thomas Philips" on May 27, 1779, but may have been a Captin in the Soldiers Delight Battalion in 1778; left service prior to February 7, 1782. His death notice stated "Capt. Benjamin Tevis, died at his plantation in Delaware Hundred on Oct. 18, 1802, aged 47 years. He leaves a large family of orphans." (ZZZ-318, HH-24, E-11, A-1/23, A-2/57, GGG-422, CCCC-71)

TEVIS, NATHAN. Non-Juror to Oath of Allegiance in 1778. (A-1/23)

TEVIS (TEVES), PETER. Oath of Allegiance, 1778, before Hon. Andrew Buchanan. (A-2/57)

TEVIS (TEVES), ROBERT SR. (c1709 - after 1796) Married ElIZABETH CURRY. He took the Oath of Allegiance in 1778 before Hon. Andrew Buchanan. (A-1/23, A-2/57, JJJ-672)

TEVIS, ROBERT JR. (March 9, 1752, Baltimore County, MD - August 25, 1846, Shelby Co.,KY) Married (1) Martha CROW (died 1807) on March 25, 1784; (2) Elizabeth DeBOIS; (3) Lucy CROW (Note: Research by John Carnan Tevis of St. Louis in 1816 indicates Robert Tevis married Lucy Crow on March 25, 1808, and does not mention Elizabeth DeBois.) Children by first wife: Matilda (born 1785), Joshua (born 1786), Samuel (born 1788), Benjamin (born 1789), John (born 1792, died 1861, became a Methodist Minister in Kentucky), and Lloyd (born 1795). Robert Tevis was an Ensign in Capt. Philips' Company in the

TEVIS, ROBERT JR. (continued)
Soldiers Delight Battalion, August 30, 1777-1778, and an Ensign in Capt. Benjamin Tevis' Company, May 27, 1779. Notes by John Carnan Tevis, 1816, state Robert was a Captain of a Maryland Company at Valley Forge in 1777-1778, and he would not allow anyone in his family to apply for pension or his pay for his Revolutionary services. He was a farmer in Baltimore County, and then in Alleghany County, near Cumberland, Maryland. He moved to Kentucky in 1807 and died in Shelby County in 1846/1848. (He is not listed in Quisenberry's Revolutionary Soldiers of Kentucky (1896) and, thus, he never filed for pension or bounty land, apparently, according to this source.) Robert Tevis, Jr. also took the Oath of Allegiance in 1778 before Honorable Andrew Buchanan. (A-1/23, A-2/57, HH-24, E-11, KK-66, BBB-350, GGG-422, XXX-699, MMM-A, and also see Westerfield's Kentucky Genealogy & Biography, Volume 7, page 252)

THACKAM, WILLIAM. Non-Juror to Oath of Allegiance in 1778. (A-1/23)

THARCY, USHER. Oath of Allegiance in 1778 before Hon. Isaac Van Bibber. (A-2/34)

THESTON, THOMAS. Recruit in Baltimore County in 1780. (H-340)

THISSELL, SAMUEL. Oath of Allegiance in 1778. (A-1/23)

THOMAS, DANIEL. Non-Juror to Oath of Allegiance in 1778. (A-1/23)

THOMAS, DAVID. Born 1738 in Gloucestershire, England. Occupation: Bricklayer. Enlisted January 31, 1776 as Private in Capt. N. Smith's 1st Company of Matrosses. Height: 5'7¼". (H-565, H-566, VV-74, QQQ-2)

THOMAS, EVAN. (January 31, 1739 - 1826) Married Rachel HOPKINS. Source JJJ-673 indicates he gave patriotic service, but Source A-1/23 states he was a Non-Juror to the Oath of Allegiance in 1778.

THOMAS, JOHN. There were two men with this name who took the Oath of Allegiance in 1778, both before Hon. James Calhoun. (A-1/23, A-2/38, A-2/65)

THOMAS, JOHN SR. Non-Juror to Oath of Allegiance in 1778. (A-1/23)
THOMAS, JOHN JR. Non-Juror to Oath of Allegiance in 1778. (A-1/23)

THOMAS, NATHANIEL. Sergeant in Capt. Furnival's MD Artillery, November 17, 1777. (H-572) There was also a Nathaniel Thomas, Private, MD Line (born 1758) who was a Revolutionary War pensioner. (YY-51)

THOMAS, PHILIP. 2nd Lieutenant in Capt. Dennis's Company, Baltimore Town Battalion, August 20, 1781. (AAAA-572)

THOMAS, SAMUEL. Private in Capt. Ewings' Company No. 4; enlisted January 27, 1776. (H-12) Non-Juror to Oath of Allegiance in 1778. (A-1/23)

THOMAS, WILLIAM. Non-Juror to Oath of Allegiance in 1778. (A-1/23)
THOMPSON, ABRAM. Non-Juror to Oath of Allegiance in 1778. (A-1/23)

THOMPSON, CHARLES. Recruited in Baltimore County Militia, April 11, 1780. (H-335)

THOMPSON, CUTHBERT. Non-Juror to Oath of Allegiance in 1778. (A-1/23)

THOMPSON (THOMSON), EDWARD. Oath of Allegiance, 1778, before Hon. Peter Shepherd. (A-1/24, A-2/49)

THOMPSON, GEORGE. Sailor on ship Defence in 1777. (H-660)

THOMPSON, JACOB. Non-Juror to Oath of Allegiance in 1778. (A-1/23)

THOMPSON, JAMES. There were two signers to the Oath of Allegiance in 1778 with this name: one before Hon. Charles Ridgely of William, and one before Hon. James Calhoun. (A-1/23, A-1/24, A-2/27, A-2/41)

THOMPSON (THOMSON), JEREMIAH. Private, Capt. Deams' Company, 7th Maryland Regiment, December 11, 1776. (H-304)

THOMPSON, JESSE. Sergeant in Capt. Gale's MD Artillery; appointed September 3, 1779; "on command at Pumpton, October, 1779." Sergeant in Capt. J. Smith's MD Artillery, 1780. Sergeant in Capt. Dorsey's MD Artillery at Camp Col. Scirvins, January 28,

THOMPSON, JESSE (continued)
1782. In Capt. Smith's rolls in 1783 it states "file has not been found" for him. He was entitled to 50 acres (lot 856) in western Maryland for his services during the war as an Artillery Sergeant. (DDDD-35, H-579, UU-232, YYY-1/113, YYY-2/47)

THOMPSON, JOHN. Served on ship Defence, January 11 to March 1, 1777. Non-Juror to the Oath of Allegiance in 1778. (H-660, A-1/24)

THOMPSON, JOHN. Enlisted in Baltimore County on July 20, 1776. Nor-Juror to the Oath of Allegiance in 1778. (H-52, A-1/24)

THOMPSON, MOSES. Non-Juror to Oath of Allegiance in 1778. (A-1/24)

THOMPSON, ROBERT. Born 1742 in Maryland. Occupation: Labourer. Enlisted January 28, 1776 as Private in Capt. N. Smith's 1st Company of Matrosses. Height: 5'9". Served as Private in Capt. Dorsey's MD Artillery, November 17, 1777, and Sergeant with that company at Valley Forge, June 3, 1778. (UU-230, H-564, H-566, H-574, VV-73, QQQ-2)

THOMPSON (THOMSON), SAMUEL. Born 1754 in Nanticoke, Maryland. Occupation: Shoemaker. Enlisted January 24, 1776 as Private in Capt. N. Smith's 1st Company of Matrosses. Height: 5'8½". Corporal in Capt. Dorsey's MD Artillery, November 17, 1777, and was Sergeant with that company at Valley Forge, June 3, 1778. (UU-230, H-563, H-566, H-574, VV-74, QQQ-2)

THOMPSON (THOMSON), THOMAS. Private in Capt. Deams' Company, 7th Maryland Regiment, January 28, 1777. (H-305)

THORNBY, JOSEPH. Private in Capt. Lansdale's Company, 4th MD Regiment; enlisted April 17, 1777; prisoner August 22, 1777; rejoined June 23, 1778; missing Aug. 16, 1780. (H-171)

THORNTON, JOSEPH. Oath of Allegiance, 1778. (A-1/24)

THORNTON, THOMAS. Non-Juror to Oath of Allegiance in 1778. (A-1/24)
THORNTON, WILLIAM. Non-Juror to Oath of Allegiance in 1778. (A-1/24)

THRIPPS, MICHAEL. Private, Capt. Sheaff's Company, June 16, 1777. (W-162)

TICE, JOHN. Oath of Allegiance, 1778, before Hon. Charles Ridgely of William. Could not write; made his mark. (A-1/24, A-2/27)

TIDE, WILLIAM. Non-Juror to Oath of Allegiance in 1778. (A-1/24)

TILGHMAN, TENCH. (December 25, 1744, Talbot County, MD - January 18, 1786, Baltimore) Son of James TILGHMAN (1716-1793) and Anne FRANCIS. He married Anna Maria TILGHMAN (cousin) in 1783, and they had two daughters: Ann Margareta TILGHMAN (born 1784) md. Tench TILGHMAN (1782-1827), son of Deborah and Peregrine Lloyd TILGHMAN; and, Elizabeth Tench TILGHMAN (1786-1852) married Nicholas GOLDSBOROUGH VI, in 1811. Called the "Paul Revere of Maryland," Tench Tilghman was a Lieutenant Colonel and Aide-de-Camp to General Washington from 1777 to the end of the Revolutionary War. When Cornwallis surrendered at Yorktown, Virginia on October 19, 1781, Tench Tilghman was called upon to make the now famous ride to the Continental Congress at Philadelphia, Pennsylvania to inform them of the victory. He made the trip in four days, spreading the news as he rode. After the war, Tench went into business with Robert Morris. At the age of 42 and suffering from tuberculosis, he died in Baltimore and was buried in St. Paul's Cemetery in Baltimore, and in 1800 he was moved to St. Paul's newer cemetery. With the permission of 78 living descendants in 1971, Tench Tilghman was removed to the family plot on Tred Avon River near Oxford, Talbot County, Maryland (Eastern Shore). Washington wrote to Jefferson when Tilghman died: "Colonel Tilghman died lately and left as fair a reputation as ever belonged to a human character." (History Trails, Vol. 9, No. 4, 1975, pp. 21-22; XXX-708, B-563/564, MMM-A) A chapter of the Maryland Society of the Sons of the American Revolution was named in Tench's honor, May, 1976.

TILL, GEORGE. Oath of Allegiance in 1778 before Hon. James Calhoun. (A-2/38)

TILLERD, WILLIAM. Non-Juror to Oath of Allegiance in 1778. (A-1/24)
TILLEY, EDWARD. Non-Juror to Oath of Allegiance in 1778. (A-1/24)

TIMAROUS, JACOB. Oath of Allegiance, 1778, before Hon. James Calhoun. (A-1/24, A-2/38)

TINGES, JOHN. (1736 - November, 1801, Baltimore, MD) Served in Baltimore Mechanical Company of Militia, November 4, 1775. Private in Capt. Cox's Company, December 19, 1776. Took Oath of Allegiance before Hon. William Lux on February 27, 1778. Died at his residence on Light Street, "an old and respectable inhabitant of Baltimore." (ZZZ-323, CCC-21, F-298, A-1/24, A-2/68)

TINKER, WILLIAM. (Died in November, 1801, at Fell's Point, Baltimore, MD) Served as Private in Baltimore Artillery Company, October 16, 1775. Took Oath of Allegiance in 1778 before Hon. George Lindenberger. (ZZZ-323, G-8, A-1/24, A-2/54)

TIPPELT, JERRARD. Matross in Capt. Brown's MD Artillery; joined November 22, 1777. Was at Valley Forge until June, 1778; at White Plains, July, 1778; at Ft. Schuyler in August and September, 1780; not listed in 1781. (UU-228, UU-230)

TIPTON, AQUILA. 2nd Lieutenant in Capt. S. Gill's Company No. 6, Baltimore County Militia, 1776. (PPP-2, RR-99, ZZZ-542) Non-Juror to Oath in 1778. (A-1/24)

TIPTON, AQUILA. Private in Capt. J. Cockey's Baltimore County Dragoons at Yorktown in 1781. (MMM-A) Non-Juror to Oath of Allegiance in 1778. (A-1/24)

TIPTON, BRYAN. Non-Juror to Oath of Allegiance in 1778. (A-1/24)
TIPTON, GERARD. Non-Juror to Oath of Allegiance in 1778. (A-1/24)

TIPTON, HESTER. Private in Capt. J. Cockey's Baltimore County Dragoons at Yorktown in 1781. (MMM-A)

TIPTON, JABEZ MURRAY (JABUS MURRY). (November 17, 1754 - December 25, 1818) Married (1) Rebeckah LEMMON, and (2) Elizabeth MITCHELL, daughter of Thomas MITCHELL and Anne PRESTON. Jabez took the Oath of Allegiance in 1778 before Honorable James Calhoun in Baltimore County. (A-1/24, A-2/41, JJJ-681)

TIPTON, JAMES. Non-Juror to Oath of Allegiance in 1778. (A-1/24)

TIPTON, JOHN. (July 6, 1726 - November 18, 1808) Married Martha MURRAY. Took Oath of Allegiance in 1778 before Hon. Robert Simmons. Could not write; made his mark ("ℲT"). (A-1/24, A-2/58, JJJ-681)

TIPTON, JONATHAN SR. Born 1723. Son of Thomas TIPTON and Sarah STEPTOE. Married in 1745 to Eleanor BRYAN (BRYANT). ChildreN: James, Bryan, Joshua, William, Jonathan married Elizabeth FORD in 1772, Benjamin, Sylvester, John, Lydia, Eleanor, and Rachel. Jonathan was Non-Juror to the Oath of Allegiance in 1778. (D-11, A-1/24)

TIPTON, JONATHAN JR. Born April 15, 1754 "fifteen miles from Baltimore, Maryland." Son of Jonathan TIPTON and Eleanor BRYAN. Married Elizabeth FORD in 1772. Took Oath of Allegiance in 1778 before Hon. James Calhoun. Enlisted in 1779 or 1780 and was a Lieutenant under Capt. Maury, Col. Thomas Gist (Guess), and Col. Decker. In 1782 he was involved in the evaluation of Baltimore County confiscated proprietary reserve lands. He applied for Revolutionary pension while living in Wilson County, Tennessee on September 25, 1832. (YY-51, OO-32, FFF-538, A-1/24, A-2/42)

TIPTON, JOSHUA. Non-Juror to Oath of Allegiance in 1778. (A-1/24)
TIPTON, MORDECAI. Non-Juror to Oath of Allegiance in 1778. (A-1/24)
TIPTON, NICHOLAS. Non-Juror to Oath of Allegiance in 1778. (A-1/24)
TIPTON, RICHARD. Non-Juror to Oath of Allegiance in 1778. (A-1/24)

TIPTON, SAMUEL SR. (1721-1804) Son of William (1696-1726) and Hannah TIPTON. Wife unknown; son, Samuel, married Ruth BOWEN. Non-Juror, 1778. (A-1/24, AAA-1258)

TIPTON, SAMUEL JR. (c1755 - 1817, Baltimore County, MD) Married Ruth BOWEN (born 1756) on December 16, 1777, and their son, Solomon TIPTON (1793-1860) married in 1819 to Jemima ANDERSON (1794-1825), and their grandson, William Bowen TIPTON (1822-1880) married in 1845 to Catherine DEETS (1823-1896). Samuel Tipton, Jr. was an Ensign in Capt. Cummin's Company, Upper Battalion, August 30, 1777 to at least 1778. (E-14, LL-66, BBB-350, AAA-1360, JJJ-681, AAA-1286)

TIPTON, WILLIAM. He applied for pension while living in Montgomery County, KY, in 1832. He was born in Baltimore County, MD, January 1, 1754 and moved to Frederick Co., VA where he enlisted. After the war he moved to Kentucky. (YY-51, OO-91)

TIPTON, WILLIAM. Non-Juror to the Oath of Allegiance in 1778. (A-1/24)

TISER, JAMES. Private in Capt. Norwood's Company, 4th MD Regiment, from April 29, 1778 to January, 1780, when reported deserted. (H-171)

TITUS, FRANCIS. Oath of Allegiance, 1778, before Hon. Richard Holliday.(A-1/24,A-2/60)

TOBIN, JAMES. Oath of Allegiance, 1778, before Hon. Richard Holliday. (A-1/24, A-2/60)

TODD, BENJAMIN. Enlisted as a Private in Capt. N. Smith's 1st Company of Matrosses on May 29, 1776; on furlough from Fort Whetstone Point in Baltimore, September 7, 1776. Member of Col. Nicholson's Troops of Horse, June 7, 1781.(BBBB-274,QQQ-2,H-568,VV-73)

TODD, JOHN. Source A-1/24 states there were two Non-Juror to the Oath of Allegiance in 1778 with this name.

TODD, RICHARD. Non-Juror to the Oath of Allegiance in 1778. (A-1/24)

TODD, THOMAS. Oath of Allegiance in 1778 before Hon. Thomas Sollers. (A-1/24, A-2/51)

TOLLEY, WALTER SR. (c1711 - September, 1782) Married (1) Mary GARRETSON (2) Mary HALL. Son of Thomas TOLLEY and Mary FREEBORN. Served in the Baltimore County legislature up to 1775 and received 14 votes for the Baltimore Committee of Observation on Sept. 12, 1775, but was not one of those elected to serve. (RR-50, JJJ-682) Source A-1/24 states he took the Oath of Allegiance in 1778.

TOLLEY, WALTER JR. (1744-1776) He represented Upper Gunpowder Hundred at the Association of Freemen on August 21, 1775, and served on the Baltimore County Committee of Observation, September 23, 1775, was a Delegate to the Provincial Convention in 1775, and served on the Baltimore County Committee of Correspondence, November 12, 1775. Took the Oath of Allegiance in 1778 before Hon. Hercules Courtenay. On May 25, 1776, he was Colonel of the Gunpowder Battalion. Son of Walter TOLLEY and Mary GARRETSON. (A-2/37, X-111, WW-443, SS-130, RR-51, SS-136, RR-47, RR-50, EEEE-1726, MMM-A)

TOMBLESON, WILLIAM. Non-Juror to Oath of Allegiance in 1778. (A-1/24)

TOMER, JOHN. Oath of Allegiance, 1778, before Hon. James Calhoun. (A-1/24, A-2/42)

TOMLIN, WILLIAM. Oath of Allegiance, 1778, before Hon. James Calhoun. (A-1/24, A-2/41)

TOMLISON, JOHN. Oath of Allegiance, 1778, before Hon. James Calhoun. (A-1/24, A-2/40)

TONEY, ABRAM. Non-Juror to Oath of Allegiance in 1778. (A-1/24)

TOOL (TOOLE), ROBERT. Born 1747 in County Kerry, Ireland. Occupation: Labourer. Was a Private in Capt. N. Smith's 1st Company of Matrosses, enlisting January 24, 1776 in Baltimore County. Height: 6' 1½" (which was quite tall for his day). He gave his deposition on enlistment term, May 7, 1779, and was a Private in Capt. McClellan's Company in Baltimore on September 4, 1780. (FFF-220,CCC-24,H-563,H-567,VV-74,QQQ-2)

TOOLE, JAMES. (1750 - July 18, 1833) Ensign, Baltimore County Troops, 1776. Became 1st Lieutenant and Quartermaster of MD Battalion of Flying Camp in Capt. Galbraith's Company No. 4, Baltimore Town Battalion, 1776. Was taken prisoner at Ft. Washington on November 16, 1776. Became Captain in Baltimore Town Battalion, April 26, 1781. and left service prior to August 20, 1781. Pensioner. (YY-52, AAAA-416, AAAA-572, B-545, GG-74, H-52)

TOOLOE, DENNIS. Marine on ship _Defence_ in 1777. (H-660)

TOOMY, JOHN. 2nd Sergeant in Capt. Ewing's Company No. 4; enlisted January 8, 1776. Ensign in 2nd MD Line, December 10, 1776; 2nd Lieutenant, April 17, 1777. Transferred to Gist's Continental Regiment, May 12, 1777. 1st Lieutenant in Capt. Gist's Company, 3rd MD Regiment, 1778. Served to Jan., 1780. (H-600, H-11, B-545)

TOON, JOHN. Oath of Allegiance in 1778 before Hon. Thomas Sollers. (A-1/24, A-2/51)

TOPET, ROBERT. Marine on ship _Defence_ in 1777. (H-660)

TORRELL (FORRELL), STEVEN. Private in Baltimore County Militia, July 19, 1776. (H-58)

TOSSUIR, CLEMENT. Loblolly Boy on ship _Defence_, September 19, 1776. (H-607)

TOWERS, JAMES. Non-Juror to oath of Allegiance in 1778. (A-1/24)

TOWNSHEND, WILLIAM. Private in Capt. Norwood's Company, 4th MD Regiment; reported as deserted in January, 1780. (H-171)

TOWNSLEY, JOHN. Made agreement to manufacture camp kettles and canteens for Baltimore Troops, February 3, 1776. (FFF-24)

TOWSEND (TOWNSEND), GEORGE. Non-Juror to the Oath of Allegiance in 1778. (A-1/24)

TOWSON, CHARLES. Non-Juror to Oath of Allegiance in 1778. (A-1/24)

TOWSON, EZEKIEL. (1735 - November 9, 1805, Baltimore County, MD) Wife, Ruth, died December 1, 1808, age 69. Her funeral was from Mrs. Rebecca Towson's near the Towson's Tavern. (ZZZ-325) Ezekiel Towson served on Baltimore County Committee of Observation, elected September 23, 1775. Became 1st Lieutenant in Baltimore County Militia Company No. 5, December 19, 1775. He was recommended by the Baltimore Committee to command the magazine guard at Armstrong's Tavern, September 23, 1776. Became a Captain, December 20, 1776. (G-10, FFF-59, RR-47, RR-50, SS-136) Source A-1/24 states he took the Oath of Allegiance in 1778. His death notice states he died at his residence on the York Turnpike Road, and he bore an active part in the Revolutionary War. (ZZZ-325) TOWSON is the Baltimore County Seat of government, and is the location of Towson State University, north of Baltimore City.

TOWSON, JAMES. Private in Capt. J. Cockey's Baltimore County Dragoons at Yorktown in 1781. (MMM-A)

TOWSON, JOHN. (1746 - September 17, 1832) Married Penelope BUCK (1753-July 28, 1794) and they are buried at Mount Paran Presbyterian Church on Liberty Road in Baltimore County. John took the Oath of Allegiance in 1778 before Hon. Edward Cockey. Also, according to Source JJJ-685, he was a Captain. (A-1/24, A-2/61, and History Trails, Volume 6, No. 3, page 10, 1972)

TOWSON, WILLIAM. Lieutenant, MD Line. Source H-335 states "2 men passed for William Towson and lost their names" in Baltimore County, April 11, 1780. As a Lieutenant he was entitled to 200 acres (lots 2431, 2432, 2433 and 2429) in western Maryland. (DDDD-4) Source RRR-6 names William Towson as wagonmaster for the Baltimore Town Committee in 1780.

TRABAUGH, MICHAL. Oath of Allegiance, 1778, before Hon. William Spear.(A-1/24,A-2/66)

TRACEY, BAZIL (BASIL). Member of Col. Nicholson's Troop of Horse, June 7, 1781. Two men with this name were Non-Jurors to the Oath in 1778, according to Source A-1/24.

TRACEY, BENJAMIN. Two men with this name were Non-Jurors to the Oath in 1778.(A-1/24)

TRACEY, EDWARD. Non-Juror to Oath of Allegiance in 1778. (A-1/24) "Edward Traisey" enlisted in Baltimore County on August 14, 1776. (H-52)

TRACEY, JAMES. Non-Juror to the Oath of Allegiance in 1778. (A-1/24)
TRACEY, JOHN. Non-Juror to the Oath of Allegiance in 1778. (A-1/24)

TRACEY, TEGO (IBGO?). Non-Juror to Oath in 1778; signed in 1781. (A-1/24, QQ-122)

TRACEY, WARNAL. Oath of Allegiance in 1778 before Hon. John Hall. (A-2/36)

TRADER, CHAPMAN. Non-Juror to the Oath of Allegiance in 1778. (A-1/24)

TRAINER, SIMON. Marine on ship Defence in 1777. (H-660)

TRANER, JOHN. Matross in Capt. Brown's MD Artillery; joined November 22, 1777. Was at Valley Forge until June, 1778; at White Plains, July, 1778; at Fort Schuyler, August and September, 1780; not listed in 1781. (UU-229, UU-230)

TRANER, TERRANCE. Private in Baltimore County Regiment No. 7, circa 1777. (TTT-13)

TRAPNELL, JAMES. 2nd Lieutenant in Gunpowder Upper Battalion, Capt. Gill's Company, August 30, 1777. Served in Col. Nicholson's Troop of Horse, June 7, 1781, and he left the service in October, 1781. Source A-1/24 states he took Oath of Allegiance in 1778. Death notice stated "James Trapnell died at his seat in Harford County, Maryland, on May 25, 1805, age 53." (ZZZ-325,BBBB-530,BBBB-274,E-12,KK-66,BBB-350)

TRAPNELL, VINCENT. Non-Juror to the Oath of Allegiance in 1778. (A-1/24)

TRAPNELL, WILLIAM SR. Non-Juror to Oath of Allegiance in 1778. (A-1/24)

TRAPNELL, WILLIAM JR. Non-Juror to Oath of Allegiance in 1778. (A-1/24)

TRAPP, ROBERT. Non-Juror to Oath in 1778; signed in 1781. (A-1/24, QQ-122)

TRASH, JACOB. Oath of Allegiance in 1778 before Hon. James Calhoun. (A-1/24, A-2/42)

TRAUT, HENRY. Private in Capt. Keeports' German Regiment; enlisted August 11, 1776.
    Was at Philadelphia, September 19, 1776. (H-263)

TRAVERS, JAMES. Oath of Allegiance in 1778 before Hon. James Calhoun. (A-2/65)

TRAVERS, MATHIAS. Submitted account and receipt for plank to Lt. Nicholas Ruxton Moore
    in Baltimore on September 6, 1776. (FFF-55, FFF-57)

TRAVERSE, JOSEPH. Private in Baltimore County Regiment No. 7, circa 1777. (TTT-13)

TRAVIS, JOHN. Non-Juror to Oath of Allegiance in 1778. (A-1/24)

TRAVIS, THOMAS. Oath of Allegiance in 1778 before Hon. Jesse Dorsey. (A-2/63)

TRAYNOD, THOMAS. Oath of Allegiance in 1778 before Hon. Andrew Buchanan.(A-1/24,A-2/57)

TRAYNOR, JOSEPH. Oath of Allegiance in 1778 before Hon. Peter Shepherd.(A-1/24, A-2/49)

TREADWAY (TREDWAY), DANIEL. (November 22, 1724, Baltimore County, MD – 1810, Harford
    County, MD) Son of Thomas TREADWAY and Christiana SAUNDERS. Married Sarah NORRIS
    (born 1727) on August 2, 1744 in Baltimore County. Took the Oath of Allegiance in
    1778. (A-1/24, AAA-2332, MMM-A)

TREADWAY (TREDWAY), EDWARD. Oath of Allegiance, 1778, before Hon. Richard Holliday.
    (A-1/24, A-2/60)

TREADWAY, THOMAS. (c1745, Baltimore County, MD – 1819, Hamilton County, Ohio) Son of
    Daniel TREADWAY and Sarah NORRIS. Married Christiana SAUNDERS (died Harford County)
    and their daughter Elizabeth TREADWAY (1780-1838) married Martin Taylor GILBERT, Jr.
    (1771-1837) on April 2, 1805 in Harford County, MD, and their grandson, John Norris
    GILBERT (1816-c1888) married Sarah Ann MITCHELL (1810-1895) on February 20, 1839 in
    Harford County, MD. Thomas Treadway (name misspelled "Freddeway") took the Oath of
    Allegiance in 1778 before Hon. James Calhoun. (A-1/24, A-2/41, AAA-2332, MMM-A)

TREADWAY, THOMAS JR. Oath of Allegiance, 1778, before Hon. James Calhoun. (A-1/8)

TREAGLE, WILLIAM. Oath of Allegiance, 1778, before Hon. James Calhoun.(A-1/24,A-2/40)

TREAKLE, GREENBERRY. Oath of Allegiance, 1778, before Hon. Geo. Lindenberger. (A-2/54)

TREAKLE (TREACKLE), STEPHEN. Oath of Allegiance, 1778, before Hon. Ed. Cockey. (A-2/61)

TREAKLE (TREACKLE), WILLIAM. Non-Juror to the Oath of Allegiance in 1778. (A-1/24)

TREGASHES, JACOB. Armourer on ship Defence in 1777. (H-660)

TREGOL (TREGAIL), GEORGE. Oath of Allegiance in 1778 before Hon. Charles Ridgely of
    William. (A-1/24, A-2/27)

TREGOL, SOLOMON. Oath of Allegiance in 1778 before Hon. James Calhoun. (A-2/65)

TREGOL (TREEGOL), WILLIAM SR. Oath of Allegiance, 1778, before Hon. James Calhoun.
    (A-2/65)

TREGOL, WILLIAM JR. Oath of Allegiance, 1778, before Hon. James Calhoun. (A-2/65)

TREVEIRS, JAMES. Oath of Allegiance, 1778, before Hon. James Calhoun. (A-2/65)

TRIMBLE, CORNELIUS. Non-Juror to Oath of Allegiance in 1778. (A-1/24)

TRIMBLE, WILLIAM. Oath of Allegiance in 1778 before Hon. Isaac Van Bibber. (A-2/34)

TRIPOLIT (TREPOLET), MRS. Her houses in Baltimore were taken over for use by the
    militia as barracks in 1776. (FFF-70, FFF-73)

TROT, STOFLE (STOPLE). Oath of Allegiance, 1778, before Hon. Frederick Decker. (A-2/31)

TROT (TROTT), THOMAS. Non-Juror to Oath of Allegiance in 1778. (A-1/24)

TROT, WILLIAM. Ordinary Sailor on ship Defence in 1777. (H-660)

TROY, JOHN. Private in Capt. N. Smith's 1st Company of Matrosses, June 29, 1776. Non-Juror to Oath of Allegiance in 1778. (A-1/24, H-567, QQQ-2)

TROYER, GEORGE. Non-Juror to Oath of Allegiance in 1778. (A-1/24)
TROYER, GEORGE JR. Non-Juror to Oath of Allegiance in 1778. (A-1/24)
TROYER, JACOB. Non-Juror to Oath of Allegiance in 1778. (A-1/24)
TROYER, MICHAEL. Non-Juror to Oath of Allegiance in 1778. (A-1/24)

TRUE, SAMUEL. Enlisted at Fort Whetstone Point in Baltimore on December 7, 1779. Discharged January 27, 1780. Recruited in Baltimore by Samuel Chester for the 3rd Maryland Regiment on March 2, 1780. (H-334, H-626)

TRUGARD, WILLIAM. Private in Count Pulaski's Legion. Enlisted in Baltimore on April 29, 1778; deserted; returned May 22, 1778. (H-592, H-593)

TRUMBO, ADAM. Private in Capt. Cox's Company, December 19, 1776. Private in Capt. McClellan's Company, September 4, 1780. (CCC-21, CCC-24)

TRUMBO, HENRY. Private in Capt. McClellan's Company, Sept. 4, 1780. (CCC-25)

TRUMBO, JOHN. Private in Capt. McClellan's Company, September 4, 1780. (CCC-25)

TRUSTEE, JOHN. Recruit in Baltimore County Militia on April 11, 1780. (H-335)

TRUX, JOHN. Married Catherine FLANNIGAN on June 10, 1811 in Frederick County, MD (Marriage proven through Maryland pension application, so this John Trux could be a son of the solider unless the soldier John Trux married late in life.) John Trux was a Private in Capt. Keeports' German Regiment; enlisted July 21, 1776; was at Philadelphia, September 19, 1776. Became a Sergeant and Pensioner and received 215 acres under Federal Bounty Land Grant Warrant 53666 (undated). (H-263, YY-52, YY-80, YY-124)

TRUX, WILLIAM. Private in Capt. Keeports' German Regiment; enlisted July 21, 1776. Was at Philadelphia, September 19, 1776. (H-263)

TUBBLE, ROBERT. Non-Juror to Oath of Allegiance in 1778. (A-1/24)

TUDER, JOHN. Enlisted in Baltimore County on July 25, 1776. (H-52)

TUDER, JOSHUA. Non-Juror to Oath of Allegiance in 1778. (A-1/24)

TUMBERSON, EVAN. Private in Capt. Oldham's Company, 4th MD Regiment, from December, 1776 to November 1, 1780. (H-171)

TUNINGLEY, JOHN. Oath of Allegiance in 1778 before Hon. James Calhoun.(A-2/41) And, Source A-1/24 states there were two men with this name, and one was a Non-Juror.

TUNIS, BOUT. Oath of Allegiance in 1778 before Hon. James Calhoun. (A-2/65)

TUNNELL, JOHN. Non-Juror to Oath of Allegiance in 1778. (A-1/24)

TUNSTILL, HENRY. Oath of Allegiance in 1778 before Hon. George Lindenberger. (A-1/24, A-2/54)

TURAN, JOSEPH. Oath of Allegiance in 1778 before Hon. William Spear. (A-1/24, A-2/66)

TURBITT, JOHN. Private in Capt. Howell's Company, December 30, 1775. (G-11)

TURLEY, DENNIS. Private in Capt. Ewing's Co. No. 4; enlisted Jan. 24, 1776. (H-12)

TURNBULL, C. GEORGE. Captain of the State Ship Defence in 1777. (H-660)

TURNBULL, GEORGE. Member of the Whig Club in Baltimore in 1776. Submitted account for salt for the ship Resolution in 1776. Took Oath of Allegiance on March 31, 1778, in Baltimore County. Signed a letter to Governor Lee, requesting the calling of the militia to protect Baltimore from the British, April 4, 1781. Served with Capt. Nicholas Ruxton Moore's Troops, June 25, 1781, and rode a five year old bay mare. (BBBB-313, FFF-7, FFF-72, S-49, BBB-559)

TURNBULL, WILLIAM. (March 10, 1751, Scotland - July 25, 1822, Baltimore, MD) Married Mary NESBIT, and their daughter Susan TURNBULL married Alexander MURDOCK. William Turnbull was a Lieutenant, 4th Company, 1st Battalion, Philadelphia PA Militia under Col. William Bradford during the Revolutionary War. (XXX-715)

TURNER, CHARLES. (April 21, 1745 - January 4, 1796) Wife named Mary, and their children were: Susanna, Edward (born 1776, married Sarah Ann RAYMOND), Charles, Jesse, Joseph, Mary, Caroline, Harriet, Samuel and Philip. Charles Turner was a Private in Captain Ramsey's Company No. 5 in 1776. (H-650, XXX-715)

TURNER, FRANCIS. Non-Juror to the Oath of Allegiance in 1778. (A-1/24)

TURNER, JOHN. Born 1747 in Nottingham, England. Occupation: Sawyer. Enlisted Jan. 26, 1776 as a Private in Capt. N. Smith's 1st Company of Matrosses. Height: 5'7". Served as Private in Capt. Dorsey's MD Artillery, November 17, 1777, and as a Gunner in that company at Valley Forge, June 3, 1778. Received 50 acres (lot 1195) in western Maryland for his services as an Artillery Matross. (DDDD-36, H-564, H-566, H-574, UU-231, QQQ-2) One John Turner took Oath of Allegiance in 1778 before Hon. Hercules Courtenay in Baltimore. (A-1/24, A-2/37)

TURNER, JOSEPH. Non-Juror to Oath of Allegiance in 1778. (A-1/24)

TURNER, MATTHEW. Private in Capt. Deams' Company, 7th MD Regiment, December 10, 1776. Non-Juror to Oath of Allegiance in 1778. (A-1/24, H-304)

TURNER, SAMSON. Matross in Capt. Gale's MD Artillery, 1779; "on command threshing" in October, 1779; "on forage guard" in December, 1779. (YYY-1/114)

TURNER, WILLIAM. Non-Juror to Oath of Allegiance in 1778. (A-1/24) One William Turner hauled flour for the Baltimore Town Committee in 1780. (RRR-6)

TURNPAUGH, CHRISTOPHER. Oath of Allegiance, 1778, before Hon. Andrew Buchanan. (A-2/57)

TURNPAUGH, JOHN. Oath of Allegiance, 1778, before Hon. Andrew Buchanan. Ensign in the Soldiers Delight Battalion in 1778. (A-1/24, A-2/57, E-10)

TURNSTIL, JOHN. Private in Extra Regt., Ft. Whetstone Point, Baltimore, 1781. (H-626)

TUTTLE, WILLIAM. Non-Juror to the Oath of Allegiance in 1778. (A-1/24)

TWIFOOT, JAMES. Oath of Allegiance in 1778 before Hon. John Cradock. (Source A-2/59 states his name was "James Twifoot" and Source A-1/24 states it was "James Turfoot.")

TWINING, NATHANIEL. Private in Baltimore County Militia in 1776. Ensign in Captain Oldham's Co., February 29, 1777, and Lieutenant, November 20, 1777. Resigned from the 4th MD Regiment, June 1, 1779. (H-59, H-171)

TYACK, THOMAS. Fifer in Capt. J. Smith's Company, MD Artillery, 1780-1783. Muster roll states "returned from N. Caro. Regt." (H-578, YYY-2/48) Source DDDD-36 indicates he was an Artillery Sergeant entitled to 50 acres (lot 1087) in western Maryland.

TYE, GEORGE. Non-Juror to the Oath of Allegiance in 1778. (A-1/24)

TYFEL, JACOB. Non-Juror to the Oath of Allegiance in 1778. (A-1/24)

TYLE, WILLIAM. Oath of Allegiance in 1778. (A-1/24)

TYLER, LITTLETON. Carpenter on ship Defence in 1777. (H-660)

TYSON, ELISHA. Non-Juror to Oath of Allegiance in 1778. (A-1/24)

U

UHLER, ERASMUS. (September 21, 1751, Germany - August 15, 1814, Baltimore, Maryland) Married Mary NEACE (1765-1795) on July 24, 1783. Children: Erasmus, Jr. (b. 1786) married Catharine HOFFMAN; John (b. 1793) married Priscilla GALLOWAY; and, George (b. 1795) married Barbara_____. Erasmus Uhler was a member of the Baltimore Mechanical Company and the Sons of Liberty in 1776. He took the Oath of Allegiance

UHLER, ERASMUS (continued)
in 1778 before Hon. James Calhoun. His death notice stated he died August 15, 1814 "at his residence on South Hanover Street, long and inhabitant of Baltimore." (ZZZ-329, XXX-718, JJJ-694, CCC-19, CCC-25, A-1/24, A-2/39)

UHLER, VALENTINE. Oath of Allegiance, 1778, before Hon. James Calhoun.(A-1/24,A-2/39)

ULENCE, MICHAEL. Private in Col. Ewings' Battalion; enlisted July 5, 1776, Baltimore County; not on muster roll in August, 1776. (H-57)

ULLRICK, PETER. Oath of Allegiance, 1778, before Hon. John Hall. (A-1/24, A-2/36) "Peter Ulricks" lived in Baltimore County's 9th Election District in 1826. (C-401)

UNDERWOOD, JAMES. Oath of Allegiance, 1778, before Hon. Isaac Van Bibber. (A-2/34)

UPERICK, JACOB. Non-Juror to Oath of Allegiance, 1778. (A-1/24 card file only)
UPERICK, JOSEPH. Non-Juror to the Oath of Allegiance in 1778. (A-1/24)

USHER, HENRY. Oath of Allegiance, 1778, before Hon. George Lindenberger. (A-2/54)

V

VALIANT, JOHN. Able Seaman on ship Defence, September 19, 1776. (H-606)

VALIANT, NICHOLAS. Received thread on April 5, 1778, and supplies on June 17, 1779, in Baltimore County. (FFF-156, FFF-228)

VALICE, JOHN. Non-Juror to Oath of Allegiance in 1778. (A-1/24)

VAN BIBBER, ABRAHAM. (1744 - August 23, 1805, near Baltimore, MD) Baltimore Privateer who, on December 28, 1777, discussed the availability of ships to facilitate trade with France. Took the Oath of Allegiance in 1778 before Hon. Isaac Van Bibber. On November 26, 1778, Captain Abraham Van Bibber was recommended as Justice for Fell's Point in Baltimore Town. Served with Capt. Nicholas Ruxton Moore's Troops, June 25, 1781, and rode a four year old bay stallion. (BBBB-313, ZZZ-330, FFF-195, FFF-134, III-207, A-1/24, A-2/34)

VAN BIBBER, ISAAC. Served on Baltimore County Committee of Inspection, March 13, 1775. Baltimore Privateer who, on February 18, 1776, offered the use of a ship if expenses were paid. Was a Justice of the Peace and Justice of the Orphans' Court in 1778 and was one of the Magistrates who administered the Oath of Allegiance in Baltimore in 1778. (A-1/24, A-2/34, GGG-242, FFF-25, RR-19, III-207)

VAN BIBBER, ISAAC. Private in Capt. J. Cockey's Baltimore County Dragoons at Yorktown in 1781. (MMM-A)

VANCE, ADAM. Non-Juror to Oath of Allegiance, 1778; signed in 1781. (A-1/24, QQ-122)

VANCE, ROBERT. Private inCapt. Howell's Company, December 30, 1775, and served in the Baltimore Artillery Company in 1777. (G-11, V-368)

VANDERFORD, CHARLES. (1755, Queen Anne County, MD - May 18, 1822, Baltimore, MD) He married Sarah MOSELY, and their son, William VANDERFORD (born 1787) married to (1) Elizabeth FRAMPTON, and (2) Margaret Ann WATTS. Charles Vanderford enlisted at Malden, Mass. in February, 1776, and served in Capt. Bell's Company of Col. Enoch Poor's New Hampshier Regiment. (XXX-719)

VANDIKE (VANDYKE), WILLIAM. Born 1747 in America. Enlisted July 5, 1776 in Baltimore County as a Private in Col. Ewing's Battn. 5'6' tall; sandy complexion. (H-56)

VANDIVORT, JOHN. Non-Juror to the oath of Allegiance in 1778. (A-1/24)

VANSICKLE, GILBERT. Seamsn on ship Defence, January 28 to June 1, 1777. (H-660)

VANSY, JOHN. Oath of Allegiance in 1778 before Hon. Robert Simmons. (A-2/58)

VANSANT (VAN ZANDT), JOHN. Enlisted in Baltimore Town on July 20, 1776. Private in Capt. Lansdale's Company, 4th MD Regiment, December 6, 1776 to November 1, 1780.

VANSANT, JOHN (continued)
Entitled to 50 acres (lot 1122) in western Maryland. (DDDD-36, H-53, H-172)

VARLIS, WILLIAM. Non-Juror to Oath of Allegiance in 1778. (A-1/24)

VAUGHAN, ABRAHAM. Marine on ship Defence, August 3 to November 19, 1777. (H-660)

VAUGHAN, BENJAMIN. Non-Juror to Oath of Allegiance in 1778. (A-1/24)

VAUGHAN, CHRISTOPHER. 1st Lieutenant in Capt. Murray's Company, February 4, 1777.
Justice of the Peace in Baltimore County in 1778. Took the Oath of Allegiance in
1778 before Hon. Robert Simmons. (A-1/24, A-2/58, GGG-242, VV-114)

VAUGHAN, GEORGE H. Lieutenant, Maryland Line; wounded at Battle of Guilford Courthouse
on March 15, 1781. Pensioned as a Lieutenant, Revolutionary Army, Baltimore County,
as follows: January 1, 1803 - $144 per annum (received $1012.80); January 12, 1810
- $160 per annum (received $1005.28); April 24, 1816 - 181.33\frac{1}{4}$ per annum (received
$353.05); April 4, 1818 - $240 per annum; and, March 4, 1820 - 181.33\frac{1}{4}$ per annum
(received $1631.99). Died December 2, 1820. (B-559, O-10, C-402, and US Pension
Rolls, 1835, page 10)

VAUGHAN, GIST. (1718 - June 27, 1800, Baltimore County, MD) Wife named Rachel, and
their children: Marie Ann (born 1741) married Richard RICHARDS (possibly); John;
Benjamin; Nancy, married a TRACY; Gist, married Mary RICHARDS; and there may have
been four other children, names not known. Gist Vaughan represented the Upper Middle
River Hundred at the Association of Freemen on August 21, 1775. He was Captain in
Baltimore County Militia, August 26, 1776, commanding 53 Privates. He was 2nd Major
under Col. Thomas Gist's Upper Battalion, February 4, 1777. He took the 1778 Oath of
Allegiance before Hon. Robert Simmons. (A-1/24, A-2/58, D-11, XXX-723, JJJ-704, RR-98
VV-114, SSS-110, EEEE-1726)

VAUGHAN, ISAAC. Private in Baltimore Artillery Company, October 16, 1775. Non-Juror to
Oath of Allegiance in 1778. (G-8, A-1/24)

VAUGHAN, JOHN. Matross in Capt. Brown's MD Artillery, joined November 22, 1777. Was at
Valley Forge until June, 1778; at White Plains, July, 1778; at Fort Schuyler, August
and September, 1780; Sergeant, August 1, 1781, at High Hills of the Santee; at Camp
Col. Scirvins, January, 1782; at Bacon's Bridge, S.C., April, 1782. Entitled to 50
acres (lot 1071) in western Maryland, and 100 acres under Federal Bounty Land Grant
Warrant 11788, September 5, 1789. Revolutionary Pensioner as Gunner, Continental Line
and marriage proven through Maryland pension application indicates that a John Vaughan
married Nancy CALLICOTT in Halifax, VA on October 16, 1794. (YY-81, YY-125, DDDD-36,
YY-52, UU-228, UU-229, UU-230)

VAUGHAN. RICHARD. Non-Juror to Oath of Allegiance in 1778. (A-1/24)

VAUN, JOHN. Marine on ship Defence in 1777. (H-660)

VERNON, GEORGE. Recruit in Baltimore County in 1780. (H-340)

VENEMMIN, ISAAC. Oath of Allegiance in 1778 before Hon. James Calhoun. (A-2/38)
Source A-1/24 states he name was "Isaac Uenemmin."

VEZEY, LEVI. Private incapt. Ewing's Company No. 4; enlisted May 24, 1776, and then
discharged May 31, 1776. Reason not stated. (H-11)

VICEBACK, MARTIN. Non-Juror to Oath of Allegiance in 1778. (A-1/24)

VICEMAN, RICHARD. Private, Capt. Deams' Co., 7th MD Regt., February 4, 1777. (H-305)

VICKERS, JAMES. Oath of Allegiance in 1778 before Hon. James Calhoun. (A-2/65)

VIDON (VIDEON), JOHN. Born 1752 in Kent, England. Occupation: Baker. Enlisted as a
Private in Capt. N. Smith's 1st Company of Matrosses on January 25, 1776. Height:
5' 7 3/4". (H-564, H-566, VV-73, QQQ-2)

VINSON, JAMES. There were two men with this name who signed the Oath of Allegiance in
1778, both before Hon. James Calhoun. One James Vinson had "Carpenter" next to his
name. (A-2/65)

VINY, THOMAS. Oath of Allegiance, 1778, before Hon. George Lindenberger.(A-1/24,A-2/54)

VITRE: See "DeVitre."

VOSHELL, AUGUSTINE. Oath of Allegiance, 1778, before Hon. Jesse Dorsey. (A-2/63)

VOSHON (VOSHANT), CHARLES. Oath of Allegiance, 1778, before Hon. Peter Shepherd. (A-1/24, A-2/50)

VOSHON (VASHON), SIMON. Oath of Allegiance, 1778, before Hon. James Calhoun. (A-2/40)

VOSLER OR VOSNER, MATHIAS. Source A-1/24 states "Mathias Vosler" took the Oath of Allegiance in 1778, and Source A-2/58 states "Mathias Vosner" took the Oath before Hon. Robert Simmons.

W

WACKER, GEORGE. Oath of Allegiance in 1778. (A-1/24)

WACKETT, JOSEPH. Oath of Allegiance, 1778, before Hon. Edward Cockey.(A-1/24, A-2/61)

WADE, WILLIAM. Private in Capt. Furnival's MD Artillery, November 17, 1777, reported "sick--flux." Matross in capt. Dorsey's MD Artillery at Valley Forge, June 3, 1778. Entitled to 50 acres (lot 1469) in western Maryland. (DDDD-36, H-573, UU-231)

WADLOW, JOHN. Non-Juror to Oath of Allegiance in 1778. (A-1/24)

WADLOW, SAMUEL. Oath of Allegiance in 1778. (A-1/24)

WADSWORTH, THOMAS. Non-Juror to Oath of Allegiance in 1778. (A-1/24)

WAGENER, HENRY. Oath of Allegiance, 1778, before Hon. John Hall. (A-1/24, A-2/36)

WAGER, FREDERICK. Private in Capt. Graybill's German Regiment, July 12, 1776. (ZZ-32)

WAGNER, JACOB. Private in Capt. Keeports' German Regiment; enlisted August 5, 1776. At Philadelphia, September 19, 1776. (H-263) Source YY-53 states "Jacob Waggoner" was a Revolutionary pensioner, born 1754, Private in German Regt., Continental Line.

WAGNER, WILLIAM. Oath of Allegiance in 1778 before Hon. John Hall. (A-2/36)

WAGSTER, ISAIAH (IZAIH). Oath of Allegiance in 1778 before Hon. George Lindenberger. (A-1/24, A-2/54)

WAIGHT, THOMAS. Stored and delivered flour for the Baltimore Committee, 1780. (RRR-6)

WAISTCOAT, NICHOLAS. Oath of Allegiance, 1778, before Hon. William Lux.(A-1/24,A-2/68)

WAITERS, MATTHIAS. Oath of Allegiance, 1778, before Hon. Andrew Buchanan. (A-2/57)

WALDON, JAMES. Recruit in Baltimore County Militia, April 11, 1780. (H-335)

WALDRON, JOSEPH. Private in Capt. Norwood's Company, 4th MD Regiment, from April 20, 1778 to September, 1780, when reported deserted. (H-179)

WALE, JOHN. Private in Baltimore Artillery Company, October 16, 1775. Private in Capt. Sheaff's Company, June 16, 1777. "John Walles" was a Private in Captain McClellan's Company, September 4, 1780. (G-8, W-162, CCC-24)

WALING, STEPHEN. Non-Juror to Oath of Allegiance in 1778. (A-1/24)

WALKER, ABRAHAM (ABRAM). Non-Juror to Oath in 1778; signed in 1781. (A-1/24, QQ-122)

WALKER, AMOS. Oath of Allegiance in 1778 before Hon. James Calhoun. (A-1/24, A-2/41)

WALKER, BENJAMIN. Oath of Allegiance, 1778, before Hon. James Calhoun.(A-1/24,A-2/41)

WALKER, CHARLES. (November 9, 1744 - November 15, 1825) Married Ann CRADOCK. Charles served on the Baltimore County Committee of Inspection, March 13, 1775, and took the Oath of Allegiance in 1778 before Hon. William Spear. (A-1/24, A-2/66,JJJ-711,RR-19)

WALKER, DANIEL. Non-Juror to the Oath of Allegiance in 1778. (A-1/24)

WALKER, DAVID. Private, Capt. McClellan's Co., 1780; Non-Juror, 1778. (CCC-25,A-1/24)

WALKER, GEORGE. Oath of Allegiance, 1778, before Hon. Peter Shepherd. (A-1/24, A-2/49)

WALKER, HENRY. Oath of Allegiance, 1778, before Hon. Charles Ridgely of William. Could not write; made his mark ("O "). (A-2/27)

WALKER, JAMES. Private in Baltimore County Militia; enlisted July 18, 1776. Took Oath of Allegiance, 1778, before Hon. James Calhoun. (H-58, A-2/41)

WALKER, JOHN. Matross in Capt. Brown's MD Artillery; joined November 22, 1777. Was at Valley Forge until June, 1778; at White Plains, July, 1778; at Fort Schuyler, August and September, 1780; not listed in 1781. (UU-228, UU-230) One John Walker signed the Oath of Allegiance in 1778 before Hon. Richard Holliday. (A-1/24, A-2/60)

WALKER, JOSEPH JR. Non-Juror to Oath of Allegiance in 1778. Involved in evaluation of Baltimore County confiscated proprietary reserve lands in 1782. (FFF-541, A-1/24)

WALKER, PHILIP. Non-Juror to Oath of Allegiance in 1778. (A-1/24)

WALKER, ROBERT. Oath of Allegiance, 1778, before Hon. Peter Shepherd. (A-1/24, A-2/49)

WALKER, SAMUEL. Master on ship Defence, April 22 to December 31, 1777. Took the Oath of Allegiance in 1778 before Hon. James Calhoun. (H-660, A-1/24, A-2/38)

WALKER, THOMAS. (September, 1742 - October 18, 1818) Married Discretion SATER (1749-1823), daughter of Henry SATER and Dorcas TOWSON, on March 3, 1766. Their children: Elijah (b. 1767) married Malinda MAGERS; Henry (b. 1769) married Hannah MAGERS; Prudence (b. 1770) married Edward WELCH; Thomas (b. 1773); Rebecca (b. 1776); Dorcas (b. 1779); Sater Thomas (1783-1786); Isaac (b. 1786); Sater Thomas (1788-1849) married Catherine Ann KELLY in 1807 and their daughter Mary Jane WALKER (1808-1884) married Benjamin Jefferson CLARK (1808-1870) in 1831; Charles (b. 1791) md. a COX; and, Joshua (b. 1793) married (1) Mary RABORG and (2) Elizabeth STOUFFER. Thomas Walker was a 1st Lieutenant on the ship Defence commanded by Capt. George Cook, as of September 19, 1776, and later became a Sea Captain. (He was Lieutenant of Marines.) Also took the Oath of Allegiance in 1778 before Hon. James Calhoun. (A-1/24, A-2/42, H-606, H-660, AAA-1601, XXX-729, XXX-730)

WALKLETTS, PETER. Recruit in Baltimore County, April 11, 1780. (H-340)

WALLACE, JOHN. (1759, Scotland - September, 1813, Baltimore, MD) Took Oath of Allegiance in 1778 before Hon. George Lindenberger. In 1780 he was coopering, hooping and trimming casks for the Baltimore Town Committee. (RRR-6, A-1/25, A-2/54, ZZZ-334)

WALLER, GEORGE. Non-Juror to Oath of Allegiance in 1778. (A-1/25)

WALLER, JOHN. Private in Col. Ewing's Battalion; enlisted July 5, 1776; not on muster roll in August, 1776. (H-57) Source A-1/25 states he took the Oath in 1778.

WALLER, RICHARD. Recruit in Baltimore County Militia, April 11, 1780. (H-335)

WALLS, RICHARD. Recruited in Baltimore by Samuel Chester for the 3rd MD Regiment on March 2, 1780. (H-334)

WALPOLE (WATPOLE), JOSEPH. Able Seaman, 1776, and Sailor, 1777, on ship Defence. (H-660)

WALSH (WELSH), DAVID. Born 1752 in Cork, Ireland. Occupation: Cooper. Height: 5' 8". Enlisted January 26, 1776 as Private in Capt. N. Smith's 1st Company of Matrosses. Private in Capt. Dorsey's MD Artillery, November 17, 1777. Sergeant with that company at Valley Forge, June 3, 1778. Sergeant in Capt. J. Smith's MD Artillery, 1780-1783. Entitled to 50 acres (lot 1817) in western Maryland for being an Artillery Sergeant. (DDDD-36, H-564, H-566, H-574, QQQ-2, VV-74, UU-230, H-579, YY-2/49)

WALSH, EDMUND (EDMOND). Born 1750 in Cork, Ireland. Occupation: Labourer. Height: 5'6½". Enlisted January 28, 1776 as Private in Capt. N. Smith's 1st Company of Matrosses, and Private in Capt. Dorsey's MD Artillery, November 17, 1777. In 1780 he stored and then delivered flour for Baltimore Committee. (RRR-6, H-573, H-567, H-564, VV-74, QQQ-2)

WALSH, JAMES. Non-Juror to the Oath of Allegiance in 1778. (A-1/25)

WALSH (WELSH), MARK. Private, 7th MD Regiment; wounded at Battle of German Town, 1777. It was ordered in August, 1786, that he be paid (Mark WELSH) 3 lbs., 15 shillings,

WALSH (WELSH), MARK (continued)
it being 3 months pay due him. Mark WALSH received 3 subsequent payments between June 15, 1787 and June 10, 1788. (J-271, K-21, K-42, K-71)

WALSH, PATRICK. Private in Capt. Smith's Company No. 8; enlisted Jan. 11, 1776. (H-18)

WALSH (WELSH), ROBERT. Appointed Assistant Surgeon, September 2, 1776, and recommended by Col. Thomas Ewing for Assistant Surgeon in the Flying Camp, Baltimore County, on March 20, 1777. Took Oath of Allegiance in 1778 before Hon. James Calhoun. (A-1/25, A-2/42, FFF-96, ZZ-253)

WALSH, STEPHEN. Oath of Allegiance, 1778, before Hon. Richard Holliday. (A-1/25,A-2/60)

WALTER, BASIL. Non-Juror to Oath of Allegiance in 1778. (A-1/25)
WALTER, JOHN. Non-Juror to Oath of Allegiance in 1778. (A-1/25)

WALTER, LEVIN. Served on ship Defence, January 21 to June 1, 1777. (H-660)

WALTER, PHILIP. Private in capt. Howell's Company, December 30, 1775. Took the Oath of Allegiance in 1778 before Hon. George Lindenberger. (G-11, A-1/25, A-2/54)

WALTER, WILLIAM. Non-Juror to Oath of Allegiance in 1778. (A-1/25)

WALTERS (WATERS), SAMUEL WRIGHT. Born 1747/1748. He came from Kent Island and by 1773 was in Anne Arundel County, MD. Later, he and his family lived at Granite, Baltimore County. He died August 24, 1786. He married Eleanor BOWEN (1744/1745-December,1813) and both are buried in a family graveyard on their farm at Granite. Eleanor WALTERS was appointed guardian of the orphan children of Samuel W. WATERS in August, 1792; all were under age 14: Rachel, Alexander, Ann, and Mary WALTERS.(L-3) Samuel Wright Walters, Esq., took the Oath of Allegiance in 1778 before Hon. Charles Ridgely of William. He was Ensign in the Hunting Ridge Company, 39th Battalion of Militia of Baltimore County on August 29, 1777 to at least 1779. (Y-61, BBB-348, E-13, F-311, A-2/27) Samuel's sister, Susannah WALTERS, married Caleb OWINGS in 1768 in Anne Arundel County, MD. Caleb was a Captain in the Severn Battalion, Anne Arundel County Militia, in 1777. Caleb was the proprietor of the Sulphur Springs in southwestern Baltimore County. He died February 26, 1816 and Susannah died September 8, 1813. Captain Jacob WALTERS was a first cousin of Samuel Wright WALTERS and he was a son of Captain Jacob WALTERS, also a Sea Captain, who came from Kent Island and lived on what is now Brooklyn, Anne Arundel County, MD. The younger Captain Jacob Walters was master of the ship Brothers in 1775. During the Revolution he served in the Navy as master of the schooner Camden, with six guns and a crew of nine, in June, 1779, and master of the schooner Harford, with 14 guns and a crew of 35, in October, 1781. He identified himself as a Mariner in his will of 1811. (This information on Samuel Wright Walters was supplied by a descendant, William J. Hollifield, III, of Towson.)

WALTON, JOHN. Non-Juror to the Oath of Allegiance in 1778. (A-1/25)
WALTON, WILLIAM. Non-Juror to Oath of Allegiance in 1778. (A-1/25)

WAND, JACOB. Oath of Allegiance in 1778. (A-1/25)

WANNELL, HENRY. Served in Baltimore Artillery Company in 1777. (V-368)

WANTLAND, THOMAS. Non-Juror to Oath of Allegiance in 1778. Involved in evaluation of Baltimore County confiscated proprietary reserve lands in 1782. (FFF-547, A-1/25)

WARD, FRANCIS. Enlisted July 25, 1776 in Baltimore County. Took Oath of Allegiance in 1778 before Hon. Andrew Buchanan. (H-52, A-1/25, A-2/57)

WARD, JAMES. Private in Capt. Gist's Company, 3rd MD Regiment, February, 1778. His son, Ignatius Pigman WARD, married Hester THOMPSON, and their son, Enoch George WARD married Jane THOMPSON. (H-600, AAA-436)

WARD, JOHN. Oath of Allegiance in 1778. (A-1/25)

WARD, JOHN. Marine on ship Defence in 1777. (h-660)

WARD, JOHN (OF RICHARD). Oath of Allegiance, 1778, before Hon. John Moale. (A-2/35) (Source A-1/25 indicates there may have been 3 men with this name as Non-Jurors.)

WARD, RICHARD. Oath of Allegiance in 1778. (A-1/25)

WARD, THOMAS. Private, Baltimore County Militia; enlisted August 15, 1776. Private in Capt. Deams' Company, 7th MD Regiment, December 27, 1776. (H-58, H-59, H-305)

WARE, EDWARD. Oath of Allegiance, 1778, before Hon. Peter Shepherd. (A-1/25, A-2/49)

WARE, FRANCIS. Lieutenant Colonel in Smallwood's MD Regiment, January 14, 1776, and stationed in Baltimore that year. Colonel, 1st MD Regiment, December 10, 1776, and resigned February 18, 1777. Pay Certificates: 82810 ($32.01); 82811 ($112.24); 82812 ($173.30); 82813 ($500); 82814 ($500); 82815 ($300); and, 82816 ($251.10). Took the Oath of Allegiance in 1778 before Hon. William Spear. (A-1/25, A-2/66, B-568, FFF-33, H-20, PP-528)

WARE, GEORGE. Stored flour for the Baltimore Town Committee in 1780. (RRR-6)

WARE, THOMAS. Oath of Allegiance, 1778, before Hon. Thomas Sollers. (A-1/25, A-2/51)

WARFIELD, CALEB. Oath of Allegiance, 1778, before Hon. Richard Holliday.(A-1/25,A-2/60)

WARHAM (WAREHAM), HENRY. 1st Lieutenant in Capt. A. Lemmon's Company, February 4, 1777. Non-Juror to Oath of Allegiance in 1778. (A-1/25)

WARINER, EDMUND. Oath of Allegiance in 1778. (A-1/25)

WARM, EDWARD. Oath of Allegiance in 1778 before Hon. John Moale. (A-2/70)

WARNELL, HENRY. Oath of Allegiance, 1778, before Hon. George Lindenberger.(A-1/25,A-2/54)

WARNER, GEORGE. (June 20, 1758 - April 30, 1836) Married Elizabeth WAGNER. "George Wearner" was a Private in Capt. Sheaff's Company; volunteered June 16, 1777. "George Warner" took Oath of Allegiance in 1778 before Hon. James Calhoun. (A-1/25, A-2/40, W-162, JJJ-717)

WARREN, JACOB. Oath of Allegiance, 1778, before Hon. Geo. Lindenberger. (A-2/54)

WARREN, JOHN. Non-Juror to Oath of Allegiance in 1778. (A-1/25 card file only)

WARRICK, ANDREW. Private, Capt. Ewing's Company No. 4; enlisted Jan. 22, 1776. (H-12)

WARRINGTON, JOHN. Non-Juror to Oath of Allegiance in 1778. (A-1/25)

WARRINGTON, WILLIAM. Non-Juror to Oath of Allegiance in 1778. (A-1/25)

WATE (WAIT), RICHARD. Married Diana CORBIN on May 10, 1772. Children: William Wilkinson WATE married (1) Susanne STANSBURY in 1792, and (2) Elizabeth PICKETT on Mar. 14, 1801; Diana WATE; and, Richard Corbin WATE, married Elizabeth BASSETT in 1811. Richard WATE took the Oath of Allegiance in 1778 before Hon. James Calhoun. (A-1/25, A-2/42, and information from Shirley Reightler of Bel Air, Maryland, 1987)

WATERS, HEZEKIA. Oath of Allegiance, 1778, before Hon. George Lindenberger. Supplied nails to the Baltimore Town Committee in 1780. (A-1/25, A-2/54, RRR-6)

WATERS (WATTERS), ISAAC. Oath of Allegiance, 1778, before Hon. John Beale Howard.(A-2/29)

WATERS (WATTERS), JOHN. Private in Col. Ewing's Battalion; enlisted July 7, 1776 in Baltimore County; not on muster roll in August, 1776. (H-57)

WATERS, JOSEPH. Non-Juror to Oath of Allegiance in 1778. (A-1/25)

WATERS, PHILIP. Oath of Allegiance in 1778 before Hon. Charles Ridgely of William. One Capt. Philip Waters died on September 20, 1798, age 55, in Baltimore. (A-2/28,ZZZ-339)

WATERS, RICHARD. (1756 - August 25, 1829) Married (1) Debora SLIFER, and (2) Elizabeth Jane BOYLE. The following records of Richard Waters as found in the papers as filed in Pension Claim W11722 based upon his service in the Revolutionary War: "Richard WATERS was appointed Lieutenant in December 1776, was commissioned April 10, 1777 from Somerset County, Maryland, Lieutenant in the 1st Maryland Regiment; April 7, 1780, he was appointed Captain and served as such until January 1, 1783, during his service he was in the battles of Brandywine, Germantwon, Monmouth, in the storming of Stony Point, Camden, and the seige of Yorktown. He was allowed pension on his application executed April 16, 1818, at which time he gave his age as 60 and upwards, and was a resident of city of Baltimore, Maryland. In 1821 he was still living in that city and gave his age as 65 with no explanation of the discrepancy. He died August 25, 1829. RICHARD WATERS

WATERS, RICHARD (continued)

married December 20, 1818 to Elizabeth Jane BOYLE at the home of Henry HOLLYDAY in
Talbot County, Maryland (no relationship stated to either the soldier or his wife).
At the time of their marriage the soldier was a resident of Baltimore, Maryland.
Soldier's widow Elizabeth Jane WATERS also referred to as Eliza Jane was allowed a
pension on her application executed May 19, 1853 at which time she was age 66 and a
resident of Baltimore, Maryland. September 10, 1863 she was living in New York Co.
New York, on account of her family having moved to New York state and she wished to
be with them. In 1821 reference was made to the following children: John, age 17,
Margaret, age 15, and Virginia Ann WATERS an infant age 7 months. Richard Waters'
brother John WATERS served as a Lieutenant in the Revolutionary War and was killed
by a cannon ball at the battle of White Plains." (I-107, H-483, YY-53, YY-125) He
received Pay Certificates 86541 ($56.12), 86542 ($13.07), 86543 ($400), and 86544
($2360). Also entitled to 200 acres (lots 2944, 2946, 2947, 2879) in western Mary-
land for services as a Captain, and Federal Bounty Land Grant Warrant 2409 for 300
acres. (DDDD-4, I-107, JJJ-721, B-575) On March 12, 1827 it was ordered to pay to
him, of Baltimore, during life, half yearly, sum equal to pay of a Captain for his
services during the Revolutionary War. On February 2, 1830 it was ordered to pay
to Elizabeth J. Waters, during life, quarterly, half pay of a Captain, in consideration of her husband Capt. Richard Waters, during the Revolutionary War. (C-404)

WATERS, SAMUEL. Oath of Allegiance in 1778. (A-1/25)

WATERS, SAMUEL WRIGHT: See "Samuel Wright WALTERS."

WATERS, THOMAS. Non-Juror to Oath of Allegiance in 1778. (A-1/25)
WATKINS, FRANCIS. Non-Juror to Oath of Allegiance in 1778. (A-1/25)

WATKINS, GASSAWAY. (1752, Anne Arundel County, MD - July 14, 1840, Anne Arundel County)
Married (1) Sarah JONES, (2) Ruth DORSEY, and (3) Eleanora Bowie CLAGGETT in 1803 in
Baltimore County (Marriage proven through Maryland pension application). Eleanora
was born in 1782 and died in 1871; a daughter Albina Charlotte WATKINS (1822-1899)
married William CLARK (1813-1887) in 1848 and their daughter, Mary Ann CLARK (1849-
1887) married William Henry GORMAN (1843-1915) in 1877; and, a son, Wm. W. WATKINS
(1810-   ) married Laura WATKINS (1818-1880) in 1837, and their daughter, Eleanor
Elizabeth WATKINS (1838-1893) married Joshua Worthington DORSEY (b. 1837) in 1862.
Gassaway WATKINS was a Corporal, Sergeant and Ensign in Smallwood's MD Regiment in
Company No. 2, in 1776; 2nd Lieutenant in Capt. Beatty's Co., 7th MD Regiment, 1777;
1st Lieutenant, 5th MD Regiment, 1781; and, Captain, 5th MD Regt., May, 1782 through
April, 1783. He received 200 acres (lots 2244-2247) in western Maryland. He was
President of the Maryland Society of the Cincinnati at the time of his death in 1840.
(H-7, H-41, H-364, YY-125, AAA-2595, AAA-1362, JJJ-721, DDDD-4)

WATKINS, JAMES. Non-Juror to Oath of Allegiance in 1778. (A-1/25)

WATKINS, JOHN. (March 1, 1758, Long Green, Maryland - May 2, 1847, Baldwin, Maryland)
Married Ruth GUYTON on June 2, 1792, and their son John WATKINS III (1803-1878) md.
(2) Minerva SLADE (1811-1898) and their son John Beale WATKINS (1838-1905) married
Clara Augusta BAGLEY (1846-1923) in 1869. John WATKINS was a Private in the company
of Capt. Dickinson in the Baltimore County Militia. (AAA-2689,JJJ-720) He was Non-
Juror to the Oath of Allegiance in 1778. (A-1/25)

WATKINS, SAMUEL. Non-Juror to Oath in 1778, but signed in 1781. (A-1/25, QQ-122)

WATKINS, WILLIAM. Oath of Allegiance, 1778, before Hon. James Calhoun. Recruit in
Baltimore County in 1780. (A-1/25, A-2/65, H-340)

WATKINS, WILLIAM. ("Stone Mason") Oath of Allegiance, 1778, before Hon. John Moale.
(A-2/70)

WATLING, ABRAHMA (ABRAM). Non-Juror to Oath of Allegiance in 1778. (A-1/25)
WATLING, JAMES. Non-Juror to Oath of Allegiance in 1778. (A-1/25)
WATLING, THOMAS SR. Non-Juror to Oath of Allegiance in 1778. (A-1/25)
WATLING, THOMAS JR. Non-Juror to Oath of Allegiance in 1778. (A-1/25)
WATSON, ARCHIBALD. Non-Juror to Oath of Allegiance in 1778. (A-1/25)

WATSON, GEORGE. Recruited in Baltimore on March 2, 1780 by Samuel Chester for the 3rd Maryland Regiment. (H-334)

WATSON, JAMES. Served on ship Defence, June 23 to August 15, 1777, and "Captain After Guard" from August 15 to November 23, 1777. (H-660)

WATSON, JOHN. Non-Juror to Oath of Allegiance in 1778. (A-1/25)

WATSON, THOMAS. Enlisted July 26, 1776 in Baltimore County, and Private in company of Capt. J. Gist, 3rd MD Regiment, in February, 1778. (H-53, H-600)

WATSON, WILLIAM SR. Non-Juror to Oath of Allegiance in 1778. (A-1/25)
WATSON, WILLIAM JR. Non-Juror to Oath of Allegiance in 1778. (A-1/25)

WATTEY, JOHN. Oath of Allegiance, 1778, before Hon. Thomas Sollers. (A-1/25, A-2/51)

WATTS, BENJAMIN. Drafted into Baltimore County Regiment No. 36, circa 1777. (TTT-13)

WATTS, EDWARD. Non-Juror to Oath of Allegiance, 1778; signed in 1781. (A-1/25, QQ-122)

WATTS, JOHN. Non-Juror to Oath of Allegiance in 1778. (A-1/25)
WATTS, JOSIAS. Non-Juror to oath of Allegiance in 1778. (A-1/25)

WATTS, RICHARD. Private in Capt. Ewing's Company No. 4; enlisted May 18, 1776. Took the Oath of Allegiance in 1778 before Hon. George Lindenberger. (H-11, A-1/25, A-2/54)

WAYTE, HENRY. Matross in Capt. Gale's MD Artillery, September, 1779. Appointed Corporal on November 7, 1779. (YYY-1/116)

WEATHERBURN, JOHN. Oath of Allegiance, 1778, before Hon. George Lindenberger. (A-1/25) Source A-2/54 mistakenly spelled his name "Weatherfurn." His death notice stated: "President of the Mechanics Bank, (he) died April 21, 1811, aged 61. Born at Kenton near Newcastle-on-Tyne, and in 1772 went to Alexandria, Virginia, and then came to Baltimore. He was a member of the Volunteer Independent Company of Militia in the Revolution." (ZZZ-341, A-1/25, A-2/54)

WEAVER, CASPER. Non-Juror to Oath of Allegiance in 1778. (A-1/25)

WEAVER, JOHN SR. Non-Juror to Oath of Allegiance, 1778; signed in 1781. (A-1/25,QQ-123)

WEAVER, JOHN JR. Non-Juror to Oath of Allegiance, 1778; signed in 1781. (A-1/25,QQ-123)

WEAVER, LEDEWICK (LUDOWICK). Oath of Allegiance, 1778, before Hon. Peter Shepherd. (A-1/25, A-2/49)

WEAVER (WEVER), PETER. Oath of Allegiance, 1778, before Hon. Geo. Lindenberger. (A-2/55)

WEAVER, PHILIP. Non-Juror to Oath of Allegiance, 1778; signed in 1781. (A-1/25, QQ-123)

WEBB, BROWN. Non-Juror to Oath of Allegiance in 1778. (A-1/25)
WEBB, JOHN. Non-Juror to Oath of Allegiance in 1778. (A-1/25)
WEBB, JONATHAN. Non-Juror to Oath of Allegiance in 1778. (A-1/25)
WEBB, THOMAS. Non-Juror to Oath of Allegiance in 1778. (A-1/25)
WEBBER, THOMAS. Non-Juror to Oath of Allegiance in 1778. (A-1/25)

WEBER, DANIEL. Oath of Allegiance, 1778, before Hon. George Lindenberger.(A-1/25,A-2/54)

WEBRIGHT (WEBUGHT), MARTIN. Non-Juror to Oath of Allegiance in 1778. (A-1/25)

WEBSTER, SAMUEL. Private, Col. Aquila Hall's Baltimore County Regiment, 1777. (TTT-13)

WEDDERFIELD, PETER. Private in Capt. Howell's Company, December 30, 1775. (G-11)

WEDGE, SIMON. Private in Capt. Sheaff's Company, June 16, 1777. Non-Juror to Oath of Allegiance in 1778. (A-1/25, W-162)

WEEKS, BENJAMIN. Baltimore Privateer and Captain of brig Cato (14 guns), owned by Samuel and William Smith of Baltimore. (III-206)

WEEMS, WILLIAM. Baltimore Privateer and Captain of sloop Porpoise (16 guns, 6 swivels). (III-206)

WEER, JOHN. Oath of Allegiance, 1778, before Hon. Peter Shepherd. (A-1/25, A-2/49)

WEER (WEEAR), ROBERT. Oath of Allegiance, 1778, before Hon. Peter Shepherd. (A-2/49)

WEER, THOMAS. Oath of Allegiance, 1778, before Hon. William Spear. (A-1/25, A-2/66)

WEER (WEEAR), WILLIAM. Oath of Allegiance, 1778, before Hon. Peter Shepherd. (A-2/49)

WEER, WILLIAM JR. Oath of Allegiance, 1778, before Hon. Edward Cockey.(A-1/25,A-2/61)

WEGER, FREDERICK. Private in Capt. Graybill's German Regiment in 1776. (H-265)

WELCH,_____AIN (part of first name torn from list) Private in Baltimore County Regiment No. 7, circa 1777. (TTT-13)

WELCH, GEORGE. Oath of Allegiance, 1778, before Hon. James Calhoun.(A-1/25, A-2/38)

WELCH (WELSH), JAMES. Matross in Capt. Brown's MD Artillery; joined Nov. 22, 1777. Was at Valley Forge until June, 1778; at White Plains, July, 1778; at Ft. Schuyler in August and September, 1780; Gunner, on August 1, 1781, at High Hills of Santee; at Camp Col. Scirvins, January, 1782; at Bacon's Bridge, S.C., April, 1782. Also, entitled to 50 acres (lot 1618) in western Maryland for his services as an Artillery Matross. (DDDD-37, UU-228, UU-229, UU-230) Non-Juror, 1778. (A-1/25 card file only)

WELCH (WELSH), JOSEPH. Enlisted August 14, 1776 in Baltimore County. (H-52)

WELCH, WILLIAM. Private, Capt. J. Gist's Co., 3rd MD Regiment, February, 1778. (H-600)

WELDERMAN, GEORGE. Oath of Allegiance in 1778. (A-1/25)

WELDERMAN, JACOB. Oath of Allegiance in 1778. (A-1/25)

WELHELM, FREDERICK. Private in Capt. Graybill's German Regt., July 12, 1776. (ZZ-32)

WELLMAN, RICHARD. Oath of Allegiance, 1778, before Hon. Charles Ridgely of William. (A-1/25, A-2/27) Could not write; made his mark.

WELLS, ALEXANDER. (March 12, 1727 - December 9, 1813) Married Leah OWINGS (1727-1815) on July 12, 1753 at St. Thomas Church. Children: Henry WELLS (1754-1814) married Jemima COE; Alexander WELLS (1756-   ) married Providence TALBOT; Ann WELLS (b. 1758) married William GRIFFITH; Michal WELLS (1759-1831) married Absalom WELLS; Nathaniel WELLS (1761-1789) married Temperance WELLS; Bezaleel WELLS (1763-1846) married (1) Rebecca RISTEAU, and (2) Sarah GRIFFITH; James WELLS (born 1765) md. Catherine OWINGS; Richard WELLS; and, Helen WELLS (b. 1775) md. Richard WELLS. Alexander Wells was 1st Lieutenant in Soldiers Delight Company No. 2, May 13, 1776 and became Captain in the Baltimore County Militia. (FF-64, JJJ-727, KKK-199)

WELLS, ALEXANDER JR. Non-Juror to Oath of Allegiance, 1778. (A-1/25 card file only)

WELLS, BENJAMIN. Oath of Allegiance, 1778, before Hon. Charles Ridgely of William. (A-2/27) Source A-1/25 indicates there was another Benjamin who was a Non-Juror.

WELLS, BENJAMIN (OF BENJAMIN). Non-Juror to Oath of Allegiance in 1778. (A-1/25)

WELLS, CHARLES. Two men with this name took the Oath of Allegiance in 1778: one before Hon. William Lux (A-2/68) and one before Hon. John Moale (A-2/70). (A-1/25)

WELLS, CHARLES. (April 6, 1745, Baltimore County, MD - April 16, 1815, Ohio Co., VA) Son of Benjamin WELLS and Temperance BUTLER. Married (1) Michal OWINGS (1745-1783) on December 27, 1764, and (2) Elizabeth PRATHER. Charles Wells moved from Baltimore County, MD to Ohio County, VA circa 1772. He signed the Oath of Allegiance there on October 6, 1777. His children: Rebecca, Joshua, Temperance, Benedict, Absalom, Mary, Elizabeth, Ephraim, and Michal. (KKK-507, JJJ-728)

WELLS, CYPRIAN. (1748/1749 - February 22, 1814) Member of the Sons of Liberty, 1776, in Baltimore, and took Oath of Allegiance in 1778 before Hon. James Calhoun.(CCC-19, A-2/39, ZZZ-343)

WELLS, EPHRAIM. Oath of Allegiance in 1778. (A-1/25)

WELLS, GEORGE. Member of Sons of Liberty, 1776, in Baltimore, and Baltimore Mechanical Company. Capt. of Baltimore Town Battalion Company No. 6 (commanding 66 men), 1776. On October 16, 1776, he requested information from the Council of Safety about the

WELLS, GEORGE (continued)
masting and rigging of a row galley. He was Captain in the Baltimore Town Artillery in 1777 (September 4), and a Non-Juror to the Oath of Allegiance in 1778. He might have been the "Mr. Wells" who built the frigate <u>Virginia</u>, containing 28 guns, at Baltimore (Fell's Point) in December, 1775. (III-201, FFF-63, CCC-19, CCC-25, BBB-362, A-1/25, E-13, GG-74)

WELLS, JAMES. Enlisted in Baltimore Town on July 20, 1776. (H-53)

WELLS, JOHN. Non-Juror to the Oath of Allegiance in 1778. (A-1/25)

WELLS, JOHN (OF THOMAS). Oath of Allegiance, 1778, before Hon. Andrew Buchanan. (A-2/57)

WELLS, RICHARD. Non-Juror to Oath of Allegiance in 1778. On June 1, 1840, one Richard Wells, age 82, was listed as a pensioner residing in the household of John G. DORCY in Baltimore City's 10th Ward. (P-128, A-1/25) He might have been the Richard Wells who served in Capt. Philip Maroney's Company in Frederick County, MD in 1776. (H-45)

WELLS, ROBERT TEVIS. Oath of Allegiance in 1778 before Hon. Andrew Buchanan. (A-2/57)

WELLS, THOMAS. (1709 - May 20, 1804, Baltimore County, MD) Married Elizabeth HOWARD (1714-1785) on September 16, 1736 in Baltimore County. Their son, Francis WELLS (1737-1769) married Ann TEVIS on March 20, 1757, and theri granddaughter Susannah WELLS (1761-c1832) married James ARMSTRONG in 1779 (he died in Knox County, Tennessee, 1813). Thomas WELLS took the Oath of Allegiance in 1778 before Hon. Andrew Buchanan. (A-2/57, JJJ-728, AAA-2745)

WELSH, GEORGE. "George Walsh" was an Ensign in Capt. Cox's Company, March 1, 1776, and "George Welsh" was a Lieutenant in that company on December 19, 1776. "George Welsh" was a Captain in the Baltimore Town Artillery in 1777, 1st Lieutenant in Baltimore Town Battalion in 1779, and Lieutenant in Capt. McClellan's Company, Sept. 4, 1780. (WW-197, CCC-21, CCC-23, MM-89, F-311, F-313)

WELSH, GRAY. Ensign in Baltimore Town Battalion on March 16, 1779. (F-311)

WELSH, HENRY. Oath of Allegiance in 1778 before Hon. James Calhoun. (A-2/65)

WELSH, JAMES. Oath of Allegiance in 1778 before Hon. Richard Cromwell. Recruit in the Baltimore County Militia, April 11, 1780. (A-2/46, H-335)

WELSH, JOSHUA. Non-Juror to Oath of Allegiance in 1778. (A-1/25 card file only)

WELSH, JOHN. Represented Delaware Hundred at the Association of Freemen on August 21, 1775. (EEEE-1726)

WELSH, JOSHUA. Ensign in Capt. H. Howard's Company No. 3 in 1776.(PPP-2, RR-99, ZZ-541)

WELSH, LABAN. Non-Juror to Oath of Allegiance in 1778. (A-1/25 card file only)

WELSH, PATRICK. Enlisted in Baltimore Town on July 17, 1776. (H-53)

WELSH, WILLIAM. Ensign in Baltimore County Militia, 6th Company, December 19, 1775. Non-Juror to Oath of Allegiance in 1778, but signed in 1781. (G-10, A-1/25, QQ-123)

WELSTET (WETSTET), WILLIAM. Private in Capt. S. Smith's Company No. 8, 1st MD Battalion, January 23, 1776. (H-641)

WELTY, JOHN. Private in Capt. Graybill's German Regiment in 1776. (H-266)

WERSHLER, MORRICE. Oath of Allegiance in 1778 before Hon. James Calhoun. (A-2/39)

WERT (WORT), CASPER. Oath of Allegiance, 1778, before Hon. James Calhoun.(A-1/25,A-2/40)

WERTINBURGER, LUDWICK. Oath of Allegiance in 1778 before Hon. James Calhoun. (A-2/40)

WEST, BENJAMIN. Oath of Allegiance in 1778 before Hon. James Calhoun. (A-2/41)

WEST, ELIJAH SR. Non-Juror to Oath of Allegiance in 1778. (A-1/25 card file only)
WEST, ELIJAH JR. Non-Juror to Oath of Allegiance in 1778. (A-1/25 card file only)

WEST, FREDERICK. Private in Capt. Norwood's Company, 4th MD Regiment. Muster roll of February, 1778, indicates "died Baltimore." (H-178)

WEST, JOHN. Recruit in Baltimore County in 1780. (H-340) Non-Juror to the Oath of Allegiance in 1778 (A-1/25 card file only).

WEST, JOSEPH. Pensioner as of June 1, 1840, age 85, residing in the household of a Joseph West in Baltimore County's 5th District. (P-127) He might have been the Joseph West who was a Private in Col. Grayson's Regiment in 1781. (H-602)

WEST, LUKE. Enlisted in Baltimore County on July 20, 1776. Took Oath of Allegiance in 1778 before Hon. John Beale Howard. (Made his mark.) (A-2/29, H-52)

WEST, THOMAS. Oath of Allegiance in 1778 before Hon. George Lindenberger. (A-2/54)

WEST, WILLIAM. Oath of Allegiance in 1778 before Hon. James Calhoun. (A-2/38)

WESTBAY (WASBAY), HUGH. Baltimore Mechanical Company of Militia, November 4, 1775. Private in Capt. Cox's Company, December 19, 1776. (F-299, CCC-21)

WESTBAY, ROBERT. Private in Capt.S. Smith's Company No. 8, 1st Maryland Battalion, January 23, 1776. (H-641)

WESTBAY, WILLIAM. Oath of Allegiance in 1778 before Hon. James Calhoun. (A-2/39)

WESTON, JOHN. On July 13, 1776, he reported to the Maryland Council of Safety that he was unable to supply guns because of the lack of a furnace blast. He became 2nd Lieutenant under Capt. Buck in the Gunpowder Battalion on August 30, 1777. Took Oath of Allegiance, 1778, before Hon. James Calhoun. Served in militia at least through 1778. (BBB-350, AA-65, E-11, FFF-42, A-2/39)

WESTON, JOSEPH. Enlisted in Baltimore County on July 20, 1776. Took Oath in 1778 before Hon. Charles Ridgely of William. (A-2/28, H-52)

WESTON, NATHANIEL. Oath of Allegiance in 1778 before Hon. George Lindenberger. Ensign in Baltimore Town Battalion on May 17, 1779. (A-2/54, F-309, F-311)

WESTON, WILLIAM. Oath of Allegiance in 1778 before Hon. Charles Ridgely of William. Could not write; made his mark ("W"). (A-2/28)

WETHER, JOHN. Oath of Allegiance in 1781. (QQ-123)

WHALEN (WHALING), JAMES. Matross in Capt. Brown's MD Artillery; joined November 22, 1777. Was at Valley Forge until June, 1778; at White Plains, July, 1778; at Fort Schuyler in August and September, 1780; Gunner on August 1, 1781 at High Hills of the Santee; at Camp Col. Scirvins in January, 1782, and Bacon's Bridge, S.C., in April, 1782. (UU-228, UU-229, UU-230)

WHARTON, REVEL. Served on ship Defence in 1777. (H-660)

WHEATON, JOSEPH. (1756, Flatbush, Long Island, N.Y. - Nov. 23, 1828, Baltimore, MD) Married Sally FLETCHER in 1786, and their daughter Mary W. P. WHARTON married to John BURKE in 1812. Joseph Wheaton was a Lieutenant in Col. Israel Angell's Rgt. in the 1st Rhode Island Line, September 1, 1779 to December 25, 1783. He also was a member of the Society of the Cincinnati. (AAA-650, which cites Rhode Island Colonial Records, Volume VIII, page 597, and Volume IX, pages 89 and 90)

WHEELAN, MARTIN. Private in Capt. S. Smith's Company No. 8, 1st Maryland Battalion, January 24, 1776. (H-641)

WHEELEN (WHEALIN), RICHARD. Private in Capt. Ewing's Company No. 4; enlisted on January 20, 1776. Private in Capt. Furnival's MD Artillery, November 17, 1777. (H-12, H-573)

WHEELER, BENJAMIN. Marine on ship Defence, June 7 to December 31, 1777. (H-660)

WHEELER, BENJAMIN SR. Non-Juror to Oath of Allegiance in 1778. (A-1/25)
WHEELER, BENJAMIN JR. Non-Juror to Oath of Allegiance in 1778. (A-1/25)

WHEELER, BENJAMIN (OF JOHN). Oath of Allegiance, 1778, before Hon. John Hall.(A-2/36)

WHEELER, EDWARD. Oath of Allegiance, 1778, before Hon. Peter Shepherd. (A-2/50)

WHEELER, ISAAC. 1st Lieutenant, Baltimore Town Battalion, September 4, 1777; deceased by January 19, 1781. (BBB-362, E-14, F-312, R-15, BBBB-29) Non-Juror, 1778.(A-1/25)

WHEELER, JOHN. (1760-1832) Married Tabitha WARRINGTON. Corporal in Capt. Furnival's MD Artillery, November 17, 1777. Sergeant in Capt. Dorsey's MD Artillery, at Valley Forge, June 3, 1778. Entitled to 50 acres (lot 1734) in western Maryland. (DDDD-37, JJJ-733, H-572, UU-230) There may have been 3 Non-Jurors, 1778, by this name.(A-1/25)

WHEELER, JOSEPH. Source A-1/25 states there were 2 Non-Jurors in 1778 with this name.

WHEELER, NATHAN. Non-Juror to Oath of Allegiance in 1778. Involved in evaluation of Baltimore County confiscated proprietary reserve lands, in 1782. (FFF-555, A-1/25)

WHEELER, RICHARD. Non-Juror to Oath of Allegiance in 1778. (A-1/25)
WHEELER, SOLOMON. Non-Juror to Oath of Allegiance in 1778. (A-1/25)

WHEELER, THOMAS. Private in Baltimore County Regiment No. 7, circa 1777. (TTT-13)

WHEELER, WAYSON (WASON). Non-Juror to the Oath of Allegiance in 1778. (A-1/25)

WHEELER, WILLIAM. Recruit in Baltimore County in 1780. (H-340) Source A-1/25 indicates there were 2 Non-Jurors to the Oath of Allegiance in 1778 with this name.

WHEELER, WILLISON. Non-Juror to Oath of Allegiance in 1778. (A-1/25)
WHELAND, EZEKIEL. Non-Juror to Oath of Allegiance in 1778. (A-1/25)

WHELAND, RICHARD. Oath of Allegiance in 1778 before Hon. James Calhoun. (A-1/25,A-2/40)

WHELLER, EDWARD. Oath of Allegiance in 1778. (A-1/25)

WHIPS (WHIPPS), JOHN. Oath of Allegiance, 1778, before Hon. Peter Shepherd. (A-2/49)

WHIPS (WHIPPS), SAMUEL. Non-Juror to the Oath of Allegiance in 1778. (A-1/25)
WHISKEY, CHRISTIAN. Non-Juror to the Oath of Allegiance in 1778. (A-1/25)

WHITAKER, WILLIAM. Private in Capt. Lynn's Company, August, 1781. "William Whitacres" was a Revolutionary War pensioner, MD Line. On February 27, 1839, it was ordered to "pay to Sarah SCRIVNER, of Baltimore City, former widow of William Whitaker, a soldier of the Revolution, or to her order, half pay of a Private of the Revolution, during her life, quarterly, commencing January 1, 1838." (C-406, YY-54, H-404)

WHITE, BENJAMIN. Seaman on ship Defence, September 20 to December 31, 1777. (H-660)

WHITE, DAVID. Born 1745 in Dublin, Ireland. Occupation: Weaver. Height: 5'5¼". He enlisted as a Private in Capt. N. Smith's 1st Company of Matrosses on Jan. 28, 1776. Private in Capt. Dorsey's MD Artillery, November 17, 1777, and Corporal in that company at Valley Forge, June 3, 1778. Entitled to 50 acres (lot 1039) in western MD for his Artillery Matross services. (H-564,H-567,H-574,QQQ-2,VV-74,UU-231,DDDD-37)

WHITE, ELISHA. Source A-2/27 states that "Elisha White" took the Oath of Allegiance in 1778 before Hon. Charles Ridgely of William (could not write; made his mark), and Source A-1/25 states it was "Elija White." This might have been two different men.

WHITE, HENRY. Non-Juror to the Oath of Allegiance in 1778. (A-1/25)

WHITE, JAMES. Born 1759. Private in Extra Regiment at Fort Whetstone Point in 1781 in Baltimore. Revolutionary War pensioner, MD Line (Invalid). (YY-54, H-627)

WHITE, JOHN. 2nd Lieutenant in Capt. Gale's MD Artillery, 1779; appointed either on September 3 or September 14, 1777; resigned February 15, 1780. (YYY-1/117)

WHITE, JOHN. Enlisted in Baltimore County on July 25, 1776. Private in Capt. Furnival's Company, MD Artillery, November 17, 1777. Took Oath of Allegiance in 1778 before Hon. Jesse Dorsey. (A-1/25, A-2/63, H-52, H-573)

WHITE, JOSEPH. Oath of Allegiance in 1778 before Hon. William Lux. Could not write; made his mark. (A-1/25, A-2/68)

WHITE, LUKE. Non-Juror to the Oath of Allegiance in 1778. (A-1/25)

WHITE, MICHAEL. Oath of Allegiance in 1778 before Hon. James Calhoun. (A-1/25, A-2/40)

WHITE, OLIVER. Oath of Allegiance, 1778, before Hon. William Spear. Could not write; made his mark. (A-2/66)

WHITE, OTHO. Oath of Allegiance in 1778 before Hon. Charles Ridgely of William. Was an

WHITE, OTHO (continued)
Ensign in Capt. Stinchcomb's Company, Soldiers Delight Battalion, February 7, 1782.
(A-1/25, A-2/27, OCCC-71)

WHITE, PETER. Seamsn on ship Defence, August 9 to November 2, 1777. (H-660) Source
A-1/25 states he took the Oath of Allegiance in 1778.

WHITE, ROBERT. Private in Col. Aquila Hall's Baltimore County Regiment, 1777. Took
Oath of Allegiance, 1778, before Hon. John Moale. (TTT-13, A-1/25, A-2/70)

WHITE, THOMAS. Oath of Allegiance, 1778, before Hon. George Lindenberger. On Feb. 3,
1828 it was ordered to pay him, of Baltimore, half yearly, for life, half pay of a
Private, as further remuneration for his services during the Revolutionary War. On
June 1, 1840, he is listed as a pensioner, age 86, residing in the household of a
Charles White in Baltimore County's 1st District. (P-127, C-407, A-1/25, A-2/54)

WHITE, ZEPHANIAH. Private in Capt. Furnival's MD Artillery, Nov. 17, 1777. (H-573)

WHITECOTTON, JAMES. Private in Capt. Lansdale's Company, 4th MD Regiment, from
May 29, 1778 to April 10, 1779, when reported deserted. (H-179)

WHITTEE, ANDREW. Oath of Allegiance, 1778, before Hon. Charles Ridgely of William.
Could not write; made his mark ("W"). (A-2/27)

WHITEFIELD, JAMES. Oath of Allegiance, 1778, before Hon. Chas. Ridgely of Wm.(A-2/28)

WHITEFIELD, THOMAS. Oath of Allegiance in 1778. (A-1/25)

WHITER, JOHN. Oath of Allegiance, 1778, before Hon. Charles Ridgely of Wm. (A-2/27)

WHITING, WILLIAM. Oath of Allegiance in 1778. (A-1/25)

WHITLEY, THOMAS. Non-Juror to Oath of Allegiance in 1778. (A-1/25)

WHITING (WIGHTING), WILLIAM. Non-Juror to Oath of Allegiance in 1778. (A-1/25)

WHITMAN, GEORGE. Involved in evaluation of Baltimore County confiscated proprietary
reserve lands in 1782. (FFF-553)

WHITTER, ANDREW. Oath of Allegiance in 1778. (A-1/25)

WHITTOM (WHITTHAM), WILLIAM. "William Whittom" was a Private in Capt. Dorsey's MD
Artillery, November 17, 1777. "William Whittem" volunteered in Baltimore County
Regiment No. 36 circa 1777. "William Whitton" took the Oath of Allegiance, 1778,
before Hon. Thomas Sollers. "William Whittham" was a Matross in Capt. Gale's MD
Artillery, 1779-1780; sick November, 1779; hospital, December, 1779. (YYY-1/119,
TTT-13, H-574, A-1/25, A-2/51)

WIDMAN, GEORGE. Oath of Allegiance, 1778, before Hon. John Hall. (A-1/25, A-2/36)

WIESENTHAL, CHARLES FREDERICK, M.D. (c1726, Baltimore or Prussia - June 1, 1789,
Baltimore) His wife, Elizabeth, died July 2, 1805; earlier, in 1792, she had been
appointed guardian of Juliana Susanna Wiesenthal, "orphan daughter of Dr. Charles
F. Wiesenthal, under age of 14." (K-246) In 1806, Julianna S. B. WIESENTHAL md.
John E. HUGHES and her daughter Maria E. HUGHES md. Henry F. REIGART. Charles F.
Wiesenthal was a German physician who settled in Baltimore circa 1755, and was
active on the American side during the entire Revolutionary War. On Marhc 13,
1775 he served on the Baltimore County Committee of Inspection, and in December,
1775 he was appointed superintendent of the manufacture of saltpeter for State of
Maryland. He was Surgeon in Smallwood's MD Regiment, February to December, 1776,
and was stationed at Baltimore, where he was Surgeon General of Military Hospitals
in 1777, as well as examiner for applicants in surgery in 1778. He also was the
Surgeon for the State Ship Defence, 1776-1777. He took the Oath of Allegiance in
1778 before Hon. George Lindenberger. Numerous letters passed from him to the MD
Council, mainly complaints, one of which was that he "is superceeded in Smallwood's
command by Dr. Toothill." (Also, earlier, in 1773, he and other German Lutherans by
aid of a lottery, built a church on Fish Street, now Saratoga, in Baltimore City.)
(H-20, B-579, A-1/25, A-2/54, K-246, RR-19, ZZZ-349, TT-146, XX-16, FFF-52, AAA-287,
ZZZ-165)

WIGGINS, JAMES. Private in Capt. Lansdale's Company, 4th MD Regiment, from March 20, 1778 to August 16, 1780 ("prisoner"). He may have served beyond that time. (H-179)

WIGHT (WHIGHT), RICHARD. Oath of Allegiance in 1778 before Hon. Peter Shepherd. (A-1/25, A-2/49)

WIGLEY, EDWARD SR. Non-Juror to the Oath of Allegiance in 1778. (A-1/25)

WIGLEY, EDWARD JR. Non-Juror to the Oath of Allegiance in 1778. (A-1/25)

WIGLEY, ISAAC. Non-Juror to the Oath of Allegiance in 1778. (A-1/25)

WIGLEY (WIGLY), WILLIAM. Stored and delivered flour for the Baltimore Town Committee in 1780. (RRR-6)

WILDERMAN, GEORGE. Oath of Allegiance in 1778 before Hon. William Lux. (A-2/68)

WILDERMAN, JACOB. Enlisted in Baltimore County on July 20, 1776. Took the Oath of Allegiance in 1778 before Hon. William Lux. (H-52. A-2/68)

WILEY, BENJAMIN. Oath of Allegiance in 1778 before Hon. Robert Simmons. Could not write; made his mark. (A-1/25, A-2/58)

WILEY, JOHN. Ensign in Capt. Shaw's Company No. 5 in 1776. (PPP-2, RR-99, ZZ-541)

WILKERSON (WILKINSON), YOUNG. "Mr. Young WILKERSON, aged 85, died at the residence of Augustine GAMBRILL on September 15, 1827. He was a Lieutenant in the Revolutionary Army." (UUU-203)(Various sources misspelled his name as Wilkinson.) On January 20, 1776 he was a Corporal in Capt. N. Smith's 1st Company of Matrosses, and was on duty at Fort Whetstone Point in Baltimore on September 7, 1776. He became a Sergeant in Capt. Dorsey's MD Artillery on November 17, 1777, and 2nd Lieutenant on Feb. 25, 1778. He was retained in the 1st Continental Artillery, May 30, 1778, and was at Valley Forge on June 3, 1778. He became a 1st Lieutenant on April 1, 1779, and served subsequently in Capt. Dorsey's 2nd Company of Matrosses under Lt.Col. Ed. Carrington, stationed at Baltimore, May 11, 1780. He also served in Capt. J. Smith's MD Artillery, and was sick in the hospital at Boon's Plantation, January 28, 1782 (S.C.). He was furloughed by General Greene for want of command in April, 1782, but did serve through June, 1783 in Capt. Smith's Company. "Lt. Young Wilkerson" was a Revolutionary Pensioner (YY-54) and "Lt. Young Wilkinson" received 200 acres (lots 2305, 2307, 2310, 2311) in western Maryland for his services. (DDDD-4, VVV-96, TT-147, H-573, H-567, H-568, QQQ-2, YYY-2/50, H-477, H-579, UU-230, UU-232, YY-54, UUU-203)

WILKES, JOSEPH. Born 1743 in England. Occupation: Labourer. Enlisted January 30, 1776 as Private in Capt. N. Smith's 1st Company of Matrosses. Height: 5'6½". He gave his deposition on enlistment terms as a Matross Soldier in Baltimore County on May 7, 1779. Served in Capt. Gale's MD Artillery and was sick in Baltimore in October, 1779, having been left sick at Fort Whetstone Point on September 15, 1779. He was claimed later by Lt. Samuel Saddler as being fit for duty on December 23, 1779. (H-626, H-567, H-565, QQQ-2, VV-74, FFF-220, YYY-1/120)

WILKINS, HAVEN (HUVEN). Oath of Allegiance, 1778, before Hon. Geo. Lindenberger. (A-2/54)

WILKINS, JOHN. Born 1742 in South Carolina. Occupation: Labourer. Enlisted February 3, 1776 as Private in Capt. N. Smith's 1st Company of Matrosses. Height: 5'9". He was a Private in Capt. Dorsey's MD Artillery on November 17, 1777, and a Corporal with that company at Valley Forge on June 3, 1778. (H-565, H-566, H-574, QQQ-2, UU-231)

WILKINS, THOMAS. Oath of Allegiance in 1778. (A-1/25)

WILKINS, WILLIAM II. (June 19, 1737, Annapolis, MD - August 21, 1817, Baltimore, MD) Married Sarah CONNANT (1742-1814) on September 28, 1765. Children: William III (born 1767) married Achsa GOODWIN; Henry (born 1770); Mary (born 1776); Joseph (born 1782) married Mary Cooke BEDFORD; and, John (born 1784). William Wilkins was a member of the committee to supervise fortifications of Annapolis in 1776. (XXX-762, XXX-763)

WILKINSON, JOHN. (1760-1825, Baltimore County, MD) Married Elizabeth MURRAY (1771-1837) on May 27, 1789. Children: Thomas (born 1789) married Rebecca HARRYMAN; John (born 1791) married Elizabeth ROLLINS; Samuel (1794-1868) married (1) Temperance CARBACK (1800-1836) in 1818 and their son William (1829-1904) married Narcissa GRAY in 1855;

WILKINSON, JOHN (continued) and (2) Susannah CLARK (1805-1900) in 1839 and their son Thomas Clark WILKINSON 91844-1921) married Emma Virginia BONN (1850-1916) in 1869; William (born 1797, died in infancy); Welthy Ann (born 1799) married John BOND: James (born 1802, died in infancy); and, Mary Ann (born 1805) married Joseph GRIFFIN. John Wilkinson took the Oath of Allegiance in 1778 before Hon. George Lindenberger, and was a Private in Capt. William Reiley's Company, 4th MD Regiment, March 13, 1778. He was a Sergeant in Capt. William reiley's Company No. 3, 1st Regiment, commanded by Col. Otho Holland Williams, from August 1, 1780 to November 13, 1783. (AAA-1523A, AAA-1247, A-1/25, A-2/54, JJJ-745, H-179, H-352, H-433, H-560, XXX-763)

WILKINSON, RICHARD. Born 1745 in Dublin, Ireland. Occupation: Sailor. Enlisted as a Private in Capt. N. Smith's 1st Company of Matrosses on January 24, 1776. Private, Capt. Dorsey's MD Artillery, November 17, 1777, and Matross with that company while at Valley Forge, June 3, 1778. (UU-231, H-564, H-567, H-574, VV-73, QQQ-2)

WILKINSON, SAMUEL. Non-Juror to the Oath of Allegiance in 1778. (A-1/25)

WILKINSON, WILLIAM. Served on Baltimore Committee of Inspection, March 13, 1775, and represented Lower Patapsco Hundred at the Association of Freemen on Aug. 21, 1775. Elected to Baltimore Committee of Observation, September 23, 1775, and served on the Baltimore Committee of Safety in 1776. Captain of Baltimore County Militia as of February 4, 1777, and Captain in Gunpowder Battalion in 1778. Took Oath of Allegiance in 1778 before Hon. William Spear. (A-2/66, VV-114, E-12, FF-64, ZZ-254, RR-19, RR-47, RR-50, SS-136, EEEE-1726)

WILKISON, HUVEN. Oath of Allegiance, 1778. (A-1/25) This is same Huven Wilkinson herein.

WILLJMED (WILLIMEA), GEORGE. Oath of Allegiance in 1778 before Hon. George Gouldsmith Presbury. (A-1/26, A-2/48)

WILLEMED (WILLIMEA), JOHN FREDERICK. Oath of Allegiance in 1778 before Hon. George G. Presbury. (A-1/26, A-2/48)

WILLEMED (WILLIAMIE), JOHN GEORGE. Oath of Allegiance in 1778. (A-1/25)

WILLEMED (WILLIMEA), PETER. Oath of Allegiance in 1778 before Hon. George Gouldsmith Presbury. (A-1/26, A-2/48)

WILLIAMS,_____AS (part of name torn off the list). Private in Baltimore County's Regiment No. 7, circa 1777. (TTT-13)

WILLIAMS, ABRAHAM. Oath of Allegiance in 1778 before Hon. Jesse Dorsey.(A-1/25,A-2/63)

WILLIAMS, BENJAMIN. Non-Juror to the Oath of Allegiance in 1778. (A-1/25)

WILLIAMS, CHARLES. Oath of Allegiance, 1778, before Hon. George Lindenberger. (A-2/54)

WILLIAMS, DAVID. Non-Juror to the Oath of Allegiance in 1778. (A-1/25)

WILLIAMS, FRANCIS. Cook's Mate on ship Defence, August 9 to November 2, 1777. (H-660)

WILLIAMS, GARRIAT. Oath of Allegiance, 1778, before Hon. James Calhoun.(A-1/25,A-2/40)

WILLIAMS, GEORGE. Non-Juror to the Oath of Allegiance in 1778. (A-1/25)

WILLIAMS, JESSE. (June 9, 1750 - September 29, 1835) Married Rachel GOTT. Ensign in Capt. Z. Onion's Company, Gunpowder Battalion, September 4, 1777. Took the Oath of Allegiance in 1778 before Hon. Jesse Dorsey. Revolutionary Pensioner, MD Militia. (A-1/25, A-2/63, YY-55, BBB-362, E-12, JJJ-747)

WILLIAM, JOHN. There were three men with this name who took the Oath of Allegiance in 1778 before Hon. James Calhoun. (A-1/25, A-2/38, A-2/40, A-2/41) Source YY-55 also lists four men who were Revolutionary War pensioners (1 Sergeant and 3 Privates). One John Williams was a Marine on the ship Defence, April 28, 1777 to Dec. 31, 1777. (H-660) Another John Williams, on February 3, 1828, received, during life, half pay of a Private, half yearly, as further remuneration for his services during the war. (C-408)

WILLIAMS, JOHN GEORGE. Oath of Allegiance, 1778, before Hon. Richard Holliday. (A-2/60)

WILLIAMS, JOSEPH. Private in Capt. Graybill's German Regiment in 1776. Revolutionary pensioner, Continental Line. Oath of Allegiance, 1778, before Honorable William Lux. (A-1/25, A-2/68, H-266, YY-55)

WILLIAMS, MARSHALL. Seaman on ship Defence, January 21, 1777 to March 21, 1777. (H-660)

WILLIAMS, MICHAEL. Oath of Allegiance, 1778, before Hon. William Spear. Could not write and made his mark. (A-1/25, A-2/67)

WILLIAMS, MORGAN. Non-Juror to Oath of Allegiance in 1778. (A-1/25)

WILLIAMS, RICHARD. Oath of Allegiance, 1778, before Hon. Charles Ridgely of William. (A-1/25, A-2/27)

WILLIAMS, ROBERT. There were two signers to the Oath of Allegiance in 1778: one before Hon. John Beale Howard (made his mark "ᘓ") and one before Hon. James Calhoun. (A-1/25, A-2/29, A-2/41)

WILLIAMS, SAMUEL. Non-Juror to Oath of Allegiance in 1778. (A-1/26)

WILLIAMS, THOMAS. Baltimore Privateer and Captain of brig Willing Lass (16 guns) owned by Henry Dennis and others of Worcester County. (III-206) Non-Juror, 1778. (A-1/26)

WILLIAMS, THOMAS. Drummer in Capt. Furnival's MD Artillery, November 17, 1777. Drummer in Capt. Gale's MD Artillery, 1779, and Drum Major, January 22, 1780. Drummer in Capt. J. Smith's MD Artillery, 1780-1783. Received 50 acres (lot 4057) in western Maryland for his services. (DDDD-38, YYY-1/121, UU-232, YYY-2/51, H-579, H-572) One Thomas Williams was a Non-Juror to the Oath of Allegiance in 1778. (A-1/26)

WILLIAMS, WILLIAM. Oath of Allegiance in 1778 before Hon. William Spear. (A-1/26, A-2/67)

WILLIAMSON, SAMUEL. Oath of Allegiance in 1778 before Hon. Edward Cockey.(A-1/26, A-2/61)

WILLIAMSON, THOMAS. Oath of Allegiance in 1778 before Hon. John Moale. (A-1/26, A-2/70)

WILLIN, JNO. Bombardier, Capt. Gale's MD Artillery, 1779-1780. (YYY-1/122)

WILLIS, JOHN. Non-Juror to Oath of Allegiance in 1778. (A-1/26)

WILLIS, LEONARD. Oath of Allegiance in 1778. (A-1/26)

WILLIS, RICHARD. Non-Juror to Oath of Allegiance in 1778. (A-1/26)

WILLS (WELLS), CHARLES DORSEY. Non-Juror to Oath of Allegiance in 1778. (A-1/26)

WILLS, JAMES. Private in Capt. Ewing's Company No. 4 in 1776. (H-13)

WILLS (WELLS), JOHN. Private in Baltimore County Militia; enlisted August 15, 1776. Revolutionary pensioner, born 1757, Private, Militia-Flying Camp. Pensioned under Act of June 7, 1785 at $40 per annum, dating from March 4, 1789 (received $1085.64). Pensioned at $64 per annum from April 24, 1816 (received $55.11) (C-410, O-11, H-58, YY-54, and U.S. Pension Rolls, 1835, page 11)

WILLSDAUGH, HENRY. Private in Capt. Graybill's German Regiment in 1776. (H-265)

WILMAN, ANDREW. Oath of Allegiance, 1778, before Hon. Frederick Decker.(A-1/26,A-2/31)

WILMOT (WILLMOTT), JOHN. (1752-1807) Oath of Allegiance, 1778, before Hon. Richard Holliday. 3rd Lieutenant, Capt. Luke Wylie's Company No. 7, Baltimore County Militia as of October 28, 1776. (A-1/26, A-2/60, PPP-2, ZZ-542, JJJ-749)

WILMOTT, JOHN (OF ROBERT). Oath of Allegiance, 1778, before Hon. Richard Holliday. (A-1/26, A-2/60)

WILMOTT, JOHN JR. Oath of Allegiance, 1778. before Hon. Richard Holliday. (A-2/60)

WILMOTT, ROBERT. (December 25, 1757 - August 5, 1839) Married Priscilla Ridgely DORSEY. Recommended by the Baltimore Committee for a commission, September 27, 1776, and was commissioned November 5, 1776 as a 2nd Lieutenant in Capt. Furnival's MD Artillery. Commissioned 1st Lieutenant in Capt. Dorsey's MD Artillery on November 24, 1777, and was at Valley Forge, June 3, 1778. Served under Lt.Col. Ed. Carrington; stationed in Baltimore, May 11, 1780. In Capt. J. Smith's MD Artillery in 1780 and was still in service as of January 28, 1782. Entitled to 200 acres (lots 2744 through 2747)

WILMOTT, ROBERT (continued)
in western Maryland, and 200 acres under Federal Bounty Land Grant Warrant 2415 on
January 28, 1800. (YY-82, DDDD-4, JJJ-749, FFF-59, H-477,UU-230,H-572,H-579,VVV-96)

WILMOTT, ROBERT. Private on ship _Defence_ on September 19, 1776. (H-607)

WILMOTT, THOMAS. Non-Juror to Oath of Allegiance in 1778. (A-1/26)

WILMOTT (WILMOT), WILLIAM. Ensign in Baltimore County Troops in 1776. 1st Lieutenant
in 3rd MD Regiment, December 10, 1776. Captain, October 15, 1777; transferred to
2nd MD Regiment, January 1, 1781. Was killed on John's Island, S.C. on November 4,
1782 by a British foraging party; his blood was the last shed in the Revolutionary
War. He was entitled to Federal Bounty Land Grant 281 for 300 acres, and 200 acres
(lots 2752-2755) in western Maryland. (DDDD-5, YY-82, B-598, H-52)

WILSHIRE, BENJAMIN. Non-Juror to Oath of Allegiance in 1778. (A-1/26)

WILSHIRE, JOHN. Private in Capt. Lansdale's Company, 4th MD Regiment, from June 18,
1779 to January 15, 1780 when reported deserted. Took Oath of Allegiance in 1778
before Hon. Andrew Buchanan. (A-1/26, A-2/57, H-179)

WILSON, ALEXANDER. Oath of Allegiance, 1778, before Hon. Thomas Sollers. (A-2/51)

WILSON, ANDREW. Oath of Allegiance in 1778 before Hon. William Lux. 2nd Lieutenant
in Capt. Douglass' Company, Baltimore County Militia, May 21, 1779. (F-309, GGG-
401, A-1/26, A-2/68)

WILSON, BARNEY. Fifer, 3rd MD Regiment, 1780; prisoner, August 16, 1780. Private, in
service to November, 1783. Bounty Land Warrant 2067-100. Died at Baltimore, 1799
or 1800. (H-178, H-430, H-560, and Raymond Clark's MD Rev. Pensioners, page 41)

WILSON, BENJAMIN. Born 1755 in America. Enlisted July 7, 1776 in Baltimore County as
a Private in Col. Ewing's Battalion. Height: 5'6 3/4"; sandy complexion. (H-55)

WILSON (WILLSON), BENKID. Oath of Allegiance, 1778, before Hon. Jesse Bussey. (A-2/44)

WILSON, CHARLES. Non-Juror in 1778 to the Oath of Allegiance. (A-1/26)

WILSON (WILLSON), EDWARD. Private in Baltimore County Militia; enl. July 5, 1776. (H-58)

WILSON, GABRIL. Enlisted July 17, 1776 in Baltimore Town. (H-53)

WILSON, GITTINGS. (January 4, 1750 - January 18, 1834, Baltimore County, MD) Married
Jane RUTLEDGE on June 23, 1779. Children: Asabel, married a GOVER; Mary (b. 1786),
married Alexander BRISCOE; John, married Sarah STANSBURY; Ruth, died in infancy;
Jane; Abraham Ruxton (1781-1802); and, Elizabeth, died in infancy. Gittings Wilson
was 2nd Lieutenant in Capt. Standiford's Company, Gunpowder Battalion, September 2,
1777. Non-Juror to Oath of Allegiance in 1778, but he signed in 1781. (A-1/26, QQ-
123, E-11, T-83, BBB-350, JJJ-750, ZZZ-354, XXX-768)

WILSON, HENRY. Non-Juror to Oath of Allegiance, 1778; signed in 1781. (A-1/26,QQ-123)

WILSON, HUGH. Oath of Allegiance in 1778. (A-1/26)

WILSON (WILLSON), ISAAC. Private, Baltimore Co. Militia; enl. Aug. 15, 1776. (H-58/59)

WILSON, JACOB. Non-Juror to the Oath of Allegiance in 1778. (A-1/26)

WILSON, JAMES. (June 8, 1732, Warwick, England - 1787, Baltimore, Maryland) Married
Elizabeth THARPE in 1760 in England. Their son, John J. WILSON (1763-1846) married
Sarah WARBURTON, and their son, James WILSON (1792-1878) married Sarah J. WICKS of
Maryland. "James Wilson served in the British Army under Duke of Cumberland and was
a Captain until 1761 when he sold his commission and emigrated to Trenton, NJ, and
then to Baltimore, MD. He obtained a commission in the American Army through the
influence of kinsman James Wilson of Philadelphia; wounded in service; present at
Valley Forge in 1778; and provided the army with money and provisions." (AAA-34)

WILSON, JAMES. Private in Col. Aquila Hall's Baltimore County Regiment, 1776-1777.
Took Oath of Allegiance in 1778 before Hon. William Lux. Private, Extra Regiment,
at Fort Whetstone Point in Baltimore, 1781. (A-1/26, A-2/68, H-627, TTT-13)

WILSON (WILLSON), JOHN. 1st Lieutenant in Capt. H. Howard's Company as of August 26, 1776. (PPP-2, RR-90, ZZ-541) Oath of Allegiance in 1778. (A-1/26)

WILSON, JOHN ("IN MINE RUN HUNDRED") Oath of Allegiance, 1778, before Honorable Jesse Dorsey. (A-2/63)

WILSON, JOHN. Corporal of Marines on ship <u>Defence</u> in 1777. (H-660) Oath of Allegiance in 1778 before Hon. James Calhoun. (A-2/41)

WILSON, JOHN SR. Non-Juror to Oath in 1778, but signed in 1781. (A-1/26, QQ-123)

WILSON, JOHN JR. Non-Juror to Oath of Allegiance in 1778. (A-1/26)

WILSON, JOHN KIDD. Private in Col.Aquila Hall's Baltimore County Regiment in 1777. Took Oath of Allegiance in 1781. (TTT-13, QQ-123)

WILSON, LEVIN. Non-Juror to Oath of Allegiance in 1778. (A-1/26)

WILSON, NATHANIEL. Ensign in Capt. Smith's Company, May 18, 1779. (GGG-401)

WILSON, RICHARD. Non-Juror to Oath of Allegiance in 1778. (A-1/26)

WILSON, THOMAS. Enlisted June 20, 1776 as Private in Capt. N.Smith's 1st Company of Matrosses; at Fort Whetstone Point, September 7, 1776. Matross in Capt. Brown's MD Artillery; joined November 22, 1777. Was at Valley Forge until June, 1778; at White Plains, July, 1780; not listed in 1781. Either this or another Thomas Wilson served as Private in Capt. McClellan's Company, Baltimore Town, September 4, 1780. Also, on October 17, 1776, a Thomas WILSON gave a shovel and hoe for use at Whetstone Point and payment was received by Hannah WILSON, as acknowledged by Capt. Nicholas Ruxton Moore. (FFF-63, CCC-24, UU-228, UU-230, VV-73, H-570)

WILSON, TOBIAS. Enlisted July 20, 1776 in Baltimore Town. Sergeant in Capt. Lansdale's Company, 4th MD Regiment, from February 11, 1777 to December 6, 1779. (H-53, H-178)

WILSON, WHITE. Enlisted July 17, 1776 in Baltimore Town. (H-53)

WILSON (WILLSON), WILLIAM. Private in Baltimore Artillery Company, October 16, 1775 and member of the Sons of Liberty in 1776. Private in Capt. Sheaff's Company, June 16, 1777. Took Oath of Allegiance in 1778 before Hon. William Lux. Source QQ-123 states a William Wilson took the Oath in 1781. (A-1/26, A-2/69, G-8, W-162, CCC-19, QQ-123)

WILTON, WILLIAM. Oath of Allegiance, 1778, before Hon. James Calhoun. (A-1/26, A-2/39)

WILSTOCK, HENRY. Private in Capt. Graybill's German Regiment in 1776. (H-265)

WILTSHIRE, SAMUEL. Private in Capt. Ewing's Co. No. 4; enlisted Jan. 24, 1776. (H-12)

WINCHESTER, GEORGE. Ensign in Capt. John Gist's 3rd MD Regiment, February, 1778, and 2nd Lieutenant in Gist's Continental Regiment, April 8, 1778; 1st Lieutenant, May 1, 1779. Taken prisoner at Charleston, S.C., May 12, 1780. Entitled to 200 acres (lots 2448, 2451, 2452, 2453) in western Maryland for services. (DDDD-5, H-600, B-600)

WINCHESTER, JAMES. (February, 1752 - July 26, 1826) Married Susan BLACK. Captain in Col. John Gist's Regiment in 1776. Captain in 8th MD Line; commissioned February 9, 1782; on duty with southern troops until August, 1782; deranged, January 1, 1783. Entitled to 200 acres (lots 2760-2763) in western Maryland for his services. (DDDD-5, JJJ-752, KKK-509, H-482)

WINCHESTER, JOHN. Oath of Allegiance in 1778 before Hon. George Lindenberger. (A-2/54)

WINCHESTER, WILLIAM (I). (December 22, 1710, London, England - September 2, 1790, Baltimore (now Carroll) County, Maryland) Wife's name not known; daughter Katherine WINCHESTER married William WELLING, and grandson William WELLING md. Mary CRAWFORD. William Winchester was a Lieutenant in Linganore Battalion, 1777. (AAA-402, GGG-145)

WINCHESTER, WILLIAM (II). (December 1, 1750, Baltimore County, MD - April 24, 1812, Baltimore, MD) Married Mary PARKS (1750-1821) in 1771. Their son George WINCHESTER (1785-1840) married Ann OWENS (1787-1840) in 1809, and their son John Marshall WINCHESTER (1821-1877) married Ann Gordon PRICE (1834-1923) in 1856. William died at residence on North Howard Street in Baltimore. He was a 1st Lieutenant in Captain David Moore's Linganore Battalion, Frederick County, MD, 1777. (AAA-1213, ZZ-356)

WINDER, LEVIN. (September 4, 1757, Somerset County, MD - July 7, 1819, Baltimore, MD) Buried in Somerset County. Married Mary Stoughton SLOSS. Children: Edward Stoughton, married Elizabeth LLOYD; William Sidney, married a BAYLEY; Marianna died young and the second Marianna married Thomas EMORY. Levin Winder was 1st Lieutenant in Smallwood's Battalion, January 3, 1776; Captain, 1st MD Regt., December 10, 1776, and Major, April 17, 1777. Prisoner and wounded at Camden, August 16, 1780 and was exchanged in June, 1781. Transferred to 4th MD Regt., January 1, 1781 and became Lt.Colonel, 5th MD Regt., June 3, 1781. Transferred to 1st MD Regt., January 1, 1783, and served to April 12, 1783. He was an Original Member of the Society of the Cincinnati of Maryland in 1783 (currently represented by Andrew Adgate Duer). Col. Winder was a Presidential elector in 1792; Major General, Maryland Militia in 1794; Speaker of the House of Delegates in 1812; Governor of Maryland, 1812-1815. As Grandmaster of the Masonic Order, he presided at the laying of the cornerstone of the Washington Monument in Baltimore on July 4, 1815. Additionally, for his war services, he received 200 acres (lots 2884, 2885, 2886, 2996) in western Maryland, and 450 acres under Federal Bounty Land Grant No. 2404, June 2, 1789. (TT-150, YY-82, DDDD-5, UUU-207, JJJ-753, XXX-770, and Albert L. Richardson (ed.) The Maryland Original Research Society of Baltimore, Bulletin No. 3 (1913), 1973 reprt., p. 19.

WINGER, PETER. Non-Juror to the Oath of Allegiance in 1778. (A-1/26)

WINGINER, PETER. Non-Juror to Oath of Allegiance in 1778. (A-1/26)

WINK, JACOB. Born 1755. Private in Capt. Keeports' German Regiment; enlisted Aug. 5, 1776; was at Philadelphia, Sept. 19, 1776. Revolutionary pensioner, Continental Line. There was also a Jacob Wink who was a Private in Baltimore County Regiment no. 15 circa 1776-1777; might be the same person. (TTT-13, YY-55, H-263)

WINK, JOSEPH SR. Non-Juror to the Oath of Allegiance in 1778. (A-1/26)

WINK, PETER. Oath of Allegiance in 1778 before Hon. John Hall. (A-1/26, A-2/36)

WINKS, JOSEPH. (c1740 - before 1804) Married (2) Elizabeth MARSH. Took the Oath of Allegiance in 1778. (A-1/26, JJJ-753)

WINNDMAN (WIUNDMAN), JOSEPH. Volunteered into Baltimore County Regiment No. 36 circa 1777. (TTT-13)

WINSLET, JOHN. Oath of Allegiance in 1778 before Hon. John Beale Howard. Could not write; made his mark. (A-1/26, A-2/29)

WINSTANLY, FRANCIS. Private in Capt. Oldham's Company, 4th MD Regiment from Dec. 15, 1776 to June 29, 1778. Deserted from the Invalids Regiment, June 11, 1781. (H-178)

WINTERBURN, JOHN. Non-Juror to the Oath of Allegiance in 1778. (A-1/26)
WINTERINGER, BARNET. Non-Juror to the Oath of Allegiance in 1778. (A-1/26)

WINTERS, E. Member of the Sons of Liberty in Baltimore in 1776. (CCC-19)

WIRE, THOMAS. 1st Lieutenant in Capt. Hurd's Company, Soldiers Delight Battalion in 1778 and served at least to May 27, 1779. (GGG-422, E-10, HH-24)

WISE, HENRY. Non-Juror to the Oath of Allegiance in 1778. (A-1/26)

WISE, LEWIS. Enlisted in Baltimore County on July 25, 1776. (H-52)

WISE, WILLIAM. Oath of Allegiance, 1778, before Hon. Isaac Van Bibber. (A-1/26,A-2/34)

WISEMAN, PETER. Non-Juror to the Oath of Allegiance in 1778. (A-1/26)

WISEMAN, THOMAS. Private in Capt. Ewing's Co. No. 4; enlisted Jan. 29, 1776. (H-12)

WITH, WILLIAM. Non-Juror to the Oath of Allegiance in 1778. (A-1/26)
WITHELL, PETER. Non-Juror to the Oath of Allegiance in 1778. (A-1/26)
WOLFE, JACOB. Non-Juror to the Oath of Allegiance in 1778. (A-1/26)

WOLFE, MICHAEL. Oath of Allegiance, 1778, before Hon. Richard Cromwell. (A-2/46)

WOLFERD, FREDERICK. Non-Juror to the Oath of Allegiance in 1778. (A-1/26)

WOLLS, W. Oath of Allegiance in 1778 before Hon. Isaac Van Bibber. (A-2/34)

WOLTT, MICHAEL. Oath of Allegiance, 1778, before Hon. John Moale. (A-1/26, A-2/70)

WONN, EDWARD. Received patent for a tract of land in Baltimore County named "Wonn's Chance" in 1745. Married Prudence MARSH in 1747. Died in 1792. His will names two sons, Edward and John, and three daughters, Rachel MILLOW, Rebecca BELL, and Prudence. Source A-1/26 states he took the Oath of Allegiance in 1778, but he is not listed in Source A-2. (Family data from Alan Virta of Hyattsville, MD, 1988)

WONN, EDWARD JR. Purchased part of "Wonn's Chance" from his father in 1771; located near Randallstown. His wife was named Rachel, and their children: Jesse WONN, Horatio WONN, John WONN, Violet WAGGONER, Comfort EBERT, and William WONN. Edward Wonn, Jr., took Oath of Allegiance in 1778 before Hon. Richard Cromwell. (A-1/26, A-2/46, and family data from Alan Virta of Hyattsville, MD, 1988)

WONN, JOHN. Son of Edward WONN, Sr., died in 1784. Wife was probably Bethia WELCH, and they had a son, William Welch WONN. John Wonn took the Oath of Allegiance, 1778, before Hon. John Beale Howard. Could not write; made his mark. (A-1/26, A-2/30, and data from Alan Virta of Hyattsville, MD, 1988)

WONOY, JOHN. Non-Juror to Oath of Allegiance in 1778. (A-1/26)

WOOD, HENRY. Matross in Capt. Gale's MD Artillery, 1779; deserted on September 11, 1779 at Annapolis, MD. (YYY-1/124)

WOOD, JAMES. Recruit in Baltimore County Militia, April 11, 1780. (H-335)

WOOD, ROBERSON. Enlisted July 25, 1776 in Baltimore County. (H-52)

WOOD, ROBERT. Oath of Allegiance in 1778. (A-1/26)

WOOD, WILLIAM. Private in Capt. Deams' Company, 7th MD Regiment, December 19, 1776. (H-305) SOurce A-1/26 indicates there were 3 Non-Jurors in 1778 with this name.

WOODCOCK, ROBERT. Non-Juror to Oath of Allegiance in 1778. (A-1/26)

WOODCOCK, THOMAS. Private in Baltimore County Regiment No. 7, circa 1777. (TTT-13)

WOODEN, BEALE BELL. Oath of Allegiance in 1781. (QQ-124)

WOODEN, JOHN. Non-Juror to Oath of Allegiance in 1778. (A-1/26)
WOODEN, SOLOMON. Non-Juror to Oath of Allegiance in 1778. (A-1/26)
WOODEN, SOLOMON (OF JOHN). Non-Juror to Oath of Allegiance in 1778. (A-1/26)
WOODEN, STEPHEN. Two Non-Jurors in 1778 with this name. (A-1/26)

WOODEN, THOMAS. Private in Col. Aquila Hall's Baltimore County Regiment in 1777. Took Oath of Allegiance in 1778 before Hon. Jesse Dorsey. (A-1/26, A-2/63, TTT-13)

WOODFIELD, JOHN. Matross in Capt. Gale's MD Artillery, 1779. Sick in October, 1779, at Annapolis; hospital in December, 1779. (YYY-1/125)

WOODING, RICHARD. Non-Juror to the Oath of Allegiance in 1778. (A-1/26)
WOODING, WILLIAM. Non-Juror to the Oath of Allegiance in 1778. (A-1/26)

WOODS, BENJAMIN. Mate on ship Defence, June 20 to August 15, 1777; 2nd Mate, August 15, to December 28, 1777. (H-660)

WOODS, ROBERT. Oath of Allegiance in 1778 before Hon. James Calhoun. (A-2/41)

WOODWARD, JAMES. Oath of Allegiance in 1778 before Hon. Richard Holliday. Private in Extra Regiment, Fort Whetstone Point in Baltimore, 1781. (A-1/26, A-2/60, H-627)

WOODWARD, JOHN. Non-Juror to Oath of Allegiance in 1778. (A-1/26)

WOODWARD, THOMAS. (February 19, 1731 - April, 1799) Married Margaret IJAMS. Source A-1/26 states he was a Non-Juror to Oath in 1778, but Source JJJ-761 states he rendered patriotic service.

WOODWARD, WILLIAM GARRETT. (1725 - August 22, 1799) Married (1) Dinah WARFIELD, and (2) Katherine _____. Oath of Allegiance, 1778, before Hon. William Spear. (JJJ-761, A-1/26, A-2/66)

WOOLFE, JAMES. Non-Juror to Oath of Allegiance in 1778. (A-1/26)

WOOLHEAD, THOMAS. Oath of Allegiance, 1778, before Hon. James Calhoun. (A-2/40)

WOOLHOUSE, JONATHAN. Oath of Allegiance, 1778, before Hon. Edward Cockey. (A-2/62)

WOOLLIN, EDWARD. Oath of Allegiance in 1778 before Hon. James Calhoun. (A-2/65)

WOOLRICH, PHILIP. Ensign in Capt. Wilkinson's Company, February 4, 1777. (VV-114)

WOOLSEY, GEORGE. Served on Baltimore Committee of Inspection, March 13, 1775, and Committee of Observation, July-August, 1775 (was not re-elected Sept. 12, 1775). Ensign in Capt. Buchanan's Company No. 1, Baltimore Town Battalion, in 1776, and applied to the Council of Safety on July 3, 1776 for captaincy of a gondola. On August 7, 1776 he purchased a vessel and requested information about serving the province of Maryland. Took the Oath of Allegiance in 1778 before Honorable James Calhoun. (A-1/26, A-2/41, FFF-41, FFF-49, GG-74, SS-130, RR-19, RR-50, EEFE-1725)

WOOLSEY, HENRY. Oath of Allegiance, 1778, before Hon. Edward Cockey.(A-1/26,A-2/61)

WOOLSEY, WILLIAM. 1st Lieutenant in Capt. N. Smith's 1st Company of Matrosses as of January 24, 1776. Took Oath of Allegiance in 1778 before Hon. William Lux. (H-563, III-192, A-1/26, A-2/68)

WORKMAN, HUGH. Private in Capt. Howell's Company, December 30, 1775. Took Oath of Allegiance in 1778 before Hon. John Moale. (G-11, A-1/26, A-2/70)

WORRELL, HENRY SR. Non-Juror to Oath of Allegiance in 1778. (A-1/26)

WORRELL, THOMAS. Oath of Allegiance, 1778, before Hon. John Moale. (A-1/26, A-2/70)

WORRELL, WILLIAM. Non-Juror to Oath of Allegiance in 1778. (A-1/26)

WORSLEY, GEORGE H. Oath of Allegiance, 1778, before Hon. James Calhoun. (A-2/42)

WORTHINGTON, HENRY. Private in Baltimore Artillery Company, October 16, 1775. Oath of Allegiance, 1778, before Hon. George Lindenberger. (A-1/26, A-2/54, G-8)

WORTHINGTON, JOHN. Non-Juror to Oath in 1778. Served in Col.Nicholson's Troop of Horse on June 7, 1781. (A-1/26, BBBB-274)

WORTHINGTON, SAMUEL. (November 19, 1733, Anne Arundel County, MD - April 7, 1815, Baltimore County, MD) Married (1) Mary TOLLEY, and (2) Martha GARRETSON. Son of John WORTHINGTON, Samuel served on the Baltimore Town Committee of Correspondence on November 12, 1775, and took the Oath of Allegiance in 1778 before Hon. Andrew Buchanan. He had 9 sons and 9 daughters: John T., Walter, Charles, Thomas T., James T., Edward, Nicholas, Samuel and Garrett, and Comfort, Martha, Charlotte, Sarah, Catherine, Susannah, Eleanor, Martha and Elizabeth. (SS-130, ZZZ-359, JJJ-763, A-1/26, A-2/57)

WORTHINGTON, THOMAS. (May 2, 1739, Anne Arundel County, MD - March 16, 1821, Baltimore County, MD) Son of John WORTHINGTON, Jr. and Helen HAMMOND. Married Marcella OWINGS (1748-1842) on April 9, 1786, and their son Rezin Hammond WORTHINGTON (1794-1884) married Rachel Owings SHIPLEY (1806-1823) in 1823. Thomas Worthington served on the Baltimore County Committee of Safety, Soldiers Delight District, 1775. And Source A-1/26 states he took the Oath of Allegiance, 1778. (AAA-799, AAA-800, 888)

WORTHINGTON, WILLIAM. (February 18, 1749 - December 15, 1802, Baltimore County, MD) Son of William WORTHINGTON and Hannah RATTENBURY (RATTENBURG). Married in 1769 to Sarah RISTEAU (1749-1805). Their daughter Catherine WORTHINGTON (died 1826) married Isaac Risteau AMOSS (d. 1821),1805, and their granddaughter, Catherine AMOSS (1809-1885) married John PLASKITT (1797-1867) in 1830. William Worthington was recruited in Baltimore County and was a Private in Col. Williams' 6th MD Regiment, August 9, 1780. (AAA-757, H-340) Source A-1/26 states he was a Non-Juror to the 1778 Oath.

WRIGHT, ABRAHAM (ABRAM). Abraham Wright was a Non-Juror in 1778 to the Oath of Allegiance, but signed in 1781. (A-1/26, QQ-124) Abram Wright took the Oath of Allegiance in 1778 before Hon. Hercules Courtenay. (A-2/37)

WRIGHT, ABRAM SR. Oath of Allegiance, 1778. (A-1/26)

WRIGHT, BLOIS. Non-Juror to the Oath of Allegiance in 1778. (A-1/26)

WRIGHT, CHRISTOPHER. Oath of Allegiance, 1778, before Hon. James Calhoun.(A-1/26,A-2/42)

WRIGHT, DANIEL. Oath of Allegiance, 1778, before Hon. Richard Holliday. (A-1/26,A-2/60)

WRIGHT, EDWARD. Private in Capt. Ewing's Company No. 4; enlisted January 24, 1776, and Private in Capt. J. Cockey's Baltimore County Dragoons at Yorktown, 1781.(MMM-A,H-12)

WRIGHT, GEORGE. Non-Juror to the Oath of Allegiance in 1778. (A-1/26)

WRIGHT, HAROLD. Private in Capt. J. Cockey's Baltimore County Dragoons at Yorktown in 1781. (MMM-A)

WRIGHT, JACOB. Non-Juror to the Oath of Allegiance in 1778. (A-1/26)

WRIGHT, JAMES. Private in Baltimore County Militia; enlisted July 5, 1776. (H-58) Source A-1/26 states he took the Oath of Allegiance in 1778.

WRIGHT, JOHN. Private in Baltimore Artillery Company, October 16, 1775. Private in Capt. Howell's Company, December 30, 1775. Took Oath of Allegiance, 1778, before Hon. John Beale Howard. Could not write; made his mark. (A-2/30, G-8, G-11)

WRIGHT, JOHN. Quartermaster on ship Defence, September 19, 1776; Seaman, in 1777; and Quartermaster in 1777. (H-606, H-660, H-661)

WRIGHT, JOSEPH. Non-Juror to the Oath of Allegiance in 1777. (A-1/26)

WRIGHT, JOSHUA. Oath of Allegiance in 1778. (A-1/26)

WRIGHT, SOLOMON. Non-Juror to Oath in 1778, but signed in 1781. (A-1/26, QQ-124)

WRIGHT, THOMAS. Oath of Allegiance, 1778, before Hon. James Calhoun. (A-1/26, A-2/40)

WRIGHT, WILLIAM. (1716-1779) Oath of Allegiance, 1778, before Hon. Charles Ridgely of William. (A-1/26, A-2/28)

WRITER, MATHIAS. Oath of Allegiance in 1778. (A-1/26)

WYLE, ABEL. Oath of Allegiance in 1778 before Hon. John Hall. Involved in evaluation of confiscated Baltimore County proprietary reserve lands in 1782. (FFF-541, A-2/36)

WYLE, WHELLER (WHALLER), Oath of Allegiance, 1778, before Hon. John Hall.(A-1/26,A-2/36)

WYLE, ZACHARIAH. Oath of Allegiance, 1778, before Hon. John Hall. (A-1/26, A-2/36)

WYLEY, JOHN. Oath of Allegiance, 1778, before Hon. Robert Simmons. (A-1/26, A-2/58)

WYLIE (WYLE), BENJAMIN (OF WILLIAM). Oath of Allegiance in 1778. (A-1/26)

WYLIE (WYLE), GREENBERRY (GREENBURY). Oath of Allegiance in 1778 before Hon. Jesse Dorsey. Ensign under Capt. Lane in the Gunpowder Upper Battalion, October 23, 1781. (A-1/26, A-2/63, AAAA-650)

WYLIE (WYLEY), JOSHUA. Source A-1/26 states Joshua Wylie took the Oath of Allegiance in 1778, but Source QQ-124 states Joshua Wyley took the Oath in 1781.

WYLIE (WYLE), LUKE. (before 1730, Baltimore County, MD - between 1778 and 1781, Baltimore County, MD) Son of Luke and Kasiah WYLE. Wife may have been Cassandra CARROLL. Their children: Comfort Rebecca WYLE (1760-1829) married Joseph PEARCE, Jr. (1760-1829) in 1781 in Baltimore County; John WYLE; Greenbury WYLE married Rachel PEARCE; Vincent WYLE; Joshua WYLE; William WYLE; Walter WYLE; _____ WYLE md. John STEVENSON; _____ WYLE md. George NORRIS; and,_____ WYLE md. William AMOS. Luke WYLE died prior to October 31, 1781 because his successor was appointed on that date to serve in the Gunpowder Upper Battalion. Luke was Captain of a Rifle Company in Baltimore Co., Company No. 7 (40 Privates) on October 28, 1776, and served under Col. Cockey's Battn. (AAA-1797, AAA-1818, ZZ-542, JJJ-766, XXX-781, PPP-2, VV-345) Took Oath, 1778.(A-1/26)

WYLIE, VINCENT. Oath of Allegiance, 1778, before Hon. Jesse Dorsey. (A-1/26, A-2/63)

WYLIE, WALTER (OF LUKE). Non-Juror to the Oath of Allegiance in 1778. (A-1/26)

WYLIE, WILLIAM. Oath of Allegiance in 1778. (A-1/26)

Y

YAETER, ANDREW. Private, Capt. Smith's Company No. 8; enl. Jan. 13, 1776. (H-18)

YARNALL, BENJAMIN. Born 1748 in England. Enlisted July 7, 1776 in Baltimore County as a Private in Col. Ewing's Battalion. Height: 5' $10\frac{1}{4}$'; pock marked. (H-55)

YATER, JACOB. Enlisted in Baltimore Town on July 17, 1776. (H-53)

YATES, RICHARD. Boatswain's Mate on ship Defence, April 28 to Dec. 8, 1777. (H-661)

YATES, THOMAS. (1740/1741 - November 15, 1815) Married Mary MYERS. Their daughter Margaret YATES married Jacob WALSH; their grandson Charles WALSH married Rebecca _____, and their granddaughter Elizabeth Ann WALSH married Archibald STIRLING. Thomas YATES was 1st Lieutenant, 2nd Battalion, Flying Camp (Baltimore County) from July 19, 1776 to August 5, 1776, when he became Captain upon the resignation of John Stevenson. He was born circa 1740 and died November 15, 1815 in Baltimore (native of England). Sources B-610 and TT-153 state he resigned on May 20, 1777, at which time he was Captain in the 4th MD Regiment; however, he was active again by September 25, 1780 (AAAA-280), militarily. He also took the Oath of Allegiance in 1778 before the Honorable George Lindenberger, and signed a letter to Governor Lee on April 4, 1781, requesting the calling of the militia to protect Baltimore against British attack. As a member of Capt. Nicholas Ruxton Moore's Troops on June 25, 1781, he is listed as "Major T. Yates" and he had one 8 year old black gelding horse and one 7 year old bay stallion. (BBBB-313, TT-153, S-49, JJJ-767, H-58, B-610, ZZZ-361, XXX-782, H-52, AAA-270, AAA-115, AAAA-280, A-1/26, A-2/55) Thomas Yates was also Captain of Baltimore County Regiment No. 46, 1776-1777, but names of his men were not listed.(TTT-13)

YATES, THOMAS. Private in Capt. Furnival's MD Artillery, November 17, 1777; reported to be "sick--sore leg." Private in 4th MD Regiment (from Baltimore County); discharged on December 3, 1781. Received 50 acres (lot 2091) for his artillery services (land in western Maryland). (DDDD-38, Q-72, H-573) One Thomas Yates was a Sergeant in Capt. Gale's MD Artillery, 1779-1780. (YYY-1/126) Name might have been spelled "Yeates."

YATES, VACHEL. Sergeant of Marines on ship Defence; Lieutenant of Marines, February 15, 1777 to October 15, 1777; Captain of Marines, Oct. 15 to December 15, 1777. (H-661)

YAUN, JOHN. Private in Capt. J. Cockey's Baltimore County Dragoons at Yorktown, 1781. (MMM-A)

YEARKS, DAVID. Baltimore Mechanical Company of Militia in 1776. (CCC-27)

YEISER, INGLEHART (ENGLEHART). Died in Baltimore in March, 1807, an old inhabitant of the city. Married Catharine KEENER in 1773, and had at least three children: John M. YEISER (1780-1896) died in Staunton, Virginia; Susan M. YEISER married George THARP on April 19, 1817 (by Rev. Dashiells); and, Engelhard YEISER, Jr., married Margaret SWOPE, daughter of Benedict SWOPE, Jr., on October 3, 1799 near Danville,(Virginia?) Englehart YEISER delievered "beef rations to the marching militia at one shilling per pound in 1777." (BBB-347) He also took the Oath of Allegiance in Baltimore County on March 16, 1778. (BBB-536, VV-536, CCC-17, ZZZ-362, ZZZ-318, BBB-347)

YEISER, PHILIP. Private in Capt. Cox's Company, December 19, 1776. Took the Oath of Allegiance in 1778 before Hon. George Lindenberger. (CCC-21, A-1/26, A-2/55)

YELLOTT, JEREMIAH. Baltimore Privateer and Captain of schooner Antelope (with 14 guns) owned by John Sterrett of Baltimore. (III-206) "Capt. Yellott, of Baltimore, died in February, 1806, and his wife Mary died March 15, 1811, age 51." (ZZZ-362)

YELLUM (YALLOME, JALLOME), JOHN. Private in Capt. Furnival's MD Artillery, Nov. 17, 1777, when reported "sick--convalescent." Matross in Capt. Dorsey's MD Artillery at Valley Forge on June 3, 1778. (H-572, UU-231)

YESSUP, WILLIAM. Oath of Allegiance, 1778, before Hon. Richard Holliday.(A-1/26, A-2/60) (Ed. Note: This name might have been "JESSOP" instead of "YESSUP" as shown in book.)

YESTER, CHRISTOPHER. Oath of Allegiance, 1778, before Hon. William Spear.(A-1/26,A-2/66)

YINGLING, JOHN. Oath of Allegiance in 1781. (QQ-124)

YOE, JAMES. Oath of Allegiance, 1778, before Hon. John Beale Howard. (A-1/26, A-2/29)

YORK, THOMAS. Private in Capt. Furnival's MD Artillery, November 17, 1777. (H-573)

YOUNG, ADAM. Non-Juror to the Oath of Allegiance in 1778. (A-1/26)

YOUNG, BENJAMIN. (1752 - August 13, 1828) Married Mary HODGSON. Sergeant in Captain Godman's Co. and later Capt. Hoops Co., 4th MD Regiment, December, 1777 to Dec. 8, 1779. In December, 1816, it was ordered to pay him, of Baltimore County, "late a Sergeant in the Revolutionary War, quarterly, during his life, the half pay of a Sgt. as further remuneration for those services by which his country has been so essentially benefitted." (C-411, H-180, JJJ-768)

YOUNG, DAVID. (April 17, 1754, Ireland - 1784/1785, Hagerstown, Maryland) Married Nancy CRUSE. Children: Mary YOUNG (born 1772) married D. Y. DAVIS; Nancy YOUNG (born 1775) married Enos RELSEY; Edward YOUNG (born 1778) married Rachel MILLER; Peggy YOUNG (b. 1781) married John VAN METER; and, Rebecca YOUNG (born 1783) married Thomas McNAUGHTON. David YOUNG was a Matross in Capt. Brown's MD Artillery; joined November 22, 1777; was at Valley Forge until June, 1778; at White Plains, July, 1778; at Fort Schuyler, Aug. and Sept., 1780; at Camp Col. Scirvins in 1782 (and High Hills of the Santee, 1781); and Bacon's Bridge, S.C., April, 1782. Received 50 acres (lot 1013) in western Maryland for his Artillery services. (DDDD-38, XXX-783, XXX-784, JJJ-768, UU-228, UU-230)

YOUNG, EDWARD. Enlisted in Baltimore County on July 20, 1776. (H-53)

YOUNG, GEORGE. Oath of Allegiance in 1778 before Hon. James Calhoun. Private in Capt. J. Cockey's Baltimore County Dragoons at Yorktown, 1781. (MMM-A, A-1/26, A-2/39)

YOUNG, HENRY. Enlisted in Baltimore County on July 20, 1776. Private in Capt. Cockey's Baltimore County Dragoons at Yorktown in 1781. Revolutionary pensioner, MD Line. (YY-56, MMM-A, H-52) Source A-1/26 states he was a Non-Juror to the Oath in 1778.

YOUNG, HUGH. 2nd Lieutenant in Capt. Sterrett's Company No. 2, Baltimore Town Battalion in 1776. Served on Baltimore Salt Committee, October 14, 1779, and took the Oath of Allegiance in 1778 before Hon. William Lux. Signed a letter to Governor Lee, Apr. 4, 1781, requesting the calling of the militia to protect Baltimore against the British. (S-49, HHH-88, GG-74, A-1/26, A-2/68)

YOUNG, JACOB. (c1725 - 1781) Married Eleanor TULLY. Oath of Allegiance in 1778 before Hon. George Lindenberger. (A-1/26, A-2/55, JJJ-769)

YOUNG, JACOB JR. (c1750-1816/1817) Married Penelope WATT. Oath of Allegiance in 1778 before Hon. James Calhoun. (A-1/26, A-2/42, JJJ-769)

YOUNG, JAMES. Member of the Baltimore Mechanical Company of Militia. Became Captain of Baltimore County Troops, 2nd MD Battalion of the Flying Camp, July to December, 1776. Oath of Allegiance, 1778, before Hon. James Calhoun. (CCC-25, FFF-45, TT-153, H-52, B-610, A-1/26, A-2/39)

YOUNG, JOHN. Captain in Gunpowder Battalion in 1778. Oath of ALlegiance, 1778, before Hon. James Calhoun. (E-12, A-1/26, A-2/40)

YOUNG, JOHN. Oath of Allegiance, 1778, before Hon. Charles Ridgely of William. Could not write; made his mark ("   "). Private in Capt. J. Cockey's Baltimore County Dragoons at Yorktown in 1781. (MMM-A, A-1/26, A-2/27)

YOUNG, JOHN TULLY. Captain of Middle River Lower Company No. 6, Gunpowder Battalion, on May 6, 1776. Oath of Allegiance, 1778, before Hon. George Gouldsmith Presbury. (X-111, EE-51, WW-413, A-1/26, A-2/48)

YOUNG, JOSHUA. Non-Juror to the Oath of Allegiance in 1778. (A-1/26)

YOUNG, MICHAEL. Non-Juror to the Oath of ALlegiance in 1778. (A-1/26)

YOUNG, SAMUEL. Non-Juror to the Oath of Allegiance in 1778. (A-1/26)

YOUNG, WILLIAM. Oath of Allegiance, 1778, before Hon. William Lux. Signed letter to Gov. Lee, April 4, 1781, calling for the militia to protect Baltimore.(S-49, A-2/39)

Z

ZARRELL, CHARLES. Private in Capt. Graybill's German Regiment in 1776. (H-265)

ZEIGLER (ZIGLER), HENRY. Oath of Allegiance in 1778 before Hon. James Calhoun.
Private in Capt. McClellan's Company, September 4, 1780. (CCC-24, A-1/26, A-2/39)

ZIMMERMAN, GEORGE. (1714, Germany - 1795, Maryland) Wife named Catherine. Their
children: George (born 1740); Michael (born 1744); John (born 1746); Peggy (born
1748) married Peter BRUNNER; Susannah (born 1750) married Nicholas HOLTZ; Elizabeth (born 1752); Andrew (born 1754); and, Catherine (born 1756) married twice:
(1) Henry BRUNNER, and (2) Peter WOLF; and, Mary Elizabeth (born 1759) married
Elias BRUNNER; Nicholas (born 1762) married Elizabeth_____; and, Benjamin (b.
1764). George Zimmerman took the Oath of Allegiance in 1778 in Baltimore County
before Hon. George Lindenberger. (XXX-785, A-1/26, A-2/55)

ADDENDUM

CHAMEAU, SIXTE. An Acadian who took the Oath of Allegiance in 1778 in Baltimore, MD.

GOTRO, JOHN. An Acadian who took the Oath of Allegiance in 1778 in Baltimore, MD.

LUCAS, FRANCOIS. An Acadian who took the Oath of Allegiance in 1778 in Baltimore, MD.

PORRIE, PETER. An Acadian who took the Oath of Allegiance in 1778 in Baltimore, MD.

WELLS, CYPRIAN. An Acadian who took the Oath of Allegiance in 1778 in Baltimore, MD.
He married Marguerite LeBLANC on September 3, 1778.

(Source: Gregory A. Wood's The French Presence in Maryland, 1542-1800, pp. 201, 204)

ACCOUNT OF POWDER AND LEAD DELIVERED OUT TO THE
BALTIMORE MECHANICAL COMPANY OF MILITIA
NOVEMBER 4, 1775

Christian Myers	Henry Lawrah
Samuel Messersmith	William Rogers
Jacob Crider	Robert Davidson
Jacob Mills	David Evins
David Smith	David Poe
David McClallum	John Poe
Christopher Reboch	Roland Smith, Jr.
James Lyston	Adam Rohebock
John Cole	George Dindenberger
George Cole	John Shrts
George Stover	Hugh Westbray
Peter MacMackenhuner	John Shlife
John Tinges	Amon Hanson
Henry Sigler	John Clements
James Holliday	James Cassan
William Stacy	Charles Shue
Aaron Mateson	Charles Kew
Joseph Sater	Nicholas Miller
Mathias Boyer	John W. Donnoho
William Duncan	Ran. Inumbrough
Jacob Mittinger	John Sprim
Frederick Humbright	Jno. Ridenbock
Balzer Fnelny	Adam Roby
Isaac Dawjon	Robt. Cox, Jr.
John Lawrah	

(Note: There are apparent spelling mistakes in this list.
For example, George Dindenberger is really George Lindenberger,
Peter MacMackenhuner is really Peter Machenheimer, Christopher
Reboch is really Christopher Reborg, and Balzer Fnelny is most
likely Balzer Finley, just to name a few of the apparent errors.)

Each of the above soldiers received two pounds of lead and a
half pound of powder.

(Source: Hodges' Unpublished Revolutionary Records of Maryland,
Vol. 2, pages 298-300, as copied from the original manuscripts
in the Daughters of the American Revolution Library in 1941.)

ELECTED OFFICERS IN SEVEN MILITIA COMPANIES
OF BALTIMORE COUNTY, DEC. 19, 1775

1st Company: Captain Andrew Buchanan
                1st Lt. William Buchanan
                2nd Lt. John Smith
                Ensign Robert Alexander

2nd Company: Captain Benjamin Nicholson
                1st Lt. John Cockey Owens
                2nd Lt. Richard Colgate
                Ensign Joshua Cockey

3rd Company: Captain James Cox
                1st Lt. John McClellan
                2nd Lt. George Lindenberger
                Ensign David McClellan

4th Company: Captain Zachariah McCubbin
                1st Lt. Elam Bailey
                2nd Lt. William Parker
                Ensign John Bailey, Jr.

5th Company: Captain Thomas Rutter
                1st Lt. Ezekiel Towson
                2nd Lt. John Eager Howard
                Ensign Michael Kramer

6th Company: Captain William Cromwell
                1st Lt. Simon Perine
                2nd Lt. Thomas Miles
                Ensign William Welsh

7th Company: Captain James Bosley
                1st Lt. William Reily
                2nd Lt. John Reily
                Ensign Elisha McCaslin

Indicates presence on rolls of 441 Privates (unnamed).

Signed by Samuel Purviance, Jr., Chairman, Committee.

(Source: The Red Books, No. 4, Part 2, Page 10)

BALTIMORE COUNTY MILITIA OFFICERS, MAY, 1776

Gunpowder Upper Hundred............................83 men
(unnamed)

      Captain James Gittings
      1st Lt. Zacheus Onion
      2nd Lt. Sutton Gudgeon
      Ensign Phillip Chamberlain

Middle River Lower Hundred.........................75 men
(unnamed)

      Captain John Tully Young
      1st Lt. John German
      2nd Lt. Philip Colvin
      Ensign William Galloway

Back River Lower Hundred...........................63 men
(unnamed)

      Captain Job Garretson
      1st Lt. John Long
      2nd Lt. William Grover
      Ensign Joseph Stansbury

Back River Lower Hundred...........................55 men
(unnamed)

      Captain John Mercer
      1st Lt. Benjamin Buck
      2nd Lt. William Clark
      Ensign Benjamin Stansbury

Patapsco Lower Hundred.............................61 men
(unnamed)

      Captain Josias Bowen
      1st Lt. William Mackubbin
      2nd Lt. Vincent Green
      Ensign Job Smith

Gunpowder Upper Hundred............................53 men
(unnamed)

      Captain John Standiford
      1st Lt. Edward Oldham
      2nd Lt. James Oglevie
      Ensign Shadrach Green

Companies reported to the Baltimore Committee:

      Samuel Purviance, Jr., Chairman
      William Lux, Vice-Chairman
      Darby Lux
      Andrew Buchanan
      John Merryman, Jr.
      James Calhoun
      Thomas Sollers

(Source: Original Manuscript in the Maryland State Archives,
Maryland State Papers, Accession No. 4574-51)

CAPTAIN NATHANIEL SMITH'S COMPANY IN BALTIMORE
FORT WHETSTONE POINT, JAN. 24, 1777

"....as we have not misbehaved since our first enlistment which was but for one year and is now at the expiration and shall rely on your honour that you will let us have a proper discharge before we enlist a second time as we are determined to enlist again and defend the libertys of the country as far as lies in our power...." (Letter to Capt. Smith)

John Curtis	Richard Burke
John Houlton	Thomas Smith
Benjamin Todd	John Clarke
Benjamin Jones	John Shly
Philip Jones	Jacob Boager
Richard Pitsland	Peter Richards
Joel Bennet	William Forbes
Freeman Newman	Jno. Forrester
Daniel Donohoe	Alexander Forrester
Edward Berry	Stephen Fennell
Anthony Barns	Henry Carroll
Robert Thompson	Thomas Connor
James Mathias	Martin Conden
George Cooper	Timothy Donovan
Richard Wilkinson	Hugh McDoole
James Jack	Frederick Pine
John Videon	Philip Sitzler
Robert Britt	John King
Thomas Wilson	Roger O'Donnell
James Rice	Mathew Kelly
Timothy Murphy	William Reed
James Rany	Joseph Wilkes
James Bradly	David Thomas
David Moroney	Robert Toole
Cornelius Forrester	John Gorman
Barny Quin	Edmund Walsh
Francis DeShields	Francis Malgawran
John Hanlon	Patrick Slaughness:
Luke Gardiner	David Walsh
John Pearson	William Culbertstan
John Howard	George Rees
David White	Edward Coughlan
James Barry	John Curtis
Robert Mitchell	Andrew Shreek
Charles Cloes	George Gitnere
Thomas Robinson	Ellack McMullin:
Samuel Thompson	John Brady
Hugh Martin	Bartholomeow Donohoe

(Source: <u>Archives of Maryland</u>, Vol. XLIII, pages 73-74)

EIGHT COMPANIES IN SOLDIERS DELIGHT, GARRISON FOREST,
BALTIMORE COUNTY, MAY 13, 1776

Company No. 1..................................... Privates
        Captain Benjamin Nicholson   (unnamed)
        1st Lt. John Cockey Owings
        2nd Lt. Richard Colegate
        Ensign Joshua Cockey (of Edward)

Company No. 2.....................................75 Privates
        Captain Samuel Owings (of Samuel) (unnamed)
        1st Lt. Alexander Wells
        2nd Lt. Thomas Owings
        Ensign David Sutherland

Company No. 3.....................................58 Privates
        Captain Richard Owings (of Samuel) (unnamed)
        1st Lt. Joshua Porter
        2nd Lt. Benjamin Lawrence
        Ensign James Barnes

Company No. 4.....................................77 Privates
        Captain Thomas Philips   (unnamed)
        1st Lt. Joshua Dorsey
        2nd Lt. John Chapman
        Ensign Richard Shipley

Company No. 5.....................................79 Privates
        Captain Charles Carnan   (unnamed)
        1st Lt. William Hudson
        2nd Lt. Richard Marsh
        Ensign Thomas Doyle

Company No. 6.....................................76 Privates
        Captain Nathaniel Stinchicomb (unnamed)
        1st Lt. Joseph Gist
        2nd Lt. John Worthington Dorsey
        Ensign Joshua Owings (of John)

Company No. 7.....................................55 Privates
        Captain Mordecai Hammond   (unnamed)
        1st Lt. Aquila Hooker
        2nd Lt. Richard Davis
        Ensign Edward Parish (of Edward)

Company No. 8.....................................75 Privates
        Captain Isaac Hammond   (unnamed)
        1st Lt. Christopher Owings
        2nd Lt. Samuel Merryman, Jr.
        Ensign William Chenoweth

Companies reported to the Baltimore Committee: Samuel Purviance, Jr.,
Chairman; Thomas Harrison; John Boyd; I. Griest; Thomas Gist; Thomas
Rutter; Andrew Buchanan; Thomas Sollers; James Gittings; John Merry-
man, Jr.; John E. Howard; William Wilkinson; James Calhoun; and,
Charles Ridgely (of William).

(Source: Original, Md. State Archives, Accession No. 4574-64)

ROSTER OF THE BALTIMORE COMPANY OF CAPT. JEHU HOWELL
DECEMBER 30, 1775
(Source: Md. State Papers-Red Books, No. 4, Pt. 2, p. 11)

Jehu Howell, Captain
David Evans, 1st Lieutenant
Cornelius Garretson, 2nd Lt.
Henry Sheaff, Ensign *

Privates

Samuel Abel

Hugh America

Thomas Baltimore

John Bast

Dennis Bryan

Michael Bruebecker

Benjamin Butterworth

John Caldwell

Joseph Cambridge

Patrick Cassaigain

William Clotraubay (?)

William Crandel

Thomas Creighton

Anthony Currier

Francis Dashield

Lewis Dashield

George Dennehaugh

Thomas Doyle

Benjamin England

William Finn

Robert Finnie

Philip Fitzler

William Froepath

Thomas Furber (Clerk)

Luke Gardner

William Graham

Samuel Grant

Andrew Greble

Thomas Green

Martin Gutterough

Hugh Hagan

John Hamilton

William Harris

Isaac James

Benjamin Jones

Stephen Joyce

David Knox

Martin Lantie

Adam Laut

William Lavely

Joseph Lawell

Adam Lindsay

Thomas Long

John McClathry

Daniel McGilton

David Nice

Christian Noddiker

Joseph Polamus

Anthony Potter

Aubrey Richardson

Wooley Ross

Masheck Samuel

Edward Saunders

Ludwick Sible

Anthony Sillister

Joseph Smith

Cunrod Smoll (Surgeon)

Benjamin Spencer

Rawleigh Spinks

Obadiah Stillwill

John Stoler

Aquila Taylor

John Turbitt

Robert Vance

CAPT JEHU HOWELL'S BALTIMORE COMPANY (cont.)

Philip Walter   Peter Wedderfield

Hugh Workman   John Wright

* A note explains that Ensign Henry Sheaff was first
chosen Captain of the Artillery Company in Baltimore.
He was with that company by September 30, 1775, for on
that day the officers of the company were chosen.

(Source: Maryland State Papers-Red Books, No. 4, pp. 8 & 11)

THE FOLLOWING MEMBERS OF THE BALTIMORE
MECHANICAL COMPANY WERE MEMBERS OF THE SONS OF
LIBERTY IN 1776

Aaron Levington	William Baker
S. Hollingsworth	William Willson
John McLane	Daniel Bowly
Caleb Hall	E. Winters
Michael Allen	George Leverly
John Dever	James Cox
David Shields	Gerard Hopkins
Geo. Lindenberger	Erasmus Uhler
Richard Moale	William Clemm
Hercules Courtney	John Sterrett
R. Adair	Benjamin Griffith
William Asquith	Melchior Keener
William Spear	James Sterrett
Arch. Buchanan	William Lyon
Isaac Grist	George Patton
William Lux	George Duvall
George Wells	James Calhoun
David Rusk	Cyprian Wells

(Source: George W. McCreary's The Ancient and Honorable
Mechanical Company of Baltimore, 1901, page 19)

BALTIMORE COUNTY MILITIA REGIMENT NO. 36
COL. EDWARD NORWOOD'S COMPANY
c1777

Capt. John Albright, Volunteer
Lt. Henry Nagle, Volunteer

Volunteers

Christian Nagle
John Sybeard
John Hegnet
John Nagle
Joseph Not
John Philin
Joseph Wiundman (?)
George Sank
Thomas Hutchison
Casper Terry
William Mitchell
Matthias Sherrad
William Robertson
John Terry
Matthias Sterad (?)
John Quinn
John Knight
David Knight
Benjamin Knight
Thomas Roach
Joseph Hook
William Whittem

Drafts

Samuel Stevens
Edward Constant (?)
Jeremiah Evans
Jacob Caball
Morris Curry
Ely Rowls
Edward Lee
David Stinchacomb
Ephraim Hamelton
William Baker
Benjamin Watts
Matthias Lightheser
William Corbet
Brian Duff
George Hammond
McCogy (?) Greenfield
Peter Shipley
Frederick Roe
Benjamin Scott
James Croxall
John Richert
(one name not legible)

(Source: Original manuscript, MS1814, Maryland Hist. Society)

BALTIMORE COUNTY MILITIA COMPANIES, OCT. 28, 1776

Company No. 1................................64 Privates
    Captain John Cockey   (unnamed)
    1st Lt. John Robert Holliday
    2nd Lt. Nathaniel Britain
    Ensign Benjamin Talbot

Company No. 2................................65 Privates
    Captain Edward Cockey   (unnamed)
    1st Lt. Beale Owings
    2nd Lt. William Harvey
    Ensign William Scarf

Company No. 3................................69 Privates
    Captain Henry Howard   (unnamed)
    1st Lt. John Willson
    2nd Lt. William Ensor
    Ensign Joshua Welsh

Company No. 4................................60 Privates
    Captain John Talbot   (unnamed)
    1st Lt. John Dunnock
    2nd Lt. James Norris
    Ensign Joshua Anderson

Company No. 5................................95 Privates
    Captain Daniel Shaw   (unnamed)
    1st Lt. John Sharp
    2nd Lt. Abraham Cox
    Ensign John Wiley

Company No. 6................................70 Privates
    Captain Stephen Gill   (unnamed)
    1st Lt. Thomas Bond
    2nd Lt. Aquila Tipton
    Ensign Nicholas Gill

Company No. 7................................40 Privates
    Rifle Company   (unnamed)
    Captain Luke Wiley
    1st Lt. Richard Cromwell
    2nd Lt. Walter Bosley
    3rd Lt. John Wilmott

                    Signed by David McMechan
                    Secretary
                    October 28, 1776

(Source: Original Manuscript, MS1814, in Maryland Historical Society Library, Maunscript Division, Box 2 (Feb.-Dec., 1776)

312

UPPER BATTALION OF BALTIMORE COUNTY
COMMISSIONS ISSUED AUG. 30, 1777

Colonel Thomas Gist

Captain Thomas Marshall
1st Lt. Philip Stilts
2nd Lt. William Davis
Ensign William Matthews

Captain Nicholas Merryman
1st Lt. Humphry Chilcott
2nd Lt. Abm: Coe, Sr.
Ensign Robinson Jones

In Capt. John Murray's Co.:
   2nd Lt. David Gist
   Ensign Henry Butler

Captain Robert Cummins
1st Lt. Abraham Hicks
2nd Lt. John Miller
Ensign Samuel Tipton

In Capt. John Showers' Co.:
   1st Lt. Stophel Shroad
   2nd Lt. Matthias Barkley
   Ensign Henry Peckly

In Capt. Robert Lemmon's Co.:
   Ensign Charles Allen

Signed by Andrew Buchanan.

(Source: Original Mansucript in Maryland State Archives,
Maryland State Papers, Accession No. 6636-8-66B)

A LIST OF OFFICERS FOR THE ARTILLERY COMPANY
BELONGING TO THE BALTIMORE TOWN BATTALION IN 1777

Captain George Wells

1st Lt. Ralph Story
   (James Morgan being unable to serve)

2nd Lt. John Steel
   (John Hayman laying sick at the time)

3rd Lt. Joseph Byas
   (James Foster being absent)

(Source: Original Manuscript in Maryland State Archives,
Maryland State Papers, Accession No. 6636-8-89)

A RETURN OF FIELD OFFICERS IN BALTIMORE COUNTY, 1777

9th Battalion, Gunpowder....................594 Privates
                                      (unnamed)
       Colonel Darby Lux
       Lt.Colonel James Gittings
       Major Thomas Sollers

Baltimore Town Battalion....................656 Privates
                                      (unnamed)
       Colonel John Moale
       Lt.Colonel Benjamin Nicholson
       Major James Cox

Soldiers Delight Battalion..................422 Privates
                                      (unnamed)
       Colonel Isaac Hammond
       Lt.Colonel Charles Carnan
       Major Joseph Gist

Gunpowder Upper Battalion...................454 Privates
                                      (unnamed)
       Colonel Edward Cockey
       Lt.Colonel Joshua Stevenson
       Major Micajah Merryman
       2nd Major Stephen Cromwell

Upper Battalion.............................405 Privates
                                      (unnamed)
       Colonel Thomas Gist
       Lt.Colonel Frederick Decker
       Major Joshua Gist
       2nd Major Gist Vaughan
           (commissioned Feb. 4, 1777)

Capt. John Sterret's Independent Company....60 Privates
                                      (unnamed)

(Source: Original Manuscript in Maryland State Archives,
Maryland State Papers, Accession No. 6636-8-110, in 1777)

ENLISTMENTS BY CAPTAIN PHILIP GRAYBILL
APPROVED BY THOMAS JONES, 2ND MAJOR, OF BALTIMORE TOWN
BATTALION OF MILITIA, JULY 12, 1776

Wolfgone Citzinger	William Libzinger
Christopher Begel	Jacob Frymiller
Frederick Welhelm	James Caple
John Moore	John Rich
Vendell Andrews	Lorance Knery
Michael Kersher	Peter Baker
George Hyalt	Rudolph Kromer
John Shlife	Adam Earbaugh
Abraham Frantz	Roland Smith
Frederick Wager	William Kemmelstone
Henry Hartman	John Shryock
John Shaffer	Joseph Stritter
David Mumma	Jacob Ruturt
Jacob Myers	Martin Lantz
Jacob Hardstone	Philip Kantz
Ferdinant Lorance	Vendell Lerance
Henry Millberger	Matthias Byer

(Source: Archives of Maryland, Volume XII, Page 32)

OFFICERS OF THE TWO GERMAN COMPANIES
TO BE RAISED FROM BALTIMORE COUNTY
JULY 11, 1776

Captain Philip Greybill
1st Lt. John Lora
2nd Lt. Christian Myers
Ensign Martin Shugarth

Captain George Peter Keyports
1st Lt. Samuel Garrock
2nd Lt. William Ritter
Ensign John Lindenberger

(Source: Copies of the original manuscripts of the Baltimore
Town and Baltimore County Committee of Observation Proceedings, 1774-1776, in the Md. Hist. Society's Library, 1931.)

THE BALTIMORE ARTIFICERS COMPANY, 1777

"We the Subscribers, being desirous to pay due Obedience
to the Directions of the Continental and Provinvial Congress,
and being Convinced that it is a duty Incumbent on each Member
of a free state to Qualify himself for the defense thereof,
have assembled and join Ourselves into a Company to be called
by the name of the Baltimore Artificers Company of Militia for
the Purpose of Aquiring and Accustoming Ourselves of Military
Knowledge and Discipline, and we do hereby bind ourselves to
Each other by all the Ties of Honour Strictly to adhere to and
Obey all such Rules of Conduct as may be by a Majority of the
Company at this or any Subsequent Meeting be deemed Necessary
for our Good Government and Regulation."

William Richardson	Ambrose Clarke
Mark Alexander	James Kean
John Caldwell	Laurence Maloney
John McCabe	Thomas Lanahan
James McFaden	John Hamilton
Patrick Keiths	Geo. S. Douglass
William Forepaugh	Clement Skerrett
Arthur Owens	Gabrile Lawyn
Anthony Ryan	Henry Wannell
Fergis McCray (?)	John Taylor
John Hawkins	Daniel Flanerey
Robert Vance	Moses Rutter
William McMillen	John Byrne
Joseph Chester	Enoch Gordon
Joseph Cambridge	Issacco M. Gordon
John Lynch	Thomas Shepard
John Howell	Gilbert Crockett
John Calder	William Grahame
Amon Hanson	Cornelius O'Leary

(Source: From the original in the collection of the Maryland
Historical Society, a copy of which is found in Filing Case A
in the Library, and also in Md. Hist. Mag., Vol. II, p. 367-8)

RETURN OF CAPT. BENJAMIN TALBOTT'S COMPANY OF MILITIA
BELONGING TO COLONEL EDWARD COCKEY'S BATTALION OF
BALTIMORE COUNTY MILITIA, MAY 31, 1779

Benjamin Talbott, Captain
Thomas Chenoweth, Lt.
Phillip G. Pearce, Lt.
Benjamin Ford, Ensign
Vincent Talbott, Sgt.
Nathan Hale, Sgt.

John Talbott
William Phillips
Joseph Chenoweth
Daniel Stansbury
Henry Hale
Loyd Ford
John Gorsuch
Josias Bowen
Caleb Owings
Thomas Cockey Deye Ford
Thomas Ford
David Stansbury
Thomas Hooper
William Linch
Walter James
Richard Gott
Richard Hiver
John Sollers
Nicholas Hale, son of G.
Nicholas Hale, Jr.
Moses Lemmon

(Source: From the original muster-roll presented to the
Maryland Historical Society by Francis B. Culver, and
printed in the Md. Hist. Magazine, Vol. VII, page 90.)

ROSTER OF BALTIMORE ARTILLERY COMPANY UNDER CAPT. HENRY SHEAFF
OCTOBER 16, 1775

(Source: Maryland State Papers-Red Books, No. 4, Pt. 2, Page 8)

Henry Sheaff, Captain
Brittingham Dickenson, Capt. Lt.
Richard Lemmon, 1st Lieutenat
Robert Moor, 2nd Lieutenat
William Hays, Standard Bearer

Privates

John Adams	Abraham Jackson
William Adams	James Jacobs
Elias Barnaby	William Jacobs
Samuel Bartis	Peter Kely
Patrick Berry	Jacob Kraber
Jacob Brown	John Lemmon
John Brown	Just Lettig
John Burk	Philip Lettig
Simon Burns	Christopher Limes (?)
John Cannon	George Litzener
John Cattle	William Litzener
Joseph Chester	William McCarte
John Craford	Roland McQuillen
Rudolph Cromer	James Morgan
Henry Evans	Furman Newman
Alexander Finlater	James Piller
David Flemming	George Prestman
John Gordon	John Proctor
Abraham Gorman	Michael Rierdan
Philip Grace	George Ross
Caleb Hall	Michael Schrily (?)
John Hall	William Scot
John Hannon	Daniel Scasebrick
Patrick Hannon	Caleb Shields
William Hays	Samuel Smith
Richard Hill	William Spencer
Thomas Stalling	Henry Stevenson
John Stuart	Richard Stuart
William Tinker	Isaac Vaughn
John Wale	William Wilson
Henry Worthington	John Wright

MUSTER ROLL OF CAPT. JOHN COCKEY'S COMPANY
BALTIMORE COUNTY LIGHT HORSE
MARCH, 1781

John Cockey, Captain
Daniel Bowley, 1st Lieutenant
John Stewart, 1st Lieutenant
Thomas Cockey, 2nd Lieutenant
Dixson Stansbury, 2nd Lieutenant
Adam Barnes, 1st Sergeant
Francis Sparks, 2nd Sergeant
Samuel Meredith, Cornet
Archibald Campbell, Blacksmith

Troopers

Archibald Campbell
Francis Morrison
James Hale
Isaac Chandler
John Chandler
Richard Owings
John Young
Hester Tipton
Aquilla Tipton
John Yaun
Morton Groom
William Lynch
John Seith
John Burnham
Charles Gorsuch
Harry Raines
William Cockey

John Barnett
William Barnett
John Richardson
Elsworth Ruxton
Thomas Jones
Henry Young
George Young
Isaac Hesterling
Patrick MacGregor
William Callahan
Michael Ballard
James Towson
Edward Wright
Harold Wright
Morris Jobe
Isaac VanBibber
Free Negro - Groom

Uniform - Scots Bonnet with white cockade, hunting boots
and trousers with blue hunting coat, sword belt over
shoulder - plaid cloak or shawl - frontal and rear body
armour - for use against the enemy.

Issue - two holster or pistol pocket with two pistols
and one broad sword of the best quality for his leather
on mount.

(Source: Copy from the DAR Files on Cavalry Dragoons in
Washington, DC in the Revolutionary Records Yorktown File
of 1781; typed and placed in Md. Hist. Soc. Filing Case A)

MUSTER ROLL OF CAPT. SHEAFF'S BALTIMORE COMPANY, JUNE 16, 1777

Henry Sheaff, Captain
Britg. Dickeson, Lt.
Robert Moore, Lt.
Caleb Shields, Ensign
William Spencer, Clerk
William Adams, Sgt.
John Brown, Sgt.
John Cannon, Sgt.
John Gordon, Cpl.
William Jacobs, Cpl., "pleads age & infirm"
Abram Jackson, Cpl.

Privates

William Hays
Patrick Hannon
Samuel Burtis
Caleb Hall
Alex. Finlater
Philip Littig
Job (?) Littig
Christopher Grisler
Henry Evans
George Prestman
Edward Allen
John Storke, "pleads infirm & doctors cert."
George Litzinger
John Gibbons, "pleads age & infirm"
Rowland McQuillan
John Wale
John Sizler
William Johnson
Andrew Granged
Francis Smith, "really sick"
Dennis Brian
Michael Thrippe
William Hobbs
Henry Philips
George Wearner (?)
William Claver (?)
John Proctor
William O'Gray
Christian Rees
Alexander Munro
William Wilson
Hammond Richards
Peter Frick, "gone to Va. for a short time"
Lewis D'Shield
Simon Wedge
John Bodden
Arthur McCarter
William Davry, "gone to Carolina a short time"
Andrew Grayble
Andrew Hooke, "pleads age"
Valentine Snieder, "gone to Carolina a short time"
John Sheller, Drummer

(Source: Original Manuscript in Maryland State Archives; Indexed as
Accession No. 4590B-47, but actually found under Acc. No. 4582-162.)

BALTIMORE COUNTY MILITIA REGIMENT NO. 15, c1777

Capt. (?) hns Company
Mathias Adrian, Sergeant
(?) yamus Clarke, Sergeant
Philip Feather, Corporal
Elias Crutchley, Corporal
Henry Branwell, Private
George Everhart, Private
Ulerk Busher
Leonard Fisher
William Starner
Conrad Long
John Sence
William Ponabaker
Elias Glooch
Peter Leighty (?)
Thomas Gain
Henry Mackey

Philip Myers
Jaba Murrey
William Johnson
John McCormsky (?)
Christopher Randall
Michael Sauble
Valentine Mankey
Joshua Bowing
Jacob Wink
Thomas Spurrier
Jeremiah Breshears
___(?)___ Cline
___(?)___ Dorsey
___(?)___ Hawkins
___(?)___ Stocksdale
___(?)___ Holmes
(rest of list torn off)

BALTIMORE COUNTY MILITIA REGIMENT NO. 7, c1777
(Colonel's name not legible)

___(?)___ s Hudson, Private
___(?)___ goe Griffith, Private
Michael Hose, Private
Stofel (?) Gants, Private
Thomas Saychas
John Grimes
George Baseman
___(?)___ Mattax
___(?)___ er Gosnell
___(?)___ as Williams
Michael Shirtail
Nicholas Merryman
___(?)___ Bond
___(?)___ Daughtery (of Richd.)
___(?)___ s Petticoat
___(?)___ N. Carnan
___(?)___ ain Welch
___(?)___ n Cahal
Thomas Woodcock
Abraham Green

Thomas Jackson
Thomas Wheeler
Terrance Traner
Calter (?) Evans
Robert Alder
Thomas Ritter
John Cockey (of Thos.)
Joseph Ford
Levin Owings
James Ranke
George Lijard
John Lewis
John Cox
John Cato
Joseph Traverse
John Lijard
Thomas Gorsuch
Patrick Kelly
Darby Corbidy
George Strawbridge

BALTIMORE COUNTY MILITIA REGIMENT NO. 46, c1777

Capt. Thomas Yates' Company (no names listed)

(Source: Original Manuscript, MS1814, Maryland Historical Society
Library, Box 13, "Baltimore County General Returns Continued.")

MUSTER ROLL OF CAPTAIN JAMES COX'S COMPANY
BALTIMORE, DECEMBER 19, 1776

James Cox, Captain
John McClellan, Lieut.
George Lindenberger, Lieut.
George Welsh, Lieut.
David Poe, Sergeant
David Evans, Sergeant
David Knox, Sergeant
Ph. Miller, Sergeant
A. Mattison, Corporal
Thos. Furber, Corporal
Henry Lorah, Corporal
W. Stacis, Corporal
John Shrim, Corporal
W. Rodgers, Corporal
M. Diffendaffer
John McDonagh
John Cooper
Chr. Loudiger
Joseph Sayter
George Poe
J. Dalrymple
D. Diffendaffer
C. Garrison
Chr. Raborg
John Pansil
James French
A. Gantz
Peter Smith
Hugh Mercer
Thos. Emmet
Jas. Makelwayn
Ad. Bennywright

John Speck
Chas. Jacob Rhume
Andrew Davidson
William Mackle
Jere Swain
Michael Miller
Ph. Yeiser
Samuel Messersmith
John Ritchey
John Stuls
John Bridenbach
William Dunkin
Jas. McCrackin
Hug. Wasbay
John Delcher
Job Davidson
John Clements
Ad. Trumbo
C. Bracker
Peter Mackenheimer
Ed. Saunders
Robert Davidson
John Tinges
George Helms
John Taylor
James Liston
Charles Kiess
Martin Segesser
Joseph Lowry
George Ducke
Charles Sayter
Peter Furney

The following was written by Capt. Cox, May 14, 1775:

"Cursed be the wretch that's bought and sold
And barters liberty for gold;
For when elections are not free,
In vain we boast for Liberty.
And he who sells his single right,
Would sell his Country, if he might;
When liberty is put to sale
For wine, for money or for ale,
The sellers must be abject slaves---
The buyers, vile designing knaves."

(Source: George W. McCreary's The Ancient and Honorable Mechanical
Company of Baltimore, 1901 Historical Sketch, pages 21 and 22)

A MUSTER ROLL OF CAPT. JOHN McCLELLAN'S COMPANY,
MILITIA OF BALTIMORE TOWN, SEPTEMBER 4, 1780

J. McClellan, Captain
G. Welsh, Lieutenant
D. Poe, Lieutenant
David Evans, Ensign
J. Boyd, Doctor
M. Swan, Clerk
W. Rodgers, Sergeant
G. Poe, Sergeant
H. Berney, Sergeant
John Martin, Sergeant
Rowland Smith
Adam Trumbo
John Walles
Alex. Grant
Joab Davidson
Jas. Lyston
John Shrim, Sr.
Chris. Reburgh
John Pinsil
Peter McInhamer
John Speck
Henry Zigler
William Davison
Martin Segauer
John Dare
John Cooper
And. Bonner
John Delcher
Adam McLean
Robert Davidson
Isaac Dorson
John Richey
Charles Sayter
Amon Hanson
William Asquew
Jonathan Butler
Joshua Pomphrey
Henry Lorah
Peter Smith
Sam. Messersmith
Stephen Bahon
George Leably (Levely)
Daniel Deady
William Cosgrove
Michael Smith
Michael Sheppard
George Rea
John Briarly
John Shrim, Jr.
Joshua Mincel
John Trumbo
Henry Trumbo
George Richardson

W. Statia
Jacob Mull
Daniel Diffend'r
David Emmit
Fred. Losbach
Thos. Emmitt
John Breidenbach
Charles Shields
Adam Gantz
John McDonagh
Balser Pensil
Michael Shrisch
Christ. Rheem
William Beecham
John Evans
Chr'n Lodiger
Jesse Follan
Bennet Ranshaw
George Jackson
William Poe
Thomas Bodley
James Bankson
John Brown
George Miller
John Dodson
Gasper Grable
Nich. Hollow
Thomas Wilson
Samuel McFadon
Matthew Hart
Chris'n Delcher
Thomas Firber
John Jinkins
Charles Snyder
Aron Mattison
Nich. Ridenoar
Cornelius Garrison
Robert Tool
Enoch Adams
John Hooper
William Hooper
William Hollar
David Walker
Joseph Smith
Abr. Drawbach
Michael Jones
George Keener
John Snider
James Flattery
Samuel Swan
Joshua Bennet
Daniel Peters
John Sprosson

(Source: George W. McCreary's The Ancient and Honorable
Mechanical Company of Baltimore, 1901, pages 23, 24, 25)

OFFICERS OF THE THREE MARYLAND COMPANIES OF ARTILLERY
IN THE CONTINENTAL FORCES, MAY 11, 1780
DATED AT BALTIMORE

Lt. Col. Ed. Carrington
Commander, Maryland Artillery

Company No. 1

Capt. William Brown, commissioned November 22, 1777
Capt. Lt. James Smith, commissioned November 22, 1777
1st Lt. James McFaden, commissioned November 22, 1777
2nd Lt. Clement Skerrett, commissioned February 5, 1778
2nd Lt. John Carson, commissioned May 1, 1779

Company No. 2

Capt. Richard Dorsey, commissioned November 24, 1777
Capt. Lt. Ebenezer Finley, commissioned November 24, 1777
1st Lt. Robert Wilmott, commissioned November 24, 1777
2nd Lt. Nicholas Ricketts, commissioned December 21, 1777
2nd Lt. Young Wilkerson, commissioned February 14, 1778

Company No. 3

Capt. Lt. Samuel Sadler, commissioned September 3, 1779
(resigned circa May 11, 1780)
1st Lt. Jacque Bacques, commissioned September 3, 1779
2nd Lt. Isaac Rawlings, commissioned September 3, 1779
2nd Lt. John Chever, commissioned September 3, 1779

Signed by Lt. Col. Ed. Carrington
Commander, Md. Artillery
Baltimore, May 11, 1780

(Source: Md. State Papers, 1776-1790, Red Book No. 23, page 96)

OFFICERS FOR THE BALTIMORE TOWN BATTALION OF MILITIA
JANUARY 19, 1781

Samuel Smith, Baltimore, to His Excellency Thomas S. Lee:

"I beg leave to recommend to your Excellency the following
Gentlemen as Officers for the Baltimore Town Battalion of
Militia, the vacancies have happened by deaths, removal and
resignations."

In Capt. Dickinson's Company:
   Jacob Brown, 1st Lieutenant
   John Hamilton, 2nd Lieutenant
   J. Cannon, 2nd Lt., resigned
   William Johnson, Ensign

Mercantile Company:
   Richard Ridgely, Captain
   Clem, Ensign

Ackerman's Company:
   Frederick Deems, Captain
   George Lux, 1st Lieutenant
   Ackerman, dead
   Wheeler, dead

A LIST OF OFFICERS WANTING IN COL. S. SMITH"S BATTALION
OF MILITIA, FEBRUARY 8, 1781

Capt. Kraner's Company:
   James Howard, 2nd Lieutenant

Formerly the Mercantile Company, but became a new
company having been entirely deprived of officers:
   Richard Ridgely, Captain
   Thomas Dewitt, 1st Lieutenant
   William Clem, 2nd Lieutenant
   Mark Alexander, Ensign

Capt. B. Dickenson's Company:
   1st Lieutenant John Hamilton, Jr., room of Caleb
     Shields, who is always drunk and some
     times crazy.
   2nd Lieutenant Jacob Brown, in room of John
     Cannon, resigned and dead
   Ensign Samuel Burtis

(Source: Archives of Maryland, Vol. XLVII, 1781, pages 29 and 61)

COL. BENJAMIN NICHOLSON'S TROOP OF HORSE
BALTIMORE, JUNE 7, 1781

"Inclosed is a roll of a Troop of Horse which I have embodied in
the Forest. They have agreed to equip themselves....(but)....if
the State could furnish pistols and swords the Troop might be
greatly enlarged and would be in immediate readiness. It was at
the solicitation of the youth in my neighborhood that I undertook
the embodying and command of the Troop.....You'll find among our
number some Veteran Officers, who have left the Continental Service
and whilst in served with reputation."   (Letter to Gov. Lee)

Benjamin Nicholson
Charles Carnan
Thomas Cromwell
Robert Lyon
Stephen Shelmerdine
John Colegate
John Cockey
Robert Carnan
Joshua Gist
Thomas Nicholson
Benjamin Todd
Richard Colegate
Bazil Tracey
Walter Bosley
Richard Britton
Edward Ford
John Dodd
Roger Boyce
Thomas Risteau
John Summers
John Gist
Joshua Cockey
Benjamin Bond
Christian Gore
James Howard
Frederick Counselman
John Worthington
James Trapnell
Joseph Butler
Ephraim Owings
Richard Johns
Thomas Cradock
John Bryson

(Source: _Archives of Maryland_, Vol. XLVII, page 274)

TROOPS AND HORSES COMMANDED BY NICHOLAS R. MOORE
OF BALTIMORE ON JUNE 25, 1781
(STATIONED IN MONTGOMERY COUNTY, MD)

Persons Names	Horse & Colour	Age
Capt. N. R. Moore	Bay Stallion	8
Capt. N. R. Moore	Black Stallion	9
Lt. Thomas Russel	Dark Chestnut Stallion	7
Lt. Thomas Russel	Grey Mare	8
Cornet Mark Pringle	Bay Gelding	12
Cornet Mark Pringle	Bay Gelding	14
Dr. Gooding (Goodwin)	Bay Gelding	9
Dr. Gooding (Goodwin)	Bay Gelding	7
Quartermaster Wm. King	Bay Mare	6
Francis Grant	Sorrell Gelding	6
John Steuart	Grey Gelding	5
John McColester	Grey Gelding	5
Alexander McCim (McKim)	Grey Gelding	5
Major T. Yates	Black Gelding	8
Major T. Yates	Bay Stallion	7
Daniel Carroll Ball	Black Mare	8
David Reese	Black Gelding	8
Robert Harris	Black Gelding	8
Nathan Levie (Levy)	Black Gelding	6
Joseph Lemon	Bay Gelding	14
James Jaffrey	Sorrell Gelding	7
George Turnbull	Bay Mare	5
Samuel Hollingsworth	Bay Gelding	6
Will. Taylor	Bay Gelding	6
Charles Myers (?)	Bay Gelding	7
John Spear	Bay Gelding	5
Joseph Foster	Bay Gelding	8
Daniel Hopkins	Sorrell Mare	10
Abraham Vanbibber	Bay Stallion	4
John Kirwin	Sorrell Gelding	6
John Jeffers	Dark Bay	10
Thorogood Smith	Iron Grey Gelding	7
James Stirling	Iron Grey Gelding	7
Will Buchanan	Bay Gelding	12
George Hamond	Sorrell Gelding	8
James Ryan	Dark Bay Gelding	6
Matthew Ridley	Bay Gelding	5
Thomas Hollingsworth	Sorrell Gelding	6
Mathew Patten	Bay	
Bryan Philpott	Dark Bay Mare	9
Luther Martin	Bay Stallion	6

(Source: "Deposition of Thomas Beall of George, Esq., Bernard
O'Neill and Leonard M. Deakins" in Montgomery County, Maryland,
Archives of Maryland, Vol. XLVII, June 25, 1781, page 312)

GUNPOWDER BATTALION OFFICERS, AUGUST 30, 1777

Colonel Darby Lux
Lt.Colonel James Gittings
Major Thomas Sollars

Captain Simon Pryor (Capt. William Cromwell
1st Lt. Thomas Miles   having resigned)
2nd Lt. Kinsey Griffis
Ensign John Griffis

Captain Benjamin Buck   (Capt. John Mercer
1st Lt. Joshua Buck   deceased)
2nd Lt. John Weston

(Source: Md. State Archives, Md. State Papers, Accession
No. 6636-8-65B, Original Manuscript)

HUNTING RIDGE COMPANY, 39TH BATTALION OF MILITIA
BALTIMORE COUNTY, AUGUST 29, 1777

Captain Elam Bailey
        in lieu of Capt. McCubbins, resigned
1st Lt. Walter S. Parker
        in lieu of Elam Bailey (chosen Captain)
2nd Lt. Joshua Carey
        in lieu of John Bailey (entered Cont. Svc.)
Ensign Samuel Wright Waters, Esq.
        in lieu of Joshua Carey (chosen 2nd Lt.)

Signed by John Moale, Lt.Col., Baltimore Town Battn.

(Source: Md. State Papers, Accession No. 6636-8-61)

SEVEN COMPANIES OF BALTIMORE COUNTY MILITIA
DECEMBER 19, 1775

Company No. 1 - Capt. Andrew Buchanan.........63 Privates (unnamed)

Company No. 2 - Capt. Benjamin Nicholson.......62 Privates (unnamed)

Company No. 3 - Capt. James Cox...............63 Privates (unnamed)

Company No. 4 - Capt. Zach: McCubbin...........60 Privates (unnamed)

Company No. 5 - Capt. Thomas Rutter............62 Privates (unnamed)

Company No. 6 - Capt. William Cromwell.........69 Privates (unnamed)

Company No. 7 - Capt. James Bosley.............62 Privates (unnamed)

Signed by Samuel Purviance, Jr., Committee Chairman

(Source: Md. State Papers, Accession No. 4574-36)

OFFICERS OF THE BALTIMORE COUNTY MILITIA
SOLDIERS DELIGHT BATTALION, 1778

Captain Ely Dorsey
1st Lt. James Barns
2nd Lt. Johnsy Selman
Ensign Tobias Talbott

Captain Joshua Hurd
1st Lt. Thomas Wines
2nd Lt. Thomas Greenwood
Ensign William Parker

Captain William Hutson
Ensign Joshua Hutson

Captain Gosnel
Ensign Thomas Chenoweth

Quartermaster Adam Shekkord

Captain Benjamin Tevis
1st Lt. John Chapman
2nd Lt. Joshua Chapman
Ensign Robert Tevis

(Source: Md. State Papers, Accession No. 6636-12-24A & 24B)

REORGANIZATION OF BALTIMORE BATTALION UNDER COLONEL
WILLIAM BUCHANAN IN JUNE, 1776

Division 1 - Captain Zachariah McCubbin

Division 2 - Captain William Galbraith

Division 3 - Captain Frederick Deams

Division 4 - Captain Thomas Rutter

Each Captain had the following men under his command:

1	1st Lieutenant
1	2nd Lieutenant
1	Ensign
4	Sergeants
4	Corporals
60	Privates

(Source: Md. State papers, Accession No. 4574-47)

COLONEL THOMAS GIST'S BATTALION, 1777
BALTIMORE COUNTY

Captain Gist Vaughan..............49 Privates
1st Lt. Thomas More   (unnamed)
2nd Lt. Nicholas Merryman, Jr.
Ensign Humphrey Chilcoat

Captain Alexes Lemmon.............37 Privates
1st Lt. Henry Warham   (unnamed)
2nd Lt. Thomas Stansbury
Ensign Peter Nace

Captain John Hall.................48 Privates
1st Lt. Thomas Marshal   (unnamed)
2nd Lt. Philip Stilts
Ensign William Davis

Captain Robert Lemmon.............40 Privates
1st Lt. Mordecai Cole   (unnamed)
2nd Lt. Peter Snap
Ensign Samuel Adams

Captain Thomas Gist, Jr...........44 Privates
1st Lt. John Murry   (unnamed)
2nd Lt. Christopher Vaughan
Ensign Joshua Gist

Captain John Cockey..............___ Privates
1st Lt. Nathaniel Brittain   (unknown)
2nd Lt. Benjamin Talbot
Ensign Nicholas Haile, son of George

Captain William Wilkinson.........___ Privates
1st Lt. Sabrit Sellers   (unknown)
2nd Lt. Nicholas Norwood
Ensign Philip Woolrich

Colonel Thomas Gist
Lt.Col. Frederick Decker
1st Major Joshua Gist
2nd Major Gist Vaughan
Quartermaster John Hall, son of Joshua

Commissioned February 4, 1777.

As the result of Capt. Thomas Gist, Jr. becoming a
Colonel, 1st Lt. John Murry became a Captain, 2nd Lt.
Christopher Vaughan became a 1st Lt., and Ensign Joshua
Gist became a 2nd Lt. And when Captain Gist Vaughan
became 2nd Major, 1st Lt. Thomas More became a Captain,
2nd Lt. Nicholas Merryman, Jr. became a 1st Lt., and
Ensign Humphrey Chilcoat became a 2nd Lt. Also, Capt.
John Showers was mentioned, but his enrollment was not.

Source: <u>Archives of Maryland</u>, Vol. XLIII, pages 105, 114)

SIX COMPANIES OF MILITIA IN BALTIMORE TOWN IN 1776

Company No. 1.................................76 Privates (unnamed)
        Captain William Buchanan   & Non-Comms.
        1st Lt. John Smith
        2nd Lt. Robert Alexander
        Ensign George Woolsey

Company No. 2.................................82 Privates (unnamed)
        Captain John Sterrett   & Non-Comms.
        1st Lt. Barnet Eichelberger
        2nd Lt. Hugh Young
        Ensign Daniel Bowly

Company No. 3.................................65 Privates (unnamed)
        Captain Henry Sheaf   & Non-Comms.
        1st Lt. Brittingham Dickenson
        2nd Lt. Robert Moore
        Ensign Caleb Shields

Company No. 4.................................58 Privates (unnamed)
        Captain William Galbraith   & Non-Comms.
        1st Lt. James Toole
        2nd Lt. John Deaver
        Ensign Joseph Getro

Company No. 5.................................71 Privates (unnamed)
        Captain William Richardson   & Non-Comms.
        1st Lt. John McCabe
        2nd Lt. George Sewil Douglas
        Ensign Fergus McIlroy

Company No. 6.................................66 Privates (unnamed)
        Captain George Wells   & Non-Comms.
        1st Lt. James Morgan
        2nd Lt. John Hayman   (Artillery Company)
        3rd Lt. James Foster

Companies reported to the Baltimore Committee:

        William Lux, Chairman
        William Buchanan
        Thomas Harrison
        Thomas Sollers
        John Boyd
        William Aisquith
        John E. Howard
        John Sterrett
        James Calhoun
        John Smith

(Source: Original Manuscript in the Maryland State Archives,
Maryland State Papers, Accession No. 4574-74)

NAMES, RANK, AND DATES OF COMMISSIONS OF THE OFFICERS
OF CAPT. RICHARD DORSEY'S COMPANY OF MARYLAND ARTILLERY
WITH A LIST OF THE PRIVATES, AS IT STOOD AT VALLEY FORGE
JUNE 3, 1778

Captain Richard Dorsey. Commissioned May 4, 1777.
Capt.-Lieut. Ebenezer Finley. Commissioned July 4, 1777.
1st Lieut. Robert Wilmott. Commissioned November 24, 1777.
2nd Lieut. Nicholas Ricketts. Commissioned Dec. 1, 1777.
2nd Lieut. Young Wilkinson. Commissioned February 25, 1778.

Sergeants for One Year

Samuel Thompson	John Wheeler
John Howard	James Rice
David Walsh	Robert Thompson

Corporals for One Year

Thomas Neilson	William Delaney
Philip Jones	Thomas Smith
David White	John Wilkins

Bombardiers for One Year

John Pierson	Alexander McMullan
David Maroney	John Clarke

Gunners for One Year

Timothy Donovan	Thomas Grainger
Daniel Donogue	John Brady
John Turner	John Ackerly

Matrosses for One Year

Dennis Flannegan	Hugh McDowell
Edward Coughland	Richard Wilkinson
James Berry	Daniel Redden
Patrick Shoughness	Freeman Newman
John Bryant	Matthew Kelly
John Jallome	Daniel Neil
John Sandall	James Jack
Howel Lewis	Thomas Randall
William Reed	Michael Connor
William Day	Thomas Pierce
William Wade	Mathew McMahan
Frederick Pine	Stephen Fennel
Andrew Shrink	John Handlin
Roger O'Donald	William Forbes
Robert Britt	Bryan Ferrel
John Pitzpatrick	

(Source: W. T. R. Saffell's Records of the Revolutionary
War, 1858, pages 230-231)

COLONEL AQUILA HALL'S BALTIMORE COUNTY REGIMENT, 1776-1777

Colonel Aquila Hall
Captain Elijah Rutledge
Lieutenant Nathaniel Standiford
Lieutenant Robert Gwynn
Ensign Samuel Standifer

Sergeant Samuel Richardson
Sergeant Thomas Gudgeon
Sergeant Richard Jones

Privates

John Howland	Samuel Webster
John McCoy	George Rhodes
Thomas Wooden	Shardrick Hurst
Patrick Develin	Mordecai Price
William Shepherd	John Johnson
James Wilson	Isaac Sampson
Jacob Shroud	John Conrad
Stephen Gorsuch	William Hall
Henry DeCoursey	John Fuller
Harry Carter	Jacob Herrington
Benjamin Gorsuch	Edward Morris
John Hawkins	John Lightfoot
Elijah Sparks	Nathaniel Evans
John Kidd Williams	Jacob Dick
Mark Coe	Peter Rutledge
John Marsh	Frederick Dick
Samuel Meridith	William Hunt (of Thos.)
Robert White	George Pocock
Thomas Hawkins	Joshua Owings
Daniel Smith	Hugh Smyth
Nathaniel Shepherd	William_____ (page torn off)

(Source: Original Manuscript, MS1814, Maryland Historical Society
Library, Box 13, "Baltimore County General Returns, Continued.")

MAGISTRATES WHO ADMINISTERED THE OATH OF FIDELITY
AND ALLEGIANCE TO THE STATE OF MARYLAND
IN BALTIMORE TOWN AND COUNTY IN 1778

HON. ANDREW BUCHANAN

HON. JESSE BUSSEY

HON. JAMES CALHOUN

HON. EDWARD COCKEY

HON. HERCULES COURTENAY

HON. JOHN CRADOCK

HON. RICHARD CROMWELL

HON. FREDERICK DECKER

HON. JESSE DORSEY

HON. JOHN HALL

HON. RICHARD HOLLIDAY

HON. JOHN BEALE HOWARD

HON. JEREMIAH JOHNSON

HON. GEORGE LINDENBERGER

HON. WILLIAM LUX

HON. JOHN MERRYMAN

HON. JOHN MOALE

HON. GEORGE GOULDSMITH PRESBURY

HON. CHARLES RIDGELY OF WILLIAM

HON. BENJAMIN ROGERS

HON. PETER SHEPHERD

HON. ROBERT SIMMONS

HON. THOMAS SOLLERS

HON. WILLIAM SPEAR

HON. ISAAC VAN BIBBER

(Source: Hodges' Unpublished Revolutionary Records, Vol. 6)

A LIST OF BALTIMORE INHABITANTS WHO ADVANCED MONEY
TO GENERAL LAFAYETTE, ON HIS SIMPLE OBLIGATION, TO ENABLE HIM TO
PROCURE CLOTHING FOR OUR ARMY

BALTIMORE, MARYLAND   –   APRIL 18, 1781

JACOB HART	$276.14
JAMES CALHOUN	272.52
RICHARD CURSON	234.06½
JAMES McHENRY	110.76½
NATHANIEL SMITH	93.56½
JOHN STERRETT	250.16½
NICHOLAS ROGERS	102.89
CHARLES CARROLL	124.76
RIDGELY & PRINGLE	234.06½
JOHN SMITH, JR	351.10
STEPHEN STEWART	379.18
WILLIAM SMITH	468.13
WILLIAM NEILL	411.87
ALEX. DONALDSON	117.03¼
DANIEL BOWLY	234.06½
STEWART & SALMON	468.13
HUGH YOUNG	458.70
WILLIAM PATTERSON	468.13
SAMUEL & R. PURVIANCE	468.13
JOHN McLURE	468.13
RUSSEL & HUGHES	234.06½
THOMAS RUSSEL	210.60
RUSSEL & GILMAN	117.03¼
SAMUEL HUGHES	702.20½
	$7,256.24

(Sources: Copied from the original document in the National
Archives in Washington and published in Niles' Register on
April 16, 1825, Vol. XXVIII, page 101, and copied by J. Alexis
Shriver in his Lafayette in Harford County, 1781, pages 28-29,
Bel Air, Maryland: Privately Printed, 1931)

LIST OF SOURCES

A = Signers of the Oath of Allegiance and Fidelity in Baltimore, Maryland in 1778.

    A-1 = Carothers, Bettie Stirling. 9000 Men Who Signed the Oath of Allegiance and Fidelity to Maryland During the Revolution, Vol. II (Baltimore, MD: Privately Printed, 1975) Also includes Non-Jurors in 1778.

    A-2 = Hodges, Margaret R. Unpublished Revolutionary Records of Maryland, Vol. 6 (Published by the Maryland Society, DAR, 1941)

B = Heitman, Francis B. Historical Register of Officers of the Continental Army During the War of the Revolution, 1775-1783 (Baltimore, MD: Genealogical Publishing Company, Inc., 1982 (originally published in 1914).

C = Brumbaugh, Gaius M. Maryland Records: Colonial, Revolutionary, County and Church, Vol. II, "Digest of Kilty's Laws Showing Maryland Revolutionary War Pensions," pp. 314-411 (Baltimore, MD: Genealogical Publishing Company, Inc., 1985) Originally published in 1928.

D = History Trails Extra Publications No. 1, December, 1975, and No. 2, July, 1976, "Revolutionary Biographies of Baltimore County." (Published by the Baltimore County Historical Society and its Genealogy Committee)

E = Hodges, Margaret Roberts. Unpublished Revolutionary Records of Maryland, Vol. 1 (Published by the Maryland Society, DAR, 1941)

F = Hodges, Margaret Roberts. Unpublished Revolutionary Records of Maryland, Vol. 2 (Published by the Maryland Society, DAR, 1941)

G = Original Manuscript of "Baltimore Town Company of Artillery, September 27, 1775" in MD State Archives (MD State Papers, Acc. No. 4574-35), and also in Calendar of Maryland State Papers: The Red Books, No. 4, Part 2, page 8.

H = Archives of Maryland, Vol. XVIII, " Muster Rolls of Maryland Troops in the American Revolution, 1775-1783" (Baltimore, MD: MD Historical Society, 1900).

I = McGhee, Lucy Kate. Maryland Pension Abstracts of Revolution, War of 1812 and Indian Wars, Vol. I (Washington, D.C.: Privately Printed, 1966).

J = Baltimore County Orphans Court Proceedings, 1777-1787 (Liber W. B. 1) Original Records in Maryland State Archives in Annapolis (Acc. No. MdHR 11814)

K = Baltimore County Orphans Court Proceedings, 1787-1792 (Liber W. B. 2) Original Records in Maryland State Archives in Annapolis (Acc. No. MdHR 11815)

L = Baltimore County Orphans Court Proceedings, 1792-1798 (Liber W. B. 3) Original Records in Maryland State Archives in Annapolis (Acc. No. MdHR 11816)

M = Baltimore County Orphans Court Proceedings, 1798-1803 (Liber W. B. 4) Original Records in Maryland State Archives in Annapolis (Acc. No. MdHR 11817)

N = Baltimore County Orphans Court Proceedings, 1803-1805 (Liber W. B. 5) Original Records in Maryland State Archives in Annapolis (Acc. No. MdHR 11818)

O = "A Statement Showing the Names, Rank. Etc. of Invalid Pensioners Residing in Baltimore County in the State of Maryland," Maryland Pension Roll (dates between 1795 and 1840). A copy of the record in the Maryland Historical Society Library.

P = Census of Pensioners for Revolutionary or Military Services Under the Act for Taking the Sixth Census. (Washington, D.C.: Blair and Rives, 1841).

Q = Original Manuscript of "List of Drafts and Substitutes of the 4th Maryland Regiment to be Discharged, December 3, 1781," in the Maryland State Archives (<u>Maryland State Papers</u> Accession No. 6636-21-72B).

R = Original Manuscript of "A List of Officers in Col. S. Smith's Battalion of Militia, January 19, 1781," in the Maryland State Archives (<u>Maryland State Papers</u> Accession No. 4596-15/16).

S = Original Manuscript of "Letter from Citizens of Baltimore Town to Gov. Lee, April 4, 1781," in the Maryland State Archives, urging the calling up of the militia to protect Baltimore. (<u>Maryland State Papers</u> Accession No. 4596-49).

T = Original Manuscript of "Officers for Capt. Standiford's Company in Baltimore County, September 3, 1777," in the Maryland State Archives (<u>Maryland State Papers</u> Accession No. 6636-8-83).

U = Original Manuscript of "Baltimore County Militia, 1779," in the Manuscripts Division of the Maryland Historical Society Library, and also published in the <u>Maryland Historical Magazine</u>, Vol. VII, page 90, in 1912.

V = Original Manuscript of "The Baltimore Artificers Company of Militia, 1777," in the Manuscripts Division of the Maryland Historical Society Library, and also in the MHS Library's Filing Case A, and published in the <u>Maryland Historical Magazine</u>, Vol. II, pages 367-368, in 1907.

W = Original Manuscript of "Capt. Sheaff's Muster Roll, June 16, 1777," in the Maryland State Archives (<u>Maryland State Papers</u>, Acc. No. 4582-162), Red Book 17.

X = Original Manuscript of "List of Officers Appointed by the Honorable Convention, May, 1776, for the Gunpowder Battalion," in the Maryland State Archives (<u>Maryland State Papers</u> Accession No. 4580A-23), Red Book 16.

Y = Original Manuscript of "Militia Officers, Hunting Ridge Company, 39th Battalion, August 29, 1777," in the Maryland State Archives (<u>Maryland State Papers</u> Accession No. 6636-8-61).

Z = Original Manuscript of "Soldiers Delight Officers, Baltimore Town, August 29, 1777," in the Maryland State Archives (<u>Maryland State Papers</u> Acc.No. 6636-8-63).

AA = Original Manuscript of "Gunpowder Battalion Officers, August 30, 1777," in the Maryland State Archives (<u>Maryland State Papers</u> Accession No. 6636-8-65B).

BB = Original Manuscript of Representatives from Baltimore who signed the document "Association of Freemen of Maryland, July 26, 1775," in the Maryland State Archives (<u>Maryland State Papers</u> Accession No. 19970-15-2/1).

CC = Original Manuscript of "Officers of Seven Companies of Militia, Baltimore County December 12, 1775," in the Maryland State Archives (<u>Maryland State Papers</u> Accession No. 4574-36).

DD = Original manuscript of "Reorganization of Baltimore Battalion Under Colonel William Buchanan, June, 1776," in the Maryland State Archives (<u>Maryland State Papers</u> Accession No. 4574-47).

EE = Original manuscript of "Militia Officers Reported by the Baltimore Committee, May, 1776," in the Maryland State Archives (<u>Maryland State Papers</u> Accession No. 4574-51).

FF = Original Manuscript of "Eight Companies in Soldiers Delight, Garrison Forest, Baltimore County, May 13, 1776," in the <u>Maryland State Papers</u> Acc. No. 4574-64.

GG = Original Manuscript of "Six Companies of Militia in Baltimore Town, 1776" in the Maryland State Archives (<u>Maryland State Papers</u> Accession No. 4574-74).

HH = Original manuscript of "Officers of the Baltimore County Militia, 1778" in the Maryland State Archives (<u>Maryland State Papers</u> Accession No. 6636-12-24A & 24B).

II = Original Manuscript of a "Letter to the Governor of Maryland on September 4, 1778," informing him that Capt. Dunscam's sloop had left Baltimore with flour intended for use by the enemy. (The signers believed it their duty "to inform his Excellency, considering our oath binding which we swore to the State (but) request our names may be kept secret." (<u>MD State Papers</u> Acc. No. 6636-12-23).

JJ = Original Manuscript of "List of Baltimore County Field Officers, September 13, 1776," in the Maryland State Archives (<u>MD State Papers</u> Acc. No. 19970-9-21/1).

KK = Original Manuscript of "Soldiers Delight and Gunpowder Upper Battalion Commsns. Issued August 30, 1777," in the Maryland State Archives (<u>Maryland State Papers</u> Accession No. 6636-8-66A).

LL = Original Manuscript of "Upper Battalion of Baltimore County, Commissions Issued August 30, 1777," in the Maryland State Archives (<u>Maryland State Papers</u> Accession No. 6636-8-66B).

MM = Original manuscript of "A List of Officers for the Artillery Company Belonging to the Baltimore Town Battalion, 1777," in the Maryland State Archives (<u>Maryland State Papers</u> Accession No. 6636-8-89).

NN = Original manuscript of "Gunpowder Battalion of Militia, 1777, Commissions," in the Maryland State Archives (<u>Maryland State Papers</u> Accession No. 6636-8-88).

OO = Armstrong, Zella. <u>Some Tennessee Heroes of the Revolution</u> (Baltimore, Maryland: Genealogical Publishing Company, Inc., 1975). Originally published in 1933.

PP = <u>Pierce's Register</u> (Register of the Certificates Issued by John Pierce, Esquire, Paymaster General and Commissioner of Army Accounts for the United States, to Officers and Soldiers of the Continental Army Under Act of July 4, 1783) "The Seventeenth Report of the National Society of the Daughters of the American Revolution," originally published as <u>Senate Documents</u>, Vol. 9, No. 988, 63rd Congress, 3rd Session, Washington, 1915 (Baltimore,Maryland: Genealogical Publishing Company, Inc., 1984 reprint).

QQ = Miller, Richard B., Ph.D. "Some Little-Known Data Regarding Maryland Signers of the Oath of Fidelity," <u>Maryland Genealogical Society Bulletin</u>, Winter, 1986, Vol. 27, No. 1, pp. 101-124. (Essentially, a "Table of Non-Jurors Petitioners in Maryland, 1780-1781," naming persons who subscribed to the Oath of Allegiance and Fidelity to the State of Maryland in 1780-1781, having failed to sign the oath for various reasons when the oath was initially administered in 1778.)

RR = <u>Baltimore Town and Baltimore County Committee of Observation Proceedings, 1774-1776.</u> (Copy of the original manuscripts in a bound volume in the library of the Maryland Historical Society in Baltimore; donated in 1931 by Ida M. Shirk.)

SS = Scharf, J. Thomas. <u>The Chronicles of Baltimore</u> (Baltimore, Maryland: Turnbull Brothers, 1874).

TT = Steuart, Rieman. <u>A History of the Maryland Line in the Revolutionary War, 1775-1783.</u> (Published by the Society of the Cincinnati of Maryland in 1969).

UU = Saffell, W. T. R. <u>Records of the Revolutionary War</u> (New York: Pudney & Russell, Publishers, 1858). (Original Manuscript of Capt. Brown's Maryland Artillery at Valley Forge, June 3, 1778, is in the Maryland Historical Society Library.)

338

VV = Archives of Maryland, Volume XLIII, "Journal and Correspondence of the Council of Safety, January 1 to March 20, 1777," and "Journal and Correspondence of the State Council, March 20, 1777 to March 28, 1778." (Baltimore, MD: The Maryland Historical Society, 1897).

WW = Archives of Maryland, Volume XI, "Journal of the Maryland Convention, July 26 to August 14, 1775," and "Journal and Correspondence of the Maryland Council of Safety, August 29, 1775 to July 6, 1776." (Baltimore, MD: The Maryland Historical Society, 1892).

XX = Berkley, Henry J., M.D. "Maryland Physicians at the Period of the Recolutionary War," Maryland Historical Magazine, Volume XXIV, No. 1, March, 1929, pp. 1-7.

YY = Newman, Harry Wright. Maryland Revolutionary Records. (Baltimore, Maryland: Genealogical Publishing Company, Inc., 1980) Originally published in 1938.

ZZ = Archives of Maryland, Volume XII, "Journal of Correspondence of the Maryland Council of Safety, July 7 to December 31, 1776." (Baltimore, Maryland: The Maryland Historical Society, 1893).

AAA = Original Applications of the Maryland Society of the Sons of the American Revolution, Baltimore, Maryland, 1889-1987 (25 Volumes containing over 2800 names).

BBB = Archives of Maryland, Volume XVI, "Journal and Correspondence of the Council of Safety, January 1 to March 20, 1777," and "Journal and Correspondence of the State Council, March 20, 1777 to March 28, 1778." (Baltimore, Maryland: The Maryland Historical Society, 1897).

CCC = McCreary, George W. The Ancient and Honorable Mechanical Company of Baltimore. (Baltimore, Maryland: Privately Published by the Author, 1901).

DDD = "Revolutionary War Pensions Applications," National Genealogical Society Qtrly., Vol. XXIII, No. 2, June, 1935 (Washington: National Gene. Soc.), pp. 51-56.

EEE = Culver, Francis B. "Merryman Family," Maryland Historical Magazine, Volume X, No. 3, September, 1915, pp. 180-185 and 286-293.

FFF = Papenfuse, Edward C., et al. An Inventory of American State Papers, Volume I, "The Era of the American Revolution, 1775-1789." (Annapolis, Maryland: Archives Division, Hall of Records Commission, 1977).

GGG = Archives of Maryland, Volume XXI, "Journal and Correspondence of the Council of Maryland, April 1, 1778 to October 26, 1779." (Baltimore, Maryland: Maryland Historical Society, 1901).

HHH = Purviance, Robert. A Narrative of Events Which Occurred in Baltimore Town During the Revolutionary War. (Baltimore, Maryland: Jos. Robinson, 1849).

III = Scharf, J. Thomas. History of Maryland from the Earliest Period to the Present Day, Volume II. (Hatboro, Pennsylvania: Tradition Press, 1967).

JJJ = DAR Patriot Index, Volume I. (Washington, D.C.: The National Society of the Daughters of the American Revolution, 1966).

KKK = Owings, Addison D. and Elizabeth S. Owings and Allied Families, 1685-1985. (Baltimore, Maryland: Gateway Press, Inc., 1985).

LLL = Lynch, Branford Gist. Gist Family History. (Westminster, Maryland: Privately Published, 1940).

MMM = Maryland Historical Society Library, Baltimore: Records in their Filing Case A.

NNN = Dorsey, Maxwell J., et al. The Dorsey Family. (Baltimore: Privately Published, 1947).

OOO = Brown, Immogene Hannan. Hammond Family of Maryland With Indiana Descendants. (Ft. Wayne, Indiana: Privately Published, 1976).

PPP = Original Manuscript of "Baltimore County Military Companies," dated October 28, 1776, in the Revolutionary War Manuscripts Division of the Maryland Historical Society Library (MS. 1814, Box 2 of 13).

QQQ = Original Manuscript of "Captain Nathan Smith's 1st Company of Matrosses," dated June 29, 1776, in the Revolutionary War manuscripts Division of the Maryland Historical Society Library (MS. 1814, Box 2 of 13).

RRR = Original Manuscript of "Commissioners of Baltimore Town Receipt Book, January and February, 1780," in the Revolutionary War manuscripts Division of the Maryland Historical Society Library (MS. 1814, Box 6 of 13), naming persons in 1780 who rendered aid and services to the military through the Baltimore Committee.

SSS = Original Manuscript of "A Return of Field Officers in Baltimore County, 1777," in the Maryland State Archives (Maryland State Papers Acc. No. 6636-8-110).

TTT = Original Manuscript of "Baltimore County Militia General Returns Continued," (undated, circa 1776-1777), in the Revolutionary War manuscripts Division of the Maryland Historical Society Library (MS. 1814, Box 13 of 13).

UUU = Barnes, Robert W. Marriages and Deaths from the Maryland Gazette, 1727-1839. (Baltimore, Maryland: Genealogical Publishing Company, 1979).

VVV = Original Manuscript of the "Present State of Three Maryland Companies of the Artillery in the Continental Forces at Baltimore, May 11, 1780," in the Maryland State Archives (Maryland State Papers Accession No. 4590-96), Red Book No. 23.

WWW = Cockey, John O. Cockey Family. (No place of publication; compiled in 1946; copy in the Maryland Historical Society Library).

XXX = DAR Directory, 1892-1965. (Washington, D.C.: The National Society of the Daughters of the American Revolution, 1965).

YYY = Maryland Revolutionary War Muster and Pay Rolls. (National Archives Microfilm No. M881.408) "Compiled Service Records of Soldiers Who Served in the American Army During the Revolutionary War."

    YYY-1 = "Capt. Gale's Company of Maryland Artillery, Muster and Pay Rolls from September 1, 1779 to April 1, 1780, with encampments at Chester, Pennsylvania from November 9, 1779, and Morristown, New Jersey from March 7, 1780."

    YYY-2 = "Capt. James Smith's Company of the 2nd and 3rd Maryland Artillery Pay Rolls, with encampments near Bacon's Bridge, South Carolina from April 1, 1782 to May 25, 1782, and Camp James Islane, South Carolina from January 31, 1783 to March 31, 1783."

ZZZ = Barnes, Robert W. Marriages and Deaths from Baltimore Newspapers, 1796-1816. (Baltimore, Maryland: Genealogical Publishing Company, 1978).

AAAA = Archives of Maryland, Volume XLV, "Journal and Correspondence of the State Council of Maryland, 1780-1781." (Baltimore: Maryland Historical Society, 1927)

BBBB = Archives of Maryland, Volume XLVII, "Journal and Correspondence of the State

Council of Maryland, Letters to the Governor and Council, 1781." (Baltimore, Maryland: Maryland Historical Society, 1930).

CCCC = Archives of Maryland, Volume XLVIII, "Journal and Correspondence of the State Council of Maryland, 1781-1784." (Baltimore: Maryland Historical Society, 1931).

DDDD = Carothers, Bettie Stirling. Maryland Soldiers Entitled to Land West of Fort Cumberland. (Baltimore, Maryland: Privately Published, 1973).

EEEE = Force, Peter. American Archives, Fourth Series, Volume IV. (Published under Authority of an Act of Congress, Washington, D.C., April, 1943).

SPECIAL ACKNOWLEDGEMENTS

For research advice, information and sharing of genealogical data:

Robert W. Barnes, of Perry Hall, Maryland

Shirley Reightler, of Bel Air, Maryland

William J. Hollifield, III, of Towson, Maryland

Alan Virta, of Hyattsville, Maryland

Edward J. Goodman, of Parkville, Maryland

Evelyn Best, of White Hall, Maryland

Raymond B. Clark, of St. Michaels, Maryland

Jon Harlan Livezey, of Aberdeen, Maryland

F. Edward Wright, of Silver Spring, Maryland

Martha Reamy, of Finksburg, Maryland

Carl F. Bessent, of Baltimore, Maryland

Veronica A. Peden, of Bel Air, Maryland

INDEX

AMOS, (?) (WYLE) 299
 Elizabeth 6
 Margaret 6
 Martha (Polly) 246
 Mauldin 246
 Mordecai 6
 Thomas 6
 William 299
AMOSS, Catherine 298
 Catherine
 (WORTHINGTON) 298
 Isaac Risteau 298
ANCKLE, Peter 6
ANDERSON, Abraham 6
 Benjamin 6
 Elizabeth 247
 Elizabeth (STIRLING)
 262
 Franklin 262
 George 6
 James 6
 Jemima 272
 John 6
 Joseph 6
 Joshiah 6
 Joshua 6, 311
 Mary (PURDUE) 7
 Nathan 6
 Samuel 6
 Sarah Elizabeth 53
 Theresa 7
 Thomas 7
 William 7
ANDREAS, Vendell 7
ANDREW, William 7
ANDREWS, Jacob 7
 Thomas, Dr. 7
 Vendell 314
 Wendell 7
ANDS, Michael 7
ANGELLY, Grace 68
ANGUS, John 7
ANTHENEY, Martain 7
ANTHONY, Martain 7
APPEL, Christian 7
APPENHAMMER, Andrew 7
APPLE, Christian 7
 Christian, Jr. 7
APPLEBY, Elizabeth
 (SHEILD) 241
 John 241
 Susan 241
 William 7
APPLEGARTH, William 7
APPLEMAN, Conrad 7
APPOLD, Andrew 7

APPOLD, Anna Maria 7
 Catherine 7
 Deitrick 7
 Elizabeth 7
 Elizabeth
 (ODENBAUGH) 7
 George 7
ARM, James 7
ARMACOST, Belinda
 (MURRAY) 192
 Elizabeth (DOYLE)
 78
 Margaret 192
 Peter 78
 Stoffel 192
ARMAGRASS, Christian
 7
ARMAND, Tuffin
 Charles, Marquis
 de la Rouerie 7
ARMATAGE, James 8
ARME, James 7
ARMISTEAD, Judith
 Carter 186
ARMN, John 8
ARMOR, John 8
ARMSTRONG, Aquilla 8
 David 8
 George 8
 Horatio G. 8
 James 8, 287
 Jereimah, Sr. 8
 John 8
 Michael 8
 Nehemiah 8
 Solomon 8
 Susannah (WELLS)
 287
 Thomas 8
 William 8
ARNOLD, Benjamin 8
 David 212
 Edward 8
 George 8
 Jacob 8
 Joseph 8
 Joshiah 8
 Joshua 8
 Peter 8
 Rebecca 212
 William 8
ARON, John 8
ARTHUS, Thomas 8
ARTIS, Thomas 8
ASHER, Abraham 8
 Mary 244

ASHERS, John 8
ASHMAN, Constant 50
 George, Sr. 50
 John 8
ASHMORE, John 9
ASHWALL, William 9
ASHWORTH, Elizabeth
 99
ASKEW, Dalrymple 9
 Keziah (HANSON) 190
 Peregrine 9
 Perrey 9
 Sarah 190
 William 190
ASKINS, William 9
ASQUEW, William 9,
 322
ASQUITH, William 309
ASTON, Peter 9
ATHENSON, William 9
ATHERTON, James, Jr.
 9
 James, Sr. 9
ATKINSON, Elizabeth
 81
 Mary Ellen 81
AUBRE, John 9
AUCHENLECK, Henry 9
AUCHENTECK, Henry 9
AUDET, Joseph 9
AUERBACH, Breinley
 190
AUGUSTINE, Henry 9
AURMAN, Maria
 Margaret 246
AUSTIN, Catherine
 229
 Isaac 9
AUSTON, John 9
AYERS, Jeremiah
 (Jr.) 9
AYLER, George 9
AYRES, Ann 9
 Jeremiah (Jr.) 9
 John 9
 Thomas 9
BACKER, John 9
BACKLEY, John 9
 Matthias 9
BACON, Elizabeth 10,
 208
 Elizabeth (LYNCH)
 10
 John 10
 Martin 10
 Mary 10

342

343

345

347

BRITTON, Temperance
  (TALBOTT) 267
BRITTON - See
  BRITTAIN
BROME, Thomas 30
BROMFIELD, Thomas 30
BROMWELL, Mary 150
BROOKE, Clement 30
  Richard 30
BROOKES, Susannah 76
BROOKMAN, George 30
BROOKS, Achsah 30, 96
  Charles 30
  Edward 30
  Humphrey 30
  James D. 30
  John, Jr. 30
  Joseph 30, 96
  Mary Magdalen
    (SMITH) 251
  Priscilla (GARDNER)
    30, 96
  Samuel, Jr. 30
  Samuel, Sr. 30
  Sidney 30
  Thomas 30
  William 30, 251
BROTHERS, Austin 30
  Thomas 30
BROTHERTON, William
  30
BROTHROCK, Andrew 30
BROUGHAM, George 30
BROWN, Abel 31
  Alexander 31
  Ann Mary (PORTS) 215
  Benjamin 31
  Colin 31
  Cornelius 31
  David 31
  Dixon 31
  Edward 31
  Garrett 31
  George 31
  Henry 31
  Hosea 247
  Isaac 31
  Jacob 31, 317, 324
  James 31
  Jane (LYNCH) 167
  John 31, 167, 215,
    317, 319, 322
  Joseph 31
  Josiah 258
  Justice 31
  Justus 31

BROWN, Luke 31
  Michael 31
  Nicholas H. 258
  Penelope (SLADE)
    247
  Ruth 51
  Ruth (STANSBURY)
    258
  Sarah (STANSBURY)
    258
  Susanna (BIAYS) 21
  Thomas 31
  William 32, 323
  William, Jr. 21
BROWNE, Henry 32
  Margaret 220
BROWNLE, Thomas 32
BRUBACHER, Michael
  32
BRUCE, John 32
  Margaret 79
BRUEBACKER, Michael
  32
BRUEBECKER, Michael
  308
BRUFF, James 197
BRUMICUM, John 32
BRUMPS, Benjamin 32
BRUMT, Peter 32
BRUNNER, Catherine
  (ZIMMERMAN) 302
  Elias 302
  Henry 302
  Mary Elizabeth
    (ZIMMERMAN) 302
  Peggy (ZIMMERMAN)
    302
  Peter 302
BRUNT, Peter 32
BRUSBANKS, Francis
  32
  Ruth 134
BRYAN, Cecilia 32
  Dennis 32, 308
  Eleanor 272
  James 32
  John 32
  Mary 32
  Mary (DRAVER/
    DRAVES) 32
  Thurbo 32
  William 32
BRYANT, Eleanor 272
  John 32, 331
  Thomas 32
BRYARLY, Mary E. 156

BRYSON, James 32
  John 32, 325
BUCHANAN, Alexander
  32
  Andrew 32, 33, 304,
    305, 307, 312,
    327, 333
  Arch. 309
  Archibald 32, 33
  Dorothy 32
  Eleanor 32, 231
  Eleanor (ROGERS)
    103
  Elenor (ROGERS) 32
  Elizabeth 103, 252
  George 33
  George, Dr. 32, 33,
    103
  James 32, 33
  Jane 175
  Letitia (MC KEAN)
    32
  Lloyd 32
  Mary 249
  Richard 33
  Robert 33
  Samuel 33
  Susan (LAWSON) 32
  Susannah 32
  Will 33, 326
  William 33, 304,
    328, 330
BUCK, Benjamin 34,
  181, 305, 327
  Catherine
    (MERRYMAN) 181
  Catherine (REESE)
    34
  Christopher 34
  Dorcas (SUTTON) 34
  Elizabeth (HICKMAN)
    34
  James 34
  Jane (HERBERT) 34
  John 34, 181
  Joshua 34, 327
  Kesiah (GORSUCH) 34
  Penelope 274
  Sarah 34, 34, 118
  Sarah (CROOK) 34
  Susana (INGRAM) 34
  Susanna 34
  Susannah 214
  William 34
  William Henry 34
BUCKINGHAM, Anne 106

348

349

350

351

COCKEY, Ann 50
Ann (LUX) 166
Charles 50
Chloe (CROMWELL) 50
Clarissa 51
Constant (ASHMAN) 50
Edward 50, 51, 307,
  311, 313, 333
Eleanor 50
Eleanor (PINDELL)
  50, 51
Elizabeth 50, 51
Elizabeth (OWINGS)
  50
Elizabeth (SLADE)
  50, 51
Elizabeth
  (ZANTZINGER) 50
Henrietta (CROMWELL)
  50, 51
James 50
John 50, 51, 311,
  318, 320, 325, 329
Joshua 50, 51, 102,
  304, 307, 325
Mary 50, 51, 182,
  201, 202
Mary (COALE) 51
Mary (JONES) 50, 51
Penelope Deye 102
Prudence (GILL) 51,
  91
Rebecca 50
Richard 51
Ruth 203
Ruth (BROWN) 51
Samuel 51
Ssuannah 102
Stephen 51
Susannah 101
Thomas 50, 51, 91,
  318, 320
Thomas Deye 166
Thomas, Jr. 51
Urath 50
Ward 51
William 50, 51, 318
William Joseph
  Cromwell 51
COCKRILL, James
  Jackson 240
  Mary Evelyn (FORD)
  240
CODY, James 51
COE, Abm., Sr. 312

COE, Cassandra
  (JONES) 146
Greenbury 51
Jemima 286
Job 51
Mark 51, 332
Mary (SEARS) 51
William 51
COERBY, James 51
COEXBY, James 51
COFFEE, (?) 51
COFIELD, Jacob 51
COGGINS, Sylvester
  51
COHOLEN, Jerry 51
COLBERTSON, William
  64
COLE, Abraham 52,
  101, 258
Abraham, Jr. 52
Aliese 40
Ann 52
Belinda 52, 258
Cassandra 100
Cecil (GIST) 101
Christopher 52
Christopher, Jr. 52
Edith 52, 169
Eleanor 52
Ezekiel 52
George 52, 303
Harriet 15
Henry 52
Hoshier 52
James 52
John 52, 303
Lewis Robert 101
Mordecai 52, 329
Patrick 52
Philip 52
Priscilla 167
Richard 52
Ruth 52
Salathiel 52
Samuel 52
Sarah 52
Sarah (HARRYMAN)
  101
Thomas 52, 52
Vincent 52
William 52
COLEGATE, Elizabeth
  (GUYTON) 114
John 52, 114, 325
Richard 52, 307,
  325

COLEGATE, Thomas 52
COLEING, John 53
COLEMAN, Duncan 52
George Stibbonds 53
John 53
Matthew 53
Patrick 53
COLEN, John 53
Thomas 53
COLGATE, Cassandra
  Cockey (DEYE) 202
Colgate Deye 202
Richard 304
Thomas 202
COLGROVE, William 53
COLINS, James 53
COLLETT, Daniel 53
Moses 53
COLLINS, Ames 53
Charity 53
David 53
Elizabeth Franklin
  (MC FEE) 53
James 53
John 53
Joseph 53
Michael 53
Sarah Elizabeth
  (ANDERSON) 53
Thomas 53
Timothy 53
William 53
COLLIS, William 53
COLLUMBER, Thomas 39
COLMAN, Duncan 52
George Stibbonds 53
John 53
Matthew 53
Patrick 53
COLOSTON, Jeremiah
  53
Joseph 53
Joshua 53
William 53
COLROE, Stephen 53
COLSON, John 53
COLVIN, Philip 53,
  305
COMBS, Coleman 54
Eleanor 54
Elizabeth (SUTHARD)
  54
John 54
Lewis 54
Mary 54
Mary (PIERCE) 54

353

354

355

357

DEARLY, Jacob 69
DEARMOND, Neal 69
DEAVE, Emanuel Kent
  70
DEAVEN, John 69
DEAVER, Ann 69
  Elizabeth (SHIPLEY)
  70
  Elizabeth Ann 70
  Emanuel Kent 69
  Honor (WORTH) 69
  Job Hunt 69
  John 69, 70, 138,
  330
  John Hunt 69
  John Talbot 69
  Margaret 131
  Margaretta Hopkins
  69
  Miriam 69
  Miriam Hunt 69
  Norah (WORTH/WROTH)
  69
  Onorah 69
  Philip 70
  Phoebe 70
  Richard 70
  Sarah (HUNT) 69, 70,
  138
  Susanna 69
  Susannah (TALBOT) 69
  William 70
DEAVERS, Martha 266
DEBURY, John 70
DECAMP, Peter 70
DECKER, Frederick 70,
  313, 329, 333
  Henry 70
DEEMS, Frederick 69,
  324
DEETS, Catherine 272
  Michael 70
DEGGAN, George 70
DEGGON, George 70
DEITCH, John
  Batholomew 70
DELAND, Roger 70
DELANEY, William 70,
  331
DELANY, William 70
DELCHER, Chris'n 322
  Christian 70
  John 70, 321, 322
DELONG, Bartholomew
  71
DELWORTH, William 71

DEMIER, Andrew 71
  Edward 71
DEMMETT, Dansbury 71
  James 71
  Stansbury 71
  William 71
DEMMITT, John 71
  Stansbury 71
  William 71
DEMMRIST, John 71
DEMPSEY, Pearce 71
DEMPSYE, Luke 71
DENCHOWER, George 71
DENMEAD, Eliza 267
DENNEHAUGH, George
  71, 308
DENNERIVAY, William
  71
DENNIS, Daniel 71
  Joseph 71
  William 71
DENNY, George 71
DENOS, Augustine
  Rouxelin 71
DENTON, John 71
DERE, Isaac 71
DESPEAUX, Frances
  Ann 83
DETTOR, Elizabeth
  (CHAPMAN) 45
  John 45
DEU, Robert 78
DEVAUGHN, Priscilla
  216
DEVELIN, Patrick 71,
  332
DEVER, John 309
DEVILBESS, George 71
DEVILBISS, Elizabeth
  (STANSBURY) 258
  Samuel 258
DEVO, Henry 71
DEW, Ann (Nancy) 258
  Charity 53
  John 71
DEWITT, Thomas 324
DEWS, Edward 71
DEYE, Cassandra
  Cockey 202
  Penelop 72
  Thomas Cockey 72
DICAS, John 72
DICK, Frederick 72,
  332
  Heart 72
  Jacob 72, 332

DICK, William 72
DICKENSON, B. 324
  Brittingham 72, 330
  George 72
  W. 72
DICKESON, Thomas 72
DICKINSON, (?) 324
DICKMAN, William 72
DICKS, Daniel 72
  Jerda 72
DICKSON, John 72
  Thomas 72
  William 73
DIDIER, Henry 72
  Maria (GIBSON) 99
DIFFEND'R, Daniel
  322
DIFFENDAFFER, D. 321
  M. 321
DIFFENDEFFER, Daniel
  72
  Mil J. 72
DILL, John 72
  Mary Ellen
  (FONDERON) 72
DILLEN, Moses 72
DILLIN, Roger 72
DILLING, Thomas 72
DILLINGS, James 72
DILLON, Andrew 72
DIMIT, John 72
DIMMETT, James 72
  Rachel (SINKLER) 72
DIMMITT, James 72
  Joshua 267
  Rachel (SINKLER) 72
  Sarah (TALBOTT) 267
DIMOT, John 72
DINDENBERGER, George
  303
DINE, John 73
DISNEY, Ezekiel, Jr.
  73
  Ezekiel, Sr. 73
DISTEL, Samuel 73
DITTO, Abraham 73
  George 73
  Henry 73
DIVERS, Annianias 73
  Christopher 73
  Denton 242
  Lucy (SHILEY) 242
DIXON, John 73
  John, Jr. 73
  Joseph 73
  Rachel (PARKS) 205

358

DIXON, Raphel 205
  William 73
DIXSON, Amos 73
  John 73
  John, Sr. 73
  Thomas 73
DOBBIN, Elizabeth
  (SWAN) 265
  George Washington,
  Jr. 265
  Robert A. 265
DOBSON, Harry 197
  John 73
DOCHTERMAN, Michael
  73
DOCKER, John 73
DODD, John 73, 325
DODGE, Samuel 73
DODSON, John 73, 322
  Michael 73
DOER, Henry 251
  Katherine (SMITH)
  251
DOICE, Dennis 73
DOLTON, Edward 73
DOMER, Christian 73
DONAL, John 73
DONALD, William 73
DONALDSON, Alexander
  73, 334
  James Lowry 60
  Jane 60
  John 73
  Mary (COX) 60
DONALLY, Michael 74
DONANS, Dennis 73
DONAVIN, John 74
DONAWAY, John 73
DONER, Christian 73
DONNELL, Elizabeth
  265
DONNELLAN, Amos 74
  Thomas 74
DONNOHO, John W. 74,
  303
DONNOVIN, Timothy 74
DONOGHUE, Daniel 74
DONOGUE, Daniel 331
DONOHOE, Bartholomew
  74, 306
  Daniel 74, 306
  John W. 74
DONOHUE, Bartholomew
  74
DONOLAN, Thomas 74

DONOVAN, Ann (COLE)
  52
  James 74
  John 74
  R. 197
  Thomas 52
  Timothy 74, 306,
  331
DOONE, Henry 74
DORAN, Barnaba 74
DORCY, John G. 287
DOREN, Michael 74
DORLING, Manns 74
DORNBAUGH, John 74
DORSET, Thomas 74
DORSEY, (?) 74, 320
  Achsah 76, 203, 204
  Andrew 76
  Anne 74
  Araminta (CUMMINS)
  75
  Ariana 203, 253
  Arnold 74
  Basil 253
  Bazel John 74
  Betsy (OWINGS) 204
  Catey 76
  Catherine 74, 76
  Catherine (WELSH)
  75
  Charles 74, 75, 76
  Clementine
  (IRELAND) 76
  Daniel Horatio 76
  Deborah 227
  Deborah (MACCUBIN)
  75
  Dorothea (HAINS) 74
  Edward 75, 76
  Edward John 76
  Eleanor Elizabeth
  (WATKINS) 284
  Elias 75
  Elinor 203
  Elisha 75
  Elizabeth 76, 203,
  227, 227
  Elizabeth (BATTY)
  16
  Elizabeth (INGRAM)
  75
  Elizabeth Keene
  (HOME) 75
  Ely 75, 328
  Eudocia 76

DORSEY, Ezekiel
  Salisbury 76
  Ezekiel Salisbury
  II 76
  Frances 76
  Frances (HUGHES) 76
  Francis 74
  Gilus 75
  Harold 75
  Henry 76
  Hezekiah 75
  James 75
  James Ireland 76
  Jane (ALLISON) 75
  Jane (CONNOR) 75
  Jesse 75, 333
  John 75, 76
  John Worthington
  307
  John, Capt. 204
  Joseph 75
  Joshua 75, 307
  Joshua Worthington
  75, 284
  Julia Elizabeth
  (ADAMS) 76
  Lakin 75
  Larkin 75
  Leaven 75
  Levin 75
  Louisa 76
  Lucretia 76
  Lydia 76
  Marcellina 76
  Margaret 76
  Martha (GAITHER) 76
  Mary 76, 227, 253
  Mary (GALE) 76
  Mary (SLADE) 75
  Mary (TALBOT) 75
  Mary (WALTERS) 74
  Mary Mitchelmore
  (MC FEE) 76
  Michael 74
  Nancy 75
  Nathan 76
  Nicholas 74, 76
  Nicholas, Jr. 76
  Orlando 76
  Orlando Griffith 76
  Priscila Ridgely
  293
  Providence 154
  Rachel 74, 76, 161
  Rachel (ODELL) 74
  Rebecca 76, 226

359

DORSEY, Richard 76, 323, 331
Robert 76
Ruth 75, 284
Ruth (TODD) 74, 76
Samuel 75, 76
Sarah 74, 75, 76
Sarah (GRIFFITH) 74, 76
Sarah (WORTHINGTON) 253
Sophia 107
Sophia (OWINGS) 76
Susannah 155
Susannah (BROOKES) 76
Thomas 76
Vachel 16, 76
William 76
Zachariah 75
DORSON, Isaac 76, 322
William 76
DOUGELS, Thomas 76
DOUGHERTY, Dennis 66
Edward 66
DOUGHLAS, William 77
DOUGLAS, Archibald 76
George 77
George Sewel 330
James 77
John 77
Robert 54
Sarah (COMBS) 54
William 77
DOUGLASS, George S. 315
George Sewell 77
James 77
William 77
DOVE, Josmas Duke 77
DOWDE, Charles 77
DOWDGE, Josiah 77
DOWLES, Samuel 77
DOWLEY, Francis 77
DOWNES, Joseph 77
Thomas 77
William 77
DOWNEY, Bartholomew 77
Edwin 204
Frederick 77
Matilda (OWINGS) 204
Thomas 77
Walter 77
DOYLE, Catherine 18
Dennis 77

DOYLE, Elizabeth 78
Francis 77
John 77
Jonathan 77
Margaret 77
Mary 78
Richard 77, 78
Sarah 77
Thomas 78, 307, 308
William 77
DRAKE, Francis 78
DRAPER, John 78
DRAVER, Mary 32
DRAVES, Mary 32
DRAWBACH, Abr. 78, 322
DREWITT, William 78
DRISCOLL, Jeremiah 78
DRISKILL, Jeremiah 78
John 78
Timothy 78
DRUMBO, Adam 78
John 78
DRURY, Sarah 59
DUCAN, Arthur 78
DUCKE, George 78, 321
DUCY, William 78
DUDLEY, Elizabeth (GILBERT) 99
John 78
Levi 99
DUE, Isaac 78
Robert 78
DUER, Andrew Adgate 296
DUESBURY, James 78
DUFF, Brian 78, 310
DUFFEY, Alex 78
DUFFY, Jno. 78
Margarett (PHARR) 78
DUGAN, Authur 78
Cumberland 78
DUGGAN, Paul 78
DUGLAS, James 77
DUGLASS, John 77
DUKE, Christopher 78
DUKEHART, Henry 78
Samuel 78
Valerius 78
DUKES, Christopher 78
William 79

DUKHART, Henry 78
DULANY, Daniel 79
Edward 79
Elizabeth 246
DUMENT, Elizabeth 227
DUMESTE, Elizabeth 227
DUMNICK, John 79
DUNACK, John 79
DUNAVAN, James 79
DUNBAR, Joseph 79
William Joseph 79
DUNCAN, Ann (SHIPLEY) 79
Benjamin 79
Elizabeth 160
Francis 79
John 79
Johnsie 79
Julia A. (GORE) 79
Patrick 79
William 79, 303
DUNGAN, Benjamin 79
Mary 35
DUNHAM, Lewis 79
DUNKIN, William 79, 321
DUNLAP, James 79
DUNN, Arthur 79
Henry 79
John 79
Samuel 79
DUNNEVAN, John 79
DUNNOCK, John 79, 311
DUNNOCKS, John 79
DUNSON, William 79
DUNSTER, John 79
DUNSYRE, William 79
DURBIN, Christopher 79
DURDIN, Thomas 79
DURHAM, Anne (TOLLEY) 79
Elizabeth 56
Margaret (BRUCE) 79
William 79
DUTER, Peter 80
DUTRO, George 80
DUVAL, George 80
DUVALL, Elizabeth 227
George 309
DUVAULL, George 80
DWEY, Samuel 80

DWYER, Hugh 80
DYCUS, John 80
DYER, William 80
EAGAN, Hugh 80
EAGER, Ruth 135
EAGLESTON, Elizabeth 110
EAGLESTONE, Abraham 80
  Charity 1
  Charity (JOHNES) 1
  Henry 1
  Jonathan 80
  Mary 1
  Salathiel (BIDDISON) 1
  Sarah (BIDDISON) 1
EARBAUGH, Adam 80, 314
EARLE, James 80
  John 80
EARNS, John 80
EARP, Ananias 80
  Ann (READ) 80
  Daniel 80
  Eleanor 80
  Eleanor (MC KINSEY) 80
  Elizabeth 80
  Honour 80
  Joseph 80
  Joshua 80
  Mary 80
  Nancy 80
  William 80
EATON, William 80
EAVENSON, Thomas 80
EBAUGH, George 46
  Sarah (CHENOWETH) 46
EBBERT, Andrew 80
  George 80
  Henry 80
  John 80
  Joseph 80
EBER, Joseph 80
EBERHARD, Martin 80
EBERT, Comfort (WONN) 297
  Philip 80
ECK, Elizabeth 258
ECKERT, Michael 80
ECKISTER, Thomas 80
EDGERLY, Edward 197
EDMONDS, John 80
EDMONDSTONE, George 80

EDMONSON, James 80
EDWARDS, Benjamin 81
  Charles 81
  Edward 81
  Elizabeth (CHILTON) 81
  Isaac 81
  James 81
  Jemima (WELSH) 81
  John 81
  Mary (CMBS) 54
  Richard 81
  Ruth (STANSBURY) 258
  William 81
EDWRDS, Henry 81
EHERT, Michael 81
EHRMAN, Johannes 81
EICHELBERGER, Barnet 81, 330
EIDER, Anne (DORSEY) 74
  Owen 74
EINSLER, Felerious 81
EISELL, John 81
ELBERT, Elizabeth (SUDLER) 81
  John L., Jr. 81
ELDER, Anne (DORSEY) 76
  Elijah 81
  Elizabeth 101, 103
  Ely 81
  John 81
  Nancy (DORSEY) 76
  Owen 76
ELLER, Nicholas 81
ELLICOTT, George 81
  John 81
ELLIIOTT, William 81
ELLIN, Frederick 81
ELLIOTT, Arthur 81
  Elizabeth 81
  Elizabeth (ATKINSON) 81
  George 7, 81
  James, Jr. 81
  James, Sr. 81
  Jemima 81, 171
  John 81, 82
  Joseph 82
  Karenhappuck 81
  Kezia 81
  Keziah (WEBB) 82
  Mary 81

ELLIOTT, Mary (WEEKS) 81
  Mary Ellen (ATKINSON) 81
  Michael 81
  Samuel 82
  Sarah 81
  Susanna 81
  Theresa (ANDERSON) 7
  Thomas 81, 82
  William 82
  William A. 81
ELLIS, Henry 82
  John 82
  Nicholas 82
  Obediah 82
  William 82
ELLOTT, Mary (PEARCE) 208
ELMS, Stephen 82
ELSEROTE, John 82
ELTON, Thomas 82
ELZEY, Arnold, Sr. 82
EMBERT, Ruth 224
EMICH, Phillip 82
EMICK, Phillip 82
EMMERSON, Mary (SHAW) 240
EMMET, Thomas 82, 321
EMMETT, David 82
EMMIT, David 82, 322
EMMITT, David 82
  Thomas 82
  Thos. 322
EMORY, Marianna (WINDER) 296
  Thomas 296
ENDERS, Jacob 82
ENGLAND, Abraham 82
  Benjamin 82, 308
ENGLGISH, Isaac 82
ENGLISH, Robert 82
ENLOES, Abraham 81, 82
  Henry 81, 82
  James 82
  Jemima (ELLIOTT) 81
  John 82
  Mary (ELLIOTT) 81
  Sophia 57
  William 82
ENLOWES, Henry 82
  William 82

362

363

FORD, Thomas Cockey
  Deye 91, 316
  Thomas, Sr. 91
  William 90, 91
FOREMAN, Leonard 91
FOREPAUGH, William
  91, 315
FORGENSON, Thorles 91
FORGESON, William 91
FORKINBRIDGE, Richard
  91
FORMAN, John 91
FORRELL, Steven 273
FORREST, Carrick 91
FORRESTER, Alexander
  91, 306
  Cornelius 91, 306
  Jno. 306
  John 91
FORSTER, James 91
  Sam 91
FORT, Loyd 91, 115
  Samuel 91
FORTT, Elizabeth 90
FORTUNE, James 91
FOSSETT, Henry 91
FOSTER, Armanelah
  (PRIBBLE) 216
  Benedict 91
  George 91
  James 91, 312, 330
  John 91, 216
  Joseph 92, 326
  Robert 92
  William 92
FOSTT, Elizabeth 90
FOUGHT, Elizabeth
  (PRIBBLE) 216
  James 216
FOUNTAIN, Collier 92
FOUSE, John 92
FOWBLE, Frederick 92
  Jacob 92
  Mary 215
  Melchior 92
  Michael 92
  Peter 92
FOWLER, James 92
  Jno. 92
  Joseph 92
  Mary (OZBORNE) 92
  Michael 92
  Susannah 209
  Thomas 92
FOX, James 92
  Thomas 92

FOY, John 92
  Michael 92
FRAMPTON, Elizabeth
  278
FRANCEWAY, John 92
FRANCH, William 93
FRANCHER, Barnett 92
FRANCIS, Ann 271
  William 92
FRANCISCUS, George
  92
FRANK, Catherine 134
  Peter 92, 94
  Philip 92, 94
FRANKEN, John 92
FRANKFORTER, John 92
FRANKLIN, Benjamin
  93
  Charles 93
  Elizabeth 93
  James 93
  Kitty 131
  Ruth (HAMMOND) 93
  Sarah 93
  Thomas 93
  Thomas Heath, Jr.
  93
FRANTZ, Abraham 93,
  314
FRAZER, John 93
FRAZIER, Daniel 93
  Henrietta M. 93
  Penelope (JOHNSON)
  93
  Priscilla 93
  Samuel 93
  William 93
FRE-LADNER, John 93
FREBURGER, Henry G.
  32
  Sarah (HODGES) 32
FREEBIRD, Julia A. 5
FREEBORN, Mary 273
FREELAND, John 93
FREEMAN, Edward 93
FRENCH, Annie
  (GIBSON) 93
  James 93, 321
  James Ormsby 93
  Lucy Ann (CULLY)
  64, 93
  Mary Elizabeth
  (WOODS) 93
  Other 93
  Otto 93
  Robert Armistead 93

FRENCH, Thomas 93
  William 64, 93
FRENSHAM, Henry 93
FREYMILLER, Jacob 93
  Joseph 93
FRICK, Harriott 94
  Peter 94, 319
FRIFOGLE, Stophel 94
FRISBY, Eleanor
  (MERRYMAN) 183
  James Edwards 183
FRISH, Francis 94
FRIZZEL, Absolom 94
FRIZZELL, Abram 94
  Jacob 94
  John 94
  John, Jr. 94
FROEPATH, William
  94, 308
FROG, Austin 94
FROLICK, Christian
  94
FRONK, Peter 92, 94
  Philip 92, 94
FROST, Rebecca 214
FRYMILLER, Jacob 314
FUCHS, Robert 94
FUCKS, Robert 94
FUGATE, Edward 10,
  94
  Elizabeth (BACON)
  10
  Martin 94
FUHRMAN, Daniel 94
FULFORD, Eleanor
  (BODKIN) 94
  Hannah (VICKERY) 94
  John 94
FULLER, John 94, 332
  Nicholas 94
  William 94
FULLUM, George 94
FUNDER, Peter 94
FURBER, Thomas 94,
  308, 321
FURLONG, Benjamin 94
FURNEY, Peter 94,
  321
FURNIVAL, Alexander
  94
  Elizabeth 95
FURNY, John 95
FUSHE, C. 95
FUSHL, G. 95
FUSS, William 95
GADD, John 95

364

GADD, Nathan 95
  Robinson 95
  Thomas 95
GADDES, James 95
GAGAN, James 95
  William 95
GAGGEN, James 95
  William 95
GAILBRAITH, William
  95
GAIN, Thomas 95, 320
  William 95
GAINER, Hugh 95
GAINSFORD, Michael 95
GAITHER, Ann 119
  Joseph 95
  Martha 76
GALA, Esther (LE
  PAGE) 159
GALBRAITH, William
  95, 328, 330
GALE, Alexander 95
  Edward 95
  George, Dr. 95
  George, Sr. 95
  Mary 76
GALL, Michael 95
GALLOWAY, Ann Taylor
  (WALLER) 96
  Aquila 95
  James 96
  John 96
  John Nicholson 96
  Mary (NICHOLSON) 96
  Mephyteca 229
  Moses 96
  Pamelia (Parnelia)
  (OWINGS) 96
  Priscilla 96, 277
  Thomas 96
  Thomas, Jr. 96
  William 96, 305
  William, Jr. 96
GALVIN, David 96
GAMBLE, Mary 96
  William 96
GAMBRILL, Augustine
  291
GAMMIL, Mary 96
  William 96
GANETSON, Job 97
GANSE, Adam 96
GANTS, Stofel 96, 320
GANTZ, A. 321
  Adam 96, 322
  John 96

GARDINER, Luke 306
GARDINER - See
  GARDNER
GARDNER, Clement 96
  George 96
  James 96
  John 96
  Luke 96, 308
  Mary 96, 106
  Priscilla 30, 96
  Priscilla
  (HAMILTON) 96
  Rachel 96
  Thomas 96
  William 96, 97
  William, Jr. 97
GAREY, John 97
GARLETS, Henry 97
GARNER, Clement 96
GARRETSN, Job 305
GARRETSON, Cornelius
  97, 308
  Job 97
  Martha 298
  Mary 273
GARRETT, Jesse 97
  William 97
GARRISON, C. 321
  Cornelius 97, 322
  David 97
GARRITSON, Cornelius
  97
  David 97
GARRITY, Jno. 97
GARROCK, Samuel 314
GARTEL, Allena 104
GARTNER, George 97
  Michael 97
GARTS, Charles 97
  John 97
  Peter 97
GARTZ, Charles 97
  John 97
  Peter 97
GARVIN, John 97
GARVIS, Benjamin 97
GASH, Ann 97
  Benjamin 97
  Benjamin Wesley 97
  Conduce 97
  Cornjuice 97
  Elizabeth 97
  Frank 97
  Frederick 97
  Godfrey 97
  Nicholas 97

GASH, Philip, Rev.
  97
  Proseliah (BURGIN)
  97
  Richard 97
  Ruth (TAYLOR) 97
  Sarah 97
  Thomas 97
  Thomas Custeman 97
GASSAWAY, Brice John
  98
  Dinah (WARFIELD) 98
  Elizabeth 135
  John 98, 197
  Rachel 203
GATCH, Benjamin 268
  Ruth (TAYLOR) 268
  Sarah 268
GATCH - See GASH
GATCOMB, John 98
GATES, Eliza 144
GATHING, Robert 98
GATTING, Robert 98
GAVEN, Roger 98
GAYPOTT, Martin 98
GEABHART, Mitchell
  98
GEDDES, David 98
  George 98
  Sarah Jean 190
GEFF, Thomas 98
GEFFARDE, James 98
GENT, Thomas 98
GEOGHEGAN, Ambm. 104
  Basil 104
GEORGE, Caleb 98
  Edmund 98
  Peter 98
GERER, John
  Valentine 98
GERHART, Adam 98
GERMAN, Abraham 98
  Benjamin 98
  John 98, 305
GEROCK, John 98
  Samuel 98
  Seigfred 98
GERROCK, John 98
  John S. 98
  Samuel 98
  Seigfred 98
GESSOP, Nicholas 143
  William, Jr. 143
GETRO, Joseph 330
GETTER, Stofel 98
GETZER, Henry 98

365

366

GIST, James 101
Jemima 101
John 101, 103, 325
John Elder 101
Joseph 101, 103,
  307, 313
Joshua 101, 102,
  313, 325, 329
Joshua Howard 101
Mary (STERRETT) 101,
  259
Mary McCall 101
Mordecai 101, 102
Mordecai, Gen. 259
Nathaniel 102
Owen 101
Penelope Deye
  (COCKEY) 102
Rachel 101, 102
Rachel (DAWSON) 101
Rebecca (HAMMOND)
  101
Rezin Hammond 101
Richard 101, 102
Ruth (BOND) 103
Sarah (HARVEY) 101
Sarah (HOWARD) 102
Sarah Harvey 203
States 101
Susanna 102
Susannah (COCKEY)
  101, 102
Thomas 101, 102,
  103, 307, 312, 313,
  329
Thomas, Jr. 102, 329
Violetta 101, 103
Violetta (HOWARD)
  101, 103
William 101, 103
Zipporah (MURRAY)
  101
GITNERE, George 103,
  306
GITTINGER, Henry 103
John 103
GITTINGS, Anne 103
Archibald 103
Benjamin 103
Clarke 103
Eleanor 103
Elizabeth 103
Elizabeth (BOSLEY)
  103
Elizabeth (BUCHANAN)
  103

GITTINGS, Elizabeth
  (REDGRAVE) 103
Hannah 103
Hannah (CLARK) 103
Harriet (STERRET)
  103
James 103, 305,
  307, 313, 327
Jesse 103
John 103
Margaret 44, 103
Mary 103
Mary (LEE) 103
Polly (STERRET) 103
Richard 103
Sarah 103
Susannah 103
Thomas 103
GIVIN, John 103
GLADMAN, Barbara 103
Cassandra 103
John 103
Michael, Jr. 103
Michael, Sr. 103
Nancy 103
Rachel 103
Rebecca 103
Thomas 103
GLANCEY, Araham 103
GLARE, Thomas 103
GLASGOW, Samuel 103
GLAVE, Thomas 103
GLEESON, Thomas 103
GLESSIN, Thomas 103
GLEVES, Thomas 104
GLISAN, Thomas 103
GLISSON, Catherine
  214
GLOOCH, Elias 104,
  320
GLOREY, William 104
GLORY, William 104
GLOVER, Samuel 104
GOAN, Mary 233
GODDARD, Ann 219
Mary Katherine 104
William 104
GODFREY, Edmund 104
William 104
GODMAN, Allena
  (GARTEL) 104
William 104
GODSGRACE, William
  104
GOFF, Richard 104
GOFFER, Richard 104

GOGHEGAN, Ambm. 104
Basil 104
GOLD, Robert 104
William 104
GOLDEN, Walter 104
GOLDSBOROUGH,
  Araminta Sidney
  (WINDER) 166
Eleanor Doll (LUX)
  166
Elizabeth Tench
  (TILGHMAN) 271
Mark 104
Nicholas VI 271
Robert III 166
Robert, Dr. 166
GOLDSBURY, John 104
Stephen 104
GOLDSMITH, Thomas
  104
GOLLIER, John 104
GOLSON, Ann 141
GOODFELLOW, William
  104
GOODING, (?), Dr.
  326
Nancy 131
GOODMAN, John 104
GOODSON, William 104
GOODWIN, (?), Dr.
  326
Abby (LEVY) 105
Achsa 291
Joseph 104
Loyd 105
Lyde, Dr. 105
Robert Morris 105
William 105
GOOSE, Adam, Sr. 105
Christopher 105
GORANE, James 105
GORCHIN, Robert 105
GORDON, Charles 105
Enoch 105, 315
Francis 105
Isaac Mount 105
Issacco M. 315
James 105
John 105, 317, 319
William 105
GORE, Andrew 105
Christian 105, 325
Christopher 105
George 105
Jacob 105
John 105

367

368

GREEN, Benjamin 109
  Clement 109
  Eleanor 234
  Elisha 109
  Elizabeth (BOERING) 109
  Elizabeth (EAGLESTON) 110
  George 109
  Greenbury 109
  Henry 109
  Isaac 109
  James 109
  Job 109
  John 109
  Joseph 109
  Josias 109
  Mashack 109
  Moses 109
  Nathan 109
  Nathaniel 109
  Nicholas 109
  Peter 109
  Rachel 109
  Richard 109
  Samuel 109
  Shadrach 109, 305
  Temperance 109
  Thomas 109, 308
  Vincent 110, 305
  William 110
GREENFIELD, James 110
  McCogy 310
  McCogy(?) 110
GREENLAND, Moses 110
GREENWAY, Joseph 110
GREENWELL, Jacob 110
GREENWOOD, Mary 262
  Thomas 110, 328
GREER, James 110
  Moses 110
GREGORY, John 110
  Robert 110
GREIST, Mary 112
GREU, John 110
GREW, John 110
GREY, James 110
  Joseph 110
GREYBILL, Philip 108, 314
GRIEST, I. 307
  Isaac 112
GRIFFEE, Elisha 13
  Martha Ann (POOL) 13
  Owen 110
  Richard 110

GRIFFIN, Charles 110
  Daniel 110
  Elizabeth D. 208
  Ignatius 110
  John 110
  John, Jr. 110
  Mary Ann (WILKINSON) 292
  Philip 110
  Rebecca (KELLY) 110
  Thomas 110
  Thomas, Jr. 110
GRIFFIS, Abraham 110
  Edward 110
  Hugh 110
  John 111, 327
  John Stone 111
  Kensey 111
  Kinsey 111, 327
  Nancy (MOORE) 111
GRIFFITH, (?)goe 111, 320
  Abraham 111
  Ann (WELLS) 286
  Benjamin 111, 309
  Benjamin C. 45
  Catherine 111
  Eleanor Ann 203
  Elizabeth (ENSOR) 111
  Evan 111
  George 111
  Greenbury 111
  Hannah 84
  Henry 111
  James 111
  James, Jr. 111
  James, Sr. 111
  John 111
  John, Dr. 111
  Jonathan 111
  Katherine (HOWARD) 111
  Kensey 111
  Kinsey 111
  Mary 111
  Mary (RIGGS) 111
  Nathan 111, 112
  Orlando 111
  Rebecca 45
  Rebecca (CHAPMAN) 45
  Richard 112
  Ruth (RIGGS) 111
  Sarah 74, 76, 171, 286

GRIFFITH, Sarah (MC BEE) 111
  William 112, 286
GRIFIN, Joseph 292
GRIGGORY, James 112
GRIGSON, John 112
GRIMES, Anthony 112
  James 112, 201
  John 112, 320
  Mary 131
  Nicholas 112
  Reason 112
  Sarah (OURSLER) 201
  Terrence 112
  W. 112
  William 112
GRIMSHAW, Edmund 112
  Edward 112
GRIMSHEAR, Richard 112
GRISLER, Christopher 112, 319
GRIST, George Gilpin 112
  Isaac 112, 309
  Mary 112
GRIZZELLE, Mary 225
GROOM, Morton 112, 318
GROOMBRIDGE, James 112
GROOME, Charles 113
GROOMRINE, Abraham 113
GROOVER, Benjamin 113
  George 113
  Josias 113
  Samuel 113
  William 113
GROSH, Charlotte 113
  Christiana (RAYMER/ROEMER) 113
  John Conrad 113
  Michael 113
GROSS, Michael 113
GROVER, Mary 4
  William 113, 305
GROVES, Ezekiel 113
  James 113
  Thomas 113
GROWLEY, Michael 113
GRUNDY, Elizabeth C. 99
  Emily 99
  John 113

369

GRUNT, Catharine 50
GUDGEON, Sutton 113, 305
  Thomas 113, 332
GULLEHAN, John 113
GULLIVER, Thomas 113
GUTHRIE, James 113
GUTRELL, Joseph 113
GUTRIDGE, Edward 113
  John 113
GUTRO, Ann 113
  Edward 113
  John 113
  Joseph 113
  Martin 113
GUTTERO, Edward 113
GUTTEROUGH, Martin 113, 308
GUYTON, Abraham 114
  Benjamin, Jr. 114
  Benjamin, Sr. 114
  Catherine 114
  Elizabeth 114
  Henry 114
  Isaiah 114
  John 114
  Nellie 114
  Priscilla (JACKSON) 114
  Rebecca 114
  Ruth 114, 284
  Sarah 114
  Underwood 114
  Vinson 114
GWIN, Hugh 114
  John 114
  Julia (STEEL/STULL) 114
GWYNN, Robert 114, 332
HAASS, Christian 114
HADLEY, John 114
HADON, William 114
HAEMMERLIN, Gerret 114
HAGAN, Charles 114
  Henry 114
  Hugh 114, 308
  James 114
HAGER, Francis 114
  John 171
  Mary (MARSH) 171
HAGERTY, John 114
HAGUE, Arthur 114
HAHN, John 114
  Paul 114

HAHN, Peter 114
  Tochim 114
  Yochim 114
HAIL, David 115
  Nicholas 115
  Stephen 116
HAILE, Deborah 116
  George 329
  John 116
  Joshua 116
  Mary (PARSONHAM) 116
  Matthew 116
  Nicholas 329
  Rebecca 116
  Rebecca (MAYS) 116
  Rebecca (ROBINSON) 116
  Thomas 116
HAILE - See also HALE
HAILES, George 115
HAILEY, Thomas 116
  William 116
HAILL, Nicholas 115
HAILTON, Eliza 118
  James B. 118
HAINES, Sarah 180
HAINS, Anthony 114
  Catherine 74
  Dorothea 74
  John 114
  Michael 74
HALDER, Charles 114
HALE, Amon 114, 115
  Amon C. 115
  Charles 115
  David 115
  Elizabeth 115
  G. 316
  George 115, 116
  George, Jr. 115
  Hannah (BAILEY) 116
  Henry 115, 316
  James 115, 318
  Jesse W. 115
  John 115
  Joseph 115
  Joshua 115
  Martha 115
  Mary 115
  Matthew 116
  Meshack 115
  Micajah B. 115
  Nathan 115, 116, 316

HALE, Neale, Jr. 115
  Neale, Sr. 115
  Neil, Jr. 115
  Neil, Sr. 115
  Nicholas 115, 316
  Nicholas, Jr. 316
  Philip 116
  Prisse 115
  Richard 115
  Robert G. 115
  Ruth 115
  Stephen 116
  Tilley 116
  Tilly 116
  Tully 116
  William 116
HALES, Charles 115
HALEY, Thomas 116
HALKINS, John 116
HALL, Ann (SPICER) 117
  Aquila 332
  Aquila, Col. 220
  Aquilla 116
  Aron 116
  Banneke (LEE) 156
  Banneker (LEE) 156
  Benedict W. 117
  Blanche Carvill 135
  Caleb 116, 309, 317, 319
  Catharine (GRIFFITH) 111
  Charles 116
  Charlotte 220
  Diana (SPICER) 117
  Edith (COLE) 52
  Edward 116
  Eleanor Brooke 220
  Elihu 116
  Elisha 116
  Elizabeth (DORSEY) 76
  Elizabeth (GORSUCH) 106
  Fanny (LEE) 156
  George Henry 219
  Hannah 117
  Hannah E. 117
  Isaac 116
  James 116
  Jane (SMITH) 117
  Job R. 111
  John 116, 117, 317, 329, 333
  Jonathan 117

372

HAYNES, Anthony 125
HAYNON, Thomas 125
HAYS, Abraham 125
  Anna 215
  James 125
  John 125
  William 125, 317,
    317, 319
HAYWOOD, Joseph 125
HAZLEHURST, Andrew
  218
  Elizabeth G.
    (BILSON) 218
  Frances (PURVIANCE)
    218
  Samuel 218
HAZLETT, Eliza Jane
  12
  Moses, Dr. 125
HEAD, John 125
HEADINGTON, Abel 126
  Eleanor (LEMMON) 157
  Nicholas 126
  Sarah (BOSLEY) 126
  William 126
  Zebulon 126
HEARLY, John 126
HEATON, John 126
HECKMAN, Lornce 126
HEDDINGTON, Abel 126
  William 126
HEDGELY, John 126
HEES, Valentine 126
HEGNET, John 128, 310
HEGNOS, Thomas 126
HELKEN, Aaron 24
  Mary (BOND) 24
HELLAM, Thomas 126
HELLAMS, Sarah 203
HELLAR, Soloman 126
HELLEN, Bazil 126
  David 126
  William 126
HELLER, Frederick 126
HELLING, William 126
HELM, Ann 126
  Elizabeth 126
  James 126
  Joseph 126
  Leonard 126
  Mary 126
  Mary (HORSEMAN) 126
  Mayberry 126
  William 126
HELMS, George 126,
  321

HENDERSON, Ann 203
  Henry 126
  James 126
  Janet 161
HENDON, Benjamin 171
  Henry 126
  Richard 126
  Sophia (MARSH) 171
HENDRICKSON, Amos
  126
  James 126
  John 126
  Joseph 127
HENESTOPHEL, Henry
  127
  John 127
HENLEY, George 127
  Peter 127
HENNEGH, Christopher
  127
HENNESSY, Edward 127
  Michael 127
HENREY, Peter 127
HENRY, Isaac 127
  James 127
HERBERT, Jane 34
HERITAGE, Benjamin
  127
HERLIHY, William 127
HERLITY, William 127
HERNE, William 127
HERON, Mary 210
HERRIAN, John 127
HERRICK, Elias 127
HERRING, Eliza
  (HOPKINS) 212
  Henry 212
  James 127
HERRINGTON, Jacob
  127, 332
HERRON, James 127
HESS, Peter 127
HESSY, Henry 127
HESTERLING, Isaac
  127, 318
HEWEITT, Jacob 127
HEWET, Edward 127
HEWITT, Edward 127
  Richard 127
  Robert 127
  Vacht 127
HICK, John 127
HICKEY, Owen 127
  Thomas 127
HICKINSON, William
  127

HICKMAN, Elizabeth
  34
HICKS, Abra 128
  Abraham 128, 312
  Elisha 128
  Henry 128
  Isaac 128
  Jacob 128
  John 128
  Laban 128
  Nehemiah 128
  Richard 128
  Stephen 128
  Thomas 128
HIDE, Henry 128
HIFFHEINS, Margaret
  266
HIGGENBOTHAM, Thomas
  128
HIGGINBOTTOM, Joel,
  Jr. 128
HIGGINS, Dennis 128
  Hugh 128
  John 128
  Mary Jane 64
  Patrick 128
HIGGS, Henry 128
  Lazarus 128
HIGH, George 128
HIGMAN, Edward 128
HIGNOT, John 128
  Thomas 128
HILL, Joseph 128
  Richard 128, 317
  Samuel 128
  Thomas 128
  Walter 128
  William 129
HILLARD, Charles C.
  129
  William 129
HILLEN, Caroline 220
  John 129
  William 129
HILLS, William 129
HILSON, Bengeman 129
HILTON, Abraham 129
  Elinor 129
  James 129
  John 129
  John, Jr. 129
  Joseph 129
  Patience 129
  Priscilla 129
  Sarah 129
  William 129

HILTRHIMER, Francis 129
HINGSTON, Richard 129
HINLEY, George 129
HIOT, Christopher 129
HIPKINS, John 129
HIPSLEY, Amelia (SHIPLEY) 242
Charles 242
Eliza (SHIPLEY) 242
Freedom 242
Mary (SHIPLEY) 242
Samuel 242
HIPWELLS, Benjamin 129
HIRED, (?) 129
HIRON, James 127
HISON, John 129
HISOR, John 129
HISS, Sarah 268
HISSEY, Charles 129
HITE, Jacob 88
HIVER, Richard 129, 316
HOALE, Samuel 129
HOBBES, Mark 129
HOBBS, Amelia 242
Sarah (STEVENS) 260
William 129, 319
HOCKELY, John 129
HOCKLY, John 129
HODGE, John 129
HODGES, John 32, 129
Mary (BRYAN) 32
Sarah 32
HODGKIN, Barbara 223
HODGSON, Mary 301
HOENIG, Christopher 134
HOFFMAN, Catharine 277
Deborah (OWINGS) 203
Jacob 129
Peter 203
W. 129
HOFSTATTER, Henry 129
HOGAN, James 129
HOGEN, Edmund 130
HOGG, James 130
HOKE, Katherine (SMITH) 251
HOKINS, Philip 133
William 133
HOLDEN, Habycuck 130
Richard 130
William 130

HOLDIN, Richard 130
HOLEBROOK, Amos 130
HOLEBROOKE, Edward 130
John 130
HOLLAND, Allen 130
Alpheus 130
Araminta B. 5
Avarilla Day 5
Daniel 130
Eliza 130
Elizabeth 130, 211
Frances 14, 136
Gabriel 130
George 130
Isaac 130
Jacob 130
Mary (SMITH) 130
Mehitable (LARKIN) 211
Otho 211
Sarah (GILBERT) 99
Sarah (HARRIMAN) 130
Solomon 130
Susannah 40
Thomas 99, 130
William 130
HOLLAR, William 130, 322
HOLLES, Mark 130
HOLLIDAY, Christiana Sim 41
Eleanor A. 130
James 130, 303
John Robert 130, 311
Mary Burrows (STONE) 130
Richard 131, 333
HOLLIFIELD, William J. III 282
HOLLINGSWORTH, Ann 131
Elizabeth 131
Elizabeth (IRELAND) 131
Elizabeth Ruth 259
Ellin Maria (MOALE) 131
Francis 131
George 131
Horatio 131
Jacob 131
Jesse 131
John 131

HOLLINGSWORTH,
Juliana 131
Martha A. (KELER) 131
Mary 131
Mary (JACOBS) 131
Mary (YELLOTT) 131
Mary Ann 131
Nancy (GOODING) 131
Parkin 131
Rachel (YELLOTT) 131
Rachel L. (PERKINS) 131
S. 309
Samuel 131, 326
Samuel, Jr. 131
Sarah 99, 131
Sarah (ADAMS) 131
Sinai (RICKETTS) 131
Thomas 131, 326
Valentine, Sr. 131
Zebulon 131
HOLLINS, Mary 27
HOLLOW, Nich 131
Nich. 322
HOLLOWAY, Eleanor (BOWEN) 26
Ella (HOUCK) 134
Katherine 26
Reuben Ross 134
Robert 26
HOLLYDAY, Henry 284
Robert 131
HOLMES, (?) 131, 320
G. 131
Gabriel 10
James 131
Mary (BACON) 10
Thomas 131
William 131
HOLTZ, Nicholas 302
Susannah (ZIMMERMAN) 302
HOLTZMAN, George 70, 131
Margaret (DEAVER) 131
Margaret Hopkins (DEAVER) 69
HOMBEY, Walter 131
HOME, Elizabeth Keene 75
HOMES, James 131
John 131

374

HONEE, James Walter
  131
HOOD, Anne (OWINGS)
  204
  Benjamin 204
  Hannah 204
  James 131, 132
  John 131, 132
  John, Jr. 131
  Kitty (FRANKLIN) 131
  Mary (GRIMES) 131
  Richard 132
  Richard, Jr. 132
  Richard, Sr. 132
  Sarah 260
  Tabitha (WOLF) 131
HOOFMAN, Isaac 132
  Jacob 132
  John 132
  Lawrence 132
  William 132
HOOK, Andrew 132
  Anne (CHANNELL) 132
  Elizabeth 132
  George 132
  Jacob 132
  Joseph 132, 145, 310
  Margaret Ann 132
  Mary 228
  Rutolph 132
  Sophia (JONES) 145
  Susan 132
  Susannah Cockley
    (BOONE) 132
HOOKE, Andrew 132,
  319
  John 132
  Joseph 132
HOOKER, Aquila 132,
  307
  Benjamin 132
  Jacob 132
  John 132
  Richard 132
  Richard, Jr. 133
  Richard, Sr. 133
  Suzanna 140
  Thomas 133
HOOKS, Jacob 133
  Jacob, Jr. 133
  Michael 133
HOOPER, Abraham 133
  Isaac 133
  Jacob 133
  James 133
  James A. 26

HOOPER, Jane (CRAGE)
  133
  John 133, 322
  Katherine
    (HOLLOWAY) 26
  Kezia (ELLIOTT) 81
  Mary (CORD) 133
  Mary (WOOLFORD) 133
  Thomas 133, 316
  William 133, 322
HOOPS, Adam 197
HOOVER, Herbert 134
HOPE, Robert 133
HOPERLY, Frederick
  133
HOPEWELL, Thomas 133
HOPKINS, Daniel 133,
  326
  Eliza 212
  Ezekiel 133
  Gerard 133, 309
  Gerard, Jr. 133
  Gerard, Sr. 133
  Gerrard 120
  Hannah (HAMMOND)
    133
  Jerrard, Sr. 133
  Joseph 133
  Margaret 138
  Mary (HALL) 133
  Rachel 270
  Richard 133
  Roger 133
  Samuel 138
  Sarah 231
HOPPAMAN, William
  133
HOPPER, Mary Louisa
  227
HOPSTATTER, Henry
  133
HORLLEY, John 134
HORN, Thomas 134
HORNE, Thomas 134
HORNER, George 134
HORNIG, Christopher
  134
HORSEMAN, John 126
  Mary 126
HORTON, Ann 240
HOSE, Michael 124,
  320
HOSEL, John 134
HOSHALL, Eleanor 134
  Isaac 134
  Jesse 134

HOSHALL, Mary Ellen
  (HURST) 134
  Sarah (KEITH) 134
HOSIER, Joshua 134
HOSTETTER, Francis
  134
HOUCK, Barbara
  (WOLF) 134
  Barnet 134
  Catherine 134
  Catherine (FRANK)
    134
  Elias 134
  Elizabeth 134
  Ella 134
  George 134
  Jacob 134
  Jacob Wever 214
  Jacob, Dr. 134
  John 134
  Margaret (WISE) 134
  Mary (WOLFE) 134
  Michael 134
  Susan 134
  Susannah Francis
    (PORTER) 214
  William 134
HOUGH, Priscilla 119
HOUK - See HOUCK
HOULT, Thomas 134
HOULTON, Eleanor
  (SOLES) 134
  Elizabeth 134
  John 134, 306
  Mary Ann 134
  Ruth (BRUSBANKS)
    134
  William 134
HOUSE, Filler 134
  Thomas 134
HOUSER, William 134
HOUSTON, Elizabeth 3
  Polly 267
HOW, Edward 134
  Robert 134
  Samuel 134
HOWARD, Agnes Young
  (DAY) 135
  Ann M. 186
  Benjamin 135
  Blanche Carvill
    (HALL) 135
  Burges 135
  Catherine (ROSS)
    135
  Charles 135

375

HOWARD, Charlotte
  (RUMSEY) 135
Cornelia (READ) 135
Cornelius 135
Edward Aquilla 135
Elizabeth 135, 235,
  287
Elizabeth (GASSAWAY)
  135
Elizabeth Gassaway
  136
Elizabeth P. (KEY)
  135
Frances (HOLLAND)
  136
Francis 136
George 135
Henry 135, 311
James 135, 324, 325
Jane (GILMORE) 135
John 135, 136, 306,
  331
John Beale 135, 333
John E. 197, 307,
  330
John Eager 135, 136,
  304
John Eager, Jr. 135
Juliana 135
Juliann 178
Katherine 111
Margaret (CHEW) 135
Margaret
  (FITZGERALD) 136
Margaret (WEST) 135
Margaretta (CHEW)
  135
Martha (TOLLEY) 136
Mary 136
Matthias 135
Parker 135
Prudence (RIDGELY)
  135
Rachel 203, 226
Rebecca (KEY) 135
Richard 136
Robert 136
Ruhama 90
Ruth 144, 242
Ruth (EAGER) 135
Sarah 102, 136
Simon 136
Sohia Catherine 135
Sophia (RIDGELY) 135
Susanna 136
Thomas 136

HOWARD, Thomas
  Gassaway 136
Thomas Henry, Dr.
  137
Violetta 101, 103
Virginia Pleasants
  59, 218
William 135, 137
HOWE, Edward 202
Elizabeth 202
William Robert 137
HOWELL, Jehu 137,
  308, 309
John 137, 315
HOWLAND, John 137,
  332
HOWLETT, Mary Ann
  167
HOWN, Joseph 125
HOY, Joseph 137
Nicholas 137
HUBBARD, Charles 137
Jafray 137
Peter 137
HUBBART, John 137
HUBBERT, William 137
HUDDLESTON, Robert
  137
HUDSON, (?) 137
(?)s 320
John 137
Jonathan 137
Robert 137
William 137, 307
HUESE, R. 137
HUETTINGER, Michael
  137
HUGGARD, William 137
HUGGINS, William 137
HUGHES, (?) 334
Ann (BOND) 24
Benjamin 137
Charles 137
Christopher 137
Clemency 205
Daniel 137
Elijah 137
Frances 76
Francis 138
Henry 138
Horatio 138
Hugh 24
James 138
John 138
John E. 290
John, Jr. 138

HUGHES, Juliana S.
  B. (WIESENTHAL)
  290
Maria E. 290
Michael 138
Nancy (BOND) 24
Samuel 138, 334
Solomon 138
Thomas 138
William 138
HUGO, Samuel B. 6
HULIHANE, John 138
HULING, Michael 138
HULLER, Nicholas 138
HULSE, R. 138
HUMBRIGHT, Frederick
  117, 303
HUMPHREY, David 26
Elizabeth 26
Elizabeth (ROBERTS)
  26
HUMPHREYS, Lewis 138
HUNGERFORD, Thomas
  138
HUNSON, Robert 138
HUNT, Ann (BOYD) 138
Benjamin 138
Elizabeth 10, 138
Elizabeth (CHEW)
  138
James 138
Jesse 138
Job 138
Jobe 138
John 138
Johns Hopkins 138
Margaret (HOPKINS)
  138
Miriam 138
Phineas 138
Samuel 138
Sarah 69, 138
Simon 138
Susanna (BOSLEY)
  138
Temperance 10
Thomas 138, 139,
  332
William 10, 139,
  332
HUNTER, George 139
George, Jr. 139
Peter 139
Samuel 139
Thomas 139
William 139

376

377

380

381

LIGHTHAUSER, George
  161
LIGHTHESER, Matthias
  310
LIGHTHISER, Matthias
  161
LIJARD, George 161,
  320
  John 161, 320
LILBON, Walter 161
LILBURN, Walter 161
LIMEBARKER, Andrew
  161
  Philip 161
  William 161
LIMES, Christopher
  317
  Elizabeth 231
LIMES (?),
  Christopher 161
LINCH, William 161,
  316
LINDENBERGER,
  Catherine 168
  George 161, 303,
  304, 309, 321, 333
  John 161, 314
  Susanna 168
LINDER, John 161
LINDIFF, John 161
LINDSAY, Adam 161,
  308
  Anthony 76, 161
  John 161
  Nancy 5
  Rachel (DORSEY) 76,
  161
LINGAN, James
  McCubbin 161
  Janet (HENDERSON)
  161
  Thomas 162
  Thomas, Jr. 162
LINKENFETTER, Ulrich
  162
LINOXE, Nathan 159
LINSAY, Anthony 161
  Rachel (DORSEY) 161
LINTHICUM, Laura
  Ellen (SMITH) 250
  Sweetser 250
LINVILLE, James
  McAllister 162
  John 162
  Maria (LONG) 162

LINVILLE, Martha (MC
  ALLISTER) 162
LION, Leonard 162
LIONS, William 162
LIPPY, Conrad 162
LISTON, James 167,
  321
LITCHFIELD, John 75
  Sarah (DORSEY) 75
LITSINGER, George
  162
LITTIE, Peter 157
LITTIG, Job 319
  Justin 162
  Peter 162
  Philip 162, 319
LITTLE, George 162
  James 162
  John 162
  Thomas 162
  William 162
LITTLEJOHN, Miles
  162
  Thomas 162
LITZENER, George
  162, 317
  William 163, 317
LITZINGER, Catherine
  156
  Elizabeth Ann 163
  George 162, 319
  Henry 163
  Joseph 163
  Mary Ann (CYPRUS)
  163
  Matilda (WRIGHT)
  163
  Peter 163
  Sarah Charlotte
  (CYPRUS) 163
  William 163
LLOYD, Elizabeth 296
LOBELE, William 163
LOCK, Isaac 163
  William 163
LOCKARD, Francis 163
  Matthew 163
  Samuel 163
LOCKERT, Nancy 165
LOCKHARD, Francis
  163
LOCKISON, John 163
LODIGER, Chr'n 322
  Christian 164
LODSECKER, Simon 163
LOEBELE, William 163

LOGAN, Thomas 163
LOGE, John 163
LOGIE, James 163
LOGSDEN, Lons 163
LOLEME, James 163
LONDAMMON, George
  163
LONG, Ann 235
  Conrad 163, 320
  Henry 163
  James 163
  John 163, 305
  Jonathan 163
  Margaret 163
  Maria 162
  Mary 63
  Peter 163
  Robert 164
  Thomas 164, 308
LONGFORD, John 164
LONGLEY, David 164
LOOCKERMAN, Fanny
  (CHASE) 45
  Richard 45
LOOGE, John 163
LOOKES, John 164
LORA, John 314
LORAH, Henry 164,
  321, 322
  John 164
  Maria E. (ZELLERS)
  164
  Maria Elizabeth 164
  Susan 164
LORANCE, Ferdinant
  314
  Fredinand 164
LORANTZ, Elizabeth
  164
  Fredinand 164
  Vendel 164
  Wendel 164
LORD, Andrew 164
LORENTZ, Ann (STEEL)
  164
  Ann E. 164
  Fredinand 164
  Jacob 164
  Vendel 164
  Wendel 164
LORENZEE, James 164
LOSBACH, Fred. 322
  Frederick 164
LOSBAUGH, Frederick
  164
LOUD, Adam 164

MC ALLISTER, Joel 174
John 174
Joseph 174
Martha 162
Robert 174
MC AVOY, Nicholas 174
MC BEE, Sarah 111
MC BOYCE, James 174
MC BRIDE, Henry 174
Janet 49, 212, 213
MC BRIED, Archey 174
MC BROOM, Elizabeth
(ELLIOTT) 81
John 81
Karenhappuck
(ELLIOTT) 81
MC CABE, John 174,
315, 330
MC CAIN, Ann 266
MC CALL, George 174
MC CALLISTER, Robert
174
MC CANDLESS, George
174
MC CANDLEY, Martha
201
MC CANE, John 174
MC CANN, John 174
MC CARNAN, Barney 174
MC CARNEL, Charles
174
MC CARREN, Barney 174
MC CARTE, William
174, 317
MC CARTER, Arthur
174, 319
William 174
MC CARTHY, Callehan
174
MC CARTY, Dennis 174
Florence 174
Jessey 174
MC CASKEY, Alexander
174
Esther Mifflin 58
MC CASLIN, Elisha
174, 304
MC CASTLIN, Elisha
174
Jacob 174
MC CAULLEY, William
174
MC CIM, Alexander 326
MC CLAIN, Ely 174
Mary C. 99

MC CLALLUM, David
175, 303
MC CLATCHIE,
Elizabeth Stowers
132
John Goodshine 132
Margaret Ann (HOOK)
132
MC CLATHRY, John
177, 308
MC CLAY, G. 175
MC CLELAND, Robert
175
MC CLELLAN, David
175, 304
Elizabeth 175
Jane 175
Jane (BUCHANAN) 175
John 38, 175, 304,
321, 322
Maria (PENNYBAKER)
175
Mary 175
Nancy 175
Robert 175
Sarah (MILLER) 175
Walter 175
William 175
MC CLENAN, Robert
175
MC CLENNAN, David
175
MC CLINTOCK, Matthew
241
Susan (APPLEBY) 241
MC CLOCKLING, John
175
MC CLUGHAN, James
175
MC CLUNG, Robert 175
MC CLURE, Elizabeth
146
John 175
MC COLESTER, John
174, 326
MC COLLESTER, Toal
175
MC COMAS, Sarah 257
MC COMISKEY, Daniel
175
John 175
MC COMKY, James 175
MC COMULL, Sarah 171
MC CONAUGHEY, Alex
175
MC CONKY, James 175

MC CONNELL, Charles
175
MC CORMACK, Dennis
175
MC CORMICK, Dennis
175
James, Jr. 166
Rachel Ridgely
(LUX) 166
MC CORMISKEY, John
175
MC CORMSKY, John 320
MC COTTOR, James 175
MC COY, George 175
John 175, 332
William 175
MC CRACKEN, Jas. 175
John 175
MC CRACKIN, Jas. 321
MC CRAE, Neal 175
MC CRAY, Fergis 175,
315
MC CREARY, John 176
MC CRUE, Neal 175
MC CUBBIN, John 176
Moses 176
Sarah (LANE) 176
William 176
Zach. 327
Zachariah 304, 328
Zachariah, Jr. 176
Zachariah, Sr. 176
MC CUBBINS, (?) 327
MC CULLOUGH, Eleanor
(HOSHALL) 134
James 176
Lysander 134
MC CURDY, Arthur 176
MC CURLEY, Elizabeth
Wallace (GRAHAM)
107
James 107
MC CUTCHIN, Samuel
176
MC DANIEL, Francis
176
James 176
John 176
Thomas 176
MC DEARMETT, John
176
MC DENNY, Thomas 176
MC DONAGE, John 321
MC DONAGH, John 322
MC DONALD, John 176
Pat 176

388

389

MERRYMAN, Thomas 182, 183
William 181, 182, 183
William, Jr. 183
MESSEROLE, Hannah M. (SHUTE) 244
John 244
MESSERSMITH,
Elizabeth 183
Matthias 183
Sam. 322
Samuel 183, 303, 321
METZER, Michael 183
MICHAEL, Abraham 183
John, Sr. 183
MIDDLETON, Gilbert 183, 184
Henry 184
Sarah 184
MIEL, Johannes 184
MIKLEWS, Mary 205
MILBURN, Joseph 184
MILDEWS, Aquila 184
Greenbury 184
MILES, Aquila 257
Elizabeth (STANSBURY) 257
Joshua 184
Moses 143
Sarah (JOHNSON) 143
Thomas 184, 304, 327
MILEY, Jacob 184
MILLAR, Peter 185
MILLBERGER, Henry 184, 314
MILLER, Anthony 184
Benjamin 184
Catherine 185
Catherine Slack (or Schleich) 5
Daniel 184
Elizabeth 184
Elizabeth Ann 109
Elizah 185
Ely 185
George 184, 185, 322
Hannah 184
Hannah (STINCHCOMB) 185
Henry 184
Hugh 184
Jacob 184
James 184
John 184, 185, 312
Joseph 38, 185, 201

MILLER, Marsiller 185
Mary 185, 208
Mary (OURSLER) 185, 201
Matthew 185
Michael 185, 321
Nicholas 185, 303
Peter 185
Ph. 321
Philip 185
Phillip 185
Rachel 185, 301
Rebeckah (BRADFORD) 185
Robert 109
Rosannah (ULRICH) 184
Ruth 185
Samuel 185
Sarah 175
Thomas 185
William 185
MILLIMAN, Charles 185
MILLIRON, Merab (LOWE) 165
Samuel 165
MILLOW, Rachel (WONN) 297
MILLS, David 185
Hannah 209
Jacob 185, 303
Jonathan 185
Leonard 185
Richard 185
Samuel 185
Thomas 185
MILNER, Francis 185
MINCEL, Joshua 185, 322
MINING, John 186
MINNEY, John 186
MINOR, Dennis 186
MINSKY, Harriet 256
MINSPAKER - See MANSPIKER
MINTSHAW, John 186
MISER, William 186
MISH, John 186
MITCHELL, Aberilla 186
Ann (PRESTON) 186
Anne (PRESTON) 272
Barnet 186

MITCHELL, Eleanor (MORGAN) 186
Elizabeth 186, 272
Elizabeth (WILLIAMS) 186
Henry 186
John 186
John V. 186
Mary 186
Priscilla (GILBERT) 186
Richard 186
Robert 186, 306
Sarah 186
Sarah Ann 186, 275
Thomas 186, 186, 272
William 186, 310
MITTER, Benjamin 186
MITTINGER, Jacob 186, 303
MOALE, Ann G. (WHITE) 186
Ann M. (HOWARD) 186
Eleanor (OWINGS) 186, 203
Elizabeth 186
Elizabeth Smith (PECK) 186
Ellen 186
Ellen (NORTH) 186
Ellin Maria 131
Ellin North 186
Frances 186
Frances (OWINGS) 186, 203
George Washington 186
John 186, 187, 313, 327, 333
Judith Carter (ARMISTEAD) 186
Lucy (MORTON) 186
Mary 186
Rachel 186
Rachel (HAMMOND) 186
Randle Hulse 186
Rebecca 186
Richard 187, 309
Richard Halton 186
Robert 186
Robert North 186, 203
Samuel 186
Thomas 186, 203

391

392

393

OATS, Peter 198
OBER, George 198
ODE, John 198
ODELL, John 74
  Providence (BAKER)
    74
  Rachel 74
ODENBAUGH, Elizabeth
    7
ODLE, John 198
  Rachel (WATERS) 198
  Reynold 198
  Walter 198
  William 198
OFFIELD, John 199
OGG, Benjamin 199
  George 199
  Mary 236
  William 199
  William Hamilton 199
OGGLE, George 199
OGILBY, James 199
  Sarah (CRISPIN) 199
OGLEBY, James 199
  Sarah (CRISPIN) 199
OGLEVIE, James 199,
    305
  Sarah (CRISPIN) 199
OLDHAM, Ann 199
  Anna (ALBRIGHT) 199
  Augustine H. 199
  Charles 199
  Charles Herman, Sr.
    199
  Edward 199, 305
  Elizabeth 199
  George Washington
    199
  Hamet 199
  John 199
  Maria 199
  Mary (ENSOR) 199
  Susan Ann (BIDDLE)
    199
OLLIVER, Samuel 200
OMANSETTER, John 200
ONION, Elizabeth
    (DAY) 200
  William 200
  Zaccheus Barrett 200
  Zachariah 200
  Zacheus 200, 305
ORAM, Benjamin 200
  Henry 200
  John 200
  Samuel 200

ORAM, Thomas 200
ORE, Marane 200
OREM, Ann Sophia
    (SHUTE) 244
  Benjamin 244
  John H. 244
  Margaret
    (STRATTNER) 244
ORM, Samuel 200
ORNANSETTER, John
    200
ORNDORFF, Elizabeth
    102
ORNONSETER, Jno. 185
ORRICK, Charles 200
  John 182, 183, 200
  Mary 227
  Nicholas 148, 183
  Nicholas, Sr. 200
  Sarah (MERRYMAN)
    182, 183
  Susan (KEENER) 148,
    200
ORRIDGE, George 200
ORSBURN, Samuel 200
ORSLER - See OURSLER
OSBORN, Joseph 200
OSBORNE, Phoebe 100
OSBURN, Daniel 200
  John 200
  Samuel 200
OSLAR, Abram 200
  Ely 200
  William 200
OSTON, Gabriel 200
  Henry 200
  John 200
  Lawrence 200
OTT, Mary 253
OTWAY, Nicholas 201
OURSLER, Abraham 201
  Ann (PEMBERTON) 201
  Catherine 201
  Catherine (DORSEY)
    74
  Charles 201
  Edward 201
  Elam 201
  Eli 201
  Elizabeth 201
  Jacob 201
  John 201
  Margaret 201
  Martha (MC CANDLEY/
    MC KINLEY) 201
  Mary 185, 201

OURSLER, Mary
    (PARKER) 201
  Miluna (TALBOTT)
    150
  Ormand 201
  Ruth (OWINGS/OWENS)
    201
  Sarah 201
  Sarah (BAKER) 201
  William 74, 201
  William W. 150
OVERCREEK, Joseph
    201
OWENS, Ann 295
  Arthur 201, 315
  Bartholamew 201
  John 201
  John Cockey 304
  Ruth 201
OWINGS, Achsah 201,
    202
  Achsah (DORSEY)
    203, 204
  Achsah (GOSNELL)
    202
  Alexander 201
  Ann 203
  Ann (HENDERSON) 203
  Ann (JOHNSON) 204
  Ann Catherine
    (ZIMMERMAN) 202
  Anna (STONESTREET)
    203
  Anna Maria
    (WARFIELD) 203
  Anne 204
  Archibald 203
  Ariana (DORSEY) 203
  Arrcy 170
  Basil 203
  Beal 203
  Beale 201, 203, 311
  Benjamin 202
  Betsy 201, 204
  Caleb 201, 282, 316
  Cassandra Deye 202
  Catherine 202, 286
  Charlotte Colgate
    202
  Christopher 201,
    307
  Churchilla Cockey
    Deye 202
  Colgate Deye
    (COLGATE) 202

394

OWINGS, Cordelia
  (HARRIS) 203
Cordelia Harris 204
Dale 201
David 203, 204
Deborah 203
Deborah (LYNCH) 203
Dorothy (STINCHCOMB)
  202
Edward 201, 202
Edward Cockey 202
Eleanor 186, 201,
  203
Eleanor (MAGRUDER)
  203
Eleanor Ann
  (GRIFFITH) 203
Eleanor Brooks 170
Eleanor Hood
  (WORTHINGTON) 203
Elihu 202
Elizabeth 50, 202,
  203
Elizabeth (DORSEY)
  203
Elizabeth (HOWE) 202
Elizabeth (LAWRENCE)
  201
Elizabeth (MUNRO)
  203
Ephraim 201, 202,
  325
Frances 186, 203
Francis Thwaites 202
George 201, 202
George Washington
  203
Hannah 263
Hannah (HOOD) 204
Hannah (STINCHCOMB)
  201
Harwood 204
Helen (STINCHCOMB)
  203
Henry 202, 203
Henry Howard 203
Isaac 204
Israel 202
Jacob 202
James 203
Jesse 204
John 201, 202, 203,
  307
John Cockey 202, 307
Jonathan 203

OWINGS, Joshua 201,
  202, 203, 307, 332
Joshua Warfield 203
Leah 286
Levin 201, 202,
  204, 320
Levin Lawrence 203
Lucy (JONES) 146
Luther 203
Marcella 202, 298
Mary 201, 202, 203
Mary (COCKEY) 201,
  202
Mary (JEAN) 202
Mary (JENNINGS) 204
Mary Ann 202
Mary Cockey 202
Matilda 204
Michal 202, 203
Miche 202
Milcah 201
Mordecai 202
Nathaniel 203
Nicholas 202, 203
Pamelia (Parnelia)
  96
Penelope Deye 202
Rachel 202, 203,
  260
Rachel (CROOKS) 202
Rachel (GASSAWAY)
  203
Rebecca 202, 203
Rebecca (MARSH) 170
Rebecca (WILLIAMS)
  204
Richard 75, 202,
  203, 307, 318
Richard Howe 202
Richard IV 203
Roger 203
Ruth 201, 202, 204,
  262
Ruth (COCKEY) 203
Ruth (LAWRENCE) 203
Ruth (WARFIELD) 203
Samuel 201, 202,
  203, 307
Samuel, Jr. 203
Sarah 202, 203
Sarah (HELLAMS) 203
Sarah (MUMMEU) 202
Sarah (WOOD) 203
Sarah Ann Brown
  (HATHERLY) 203

OWINGS, Sarah Harvey
  (GIST) 203
Sophia 76
Stephen 203
Stephen, Jr. 146
Susan 201
Susanna 253
Susanna (WALTERS)
  201
Susannah 201, 204
Susannah (WALTERS)
  282
Thomas 139, 203,
  204, 307
Thomas Beale 203
Thomas Deye 202
Thomas Isaac 203
Urath 201, 203
Urath (KELLEY) 203
Urath (RANDALL)
  201, 203
Urath Randall 155
William 203, 204
OZBORNE, Mary 92
PACA, Abraham 204
Peter, Jr. 204
Peter, Sr. 204
PACKER, Branford 101
States (GIST) 101
PAGE, John 204
Richard 204
PAIN, George 204
J. George 204
PAINE, Charles
  Thomas 143
Clara Mussard
  (JOHNSON) 143
Joshua 204
Sarah 190
PAKER, John 204
PALFREY, Edward 204
PALLAN, Richard 204
PALMER, George 204
John 204
Thomas 204
PANNELL, Edward 204
John 204
PANSIL, John 321
PANTEL, Thomas 204
PANTSE, Thomas 204
PARISH, Edward 307
PARK - See PARKS
PARKER, Alexander
  204
John 204
Mary 201, 205

395

PEARCE, Phillip
  Grafford 208
  Rachel 208, 299
  Rachel (SLADE) 208
  Rebecca (WYLE) 299
  Ruth (SPARKS) 208
  Sarah 208
  Sophia (WILEY) 208
  Thomas 10, 208
  Walter 208
  William 208
  William, Sr. 208
PEARSON, John 208,
  306
  Thomas 208
PEASLEY, David 208
  William 208
PECK, Elizabeth Smith
  186
  Nathaniel 208
PECKHAM, John 208
PECKLEY, Henry 208
PECKLY, Henry 312
PECOCK, John 207
  Joshua 207
PEDDECOAT, William
  210
PELKONTON, Thomas 208
PEMBERTON, Ann 201
  Henry 208
PENDLETON, Richard
  197
PENEBAKER, Peter 208
PENINGTON, John 209
PENN, John 208
  Nathan 208
  Resin 208
PENNIFIELD, Esther
  (BEANE) 208
  Thomas 208
PENNINGTON, Daniel
  209
  James 209
  Sarah 253
  William 209
PENNY, Alexander 90
  Henry 209
  Susanna (FORD) 90
PENNYBAKER, Maria 175
PENNYWIT, Adam 208
PENSIL, Balser 211,
  322
  John 211
PENTZ, Barbara
  (GOULD) 209

PENTZ, Catherine
  (ROTHROCK) 209
  John Joseph 209
  Philip Henry 209
  Virginia (WILSON)
  209
  William Hamilton
  209
PERCIVAL, Samuel 209
PERDUE, Laban 209
  Walter 209
  William 209
  William, Jr. 209
PERES, Anthony 209
PERIN, William 209
PERINE, Elisha 209
  Hannah (MILLS) 209
  Henry 209
  James 209
  Jane 209
  Joseph 209
  Micha 209
  Sarah 209
  Simon 209, 304
  Susannah (FOWLER)
  209
  William 209
PERKERSON, Abraham
  205
PERKINS, Rachel L.
  131
PERRIGO - See
  PERRIGOE
PERRIGOE, Delilah
  245
  Elisha 209
  Henry 209
  James 209
  John 209
  Joseph 209
  Moses 209
  Nathan 209
  William 209
PERRIN, Simon 209
PERRY, Francis 209
  Richard 209
PETERS, Daniel 209,
  322
  George 209
  Jacob 210
  Mary 135
  Nicholas 210
PETERSON, Joseph 210
PETTICOAT, (?) 210
  (?)s 320
  Humphry 210

PETTICOAT, William
  210
PETTY, Francis 210
  John 210
PHARR, Margarett 78
PHELAN, Frances
  (SCOTT) 210
  John 210
  Mary (HERON) 210
  Matthew 210
PHELPS, Asahel 125
  George A. 267
  Rebecca (TALBOTT)
  267
PHILE, John 210
PHILIN, John 310
PHILIN - See also
  PHELAN
PHILIP, Isaac 210
  William 210
PHILIPS, Thomas 307
PHILIPS - See also
  PHILLIPS
PHILLIPS, David 210
  Elizabeth 210
  Henry 210, 319
  John 210
  Jonas 210
  Thomas 210, 269
  William 210, 316
PHILPOT, Brian 144,
  210
  Bryan 210
  Elizabeth (JOHNSON)
  144, 210
  John 211
PHILPOTT, Bryan 326
PHINNIMORE, John 211
PHIPPS, James 211
PICKARD, John 211
  William 211
PICKED, Charles 211
PICKERING, Nancy
  (PRIBBLE) 216
  Thomas 216
PICKETT, Elizabeth
  283
  John 268
  Mary (TAYLOR) 268
  William 211
PICKRON, John 211
PICKSLER, Jacob 211
PIERCE, Elizabeth
  (STEVENS) 260
  Frances 54
  John 54

PIERCE, Mary 54
  Thomas 331
PIERCY, William 211
PIERLY, Conrad 211
  Lodowick 211
PIERPOINT, Charles,
  Sr. 211
PIERPONT, John 211
  Joseph 211
PIERSON, John 208,
  331
PIKE, John 211
  Matthew 211
  Sally 60
PILASH, Joseph 211
PILL, George 211
PILLER, James 211,
  317
PIMBARTON, Henry, Jr.
  211
PINDELL, Catherine
  211
  Catherine (WALKER)
  211
  Charles Ridgely 211
  Eleanor 50, 51, 211
  Eleanor (BOND) 211
  Eleanor (GILL) 100,
  211
  Elizabeth 211
  Elizabeth (HOLLAND)
  211
  John 100, 211
  John Larkin 211
  John, Jr. 211
  John, Sr. 211
  Joshua 211
  Margaret (GORSUCH)
  211
  Mary 211
  Mary (LAUDAMAN) 211
  Philip 50, 211
  Sarah 211
  Susannah (LOUDERMAN)
  211
  Thomas 211
PINE, Frederick 211,
  306, 331
PINES, Charles 211
  William 211
PINGLE, Peter 211
PINSIL, Balser 211
  John 211, 322
PIPER, William 211
PITCHED, Charles 217

PITSLAND, Richard
  211, 306
PITTS, John 212
  Lewis 212
  Louis 212
PLASKITT, Catherine
  (AMOSS) 298
  John 298
PLATT, James 212
PLOWMAN, Edward 212
  James 212
  John 212
  Jonathan 212
  Rebecca (ARNOLD)
  212
  Richard 212
PLUM, William 212
PLUMLY, Jacob 212
PLUNKET, David 212
POAGUE, Joseph 212
POCOCK, Ashel 212
  Daniel 212
  Diley 212
  Elizabeth 212
  George 212, 332
  James 212
  John 212
  Joshua 212
  Ruth (GOTT) 212
  Susanne 212
  Sutton 212
  Thomas 212
POE, Bridget Amelia
  Fitzgerald
  (KENNEDY) 213
  Catharine (DAWSON)
  49, 212, 213
  D. 322
  David 49, 212, 213,
  303, 321
  David, Jr. 212
  Edgar Allan 212
  Edward 213
  Eliza (HOPKINS) 212
  Elizabeth (CAIRNS)
  49
  Elizabeth (CAIRNS/
  CAIRNES) 212, 213
  G. 322
  George 213, 321
  George, Capt. 49,
  212
  Harriet 49, 212,
  213
  Jacob 213
  Jane (MC BRIDE) 49

POE, Janet (MC
  BRIDE) 212, 213
  John 49, 212, 213,
  303
  Joseph 213
  Josephine Emily
  (CLEMM) 213
  Maria 49, 212
  Neilson 213
  Stephen 213
  Virginia (CLEMM)
  212
  William 213, 322
POGUE, Joseph 212
POLAMUS, Joseph 213,
  308
POLAND, William 213
POLEMUS, Joseph 213
POLK, Josiah 213
POLLARD, William 213
POLLICE, Martin 213
POLLY, Christopher
  213
POMPHREY, Joshua
  213, 322
PONABAKER, William
  213, 320
POND, Jane 214
POOL, Basil 214
  John 214
  Lloyd 13
  Martha Ann 13
  Matthew 214
  Naomi (BARNES) 13
  Peter 214
  Richard 214
  William 214
POOLE, John 214
POOR, Samuel 118
POORE, John 214
POPHAM, Francis 214
PORKAPINE,
  Christopher 214
  William 214
PORM, Rezin 214
PORRIE, Peter 302
PORT - See PORTS
PORTER, Andrew, Dr.
  214
  Ann (MACKENZIE) 214
  Catherine (GLISSON)
  214
  Charles 214
  Daniel 214
  David 214

RICHARDS, Richard,
  Jr. 225
RICHARDSON, Alexander
  225
  Aubrey 225, 308
  Beale Howard 135
  Benjamin Vincent 135
  Daniel 225
  David 225
  Elizabeth (HOWARD)
    135
  Elizabeth (RIDGELY)
    227
  George 132, 225, 322
  James 225, 226
  John 225, 318
  Mary (GRIZZELLE) 225
  Mary (PETERS) 135
  Robert Ridgely 227
  Samuel 225, 332
  Susan (HOOK) 132
  Thomas 226
  Will 226
  William 226, 315,
    330
  Zachariah 226
RICHART, Abram 226
  John 226
  Michael 226
RICHARTS, Michael 226
RICHERT, John 226,
  310
RICHEY, John 226, 322
  William 226
RICK, John 226
  Robert 226
RICKETTS, David 226
  Martha (WILSON) 226
  Nicholas 226, 323,
    331
  Ruth (ADAMSON) 226
  Sinai 131
  Thomas 226
RICKEY, William 226
RICKHART, John 226
RID, James 226
RIDDELL, William 226
RIDDLE, Alexander 226
  Robert 226
RIDENBOCK, Jno. 226,
  303
RIDENHOUR, Nicholas
  226
RIDENOAR, Nich. 322
RIDENOUR, Nicholas
  226

RIDER, John 226
  Mary (CHAPMAN) 45
  Mathias 45
RIDGELY, (?) 334
  Ann 227
  Camilla Hammond (MC
    KEAN) 188
  Charles 226, 227,
    307, 333
  Charles Carnan, Dr.
    227
  Charles S. 131
  Charles Washington
    227
  Charles, Capt. 226
  Charles, Jr. 227
  Daniel 227
  Deborah 227, 259
  Deborah (DORSEY)
    227
  Deborah Ridgely
    (BAER) 227
  Dorothy 227
  Edward 227
  Elizabeth 227
  Elizabeth (DORSEY)
    227
  Elizabeth (DUMESTE/
    DUMENT) 227
  Elizabeth (DUVALL)
    227
  Elizabeth
    (HOLLINGSWORTH)
    131
  Elizabeth (SHORT)
    227
  Elizabeth
    (WARFIELD) 227
  Frank 227
  Frederick, Dr. 227
  Greenberry 227
  Greenberry, Dr. 266
  Greenbury 227
  Gustavus Warfield
    188
  Harriet (TALBOTT)
    227, 266
  Henry, Judge 45
  Isaiah 227
  James 227
  John 227
  Joseph Graham 227
  Julia 227
  Julia Ann 205
  Lloyd 227
  Lot 227

RIDGELY, Lucy
  (STRINGER) 227
  Maria (SOLENO) 227
  Mary 195, 227, 259
  Mary (DORSEY) 227
  Mary (ORRICK) 227
  Mary Hodges
    (FISHER) 227
  Mary Louisa
    (HOPPER) 227
  Matilda 227
  Matilda (CHASE) 45
  Nicholas 227
  Noah 227
  Priscilla 226
  Prudence 135
  Rachel 166, 227
  Rachel (HOWARD) 226
  Rachel (RYAN) 227
  Rebecca 15, 227
  Rebecca (DORSEY)
    226
  Rebecca (LAWSON)
    227
  Rhoada 227
  Richard 227, 324
  Robert 227
  Ruth 227
  Ruth (NORWOOD) 227
  Ruxton Moore 188
  Samuel 227
  Sarah 227
  Silas 227
  Sophia 135, 227
  Susan 227
  Thomas Graham 227
  Thomas P. 227
  Washington 227
  William 307, 333
  William A. 227
  William III 227
  William, Capt. 227
RIDGEWAY, William
  227
RIDLEY, Matthew 228,
  326
RIEF, Daniel 228
RIELEY, Charles 223
  John 223, 228
RIELY, John 228
  Stephen 228
RIERDAN, Michael
  228, 317
RIFFETT, Nicholas
  228
RIGDON, William 228

402

RIGGS, Mary 111
Ruth 111
RIGHT, Christopher 228
James 228
Thomas 228
RIGHTER, Hannah 159
RILEY, Dennis 228
James 228
Mary (HOOK) 228
Mary R. P. (PRICE) 224
Michael 228
Tim 228
William 223
William Leonidas 224
RIM, Nicholas 228
RIMMER, John 228
RINEHART, Simon 228
RINGFIELD, James 228
RINGGOLD, Mary (GITTINGS) 103
Thomas 103
RISTEAU, Abraham 228
Ann 143
Ann (LUX) 166
Eleanor 228
Frances (TODD) 228
Francis 228
George 166, 228
John 228
Katherine 41, 61, 228
Rebecca 228, 286
Sarah 298
Thomas 228
RISTEAY, Thomas 325
RISTEN, Benjamin 228
RISTER, John 223
John, Jr. 223
Philip 224
RISTON, Benjamin 228
John 228
RITCHEY, John 226, 321
RITCHIE, Matthew 228
RITTER, Anthony 228
John 228
Lodowick 228
Michael 228
Thomas 228, 320
William 229, 314
RITTLEMYER, George 229
ROACH, John 229
Thomas 229, 310

ROAD, William 229
ROADS, Christopher 229
ROAN, Daniel 229
ROANE, Edward 229
ROBBINS, Philip 229
ROBERSON, George 229
ROBERTS, Benjamin 229
Catherine (AUSTIN) 229
Elizabeth 26
George, Dr. 159
John 229
Mary Ann (SADLER) 235
Patrick Henry 229
Rachel 119
Richard 229
Susannah (LE PAGE) 159
Thomas 229, 235
Zahcariah 229
ROBERTSON, George 229
Thomas 229
William 229, 310
ROBEY, Thomas 233
ROBINSON, Ann 24
Charles 229
Elizabeth 229
George 229
James 229
John 229
Joseph 229
Mephyteca (GALLOWAY) 229
Peter 229
Rebecca 116, 229
Robert 229
Roger 229
Sarah (ELLIOTT) 81
Solomon 230
Standly 230
Thomas 230, 306
William 229, 230
ROBOSSON, Charles 230
Hanwital (SHIPLEY) 242
Margaret (SHIPLEY) 242
O'Neal 242
Rebecca 230
Thomas 242
ROBY, Adam 230, 303

ROCK, Fiddle 230
George 230
Samuel 230
ROCKHOLD, Asael 230
Charles 230
Jacob 230
ROCKWELL, Isah 230
Isaiah 230
RODDEN, Daniel 230
RODDIN, John 230
RODGERS, James, Jr. 230
John 230
W. 230, 321, 322
RODMAN, Sophia 219
RODWALL, Godfrey 230
ROE, Frederick 310
Fredericks 230
Manna 230
Marma 230
Walter 230
William 230
ROEBUCK, William 230, 231
ROEMER, Christiana 113
ROGERS, Ann 231
Benjamin 231, 333
Catherine 231
Charles 231
David 231
Edmund Law 231
Eleanor 100, 103
Eleanor (BUCHANAN) 231
Elenor 32
Eliza (LAW) 231
Elizabeth (LIMES) 231
Jacob 231
James 231
John 231
John H. 193
Joseph 231
Joshua 231
Julia A. 193
Julia A. (NAGLE) 193
Lloyd Nicholas 231
Mary 99, 100, 231
Nicholas 100, 231, 334
Philip 231
Ruth 231
Sarah 181, 182, 231
Sarah (HOPKINS) 231

ROGERS, Thomas 231
William 231, 303
ROHEBOCK, Adam 303
ROHRBACK, Adam 231
ROLAND, John 232
Thomas 232
ROLES, David 232
Jacob 232
Thomas 232
ROLLINGS, Richard 232
ROLLINS, Elizabeth
291
ROLPH, William 232
ROMMELSEM, William
232
RONEY, James 232
ROOD, William 232
ROODS, Christopher
232
ROOK, George 232
Jacob 232
Martin 232
ROONEY, John 232
ROSE, Elizabeth
(MARTIN) 232
William 232
ROSS, Catherine 135
George 232, 317
James 232
Nathan 232
Peter 232
Wooley 232, 308
ROSSITER, Thomas 232
ROTHROCK, Catherine
209
ROUSE, James 232
ROWAN, John 232
ROWDON, John 232
ROWE, John 232
ROWELL, James 232
ROWEN, George 232
ROWLAND, Samuel 232
Thomas 232
William 232
ROWLES, Asa 233
Ely 233
John 233
Richard 233
ROWLS, Ely 233, 310
ROWNS, James 233
ROYNORLD, Thomas 233
ROYSTON, James 233
Mary (GOAN) 233
ROYTSON, John 233
Thomas 233
RUBEY, John 233

RUBEY, Thomas 233
Thomas, Sr. 233
RUBOTHAM, Thomas 233
RUBY, John 233
Thomas 233
Thomas, Sr. 233
RUMFIELD, Henry 233
RUMSEY, Charlotte
135
RUPERT, John 233
RUPPERT, Jacob 233
John 233
RUSH, Benjamin, Dr.
178
Elizabeth (FORD) 90
William 233
RUSHO, John 233
RUSK, David 233, 309
Richard 233
Thomas 233
William 233
RUSSEL, (?) 334
Thomas 326, 334
RUSSELL, Andrew 233
Mary Ann 159
Rebecca (MOALE) 186
Thomas 186, 233
William 233
RUTH, William 233
RUTLEDGE, Abraham
234
Abram 233
Abram, Jr. 233
Augustine Ann
(BIDDLE) 234
Elijah 233, 332
Ephraim 233
Jane 294
John 234
Joshua 234
Michael 234
Penelope 150, 234
Peter 234, 332
Thomas 234
William 234
RUTTER, Henry 234
Moses 234, 315
Richard 234
Thomas 234, 304,
307, 327, 328
RUTURT, Jacob 234,
314
RUXTON, Elsworth
234, 318
RYAN, Anthony 234,
315

RYAN, Edmon 234
Eleanor (GREEN) 234
James 234, 326
John 234
Rachel 227
Thomas 234
William 235
RYANT, James 235
RYE, Henry 235
RYLAND, Nicholas 235
RYON, Thomas 234
RYSTON, Abraham 235
SADDLER, Joseph 235
Samuel 235
SADLER, Ann (LONG)
235
Elizabeth (HOWARD)
235
Elizabeth Gassaway
(HOWARD) 136
Joseph 235
Mary Ann 235
Samuel 235, 323
Sewell Long 235
Thomas 136, 235
William 235
SAFFLE, Sarah 122
SALMON, (?) 334
George 235
George, Capt. 235
Rebecca (MERCER)
235
SAMPSON, Abram 235
David 235
Emanuel 235
Isaac 235, 332
Isaac, Jr. 235
Isaac, Sr. 235
Richard 235
SAMUEL, Masheck 235,
308
SANDALL, Jno. 235
John 331
SANDERS, Benjamin
235
John 235
Robert 236
SANDERSON, Francis
236
Joseph 236
SANDLANT, William
236
SANDLE, Jno. 235
SANK, George 236,
310
John 236

404

405

SHIPLEY, Rosanna 214
  Ruth 13, 239
  Ruth (HOWARD) 242
  Samuel 243
  Samuel, Jr. 243
  Samuel, Sr. 243
SHIRE, Nicholas 243
SHIRTAIL, Michael
  243, 320
SHIRWELL, William 243
SHLEY, John 237
SHLIFE, John 243,
  303, 314
SHLY, John 306
SHOLL, Philip 243
SHOOK, Peter 243
SHOPE, Catherine 255
SHORT, Christopher
  243
  Elizabeth 227
  Patrick 243
SHOUGHNESS, Patrick
  331
SHOURS, John 243
SHOWERS, John 243,
  312, 329
  Thomas 243
SHRACK, Piter 243
SHRANK, Catherine 243
  Elizabeth 243
  John 243
SHREAGLEY, Michael
  237
SHREEK, Andrew 306
SHRIACK, John Michael
  243
  Michael 243
  Michael, Sr. 243
SHRIER, Lodowick 243
SHRIKE, Andrew 244
SHRIM, Johannes 243
  John 243, 321
  John, Jr. 243, 322
  John, Sr. 243, 322
SHRINK, Andrew 244,
  331
SHRIOCK - See SHRIACK
SHRISCH, Michael 322
SHRIVER, Jacob 244
SHROAD, Jacob 244
  Stohel 312
  Stophel 244
  Valentine 244
SHROUD, Jacob 332
SHROVER, Peter 244
SHRTS, John 244, 303

SHRYOCK, John 314
SHRYOCK - See also
  SHRIACK
SHUBUT, Christr 244
SHUE, Charles 244,
  303
SHUGART, Martin 244
SHUGARTH, Martin
  244, 314
SHUSTER, Joshua 244
SHUTE, Ann Sophia
  244
  Hannah M. 244
  John H. 244
  Mary (ASHER) 244
SHY, John 244
SIBLE, Ludwick 252,
  308
SIDDAN, John 252
SIEGLER, John 252
SIGLER, Henry 252,
  303
SIGNER, George 252
SILISTER, Anthony
  252
SILLISTER, Anthony
  308
SILLMAN, John 238
SILVER, James 244
  John 244
SILVESTER, John 244
SIM, Barbara 247
  Jane 244
SIMISTER, Thomas 244
SIMMONDS - See
  SIMMONS
SIMMONS, Alexis, Jr.
  244
  Alexis, Sr. 244
  Jacob 244
  James 244, 245
  John 245
  Joshua 245
  Moses 245
  Rebecca (SHEKELLS)
  244
  Robert 245, 333
  Sarah (DARTON) 245
  William 245
SIMMS, Charles 245
  Thomas 245
SIMONS, Thomas 245
SIMPERS, Emily Tyson
  40
SIMPSON, (?), Mrs.
  245

SIMPSON, Ann 245
  Benjamin 245
  Francis 119
  James 245
  John 245
  Tomasis
  (WORTHINGTON) 119
  Tomsey 119
  William 245
SIMSON, James 245
SINCLAIR, Edward 245
  William, Sr. 245
SINCLARE, William,
  Sr. 245
SINDALL, David 245
  Delilah (PERRIGOE)
  245
  Elizabeth 245
  Jacob 245
  Ureth (COOK) 245
SINDELL, David 245
  Jacob 245
  Nathan 245
  Philip 245
  Rebecca 245
  Samuel 245
  Samuel, Jr. 245
  Samuel, Sr. 245
SINGERY, Christian
  245
SINGLETON, Joseph
  245
SINKLAIR, Moses 245
SINKLE, Nathaniel
  245
SINKLER, Rachel 72
SIPES, Miche
  (OWINGS) 202
  Peter 202
SITTLER, Matthias
  245
SITZLER, Philip 245,
  306
SITZLEY, Philip 245
SIZLER, John 245,
  319
  Philip 245, 246
SKERRETT, Clement
  315, 323
SKERRITT, Clement
  246
SKIFFINGTON, Mathew
  246
  Roger 246
SKINNER, Francis 246
  John 246

407

SKINNER, Thomas 246
SKIPPER, James 246
  Thomas 246
SKULL, William 246
SLACK, Henry 246
  John 246
  Maria Margaret
    (AURMAN) 246
  Sarah 246
SLADE, Abraham 208
  Belinda 246, 247
  Charlotte 246
  Dixon 246
  Elizabeth 37, 50,
    51, 247
  Elizabeth (ANDERSON)
    247
  Elizabeth (DULANY)
    246
  Elizabeth (PEARCE)
    208
  Elizabeth (STANS-
    BURY) 246, 257
  Josiah 246
  Josias 246
  Martha (Polly)
    (AMOS) 246
  Mary 75, 246
  Mathilda 247
  Minerva 284
  Nancy 246
  Nicholas 246
  Patsy 246
  Penelope 247
  Polly 246
  Rachel 208
  Rebeckah 246
  Sally 246
  Surena (MORGAN) 246
  Susanna 246
  William 246, 247,
    257
  William, Jr. 246,
    247
SLAGELL, Chris 247
SLAGLE, Peter 247
SLAKER, Henry 247
SLARP, Peter 247
SLATER, Hannah
    (JAMES) 142
  Robert 247
  William 142, 247
SLAUGHNESS, Patrick
    306
SLAYMAKER, John 247
SLIDE, Nicholas 247

SLIDER, Christ 247
SLIFER, Debora 283
SLOCAM, Elezer 247
SLOSS, Mary
    Stoughton 296
SLUPS, Stephen 247
SLUTS, John 247
SLY, John 247
SLYSER, Jno. 247
SMALL, Conrad 247
  Susanne Emily Adam
    190
SMETHEREST, Robert
    247
SMILIE, John 247
SMITH, Adam 247
  Alice 248
  Andrew 247
  Annie 247
  Anthony 249
  Aquila 247
  Barbara 250
  Barbara (SIM) 247
  Bill 247
  Cary Anne
    (NICHOLAS) 251
  Catherine (CONWAY)
    247
  Catherine (REISTER)
    251
  Cecia 249
  Charles 247
  Clement 247
  Conrad 247
  Daniel 247, 332
  David 247, 303
  Edmund Law Rogers
    231
  Edward 248
  Elijah 248
  Elizabeth 247, 249
  Elizabeth
    (BUCHANAN) 252
  Elizabeth
    (GITTINGS) 103
  Ephraim 248
  Esther 249
  Francis 248, 319
  Hannah 195, 196
  Hannah Henrietta 62
  Harriet 249
  Henry 248
  Hugh 248
  Jacob 248
  James 248, 249, 323
  James Hawkins 250

SMITH, Jane 117
  Job 248, 305
  John 141, 248, 249,
    304, 330
  John, Jr. 334
  John Addison 182,
    249
  John Spear 251
  Jonathan 249
  Joseph 249, 250,
    308, 322
  Joshua 185
  Katherine 251
  Lambert 103
  Laura Ellen 250
  Lucy 249
  Margaret 143, 248,
    249, 251, 252
  Margaret (SPEAR)
    249, 251
  Martha 266
  Mary 130, 249, 251
  Mary (BUCHANAN) 249
  Mary Magdalen 251
  Matilda 195
  Michael 250, 322
  Middleton (BELT)
    249
  Nancy 250
  Nancy (BISHOP) 250
  Nathaniel 250, 306,
    334
  Nicholas 250
  Patrick 250
  Peter 250, 321, 322
  Phil 250
  Polly 99
  Priscilla (ABBOTT)
    248
  Rachel (MILLER) 185
  Richard 250
  Robert 249, 250,
    252
  Robert, Jr. 251
  Roland 314
  Roland, Jr. 251,
    303
  Roland, Sr. 251
  Rosana (JACKSON)
    141
  Rowland 322
  Rowland, Sr. 251
  Samuel 249, 251,
    317, 324
  Sarah 99, 250
  Sarah (ROGERS) 182

408

SPROSSON, John 256,
  322
SPROUL, Ann
  (STANSBURY) 258
  Mary 17
SPURRIER, Green 256
  Levin 256
  Thomas 256, 320
SQUIB, John 256
SQUIRES, Peter 256
STACEY, William 256
STACIA, William 258
STACIS, W. 321
STACK, John 256
STACY, Robert 256
  William 256, 303
STAFFORD, John 256
STAHL, George 256
  William 256
STAINS, Thomas 256
STALEN, John 256
STALKER, William 256
STALLING, Thomas 256,
  317
STALLINGS, Thomas 256
STANDIFER, Samuel
  256, 332
STANDIFORD, Abraham
  256
  C. 256
  Jacob 256
  John 256, 305
  John, Capt. 225
  Nathaniel 256, 332
  Sarah 143
  Skelton 256
  Skelton, Jr. 256
  Skelton, Sr. 256
  Vincent 256
STANDLEY, John 257
  Thomas 257
STANDSBURY, Luke 257
  Thomas 258
STANLEY, John 257
  Thomas 257
STANSBERRY, Luke 257
STANSBURY, Abraham
  257, 258
  Ann 258
  Ann (Nancy) (DEW)
  258
  Anna D. 258
  Ariana (SOLLERS) 253
  Belinda 258
  Belinda (COLE) 52,
  258

STANSBURY, Belinda
  (SLADE) 246
  Belinda Slade
  (TALBOTT) 257
  Benjamin 257, 305
  Caleb 257
  Catherine 268
  Charity 258
  Charles 257
  Daniel 257, 258,
  316
  Daniel, Rev. 138
  David 257, 316
  Deborah 258
  Dixon 257
  Dixon, Jr. 257
  Dixson 318
  Edmund 246, 257
  Elijah 258
  Elizabeth 24, 246,
  257, 258
  Elizabeth (ECK) 258
  Elizabeth (ENSOR)
  258
  Elizabeth (HUNT)
  138
  George 167, 257
  Hannah 236
  Isaac 257, 258
  Jacob 258
  James 257
  Jane 167
  Jemima 167
  Jemima (GORSUCH)
  257
  John 257
  John Ensor 258
  Joseph 257, 305
  Luke 257
  Mary (BUFFINGTON)
  258
  Micajah 258
  Nathaniel 257
  Patience 62
  Penelope (BODY) 257
  Rachel 157
  Rebecca 24, 258
  Richard 257
  Richardson 257
  Richardson, Jr. 257
  Ruth 167, 258, 268
  Ruth (GHANT) 258
  Ruth (LEMMON) 157
  Samuel 258
  Sarah 157, 158,
  241, 258, 294

STANSBURY, Sarah (MC
  COMAS) 257
  Sophia (LEVY) 257
  Susanne 283
  Thomas 167, 258,
  329
  Thomas, Jr. 258
  Tobias Emerson 258
  Tobias, Rev. 253
  William 52, 258
STANTON, Alexander
  258
STANTRE, George 258
STANTRO, George 258
STAPLES, John 258
  Margaret (TEEPLE)
  258
STARNER, John 258
  William 258, 320
STARR, Obediah 258
STATIA, W. 322
  William 258
STATTON, Henry Adams
  258
STAUFFER, George 258
STAYTER, William 258
STEAD, William 258
STEEL, Ann 164
  James 259
  John 259, 312
  Julia 114
  William 259
STEELE, George 259
STEIN, Jacob 258
STEINBECK, Anna D.
  258
STELL, Benjamin 259
  Gabriel 259
STENHOUSE, A. 259
STENSON, William 259
STEPHEN, Nathan 259
  Thomas 259
STEPHENS, Abraham
  259
  Abram 259
  Edward 259
  Ephraim 259
  John 260
  Rezin 259
  Thomas 259
STEPHENSON, John 259
STEPLETON, Richard
  259
STEPTOE, Sarah 272
STERAD, Matthias
  259, 310

410

411

412

414

415

417

WATERS, Rachel 198
Richard 283, 284
Samuel 284
Samuel Wright - See
WALTERS, Samuel
Wright
Thomas 284
Virginia Ann 284
WATKINS, Albina
Charlotte 284
Clara Augusta
(BAGLEY) 284
Eleanor Elizabeth
284
Eleanora Bowie
(CLAGGETT) 284
Francis 284
Gassaway 284
James 284
John 114, 284
John Beale 284
John III 284
Laura 284
Minerva (SLADE) 284
Ruth (DORSEY) 284
Ruth (GUYTON) 114,
284
Samuel 284
Sarah (JONES) 284
William 284
William W. 284
WATLING, Abrahma 284
Abram 284
James 284
Thomas, Jr. 284
Thomas, Sr. 284
WATPOLE, Joseph 281
WATSON, Archibald 284
George 285
James 285
John 285
Mary 10
Thomas 285
William, Jr. 285
William, Sr. 285
WATT, Penelope 301
WATTERS, Isaac 283
John 283
WATTEY, John 285
WATTS, Benjamin 285,
310
Charles R. 143
Edward 285
John 285
Josias 285
Margaret Ann 278

WATTS, Mary
(JOHNSON) 143
Richard 285
WAYMAN, Margaret
(ALLEN) 5
WAYTE, Henry 285
WEARNER, George 319
WEATHERBURN, John
285
WEAVER, Casper 285
John, Jr. 285
John, Sr. 285
Ledewick 285
Ludowick 285
Mary 260
Peter 285
Philip 285
WEBB, Brown 285
John 285
Jonathan 285
Keziah 82
Thomas 285
WEBBER, Thomas 285
WEBER, Daniel 285
WEBRIGHT, Martin 285
WEBSTER, Aliceanna
149
Amelia Ross
(WEBSTER) 21
John Adams 21
John Adams, Jr. 21
Rachel (BIAYS) 21
Samuel 285, 332
WEBUGHT, Martin 285
WEDDERFIELD, Peter
285, 309
WEDGE, Simon 285,
319
WEEAR, Robert 286
William 286
WEEKS, Benjamin 285
Mary 81
WEEMS, William 285
WEER, John 285
Thomas 286
William 286
William, Jr. 286
WEET, Robert 286
WEGER, Frederick 286
WELCH, (?)ain 286,
320
Bethia 297
Edward 281
George 286
James 286
Joseph 286

WELCH, Margaret
(SMITH) 251
Patty (SELLMAN) 239
Polly (SELLMAN) 239
Prudence (WALKER)
281
Robert 239
William 286
WELDERMAN, George
286
Jacob 286
WELHELM, Frederick
286, 314
WELKER, Susanna 266
WELLER, Elizabeth
165
WELLING, Esther (LE
PAGE) 159
Katherine
(WINCHESTER) 295
Mary (CRAWFORD) 295
Mary (OWINGS) 203
William 159, 203,
295
WELLMAN, Richard 286
WELLS, Absalom 286
Alexander 286, 307
Alexander, Jr. 286
Ann 286
Ann (TEVIS) 287
Benedict 286
Benjamin 286
Bezaleel 286
Catherine (OWINGS)
286
Charles 286
Charles Dorsey 293
Cyprian 286, 302,
309
Elizabeth 286
Elizabeth (HOWARD)
287
Elizabeth
(LAWRENCE) 201
Elizabeth (PRATHER)
286
Ephraim 286
Francis 287
George 286, 287,
309, 312, 330
Helen 286
Henry 286
James 286, 287
Jemima (COE) 286
John 287, 293
Joseph 201

420

421